Quantitative Financial Analytics
The Path to Investment Profits

Quantitative Financial Analytics
The Path to Investment Profits

$$P = \sum_{t=0}^{\infty} \frac{D_t}{(1+k_e)^t}$$

Edward E. Williams
John A. Dobelman

Rice University, USA

World Scientific

NEW JERSEY · LONDON · SINGAPORE · BEIJING · SHANGHAI · HONG KONG · TAIPEI · CHENNAI · TOKYO

Published by

World Scientific Publishing Co. Pte. Ltd.
5 Toh Tuck Link, Singapore 596224
USA office: 27 Warren Street, Suite 401-402, Hackensack, NJ 07601
UK office: 57 Shelton Street, Covent Garden, London WC2H 9HE

Library of Congress Cataloging-in-Publication Data
Names: Williams, Edward E., author. | Dobelman, John A., author.
Title: Quantitative financial analytics : The path to investment profits /
    Edward E Williams (Rice University, USA), John A Dobelman (Rice University, USA).
Description: New Jersey : World Scientific, [2017] |
    Includes bibliographical references and index.
Identifiers: LCCN 2017030460| ISBN 9789813224247 | ISBN 9789813224254 ((pbk))
Subjects: LCSH: Technical analysis (Investment analysis)
Classification: LCC HG4529 .W5395 2017 | DDC 332.63/2042--dc23
LC record available at https://lccn.loc.gov/2017030460

British Library Cataloguing-in-Publication Data
A catalogue record for this book is available from the British Library.

Copyright © 2018 by World Scientific Publishing Co. Pte. Ltd.

All rights reserved. This book, or parts thereof, may not be reproduced in any form or by any means, electronic or mechanical, including photocopying, recording or any information storage and retrieval system now known or to be invented, without written permission from the publisher.

For photocopying of material in this volume, please pay a copying fee through the Copyright Clearance Center, Inc., 222 Rosewood Drive, Danvers, MA 01923, USA. In this case permission to photocopy is not required from the publisher.

Desk Editor: Shreya Gopi

Typeset by Stallion Press
Email: enquiries@stallionpress.com

Printed in Singapore by B & Jo Enterprise Pte Ltd

Dedication

To the memory of M. Chapman Findlay, William Price Baker, and William E. Gordon — outstanding scholars, good friends, and mentors all.

Preface

Quantitative Financial Analytics: The Path to Investment Profits is written to provide a comprehensive treatment of the important aspects of investment theory, security analysis, and portfolio theory and selection. Entrepreneurs will find the volume to be especially useful, and the book is written from the perspective of an individual who has owned and operated a business. It also contains a clearly detailed explanation of many recent developments in portfolio and capital market theory as well as a thorough procedural discussion of security analysis. Professionals preparing for the certified public accounting (CPA), chartered financial analyst (CFA), and/or chartered financial planner (CFP) examinations may benefit from a close scrutiny of the many problems following each chapter.

The explication progresses from reasonably simple institutional description to somewhat more complicated analytical material. This book should be comprehensible even to the financially uninitiated, but it will prove most beneficial to readers with some financial background, either academic or professional. The level of difficulty progresses with more advanced treatment appearing in the latter sections of each chapter, and the last chapters of the volume. Concise English prose is the major vehicle for communicating.

The book is divided into 10 chapters. Chapter 1 begins by posing the challenges of managing risk and reward. It considers the scope of investment management, financial information sources, the organized securities markets, and the instruments of the money and capital markets. Chapter 2 outlines the basics of financial mathematics (compound interest, present values, and so on) and statistics, while Chapter 3 summarizes the macroeconomic influences on the money and capital markets. The analysis is not confined to vague generalities about the exogenous variables that affect security prices, but rather explores the financial aspects of the simplified Keynesian, monetary, and supply-side approaches to macro-economics. Chapter 4 begins the process of evaluation with classical ratio analysis and complements the material that follows. Chapter 5 provides a summary discussion of various forecasting techniques and provides an explication of data analysis. Chapter 6 outlines specific methods for examining fixed-income securities, while a comprehensive scheme for analyzing equities is constructed in Chapter 7. The characteristics of futures, options, and derivatives securities are detailed in Chapter 8. Risk-bearing characteristics and profiles of investors are assessed in Chapter 9 together with the elements of portfolio theory in a Markowitz-Sharpe framework. These constructs are extended into capital market theory in Chapter 10, along with a final assessment of the question of capital market efficiency in light of earlier work by Benjamin Graham, David Dodd, J.B. Williams, and others.

The authors are indebted to a number of people for their help in the preparation of the volume. We first thank the skillful editors at World Scientific for their leadership and fastidious production of this text. Linda Werckle, Prof. Williams' administrative assistant, typed and proofed early editions of this manuscript numerous times with her usual exceptional efficiency. We acknowledge the skillful and adept creation of the figures and diagrams done by Sarah R. Neill and Robyn Tinsley. During the time that Wei Fu was a graduate assistant, he provided tremendous assistance with the formulas, examples, and problems. We thank Lynn Lewis for her astute insights into the institutional trading aspects of the markets. Kim Raath and the late Sarah Tooth consolidated student feedback of the preliminary chapters used in various statistical finance classes at Rice University, Houston, Texas. Finally, a special note of appreciation is reserved for the late M. Chapman Findlay, III, who provided us with many of the skills and much of the philosophy found in these pages. Chap's wit and insights made him a very special financial economist.

As a final note, with the advent of the Trump Administration, major changes in tax laws and regulations in the United States are quite likely. Thus, some of the explication and analysis to follow may need adjustment accordingly.

The Woodlands, TX	Edward E. Williams
Summer 2017	John A. Dobelman

About the Authors

Dr. Edward E. Williams is Professor Emeritus at Rice University where he taught for 36 years (1978–2014). He received his B.S.E. from the Wharton School at the University of Pennsylvania in 1966 and his Ph.D. from the University of Texas at Austin in 1968. Over the years, he has written 12 books and numerous articles and scholarly papers. He was one of the original critics of the Efficient Market Hypothesis (EMH) when it first appeared five decades ago. At Rice, he began its entrepreneurship program which is now rated as one of the top such endeavors in the world. During his teaching career, he received many awards for teaching excellence and was named by *BusinessWeek* as the second best entrepreneurship professor in the U.S. He has also been Professor of Statistics at Rice where he has published numerous works in financial economics and investments.

Dr. John A. Dobelman is Professor in the Practice in Statistics and Director of the Professional Master's Program at Rice University, Houston, Texas; he has taught at Rice since 2004. Prior to that he was a pricing scientist at PROS Holdings, Inc., and held various engineering and management positions in aviation facilities engineering and construction. His current research interests include investments analysis, stochastic modeling for markets and finance, simulation-based and quantitative portfolio selection and management, deception in patterns of noise, optimal display of quantitative information, improved communication, and applications of statistics to engineering models and vice versa. He has worked with Dr. Williams on numerous projects dating back several decades.

About the Cover

The cover of this book was adapted from the cover of a work by M.C. Findlay and E.E. Williams written over 40 years ago. It attempts to portray in very simple equations the evolution of the pricing of common stock going back a century. From the definition of book value per share as being "value" (1910) to the speculative excesses of the 1920s ("whatever a bigger fool will pay"), the equations settle on the true value of stocks as being determined by their earnings and dividend paying potential.

Along the way, we encounter the equation used by Benjamin Graham and David Dodd in the early editions of their famous book *Securities Analysis* first published in 1934. Graham developed a formula which gave particular value to dividends (based on the "bird-in-the-hand" philosophy) weighing them three times the value of earnings. He also described what he considered to be a proper "multiple" to be paid for a stock given its status as a "growth" stock, "value" stock, "cyclical" stock, etc. Thus, if, say the Southern Pacific Co. (at the time the largest corporation west of the Mississippi) earned $3 per share and paid out $1 in dividends, it could be valued with a multiple (M) of, say, ten times as: $P = 10 \left(\frac{\$3}{3} + \$1 \right) = \$20$ per share (see 1930 equation).

Later formulations (even by Graham and Dodd) were influenced by J. B. Williams who wrote *The Theory of Investment Value* in 1938. Williams (and others) emphasized earnings and dividend growth such that by the 1940s many authorities valued earnings with what has become known as P/E or price-to-earnings multiples. These formulations were also presented as earnings capitalizations where k_e was the capitalization rate. By the 1960s, growth was specifically taken into account. Say a stock earned $3 per share, had an earnings capitalization rate of 10%, and earnings were expected to grow at 3% per year. The valuation would be: $P = \frac{\$3}{0.10-0.03} = \$42.86$ (see 1960 equation). Of course, this would correspond to a P/E multiple of $\$42.86/\$3 \cong 14.3X$.

In modern times (∞), financial economists have returned to J. B. Williams' original formula, arguing that a stock is worth the discounted present value (P) of an infinite duration dividend stream capitalized at an appropriate discount rate derived from what has become known as the Capital Asset Pricing Model (CAPM). The history and underlying theory of all of these equations (even that of the 1920s) are the theme of this book.

Contents

Dedication	v
Preface	vii
About the Authors	xi
About the Cover	xiii
1. The Challenge: Can You Attain Wealth in Today's Investment Environment?	1
INTRODUCTION	1
THE NATURE OF INVESTMENT MANAGEMENT	3
INVESTMENT MEDIA AND THE ENVIRONMENT	5
CAN YOU MAKE MONEY IN THE STOCK MARKET?	6
THE STOCK MARKET AS A SPECULATIVE INSTITUTION	8
FINANCIAL INFORMATION	13
THE SECURITIES MARKETS	15
TRADING SECURITIES	18
REGULATION OF SECURITIES MARKETS	20
MARGIN PURCHASES	22
INSIDER TRADING	23
SHORT SELLING	26
STOCK MARKET INDICATORS	27

xvi *Contents*

THE 1929 CRASH	30
SUMMARY	32
REFERENCES	35

2. Financial Mathematics — 37

INTRODUCTION	37
Axiom of Value	38
Axiom of Time	38
Axiom of Time Value of Money (TVOM)	40
FUTURE AND PRESENT VALUE	41
Simple and Compound Interest	41
Continuous Compounding	42
Annuity Values	43
Present Value and Discounting	44
Capitalization of an Income Stream	46
FINANCIAL RETURNS	46
Gross Returns	47
Incremental Returns	49
Summary Measures	51
SUMMARY	56
PROBLEMS	57
REFERENCES	58

3. The Securities Markets and Macroeconomics — 59

THE SECURITIES MARKETS	59
Securities of the U.S. Government	60
Municipal Securities	61
Bankers' Acceptances	62
Negotiable Certificates of Deposit and Commercial Paper	63
Eurodollars and Non-U.S. Money-Market Instruments	64
THE CAPITAL MARKET	65
Long-Term Debt Instruments	67
Equity Securities	73

MACROECONOMIC INFLUENCES UPON THE MONEY AND CAPITAL MARKETS	74
Investment and Saving Equilibrium	78
THE NEOCLASSICAL MONETARIST VIEW	85
INTEREST RATE TERM STRUCTURE	91
Example	95
Term Structure Theory: Other Hypotheses and Implications	96
Examples	99
SUMMARY	100
PROBLEMS	101
REFERENCES	107

4. Financial Statement Analysis   109

RATIO ANALYSIS	109
FINANCIAL STATEMENTS	111
Group I — Liquidity	114
Group II — Profit Ratios	115
Group III — Turnover Ratios	116
Group IV — Return on Investment Ratios	117
Group V — Leverage and Capital Structure Ratios	118
Group VI — Asset-Relation Ratios	120
Group VII — Common Stock Security Ratios	121
Group VIII — Yield and Price Ratios	122
Common Size Analysis	123
ADJUSTMENTS TO FINANCIAL STATEMENTS	132
FINANCIAL STATEMENTS AND ACCOUNTING DATA	138
FINANCIAL ANALYSIS FOR MERGERS AND ACQUISITIONS	139
DEAL STRUCTURE	140
INSTALLMENT SALES ANALYSIS	140
CORPORATE STRUCTURE FOR MERGERS AND ACQUISITIONS	144
ACCOUNTING FOR MERGERS AND ACQUISITIONS	150

xviii Contents

SPECIAL INDUSTRY RATIOS 151
    Railroads................................ 151
    Regulated (Public) Utilities.................. 152
    Airlines................................. 153
    Commercial Banks 153
    Life Insurance Companies 154
    Property and Casualty Companies 154
    Mutual Funds............................ 155
SUMMARY.................................... 157
PROBLEMS................................... 160
REFERENCES 168

5. Forecasting Techniques   171

INTRODUCTION TO FORECASTING 171
FORECAST ACCURACY MEASURES 172
NAÏVE FORECASTS 173
SMOOTHING TECHNIQUES 177
STOCHASTIC MODELING....................... 179
TIME SERIES ANALYSIS........................ 185
REGRESSION AND CORRELATION ANALYSIS 186
    Examples 187
INDEPENDENT VARIABLES AND SENSITIVITY
    ANALYSIS............................... 188
SUMMARY.................................... 191
PROBLEMS................................... 193
REFERENCES 194

6. Analysis of Fixed Income Securities   195

FORECASTS AND BOND ANALYSIS 195
COVERAGE RATIOS AND INCOME SECURITY 200
PROTECTION IN CASE OF FINANCIAL
    DIFFICULTY 203
THE RISK STRUCTURE OF INTEREST RATES 208

METHODS OF PRINCIPAL REPAYMENT	217
PREDICTION OF FUTURE DEFAULT	221
HOLDING PERIOD RISKS	223
BOND TABLES AND BOND-RATING AGENCIES	226
ANALYSIS OF MUNICIPAL BONDS	232
ANALYSIS OF PREFERRED STOCK	234
CONTINUING THE ANALYSIS OF AMERICAN FUNERAL SUPPLIES	236
SUMMARY	246
PROBLEMS	248
REFERENCES	259

7. Analysis of Common Stocks — 261

COMMON STOCK BASICS	261
Determining Capital Outlays and Future Financing	263
Common Stock Valuation Models	268
Holding-Period Returns	272
The Dividend Stream — Earnings Multiplier Model	274
An Illustration of Estimating Common Stock Returns	277
GROWTH AND RISK ANALYSIS	279
MERGERS AND GROWTH	287
After-Tax Returns and Growth	292
RISKINESS OF STOCKS	294
RISK MEASURES FOR COMMON STOCK RETURNS	300
Growth-Rate Equations for the Levered Firm	305
Common Stocks: Further Considerations	308
Example	310
STOCK PRICES AND THE ISSUANCE OF NEW SHARES	312
Example	314
Example	318
FINANCIAL ANALYSIS AND ACCOUNTING DATA	319

CONVERTIBLE SECURITIES	321
SUMMARY	330
PROBLEMS	338
REFERENCES	357

8. Futures and Options — 359

INTRODUCTION	359
A Famous Example	361
Futures	363
WARRANTS	368
Common Stock Subscription Rights	380
Example	382
Warrants, Convertibles, and Dilution	383
Options	384
SUMMARY	388
PROBLEMS	391
REFERENCES	395

9. Risk, Uncertainty, Utility and Portfolio Theory — 397

UTILITY THEORY	397
VON NEUMANN–MORGENSTERN UTILITY	403
INDIFFERENCE CURVES	406
PORTFOLIO THEORY	415
Example	434
SUMMARY	435
PROBLEMS	438
REFERENCES	443

10. Capital Market Theory, Efficiency, and Imperfections — 445

CAPITAL MARKET THEORY	445
THE CAPITAL MARKET LINE (CML)	450
THE SECURITY MARKET LINE (SML)	452

PORTFOLIO EVALUATION	455
ADDITIONAL TOPICS IN PORTFOLIO MANAGEMENT	461
CAPITAL MARKETS: EFFICIENCY AND IMPERFECTIONS	477
CAPITAL MARKETS AND THE REAL WORLD	482
EXPECTATIONS, CONVERGENCE, AND THE EFFICIENT MARKET HYPOTHESIS	485
Example: AFS, A Graham & Dodd Approach	492
CAPITAL ALLOCATION EFFECTS	499
SUMMARY	502
PROBLEMS	504
REFERENCES	508

Appendix A.   Time Value of Money — 511

PRESENT AND FUTURE VALUE FACTORS	511
INTERNAL RATE OF RETURN (IRR) CALCULATION	513
PROBLEMS	518

Appendix B.   Financial Statistics — 521

PROBABILITY, RANDOM VARIABLES, AND MEASURES OF LOCATION, DISPERSION AND SHAPE	521
Examples	525
THE NORMAL DISTRIBUTION	527
Examples	529
SAMPLING AND THE t-DISTRIBUTION	529
Examples	530
COVARIANCE	532
REGRESSION AND CORRELATION ANALYSIS	534
CONDITIONAL PROBABILITY DISTRIBUTIONS	541
EXPECTED VALUES AND VARIANCES OF TWO OR MORE RANDOM VARIABLES	543
PROBLEMS	545
REFERENCES	551

Appendix C. Company Data   **553**

IMPORTANCE OF REAL WORLD DATA   553
SERVICE CORPORATION INTERNATIONAL (SCI) . . .   553

Appendix D. Selected Snapshot Data   **583**

SELECTED SNAPSHOT DATA   583

Index   **593**

Chapter 1

The Challenge: Can You Attain Wealth in Today's Investment Environment?

> *"You ought never to take your little brother's chewing gum away from him by main force; it is better to rope him in with the promise of the first two dollars and a half you find floating down the river on a grindstone. In the artless simplicity natural to his time of life, he will regard it as a perfectly fair transaction. In all ages of the world this eminently plausible fiction has lured the obtuse infant to financial ruin and disaster."*
>
> Mark Twain

Introduction

The discussion in the coming chapters may well leave the reader under the impression that it is virtually impossible to attain great wealth from investing in the stock market. At best, it may appear that investors should be able to earn no more than average returns. This conclusion is not unwarranted, although the reader should bear in mind that all the evidence is not yet in. Our understanding of investments as an economic phenomenon is still limited, and only recently have scientific tools been employed to analyze the process. Furthermore, the discipline of investment analysis and its underlying theoretical constructs are being reconsidered in the light of an ever-expanding body of literature. The learned opinions of many leading scholars in the area differ widely even after surveying similar documentation.

On the one hand, there are those who argue that above-average market returns may be achieved by the investor who acquires sufficient expertise. The job of asset management, though interdisciplinary and frustrating, can be performed. It appears that through the use of a judicious combination of expert judgment and objective analysis, one can achieve superior returns consistently. The example of Warren Buffett immediately comes to mind.

At the other end of the spectrum, many academic financial economists suggest that the Warren Buffetts of the world are a rare breed. They maintain that, although some investors think that fundamental analysis may hold the key to beating the market, in reality stock markets are intrinsic-value, random-walk phenomena. As a result, most fundamental analysts will not be able to beat the market. Only a very few expert fundamental analysts who uncover hard to detect data will be able to earn above market returns. It takes years of hard work to become such an expert, and it is unlikely that any particular person will be able to consistently discover such data. In light of efficient market evidence, one may reflect upon the work required to analyze and select securities and ask: Why bother?

The answer should be clear. If investors see no need to insure that potential risk is balanced by potential return, then perhaps there is no need to bother. But many elements relevant to the behavior of companies, industries, and markets can be learned. Probabilities about the future behavior of those elements can also be quantified. Inputs determined by security analysis and manipulated by portfolio managers should lead to an optimum balance between risk and return in order to achieve maximization of long-run portfolio wealth.

In the effort to follow, we feel some obligation to apprise the reader of our views since we shall ask him or her to patiently traverse many pages of somewhat difficult (and perhaps even occasionally tedious) material. Although we will try to make our work as entertaining as possible, diversion is certainly no justification for spending the money required to buy this book.

First, we do believe that security analysis is a necessary task for every investor. There is no other way that one can make determinations of risk and return. Even if it is impossible to gain above-average rewards (a point on which we shall reserve judgment for the time being), forecasts of expected risk–return relationships are required for all but the most simple-minded decision algorithms. Moreover, we believe that entrepreneurs are especially qualified to be good investors. People who have operated businesses tend to take a longer term view and try to understand the real economic value of a business. This is the approach adopted by Warren Buffett, and it has proven to be very successful.

Second, we would argue that portfolio analysis is also a required activity if one is to decide in a rational framework which securities should be purchased. Although some aspects of portfolio analysis in the current state-of-the-art are rather abstract, we maintain that operational decisions can be made using the tools we will suggest. Entrepreneurs should pay particular attention to their portfolio of investments since they tend to have a major asset holding in the business(es) they own. Risk is an important aspect of portfolio construction, and the investor must be able to determine his or her personal risk preferences in order to make optimal selections.

Finally, an understanding of the constructs of capital market theory is essential if one is to grasp clearly the significance of many of the issues that we will raise in the pages to follow. Although capital market theory may not be as yet a completely accurate description of the operations of the capital markets, if markets become more efficient the theory becomes a better depiction of reality.

The Nature of Investment Management

Every individual who has more money than he or she needs for current consumption is potentially an investor. Whether surplus funds are placed in a bank at a guaranteed rate of interest or used to invest in an oil well, an investment decision must be made. These decisions may be made wisely or foolishly, but the intelligent investor will seek a rational, consistent approach to managing one's money. The best method for many is simply to turn their funds over to someone else for management. A significant number of investors do indeed follow this policy, and it is quite likely the correct decision for them. Others, however, manage their own money or even become professionals and manage other people's. This book is written for these individuals.

In the succeding chapters, any mysteries about getting rich quickly are not obviated. Indeed, if such secrets existed, it is doubtful that anyone would be willing to reveal them. There are systematic procedures for making decisions, however, that can enable the intelligent investor to achieve solid performance. There is generally a positive correlation between the returns one expects from an investment and the amount of risk that is assumed. Thus, decisions must be made that reflect the ability and desire of the investor to assume risk. In the final portions of this volume, we shall examine in both theoretical and practical terms the nature of this correlation.

As has been observed elsewhere (Thompson, Williams and Findlay, 2003, p. 2):

> "Although intelligence is about the only important requisite for any kind of decision making, there are other traits that may be helpful to the money manager. In particular, a certain amount of scientific curiosity may be very important to successful investors. By scientific curiosity we do not mean knowledge or even interest in disciplines generally considered 'science,' such as biology or chemistry, although the scientifically trained analyst may have an advantage in scrutinizing the stocks of high-technology companies. Rather, scientific curiosity refers to the systematic pursuit of understanding. An investor should be willing to take the time and spend the energy to know himself and his environment."
>
> "It is unfortunately true that many otherwise successful people make poor investors simply because they do not have a logical investment policy. They have only vague objectives about what they want (such as 'capital appreciation' or 'safety of principal'), and they often substitute general impressions for solid fact gathering. How many highly competent doctors, for example, go beyond the recommendations of their brokers (friends, relatives, or patients) when selecting a security? How many business people take the time to familiarize themselves with the income statements and balance sheets of the firms in which they hold stock?"

We might add: How many professional portfolio managers make decisions based on a well-researched, documented effort to uncover investments that others have not discovered? Even in the case of professional portfolio managers, other factors than solid analysis may be allowed to dominate. Of course, the doctor may not have the time or knowledge to make a sound investment decision and the business person may be too occupied with his or her own company to do the required due diligence. If so, these individuals should not attempt to manage their own money. The professional manager who bases decisions on what one "feels" the market will do, however, is being negligent. Although knowledge of what other managers are doing may be important and an experienced person's market "feel" may be superior to any professor's theoretical model, too often even the professional tends to substitute rumor and hunch for sound analysis and thorough investigation.

The sophisticated investor needs to be reasonably versed in mathematics and statistics. In this book, we provide a review for those who are somewhat hazy on these subjects. This review is not intended as introductory expositions to the investor who has never heard of compound interest or a standard deviation, but it should serve as an adequate guide and handy reference for those who have a basic knowledge of mathematics and statistics.

Investment Media and the Environment

Numerous investment media exist that the investor may consider. The simplest is the insured deposit at a commercial bank. Such accounts provide safety of principal and liquidity. Historically, they have also provided yields that closely track the rate of inflation. The insured bank deposit account requires little analysis as an investment vehicle, but it is not entirely riskless. A failed bank may be taken over by the government, and the depositor may be required to wait weeks or longer to get his or her money back. Moreover, deposit insurance offered by the Federal Deposit Insurance Company (Uncle Sam) is limited in amount, and this makes it impossible for managers of large amounts of money to take advantage of this opportunity. Investors of this sort typically invest in U.S. Treasury Bills, or equivalents, which will be discussed later in Chapter 2.

At the opposite end of the asset spectrum are highly illiquid investments (real estate, oil well interests, paintings, coins, stamps, antiques, and even ownership of business enterprises). These investments require very specialized due diligence, and are beyond the scope of this book. In between the insured bank deposit (or Treasury Bill) and the very illiquid assets are a host of investments that can generally be described as securities. A security is an instrument signifying either ownership or indebtedness that is negotiable and that may or may not be marketable. Securities are by far the most popular form of semi-liquid investment (that is, an investment that is marketable but that may not be salable near the price at which the asset was purchased). Moreover, they can be analyzed in a systematic, consistent fashion.

Pension fund assets, life insurance reserves, bank portfolio holdings, and so on are far more heavily invested in bonds than equities. Thus, the bond markets are far more important to both issuing corporations and many investors than equities (stocks). Bond analysis is not simple or even uninteresting. Indeed, some of the most sophisticated minds in the investments business are engaged in the bond market. We shall devote a chapter of this book to bond analysis, and the reader will be convinced that bonds have a place in many portfolios. However, it is the stock market that engenders the interest of most investors. This is undoubtedly true because the rewards (and penalties) of stock market investment well exceed those obtainable in the bond market. Furthermore, equity analysis is more complicated than bond appraisal, and greater skill is required in selecting common stocks than fixed income securities.

Can You Make Money in the Stock Market?

For 50 years now, a school of thought has developed that argues that only insiders and those privileged to have information not known to the rest of us can make large profits in the stock market. These people subscribe to a theory of stock prices called the efficient market hypothesis (EMH). EMH advocates argue that the current price of a stock contains all available information possessed by the market and only new information can change stock prices. Since new information becomes available randomly, there should be no reason to expect any systematic movements in stock prices or returns.

Believers in the strongest form of the EMH feel that the stock market is perfectly efficient and the cost of research and investigation cannot be justified by any "bargains" (that is, undervalued stocks) that can be found. The efficient market hypothesis was initially tested many years ago by a number of scholars (see Fama, 1965, 1970). These researchers have considered various hypotheses about the behavior of the stock market, from notions that past stock prices can be used to forecast future prices (the belief held by stock market chartists or "technicians") to opinions that there are stocks that are undervalued by the market and that these stocks can be uncovered by a thorough investigation of such fundamental variables as reported earnings, sales, price-to-earnings multiples, and other economic, accounting, or financial data.

The latter view of the market has long been held by most investors, and the whole profession of security analysis is founded on it. From the early days of the first edition of Graham and Dodd (1934) down to the present (see Graham and Dodd, 2008) analysts believed that there are overpriced stocks, and underpriced stocks, and the securities analyst searches to determine both. EMH advocates have maintained, however, that the presence of so many analysts trying to find bargains (and overpriced stocks to sell short, a technique discussed later in this book) makes it impossible for any one of them to outperform the general market consistently. Thus, as the economy grows and corporate earnings increase, it is possible to make money in the stock market, but it is not reasonable to expect to earn more than "average" (risk-adjusted) returns over the long run.

The EMH hypothesis is based on the observation that there are many buyers and many sellers in the market who have a great deal of similar information about stocks. If any one stock were "worth" more than the price for which it was currently selling, analysts would recommend buying until its price rose to the point at which it was no longer a bargain. Similarly, if a stock were selling for more than its intrinsic value, analysts would recommend selling. The price of the security would fall until it was no longer overpriced.

The efficient market hypothesis became quite popular among academic economists over the past 50 years. Nevertheless, most practitioners have rejected it for a number of reasons. In the first place, if the EMH were correct, it would be hard for professionals to justify the salaries that they are paid to find better-than-average performers. Second, many analysts have suggested that their very presence is required for the EMH to work. If they could not find undervalued stocks, they would not come to their desks each day, and if they did not appear, there would no longer be that vast army of competitors to make the stock market efficient and competitive!

Moreover, many analysts point out that there are substantial differences of opinion over the same information. Thus, although every investor may have available similar information, some see favorable signs where others find unfavorable ones. Furthermore, various analysts can do different things with the same data. Some may be able to forecast future earnings, for example, far more accurately than others simply because they employ a better analytical and more systematic approach.

The Stock Market as a Speculative Institution

Others (including many academic historians) maintain that the stock market is neither competitive nor efficient. It has been observed that securities speculation in the past has been far from scientific and that emotion rather than reason has usually guided the path of stock prices. These inefficiency proponents believe that people are governed principally by their emotions and that bull and bear markets are merely reflections of the optimism or pessimism of the day. Most of us have been tempted by the thought that economics plays an unfortunately slight role in the market and that investor psychology may in fact be more important. Indeed, there is good historical reason for one to feel that people are anything but rational when it comes to investing. Charles Mackay, in his *Memoirs of Extraordinary Popular Delusions and the Madness of Crowds*, points out (1869, pp. vii–viii):

"In reading the history of nations, we find that, like individuals, they have their whims and their peculiarities; their seasons of excitement and recklessness, when they care not what they do. We find that whole communities suddenly fix their minds upon one object, and go mad in its pursuit; that millions of people become simultaneously impressed with one delusion, and run after it, till their attention is caught by some new folly more captivating than the first. We see one nation suddenly seized, from its highest to its lowest members, with a fierce desire of military glory; another as suddenly becoming crazed upon a religious scruple; and neither of them recovering its senses until it has shed rivers of blood and sowed a harvest of groans and tears, to be reaped by its posterity. ... Money, again, has often been a cause of the delusion of multitudes. Sober nations have all at once become desperate gamblers, and risked almost their existence upon the turn of a piece of paper."

Mackay's history outlines a number of remarkable financial events in history (1869, pp. 1–92). First, there was John Law's Mississippi scheme, which sold shares to the French public in a company that was to have a monopoly of trade in a province of French Louisiana called Mississippi. Shares in the Mississippi scheme were eagerly bought up by French investors who knew that this "growth stock" could not help but make them rich. After all, it was common knowledge that Louisiana abounded in precious metals. They were correct in the long run. Two hundred fifty years later, Louisiana was one of the oil centers of the world!

Next, there was the South Sea Bubble which induced Englishmen to speculate on a trading monopoly in an area (the South Atlantic) owned by a foreign power (Spain) that had no intention of allowing the English into the area for free-trading purposes. The fevers produced by the South Sea spilled over into other "bubbles," one of which proposed to build cannons capable of discharging square and round cannon balls ("guaranteed to revolutionize the art of war") and another that sought share subscribers to "a company for carrying on an undertaking of great advantage, but nobody to know what it is" (1869, p. 53).

The Tulipomania, which engulfed 17th-century Holland, provides yet another example. Fortunes were made (and later lost) on the belief that every rich man would wish to possess a fine tulip garden (and many did, for a while at least). Tulip bulb prices reached astronomical levels, as one speculator bought bulbs to sell at higher prices to a second speculator who purchased to sell at even higher prices to yet another speculator. The term "bigger fool theory" of investing was coined based on this history.

Even as Mackay was writing, Jay Gould and Jim Fisk were busily manipulating the value of the shares of the Erie Railroad in the United States. After the War Between the States (1861–1865), northern financial speculators rode roughshod over the South. It was common practice at this time for directors in many companies to buy up war-ravaged properties cheaply in order to "build" railroads that had no chance of being successful. With the success of the government-sponsored transcontinental railroad (Union Pacific/Central Pacific), the idea was to raise money on the stock exchange, fool investors, and then issue information causing the price of their firm's stock to rise. They then sold their shares at inflated prices to the unsuspecting public. Some months later, they would release discouraging information about the company's prospects, in the meanwhile selling short the shares of their company. When the new information drove the price of the shares down, the directors would cover their short positions, again reaping nice profits at the expense of the unaware (see Adams and Adams, *Chapters of Erie*, 1956).

These shenanigans followed throughout the rest of the 19th century and into the decade of the 1920s. After the First World War, the United States entered a recession that was followed by an incredible financial boom. As Frederick Lewis Allen has pointed out in *Only Yesterday* (1964), it was a time when "the abounding confidence engendered by Coolidge Prosperity ... persuaded the four-thousand-dollar-a-year salesman that in some magical way he too might tomorrow be able to buy a fine house and all the good things of earth" (1964, p. 227). The binge started in 1924 with the Florida land boom, where "investors" paid large sums of money for plots that turned out in many cases to be undeveloped swampland, and ended in October 1929, with the stock market crash (see Galbraith, *The Great Crash*, 1954).

It was with the background of these speculative binges, and the Great Depression that followed, that John Maynard Keynes wrote *The General Theory of Employment, Interest, and Money* (1936). Keynes believed that much of man's endeavors (including the stock market) were not well explained by economic theory. He felt that "animal spirits" exercised greater influence on many economic decisions than the "invisible hand." His reasoning was based partly on a very acute understanding of human nature and a lack of faith in the credibility of many of the inputs that go into economic decision making. He argued, "... our existing knowledge does not provide a sufficient basis for a calculated mathematical expectation. In point of fact, all sorts of considerations enter into the market valuation which are in no way relevant to the prospective yield" (1936, p. 152). He would thus condemn many of the procedures to be outlined in the following pages of this book on the grounds that "... the assumption of arithmetically equal probabilities based on a state of ignorance leads to absurdities" (1936, p. 152).

Keynes felt that the stock market was a battle of wits more like a game of Snap, Old Maid, or Musical Chairs than a serious means of resource allocation. One of his favorite metaphors was to compare the "game" to the newspaper competitions in which contestants try to pick the prettiest faces, a prize being given to the person who comes closest to choosing the girls most often selected by the other competitors. In this instance, each competitor is not really interested in selecting the prettiest girls. He is, rather, trying to assess which girls *everyone else* will think are the prettiest. In the stock exchange, pretty girls are replaced by equities that one speculator believes will appeal to other speculators. He said, "A conventional valuation which is established as the outcome of the mass psychology of a large number of ignorant individuals is liable to change violently as the result of a sudden fluctuation of opinion due to factors which do not really make much difference to the prospective yield; since there will be no strong roots of conviction to hold it steady" (1936, p. 154).

Many practitioners even today (eight decades later) agree with Keynes' arguments. They feel that the lessons of history reveal economic analysis to be a bankrupt approach to making an investment decision. It is suggested that esoteric discussions of whether or not the stock market is efficient are meaningless because whim and fancy are more important than yield calculations in setting the prices of securities. Stock prices move up or down depending on the mood of the public. Frenzy and unbridled optimism make for bull markets, and gloom and severe pessimism produce bear markets. The states of optimism and pessimism often have little basis in economic fact.

Although much of what has been said above would appear to have a great deal of merit, the reader would be ill-advised to throw his or her hands up in despair at the impossibility of making rational investment choices. We believe that one still can learn more about investments from an analytical study of the subject than one would if he became a psychologist or metaphysician. The very presence of Keynes and others like him has forced a re-examination of many of the assumptions underlying the investment process. Keynes' contribution in aggregate economic policy has led to a less volatile business cycle than in the past, and this has made it easier for those who do attempt to make superior long-run forecasts to at least influence (if not govern) the market.

The advent of the computer also made it possible for analysts to engage themselves in the task of interpreting large quantities of data. Although it may be doubtful that we have entered the world of perfectly efficient capital markets, it is likely that the very chaotic world that Keynes described has passed. In some respects, we live in ideal times for the modern, well-versed analyst. Markets are not so perfect that all opportunities for better-than-average returns are eliminated, and they are not so imperfect as to render impossible the task of making rational choices. Ironically, however, it is also massive computational power which has enabled rapid calculations to contribute to systemic financial crashes and contagion of scale sufficiently large to capture even the most detached observer's attention in the 21st century. More will be said about this in the coming chapters.

Financial Information

To a degree, the EMH rests on the assumption that all investors (except insiders) have similar information at their disposal. Moreover, the EMH is predicated on the notion that all data have been digested by the market and that the current price of a security reflects all available information. Opponents of the efficient market view advise that information is neither perfectly nor equally available and investors may interpret information differently. Since information is clearly important as a foundational input for both pro and anti EMH views, we shall examine several major sources.

First, a great deal of information is generated by agencies and services that prepare reports for the investing public. These reports vary from general economic forecasts to very concrete analyses of industry and corporate prospects. Moody's and Standard & Poor's (S&P) both supply numerous bulletins and reports on a regular basis. They prepare substantial reference papers and online research, which are updated regularly to include the most recent financial information about thousands of companies. Moody's and S&P also publish detailed reports on individual corporations including informative reports on thousands of stocks in detail. Charts of price performance over time as a history of important financial statistics and an analysis of the background and prospects for individual companies are updated regularly (about once every 3 months as new quarterly reports are published by companies) and are available from most stockbrokers and online.

Value Line publishes ratings and reports on hundreds of stocks that are somewhat more specific than either Moody's or S&P. Value Line ranks stocks in terms of quality, potential short-term and long-term price performance, and yield. Securities are appraised by Value Line analysts and are given a normative market value.

Brokerage and investment banking firms also publish reports that analyze and evaluate individual companies and securities. These reports are normally provided to customers at no specific charge (the cost is actually included in commissions and other fees that are generated from their customers). Many firms maintain staffs of analysts who specialize in one or more industry.

In addition to the reports catalogued above, there are a number of private investment letters that are distributed to paid subscribers. These letters often cost hundreds of dollars, and some have been prepared for years and are widely respected.

Much of the data and most of the reports previously outlined are available to a large audience. Thus, if one of the leading investment firms puts out a "buy" recommendation on a particular stock, that knowledge would most likely be made available to most other participants in the market. Thus, there would be a tendency for this information to be fairly rapidly incorporated into the price of this stock, and it might advance accordingly. If only data of this sort existed, there would be good reason to accept the EMH. There are other kinds of information, however, that may not be easily gained or understood. Important data are not always available to the general public, and even when widely disseminated some information is not easily interpreted. Data in the latter category often appear in the financial press and require specialized knowledge for proper understanding.

For example, many of the articles that are found in *The Wall Street Journal*, *Barron's*, *Forbes*, *Investors' Business Daily*, and other such publications are very specific and provide obvious inputs for the appraisal of a firm. Frequently, however, it is not easy to make sense of an isolated fact that may be reported about a particular company. Consider the case of a firm reporting its most recent quarterly earnings. Suppose that the results are immediately carried by *The Wall Street Journal* and that the reported earnings were up significantly from the previous quarter and from the same period (quarter) in the previous year. What does this mean? The average reader might assume that the report is bullish and that the firm has done well. However, he or she looks at the price of the firm's stock and finds that it went down with the publication of the information. How can this be explained? One possibility is that professional analysts who had been scrutinizing the company very carefully for years had expected the firm to do even better than the reported figures and were disappointed by the result. Another possibility is that the market had discounted the good news (that is, the improvement was expected and the price of the stock had been previously bid up accordingly). When the news was not quite as good as expected, the market realized that it had over-anticipated the result, and the price thus had to fall.

Information of this sort can often bewilder the "little" investor, and even the seasoned analyst is sometimes surprised by the way the market reacts to certain new information. Of course, it is situations such as these that make possible above-average stock market performance. The investor who went against the crowd with the belief that the firm was not going to do as well as others expected and sold his shares (or took a short position) would have profited. Here, of course, superior forecasting or a better understanding of the situation would have enabled the shrewd investor to realize better-than-average returns.

The inputs that go into independent appraisals may include publicly available information, such as a corporation's annual report, but these data will be uniquely interpreted. Moreover, the professional analyst may have access to certain inputs that are not generally known to the public. Competent securities analysts spend many hours each week interviewing corporate officers and employees of the firms that they follow. The capable analyst learns how to take clues from what managers say and use these clues to good advantage. This is not quite as good as inside information (which is illegal to provide or receive), but the really top analysts can sometimes deduce facts from evidence garnered that equals that possessed by management. These fellows are rare, however, and they are very highly paid. Because there are so many pieces of information available, it is fortunate that computers that have large memory banks and can perform sophisticated calculations rapidly and accurately are available.

The Securities Markets

A market exists whenever there is an exchange of goods, services, or other property. For a market to be competitive, it usually must be sufficiently large so that any buyer (seller) can purchase (sell) whatever quantity he or she wishes at the going price (that is, the price set through the interaction of all buyers and sellers together).

The U.S. securities markets generally satisfy the size requirement since billions of dollars worth of stocks and bonds are traded daily here. This does not mean that there is a good market for every stock or bond outstanding. If there is sufficient trading volume (numerous transactions) in a particular security, it may be possible for trades to take place at a price very near the most-recent past transaction price. However, there are numerous stocks (and many more bonds) that trade in very thin markets where the number of transactions is so small that one may have to bid well above the last price to buy or ask well under that price to sell. Such a market is neither perfect nor efficient. Whether or not a particular stock or bond is traded in a mostly efficient market may depend on the "floating supply" of the issue outstanding. A stock with only 100,000 shares in the public hands that "turns over" only 10 percent of the issued and outstanding shares annually (that is, 10,000 shares) will probably not have market depth. Such a security may show rather substantial price volatility from one transaction to the next, and no one buyer (seller) could accumulate (sell) more than a few shares at any one time without affecting the price.

Most stocks that are traded on an organized exchange have some degree of market depth. Although the total dollar volume of securities transactions on exchanges is less than in the over-the-counter-market (i.e., unorganized markets), it is generally the case that the dollar volume per security is greater for listed securities. However, this will not always be true. The government bond market is conducted almost exclusively over-the-counter, and the dollar volume of specific government issues can be quite large. Furthermore, some stocks that are widely held and actively traded are not listed on any exchange. Also, most exchanges have listing requirements that are designed to guarantee market depth. The New York Stock Exchange (NYSE), for example, requires that a firm have a minimum number of shares outstanding in the hands of a minimum of record shareholders. Additionally, a stock which trades only infrequently would not usually be a candidate for listing.

Organized securities markets have existed for some time. Securities were trading as early as 1602 in Antwerp, and an organized exchange existed in Amsterdam by 1611. Almost all major countries (including Communist China) have at least one major exchange. In North America, the NYSE and the NASDAQ are by far the most important exchanges. In Canada, the Toronto Stock Exchange lists most leading Canadian industrial securities and a large number of mining and oil and gas securities as well. Other exchanges in foreign markets are even more important. Many securities are traded on more than one exchange. An advantage of dual listing is that extra trading hours may be secured for a firm's stock. Some securities also trade in the "third market," which is the over-the-counter (OTC) market for stocks that are also listed on an exchange. Both dual listing and third market trading tend to increase the depth of the market for a stock and hence contribute to greater market efficiency.

Any securities transaction that does not take place on an exchange is said to be an OTC trade. The OTC market consists of numerous brokers, traders, and dealers who "make a market" in bonds and shares and are ready to buy or sell to each other and the investing public. Business is conducted via telephone or computer, and there may be no formal signal to other investors when a transaction has taken place. On an exchange, there is a record for each transaction, and an investor can observe the last price at which the security was traded. He or she may call a broker or follow the market online and find out at what price a particular stock opened (its first price for the day) and obtain the current quotation. In the OTC market, there may be no information available about the most recent transaction, and one's broker can only secure bid and ask prices on a security. A bid price is the amount that is offered for the purchase of a security; an ask price is the amount required by a seller. A "spread" between the bid and ask prices that serves to compensate those who make a market in the issue will typically exist. Depending upon the depth of the market, spreads may vary from 1 or 2 percent to as large as 5 percent.

Transactions in the primary market are OTC trades. The primary (new issue) market is the first sale or new issue market. All Initial

Public Offerings (IPOs) are new issues. When a firm (or government) sells its securities to the public, it is a primary transaction. After a bond or share is in the hands of the public, any trading in the security is said to be in the secondary market. Both exchange and OTC transactions can be secondary trades. Purchases of securities in the primary markets are usually made through investment bankers who originate, underwrite, and market new issues to the public. A corporation will arrange to "float" an issue through its investment bankers and is given a price for its securities that reflects market conditions, prices on equivalent securities (either the company's or those of similar concerns), and the costs involved to the investment bankers to distribute the securities. Title is customarily taken by the underwriting syndicate (several banking houses) on a "firm commitment" basis where the bankers "underwrite" or guarantee the price, although small corporations usually have to settle for a "best efforts" distribution in which the bankers merely act as selling agents for the company. The primary IPO market has been quite popular in recent years for speculative investors. The reason for this popularity is the fantastic upward price movement experienced by many stocks after initial sale. The primary markets, particularly for unseasoned firms, are clearly affected by investment banking practices that do not encourage market efficiency. Nevertheless, it is very difficult to price an issue that has never before traded.

Trading Securities

Technically speaking, a securities dealer maintains an inventory of securities in which he makes a market by purchasing and selling from his own account as a principal; thus, the OTC market is maintained by dealers. A broker acts as an agent for his customer in purchasing or selling securities on the floor of the exchange or from a dealer in the OTC market and he or she is expected to obtain the best available price for the customer. A commission is paid for these services. The investment banker advises issuers of securities and purchases such issues for resale to syndicates of dealers (the banker is generally prominent in such a syndicate) and ultimate resale to the public (with a commission allowance for brokers and dealers who are not members of the syndicate). The simplest order to a broker to buy or sell a security at the best available price is a "market order." In the OTC market, the broker would check dealer quotes and execute the order at the best available price. On an exchange, the broker would typically determine the best available price and execute the order.

There are other types of orders. A "limit order" specifies a maximum (minimum) price that the customer is willing to pay (receive) to buy (sell) the stock. A "stop order" provides a price above (below) the current market price of the stock that, if reached by the market, the customer desires to trigger a buy (sell) market order. For example, a "stop loss" order might be entered at a price a few points below the current market price to limit downside risk exposure. If that price is reached, the order is reached, the order is put in line for execution.

The brokerage business has changed a lot over the past few decades. Stocks used to be traded in "eighths" and "quarters" ($12^1/_2$ cents and 25 cents). For example, the price of a stock might be quoted at "$10^1/_2$ bid, $10^5/_8$ asked." This meant bidders were willing to pay $10.50 per share and sellers wished to receive $10.625 per share. The resulting spread of $0.125 often went into the pocket of the brokers making the trade. Today, stocks are traded in pennies ($10.50 bid, $10.51 asked) so that spreads are much lower. Also, decades ago the practice was to charge fixed commission rates per 100 shares of stock traded. This often meant that large quantities of shares (say 100,000 share orders) generated huge commissions for brokers.

With the advent of negotiated commissions and substantial price competition, trades are often made at almost no spread and at commissions of less than a penny per share at discount brokers. Reduced revenues resulting from negotiated commissions coupled with the higher costs of doing business have altered the structure of the brokerage industry. A number of less efficient houses have failed, been merged with stronger concerns, or undertaken voluntary liquidation. Several large investment banking firms have collapsed as well (e.g., Lehman Brothers, Bear Stearns, etc., in the 2008–2009 crash).

The old days of getting an MBA, going to Wall Street, and getting rich in the brokerage business have passed. However, this increased competition has undoubtedly improved the efficiency of the stock market. (The bond market is another matter about which we address later in this book.)

Regulation of Securities Markets

A major element that also may have contributed to the increased efficiency of the U.S. securities markets is the regulation of those markets by the federal government. Before 1933, there were no federal laws governing stock exchanges or investment house activities, and widespread manipulation and questionable practices abounded. Although some states had adopted securities laws (called "blue sky" laws), in general corporations were not required to provide information to investors, and fraudulent statements (or no statements at all) were regularly issued by many companies. With the advent of the New Deal (the policies adopted by Franklin Roosevelt after his election as President of the United States in 1932), a number of laws were passed to prevent a recurrence of the events that led to the 1929 crash. Among these were major reforms of the securities business.

The Securities Act of 1933 was passed early on in the Roosevelt administration. It required full and complete disclosure of all important information about a firm that plans to sell securities in interstate commerce. Issues of securities exceeding a minimum in dollar value, and all issues sold in more than one state, must be registered with an agency of the federal government. (That agency became the Securities and Exchange Commission, or SEC, under another act passed the next year.) A prospectus must be prepared by the issuing company and distributed to anyone who is solicited to buy the securities in question. The prospectus must include all pertinent facts about the company, such as recent financial reports, its current position, a statement about what will be done with the funds raised, and a history of the company. Data about the officers and directors of the company are also required. Details about the firm's objectives, its primary business activities, projected financial statements (including any assumptions made), foreseeable risks to the enterprise, and the offering price of the shares must be spelled out. In the case of a new bond or note issue, how interest and principal will be paid must also be outlined.

The Securities Exchange Act of 1934 created the SEC. The Act was designed to regulate the securities markets and institutional participants in the market, such as brokers and dealers. All exchanges are required to register with the SEC, although much of the supervision of individual exchanges is left up to the governing bodies of each exchange. The 1934 Act also regulates the governance of publicly held entities. Regulations require any company with a given amount of assets and a minimum number of shareholders of record, or any listed on an exchange, to file numerous reports with the SEC. Included are Forms 10-K (a detailed annual filing which will be discussed later in this book), 10-Q (a somewhat less detailed quarterly filing), and 8-K (a filing required in the case of a special event or change in the firm's circumstances such as the resignation of a member of the company's board of directors). A "Proxy Statement" is also required indicating when and where the firm's annual meeting is to take place. The Statement contains much detailed information that we will further address later. (For a more complete discussion on the issues of "going public" from the firm's perspective, see Williams and Napier, *Essentials of Entrepreneurship*, 2013, pp. 257–268.)

Other important legislation regarding securities and the securities business include the Public Utility Holding Company Act of 1935, the Trust Indenture Act of 1939, the Investment Company Act of 1940, and the Investment Advisors Act of 1940. These acts regulate the operations and financial structure of gas and electric holding companies; require that bonds (and similar forms of indebtedness) be issued under an indenture that specifies the obligations of the issuer to the lender and that names an independent trustee to look after the interests of lenders; regulate the management and disclosure policies of companies that invest in the securities of other firm; and require the registration of investment counselors and others who propose to advise the public on securities investment.

Margin Purchases

It is possible to buy or sell stock (deemed a "short sale" discussed below) without putting up the entire purchase price. Such a transaction is called buying "on margin" or a "margin purchase." For example, suppose Mr. Brown bought 400 shares of Apple at 149.90 on 50 percent margin. The purchase would be $59,960 plus brokerage commissions. Say Brown used a discount broker and the commission was $40. His total cost would be $60,000. Brown would only be required to put up $30,000. The remaining $30,000 would be borrowed either from his broker, a bank, or other financial institution. Margin purchases may increase (or decrease) the rate of return earned by an investor. If Apple went up 15 points, Brown would have made $6,000. Without leveraging the purchase, his gain would have been $6,000/$60,000 = 10 percent. If he had paid 5 percent interest on the margin balance and held the stock for a year, his net gain would be: $6,000 − (0.05)($30,000) = $4,500, or $4,500/$30,000 = 15 percent (less commissions if he sold the stock). Of course, margin purchases increase one's risk exposure as well. If Apple went down 15 points Brown's loss would be −($6,000 + $1,500), or −$7,500/$30,000 = 25 percent (again, with commissions further subtracted if he sold the stock).

Prior to the New Deal reforms of the 1930s, investors could buy stock on less than 10 percent margin. Substantial leveraged returns were earned so long as stock prices were advancing. When prices began to collapse in late 1929, however, many people were wiped out in a matter of days. Adding to the problem, investors tended to build their margin positions as prices rose by buying more shares with the profits earned. Thus, one might have put $1,000 into stock worth $10,000 in January 1929. As prices advanced by 20 percent, say, in February, he or she might have used the $2,000 profit to buy another $10,000 worth of stock. The commitment was still the original $1,000, but the investor now owned $20,000 in stock. As prices rose further, he or she might have increased his or her position to, say, $25,000. The margin in the investor's account, however, remained at only $1,000 (or 4 percent of the value of the stock). Even a small decline in price (say 1 percent, or $250) would prompt a "margin call," and the investor would have to come up with another $250 in cash, typically by the next trading day. If the investor could not raise the $250, enough stock would be sold to cover that amount. Now suppose prices fell just a little more, say 4 percent. This decline would be enough to wipe out the investor's entire investment. Furthermore, if many investors were "playing the market" on margin at the same time, their collective selling might tend to drive the market down by even more than it would have gone down otherwise.

The 1929 crash caused many investors to be sold out of their stocks as prices fell. The process of liquidating shares as prices went below margin levels caused further price declines which resulted in more liquidations. As Thompson, Williams, and Findlay observe (2003, p. 22), "The snowballing effects of this phenomenon produced the major crash of October 29, 1929 and contributed to the subsequent collapse of both the stock market and the American economy." As a consequence of the problems directly traceable to margin purchases, the Securities Exchange Act of 1934 gave the Board of Governors of the Federal Reserve System the power to set margin requirements for all stocks and bonds. Thompson, Williams, and Findlay continue (2003, p. 22), "Since 1934, margins have been allowed as low as 40 percent but have also been as high as 100 percent (no borrowing permitted). To some extent, the sobering experiences of 1929 caused a natural reaction against margin purchases in subsequent years." Nevertheless, there are those in the market today who have only read about 1929 and would, if given the chance, follow their grandfathers and great-grandfathers down the same speculative path. Thus, "Big Brother" (Uncle Sam) considers it his job (among thousands of other such assignments) to protect these people from themselves. In so doing, perhaps the economy in general is saved from the effects of stupid people making bad decisions.

Insider Trading

The Securities Exchange Act of 1934 regulates "insider trading." The Act defines officers, directors, and holders of more than 10 percent of the shares of a firm as insiders. Such persons are required to file a statement of their holdings of the firm's stock and any changes in such holdings with the SEC (this is done on a Form 4, which must be filed within days of any purchases or sales). Insiders are also required to file a Form 144 with the SEC indicating an intention to sell securities. Form 144 contains information about prior sales of the company's shares as well as a statement on how the shares being sold were acquired (market purchases, options exercised, stock grants, etc.).

Profits made by insiders on shares held less than 6 months must also be reported and may be legally recovered by the firm (through a shareholders' derivative suit if necessary); in addition, malfeasance suits could be filed for other injuries to shareholder interests.

Over the years, holdings of related persons have come to be included in the determination of whether the 10 percent rule was met and persons related to insiders were also considered to be insiders for the purpose of the law. In general, the principle was established that insiders and their relatives should not gain a special benefit over other shareholders by virtue of the information about the firm they possess. The Texas Gulf Sulphur case of the mid-1960s, in which corporate insiders withheld information about a mineral's discovery until they could obtain stock, clearly re-established this point through both civil and criminal action.

Other cases have greatly expanded the concept of insider information. During the 1970s, in the Douglas Aircraft and Penn-Central cases, brokerage houses obtained insider information (of bad earnings and impending bankruptcy, respectively) and informed selected institutional investors before the general public. Subsequent suits and SEC and stock disciplinary actions against the brokerage houses involved (and suits against the institutions) found that second and even third-hand possessors of inside information may be classed as insiders. In the Equity Funding case, information which did not even originate from the company itself but rather from former employees was considered inside information. It is more or less true today that insiders are deemed such, more on the basis of the information they possess than the positions they hold in regard to the firm. The rule best to keep in mind is, if one knows something about a company that has not been announced publicly, it is best NOT to trade (or even tell others) about such until the information is made public.

The current state of insider trading was in major flux just prior to the writing of this book, with a pending U.S. Supreme Court decision which would decide how much "tooth" is still in the insider trading law. In 2014, the Second Circuit Federal Appeals Court in Manhattan upended the government's campaign to quash insider trading, imposing the greatest limits on prosecutors in a generation.

It reversed the conviction and threw out the case conviction for U.S. v. Newman, against two former hedge fund traders Todd Newman and Anthony Chiasson. This decision was based on the doctrine of insider trading rules articulated in 1983 as a result of Dirks v. SEC, known as the cornerstone of insider trading law. Raymond Dirks was a star security analyst, and he heard from a whistle blower that an insurance company Equity Funding was hiding insolvency; he informed the SEC, which did nothing; he told journalists, who did nothing; so, he told clients, who then dumped their stock, depressed the price, making the press pay attention. The SEC was embarrassed. It went after Dirks, and the case was taken to the Supreme Court, which defined "safe harbor" as follows: the tippee who is given the inside information is liable only when the tipper receives a direct or indirect personal benefit from the disclosure". U.S. v. Newman was challenged by the Second Circuit but was denied a ruling by the Supreme Court on October 2, 2015. Critics of the 2nd Circuit court decision said it reflected a naive view of how information is now traded on Wall Street. Wall Street can be described as a big "favor bank" with a culture of reciprocity.

On the other hand, a former investment banker for Citigroup, Mahar Kara, leaked confidential info about takeover deals to his brother Mounir Kara, who passed them to their sister's fiance, Bassam Salman, who made $1.3 million on trades. These are essentially the same facts found in U.S. v. Newman, but with a conviction. Salman was found guilty on September 1, 2011, and appealed to the 9th Circuit U.S. Court of Appeals in California, which upheld the guilty verdict in Salman v. U.S. (2014), rejecting the Newman reasoning. At that time, there were two sets of law in the country governing the same conduct. The dispute between the two federal appellate courts was resolved, when the U.S. Supreme Court affirmed the conviction on December 6, 2016.

As an interesting aside, given the increasingly important role of government regulation, it was not illegal for U.S. Congressmen and Senators and their staff members to trade on not-publicly announce information about the progress of legislation until 2012. One Democratic Senator (well known for his bombastic defense of the "little man" from Wall Street and corporate greed) knew that legislation was going to be passed which would change patent law and harm the drug industry. This great defender of the public good (and a multi-millionaire to boot due to his shrew investment in a rich widow) sold all of his drug stocks BEFORE the public knew these facts. For an act that would have sent a corporate insider to prison, the Senator was not even subject to reprimand by his colleagues.

Short Selling

When one sells a security, he or she does not own but borrows from someone else to make delivery, he or she is said to sell that security "short." The device has been used for years and can be defended on economic grounds even though it does sound a bit immoral to be selling something one does not own. An investor might consider selling a security short if he or she believes its price is going to decline. One would simply call his or her broker and ask to sell so many shares of such and such company short at a given price. If the broker could find the shares for the customer to borrow (usually from securities held by the broker in its own account or securities margined with the broker), the transaction could be effected. This can even be done in online accounts for most large companies where the public float is large. Because short selling can tend to exacerbate downward movements in stock prices, it is easy to see how speculative excesses could occur through unregulated use of the device. Thus, the Securities Exchange Act of 1934 allows the SEC to set rules for short selling.

Stock Market Indicators

Investors need to have benchmarks to measure how their respective efforts compare with the "market" in general. Professional money managers are often paid by how much they can beat "the market." Perhaps the most widely known benchmark is the Dow Jones Industrial Average (DJIA). This stock price comparative is an arithmetic average that appears in *The Wall Street* each day. The DJIA is computed by taking the price of each of 30 selected blue-chip stocks, adding them, and dividing by a divisor. The divisor initially was the number of stocks in the average (originally 12); but because of the obvious biases of stock splits (a two-for-one split would tend to cause the price of a share to fall by one half), the divisor was adjusted downward for each split. The divisor is now just above 0.16 (yes, it is actually a multiplier since it has been reduced to a number below 1 for many years).

In addition to the DJIA, there is a Dow Jones Transportation average of 20 stocks, a Dow Jones Utility average of 15 stocks, and a composite average of all 65 stocks. Each is computed in the same manner as the DJIA.

For many investors, the Dow Jones averages are the market. When an investor checks the market or asks his or her broker to ask what the market is doing, he or she is very likely to get a response such as "down 105." The broker means, of course, that the DJIA is down 105 points. This information may have very little to do with what the investor really wants to know (that is, how are my stocks doing?). The DJIA is not an overall indicator of market performance, although many use it as if it were. In fact, only blue-chip stocks are included in the average. The thousands of other stocks that are not blue chips are not represented. Moreover, the DJIA has been criticized by many even as a measure of blue-chip performance. Because the DJIA merely adds the prices of all included stocks before applying the "divisor," a stock that sells for a higher price receives a larger weight in the measurement.

Most professional investors follow the S&P Indices. S&P computes a number of indices including the S&P 500, S&P 100, and specialized indices for foreign and specific industries. These indices include both the price per share of each stock and the number of shares outstanding. These figures thus reflect the total market value of all the stocks in each index. The aggregate number is expressed as a percentage of the average value existing during 1941–1943 in the case of the S&P 500, and the percentage is then divided by 10. The S&P Indices are better overall measures of stock market performance than the Dow because more securities are included. Furthermore, the statistical computation of the S&P indexes is superior to the Dow Jones method.

It should be remembered that the major U.S. and global stock indexes are in fact a filter on the investable universe. Although some indexes such as the Russell indexes and others are managed entirely on quantitative criteria, the most widely followed indexes have the most powerful filter, and are managed by the Index Committees of S&P Global Inc., headquartered in New York City, NY. The committees meet monthly; according to the S&P Global index methodology documentation, "the Index Committee reviews pending corporate actions that may affect index constituents, statistics comparing the composition of the indices to the market, companies that are being considered as candidates for addition to an index, and any significant market events. In addition, the Index Committee may revise index policy covering rules for selecting companies, treatment of dividends, share counts or other matters." Components of the Dow Jones Indexes are selected from the S&P 500 universe and maintained in accordance with committee rules such as company reputation, demonstrated sustained growth, and potential interest to a large number of investors. Maintaining adequate sector representation within the indices is also a consideration in the selection process. The

DJIA index committee's changes since 2000 are summarized below:

DJIA Constituent Changes Since 2000
Current to October 31, 2016

Date of Change	Dropped from Average	Added
January 27, 2003	Name changes only	Name changes only
April 8, 2004	AT&T, Eastman Kodak, and International Paper	American International Group, Pfizer, and Verizon
November 21, 2005	SBC renamed AT&T Inc.	AT&T through SBC acquisition
February 19, 2008	Altria Group and Honeywell	Bank of America and Chevron
September 22, 2008	American International Grouip	Kraft Foods Inc.
June 8, 2009	Citigroup and General Motors	Cisco Systems and Travelers
September 24, 2012	Kraft Foods Inc.	UnitedHealth
September 23, 2013	Alcoa, Bank of America, and Hewlett-Packard	Goldman Sachs, Nike, and Visa
March 19, 2015	AT&T	Apple

In this timeframe, it would appear that the index committee did not perform a service in making these changes, although some of them were inevitable given the bankruptcy of firms like General Motors and Eastman Kodak. The compound annual growth rate (CAGR) for the DJIA from 1/3/2000 to 12/15/2016 was around 2.6 percent (excluding dividends); however, had the constituents been left alone, the CAGR would have been 3.5 percent. Incidentally, the decade 2000–2009 is called the "lost decade" on Wall Street, for its lackluster decade performance.

30   *Quantitative Financial Analytics*

Although there is no single perfect indicator of average performance (at least for measurement purposes), there is a high correlation between the price movements of all stocks. Thus, if most stocks are going up (or down), almost any measure will indicate this. In fact, the 88 year correlation of returns for the DJIA, S&P 500, and NYSE indexes are all over 96 percent.

The 1929 Crash

Several times in this chapter, we have made reference to the stock market collapse of 1929. As an event, it rivaled both world wars and the Great Depression that followed. Figure 1.1 portrays movements in the DJIA from 1920 to 2016 (almost a century). Notice the upward trend throughout most of the 1920s. The trend was snapped in the late 1920s, but most analysts thought this was a normal correction to the bull market that came earlier. Opinion changed dramatically on October 24, 1929, a day that became known as "Black Thursday."

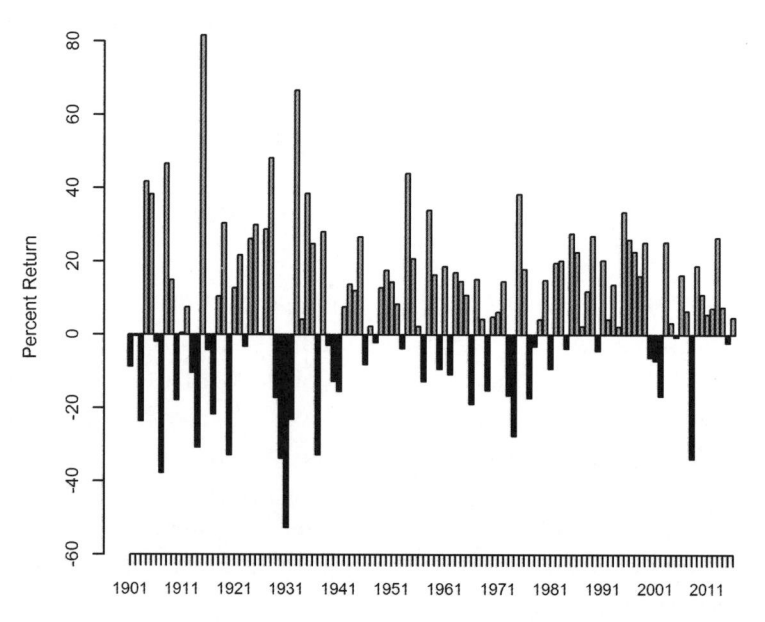

Figure 1.1. Changes in the DJIA, 1901–2016

The DJIA opened at 306 that day and fell about 11 percent during intraday trading. It closed down only 2 percent, but the decline capped a down movement from the record high close of 381 reached on September 3. Even though the market had witnessed 20 percent negative changes in the past, such a dramatic collapse in just a few weeks was cause for alarm. Commercial banks were allowed to buy common stock in those days, and a consortium of New York banks including Morgan, Chase, and National City Bank began buying on Friday to inspire confidence. Such measures had been taken during earlier panics when the House of Morgan alone could stem a bear tide. This time things were different. The market was simply too large for one bank or even three of the largest in the country to keep the collapse from getting worse. Although the market rose on Friday, by Monday it fell to 260. On Tuesday, October 29, 1929, the DJIA entered what became the largest rout in its history, falling 11 percent alone that day to 230. The date became known as "Black Tuesday" and market participants noted the drop from 381 to 230 (40 percent) in less than two months. Many a fortune was lost on this single day alone as margin calls came flooding in.

The market did not bottom until July 8, 1932, closing at 41.22. By then, the market had lost about 90 percent of its value. The Great Depression was in full swing at this point and numerous previously quite wealthy people were reduced to poverty (even selling apples on the street to earn a crust of bread). Some even committed suicide. Causes for the crash were many, including institutional flaws in the system. However, "irrational exuberance" was certainly one of the most important. Many of the institutional flaws were corrected by New Deal legislation in the 1930s (see above), but irrationality remains even to this day. This is evidence that market efficiency may prevail but only in a world where market participants are not at all rational. We shall return to this conclusion many times in this book.

By the way, those who say not to panic but wait out the bottoms would have had quite a time back in the 1930s, 1940s, and 1950s (see Figure 1.1). The market did not get back to its former high of 381 until November 23, 1954! A man born, say, in 1897 would have been 32 when the crash occurred. He would have been 57 before he got even (ignoring dividends, which were mostly eliminated during the 1930s but were paid in the 1940s through 1954). One of the author's father was just such a person. He wound up putting most of his savings into U.S. Savings Bonds and eventually federally insured savings deposits. He and most of the people he knew never trusted the stock market again as an investment vehicle.

Summary

Every individual who has more money than he or she needs for current consumption is potentially an investor. Whether surplus funds are placed in a bank at a guaranteed rate of interest or used to invest in an oil well, an investment decision must be made. These decisions may be made wisely or foolishly, but the intelligent investor will seek a rational, consistent approach to managing one's money.

Numerous investment media exist that the investor may consider. The simplest is the insured deposit at a commercial bank. Such accounts provide safety of principal and liquidity. At the opposite end of the asset spectrum are highly illiquid investments (real estate, oil well interests, paintings, coins, stamps, antiques, and even ownership of business enterprises). These investments require very specialized due diligence, and are beyond the scope of this book. In between the insured bank deposit (or Treasury bill) and the very illiquid assets are a host of investments that can generally be described as securities. A security is an instrument signifying either ownership or indebtedness that is negotiable and that may or may not be marketable.

For 50 years now, a school of thought has developed that argues that only insiders and those privileged to have information not known to the rest of us can make large profits in the stock market. These people subscribe to a theory of stock prices called the EMH. EMH advocates argue that the current price of a stock contains all available information possessed by the market and only new information can change stock prices. Since new information becomes available randomly, there should be no reason to expect any systematic movements in stock prices or returns.

Others (including many academic historians) maintain that the stock market is neither competitive nor efficient. It has been observed that securities speculation in the past has been far from scientific and that emotion rather than reason has usually guided the path of stock prices. These inefficiency proponents believe that people are governed principally by their emotions and that bull and bear markets are merely reflections of the optimism or pessimism of the day. Most of us have been tempted by the thought that economics plays an unfortunately slight role in the market and that investor psychology may in fact be more important. Indeed, there is good historical reason for one to feel that people are anything but rational when it comes to investing.

To a degree, the EMH rests on the assumption that all investors (except insiders) have similar information at their disposal. Moreover, the EMH is predicated on the notion that all data have been digested by the market and that the current price of a security reflects all available information. Opponents of the efficient market view advise that information is neither perfectly nor equally available and investors may interpret information differently. A major form of such information is that supplied by research agencies and services. A number of reports are also periodically prepared by investment advisory companies. These are designed to aid the investing public in making decisions. An important feature of the established service and agency reports is that they are available to large audiences. Thus, the data that are contained in them could be expected to be incorporated in stock prices just as soon as the information is published.

Another EMH implicit assumption is the presence of large, well-behaved securities markets. A perfectly competitive market is one where there are many buyers and sellers, no one of which can influence price; where perfect information is available to all participants in the market; where a homogeneous commodity is traded in the market; and where free entry of sellers and buyers into the market is observed. The securities markets may satisfy these requirements for some securities but not for others. In general, stocks traded on an organized exchange will have a more efficient market than those that are traded OTC, because exchanges have listing requirements designed to guarantee market depth.

A major element that also may have contributed to the increased efficiency of the U.S. securities markets is the regulation of those markets by the federal government. Before 1933, there were no federal laws governing stock exchanges or investment house activities, and widespread manipulation and questionable practices abounded. Although some states had adopted securities laws (called "blue sky" laws), in general corporations were not required to provide information to investors, and fraudulent statements (or no statements at all) were regularly issued by many companies. With the advent of the New Deal (the policies adopted by Franklin Roosevelt after his election as President of the United States in 1932) a number of laws were passed to prevent a recurrence of the events that led to the 1929 crash.

The Securities Act of 1933 was passed early on in the Roosevelt administration. It required full and complete disclosure of all important information about a firm that plans to sell securities in interstate commerce. Issues of securities exceeding a minimum in dollar value, and all issues sold in more than one state, must be registered with an agency of the federal government. (That agency became the Securities and Exchange Commission, or SEC.)

The Securities Exchange Act of 1934 created the SEC. The Act was designed to regulate the securities markets and institutional participants in the market, such as brokers and dealers. All exchanges are required to register with the SEC, although much of the supervision of individual exchanges is left up to the governing bodies of each exchange. The 1934 Act also regulates the governance of publicly-held entities. Other important legislation regarding securities and the securities business include the Public Utility Holding Company Act of 1935, the Trust Indenture Act of 1939, the Investment Company Act of 1940, and the Investment Advisors Act of 1940.

It is possible to buy or sell stock without putting up the entire purchase price. Such a transaction is called buying "on margin" or a "margin purchase." As a consequence of problems directly traceable to margin purchases during the 1920s, the Securities Exchange Act of

1934 gave the Board of Governors of the Federal Reserve System the power to set margin requirements for all stocks and bonds. Another practice that caused problems prior to 1933 was the short sale. This process is still permitted, although the SEC may make rules governing its use.

In order to determine whether one has earned above (or below) market returns, one must have a good measure of the average performance of stocks in general. No perfect indicator exists. The most widely used average is the DJIA. The DJIA is primarily a blue-chip measure, although many investors use it for overall market activity. S&P computes indices that have a larger base than the Dow Averages. The S&P measures are also statistically superior to the Dow calculation.

References

Adams, C. F. and Henry Adams, *Chapters of Erie*. Ithaca: Great Seal Books, 1956.

Allen, F. L., *Only Yesterday*. New York: Harper & Row, 1964.

Cootner, P. H., ed., *The Random Character of Stock Market Prices*. Cambridge: The M.l.T. Press, 1964.

DePamphilis, D. M., *Mergers, Acquisitions, and Other Restructuring Activities*, 6th ed. New York: Academic Press, 2012.

Fama, E. F., "Random Walks in Stock Market Prices," *Financial Analysts Journal*, September–October 1965, pp. 55–59.

Fama, E. F., "Efficient Capital Markets: A Review of Theory and Empirical Work," *Journal of Finance*, May 1970, pp. 383–423.

Galbraith, J. K., *The Great Crash*. Boston: Houghton-Mifflin Co., 1954.

Graham, B. and D. Dodd, *Security Analysis*. New York: McGraw-Hill, 1934.

Graham, B., D. Dodd, and S. Cottle, *Security Analysis*, 6th ed. New York: McGraw-Hill Book Company, 2009.

Keynes, J. M., *A Tract on Monetary Reform*. London: McMillan & Co., 1923.

Keynes, J. M. *The General Theory of Employment, Interest, and Money*. New York: Harcourt, Brace, and World, 1936.

Lee, Ruben, *What is an Exchange? The Automation, Management, and Regulation of Financial Markets*. New York: Oxford University Press, 1998.

Mackay, C., *Memoirs of Extraordinary Popular Delusions and the Madness of Crowds*. London: George Routledge and Sons, 1869.

Rubinstein M., *A History of the Theory of Investments*. New York: John Wiley & Sons, 2006.

Taleb, N., *The Black Swan*. New York: Random House, 2007.

Thompson, J. R., E. E. Williams, and M. C. Findlay, *Models for Investors in Real World Markets*. New York: John Wiley & Sons, 2003.

Williams, E. E. and H. A. Napier, *Essentials of Entrepreneurship*. Chicago: T.&N.O. Book Co., 2013, pp. 257–268.

Chapter 2

Financial Mathematics

Gentlemen, if the man who invented compound interest had of secured a patent on his idea he would have had without any doubt the greatest invention the world has ever produced.
                              Security Investment Co., 1916

Introduction

The financial economics texts typically begin with a discussion of compound interest, yields, and returns. Others then turn to probabilistic considerations such as stochastic finance. Here, we step back a bit and consider the underpinnings of financial mathematics and some of its applications.

Although some of the techniques in this book require the use of computers and programming languages, with Monte Carlo resampling techniques, the bulk of financial mathematics is still performed in spreadsheets, or with high-powered hand calculators. Indeed, soon these calculations will be carried out on the reader's handheld communication device. It is nonetheless humbling to note that many multi-billion dollar deals are estimated, calculated, and "what-if-ed" with the lowly HP-12C financial calculator.

In essence, there is nothing out of the ordinary in financial mathematics not encountered in usual practice, except for the following three additional axioms which are generally not stated: the axioms of Value, Time, and of the Time Value of Money (TVOM). Although the following concepts deliver the reader to a minefield of philosophical considerations, we hope that he or she will absorb the basic ideas and consult appropriate texts for the other nuances which will arise.

Axiom of value

There exists an asset X, which can be exchanged for another asset Y. We may possess $2X$ irrespective of the value of X expressed in terms of the reference asset Y. Suppose X may be exchanged for $3Y$. We say the *price* of the asset in terms of Y is 3. Then the value of X with respect to Y is $3Y$, or $V_Y(X)X_Y = 3$. In this case, the holding of $2X$ is worth $6Y$.

The formal name for this framework is numeraire analysis, and it is mostly outside the scope of this text. However, this and other concepts are not unusually hard to grasp, so we will mention them here. The fundamental point of numeraire analysis is that the asset valuation for non-arbitrage assets can be made in terms of any convenient reference asset. A non-arbitrage asset is any asset which retains its fundamental existence irrespective of any reference asset valuation, such as physical gold, or (non-dividend paying) shares in a company, or a bond which pays a terminal value at time $t = T$. In contrast, an outright holding of currency (for example dollars, $) is considered an arbitrage asset since another buyer can buy back the asset using funds upon which interest has been earned.

For our purposes, we are generally concerned with the reference asset of currency, i.e., we exchange X for $/€/¥/£, etc., and we normally hold such assets over multiple periods of time. For convenience and consistency with the majority of texts, therefore, we will usually express assets $X(t)$ valued in a home currency with customary symbols, such as F (futures), S (stocks), C/P (calls and puts), V (derivative contracts), B (bonds), or D (dividends of cash flows).

Axiom of time

We treat time in a unidirectional sense, i.e., time moves "forward," in most systems it progresses "to the right." Indeed, almost all physical systems have in their implicit axioms the rule that future states are not known, i.e., the system is *causal*. Thus, $\forall s, t$ and $t \geq s$, we say

t is a later time than s; or, from an outside perspective, t is "in the future with respect to s."

As we discuss in Chapter 9, utility can be applied to time and value. In this book, our concern is generally about making allocation decisions at the present for cash flow streams occurring in the future, or *vice versa*. We do not generally spend too much time on past allocations. These are considered in accounting terms as sunk costs/opportunities. So, most cases in finance deal with present and future values.

We are again ignoring the philosophical aspects of the existence, definition, and progression of time. Occasionally, we might make a distinction between spatial dimensions (the world we live in) and a set of spatial dimensions onto which the time dimension is added.

(a) Beginning points: For making a reference to a beginning point in time we say $t = t_0$. For $s, t \in R$, there are applications where $t = (s, t) \in R^k, k > 1$.

(b) "Ending" (Horizon) time: $t = h$ or $t = T$. For any two points in between, $t \geq s$, we can define $\Delta t = t - s \geq 0$, which is often notated as $\tau = t - s \geq 0$, although we normally reserve τ for continuous time, or time-to-horizon presentations. In many applications, $\tau = h - t_0, t_0 = 0$ and $h \equiv T$ such that $\tau = (T - 0) = T$.

(c) Increments of time: In general, $\tau \in \mathcal{T}$, is an index set, giving $\Delta \tau = \tau_n - \tau_m$. There are various ways to deal with increments in this notation. The simplest way is to restrict ourselves to "periods" of variable lengths of time, not necessarily equal, or $\Delta t = t_k - t_{k-\tau}$. Here, "$\tau$" has developed a new use, as an increment.

An even simpler way to express increments is to use countable index sets $\mathcal{T} \equiv T$ so that $\Delta t = t_k - t_{k-l}$, where l is an integer. This has the added benefit of freeing up our symbol τ for more widely used definitions (see below).

Yet another simplification is to restrict attention to $l = 1$, or $\Delta t = t_k - t_{k-1}$. This permits a simple, intuitive, and discrete system.

Suppose we translate our time frame of reference to $t_0 = 0$, and consider n periods of equal length Δt. Then our horizon $h = n\Delta t$, which we can also write as $t = t_N$. Using years, for example.

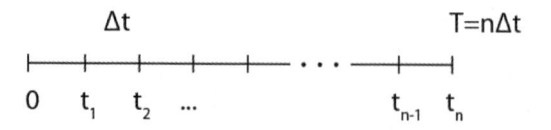

```
        Δt                              T=nΔt
   |----+----+----+----+-- ... --+----|
   0    t₁   t₂                 t_{n-1}  t_n
```

Here, we have $t_0 = 0$ years, $\Delta t = 1$ year, and $h = n\Delta t$, sometimes written with N being the maximum number of periods. Note that with $t_0 = 0$, $T - t_0 = n$ (or N).

(d) Arbitrary point with respect to T: For an arbitrary point t:

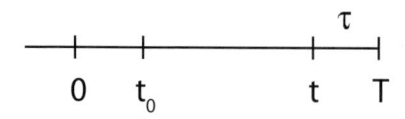

```
                        τ
   |----+----------+----|
   0    t₀         t    T
```

We can define a "time remaining" in an analysis as $\tau = T - t$. For $t = t_0$, $\tau = T - t_0$ is the "full" horizon time.

For example, suppose a time-dated instrument is scheduled to expire 1 month from the day it comes into existence. Then at the outset the time to expiration (TTE) is 1 month, or 100% of its lifetime. Thus, $t_0 = 0$, $T = 1$, so $\tau = T - t = 1$(month). One week later, $t = \frac{1}{4}$ and $\tau = T - t = \frac{3}{4}$(month). Note that 1 second before trading stops on this option, $\tau \approx 0$ (1 trade-second).

For another example, a time-dated instrument with 90-day (3-month) maturity changes hand 1 month from issue. Thus, $\tau = T - t = 3 - 1 = 2$ months $= 60$ days.

Axiom of time value of money (TVOM)

For a currency (for example, a dollar), $\$(t) > \$(t+k), \forall k > 0$. That is, the value of a dollar today is more than the same dollar at some time in the future, since in general it may have been invested in a money market instrument earning a positive rate of interest. Time has a price, denominated in percent of principal involved. This relation has been in operation for millennia and has been mathematically described at least since Fibonacci in 1202 AD. This is also true in spite of the near zero-interest rate environment that prevailed from 2009–2016. Even in a zero-rate regime, statistical considerations require the TVOM axiom, since events which decrease the asset's reference value (price) can always occur in the time interval $[t, t+\Delta t)$.

Future and Present Value

Simple and compound interest

A good part of financial analysis depends upon calculations of compound interest. This is because the time horizon in finance is usually long, and so some method must be obtained to compare financial flows over time. Because of the TVOM axiom, and the fact that financial flows may be "invested" at some positive rate of interest, a flow received today is worth more than an equal flow received in the future. This idea may be expressed as a very simple equation:

$$D_n = D_0 \overbrace{(1+i)(1+i)\cdots(1+i)}^{n}, \qquad (2.1)$$
$$D_n = D_0(1+i)^n,$$

where D_0 is a financial flow (number of dollars) invested today; D_n is the value n periods from now of the invested flow D_0; and i is the periodic rate of interest by which D_0 will grow for n periods, held constant in this equation.

Thus, if $1,000 is put into a savings account today and is left there for one year at a rate of interest of 5 percent compounded and paid annually, that sum will be worth $1,050 after one year. If the $1,000 is left on deposit for two years, at the end of the second year it would be worth:

$$D_n = \$1{,}000(1.05)^2 = \$1{,}102.50.$$

The factor $(1+i)^n$ may be obtained immediately using a calculator, a spreadsheet, or the formulas in Appendix A. Thus, if $1,000 is left on deposit for 20 years (assuming annual compounding), at the end of that period it would be worth:

$$\$1{,}000(2.653) = \$2{,}653.00.$$

Continuous compounding

Interest may be compounded more often than once per year. When interest is compounded several times during the year, we interpret as follows:

Let:

t = number of years
T = horizon time $(n \cdot t)$
r = annual interest rate (using 12% in the example)
D_0 = $1,000 initial investment
m = Compounding frequency

Annual: $m = 1$

$$D_T = 1{,}000(1+r)^1 = \$1{,}120.$$

Semi-annual: $m = 2$

$$D_T = D_0\left(1+\frac{r}{m}\right)^{mt} = D_0\left(1+\frac{r}{2}\right)^{2t}$$
$$= \$1{,}000 \cdot (1.06)^2 = \$1{,}123.60.$$

Quarterly: $m = 4$

$$D_T = D_0\left(1+\frac{r}{4}\right)^{4t} = \$1{,}000 \cdot (1.03)^4 = \$1{,}125.51.$$

Daily: $m = 360$.

There are various conventions for the number of days in the year. For fixed income investments, the most common numbers in use are 360 and 365 (calendar days). Which one is intended will be specified in context, or by industry standard. Business (trading) days are about 252 per year. The actual number of days in a year, 365.25, is almost never used

$$D_T = \$1{,}000 \cdot \left(1 + \frac{r}{360}\right)^{360t} = \$1{,}127.47.$$

Note that although the terminal value is going up with the compounding frequency, it appears to be approaching a limit, which it is, and may be written as

$$\lim_{m \to \infty} (1 + r/m)^{mt} = \lim_{m \to \infty} \left(1 + \frac{rt}{mt}\right)^{mt} = e^{rt}. \qquad (2.2)$$

Thus, $D_T = D_0 e^{rt}$.

Continuous compounding is an unusual species. It even reportedly puzzled the great Einstein. In our example, $D_T = \$1{,}000 e^{0.12t} = \$1{,}000 e^{0.12} = \$1{,}127.50$. We first note that the change from 360 to continuous compounding did not make much difference. Although some rules such as the *rule-of-72* give rough ideas of the compounding relationship, they result in terminal values which invariably are non-intuitive. (The *rule-of-72* posits that dividing an interest rate into 72 will result in the approximate number of years required for an investment to double.) In our 1-year example, if we were to calculate this amount over a 20-year period, the compound factor would be $e^{0.12 \cdot 20} = 11.0231$; yet, it takes 48 years at an interest rate of 5 percent to attain the same terminal value of 11.0231.

In most practical finance applications, semi-quarterly, quarterly, or perhaps monthly compounding is typically sufficient, continuous compounding is mostly used for approximating and for mathematical and conceptual reasons. It is, however, widely used in financial engineering.

Annuity values

When funds are deposited periodically to an account, the terminal or annuity value of the payments is given by a series of the following type:

$$V_n = D_0(1+r)^n + D_1(1+i)^{n-1} + \cdots + D_n(1+i)^{n-n},$$

$$V_n = \sum_{t=0}^{n} D_t(1+i)^{n-t}. \qquad (2.3)$$

Each payment has its own terminal value of $D_t(1+i)^{n-t}$, until the final payment at D_n which earns no interest, and indeed would be withdrawn as soon as it is deposited. An alternate annuity value is made by excluding this final payment, or

$$V_n = \sum_{t=0}^{n-1} D_t(1+i)^{n-t}. \tag{2.4}$$

If the deposits are equal over time, i.e., $D_0 = D_1 = D_t = D$, we have

$$V_n = D\sum_{t=0}^{n-1}(1+i)^{n-t},$$

or

$$\frac{V_n}{D} = \sum_{t=0}^{n-1}(1+i)^{n-t}.$$

This latter term is the compound value of an annuity and can be calculated with some small amount of additional work, or can be calculated using Appendix A.

In the case of continuous compounding, Equation (2.3) becomes

$$V_n = \int_0^n D(t)\left(1+\frac{i}{m}\right)^{m(n-t)} dt.$$

In the limit we find

$$V_n = \int_0^n D(t)e^{i(n-t)} dt.$$

Assuming i and D are constant we may integrate to obtain

$$V_n = \frac{D}{i}(e^{in} - 1). \tag{2.5}$$

Present value and discounting

A *present value* (PV) is the value today of funds received in the future. It is, in effect, the reverse operation of a compounded sum. Thus, if we know D_n dollars will be received n periods from now, and if we know the rate of interest, we can determine the PV, D_0, of that future sum. This process is described simply by rewriting

Equation (2.1) in the following form:

$$D_0 = \frac{D_n}{(1+i)^n} = D_n(1+i)^{-n}. \tag{2.6}$$

Again, the PV factors may be easily calculated, or the reader may refer to an appropriate PV table. This interest rate i is often referred to as a *discount rate* since it is the factor which deflates a future value to the present, reflecting the fundamental axiom of TVOM. Determination of the appropriate discount rate is a thorny issue.

Discounting can also be calculated based on a more frequent discounting program, or even continuously, exactly as we did for future value. For continuous discounting, we have

$$D_0 = D_t e^{-rt}. \tag{2.7}$$

For annuities, the PV of future payments is

$$\text{PV} = V_0 = D_0(1+r)^{-0} + D_1(1+i)^{-1} + \cdots + D_n(1+i)^{-n}, \quad \text{or}$$

$$V_0 = \sum_{t=0}^{n} D_t(1+i)^{-t}. \tag{2.8}$$

When the payments D_t vary from year to year, the PV must be obtained after some computer programming, or by manually adding each term using discount factors. Most financial calculators and other applications have built-in routines to accommodate the user input of differing incomes streams.

If the payments are constant over time, however, Equation (2.8) may be simplified to

$$V_0 = D \sum_{t=0}^{n} (1+i)^{-t}. \tag{2.9}$$

Similar to how we obtained (2.4), if we assume that the first payment is received 1 year from now, then the equation becomes

$$\frac{V_0}{D} = \sum_{t=1}^{n} (1+i)^{-t}. \tag{2.10}$$

The factor on the right-hand side of (2.10) may be computed.

Capitalization of an income stream

Under continuous compounding assumptions, the basic PV Equation (2.6) becomes

$$V_0 = \int_0^n D(t)e^{-it}dt. \tag{2.11}$$

If $D(t)$ and i are constant, Equation (2.11) can be integrated to give

$$V_0 = \frac{D}{i}(1 - e^{-in}). \tag{2.12}$$

Note that if the constant income stream continues indefinitely, as $n \to \infty$ the equation reduces to

$$\text{PV} = V_0 = \frac{D}{i}. \tag{2.13}$$

This last equation is a very important one, and the process underlying the equation is frequently referred to as capitalization. A number of financial instruments have very long (or infinite) lives. A perpetual bond, for example, promises to pay a coupon of a constant amount forever. Such an instrument may be evaluated very quickly with Equation (2.13). In forecasting cash flows of a company, for example, detailed predictions may be made for a near-term horizon, with the out-years being modeled by (2.13), using an economic growth rate for perpetuity. Common stocks may also be valued with this equation, but one must be careful about growth assumptions in this case. For a firm that pays a reasonably constant dividend, the equation is adequate. For a growth stock where D is increased over time, the assumption of a constant $D(t)$ is violated, and the equation is inappropriate.

Financial Returns

Jokes about return "of" capital aside, return on investment is one of the underpinnings of the investment paradigm. As we stated in Chapter 1, we have the expectation of a return in a reasonable period of time, along with safety of that return, as well as safety of the investment itself.

Gross returns

These are also called *total returns*. Financial returns can be considered a growth factor of an investment S, and are quite similar to future value, depending on the compounding scheme. To make a working definition, for time t, we define a 1-period return as

$$R_t = \frac{S_t}{S_{t-1}}. \tag{2.14}$$

Clearly, $S_1 = S_0 R_1$. Here, the "return" R_1 represents the growth of the investment. Although it is not necessary to do so, one can decompose this *gross return* into a return of principal plus a simple growth rate (which could be an interest rate) r in 1 period, we have that $S_1 = S_0(1+r)^1$. However, that is an example of a definition of a marginal return; we will see that gross returns provide a much simpler analysis framework.

Suppose we have a dollar-denominated asset $S(t) \equiv S_t$ which exhibits the following growth factors over 4 periods:

$$R_1 = 1.10$$
$$R_2 = 1.05$$
$$R_3 = 0.95$$
$$R_4 = 1.20.$$

Assuming observable market prices, these growth factors are easily obtained using (2.14). Since $R_t = S_t/S_{t-1}$ and $S_t = S_{t-1}R_t$, and beginning with $S_0 = 100$, we have

$$\begin{aligned} S_1 &= S_0 R_1 = 100(1.10) = 110, \\ S_2 &= S_1 R_2 = S_0 R_1 R_2 = 110(1.05) = 115.5, \\ S_3 &= S_2 R_3 = S_0 R_1 R_2 R_3 = 115.5(.95) = 109.725, \\ S_4 &= S_3 R_4 = S_0 R_1 R_2 R_3 R_4 = 109.725(1.20) = 131.67. \end{aligned} \tag{2.15}$$

The terminal value is quite easy to determine given the gross returns. We state our terminal asset value as S_T, and note from the above that $S_T = S_0 \prod_{t=1}^{T} R_t = S_0 R_T$, where the terminal gross return is R_T. Again,

$$\begin{aligned} R_T &= (S_1/S_0)(S_2/S_1)\cdots(S_4/S_3) \\ &= S_4/S_0 = S_T/S_0 = \Pi R_t. \end{aligned} \quad (2.16)$$

In our example, we have $R_T = 1.3167$. It is rather pleasant that the terminal gross return is independent of the time granularity of the price series; neither is it sensitive to unequal increments. Using, for example, the commodity cotton, from 9/8/11 to 9/6/12, there were 252 trading days which saw the price descend from 105.02 to 75.59 (¢/lb), giving a terminal return of 0.736. This will be the same regardless of whether the prices are monthly, yearly, daily, or sporadic, so long as the beginning and ending dates have data and are properly recorded.

Since the gross returns are always greater than or equal to 0, discounting and compounding is somewhat more straightforward with returns as opposed to the general PV or future value of varying income streams. The fundamental value of study is the terminal value of an investment, which is easily observable for historical data, and its analysis follows below. Determining a future terminal value, however, is the essence of the problem of investments analysis.

As an aside, however, it should be noted that the return calculation can be difficult if the payment streams change sign over the time period in question. This rarely happens for financial instruments like bonds and stocks where investors pay for an income stream and the only sign change takes place from the time of investment ($t = 0$) with a negative sign and the payments received (all future t's) with positive signs. However, this same procedure can apply to the purchase of any asset (say a machine or plant and equipment) which may require infusions of cash in future periods that might result in a negative net payment (additional investment). Each time there is a sign change there may be another return solution. In essence, we have a polynomial with n roots, and a solution for each root. If there is only one sign change, there will only be one solution (positive or negative). With many sign changes, there may be many solutions, including positive and negative real numbers, irrational numbers, or imaginary numbers. For additional discussion and examples, see Appendix A.

Incremental returns

While gross returns are quite useful, it is however completely natural to want to have at our disposal measures of *incremental return*. We examine the relative merits of 3 useful definitions of incremental returns. Each one of them is applicable in individual periods, or over an entire time horizon.

(a) Absolute differences: We could define an incremental return as $\Delta S_t = S_t - S_{t-1}$. This would give us a series of the absolute changes in the asset price, from which we could reconstruct the terminal value. However, apples/oranges problems arise if you try and compare say changes in cotton prices with those of other assets. In the case of cotton in the previous example, ΔS is -29.43, but for median home sale prices in a neighborhood, or for yacht prices, the difference could easily be $50,000.

(b) Relative returns: The most widely used method of relative comparison is to scale the change by the initial asset value, i.e., $\Delta S/S$. This is $\frac{S_t - S_{t-1}}{S_{t-1}} = R_t - 1 = r_\%$, or what we call the *percent change* in the asset price (*percent return*), and is highly engrained in the most quantitatively literate people's psyche. If you start with an asset at $50, and sell at $55, you have made a 10% "*return.*" Colloquially we use r, or r_{pct}, instead of $r_\%$. In fact, you have made a 10 "*percent return.*" Unfortunately, neither the sum nor the average of percent returns applied to the original asset price will recover the terminal value, which feature we need for subsequent, consistent analysis.

(c) Mathematical returns: We define a mathematical return

$$r = \ln(R) = \ln(S_t/S_{t-1}) = \ln S_t - \ln S_{t-1} = \Delta \ln S.$$

This return r, sometimes written as r, is close to but not exactly the same as $r_\%$ and is vastly different for large differences. That they are close is seen by the mathematical approximation for the log function, as $r = \ln(R) \approx \ln(1 + r_\%) = r_\% - \frac{r_\%^2}{2} + \frac{r_\%^3}{3} - \cdots \approx r_\%$. Using the second-order term makes for quite a nice approximation, and also shows that $r < r_\%$. Note that this approximation is only good in the range $|r_\%| < 1$; however, since in many years there are hundreds of stocks which lose 50 percent or more of their value, and there may be many dozens which experience more than 100 percent positive returns, a symmetric relative return is compelling. The log function transforms the gross return into symmetric excursions as we will later show.

(d) Useful identities: Given $r_\%$ and r, some identities are as follows:

$$R = 1 + r_\% = e^r, \tag{2.17}$$

$$R = \frac{S_t}{S_{t-1}} = 1 + r_\% = 1 + \left(\frac{S_t}{S_{t-1}} - 1\right) = e^{\ln(S_t/S_{t-1})} = e^r. \tag{2.18}$$

(e) Rates of return: The arithmetic rate of return μ over an interval $[t, t + \Delta t]$ is defined as

$$\frac{r_\%}{\Delta t} = \frac{S_{t+\Delta t} - S_t}{\Delta t \cdot S_t}.$$

The *instantaneous rate of return* is obtained as $\Delta t \to 0$, where we have

$$\frac{dS_t}{dt} \cdot \frac{1}{S_t} = \mu,$$

or

$$\frac{dS_t}{dt} = \mu S_t.$$

Similarly, the log rate of return is defined as

$$\frac{\ln R}{\Delta t} = \frac{\ln(S_{t+\Delta t}/S_t)}{\Delta t} = \mu,$$

with $\Delta t \to 0$ giving the *instantaneous log rate of return*

$$\lim_{\Delta t \to 0} \frac{\ln S_{t+\Delta t} - \ln S_t}{\Delta t} = \frac{d \ln S}{dt} = \frac{dS_t}{dt} \cdot \frac{1}{S_t} = \mu,$$

again with $dS_t/dt = \mu S_t$. When μ is a constant, the solution for S_t is obtained by an elementary guess and is $S_t = S_o e^{\mu t}$, the formula for compound interest. Note that both instantaneous arithmetic and log rates of return give the same progression formula for S_t.

Summary measures

Since we normally deal with large data sets, or at least reasonably lengthy series of data, a way of summarizing the period returns is necessary for gauging how well one investment performs relative to another. What we need is a summary growth rate for comparative purposes. Consider the example returns in Table 2.1.

There is no doubt that the terminal return is 1.3167, obtained as $\prod_i R_i$, but how might we summarize the period incremental returns? We will examine the expected, average, and compound average growth rates.

(a) Expected (mean) growth rate: A logical statistical solution to the summary growth issue is to use expected return, $E(R)$. Unfortunately, in this configuration, R is a random variable with an unknown probability distribution. If we knew the distribution we might be able to estimate its parameters, but great minds have been trying to determine this distribution of R for over 60 years, without success, and not without great effort. So we will agree to defer developing some new theory of market return distributions for another time.

Table 2.1. Comparison of Returns

R	$r_\%$	r
1.1	0.1	0.095
1.05	0.05	0.049
0.95	−0.05	−0.051
1.20	0.2	0.182
R_T 1.3167	?	?

52 *Quantitative Financial Analytics*

(b) Average (sample mean): This is quite a logical choice we have, using percent returns, here denoted as r,

$$\bar{R} = \frac{1}{n}\sum_{i=1}^{n} R_i = \frac{1}{n}(1 + r_1 + \cdots + 1 + r_n)$$

$$= \frac{1}{n}\left(n + \sum r_i\right) = 1 + \bar{r}. \quad (2.19)$$

Using our data in Table 2.1, $\bar{R} = 1.075$. This measure is useful in some applications but has the disadvantage that it will not recover R_T. That is, $R_T \neq \Pi\bar{R} = \bar{R}^N$. Using $\bar{R}$, we obtain for the terminal value $R'_T = 1.3355$. It is always the case that:

$$R_T \leq \bar{R}^N, \quad (2.20)$$

which can be verified mathematically.

(c) Compound annual growth rate: Consider the geometric mean $\widehat{R} = (\Pi R_i)^{1/N}$ of the gross returns:

$$\widehat{R} = (\Pi R_i)^{1/N} = (R_T)^{1/N} = \sqrt[N]{R_T}. \quad (2.21)$$

$\widehat{R}$ has the definitional property that $\widehat{R}^N = R_T$, and that the compound average growth rate (CAGR), $r' = \widehat{R} - 1$, is such that the terminal value is always recovered as R_T. This r' is sometimes called the *internal rate of return* (IRR) of an investment, but the IRR is not perfectly suited to this simple analysis, so we prefer the standard term CAGR.

Using the definitions, we have the following tautology:

$$R_T = \frac{S_T}{S_0} = (1 + r')(1 + r') \cdots (1 + r') = (1 + r')^N,$$

$$= \widehat{R}^N = (\Pi R_i)^{\frac{1}{N}N} = \Pi R_i = R_T. \quad (2.22)$$

We also have the following constraint:

$$\widehat{R} \leq \bar{R} \Rightarrow r' \leq \bar{r}. \quad (2.23)$$

So in summary, our CAGR is calculated as

$$r' = \sqrt[N]{R_T} - 1. \quad (2.24)$$

And using our Table 2.1 data, we calculate $\widehat{R} = 1.07123$, giving $r' = 0.07123 < \bar{r} = 0.075$. Of course, $(1 + r')^4 = 1.07123^4 = 1.3167 = R_T$.

(d) Other considerations: Using the notation that $\ln R_t = r_t$, we have

$$\ln \widehat{R} = \frac{1}{N} \ln(\Pi R)_i = \frac{1}{N} \sum \ln R_i = \overline{\ln R},$$

or the average log return $\bar{r}$. Thus, $\widehat{R} = e^{\bar{r}}$, and

$$R_T = \widehat{R}^N = e^{n\bar{r}} = e^{\sum r} = e^{r_1} e^{r_2} \cdots e^{r_N} = R_1 R_2 \cdots R_N.$$
(2.25)

The symmetry of log returns is very compelling. Consider the table of realistic returns found in Table 2.2. The shaded section of the table clearly shows the symmetry; the non-shaded areas depict the percent returns which have no symmetry.

Table 2.2. Symmetry of Log Returns.

R	r (%)	r
100	9,900	4.605
10	900	2.303
5	400	1.609
2	100	0.693
1.333	33.333	0.288
1.25	25	0.223
1.10	10	0.095
1.05	5	0.049
1.01	1	0.01
1	0	0
0.99	−1	−0.01
0.95	−5	−0.051
0.90	−10	−0.105
0.85	−15	−0.163
0.667	−33.333	−0.405
0.5	−50	−0.693
0.2	−80	−1.609
0.1	−90	−2.303
0.01	−99	−4.605

54   Quantitative Financial Analytics

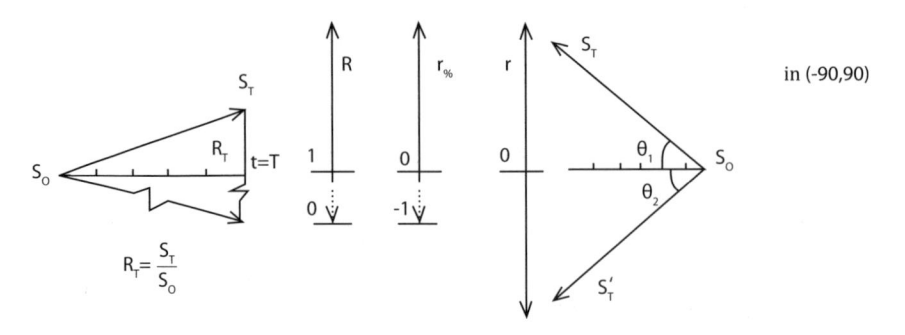

Figure 2.1. Geographical Relationship of Returns

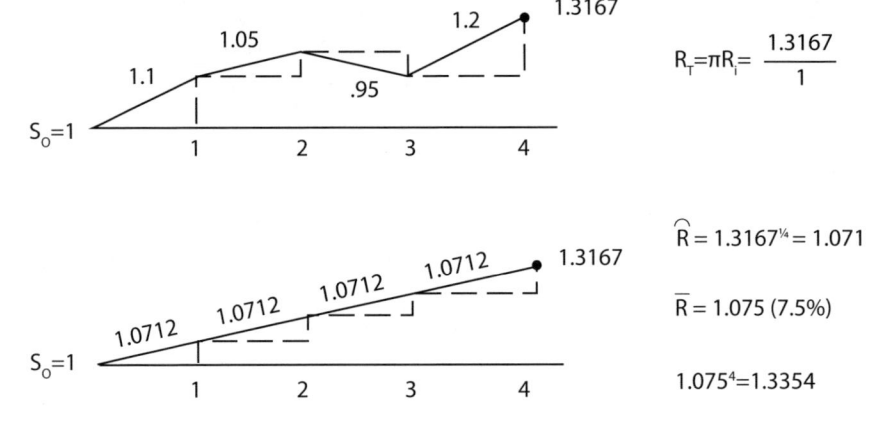

Figure 2.2. Equivalent Terminal Values

This symmetry is easily explained as $\ln(1/R) = \ln R^{-1} = -\ln R$. Again considering $t = T$, and $R_T = S_T/S_0$, the returns can be diagrammed as shown in Figure 2.1 (assuming $S_0 = 1$).

The resulting reconstitution of the terminal values is illustrated in Figure 2.2.

Although log returns are mathematically useful and interesting, their use is not as widespread in finance as are percent returns. We argue that percent returns of 10,500 percent are cognitively meaningless and that another approach should be used. Note from Table 2.3 that for any given year, there are a large number of stocks

Table 2.3. 1-year Extreme Returns[a]

Date	Total	Worse Returns			Better Returns		
		Returns	Num	Percent	Returns	Num	Percent
Jan-85	230	−50%	4	1.70	100%	10	4.30
		−75	1	0.40	200	3	1.30
		−90	1	0.40	300	1	0.40
		−99	0	0	500	0	0
Jan-87	466	−50%	17	3.65	100%	8	1.72
		−75	5	1.07	200	0	0
		−90	1	0.21	300	0	0
		−99	0	0	500	0	0
Jan-99	4,096	−50%	378	9.20	100%	518	12.60
		−75	88	2.10	200	223	5.40
		−90	26	0.60	300	121	3.00
		−99	4	0.10	500	61	1.50
Jan-01	4,186	−50%	577	13.80	100%	224	5.40
		−75	205	4.90	200	66	1.60
		−90	73	1.70	300	23	0.50
		−99	24	0.60	500	7	0.20
Jan-05	4,787	−50%	277	5.80	100%	178	3.70
		−75	53	1.10	200	25	0.50
		−90	19	0.40	300	6	0.10
		−99	3	0.10	500	1	0
Jan-08	5,050	−50%	2,080	41.19	100%	15	0.30
		−75	783	15.50	200	2	0.04
		−90	223	4.42	300	1	0.02
		−99	18	0.36	500	0	0
Jan-10	4,641	−50%	133	2.90	100%	239	5.10
		−75	33	0.70	200	32	0.70
		−90	11	0.20	300	9	0.20
		−99	2	0	500	0	0

[a]Extreme returns formed from January holdings for all U.S./Canadian stocks exceeding marketcap and liquidity constraints.

whose 1-year returns exceed either a 100 percent gain or a 50 percent loss. Other scalings are possible which have more intuitive appeal than extreme percent units.

One such scaling is the "decibel" scale, indicated in the third column in Table 2.4. This has been shown to be a natural scaling

Table 2.4. Presentation of Extreme Returns.

R	r (%)	Ln R	10 $\text{Log}_{10} R$
101	10000	2.004	20.04
21	2000	1.322	13.22
10	900	1.000	10.00
6	500	0.778	7.78
5	400	0.699	6.99
4	300	0.602	6.02
3	200	0.477	4.77
2	100	0.301	3.01
1	0	0.000	0.00
0.50	−50	−0.301	−3.01
0.33	−67	−0.477	−4.77
0.25	−75	−0.602	−6.02
0.10	−90	−1.000	−10.00
0.05	−95	−1.301	−13.01
0.01	−99	−2.000	−20.00

when perceived by the human mind, although there are still surprises with that. More work needs to be done in this area; a better scaling is required in order to handle changes in the negative area, as well as from negative to positive values, or from very small to moderate values, etc.

Summary

There is nothing out of the ordinary in financial mathematics not encountered in usual practice, except for the following three axioms which are generally not stated: the axioms of Value, Time, and of the TVOM. Although the following concepts deliver the reader to a minefield of philosophical considerations, we hope that he or she will absorb the basic ideas and consult appropriate texts for the other nuances which will arise.

A good part of financial analysis depends upon calculations of compound interest. This is because the time horizon in finance is usually long, and so some method must be obtained to compare financial flows over time. Because of the TVOM axiom, and the fact that financial flows may be "invested" at some positive rate of interest, a flow received today is worth more than an equal flow received in the future. In most practical finance applications, semi-quarterly, quarterly, or perhaps monthly compounding is typically sufficient; continuous compounding is mostly used for approximating and for mathematical and conceptual reasons. It is however widely used in financial engineering.

A PV is the value today of funds received in the future. It is, in effect, the reverse operation of a compounded sum. Thus, if we know X dollars will be received n periods from now, and if we know the rate of interest, we can determine the PV, Y, of that future sum.

Return on investment is one of the underpinnings of the investment paradigm. We have the expectation of a return in a reasonable period of time, along with safety of that return, as well as safety of the investment itself. Gross returns are also called total returns. Financial returns can be considered a growth factor of an investment and are quite similar to future value, depending on the compounding scheme. While gross returns are quite useful, it is however completely natural to want to have at our disposal measures of incremental return. We examined the relative merits of 3 useful definitions of incremental returns. Each one of them is applicable in individual periods, or over an entire time horizon. These are absolute differences, relative returns, and mathematical returns.

Problems

1. How much will $5,000 be worth in 10 years if the rate of interest is 10 percent under conditions of annual compounding? Quarterly compounding? Continuous compounding?
2. Let $250 be placed in a savings account that pays interest of 1 percent per quarter compounded quarterly. How much will it be worth after 1 year (4 compounding periods)?
3. Plot the compound growth factor of $1 over 10-, 20-, and 50-year periods for the interest rates $r = (0.01, 0.02, 0.05, 10)$.
4. A savings account in Mexico pays interest of 12.5 percent compounded annually. If $100,000 is put into this account today, how much will be on deposit 20 years from now? (Solve through

interpolation and the use of common logarithms. Account for the rather large difference in your results.)

5. Schmidt places $50 in the bank each quarter. His bank pays interest quarterly at an annual rate of 4 percent. How much will Schmidt have on deposit after three years?
6. Gormann puts $600 in a savings account each year. He is paid interest of 6 percent per annum compounded annually. How much will he have after 5 years?
7. A special depository account requires annual payments of $1,000. After 8 years, the account matures and pays to the holder $10,000. At what annual rate of interest do funds grow in this account?
8. Determine the present value of $10,000 received in 20 years when interest is compounded at 5 percent:

    a. Annually
    b. Continuously (Hint: $1/e \sim 0.368$)

9. Verify using an online data provider that the monthly and daily returns for stock indexes such as the S&P 500, DJIA, or NASDAQ provide the same 20-year CAGR.
10. Verify (prove) the *rule-of-72*: a rough translation of Pacioli's 1494 summary goes something like, "In wanting to know of any capital, at a given yearly percentage, in how many years it will double adding the interest to the capital, keep as a rule [the number] 72 in mind, which you will always divide by the interest, and what results, in that many years it will be doubled."

References

Rubinstein, M., *A History of the Theory of Investments: My Annotated Bibliography*. Hoboken, NJ: John Wiley & Sons, 2006.

Ruppert, D., *Statistics and Data Analysis for Financial Engineering*. New York, NY: Springer, 2011.

Vecer, J., *Stochastic Finance: A Numeraire Approach*. Boca Raton, FL: Chapman and Hall/CRC, 2011.

Chapter 3

The Securities Markets and Macroeconomics

This [financial] crisis... has turned out to be much broader than anything I could have imagined...

Alan Greenspan, October 23, 2008

The Securities Markets

Negotiable financial assets are traded in the money and capital markets. The distinction between the two is based upon the maturity of the financial asset under consideration. The money market is generally defined as consisting of negotiable securities with a maturity of one year or less; the capital market is composed of the longer-term securities (including equities, which have a theoretically perpetual life). The distinction, however, is generally more significant than the mere artificial division at the one-year maturity level.

The instruments of the money market, aside from being less than a year in maturity, are also generally of high investment quality and are purchased as a means of obtaining some return on temporarily idle funds; in other words, the money market is a market in near-money instruments where safety of principal and liquidity are the primary considerations.

The capital market, on the other hand, not only includes securities of all degrees of risk but also tends to be utilized by investors with funds to be committed for substantial periods. Finally, long-term debt securities constitute a portion of the capital market at the time of their issuance, but as they approach maturity they become money-market instruments. We shall begin the discussion with the more traditional money-market instruments, which, in the context of this book, may be viewed as possible interest-earning cash substitutes in the investment portfolio.

Securities of the U.S. government

The *U.S. treasury bill* is one of the most significant money market instruments. This short-term U.S. government obligation is offered in 28-, 91-, and 182-day maturities. Bills do not carry an interest coupon but are sold at less than their face value. Because of the large amount of bills outstanding, the narrow spreads between bid and asked prices, and the lack of credit risk, treasury bills are viewed as very desirable liquidity instruments. Bills of nine- and twelve-month maturity are also offered. Some of the government agencies discussed below issue short-term debt as well that would qualify as money market instruments. Also, as mentioned before, the longer-term government and agency securities become money-market instruments when they approach maturity.

Suppose that an investor desired to find the price and yield on a treasury bill due in 300 days on a 3 percent basis. Since treasury bills are quoted on a "discount" basis, the price would be:

$$3\% \times (300/360) = 2.5\% \text{ "discount."}$$

Price = \$975 per \$1,000 face value of the bill, and the approximate true rate would be:

$$(25/975) \times (365/300) = 3.12\%.$$

The latter is an approximation because it assumes annual compounding. The government has devised a more complicated computation for equivalent bond yield assuming semiannual compounding. Bill rates are quoted every business day in the financial press and online so it is not even necessary to make specific calculations. Since 1926, the average 30-day bill has yielded about 3 percent. After the 2007 collapse, the Federal Reserve Board (see discussion below) has maintained a policy of keeping rates at extremely low levels. Indeed,

30-day bills have regularly yielded only a few basis points (a basis point is 1/100 of 1 percent). In fact, yields actually went negative for a few days, meaning that investors were willing to *pay* Uncle Sam for the privilege of lending him money!

Because we shall continually refer to U.S. federal government securities as devoid of credit (default) risk, we shall explain this point. It does not mean that we feel an entity with almost $20 trillion in debt (with additional unfunded liabilities such as Social Security and Medicare) is a great credit risk by normal standards of evaluation. What it does mean is that, because the government has the power of money creation, it would undoubtedly create enough new money to repay any bondholder who demanded redemption. Only events like war, revolution, or, by some definitions, hyperinflation, could prevent this and would cause all other dollar-denominated obligations to become worthless anyway.

It is interesting to note that in 2012, one might obtain a yield of only, say, 20 basis points on a treasury bill. This means that a purchaser of $100,000 in bills would have earned just $200 over the span of a year. If that investor paid federal income taxes of 36 percent, he or she would have a net after-tax return of only $128 (or 0.128 percent). The inflation rate has been above 2.50 percent recently, meaning that an investor in treasury bills has actually lost about 2.37 percent on an annualized basis. Why would intelligent investors accept such miserable returns? Part of the answer to this question will be revealed later in this chapter.

Municipal securities

Securities issued by states and their political subdivisions are usually known by the broad term municipals or "Munis" and are distinguished by the fact that their interest is, in most cases, exempt from federal income taxes. Although municipals are generally long term in maturity and are considered later in the chapter, certain situations give rise to short-term obligations. A city or state may borrow in anticipation of tax receipts or the proceeds of a bond issue. A municipal bond issue itself may have a portion that matures within a year and thus might qualify as a money-market instrument. The quality of these issues can vary widely, and the ratings (see discussion below) on the bonds of the issuing entity will give some indication of credit-worthiness. Only the issues of bodies having one of the top two or three bond ratings would be of sufficiently high quality to be considered a true money-market instrument. The short-term municipal market is also fed by the interim financing needs of various housing and renewal authorities. The notes of state and local housing authorities are generally treated as obligations of the appropriate government body, and their quality is judged accordingly.

An additional advantage of municipals is that they are also usually exempt from state taxes in the state of issuance. A disadvantage is that the issues may be small, thus the secondary markets are often rather illiquid. To illustrate the tax effect of municipals, consider the Treasury bill analyzed above. Its yield was only 0.20 percent, or 0.128 percent after-tax. Thus, if an otherwise similar municipal security offered a return in excess of 0.128 percent, the after-tax return to the holder would be more attractive. Since many munis are below the credit-worthiness of the U.S. government (California cannot print money but Uncle Sam can), these instruments often have to yield more, say somewhere between 0.128 and 0.20 percent.

Bankers' acceptances

A *bankers' acceptance* arises from a commercial transaction, often involving international trade. An American importer may send a letter of credit with an order for goods to a foreign exporter. The exporter may then draw a *time draft* (an order to pay in the future) against the importer and sell it to his local bank at a discount in order to receive immediate payment. The foreign bank will then send the draft and title to the goods to the importer's bank. The importer's bank accepts the draft by indicating that it will guarantee payment. The time draft is now a bankers' acceptance that is sold in the money market to pay the foreign bank. Because the bank is obligated on the instrument, acceptances tend to trade on the basis of the bank's credit rather than that of the company primarily obligated. In a very crude sense, an acceptance may be viewed as a postdated certified check sold at a discount. Most large banks and bond dealers carry a wide range of sizes and maturities in acceptances, although it may not be possible to match desires exactly.

Negotiable certificates of deposit and commercial paper

Negotiable Certificates of Deposit (CDs) are claims upon time deposits at banks that may be sold prior to the maturity of the deposit. The deposit itself is made for a specified period (at a rate tied to the maturity) and may not be withdrawn early. The ability to negotiate the ownership of the deposit, however, provides essentially the same liquidity benefits as withdrawal to the owner and allows the higher rates associated with longer-term deposits to be earned. These deposits are backed by the Federal Deposit Insurance Corporation (FDIC) to $250,000; but because negotiable CDs are rarely smaller than multiples of $1 million, this is little comfort. Beyond FDIC insurance, the only security is the size and quality of the issuing bank. As a result, only the CDs of the larger money-market banks really qualify as money-market instruments.

The commercial paper market consists of the short-term, unsecured promissory notes of industrial and financial companies. Directly placed paper is that sold directly by the borrower to the lender. Sales finance and consumer finance companies are the major sellers of directly placed paper, using the proceeds to carry the inventory of dealer and consumer loans they hold. Directly placed paper is generally sold to mature on any day desired by the lender from 3 to 270 days hence (an obvious advantage if the lenders know exactly when they want their money back). A disadvantage of directly placed paper is that there is no secondary market, although in cases of hardship the issuer may buy it back early.

Dealer-placed commercial paper is sold in the form of a one-time issue through a bond dealer. Finance companies also use this approach, and industrial companies employ it for seasonal working capital needs or as an alternative to bank borrowing. In all cases, and especially with dealer-placed paper, the issuer will be required to keep open bank lines of credit to secure the retirement of the issue.

Eurodollars and non-U.S. money-market instruments

From the lender's point of view, the *Eurodollar market* merely presents the opportunity to buy negotiable CDs, expressed in dollars, from non-U.S. banks (either foreign banks or foreign branches of U.S. banks). A major disadvantage of this form of short-term investment is that the regulation, disclosure, and deposit insurance in this market leave much to be desired, so the possibility of a panic or default cannot be ignored. This possibility is enhanced by the fact that the bank of deposit is creating a liability in a currency (the dollar) that its own government is under no obligation to provide in times of crisis.

In theory, there is no reason why an American investor should not consider the liquidity instruments of any major foreign country if the credit standing is adequate. To minimize the risk of the transaction, however, it is necessary to "cover" it in the forward exchange market (which merely involves reaching an agreement in the present as to the price at which one will buy or sell an amount of foreign money at some point in the future).

To illustrate covered arbitrage, suppose that the NKV Trust wished to buy $1 million of 10 percent, 180-day securities of the Dak government. The Dak currency is currently exchanging at 30 to the dollar. The 180-day forward Dak is quoted at 31 to the dollar (the rate at which it would be possible to contract now for delivery in six months). The return to be earned by NKV on a covered transaction would be given as follows:

Now: (a) Sell $1M to obtain Dak (@30:1) = 30M Dak
(b) Buy 30M Dak securities (will earn interest of 1.5M Dak)
(c) Sell 31.5M Dak for delivery in 180 days against the dollar (@31:1)

In 6 months: (a) Redeem bonds = 31.5M Dak
(b) Deliver on forward contract

$$(31.5M/31) = \$1,016,130$$

$$\text{Return} = \frac{\$16,130}{\$1,000,000} \times \frac{360}{180} \approx 3.2\%.$$

The Capital Market

The capital market may be distinguished from the money market in several ways. The securities involved are far more numerous and varied. The markets themselves generally lack the breadth and depth of the money market in the technical sense that the spread between bid and asked prices is greater and the change in price on consecutive transactions is also generally greater. Finally, the capital market is regulated by the government (primarily through the Securities and Exchange Commission and its various self-regulatory arms) in many more specific ways than the money market.

The major distinction between the money and capital markets is the maturity of the instruments. Because capital market instruments have maturities beyond one year, the measurement of yield on these securities depends upon time value of money calculations. From Chapter 2, we know that the basic equation for the yield on any asset is:

$$P_0 = \frac{A_1}{(1+i)^1} + \frac{A_2}{(1+i)^2} + \cdots + \frac{A_n}{(1+i)^n}, \qquad (3.1)$$

where P_0 is the current price of the asset; A_1 is the dollar return from the asset one period (year) from now; A_2 is the dollar return two periods from now, and so on; n is the number of periods the asset will generate payments; and i is the yield on the asset.

This equation may be rewritten as:

$$P_0 = \sum_{t=1}^{n} \frac{A_t}{(1+i)^t}. \qquad (3.2)$$

The computation of a rate of return is easy if the dollar payments in the future are constant. All one need to do is divide the dollar payments into its current value. Either present value factor tables or direct calculator (computer) computations demonstrate this. For example, if a mortgage obligates the borrower to pay a sum of $1,000 per year for 18 years, and the face value of the mortgage is $10,000, the factor is:

$$\$10{,}000/\$1{,}000 = 10.$$

Using the factor calculations in Appendix A, we find that a factor 10.059 exists for an 18-year present value if the rate of return is 7 percent. Thus, the mortgage has a yield of about 7 percent. In many cases, the solution for a rate of return will not be found directly from the tables but will require interpolation. Using a calculator or computer provides more accurate results and is much easier.

When the future payment stream is not constant but differs from year to year, the solution is more tedious and requires a trial and error approach. Bonds pay an annual (or more frequently, semiannual) coupon. At the date of maturity of the bond, the principal sum (par value) of the bond is repaid to the holder. Thus, Equation (3.1) could be rewritten in this case as:

$$P_0 = \sum_{t=1}^{n} \frac{C_t}{(1+i)^t} + \frac{P_n}{(1+i)^n}, \qquad (3.3)$$

where P_0 is the current market price of the bond; C_t is the annual dollar coupon payment on the bond; P_n is the par value of the bond; n is the number of years until the bond matures; i is the yield to maturity on the bond.

Suppose a bond will mature in five years. The bond will pay $1,000 upon maturity and pays $70.00 per year each year for the five-year period. What is its yield to maturity? To find the answer, we must know the current price of the bond, which we shall assume is 95. Since bond prices are quoted in percentages of par, this means that for a $1,000 par bond one pays $950.00 for a stream of payments of $70.00 for five years plus $1,000 at the end of the fifth year. Because the bond is selling at a discount, we know that its yield must be greater than its coupon yield of 7 percent (that is, $70.00 on a par of $1,000). From factor calculations, we find that at 8 percent, the present value of this stream is:

$$3.993 \times \$70.00 = \$279.51$$
$$0.681 \times \$1000.00 = 681.00$$
$$\$960.51.$$

This present value is too high. Hence, the yield must be greater than 8 percent. Let us try 9 percent:

$$3.890 \times \$70.00 = \$272.30$$
$$0.650 \times \$1000 = 650.00$$
$$\$922.30.$$

The value of $950.00 is between $960.51 and $922.30. Thus, by interpolation we may find the yield to maturity:

$$8.0 \text{ percent} = \$960.51$$
$$9.0 \text{ percent} = \$922.30$$
$$8.3 \text{ percent} = \$950.00.$$

For a bond, there is a shortcut formula that will give the yield to maturity rather closely if the bond is selling reasonably near par and if there are only a few years before it matures. This equation is:

$$i = \frac{C + (P_n - P_0)/n}{(P_n + P_0)/2}. \tag{3.4}$$

We may use Equation (3.4) to solve for the yield in the previous example:

$$i = \frac{70 + (1000 - 950)/5}{(1000 + 950)/2}$$
$$= \frac{80}{975} = 8.2\%.$$

Thus, the shortcut formula comes close to the actual yield to maturity of 8.3 percent. This computation is again most easily made on a calculator or computer.

Long-term debt instruments

The long-term marketable debt of the federal government consists of *treasury notes* and *treasury bonds*, both of which usually pay interest semiannually. The notes are issued with an original maturity of one to ten years and are generally sold quarterly. Although the bonds have no maturity restrictions, they are presently sold in 20 and 30 year maturities.

Government agencies and sponsored corporations also issue short- and long-term debt in their own names. This group includes the Federal National Mortgage Association ("Fanny Mae"), the Government National Mortgage Association ("Ginny Mae"), the Student Loan Marketing Association ("Sallie Mae"), the Tennessee Valley Authority (TVA), the Federal Home Loan Mortgage Corporation ("Freddie Mac"), the Federal Land Banks, the Farmers' Home Administration, and the Export–Import Bank and other agencies that seem to be created regularly by the federal government. None of the debts of these agencies is a direct obligation of the government, although it has been assumed by the investment community that none of them would be allowed to default. As a result, *agency issues* command a rate only slightly higher than treasury securities. The securities are generally issued originally following an announcement by the fiscal agent and trade in a reasonably active secondary market.

One aid in market efficiency is size of issue. Even with the best of intentions, it is very difficult to maintain an active secondary market in a security of which there is little outstanding. This is one reason that treasury bills are such good liquidity instruments; every weekly offering is for several billion dollars, and therefore a transaction involving several million dollars worth of bills should not upset the market greatly. The longer-term issues, however, are smaller, raising the possibility of a large transaction influencing the price. For example, if an investor wished to acquire in the market $10 million of a $200 million corporate bond issue, he or she might need to bid the price up significantly to fill the order. Fortunately, ratings come to the rescue. Instead of seeking a particular issue, the investor might simply specify that he or she wished to buy $10 million of Aa-rated industrials maturing in the next 10–15 years. His or her broker could then obtain whichever bonds of this type were offered, and the investor would receive several different bonds at a far more reasonable price. Thus, ratings help make "thin" markets more efficient (See Chapter Six for more details.).

Finally, bonds are also offered by international institutions of which the U.S. is a member. Included in this group are the

International Bank for Reconstruction and Development ((IBRD) or simply, World Bank) and the Inter-American Development Bank. These issues are secured by the assets of the banks and, beyond that, by the right of the banks to call upon their members for additional contributions to meet debt requirements. The investment community has viewed this "back door" guarantee as only slightly weaker than the implicit guarantee of the agency issues and has priced the securities accordingly.

Municipals were introduced earlier in this chapter, and the point was made that they are currently generally exempt from federal income taxes. These bonds are often in serial form, meaning that a specified portion of an issue matures each year. They may also be identified as either *general obligations* or *revenue bonds*. General obligation bonds (GOs) pledge the "full faith and credit" of the government entity to the payment of the bonds. In analyzing such bonds (discussed in detail in Chapter 6), aside from the ratings given by the bond agencies and the default record of the community, one often looks at the value of property, the tax rate, debt per capita, debt service as a proportion of the operating budget, and various demographic factors. Is the community growing? Or is it dependent upon one industry, so on?

Revenue bonds, on the other hand, do not pledge the credit of the community but only the proceeds from the project being financed by the bonds (everything from toll roads to college dormitories). In this case, therefore, the investor looks at the need for the project, the adequacy of the expected usage and charges, and so on. Confusion can arise because there have been cases of quite credit-worthy communities defaulting upon revenue bonds when proceeds were inadequate because they were not obligated to pay the bonds; the Calumet Skyway bonds issued by Chicago several decades ago is a case in point, and this example also illustrates some additional protection offered by the bond market. It is almost an unwritten rule that an issuer who has defaulted will find it virtually impossible to raise new funds until settlement is made with the old holders. Even though Chicago was not legally obligated on the Calumet bonds, it found the reception for its other bonds after the default sufficiently cold that officials for some years seriously considered paying them off and ultimately did so.

Several factors frustrate the efforts of American investors to purchase foreign stocks and bonds. First, of course, is the currency risk — the possibility that the currency in which the foreign security is denominated will change its parity vis-à-vis the dollar. In the short-term area, it is suggested that a covering transaction in the forward exchange market could eliminate this risk. Unfortunately, however, the forward market in most currencies becomes quite thin beyond six months, and even in the most active currencies it is difficult to obtain a commitment beyond a few years.

Taxes in foreign countries also present an additional burden. Most long-term foreign securities are subject to withholding tax on interest and dividends paid (most of the short-term foreign instruments are exempted). Depending upon the tax treaty between the U.S. and the foreign country involved, taxes withheld abroad may serve as either a credit or deduction on American tax returns. If only a deduction is allowed, a greater total tax is paid. Even if a full tax credit is allowed, a loss may occur if the foreign withholding rate is greater than the American rate paid (often the case for financial institutions and obviously so for tax-exempt organizations).

Corporate debt may take the form of either a publicly offered bond issue or a privately placed note. The private placement is generally made with one or a few large institutional investors and is, as a rule, held until maturity by the original purchasers. In return for this lack of marketability, the lenders generally receive a slightly higher coupon and are able to obtain a larger portion of the issue (an advantage to institutions such as insurance companies that have small staffs and much money to invest).

Bonds are sold to the public through an underwriting, by which an investment banker buys the bonds from the issuer, marks them up, and attempts to sell them to the general public. The bonds can be bought from the issuer by the investment banker either at a price negotiated by the parties involved, or by competitive bid. Most companies regulated by agencies of the government (power companies, railroads, and so on) are required to sell their securities by competitive bid; most others negotiate. The bonds are issues and sold under an *indenture*, which is a statement of rights and obligations negotiated between the issuing company and the trustee (often the trust department of a bank) as representative of the lenders. The importance of the indenture, and its salient features printed in the prospectus, cannot be overstated; it is the final arbiter of the rights and duties of borrowers and the lender, as many bond buyers have subsequently discovered to their sorrow.

Among the facts to be found in an indenture are the provisions for retirement and refunding of the issue. For example, a portion of the bond issue may be retired each year prior to maturity. This may be done by having the company pay the trustee, who, in turn, determines by lot which bonds will be called for redemption or by merely having the company enter the market to buy the required number of bonds. These two methods may usually be employed at the company's option, which is a disadvantage to the bondholder.

If rates rise and the bonds go to a discount, the company can buy them in the market; if rates fall, the company can have the trustee call the bonds at or above par. In like manner, the refunding (or *call*) provisions also work to a disadvantage to the lender. In a reasonably efficient market, of course, the bondholder would receive a higher return in compensation for these disadvantages. If interest rates decline, the issuer invariably has the right to call the bond issue and refund it at the lower rate. The only protection to the bondholder is that such a call must generally be made at a slight premium over par and that there may be an interval of 5 or 10 years after the bonds are issued (the *no-call period*) during which a call is not allowed.

Finally, the company may be allowed to call the issue at a very small premium if the funds do not come from a cheaper bond issue (for example, if the company sells assets). The issuer can generally be expected to undertake its most advantageous option, which is also generally the least advantageous to the holder.

The indenture will also indicate the security of the issue. *Mortgage bonds* are secured by a lien on all or part of the property of the issuer. In bankruptcy, the mortgage bondholders have first claim upon the proceeds of the property against which they hold a lien;

to the extent that these proceeds are inadequate, the bondholders become general creditors for the rest. It is also possible to issue second (and even lower priority) mortgage bonds; these holders have a claim on any proceeds from the mortgaged property after the prior mortgage holders are satisfied (and become general creditors for any of the remainder).

A very strong mortgage bond would include an *after-acquired clause*, indicating that not only is all current property of the company subject to the mortgage but all new property acquired later is also encumbered; this provision is so strong that it would require the company to make any new debt second mortgage or lower in priority. The open-end indenture is less rigid in that the company is allowed to issue additional debt on the same mortgage; to protect the old holders; however, the new debt is generally limited to some fraction (often 50–66 percent) of the net increase in property subject to the mortgage.

Two other types of secured bonds are the *collateral trust bond* and the *equipment trust certificate*. For the first type, the borrower places the securities of other companies into a trust and then issues securities against the trust. For the second type, used extensively by railroads and airlines, title to the equipment is held by a trustee for the benefit of the lenders until the company has redeemed the debt; thus, the lenders can obtain immediate possession of the equipment and resell it if the borrower goes into bankruptcy.

Debentures are not secured by any particular piece of property and are only covered by the general credit of the borrowing corporation. In bankruptcy, the debenture holder ranks as a general creditor of the corporation. *Subordinated debentures* are of even lower priority, in that the proceeds that the holders would receive as general creditors in bankruptcy must go to satisfy the claims of the issues to which they are subordinated. Even junior subordinated debentures have been issued.

Income bonds obligate the issuer to pay interest only if the firm's earnings are sufficient to make payment. The income bond has been used historically by trustees in many railroad reorganizations. As a result, these bonds have achieved a relatively poor reputation. It might also be noted that, in the purchase of most bonds, the investor pays the price quoted plus accrued interest on the bond; in the case of income bonds and bonds in default, no accrued interest is included (the bonds are said to trade "flat"). Finally, convertible bonds, which grant the holder the option to exchange the bond for stock at a specified ratio, are also issued in debenture form. These subjects are discussed in greater detail in Chapter 7. In conclusion, it must be stressed that only an examination of the indenture will reveal the attributes of any given issue.

Equity securities

Equity instruments are also a part of the capital market. *Preferred stock* represents a curious combination of various features of debt and common stock. It is like common stock in that the instrument is called stock and is included in the equity section of the balance sheet of a corporation. Payments are called dividends and are not deductible for tax purposes by the corporation; the payment of dividends is not legally required, and the issue typically has no given maturity. Preferred stock is like debt in that the dividends have a fixed maximum rate. Preferred holders generally have no vote on corporate matters unless a specified number (often four to six quarterly) of dividends are passed, in which case they may typically elect a minority of the board of directors. Preferred stockholders are entitled to no more than the amount paid in to the firm in case of liquidation, and preferred stock may contain the same call, sinking fund, or conversion features as any debenture. A rare type, called *participating preferred*, provides that after preferred dividends have been paid and common shareholders have received a like return, both classes may participate by some formula in any additional dividends to be paid.

Cumulative preferred requires that all past, unpaid dividends be paid (although not with interest) before any common dividend may be paid; *noncumulative preferred* only requires that the current year's dividend be paid before a common dividend is paid. Companies with either large arrearages on their preferred stock or high-dividend non-callable preferred are often forced to make an exchange offer for cash or other securities in order to retire the preferred. The yield on preferred is simply dividend/price; the computation is meaningless for preferred in arrears. The tax law allows Subchapter "C" corporations that hold stock (either preferred or common) of other corporations to exclude 70 percent of any dividends received from taxes. Since this causes preferreds to be almost tax exempt to a corporate holder, it may appear in some cases that a company's preferreds yield less in the market than its bonds.

The residual owners of the firm are the *common stockholders*. As such, they have claim on the earnings of the firm after all creditors are paid. In case of the dissolution or liquidation of the firm, the common stockholders are entitled to the net assets remaining after the claims of creditors are satisfied. They have the right to examine the books of the company (usually deemed satisfied by having the company send out the annual report containing audited statements) and may have the right to maintain their proportionate ownership. They also have the right to elect a board of directors to act as their agent in running the firm.

Macroeconomic Influences upon the Money and Capital Markets

One of the major developments of economic theory over the past 80 years has been an increased awareness of the impacts of real investment and, especially, government spending upon the level of aggregate economic activity. Because the return to be earned on securities in the long run and the level of their market prices in the short run are related to the level of economic activity, the latter must be a matter of continuing interest to the security analyst and portfolio manager. Prior to the 1930s, economists assumed that the macro markets (consumption, saving, business investment, and the like) were merely aggregations of micro markets. As a consequence of the Great Depression, thinking began to change. With the appearance of John Maynard Keynes' *General Theory of Employment, Interest, and Money* (1936), a whole new branch of economics called *macroeconomics* came into being.

Macroeconomics deals with large issues such as the output (income) of an economy, the aggregate prices level, unemployment, so on. National income is a central focus since more national income typically results in higher standards of living. The notion of national income goes back to the mid-seventeenth century when nation states were flourishing and needed some notion of an aggregate measure of production. Taxation issues were mostly responsible for its creation. Previously, kings (and queens) would try to assess taxes based on the "wealth" of nobles but wealth was hard to measure. Land counted heavily in these taxation calculations but land was illiquid and could not be converted to cash easily. Of course, some kingdoms just created money out of nothing (called fiat money) but those straying far from standards based on precious metals (gold and often silver) were typically brought down by hyper-inflation and complete destruction of the national economy (and usually the monarchs in charge as well). Often kings simply took what they could from nobles, especially to fight wars, but even the nobility tended to rebel if taxes were too high or unfairly collected. Thus, there was a need to define income (both personal and national) in order to maintain the legitimacy of both nation-states and their monarchs.

The idea of taxing income was hit upon well before the seventeenth century. Even in the early Christian period, Jesus was to have said, "Render unto Caesar what is Caesar's." Usually a 10 percent tax rate was applicable, and even Caesar (any one of them) would have faced a revolution if he tried to implement tax rates of modern portions (which, interestingly enough, often exceed 100 percent at the margin). In Great Britain after World War II, a socialist government put marginal rates at over 100 percent to "soak the rich." And even in the U.S. today, rates can be that high for those seeking to get out of poverty. That happens because many government benefits are reduced or eliminated as people get jobs and actually make an honest living. Oh well, as the saying goes, "The only things certain in the world are death and taxes."

The modern concept of gross national product (GNP) was first developed by economist Simon Kuznets in 1934 for a U.S. Congressional Report. At the time, GNP was the preferred measurement of aggregate output but it was replaced in the 1980s by a slightly different notion called gross domestic product (GDP). It should be warned, however, that: "The actual number for GDP is ... the product of a vast patchwork of statistics and a complicated set of processes carried out on the raw data to fit them to the conceptual framework" (Coyle, 2014).

The basic Keynesian model postulated that the level of aggregate economic activity (Y) is the sum of all consumer spending (C), business investment (I), government spending (G), and net exports ($\bar{X}$) that take place over a period of time (say, a year). Symbolically,

$$Y = C + I + G + \bar{X}. \tag{3.5}$$

Consumer spending is related to the overall level of income, however. If we assume that consumers pay T dollars per year in total taxes, that they receive T_r dollars from the government in transfer payments (for example, social security, unemployment compensation, and so on), and that they spend a constant proportion (b) of each extra dollar of disposable income $b = \Delta C / \Delta (Y - T + T_r)$, then changes in consumption spending may be viewed as:

$$\Delta C = b \Delta (Y - T + T_r). \tag{3.6}$$

Furthermore, if we postulate a world in which taxes and transfer payments are not a function of the level of income, it is possible to derive what Keynes called the simple investment multiplier. We shall ignore $\bar{X}$ since it is a relatively small number and complicates the analysis which follows.

$$\Delta Y = \Delta C + \Delta I + \Delta G$$

$$\Delta Y = b \Delta (Y - T + T_r) + \Delta I + \Delta G.$$

Letting $\Delta T = \Delta T_r = \Delta G = 0$, then:

$$\Delta Y = b \Delta Y + \Delta I$$

$$\Delta Y = \frac{1}{1-b} \Delta I. \tag{3.7}$$

The quantity $1/(1-b)$ is the simple investment multiplier. It indicates the amount by which the total level of income would rise (fall) if there were an exogenous increase (decrease) in business investment for plant and equipment. Thus, if we considered a simplified economy without income taxes in which consumers had a *marginal propensity to consume* (b) of 0.8, autonomous investment would increase income not just by ΔI but rather by $[1/(1-.8) = 5]\Delta Y$. A $10 billion increase in business investment would not only add this amount to total aggregate income, but because such spending would induce further spending in the consumer sector, the total increase to total income would be:

$$\Delta Y = \frac{1}{1-b}\Delta I = 5(\$10 \text{ billion}) = \$50 \text{ billion}.$$

The reader will note that an exogenous increase in government spending (or consumption for that matter) would produce the same result. If $\Delta I = 0$ but $\Delta G = \$10$ billion, the same $50 billion increase in aggregate income would be effected. Admittedly, the economy postulated above is greatly simplified. In the first place, it is very likely that higher levels of income may not only stimulate consumers to spend more but may also encourage businesses to invest extra amounts. Hence, we may conceive of a *marginal propensity to invest* $Z = \Delta I/\Delta Y$. The presence of this factor may add an "accelerator" effect to economic activity such that:

$$\Delta Y = \Delta C + \Delta I + \Delta G.$$

Let $\Delta T = \Delta T_r = 0$, then

$$\Delta Y = b\Delta Y + Z\Delta Y + \Delta G$$

$$\Delta Y = \frac{1}{1-b-Z}\Delta G.$$

Suppose in the previous example $Z = 0.1$. The change in national income, given an increase in government spending (or investment) of $10 billion, would be:

$$\Delta Y = \frac{1}{1-.8-.1}(\$10 \text{ billion}) = \$100 \text{ billion}.$$

In a world of proportional income taxes, total taxes (T) could be expressed as (tY), where t is the rate of taxation. If we assume that transfer payments are inversely proportional to income, changes in total payments (ΔT_r) may be expressed as $-t_r \Delta Y$, where $t_r = -\Delta T_r / \Delta Y$. The government expenditure multiplier (in the absence of induced investment) then becomes:

$$\Delta Y = \Delta C + \Delta I + \Delta G$$
$$\Delta Y = b(\Delta Y - \Delta T + \Delta T_r) + 0 + \Delta G$$
$$\Delta Y = b[\Delta Y - t\Delta Y - t_r \Delta Y] + \Delta G$$
$$\Delta Y(1 - b - bt - bt_r) = \Delta G$$
$$\Delta Y = \frac{1}{1 - b(1 - t - t_r)} \Delta G.$$

For the society discussed above, let the rate or taxation (t) be 30 percent and the marginal rate of transfer payments (t_r) be 0.1. Then,

$$\Delta Y = \frac{1}{1 - .8(1 - .3 - .1)} \$10 \text{ billion}$$
$$= \frac{1}{1 - .48} \$10B = \$19.2 \text{ billion}.$$

Notice that the multiplier effect is greatly reduced because added taxes and lower transfer payments tend to dampen the stimulating aspects of the increase in government spending.

Investment and saving equilibrium

Now that some of the implications of the income-constrained multiplier process have been demonstrated, let us consider more concretely the equilibrium conditions that the economy will reach. The Keynesian system specifies not only that $Y = C + I + G$, but also that $Y = C + S + T$ (where S = savings). For the two definitions to be the same, and thus for equilibrium conditions to exist, it is necessary that $I + G = S + T$.

Let:

A = amount of consumption if $Y = 0$
S = saving
i = interest rate
B = level of investment if $i = 0$
g = interest elasticity of investment $-\left(\dfrac{\Delta I}{\Delta i}\right)$

Then

$$S = -A + (1-b)(Y - T + T_r)$$
$$S = -A + (1 - b - t + bt - t_r + bt_r)Y$$
$$T = tY. \qquad (3.8)$$

It follows, therefore, that

$$S + T = -A + (1 - b + bt - t_r + bt_r)Y. \qquad (3.9)$$

This relationship is graphed as Figure 3.1. It shows that as the level of income rises, the volume of saving generated and taxes paid in the economy also increase.

To add further realism to the model, we may postulate that the level of investment is inversely related to the rate of interest. This is intuitively obvious, since higher interest rates increase the overall cost of capital to businesses. A higher cost of capital, *ceteris paribus*,

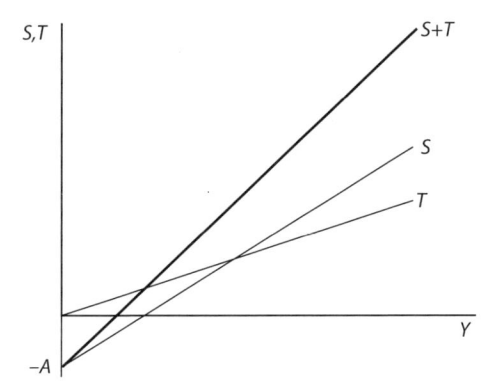

Figure 3.1. Savings and Taxes as a Function of Income

80 Quantitative Financial Analytics

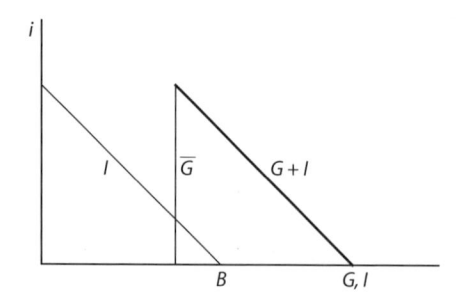

Figure 3.2. Investment and Government Spending as a Function of the Interest Rate

should reduce the willingness of firms to invest in plants, equipment, so on. Hence:

$$I = B - gi. \tag{3.10}$$

If G is exogenously determined by the government, then:

$$G + I = G + B - gi. \tag{3.11}$$

This relationship is graphed in Figure 3.2 with the axes reversed (to correspond to Figure 3.3).

The issue of government expenditures is worth a bit of discussion at this point. According to the Keynesian view, spending by all levels of government (federal, state, and municipal) is required to supply needed services such as roads, highways, schools, national defense, so on. In addition, federal spending may be enhanced in order to stimulate a sluggish economy or one in recession. Even deficits may be required. Indeed, over the years the notion of incurring large deficits to stimulate economic growth has resulted in a cumulative U.S. national debt approaching $20 trillion. This is a controversial issue to which we shall return later in this chapter. For the present, we shall be content to develop the basic Keynesian model.

By equating Equations (3.6) and (3.8), it is possible to determine the equilibrium conditions:

$$-A + (1 - b + bt - t_r + bt_r)Y = \bar{G} + B - gi.$$

$$i = \frac{1}{g}(A + B + \bar{G}) - \frac{(1 - b + bt - t_r + bt_r)}{g}Y. \tag{3.12}$$

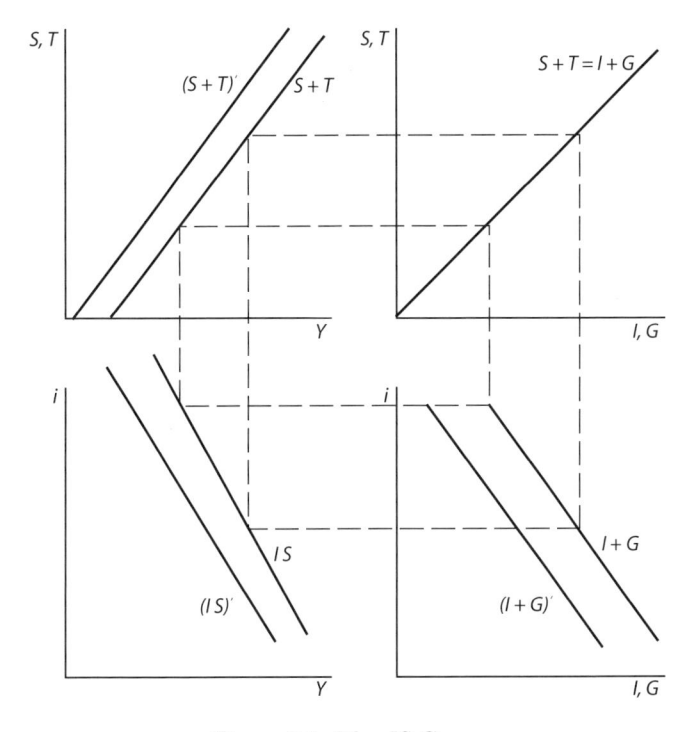

Figure 3.3. The IS Curve

These conditions are also graphed in Figure 3.3. It will be observed that no unique solution exists, but rather a set of income and interest rate levels where $S+T=I+G$. The resulting function is called an *IS* curve.

A second equilibrium condition, introduced below, is required before a specific solution may be obtained. It will be noted, however, both from the graph and Equation (3.9) that an upshift in the $S+T$ function $(S+T)'$ or a downshift in the $I+G$ function $(I+G)'$ will cause a downshift in the *IS* function $(IS)'$ and vice versa. The implication is that as the rate of saving or taxation rises or the level of government spending or the efficiency of investment falls, the equilibrium level of the interest rate and/or the income level tends to fall; the reverse is also true.

In light of the above, it should be anticipated that an increase in government spending, a reduction in taxes, an increased propensity to consume, or improved expectations for investment should cause national income to rise. Assuming that industry sales keep pace and a company can maintain its market share, the increase in national income should be reflected in larger company cash flows. Larger company flows, in turn, cause its bonds to be more secure and the dividend-paying potential of its stock to be enhanced. Thus, an initial impact (subject to qualification below) of such changes should be upward pressure on the prices of both shares and bonds, especially in the case of companies that would benefit the most from the increase in aggregate demand. The use of aggregate data to predict company flows is considered in more detail later in this book.

In addition to the requirement that $S+T = I+G$, equilibrium in the Keynesian system also requires that the supply of money equal the demand for money. The supply of money $(\bar{M})$, which consists of all currency and demand deposits held by the public, is essentially fixed by policy actions of the Federal Reserve and is therefore treated as an exogenous variable in the analysis. The demand for money (L) has historically been divided into two parts. The combined Keynesian transactions and precautionary demand for money (L_1) is generally assumed to be a direct function of income $(L_1 = lY)$; this demand constitutes the need for money to purchase goods in the normal course of events and to hold against a "rainy day." The Keynesian asset or speculative demand for money (L_2) is generally assumed to be an inverse function of the rate of interest $(L_2 = J - mi)$; this demand for money can most easily be viewed as a lack of demand for long-term bonds when interest rates are low (bond prices high) and there is a high probability that rates will rise (prices fall). Therefore:

$$L_1 = lY$$

$$L_2 = J - mi$$

$$L = L_1 + L_2 = lY + J - mi. \qquad (3.13)$$

In equilibrium, $L = \bar{M}$.

$$\bar{M} = J + lY - mi$$

$$i = \frac{J - \bar{M}}{m} + \frac{l}{m}Y. \qquad (3.14)$$

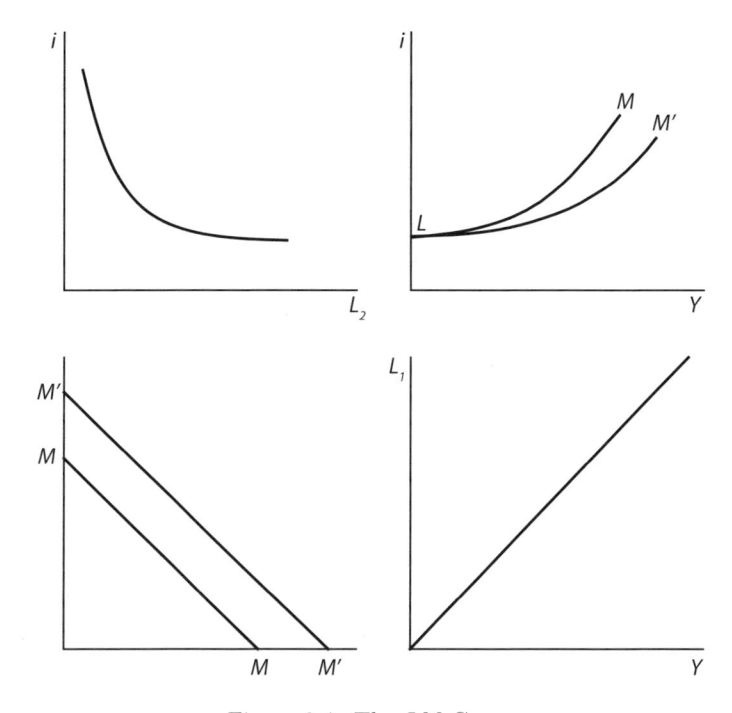

Figure 3.4. The *LM* Curve

These relationships are graphed in Figure 3.4. It will again be noted that no single answer emerges but rather a set of Y, i combinations at which $L = M$. will also be noted that an increase in the money supply (to $M'M'$) causes outshift in the *LM* curve (to LM'). It should also be observed that the L_2 function is graphed as curvilinear even though it is expressed in the formula as linear. This is done to allow for the possible existence of the "liquidity trap" discussed later in this chapter.

It is now possible, at a given price level, to equate Equation (3.11) with Equation (3.9) in order to obtain a unique equilibrium level of i and Y. This level corresponds to the point of intersection of the *IS* and *LM* curves, as shown in Figure 3.5 as Y_0, i_0.

From this initial equilibrium position, an increase in the money supply (L', M') will shift the new equilibrium position to Y_1, i_1 with higher income (which will be a real gain to the extent unemployment

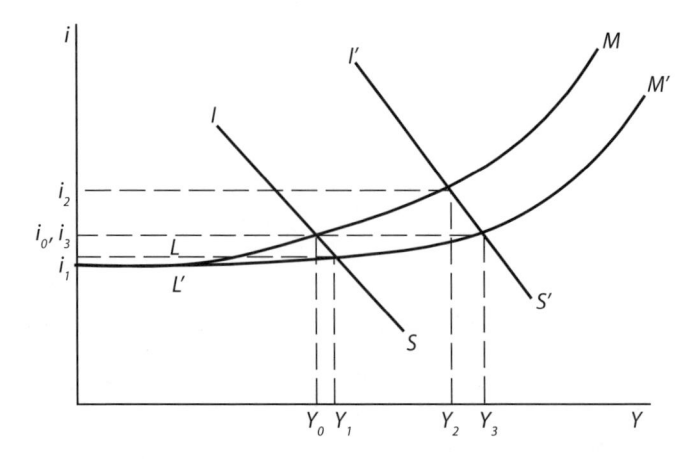

Figure 3.5. Equilibrium in IS–LM Analysis

existed) and lower interest rates. An increase in government spending or investment ($I'S'$) will also raise income (Y_2) but at the expense or higher interest rates, or (i_2); the higher income will raise L_1, but, because $\bar{M}$ is held constant, L_2 must be reduced (which requires the higher rates of interest).

Finally, the simultaneous application of an easier monetary policy ($L'M'$) and an expansionary fiscal policy ($I'S'$) should definitely raise dollar income (Y_3) and will raise real income to the extent Y_3 lies below the full employment level of output. But the effect upon the interest rate (i_3) cannot be foretold in the Keynesian analysis (whether $i_3 >=< i_0$): this will depend upon the relative magnitude of the two effects.

A secondary effect upon security markets resulting from increased spending can now be seen with the addition of the LM curve. To the extent that the money supply remains constant, the securities sold to finance government and business spending must put upward pressure on the general level of interest rates. Such an increase in the required return upon securities puts downward pressure on their prices. As indicated above, this effect can be mitigated if the money supply is also increased (subject to the qualification on inflation discussed later in this chapter).

The Neoclassical Monetarist View

The Keynesian model developed thus far makes some rather specific assumptions about the chain of events following an increase in the money supply. It posited that investors, finding themselves with more money in relation to bonds than they want at the going rate of interest, will attempt to use the extra money to buy bonds, thus bidding up the price of bonds (reducing the rate of interest). Because investors as a group must hold the new money supply, the above process will continue until the rate of interest is reduced to the point that they are willing to hold the total money supply (remember that the asset demand for money increases as the rate of interest declines). The lower rate of interest will cause increased investment, which through the multiplier process will cause increased income and consumption. Keynesians suggested that this process could break down if either (1) interest rates were already so low (bond prices so high) that nobody would want to risk a capital loss when bond prices came down and would thus not buy more bonds (the so-called "liquidity trap"), or (2) investment spending was insensitive to changes in the interest rate. Indeed, it was on the basis of these limitations that followers of Keynes were more enthusiastic about fiscal than monetary policy for a quick recovery from depression.

A different school of thought (the so-called monetarist view) took exception to the above chain of causation and some of the major conclusions of the Keynesians. This view was traceable from Yale's Irving Fisher (1922) to the budding Chicago School whose Milton Friedman was developing a small but intellectually powerful argument against the Keynesians. In a seminal work, Friedman and Anna Schwartz (1963) produced evidence on the monetary policy and the relationship between money and output in the U.S. for over a century.

The Keynesians felt that fiscal policy (lowering taxes and/or increasing government spending) was more effective in combating recessions than monetary policy. This was due to their belief that the IS curve is quite inelastic (steep) and changes in interest rates have little effect on business investment. (Interestingly, this view has been resurrected in recent years as monetary policy has been forced to do the job alone with almost no help from fiscal policy due to politics. Democrats want to raise taxes to soak the rich even if it harms the economy and Republicans want to cut government spending due to fears of out-of-control federal deficits.) Professor Friedman argued quite the opposite and maintained that changes in the money supply explain most of the fluctuations in the economy (called "the business cycle") in the postindustrial revolution era.

It is important at this juncture to understand some history of central banking. From its beginnings, it was argued that there needed to be some sort of "big" bank that was controlled by the U.S. Federal Government to regulate the currency. Congress was charged to do this indirectly by the American Constitution. There was a great debate on the subject led by Federalists such as Alexander Hamilton on the side of having such a bank (and there were two created prior to the 1830s) and opposed by Democrats such as Andrew Jackson who held the populist view that a big national (or central) bank would be manipulated by special interests (eventually to be called Wall Street). The populist view prevailed and until 1913, the U.S. had no central bank (England's, by the way, dates back over three centuries.) There were numerous recessions, depressions, and collapses in the nineteenth century as the economy transformed from almost purely agricultural to more industrial. The U.S. coped, but barely. The big American banks in New York, controlled by the Morgan interests, Kuhn Loeb, and the Rockefellers, among others, were able to keep the economic ship from sinking until the Panic of 1907. At this point, even J.P. Morgan worried that help from the federal government was required. This set in motion events that led to the creation of the Federal Reserve System in 1913.

It is beyond the scope of this book to discuss the complete operations of the Federal Reserve (the "Fed"). Suffice it to say that historically at least the Fed through its Federal Open Market Committee could more or less control the supply of money by buying and selling short-term treasury securities, setting the interest rate it pays to member commercial banks (nearly all banks are included), and dictating the federal funds rate. This rate has been subject to widespread controversy in recent years as the Fed reduced it to near zero and now is raising it ever so slightly. Incidentally, federal funds are reserves in excess of those required by the Fed for member banks. These funds may be lent to other market participants that have insufficient cash on hand to meet their lending and reserve requirements. These loans are unsecured and are lent for an overnight period.

The system put in place in the early twentieth century seemed to work well, until it didn't! Professor Friedman argued, indeed, that the Fed could be at least as destabilizing a force as a stabilizing one. He suggested that the Great Depression was not the result of a stock market collapse or falling demand (these were symptoms not the cause). The real culprit was a big mistake in monetary policy which resulted in a decrease in the money supply as a consequence of bank failures. The Fed should have increased the monetary base but it did not. Friedman's approach is based on what is called the *quantity theory of money*. In turn, that theory follows the *equation of exchange* which can be expressed as follows:

Let:

M = money supply
V_0 = output velocity of money (number of times the money supply "turns over" in purchase of final output)
P = price level
O = output of final goods and services
PO = surrogate for GDP

Then:

$$MV_0 = PO. \qquad (3.15)$$

The equation of exchange as expressed above is simply definitional. The equation can also be expressed for all transactions where V_t = transactions velocity and T = transactions, then $MV_t = PT$. It can be used, however, to illustrate several forms of the quantity theory of money. In its crudest form, the quantity theory assumes that V_0 is determined by institutional means of payment and thus is constant.

Under the assumption of full employment, O is at a maximum and constant in the short run. It follows that any changes in the money supply will have direct and proportional effects upon the price level. In such a world, monetary policy is not only ineffective, but positively harmful. More modern versions of the quantity theory allow V_0 to vary inversely with M (but not by so much as to cancel the net effect) and O to vary as well (depending upon employment levels). A simple statement of the modern quantity theory might be that an increase in the money supply will put pressure on both P and O, the proportions being determined by how near the economy is to full employment.

A model of interest rate determination consistent with this view that takes explicit account of flow variables is the *loanable funds* theory. In this model the supply of loanable funds over a period consists of (1) changes in the money supply (ΔM), plus (2) saving (here considered a function of both income and interest, or $S = S(Y, i)$), less (3) changes in the demand for money (L) or, as it is sometimes called in this literature, the demand for hoards. The supply schedule or loanable funds is illustrated in Figure 3.6.

The demand for loanable funds consists of business investment, plus net federal government borrowing, plus net borrowings by state and local governments. Investment is given by: $I = I(i)$ and net federal borrowing is: $B_f = G + T_r - T = B_f(Y)$. Net borrowings by state and local governments is given by: $B_f = G + T_r - T = B_f(Y)$. Notice that federal government borrowing is assumed to be not interest sensitive. That is, the federal government pursues policies without regard to the cost of its funds. Indeed, it is often the case that

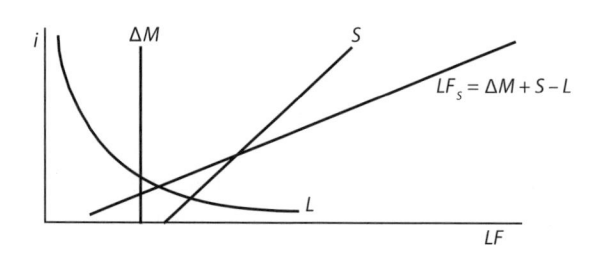

Figure 3.6. Supply of Loanable Funds

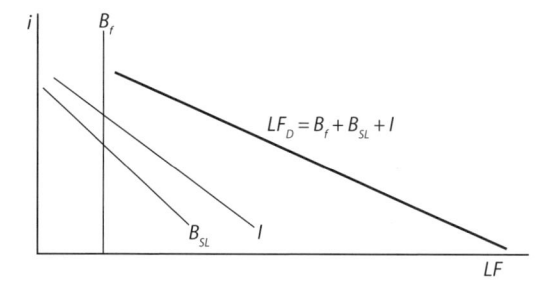

Figure 3.7. Demand for Loanable Funds

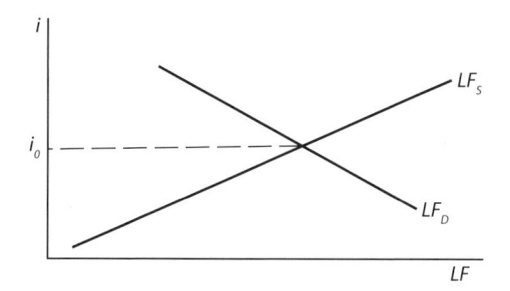

Figure 3.8. Loanable Funds Equilibrium

the federal government borrows *more* when interest rates are high than when they are low. The demand for loanable funds is graphed in Figure 3.7. The intersection of the supply and demand curves provides the equilibrium rate of interest (i_0) in the loanable funds market, as shown in Figure 3.8.

It should be noted that the monetarists assume that changes in the money supply operate directly upon the demand for output (rather than indirectly through the interest rate and investment as posited by the Keynesians). They contend that an increase in the money supply makes money less desirable in relation to all goods and services, not just bonds. The monetarists would agree that the first observable effects might be an increase in bond prices (and lower interest rates), as suggested by the Keynesians. But, the monetarists claim, a much more important secondary effect then occurs. Not only will the public increase consumption because of their greater liquidity with the additional money but also the higher prices for financial assets will cause the public to feel wealthier and also increase consumption.

These points could be incorporated into the consumption function by including a liquidity–asset effect, such that $C = f(Y(M*/P) - (M/P))$ where M/P represents real money balances and the asterisk indicates the desired level. The increased consumption will induce additional investment, and all these factors will increase the demand for loanable funds and put upward pressure on interest rates. Should this process be continued to the point of full employment and beyond, the effects of inflation cause even more pronounced upward pressure on the interest rate. In an inflationary period, everybody wants to be a borrower so as to pay back "cheaper" dollars out of higher incomes in the future. Because lenders are quite hesitant in such periods, only ever-higher rates of interest will clear the market.

Because it is not the goal or function of this book to resolve the Keynesian–monetarist controversy, let us merely consider several points raised by the monetarists that are relevant to the field of investments:

(1) *Money-supply increases in excess of real-output increases tend to result in inflation*

Stated in crude form, the above implies that $\Delta M - \Delta O \cong \Delta P$. A fairly impressive body of evidence from many countries and many periods of history exists to demonstrate this tendency. It also contributes to the reasons for the advocacy by Friedman and others that the money supply be increased automatically in line with productivity and real-output increases [see Friedman (1958) and Friedman (1960).]

(2) *Large rates of increase in the money supply tend to be associated with high, not low, rates of interest*

The theoretical justification for this phenomenon is the increased demand for loanable funds caused by the monetarists' secondary effect discussed above. Empirical evidence of this effect also exists,

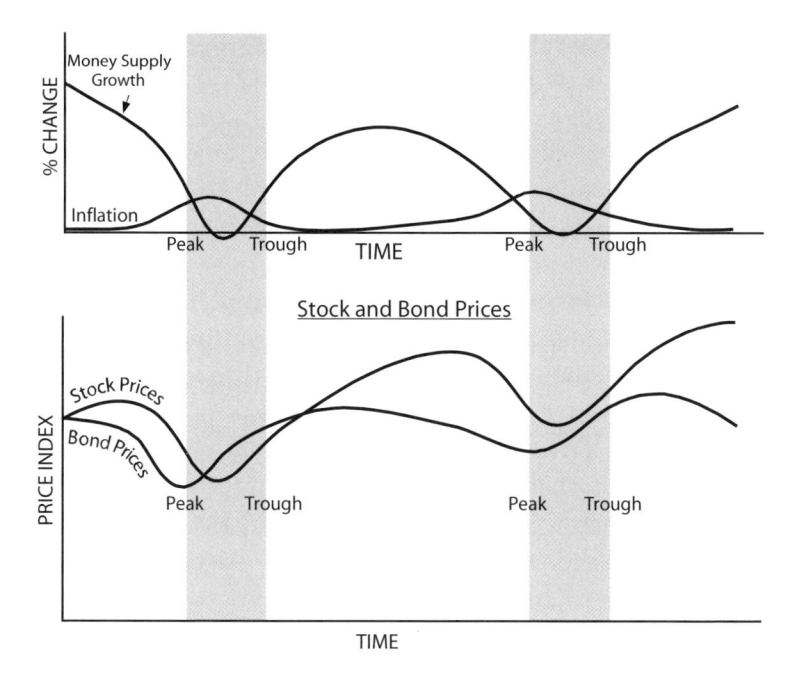

Figure 3.9. Monetary Change and Markets

although it is subject to some dispute. Another implication of this hypothesis is that much of the change in the interest rate on riskless securities can be attributed to inflationary expectations.

(3) *Changes in the rate of growth of the money supply affect the business cycle and, hence, the price and yields of securities*

It has been observed that business cycles may be anticipated by markets and are hence reflected in securities prices, as noted on Figure 3.9.

Interest Rate Term Structure

The ideas discussed above deal with the effects of monetary and fiscal policy upon the level of aggregate economic activity and interest rates. With regard to the latter, the nature of monetary policy and governmental finance causes the rate on treasury securities (and especially bills) to be among the first influenced. From the earlier discussion, it should be obvious that money-market instruments possess a fairly high level of substitutability for each other (on both the supply and demand sides of the market), and thus any change in treasury bill rates would be quickly reflected in the rates of the other instruments. The basic topic of this book, however, is long-term securities. Even here, as it was shown above, actions of the government will affect dividend- and interest-paying ability. A question arises, however, as to whether such policy actions have a direct effect upon long-term security prices, and the market rates of return. To be specific, is there a mechanism through which changes in short-term rates (or security prices) are also reflected in changed long-term rates? This section is directed to that question.

The theory of the term structure of interest rates holds that the observed market yield on otherwise identical securities may be a function of the securities' term to maturity. In other words, market return may be dependent upon maturity as well as all the other factors determining yield. Acceptance of this theory allows a yield curve to be drawn as a valid functional relationship. Three hypothetical yield curves are shown below. It is assumed that the securities depicted on a given curve differ only by maturity, not by other risk factors (U.S. government bonds are often used in the analysis for this reason). Curve A is called a flat yield curve, curve B is upward sloping, and curve C is downward sloping. The implications of the slope of the curve and the exact relationship of maturity to yield will depend upon which of the several term structure hypotheses one is prepared to accept.

The *pure expectations hypothesis* of the term structure is the simplest to understand. Let it be assumed that taxes and transaction costs do not exist, all securities are riskless as to income (the coupon will be paid), and all investors have identical expectations as to future short-term interest rates (the model should also work if enough investors at the margin share common expectations). It should then follow that an individual wishing to invest in bonds for 10 years could buy a series of 10 one-year issues, two five-year issues, a single 10-year issue, or a 20-year issue to be sold at the end of 10 years. Assuming the individual wishes to maximize profits, such an investor would

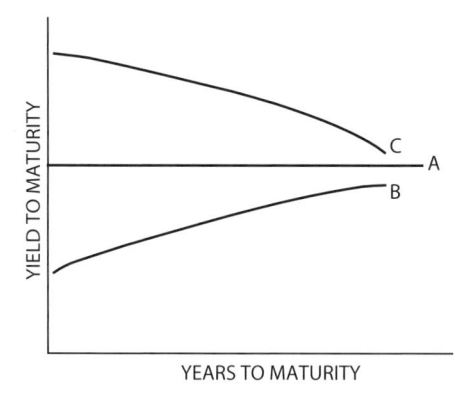

Figure 3.10. Three Hypothetical Yield Curves for Homogeneous Bonds which Differ Only by Maturity

presumably engage in that series of bond transactions promising the greatest return.

Because everyone has been assumed to hold the same expectations, equilibrium would not be established until the returns on all such courses of action were the same. At this point, one would earn the same return for a 10-year investment in bonds whether he or she bought a 10-year issue, a series of one-year issues, and so on. As the expected short-term rates have been assumed to be agreed upon, the pure expectations hypothesis essentially posits that long-term rates will adjust accordingly to maintain holding-period returns constant.

Let:

R_n = average rate of return, compounded once per period, on a bond maturing at the end of period n if purchased at the beginning of period t;

r_j = expectation in period t of the rate of interest on one-period bonds purchased at the beginning of period j (note that if $t = j$, the rate is known);

$\rho_{p,n}$ = expectation in period t of the average rate of return, compounded once per period, on bonds bought at the beginning of period p to mature at the end of period n.

94   Quantitative Financial Analytics

Then, for an investment of n years to have a uniform expected return regardless of maturity purchased:

$$(1 + R_n)^n = (1 + r_t)(1 + r_{t+1}) \cdots (1 + r_n). \tag{3.16}$$

Equation (3.16) merely reaffirms that the value of the investment after n years should be the same whether an n year bond or n one-year bonds were bought; this equation is restated in more general form as Equation (3.17). It illustrates that the average annual return on the long-term bond is the geometric mean of the intervening expected short-term rates:

$$R_n = \left(\prod_{j=1}^{n} (1 + r_j) \right)^{1/n} - 1. \tag{3.17}$$

It should follow for any length of time $n - k (k < n)$:

$$(1 + R_{n-k})^{n-k} = (1 + r_t)(1 + r_{t+1}) \cdots (1 + r_{n-k}). \tag{3.18}$$

Dividing Equation (3.16) by Equation (3.18) and rearranging terms, we obtain:

$$(1 + r_{n-k+1})(1 + r_{n-k+2}) \cdots (1 + r_n) = \frac{(1 + R_n)^n}{(1 + R_{n-k})^{n-k}}. \tag{3.19}$$

The information in Equation (3.19) tells us that, given the assumptions above, if we can observe the market rate on n-year (say, 10-year bonds) and on $n - k$ (say, seven-year bonds), then we have also obtained information about the currently expected one-year yields for the intervening period (years 8, 9, and 10). Furthermore, the pure expectations hypothesis would imply that it is currently expected that bonds with a maturity of k (three) years bought at the beginning of year $n - k + 1$ (eight) would have an average yield equal to the geometric mean of these expected one-year yields. Therefore:

$$(1 + \rho_{n-k+1,n})^k = (1 + r_{n-k+1})(1 + r_{n-k+2}) \cdots (1 + r_n). \tag{3.20}$$

Substituting Equation (3.19) into Equation (3.20) we obtain:

$$(1 + \rho_{n-k+1,n})^k = \frac{(1 + R_n)^n}{(1 + R_{n-k})^{n-k}}, \tag{3.21}$$

or

$$\rho_{n-k+1,n} = \sqrt[k]{\frac{(1+R_n)^n}{(1+R_{n-k})^{n-k}}} - 1. \tag{3.22}$$

Under the assumptions made, the investor could input the current market rate on 10-year and seven-year bonds to the right side of Equation (3.22) and obtain the market's current expectation of the rate on three-year bonds seven years from now. Before the reader becomes unduly excited about the interest rate prediction implications of Equation (3.22), a strong caveat is required. In the first place, it is necessary that the long-term rates be unbiased estimators of expected intervening short-term rates (for example, Equations (3.16)–(3.18) must hold); possible causes for this assumption to be unrealistic are considered below. Even if this condition holds, however, Equation (3.22) solves only $\rho_{p,n}$ (the rate currently expected on bonds sold in p to mature in n), not $R_{p,n}$ (the actual rate in year p on bonds maturing in n). Thus, as a practical matter, expectations may change over time or be wrong in the first place (possibilities assured away in formulating the model) such that $\rho_{p,n} \neq R_{p,n}$.

Example

Assume that riskless securities are available in five-year maturities to yield 6 percent and three-year maturities to yield 5 percent. Under all the assumptions of the pure expectations hypothesis, what is the rate currently expected on two-year bonds three years hence?

$$n = 5; \quad n - k = 3; \quad k = 2; \quad R_n = .06; \quad R_{n-k} = .05$$

$$\rho_{n-k+1,n} = \sqrt[k]{\frac{(1+R_n)^n}{(1+R_{n-k})^{n-k}}} - 1$$

$$\rho_{4,5} = \sqrt[2]{\frac{(1.06)^5}{(1.05)^3}} - 1 = \sqrt{\frac{1.338}{1.158}} - 1 = \sqrt{1.1554} - 1 \approx 7.5\%.$$

Thus, it is currently expected that two-year bonds will sell at an annual return of about 7.5 percent at the beginning of year four.

Term structure theory: Other hypotheses and implications

In view of the discussion earlier in this chapter, the reader may be wondering what impact inflation would have on the pure expectations model. It should be borne in mind that the theory deals only with nominal (market) rates of interest, not real rates. To the extent that future inflation is anticipated, then, by the monetarist view the expected one-year rates (r_j) would be adjusted accordingly and, if all the other assumptions held, the model would remain valid. The problem arises, of course, if future inflation is incorrectly estimated. In this case, unexpected inflation merely becomes another factor that can cause expectations to change over time and cause the failure of predictions made with Equation (3.22) to be fulfilled.

Another complication has been raised by a school of thought associated with Sir John Hicks (1939). It can be shown that a given change in the market rate of interest will have a greater effect upon the price of a bond the longer its term to maturity (see the example below). Sir John and his followers argued that the increased capital risk on long-term bonds makes lenders prefer short-term issues and requires a liquidity premium in order to lend on a long-term basis. Although short-term lending does reduce principal risk, it increases income risk (the risk or what will be earned in future periods) because the investor is then at the mercy of future short-term rates. Hicks assumed the former is more compelling than the latter. It is also maintained that borrowers prefer the security of having money for long periods (thus not being forced into the market at unseemly times) and are willing to pay this premium. The result is the Hicksian *liquidity preference version* of the expectations hypothesis. This version contends that long-term rates reflect expected future short-term rates plus a liquidity premium for lending long and as such, are biased estimates upward of the expected future short-term rate. Let:

$L_j =$ liquidity premium required in period t to lend long term rather than short term in period j.

Then Equation (3.13) in liquidity preference form becomes:

$$(1+R_n)^n = (1+r_t+L_t)(1+r_{t+1}+L_{t+1})\cdots(1+r_n+L_n). \quad (3.23)$$

The simplest comparison is with bonds maturing in year $n-1$:

$$(1+R_{n-1})^{n-1}$$
$$= (1+r_t+L_t)(1+r_{t+1}+L_{t+1})\cdots(1+r_{n-1}+L_{n-1}). \quad (3.24)$$

Dividing Equation (3.13) by Equation (3.15) and simplifying, we obtain:

$$r_n = \rho_{n,n} = \frac{(1+R_n)^n}{(1+R_{n-1})^{n-1}} - L_n - 1. \quad (3.25)$$

It thus becomes obvious that we cannot even predict currently expected rates much less actual future rates, without a complete schedule of the liquidity premiums embodied in the long-term rates.

It can be shown from Equation (3.16) that, if future short-term rates are expected to be constant ($r_t = r_{t+1} = \cdots = r_n$), then the long-term rate should be equal to the short-term rate ($R_n = r_t = \cdots = r_n$) for any term selected. This implies a flat yield curve for neutral expectations under the pure expectations hypothesis. In like manner, if future short-term rates are expected to rise from the current level ($r_t < r_n$), then the long-term rate, as the geometric mean of the short-term rates, should be greater than the current short-term rate (R_n). This implies an upward sloping yield curve. The liquidity preference version implies an upward sloping yield curve even under neutral expectations, however. Remember that even if short-term rates are assumed constant in Equation (3.23) the existence of the liquidity premiums (the L terms, assumed to be positive increasing with n) assures that R_n will rise as n increases. Thus, an upsloping yield curve does not mean that rates must rise in the future or necessarily that people think they will; it may merely represent neutral expectations and liquidity preference.

Note should be taken of the behavior of the yield curve over an interest rate cycle. If there exists some concept of the "normal" level of interest then it should follow that when rates are "low" relative to the norm, the yield curve should be upward sloping. The mere fact that future short-term rates are expected to be higher than current rates would cause the long-term rate to exceed the short-term rate by the analysis given above for the pure expectations case. Under the Hicks' version, the upslope should be greater than that for liquidity preference under neutral expectations. Likewise, at "high" interest rate levels, the curve would be downward sloping under the pure expectations model and moderately upward sloping, flat, or downward sloping (depending upon how "high" the rates are) under the liquidity preference version.

The null hypothesis with regard to term structure theory is the *market segmentation*, or *institutional pressure*, theory. Advocates of this theory contend the market at each maturity level (especially long-term versus short-term) is populated by borrowers and lenders who, because of the nature of their operations, legal restrictions, and so on, find it very difficult to operate at any other maturity level. As a result, it is contended, the markets at different maturity levels are segmented from each other. Long and short rates would thus be determined by supply and demand conditions within their respective markets and, at least within broad limits, would have no necessary relationships to each other. A yield curve would represent a specious functional relationship, and no information at all could be derived from its slope.

Now that we have come full circle from establishing the concept of term structure to discrediting it, perhaps it is time to reassess. The yield curve in the U.S. has been fairly generally upward sloping since the end of World War II. Rates have risen during this period, but not by enough to justify the slope. During the late 1970s, the hyperinflation induced by the fiscal and monetary policies of the Carter administration produced an incredible yield curve inversion with short rates being many basis points above long rates. With this exception, however, the downslope when rates were at cyclical peaks has not been nearly as steep as the upslope when rates were "low." This casual evidence, plus a good bit of empirical work, tends to indicate that the liquidity preference version may be more useful than the unmodified pure expectations hypothesis.

Predictions made on the basis of even the liquidity preference version have turned out badly, however. The fact that the implied rates differ from the actual rate ($\rho_{p,n} \neq R_{p,n}$) does not disprove the theory, of course; people could simply be wrong in their expectations. To assume that they are wrong consistently, however, is not very appealing. Nor is it terribly inviting to join the market segmentationists; it is difficult to accept that the most fungible of all commodities could be traded in such imperfect markets. Other models have assumed that people change their expectations of future rates on the basis of errors they make in estimating past rates. This error-learning model is fairly successful in explaining rate changes. Although these models are based on the pure expectations hypothesis, they are consistent with the liquidity preference version as well.

Examples

1. Assume that a 3 percent bond, paying interest semiannually, is selling at par. If the rate of interest goes to 4 percent, what would happen to price of the bond if its maturity were:

   a. one year
   b. 10 years
   c. never (a perpetual bond)

	Period	Payment	@2%/Period	P.V.
a.	1	$15	0.98	$14.70
	2	1,015	0.961	975.42
				990.12
b.	1–19	$15	15.678	$235.17
	20	1,015	0.673	683.1
				$918.27
c.	$15/.02 = $750			

2. Assume that expected one-year rates are as follows: Year one, 4 percent; year two, 5 percent; and year three, 6 percent. Assume

further that a lender requires a liquidity premium of 0.2 percent to lend two years instead one and that this premium grows at a compounded rate of 6 percent as the term of the loan increases.

a. What are the market rates on two- and three-year bonds?

$$(1 + R_n)^n = (1 + r_t + L_t)(1 + r_{t+1} + L_{t+1})$$
$$(1 + R_2)^2 = (1 + .04 + 0)(1 + .05 + .002)$$
$$R_2 = \sqrt{1.09408} - 1 = 4.6\%$$
$$(1 + R_3)^3 = (1 + .04 + 0)(1 + .05 + .002)(1 + .06 + .00212)$$
$$(1 + R_3)^3 = (1.04)(1.052)(1.06212) = 1.162044$$
$$R_3 = \sqrt[3]{1.162044} - 1 = 5.1\%.$$

b. If four-year bonds are yielding 6 percent, what is the implied one-year rate for year four?

$$\rho_{4,4} = \frac{(1 + R_4)^4}{(1 + R_3)^3} - L_4 - 1$$

$$\rho_{4,4} = \frac{(1.06)^4}{1.1620} - (.002)(1.06)^2 - 1$$

$$\rho_{4,4} = \frac{1.262}{1.162} - (.002)(1.124) - 1$$

$$\rho_{4,4} = 1.086 - .002 - 1 = 8.4\%.$$

Summary

In this chapter, we have outlined the major characteristics of the money and capital markets. We have also observed the conflicting effects of both monetary and fiscal policies upon the securities markets. Increases in government spending (or business investment), by increasing aggregate demand, tend to put upward pressure on security prices; yet, the increased supply of securities issued to finance such spending exerts downward pressure on prices. Likewise, increases in the money supply, by making money more plentiful in the portfolio relative to securities, tend to push security prices upward (rates downward); yet, constant infusions of money can fuel inflationary expectations and drive rates up.

All the above contradictions indicate the difficulty of determining the final effects of changes in macroeconomic variables. Nevertheless, because these variables are essential determinants of the risk and return patterns evidenced by individual securities, the analyst must assess them as best he or she can. The issue of the term structure of interest rates continues to be a debatable one with economic, econometric, and statistical models all failing to really capture the observed shapes and dynamics as the interest rate cycles unfold.

Problems

1. Find the price and yield on a treasury bill:

   a. due in 30 days on a 4 percent basis.
   b. due in 180 days on a 5 percent basis.
   c. due in 150 days on a 6 percent basis.

2. Refer to 1, above:

   a. Suppose you bought the bill in 1(b) and were selling it 30 days later as per 1(c). What return did you earn?
   b. Would you have been wiser to elect 1(a)?
   c. Would your answer to 1(a) change depending upon whether the bill were originally a 91- or 182-days bill? Why?
   d. What return on a tax-exempt security would be equivalent to 1(a), (b), and (c) if the investor's tax rate were 30 percent and 60 percent?

3. In the example of the NKV Trust in the chapter, suppose it decided not to cover the transaction and instead to sell the Dak at the end of six months for whatever the going rate was at the time. What would their return have been if the exchange rate at the time were 30:1? 35:1? 50:1? Why is an uncovered transaction inconsistent with the basic function of the money market?

4. Compute the annual return, on both a covered and uncovered basis, of the purchase of $10M, 90-day U.K. Treasury bills at

9 percent if the spot pound is $2.40 = £1, and the 90-day forward pound is $2.35, if the actual spot rate in 90 days is:

a. $2.40 = £1
b. $2.30 = £1
c. $2.50 = £1.

5. A bond has a coupon yield of 5 percent (that is, pays $50.00 per year on a par of $1,000), matures in 20 years, and sells for 80. Compute the yield to maturity of the bond using the discount tables and the shortcut formula. Compare your results.
6. Mr. Elgar has bought stock in the Pomp and Circumstance Corp. The firm pays a dividend $1.00 per share per year. Elgar feels that this dividend will be maintained over the 10 years he plans to hold the stock. If Elgar paid $25.00 per share and sold his stock for $30.00 per share in 10 years what is his expected yield from holding the stock?
7. Suppose Mr. Aged (see the example in the chapter) is expected to live 10 years and 10-year securities yield 8 percent. Would this change the solution?
8. Mr. Ronson (see example in the chapter) is also contemplating the purchase of a 10-year security of the Ziff government. The Ziff trade at 50 to the dollar and could trade at 40 to the dollar at the end of 10 years with a probability of 0.2. Gross yield is 12 percent, with 30 percent withholding treated as a credit on U.S. taxes. The IET is 5 percent. Determine Mr. Ronson's expected return.
9. The Lafarge Corporation has a 40 percent tax rate and is contemplating the purchase of securities of the Camus Corporation. Camus's 20-year, 7 percent debentures are selling at 95, while the preferred (6 percent) is selling at par. What is the return on each security? Which should be purchased? Why? Would your answer change if Lafarge were a tax-exempt institution?
10. Ignoring taxes and transfers, if $b = 0.9$ and $\Delta I = \$5$ billion, what is ΔY?
11. If $b = 0.7$, $Z = 0.1$, and $\Delta G = \$1$ billion, what is ΔY?
12. If $b = 0.7$, $t = 0.2$, $t_r = 0$, and $\Delta G = \$5$ billion, what is ΔY?

13. Answer 12 assuming $t_r = 0.1$.
14. If $A = \$100$ billion, $b = 0.8$, $t = 0.2$, and $t_r = 0$, plot the $S + T$ curve.
15. If $\bar{G} = \$50$ billion, $B = \$40$ billion, and $g = \$3$ billion per 1 percent Δi, graph the $G + I$ curve.
16. Given the data in Problems 14 and 15, graph the IS curve.
17. What would happen to the IS curve derived in Problem 16 given each of the following:
    a. t becomes 0.25;
    b. $\bar{G}$ becomes \$60 billion;
    c. G becomes \$4 billion per 1 percent Δi;
    d. b becomes 0.85?
18. In a loanable funds framework, determine the effect of each of the following changes upon the equilibrium rate of interest:
    a. an increase in the federal government's deficit;
    b. an increase in the marginal propensity to consume;
    c. an increased aversion on the part of localities to go into debt to pay for trains that "go to nowhere;"
    d. a decrease in businessman's expectations of future profit to be earned from investment projects;
    e. a public lack of confidence in the future manifesting itself in the form of an increase asset demand for money;
    f. a federal deficit partially financed by the sale of bonds to the Federal Reserve, causing an equivalent increase in the money supply.
19. Interpret the above events in a Keynesian framework, what differences, if any, do you find? Why?
20. If $l = 0.2$ and $m = \$10$ billion per 1 percent Δi, $J = 170$ billion, and $M = \$200$ billion, construct the LM curve.
21. Given the data in the Problems 16 and 20, determine the equilibrium level of Y and i.
22. Assume the GDP $= \$800$ billion, $M = \$200$ billion, V_o is constant, and the current level of output represents 95 percent of full employment. Give a monetarist explanation of what would happen if M were increased to \$200 billion.

104   Quantitative Financial Analytics

23. Assuming the facts in Problem 22:

   a. If the long-run real rate of interest is 3 percent and the former pure rate of interest was 5 percent, what should happen as a result of the increase in M?
   b. What should happen if a 10 percent increase in M were expected to become an annual event, while the increase in real output at full employment (caused by improved technology and population growth) were estimated at 4 percent?

24. A former U.S. Secretary of the Treasury analyzed a stock market collapse this way: "The stock market decline reflects the smart people being convinced they don't need common stocks as a hedge against inflation. Our economic policies have broken the back of the rampant price increases of recent years." Discuss the merits of the secretary's argument.

25. Assume that the following one-year interest rates are anticipated:

Year	Rate
1	5%
2	10%
3	5%
4	20%

   a. If $100 were invested in one-year bonds at the beginning of year one, to what amount will it grow by the end of year four?
   b. What annual rate of interest would a four-year bonds need to offer to be competitive?
   c. Answer b for a three-year bond sold at the beginning of year two.
   d. Answer b for a two-year bond sold at the beginning of year three.
   e. Answer b for a three-year bond sold at the beginning of year one.
   f. At what price would bond in b sell at the end of year two? Year three?

g. How would your answer to f change if, during year two, the expected rate in year four declined to 15 percent?

26. Riskless bonds are currently selling as follow:

Yield	Maturity
6%	5 years
7%	6 years
8%	7 years

Employing the pure expectations hypothesis:

a. What is the expected one-year rate five years from now?
b. What is the expected two-year rate five years from now?
c. What is the expected one-year rate six years from now?

27. If 25-year riskless bonds yield 4 percent, and 10-year bonds yield 6 percent, what is the expected 15-year rate 10 years hence under the pure expectations hypothesis?

28. Suppose the long-run real rate of interest is expected to be 3 percent. In addition, there is expected to be inflation of 3 percent in year one, 2 percent in year two, 1 percent in year three, and none thereafter. In a monetarist pure expectations framework, what rate of interest would be currently observable in the market on (a) one-year bonds; (b) three-year bonds; (c) 10-year bonds? If, in the next instant, the market also began to expect 2 percent inflation in year four, what would happen to the price of the three bonds?

29. Suppose that a 6 percent riskless security is currently selling at par and pays interest semiannually. If the interest rate were to drop to 4 percent, what would be the effect upon the price of the bond if its maturity were (a) six months; (b) one year; (c) five years; (d) 10 years; (e) 15 years; (f) perpetual?

30. a. Rework Problem 29 under the assumption that the interest rate went from 6 to 8 percent.
    b. Graph both sets of prices obtained against maturity.

c. Suppose that in the next instant there is a 0.5 probability that the rate will stay at 6 percent, a 0.25 probability that it will go to 8 percent, and 0.25 probability that it will go to 4 percent.

   (1) What is the expected value of the interest rate level and the price of the 6 percent bond that corresponds to it?
   (2) What is the expected value of the price of the 6 percent bond at each maturity level?
   (3) Which maturity would you prefer to hold in this case?

d. Can you now explain what financial economists mean when they discuss how asymmetrical distribution of expected interest rates will result in an asymmetrical distribution of expected bond prices?

e. What slope of the yield curve has been assumed in this problem? Are the assumptions concerning interest rate expectations consistent with this slope? Does it seem likely that this slope could be maintained? Why?

f. May changes in interest rates and inverse changes in bond prices be used interchangeably in capital market analysis as though they were equivalent?

31. Under the liquidity preference version, assume that lenders require a premium of 0.1 percent to lend for two years instead of one (L_2 = 0.1 percent) and that this premium grows at a compound rate of 10 percent per year for each additional year they must lend long (that is, L_3 = (0.1 percent)(1.10) = 0.11 percent). Under this assumption, rework Problem 26.

32. In a pure expectations framework, assume that currently expected one-year rates are:

Year	Rate
1	3%
2	4%
3	5%
4	6%
5	7%

Graph the yield curve (up to five-year bonds) implied by the data. Rework assuming the order of the rates is reversed. Assuming that expectation are fulfilled, what will the first four years of the yield curves drawn in a and b look like next year?
33. Rework Problem 32 employing the liquidity preference assumptions of Problem 31. Compare your results by placing the corresponding curves on the same graph. What is the effect of the presence of liquidity preference?

References

Barro, R. J., *Modern Business Cycle Theory*. Cambridge, MA: Harvard University Press, 1989.

Coyle, D., *GDP: A Brief but Affectionate History*. Princeton: University Press, 2014.

Davidson, P., *Post Keynesian Macroeconomic Theory: A Foundation for Successful Economic Policies for the Twenty-First Century*, 2nd edn. London: Edgar Elgar, 2011.

Friedman, M., *The Supply of Money and Changes in Prices and Output*, Testimony of Congress, 1958.

Friedman, M., *A Program for Monetary Stability*. New York: Fordham University, 1960.

Friedman, M. and Anna Schwartz, *A Monetary History of the United States, 1867–1960*. Princeton, NJ: Princeton University Press, 1963.

Fisher, I., *The Purchasing Power of Money*. New York: Macmillan, 1922.

Gilman, M., *Robert E. Lucas, Jr.'s Collected Papers on Monetary Theory*. Cambridge: Howard University Press, 2013.

Hicks, J., *Value and Capital*, 2nd edn. London: Oxford University Press, 2001 (first published 1939).

Keynes, J. M., *The General Theory of Employment, Interest and Money*. New York: Harcourt, Brace and World, 1936.

Marshall, A., *Money, Credit and Commerce*. London: Macmillan, 1922.

Sargent, T. J., "Robert E. Lucas, Jr.'s Collected Works on Monetary Theory," Review Article, *Journal of Economic Literature*, March 2015, pp. 43–64.

Taylor, J. B. and M. Woodford, eds. *Handbook of Macroeconomics*. Amsterdam: North Holland, 1999.

Chapter 4

Financial Statement Analysis

Now what I want is, Facts. Teach these boys and girls nothing but Facts. Facts alone are wanted in life. Plant nothing else, and root out everything else. You can only form the minds of reasoning animals upon Facts; nothing else will ever be of any service to them... Stick to the Facts, sir!

Charles Dickens, *Hard Times* (1854)

Ratio Analysis

In this chapter, we begin the process of analyzing individual securities. The culmination of our efforts will be the estimation of the variables needed to build an optimal portfolio: expected returns, variances, and covariances. In Chapter 5, some useful techniques for obtaining measures of these variables will be discussed. Additional procedures will be developed in later chapters.

The art of financial analysis has depended for years on the computation of ratios of data from the published financial statements of corporations (for example, balance sheets, income statements, cash flow statements, and so on). The earliest attempts at evaluating a firm and its securities were mainly qualitative assessments and shrewd guesses. These early attempts were succeeded by the computation of a growing battery of comparative financial statistics. These comparisons were of two kinds: comparisons over time and comparisons among different variables at the same time. The first form yielded simple but important information. As an example, suppose ABC Corp. earned $125,000 last year and $150,000 this year. The computation of a simple ratio [(This Year Sales − Last Year Sales)/(Last Year Sales)] would show that sales were up by 20 percent [($150,000−125,000)/($125,000)]. Although such a comparison is extremely crude in that it gives no clue as to why sales increased or whether such an increase will be sustained in the future, it is nonetheless a very significant first step in analyzing the financial position of the company. The second form of comparison is one among variables. Suppose ABC had sales this year of $150,000 and net income of $15,000. A comparison of these data would show that net income was 10 percent of sales. This information by itself may not be terribly useful, although if it were observed that such a relationship had held fairly steadily over time, perhaps a meaningful conclusion could be drawn.

Ratio comparisons have been made and can be made whenever it makes sense to examine the relationship between two or more financial numbers. There is nothing sacrosanct about any given set of ratios, and different comparisons may be necessary when conditions differ. Nevertheless, there is some advantage in attempting to standardize the computation of ratios whenever possible. Hence, financial analysts have developed a core of ratios that may be used in determining such things as the current financial condition of the firm, the trend in the firm's financial condition, and the financial condition of the firm in relationship to the position of other firms.

The information content of ratios and their use in determining the risk position of the firm and the expected rates of return on the firm's securities will be the focal point of this chapter. In the paragraphs that follow we present most of the basic ratios that the financial analyst may require. Additional ratios for unique industries are also given.

A number of interest groups, including internal management, may find ratios a useful guide for policy making. We shall focus here, however, on the use made of them by investors. Hence, we shall examine each category of ratios as they may apply to the evaluation of the securities of the firm. We name the ratio and provide a brief description of what its purpose is.

It should be observed that there was a time when searching for data and calculating ratios occupied most of an analyst's time.

Today, however, the ubiquity of cheap computing power has made the collection, dissemination, recapture, and possibly subsequential analysis much, much easier. Computers record vast quantities of company information and relay these data to the analyst upon command. Data providers such as Standard & Poor's Corporation, Compustat, Capital IQ, Factset, and many others can provide data such as 25 years of all balance sheet, income statement and statements of cash flow data at the press of a button. It is now possible to compute all 45 ratios (and more) given below, along with hundreds of other data elements, in seconds. Hence, the unpleasant effort of collection can be done painlessly in virtually no time. The analyst, must therefore spend more time analyzing and thinking how applicable the data in hand really is.

Financial Statements

Before we can delve into even the most common ratios, it is necessary to understand the basics of financial statements. These documents show the flow of revenues and profits for a company over a period of time, say a year, and the financial position of the company at a given date in time. The first of these is called an income statement and the second is called a balance sheet. The best way to become familiar with both statements is by examining a set. On the two pages to follow are income statements and balance sheets for American Funeral Supplies (AFS), Inc. This fictional company was founded in 1984 to supply various fluids, clothing, caskets, burial markers, and monuments to independent funeral directors. AFS went public in 2010, and has reported four complete years of statements filed with the SEC.

The company is headquartered in New Orleans and has sales of just under $7 billion. From its founding over 30 years ago, revenues (sales) have grown from less than $10 million to the present levels, or a compounded rate (taken from an HP-12C calculator) of 24.4 percent. Much of this growth has come from acquiring smaller companies in the same line(s) of business. The remaining sales growth has been generated by internal revenue development efforts and extensive marketing. Local funeral directors are called on regularly by American salesmen. Extensive entertainment is also done to cement personal relationships which are vital in this business.

The financial statements below are prepared following *Generally Accepted Accounting Principles* (GAAP). These principles are established by the *Financial Accounting Standards Board* (FASB), which is an independent, private *self-regulatory organization* (SRO). The SEC required public companies to use GAAP measures in their regular (annual, quarterly, etc.) filings. Given this, we may begin the process of calculating a number of ratios. The definition and purpose of each ratio will be explained first before we begin the number crunching.

American Funeral Supplies, Inc.
Statement of income and retained earnings for
the year ending December 31

(Millions of Dollars)

	2013	2012	2011	2010
Net sales	$6,883	$5,976	$4,814	$4,666
Cost of goods sold	4,320	3,600	2,882	2,895
Gross profit	$2,563	$2,376	$1,932	$1,771
Selling, general, and administrative expenses	874	788	677	648
Provision for amortization	173	128	170	175
Operating profit	$1,516	$1,460	$1,085	$948
Other income/expenses:				
Interest expense	(6)	(42)	(63)	(92)
Interest income	20	141	47	65
Earnings before taxes	$1,530	$1,559	$1,069	$921
Provision for federal income and state franchise tax	673	683	469	326
Net profit for the Year	$857	$876	$600	$595
Retained earnings, January 1	$2,542	$1,666	$1,066	$471
Dividends	219			
Retained earnings, December 31	$3,180	$2,542	$1,666	$1,066

American Funeral Supplies, inc.
Balance sheet as of December 31
(Millions of Dollars)

	2013	2012	2011	2010
ASSETS				
Current assets:				
Cash	$951	$898	$818	$706
Note receivable	239			
Accounts receivable (less allowance for doubtful collections)	630	455	357	281
Inventories	910	757	591	593
Prepaid expenses	91	61	47	22
Total current assets	$2,821	$2,171	$1,813	$1,602
Furniture, fixtures, machinery and equipment, motor vehicles	$227	$176	$153	$151
Less: accumulated depreciation	139	103	96	64
	$88	$73	$57	$87
Patents and trademarks	$1,178	$1,077	$853	$753
Less: accumulated amortization	751	578	450	280
	$427	$499	$403	$473
Goodwill	800	900	1,000	1,100
	$4,136	$3,643	$3,273	$3,262
LIABILITIES				
Current liabilities:				
Note payable	$0	$275	$1,000	$1,750
Accounts payable and accrued liabilities	224	196	118	100
Income tax payable	712	610	469	326
	$936	$1,081	$1,587	$2,176

(*Continued*)

(*Continued*)

	2013	2012	2011	2010
Capital stock:				
Authorized 100,000,000 shares of common no par value — issued and outstanding	$20	$20	$20	$20
Retained earnings	3,180	2,542	1,666	1,066
Total capital stock and retained earnings	$3,200	$2,562	$1,686	$1,086
	$4,136	$3,643	$3,273	$3,262

Group I — Liquidity

Short-term creditors, bondholders, and stockholders are all concerned with the liquidity of the firm (group I ratios). Liquidity is important to short-term creditors because payment of their claims may depend on the cash-conversion ability of the firm. Bondholders are concerned because deteriorating liquidity may impair the security of the firm's debt. If the firm's cashable assets (cash, accounts receivable, and in some cases, inventory) are low in comparison with liabilities soon to come due, then the payment of creditor interest may be jeopardized. Even if the firm has adequate fixed assets, the conversion of these assets into cash in order to meet liabilities may be expensive (the assets may have to be liquidated by the firm at prices below their economic values) and time consuming. Stockholders are also concerned with corporate liquidity because dividend payments, like interest payments, may be jeopardized if the firm is short of cashable assets. Furthermore, the long-run earning power of the firm may be impaired if it becomes necessary to liquidate fixed assets to meet current liabilities.

Even more importantly, if a company runs out of cash, it may be forced to make suboptimal decisions regarding both operational and financial matters. Indeed, a firm may be deemed "technically insolvent" even if its balance sheet shows total assets exceeding total liabilities. Obligations to pay everyone from employees to long-term creditors depend upon having cash and not a positive net worth (total assets in excess of total liabilities). Just try to make next Friday's payroll with a notice that the company has a positive net worth but is temporarily out of cash. The firm might as well have prepared for a bankruptcy filing instead.

a. <u>Current ratio</u>. Ability to meet current debts with current assets.

$$\frac{\text{Current assets}}{\text{Current liabilities}}.$$

b. <u>Cash ratio</u>. Ability to meet current debts with cash on hand.

$$\frac{\text{Cash + short-term securities}}{\text{Current liabilities}}.$$

c. <u>Quick (acid test) ratio</u>. Ability to meet current debts with more liquid current assets.

$$\frac{\text{Cash + short-term securities + receivables}}{\text{Current liabilities}}.$$

d. <u>Basic defensive interval</u>. How long the firm could meet cash obligations from liquid assets.

$$\frac{\text{Cash + short-term securities + receivables}}{\text{Daily operating expenditures}}.$$

e. <u>Working capital to total assets</u>. Liquidity of total assets and working capital position.

$$\frac{\text{Current assets} - \text{current liabilities}}{\text{Total assets}}.$$

Group II — Profit ratios

The maintenance of profit margins is necessary if the firm is to be able to service its debt obligations, pay dividends, and increase earnings. The ratios in group II are designed to test the ability of the firm to control costs and keep profit margins intact. The long-run profitability of the firm is clearly far more important to bondholders and stockholders than the asset security of the firm's debt and equity. Because asset liquidation is only a final resort relied upon by the unprofitable firm, profit-margin indicators assume the most important role for all the firm's investors.

a. Gross profit margin. Gross profit per dollar of sales.
$$\frac{\text{Net sales} - \text{cost of goods sold}}{\text{Net sales}}.$$

b. Operating income ratio. Operating profit before interest and taxes per dollar of sales.
$$\frac{\text{Net sales} - \text{CGS} - \text{selling \& adm. expenses}}{\text{Net sales}}.$$

c. Earnings before interest and taxes (EBIT) ratio: EBIT per dollar of sales.
$$\frac{\text{Net sales} - \text{CGS} - \text{S\&A expenses} + \text{nonoperating income}}{\text{Net sales}}.$$

d. Operating ratio. Operating expenses per dollar of sales.
$$\frac{\text{Operating expenses (CGS} + \text{S\&A expenses)}}{\text{Net sales}}.$$

e. Net profit margin. Net income per dollar of sales.
$$\frac{\text{Net income}}{\text{Net sales}}.$$

Group III — Turnover ratios

Turnover ratios (group III) indicate the ability of the firm to generate revenues from its asset investment. Even if profit margins are high, the firm may be unprofitable if a large investment in assets is required to generate a meager sales volume.

In addition to indexing the revenue-generating capacity of the firm, turnover ratios may also serve to portray the liquidity of the firm along with the ratios in group I. In particular, the working capital ratios IIIb through IIIf may give clues to the cash cycle of the firm, that is, its ability to convert receivables and inventories into cash.

a. <u>Total asset turnover</u>. Ability of invested capital to produce gross revenue.

$$\frac{\text{Net sales}}{\text{Total assets}}.$$

b. <u>Receivables turnover</u>. Quality and liquidity of receivables.

$$\frac{\text{Net credit sales}}{\text{Average receivables}}.$$

c. <u>Average collection period</u>. Period required to collect average receivables.

$$\frac{\text{Average receivables} \times 365 (\text{or } 360)}{\text{Net credit sales}}.$$

d. <u>Inventory turnover</u>. Liquidity of inventory and tendency to overstock.

$$\frac{\text{Cost of goods sold}}{\text{Average inventory}}.$$

e. <u>Average day's inventory</u>. Holding period of average inventory.

$$\frac{\text{Average inventory} \times 365 (\text{or } 360)}{\text{Cost of goods sold}}.$$

f. <u>Working capital turnover</u>. Indication of the cash cycle of the firm.

$$\frac{\text{Net sales}}{\text{Current assets} - \text{current liabilities}}.$$

Group IV — *Return on investment ratios*

Profit and turnover ratios lie behind the most-important group of comparisons — those describing return on investment. Indeed, the earning-power-of-total-investment is simply the EBIT ratio times the total-asset turnover ratio. Because a firm's return on investment is a function of both its ability to produce cheaply (margins) and sell in quantity (turnover), the rates of return on investment ratios are good summaries of the overall earning position of the firm.

a. <u>Net-earning-power ratio.</u> Net earning power of invested capital.

$$\frac{\text{Net income}}{\text{Total assets}}.$$

b. <u>Earning power of total investment.</u> Ability of invested capital to produce income for all investors (bondholders and stockholders) — eliminates "leverage" effect from net profit-to-total-assets ratio.

$$\frac{\text{EBIT}}{\text{Total assets}}.$$

also,

$$(\text{EBIT ratio}) \times (\text{total asset turnover}).$$

c. <u>Net profit to common equity.</u> Net earning power of common capital.

$$\frac{\text{Net income}}{\text{Total common equity}}.$$

Group V — Leverage and capital structure ratios

The use of debt by the enterprise to improve earnings for shareholders is demonstrated by the ratios in group V (leverage and capital-structure ratios). These ratios serve further to test the asset security of debt sources and the risk accruing to bondholders and stockholders from financial leverage. The income security of bondholders and preferred-stock holders is also indicated by these ratios.

a. <u>Total debt to equity ratio.</u> Total amount of debt leverage per dollar of common equity.

$$\frac{\text{Current liabilities} + \text{long-term debt}}{\text{Total common equity}}.$$

b. <u>Total debt to total capital.</u> Debt financing per dollar of total finance.

$$\frac{\text{Current liabilities} + \text{LTD}}{\text{CL} + \text{LTD} + \text{Pfd.stk.} + \text{Total common equity}}.$$

c. <u>Total debt to total assets</u>. Asset security of debt sources of finance.

$$\frac{\text{Current liabilities} + \text{LTD}}{\text{Total assets}}.$$

d. <u>Long-term debt (LTD) to equity ratio</u>. LTD leverage per dollar of common equity.

$$\frac{\text{LTD}}{\text{Total common equity}}.$$

e. <u>Tangible assets debt coverage</u>. Asset security of LTD sources of finance.

$$\frac{\text{Total assets} - \text{intangibles} - \text{current liabilities}}{\text{LTD}}.$$

f. <u>Total debt plus preferred to equity ratio</u>. Debt and preferred leverage per dollar of common equity.

$$\frac{\text{Current liab.} + \text{LTD} + \text{pfd. stk.}}{\text{Total common equity}}.$$

g. <u>Times interest earned ratio</u>. Income security of LTD.

$$\frac{\text{EBIT}}{\text{Long-term debt interest}}.$$

h. <u>Cash flow-times interest earned ratio</u>. Short-run ability to meet interest payments.

$$\frac{\text{EBIT} + \text{depreciation}}{\text{Long-term debt interest}}.$$

i. <u>Coverage of interest and sinking fund payments (I)</u>. Coverage of interest and sinking fund payments when depreciation exceeds sinking fund payments.

$$\frac{\text{EBIT} + \text{depreciation}}{\text{Interest} + \text{sinking fund}}.$$

j. Coverage of interest and sinking fund payments (II). Coverage of interest and sinking fund payments when depreciation is less than sinking fund payments.

$$\frac{\text{EBIT} + \text{depreciation}}{\text{Interest} + \frac{\text{sinking fund} - (\text{tax rate})(\text{depreciation})}{1 - \text{tax rate}}}.$$

k. Times-interest-earned plus preferred dividends. Income security of the preferred stock.

$$\frac{\text{EBIT}}{\text{Long-term debt interest} + \frac{\text{preferred dividends}}{1 - \text{tax rate}}}.$$

Group VI — Asset-relation ratios

The asset-relation ratios (group VI) may be used to supplement some of the previously outlined groups. The composition of assets into earnings and liquid parts is suggested by VIa. The ratios VIb and VIc are useful supplements to the liquidity and turnover ratios of groups I and III. Ratio VId is an indicator of the regularity and uniformity of depreciation allowances and may imply the necessity of adjusting the firm's depreciation accounts (see the "Adjustments to Financial Statements" section). Ratio VIe provides information about the average life of plant and equipment. It can also be used to determine whether reported earnings have been overstated (understated) when book depreciation has been inadequate (excessive).

a. Plant and equipment to total assets. Proportion of operating-earning assets to total assets.

$$\frac{\text{Net plant} + \text{net equipment}}{\text{Total assets}}.$$

b. Inventory to total assets. Size of inventory and tendency to over stock.

$$\frac{\text{Average inventory}}{\text{Total assets}}.$$

c. Receivables to total assets. Size of receivables and credit policy.

$$\frac{\text{Average receivables}}{\text{Total assets}}.$$

d. Annual depreciation to plant and equipment. Regularity and uniformity of depreciation allowances.

$$\frac{\text{Annual depreciation}}{\text{Gross plant and equipment}}.$$

e. Approximate average asset life. Average life of plant and equipment.

$$\frac{\text{Net plant and equipment}}{\text{Normalized depreciation}}.$$

Group VII — Common stock security ratios

The security of common stock may be determined from the ratios in group VII. The asset security, income security, dividend security, and leverage risk to shareholders are indexed by the ratios in this group.

a. Book value per share of common stock. Asset security of the common stock.

$$\frac{\text{Total common equity}}{\text{No. of shares outstanding}}.$$

b. Net tangible assets per share. Tangible asset security of the common stock.

$$\frac{\text{Total common equity} - \text{intangible assets}}{\text{No. of shares outstanding}}.$$

c. Leverage and capital structure ratios. Leverage risk of the common stock.

See group V ratios above.

d. Earnings per share (EPS) ratio. EPS of common stock.

$$\frac{\text{Net Income available for common}}{\text{No. of shares outstanding}}.$$

122 *Quantitative Financial Analytics*

e. Dividends per share (DPS) ratio. DPS of common stock.

$$\frac{\text{Dividends paid on common}}{\text{No. of shares outstanding}}.$$

f. Cash flow per share ratio. Cash flow per share retainable of investment in assets.

$$\frac{\text{Net income} + \text{depreciation}}{\text{No. of shares outstanding}}.$$

g. Payout ratio. Dividend security of the common stock and the dividend policy of the corporation.

$$\frac{\text{Dividends paid on common}}{\text{Net income available for common}}.$$

Group VIII — Yield and price ratios

The final group ratios (VIII) describe the yields of the securities of the firm. As such, these ratios are the most important single group. The percentage rates of return to bondholders, preferred stock holders, and common stockholders are computed with these ratios. Hence, they play a very important role in the selection of the optimal portfolio of securities.

a. Net yield to maturity. Expected annual rate of income return on funds invested in bonds.

To be read from bond table or computed (see Chapter 6).

b. Current yield of preferred. Expected annual rate of income return on funds invested in preferred.

$$\frac{\text{Annual cash dividends}}{\text{Market price of pfd}}.$$

c. Current yield of common (dividend yield). Expected annual rate of income return on funds invested in common.

$$\frac{\text{Annual cash dividends}}{\text{Market price of common}}.$$

d. *Price to earnings ratio.* Price of common relative to earnings.

$$\frac{\text{Market price of common}}{\text{Dollars earned per share of common}}.$$

e. *Earnings yield ratio.* EPS relative to price of common stock.

$$\frac{\text{Dollars earned per share of common}}{\text{Market price of common}} \times 100\%.$$

Common size analysis

Another presentation of income-statement and balance-sheet ratios is on a common size basis. This form breaks down each category of income, expense, asset, liability, and so on into percentages. Thus, all revenue and cost items are expressed as percentages of net sales. All asset items are expressed as percentages of total assets, and all liability and net worth items are expressed as percentages of total liabilities and net worth. This form of computation allows the analyst to make immediate comparisons of all items in the income statements and balance sheets of a firm over time and among firms at a point in time.

Now, let us review the income statements and balance sheets for American Funeral Supplies, Inc. (AFS, see statements above). We shall examine all ratios, interpret them, and attempt to consider their implications for the future. Common-sized statements will also be prepared. Assume our analysis is done in 2014.

Let us begin with the liquidity ratios. In 2013, AFS ended the year with $2.82 billion in current assets and had $936 million in current liabilities. This would result in a current ratio of just over 3:1. Historically, analysts have considered a 2:1 ratio to be good. Higher ratios would indicate greater relative liquidity, although much depends on the nature of the firm. Some businesses end the year with lots of cash and receivables soon to be collected. The current ratio for these businesses might tend to go down as receivables are collected and cash is spent during the year. From our knowledge of AFS' business, we understand that the winter months experience higher death rates than the summer, so a high level of current assets for funeral home suppliers might be expected. Next, we may compute AFS' cash ratio for 2013. In this case, the only non-cash securities are the note. Adding this to cash and dividing by current liabilities results in a cash ratio of 1.27. (Note that cash is the only items that would appear in this ratio in prior years.) The quick or "acid test" ratio combines the cash ratio numerator plus receivables. For AFS in 2013, this would be (in millions): [($951 + $239 + $630)/($936)] = 1.94.

Calculating the basic defensive interval (BDI) for AFS depends on knowing the daily cash expenditures. This might be approximated by summing the cost of goods sold expenditure and the selling, general, and administrative expenses expenditure and dividing by 365, or (in millions): [($4,320 + $874)/(365)] = $14.2 million per day. This amount would then be divided into the sum of the cash, short-term securities and receivables, or, in millions: [($951 + $239 + $630)] = $1,820. The BDI would thus be: $1,820/$14 million = 128 days. In other words, AFS should be able to operate without any new cash flows from future sales for about four months before running out of cash (assuming all receivables could be collected during this period). The working capital to total assets ratio for AFS in 2013 would be (millions): [($2,821 − $936)/($4,136)] = 0.46.

At this point, we could determine the five liquidity ratios for AFS from 2010 to 2013 as follows:

	2010	2011	2012	2013
Current	0.74	1.14	2.01	3.01
Cash	0.32	0.52	0.83	1.27
Quick	0.45	0.74	1.25	1.94
BDI (days)	102	121	113	128
WC/TA	(0.18)	0.07	0.30	0.46

Summarizing, the liquidity ratios suggests that AFS has become much more liquid over the past four years. The cash position has improved greatly, and the note payables have been completely paid off. The current, cash, and quick ratios have all become substantially more positive. The BDI has increased as well and the net working capital (current assets less current liabilities) has gone from being negative in 2010 to very positive in 2013. As a result, net working capital has become a fairly large percentage of total assets. All in all, it may be said that AFS has strong liquidity and could even reduce such if an attractive acquisition candidate came along.

Next, we turn our attention to AFS' profitability. The five ratios for 2013 are computed below (dollar figures in millions):

Gross profit margin	(($6,883 − 4,320)/$6,883	= 0.37
Operating profit ratio	$1,516/$6,883	= 0.22
EBIT ratio	($1,516 + $14)/$6,883	= 0.22
Operating ratio	($4,320 + $874 + $173)/$6,883	= 0.78
Net profit margin	($857)/($6,883	= 0.12

Notice that the "provision for amortization" is included as part of "selling, general, and administrative" expenses such that the ratio is simply "operating profit" divided by net sales. The reason for this will be explained in the "Adjustments to Financial Statements" section later in this chapter. The subsequent ratios are adjusted as well, so that the EBIT ratio merely adds "other income/expense" to operating profit and the operating ratio is operating expenses (including "provision for amortization") divided by net sales. At this point, we could determine the five profitability ratios for AFS from 2010 to 2013 as follows:

	2010	2011	2012	2013
Gross margin	0.38	0.40	0.40	0.37
Oper. profit	0.20	0.23	0.24	0.22
EBIT ratio	0.20	0.20	0.20	0.22
Oper. ratio	0.80	0.77	0.76	0.78
Net margin	0.13	0.12	0.15	0.12

An analysis of the profitability ratios indicates that AFS maintains fairly stable margins. These ratios should be compared with the same ratios for similar businesses to see if AFS is more, less, or about as profitable as its competitors.

Next, we examine AFS' turnover ratios. The six ratios for 2013 are computed below (dollar figures in millions):

Total asset turnover	$6,883/$4,136	= 1.66
Receivables turnover	$6,883/$630	= 10.93
Average collection period	($630)(365)/$6,883	= 33
Inventory turnover	$4,320/$910	= 4.75
Average day's inventory	($910)(365)/($4,320)	= 77
Working capital turnover	($6,883)/($2,821 - $936)	= 3.65

Observe that the average collection period is expressed in days as is the average day's inventory. This means the typical account receivable for AFS was outstanding for 33 days (from invoice to collection). Inventory remained in house an average of 77 days. At this point, we could determine the six turnover ratios for AFS from 2010 to 2013 as follows:

	2010	2011	2012	2013
Total asset turnover	1.43	1.47	1.64	1.66
Receivables turnover	16.60	13.48	13.13	10.93
Average collection	22	27	28	33
Inventory turnover	4.83	4.88	4.76	4.75
Average inventory	76	75	77	77
Working capital turn	N/A	21.30	5.48	3.65

An analysis of the turnover ratios portrays AFS as having fairly stable relationships. Once again, these ratios should be compared with those of similar businesses to see if AFS maintains more, less or similar sales generation per dollar of assets invested as its competitors. Note that the working capital turnover ratio is not applicable in 2010, due to the fact that net working capital is negative.

AFS' return on investment ratios is now considered. The three ratios for 2013 are computed below (dollar figures in millions):

Net earning power	$857/$4,136	= 0.21
Earning power of total investment	$1,530/$4,136	= 0.37
Net profit to common equity	$857/$3,200	= 0.27

The three return on investment ratios for AFS from 2010 to 2013 are as follows:

	2010	2011	2012	2013
Net earning power	0.18	0.18	0.24	0.21
Earning power of total investment	0.28	0.33	0.43	0.37
Net profit to common equity	0.55	0.36	0.34	0.27

The return on investment ratios for AFS are quite strong. Few publicly held companies earn as much money on their asset investment as does this company. One of the reasons for this is the fairly strong profit ratios combined with almost equally strong asset turnovers. Put another way, the economic position of the company is such that it can charge reasonably high prices (resulting in strong profit margins) on an asset base that is relative small. Not many firms are so fortunate. Lurking behind this positive situation is an indication that AFS may have relatively few competitors, and those it has may have cost structures less efficient than that of AFS. Many businesses have high profit margins, but their asset base must be very high to earn those margins (steel companies, auto manufacturers, and even railroads currently). Other, such as retailers, smaller manufacturers, etc. have low profit margins but still make a good profit by turning over their asset base several times a year. Grocery stores typically operate on very thin margins (often under 3 percent) but turn their major asset (inventory) over many times a year and thus achieve nice returns on investment. One concern for AFS is the decline in all three ratios in the latest year.

Although there are 11 "Group V" ratios provided, several are not in extensive use today. Many bond issuers still require sinking funds, but required redemptions (by call or market purchase) are increasingly popular. Sinking funds are a means of making sure companies can repay their debts by having money regularly deposited in a "fund" to pay off the debt. Also few publicly held firms except for banks and certain other financial institutions issue preferred stock. AFS has no LTD outstanding; so, for calculation purposes, only three ratios remain. As AFS adds LTD to its capital structure (Chapter 6), we shall return to a more extensive list of leverage and capital structure ratios.

Total debt to equity	$936/$3,200	= 0.29
Total debt to total capital	$936/($936 + $3,200)	= 0.23
Total debt to total assets	$936/$4,136	= 0.23

Notice that the last two ratios provide the same result. This is because AFS has no LTD. Also, note that the definition of "equity" in the AFS statements is the "capital stock" account plus accumulated retained earnings. Thus, total capital equals total assets in this case. At this point, we could determine the three ratios for AFS from 2010 to 2013 as follows:

	2010	2011	2012	2013
Total debt to equity	2.00	0.94	0.42	0.29
Total debt to total capital	0.67	0.48	0.30	0.23
Total debt to total assets	0.67	0.48	0.30	0.23

An analysis of the above ratios indicates that AFS has reduced its note payable over the past four years from $1.75 billion to zero. Additionally, it has increased its equity from $1.1 billion to $3.2 billion over the 2010–2013 period. As a consequence, all of the leverage ratios have improved dramatically. Indeed, it may be argued that AFS is insufficiently leveraged at this point. One way to balance this would be to borrow money to re-purchase its common stock. Another would be to borrow to make future acquisitions. Both measures augur well for existing stockholders and are quite positive for the future of the company.

The five asset-relation ratios for 2013 are computed below (dollar figures in millions):

Plant and equipment to total assets	$88/$4,136	= 0.02
Inventory to total assets	$910/$4,136	= 0.22
Receivables to total assets	$630/$4,136	= 0.15
Annual depreciation to plant and equipment	$36/$88	= 0.41
Approximate average asset life (in years)	$88/$36	= 2.44

The plant and equipment account for AFS is indicated as "furniture, fixtures, machinery, motor vehicles" on the balance sheet. The depreciation of $15 million is not specifically found on either the balance sheet or income statement. Some depreciation is most likely included in both the "cost of goods sold" account and the "selling, general, and administrative expense" account. Information of this sort is usually found in more detailed financial statements or in footnotes to the statements which will be discussed later in this chapter (under the "Adjustments to Financial Statements" section).

The five asset-relation ratios for AFS from 2010 to 2013 are calculated as follows:

	2010	2011	2012	2013
Plant and equipment to total assets	0.03	0.02	0.02	0.02
Inventory to total assets	0.18	0.18	0.21	0.22
Receivables to total assets	0.09	0.11	0.12	0.15
Annual depreciation to plant and equipment	0.34	0.56	0.34	0.41
Approximate average asset life (in years)	2.94	1.79	2.94	2.44

The asset structure of AFS shows a heavy emphasis on inventories. This is not surprising given the nature of the business. Much of the inventory (fluids, clothing, and caskets) is purchased from other manufacturers, and AFS only makes a limited product line of cemetery grave markers. The company sells directly to funeral homes on terms (either cash up front, or for long-time customers, payment due 30 days after the shipment of goods). Receivables are not large given the sales volume of the business. There is very little in the way of fixed assets. Mostly this is office furniture, fixtures, etc., and vehicles. A small amount of manufacturing equipment is maintained for the production of grave markers. Given the nature of the operations, the fixed assets are depreciated over a fairly short time frame. This is true despite the fact that the actual physical life of much of the fixed assets is longer than that required for accounting (and tax) write-offs.

Next, we examine AFS' common stock security ratios. The six ratios for 2013 are computed as follows (dollar figures and number of shares in millions):

Book value per share of common stock	$3,200/100	= $32.00
Net tangible assets per share	($3,200 − $800)/100	= $24.00
EPS ratio	($857)/100	= $8.57
DPS ratio	$219/100	= $2.19
Cash flow per share	($857 + $36)/100	= $8.93
Payout ratio	$219/$857	= 0.26

Summarizing, AFS had a book value of $32.00 per share at the end of 2013. After subtracting the "goodwill" intangible (to be discussed later in the "Adjustments to Financial Statements" section below), the tangible assets per share were $24.00. The firm earned $8.57 per share, had cash flow of $8.93 per share, and paid out a dividend of $2.19 per share. The balance ($8.57 − $2.19) was retained and added to the "retained earnings" account. The dividend of $2.19 per share was 26 percent of the earnings for the year and was the first dividend paid since AFS went public. Examining the quarterly financial statements of the company (not included in the text), we find that the dividend was originated in the first quarter of 2013 at $.50 per share. This amount was also paid in the second and third quarters and was raised to $.69 per share in the fourth quarter.

The ratios for 2010–2013 are indicated as follows:

	2010	2011	2012	2013
Book value per share of common stock	$10.86	$16.86	$25.62	$32.00
Net tangible assets per share	($.14)	$6.86	$16.62	$24.00
EPS ratio	$5.95	$6.00	$8.76	$8.57
DPS ratio	Nil	Nil	Nil	$2.19
Cash flow per share	$6.02	$6.32	$9.06	$8.93
Payout ratio	Nil	Nil	Nil	0.26

These ratios suggest the asset and income security of AFS' common stock have improved over the past four years. Book value per share has tripled while tangible book has gone from a negative to a substantial positive. Earnings and cash flow per share have also advanced. The initiation of a dividend in 2013 seems prudent given the increasingly positive cash and earnings position of the company. The $2.19 dividend is protected by almost four times in earnings, such that the payout ratio is conservative at 0.26. Further dividend increases might be expected in the future.

Finally, AFS' yield and price ratios are considered. Of the five ratios, only three are applicable since the company has no outstanding bonds or preferred stock. The remaining ratios for 2013 require information on the price of AFS common stock, and there are a number of ways to make the calculation. For example, we might use the price of the stock at the present. For past calculations we could use an average of the high and low price for the year or the price at the end of the year. Research analysts typically use the high/low average for the past and the current price for the present. Suppose we are examining the stock just after earnings were announced to the public early in 2014. Suppose further that the high/low prices in the past were as follows (dollars per share):

	2010	2011	2012	2013
High	$47.86	$56.86	$65.62	$92.03
Low	$27.80	$36.06	$45.22	$52.09
Average	$37.83	$46.46	$55.42	$72.06

Based on the average prices, the yield and price are computed below (dollar figures in millions):

Dividend yield of common stock	$2.19/$72.06	= 3.3 percent
Price to earnings ratio	$72.06/$8.57	= 8.4X
Earnings yield ratio	$8.57/$72.06	= 11.9 percent

The three return on investment ratios for AFS from 2010 to 2013 are as follows:

	2010	2011	2012	2013
Dividend yield of common stock	Nil	Nil	Nil	3.3%
Price to earnings ratio	6.4X	7.7X	6.3X	8.4X
Earnings yield ratio	15.7%	12.9%	15.8%	11.9%

Adjustments to Financial Statements

By necessity, ratio analysis depends on the use of externally reported accounting data. To the extent that accounting data do not accurately depict the real economic condition of the firm, ratios do not give a good picture of the position of the firm. Accounting practices do not always produce numbers that the financial analyst regards as adequate or useful. Hence, adjustments have to be made frequently to accounting reports so that the analyst can get the information one wants. When accounting practices vary among firms or industries, the analyst must also make adjustments in order to get comparable results.

We may divide the various adjustments to financial statements into several categories. Perhaps the most important type of adjustment is that resulting from the presence of nonrecurring items on income statements. The payment of back taxes or receipt of tax refunds, the results of litigation or renegotiation, profits or losses on the sale of fixed assets, adjustments to the market value of securities, the write-down or recovery of foreign assets, and the proceeds of life insurance policies collected are all income statement entries that cannot be expected to recur. The appropriate adjustment for these items is to transfer them from the income statement to a schedule of capital charges and credits and to adjust the deduction for income taxes accordingly.

A second type of adjustment may be required when allocations have been made from income to reserve accounts. Examples of this practice are commonly found in the establishment of valuation reserves, liability reserves, and net-worth reserves. As a rule, the analyst should add back to income all reserve appropriations that are not allowed as deductions for income tax purposes.

A reconciliation of reported taxable income with the income tax deduction indicated in the income statement is required when any substantial deviations exist. The U.S. corporate tax rate is 35 percent for most publicly held firms. The average state corporate income tax typically brings the total income tax rate to about 40 percent. There are a number of explanations for deviations, and the analyst should explore all possibilities. Common examples include: (1) loss carry-backs and carry-forwards; (2) tax-exempt income; (3) dividends from domestic corporations; (4) profits and losses from the sale of capital assets; (5) minerals depletion allowances; (6) investment company exemptions, plus many more. In the U.S., municipal bonds are generally exempt from federal income taxes. Thus, corporations that carry these items (such as banks and insurance companies) may have a lower average tax rate than companies that hold no such bonds.

Only 30 percent of the dividend income received by domestic corporations paid by other domestic corporations is taxable in the U.S.. Firms that carry substantial holdings in common stocks (such as property and casualty insurance companies and entities like Berkshire Hathaway) may thus have their taxes reduced by this exclusion. In the U.S., oil, gas and mining companies are given depletion "allowances" that are deductible from taxes. These allowances are based on a percentage of revenues. Other tax discrepancies may result from management decisions. When depreciation is charged at a higher rate for tax purposes than on financial statements, the tax deduction item will be lower than expected. This typically results in a balance sheet account called "deferred tax liabilities." Capital charges and credits that should be reflected in the equity accounts may affect the taxes paid by the corporation. Taxes may be higher or lower depending on whether a charge or a credit is involved. Interest payments made during the construction of plant (particularly for public utilities) are not a legitimate charge to income, although they may be allowed as a deduction for tax purposes. This item should be capitalized as a construction cost (by adjustment if necessary), and shown as a discrepancy in the tax reconciliation.

The analyst's attitude toward tax discrepancies should be the following: Determine the reason for the difference. If the discrepancy is due to tax-exempt income or depletion allowances, the results should be accepted as reported. If the difference is due to capital gains, these transactions should be separated from the income statement as nonrecurring items and taxes should be adjusted accordingly. If the firm has a small tax or no tax due to loss carryforwards, earnings should be computed on the basis of full tax assumption for that year. When discrepancies result from allocations to reserves that are not deductible, earnings should be restated after adding back these allocations.

Intangible assets (patents, goodwill, and so on) should be treated with great care, as their value on the books often has no relation to their market value or future income-generating capacity. If a company leases a substantial amount of its assets (which may often be detected by the presence of sizable leasing expenses on the income statement), it may appear to have little debt and yet be heavily obligated by leasing contracts. Accounting rules now provide that most lease payments be capitalized and booked as both an asset and a liability, generally increasing fixed assets and LTD.

Adjustments to financial statements should be made with caution. Although one goal of adjusting statements is the assurance of uniform data for making comparisons, the analyst should not adopt a doctrinaire approach. When it is felt that an adjustment is required in order to reflect more accurately the true economic position of the firm, the adjustment should be made. If the analyst is considering an adjustment because it is believed the data for one firm over time or for a group of firms at a point in time are not comparable, it should be asked whether the adjustment is being contemplated for sake of convenience or because it is really needed. In no case should an adjustment be made if the result is small. As a rule, if the impact of an item is less than 5 percent of the pertinent result (net income, total assets, and so on), it can safely be ignored.

Another form of adjustment is almost always made by the firm in the preparation of its financial statements. These are adjustments made necessary by common stock splits and dividends paid in stock rather than cash. If data are not adjusted for these changes, gross distortions may result. In the case of small dividends paid in stock (i.e., less than 5 percent), analysts frequently ignore the adjustment. It should be pointed out, however, that the cumulative effect of a large number of such dividends of less that 5 percent can be significant. The payment of dividends in stock from issuing more shares to existing stockholders (rather than paying dividends in cash) is increasingly uncommon, however.

An income statement and a balance sheet for Raw Data, Inc., are provided below:

Raw Data, Inc.
Consolidated Statement of Income
(thousands)

Net sales	$250,000
Cost of goods sold[1]	200,000
Gross Income	50,000
Selling and adminstrative expense	20,000
Net operating income	30,000
Other income[2]	30,000
Earnings before interest and taxes	60,000
Interest	5,000
Earnings before taxes	55,000
Taxes	21,250
Net Income	33,750

[1] Includes $10 million reserve for replacement of plant.
[2] Includes a $5 million tax refund, $10 million profit from sale of securities, $5 million in municpal bond interest, and $10 million in dividends from subsidiaries.

Raw Data, Inc.
Consolidated Balance Sheet
(thousands)

Current assets	$200,000
Net plant	400,000
Other assets [1]	300,000
Total Assets	900,000
Current liabilities	200,000
Long-term debt	100,000

(*Continued*)

(Continued)

Net worth	
Common stock	200,000
Retained earnings	250,000
Reserve for plant replacment	150,000
Total net worth	600,000
Total liabiliaites and net worth	900,000

[1] Includes $100 million in municipal bonds (at market) and a $200 million investment in subsidiaries.

Appropriate adjustments to the income statement and balance sheet would be the elimination of nonrecurring items from the income statement. The profit on the sale of securities should be reduced. Assuming a marginal tax rate of 30 percent, the result would be a change in the reserve for the replacement of plant. It should be deducted from cost of goods sold (that is, added back to income). The adjusted income statement would appear as follows:

Raw Data, Inc.
Adjusted Consolidated Statement of Income
(thousands)

Net sales	$250,000
Cost of goods sold	190,000
Gross Income	60,000
Selling and adminstrative expense	20,000
Net operating income	40,000
Other income	15,000
Earnings before interest and taxes	55,000
Interest	5,000
Earnings before taxes	50,000
Taxes	18,250
Net Income	31,750

Financial Statements and Accounting Data

There are times when simply adjusting a firm's financial statements is insufficient to make them useful to the analyst. Even though the auditors may have given the opinion that a document has been prepared "according to generally accepted accounting principles," this reassurance may mean very little. Unfortunately, accounting is an art and not a science, and there is no single "correct" way of recording business transactions. The accounting community frequently attempts to achieve verifiable results, which implies that reasonable people examining the same data would come to the same conclusions. These data are supposed to be supported by formal business documents that evidence "arm's-length" transactions and that leave little room for interpretation. Of course, if perfect verifiability were achieved (which never happens), it would be at the expense of the usefulness of statements. Many transactions do require interpretation for meaningful presentation, and judgment may play an important role. On the other hand, when opinions, estimates, and judgment become significant in interpreting financial events, the objectivity and consistency of reporting may suffer.

Consider an asset which was purchased two years ago for $100,000 with an estimated life of 10 years and no salvage value. Under the accounting principle of verifiability, it could objectively and consistently be determined that the asset cost $100,000, that under straight-line depreciation it would be valued at $80,000 today, and that the annual depreciation expense for the asset is $10,000. Unfortunately, only the first of these numbers may have any real economic meaning. The asset may be worth $90,000 today (due to price changes) and the replacement depreciation might be closer to $11,250. Nevertheless, the current value of the asset and its replacement depreciation are very subjective numbers. Reasonable persons may have differing opinions on these figures, and herein lies the dilemma. Verifiable, objective, and consistent statements are not terribly useful. On the other hand, statements in which opinion and judgment play a substantial role may lose comparability over time for a firm and across firms at an instance in time. Moreover, statements that are subjective in nature are much more easily abused in evaluation than those conservatively prepared. An unscrupulous management may prevail upon accountants to prepare (and its auditors to certify) reports that are blatantly misleading if too much interpretative leeway is allowed. We shall return to the issue of adjustments in Chapter 6, when the security analysis element for AFS is considered.

Financial Analysis for Mergers and Acquisitions

A major set of problems develops for the analyst when a merger occurs. It is clear that the combination of two firms during an accounting period may distort the financial reports of the surviving company, particularly with regard to such general figures as sales, net income, and so on. Of course, arranging the figures on a per share basis may reduce some of the distortion; but even per share numbers can differ widely after a merger, even though the firm's position may not have altered considerably. The biggest problem for the analyst is making the figures comparable before and after the merger. This task is becoming more and more difficult as corporate acquisitions assume a more important role in business.

Technically speaking, a combination of two or more companies in which one is the survivor is called a merger; if a totally new company absorbs the old companies, a consolidation has been effected. A combination of firms involved in different stages of the production of the same product is a vertical merger, and the combination of firms in totally unrelated lines of business is called a conglomerate merger. A combination of companies in the same business is called a horizontal merger.

A merger may be effected either by the purchase of a firm's assets or by the purchase of its stock. A purchase of assets generally requires only the approval of the board of directors of the purchasing company. In both cases, some form of approval by the stockholders of the selling company is required. A purchase of stock also generally involves the acquisition of the liabilities and assets of the firm. If the purchase is made in the form of cash or debt securities, any gain is taxable immediately either to the firm or to the shareholders (if distributed under a plan as a dividend in total or partial liquidation).

The acquiring company, however, is often able to write up the assets for additional depreciation if a cash purchase is made. A purchase for stock will usually defer taxation to the holder until the stock is disposed of, but the purchasing company will only acquire the assets at their book value. In any case, the purchase may result from negotiations with the company or a direct tender offer to the stock holders for their shares. Dissenting stockholders may go to court to have a fair market value of their shares determined and demand payment in cash.

Deal Structure

In terms of deal structure, there are really only two alternatives: an asset purchase or a stock purchase. Buying a proprietorship or a partnership must always involve an asset purchase for obvious reasons. These entities do not issue stock. The purchase of a corporation, however, may be done either through a stock purchase or though an asset purchase. Purchasing the stock of an existing corporation involves risks that may be avoided by doing an asset purchase. Although one gets the entire business "lock, stock, and barrel" when buying a corporation's common stock, part of the "barrel" may include liabilities that are not presently on the company's balance sheet. These liabilities are often called "contingent" liabilities and may result from events that have taken place in the past. These liabilities may turn out to be substantial and identifying them is a major part of the due diligence process done when one company is considering the purchase of another.

Installment Sales Analysis

Often sellers are willing to accept a note as part (or total) payment for the sale of a business. The note represents the purchaser's promise to pay cash to the seller over a specified future period rather than on the date of sale. In an "arm's length," seller financed deal, the seller will typically require the purchaser to pay a market rate of interest on the note. As a general rule, the seller will then include the principal amount of the purchaser's note in the amount realized on sale and compute a gain or loss accordingly. In this case, the seller may use a statutory tax method of accounting for gains (or losses) realized called an installment sale.

Under the installment sale method, the seller does not recognize the entire realized gain or loss in the year of sale. Instead, income recognition is linked to the seller's receipt of cash over the term of the note. The seller calculates the gain recognized in the year of sale and each subsequent year by multiplying the cash received during the year by a profit percentage. This percentage is calculated by taking the gain realized and dividing by the sale price. Thus, if Jones has a tax basis in his business of $1 million and he sells the business for $1.5 million, his gain would be $500,000. The profit percentage would be: $500,000/$1,000,000 or 50 percent. As principal payments are made, this percentage is applied to calculate tax. Suppose Jones received $100,000 at the closing of the sale, his taxable gain would be: (0.50)($100,000) or $50,000. Assuming he has owned the business for longer than one year, this $50,000 would be subject to being taxed as a long-term capital gain.

It should be observed that the annual interest payments that the seller receives on an installment note are not part of the computation of recognized gain. Instead, the seller recognizes these interest payments as ordinary income. When a seller receives a purchaser's note in a seller financed sale, the seller generally takes a basis in the note equal to its face value. This basis represents the dollars that the seller will recover as tax-free principal payments.

Let us consider a more complicated example. Smith is contemplating an offer to sell his business to Brown International, Inc., a Texas corporation. Brown has offered $1 million in cash or a payout of $100,000 each year with interest at 10 percent on the unpaid balance. What should Smith do? Assume the following:

1. A stock sale is contemplated.
2. Smith has tax basis of $10,000 in his stock.
3. Smith could reinvest all his cash in treasuries at 3 percent.
4. Smith has a long-term gain on his stock and will pay 15 percent capital gains tax.
5. Smith pays tax at a 35 percent rate on ordinary income.

The solution to Smith's problem is as follows: First, Smith would have a realized gain of $990,000 on the sale of his stock. At a 15 percent tax rate, Smith could pay his capital gains taxes and have the following left over:

$$[\$1,000,000] - [0.15][\$990,000] = \$1,000,000 - \$148,500$$
$$= \$851,500.$$

Investing at 3 percent, this would give Smith an annual income before tax of:

$$[0.03][\$851,500] = \$25,545,$$

which after paying 35 percent income tax would leave:

$$[0.65][\$25,545] = \$16,604.$$

In the alternative, Smith could accept Brown's installment offer. Assuming an initial payment at closing of $100,000 plus $100,000 each year over the next nine years, Smith would receive installment payments net of tax of $85,150. He would also receive interest on the unpaid balance of his note as follows:

Year	Balance	Interest	Net of tax (0.65)
0	$1,000,000	0	0
1	$900,000	$90,000	$58,500
2	$800,000	$80,000	$52,000
3	$700,000	$70,000	$45,500
4	$600,000	$60,000	$39,000
5	$500,000	$50,000	$32,500
6	$400,000	$40,000	$26,000
7	$300,000	$30,000	$19,500
8	$200,000	$20,000	$13,000
9	$100,000	$10,000	$6,500

Smith's total after-tax cash flows from the installment would thus be:

Year	Principal	Interest	Total
0	$85,150	0	$85,150
1	$85,150	$58,500	$143,650
2	$85,150	$52,000	$137,150
3	$85,150	$45,500	$130,650
4	$85,150	$39,000	$124,150
5	$85,150	$32,500	$117,650
6	$85,150	$26,000	$111,150
7	$85,150	$19,500	$104,650
8	$85,150	$13,000	$98,150
9	$85,150	$6,500	$91,650

which might be compared to the cash flows from the cash sale:

Year	Cash	Installment	Difference
0	$0	$85,150	($85,150)
1	$16,604	$143,650	($127,046)
2	$16,604	$137,150	($120,546)
3	$16,604	$130,650	($114,046)
4	$16,604	$124,150	($107,546)
5	$16,604	$117,650	($101,046)
6	$16,604	$111,150	($94,546)
7	$16,604	$104,650	($88,046)
8	$16,604	$98,150	($81,546)
9	$868,104*	$91,650	$776,454

*$851,500 + $16,604.

Now suppose Smith invested the difference at the after-tax treasury return of: $(0.65)(3 \text{ percent}) = 1.95$ percent. The resulting differential cash flow would be:

Year	Difference	FV@1.95 percent
0	($85,150)	
1	($127,046)	($213,856)*
2	($120,546)	($338,573)
3	($114,046)	($459,221)
4	($107,546)	($575,722)
5	($101,046)	($687,994)
6	($94,546)	($795,956)
7	($88,046)	($899,523)
8	($81,546)	($998,610)
9	$776,454	($241,629)

*$85,150(1.0195) + $127,046$, etc.

Thus, given these assumptions, the installment deal is "worth" $241,629 in future value dollars more than the all cash deal. This should be weighed against the risk differences to make the decision.

Corporate Structure for Mergers and Acquisitions

Acquisition transactions may be either taxable or tax deferred (to the seller). Tax-deferred exchanges must meet the criteria discussed below and are classified as Type "A", Type "B" or Type "C" reorganizations (see Figures 4.1–4.3).

Type "A" reorganizations include both consolidations and mergers. Under a *consolidation*, a new corporation is organized to assume all the assets and liabilities of the combining firms. The separate firms are then dissolved. A *merger* involves the absorption by an existing corporation of the assets and liabilities of another corporate entity. The acquired firm is then dissolved. The merger need not involve the formation of a new corporation. An existing corporation may absorb

Financial Statement Analysis 145

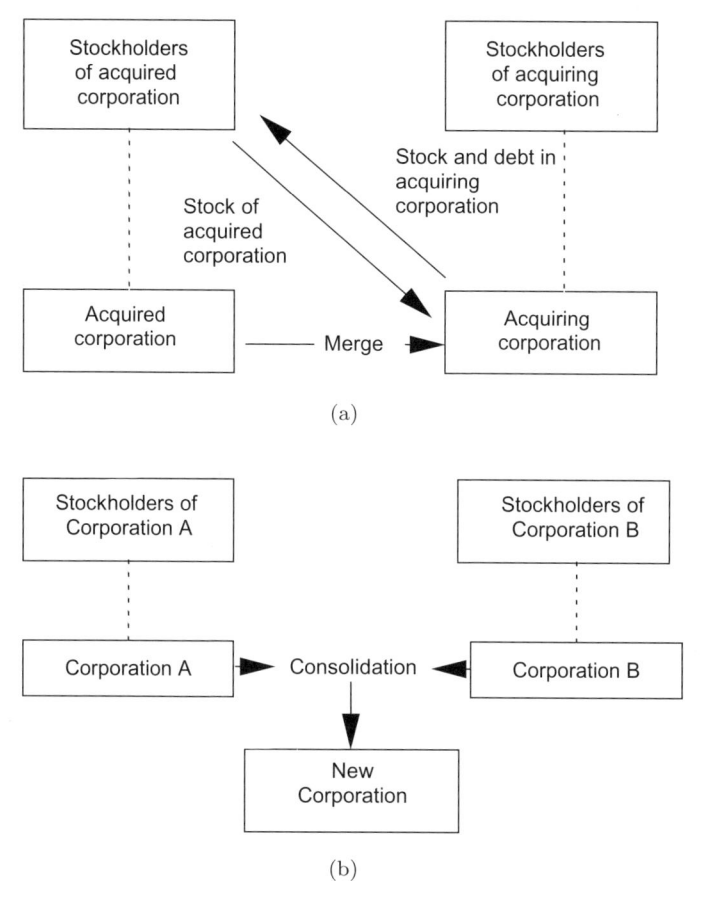

Figure 4.1. Type A Reorganization (Statutory Merger and Consolidation)

another existing corporation, which then ceases to exist. However, corporate names can and do frequently change.

The advantages of the Type "A" consolidation/merger route include the following: (a) The transaction can be set up to qualify as a tax-deferred reorganization. (b) The transformation is permanent and gives the management of the surviving corporation complete control. (c) The method favors the exercise of centralized authority. The offsetting factors are as follows: (a) The arrangement is inflexible. The acquiring company must assume all the assets and liabilities of the selling firm, including those adverse to its primary

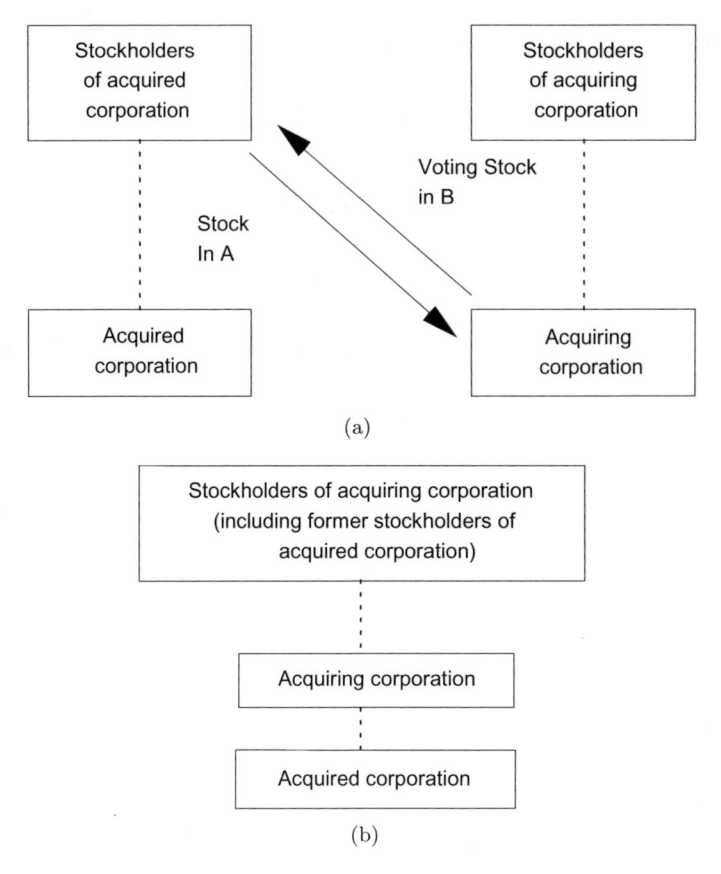

Figure 4.2. Type B Reorganization (Stock for Stock)

strategy. (b) Stockholders of both corporations must consent to the combination. Dissenting stockholders may demand an appraisal of their holdings and payment in cash. Dissenters also may sue to test compliance with the legal formalities stipulated by the state law. (c) Negotiators must wrestle with the issues of valuation, the choice of accounting method, and the tax status of the two firms and their stockholders. (d) The behavioral problem of blending two management teams with separate corporate loyalties can be a formidable task. (e) The permanent nature of the arrangement makes dismantling difficult if the acquisition should subsequently prove to be an unfortunate decision.

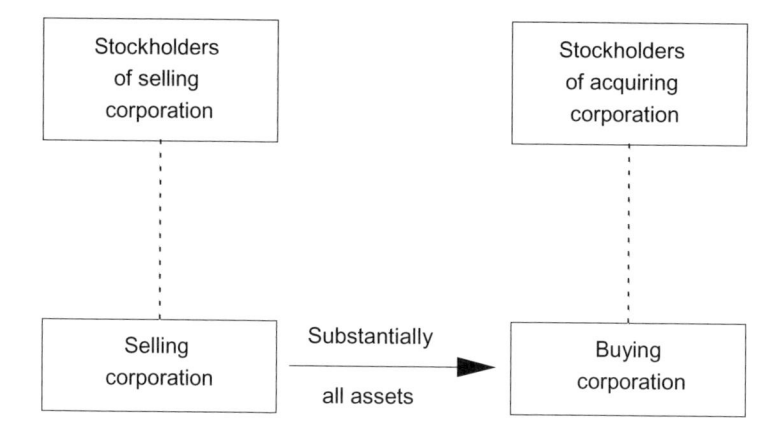

Figure 4.3. Type C Reorganization (Stock for Assets)

Under a Type "B" reorganization, the acquired corporation remains as a subsidiary of the acquiring corporation. The advantages are the same as for the Type "A" reorganization (above) with the added advantages that contracts with that corporation generally are not voided and another layer of protection may be provided in case of lawsuits (although "alter ego" assertions are frequently made with success by plaintiff attorneys). The disadvantages are also the same as for the Type "A" reorganization with the added disadvantages that records must be kept separately for the subsidiary corporation and additional state franchise taxes must be paid.

Under a Type "C" reorganization, voting stock in the acquiring corporation is issued for substantially all of the assets of the acquired corporation. The advantages are generally the same as for the Type "A" reorganization except that the Type "C" is more easily accomplished if the acquired company has many stockholders. The disadvantages are also generally the same as for the Type "A" reorganization except that the arrangement is more flexible (liabilities are not assumed but substantially all assets must be purchased).

The term "boot" frequently appears in tax deferred reorganizations. One definition of boot is: "that which is 'thrown in,' or given in addition, to make up a deficiency of value; a premium, compensation." 1483 Cath. Angl. 49 Bute [v.r. Buyt], auctorium, augmentum. 1593 G. FLETCHER Licia (1876). Were all the world offered to make a change, yet the boote were too small. 1597 SKENE Expl. diffic. Wds. s.v. Bote (Jam.), The aine partie that gettes the better, giues ane bote, or compensation to the vther. 1600 HEYWOOD1 Edw. IV, III. i. Wks. 1874 I. 44 If I were so mad to score, what boote wouldst thou giue me? a1652 BROME Queen IV. iv, Doct. Too many a man. .will change with thee And give good Boot. 1726 CAVALLIER Mem. IV. 313 Now I am convinced that my Religion is better than yours since you give me so much Boot. The term evidently first appeared in print as a translation in a 1483 Bible as Middle English for the Latin "Augmentum," "That which augments, makes up a deficiency of value."

With a type "A" reorganization, the issuance of stock plus "boot" is possible. The stock does *not* have to be voting stock (preferred stock is also permitted). Boot must be less than 50 percent of purchase price to preserve the continuity of interest doctrine. Any boot is taxable. With a type "B" reorganization, the deal must be all stock for stock. Only voting stock for at least 80 percent of each class of stock of acquired corporation is a requisite. The acquired corporation remains "alive" as a subsidiary of the acquirer. Net operating loss carryforwards cannot be appropriated without additional reorganization. A type "C" reorganization results when only voting stock is used to acquire the assets of the seller. This method is useful when stock is widely held. Boot is acceptable for up to 20 percent of purchase price.

It should be noted that tax-deferred reorganizations do not result in tax never being paid by the seller. Tax is merely postponed until the stock of the acquiring corporation is eventually sold, and the tax basis of the seller remains at his or her original basis. For example, suppose the stockholders in the DEF Corp. sold all of their shares to ABC Corp. and DEF became a wholly owned subsidiary of ABC. This transaction would probably qualify as a Type "B" reorganization. No tax would be paid by DEF shareholders until they sold their ABC stock. Suppose Mr. and Mrs. Smith owned all of the stock in DEF and had a basis of $50,000 in their stock. Suppose they received 11,150 shares in ABC, for a new basis of $50,000 \div 11,150 = \$4.4843$ per share. When the Smiths sold their ABC stock, their capital gain tax would be paid using the $4.4843 basis to calculate the gain. If they sold stock at say, $100 per share, their taxable gain would be: $100.00 - \$4.4843 = \$95.5157$ per share.

If a seller takes all cash for the sale of his or her business, the capital gains tax is due the year the sale takes place. If a deal qualifies as a tax-deferred reorganization, tax payments are as outlined above. If notes are taken, or if the deal fails to qualify as a reorganization, the selling taxpayer(s) may receive installment sale treatment taxation on the sale. Under an installment sale, tax is paid only to the extent that cash (or its equivalent) is received.

For example, suppose the Smiths (above) sold all of their stock in DEF to ABC for the following:

Cash	$200,000	
Notes	315,000	
Stock in ABC	600,000	(6,000 shares @ $100)
	$1,115,000	

Since boot (cash + notes) is still less than 50 percent of the purchase price, part of the deal would still be tax-deferred. (The deal would have to be a Type "A" reorganization rather than a "B" however.) The Smiths would have to pay tax on the $200,000 received in the year of the closing. This would represent $\$200,000/\$1,115,000 = 17.937$ percent of their total gain. Thus, their gain for the first year would be:

Selling price	$1,115,000
Basis	50,000
Total gain	$1,065,000

The capital gain due the year of closing would be: (0.17937) $(\$1,065,000) = \$191,029$. The stock portion of the transaction would still have a basis $4.4843 per share, and tax would be due on the difference between the ultimate selling price of their ABC stock and $4.4843. The $315,000 in notes would be taxed as the notes were paid down (hence, "installment" sale). Also, interest on the notes would be taxed as earned. Suppose the notes were at 7 percent and $100,000 was paid at the end of one year after the closing. Interest of $(0.07)(\$315,000) = \$22,050$ would be paid by ABC to the Smiths. This would be taxed at ordinary (not capital gains) rates to the Smiths (and deductible as an expense to ABC). Also, the Smiths would pay capital gains tax on: $\$100,000/\$1,115,000 = 8.9686$ percent of their gain, or: $(0.089686)(\$1,065,000) = \$95,515.70$ in that year. Future interest and capital gains would be computed according to the repayment schedule of the notes. Observation: It is important for the Smiths to maintain the tax deferred status of this deal. If over 50 percent of the $1,115,000 were received in cash + notes, *none* of the stock portion would be tax-deferred. Worse still, the entire amount received in stock would be treated as if it were cash! (The basis of the stock received would become its fair market value, however, or $100.00 per share rather than $4.4843.)

Accounting for Mergers and Acquisitions

The assets and liabilities of an acquired firm are reported after the merger on the books of the acquiring firm at their "fair market value" (usually determined by appraisal). Individual assets are carried at their separate "fair values," and liabilities are similarly appraised and carried. Any difference between the actual price paid for the acquisition and its net (assets less liabilities) fair value is reported as "goodwill from acquisitions." At the date of combination, the retained earnings balance of the surviving company is carried forward, and the balance of the acquired firm is eliminated. After the combination, future financial statements depict only the historical data of the acquiring company.

When the analyst encounters a merger, an examination of the reasonableness of the transaction should be made. The acquired assets may be worth a higher purchase price (than their book value) because of the synergism of the combination (the 2 + 2 = 5 effect). Equally possible, however, is that inflation and higher replacement costs account for at least part of the difference. In any event, the analyst should accept the transaction (market) price of the assets. Under current accounting rules, "goodwill" is permanently placed on the books of the acquiring company, and "goodwill" is only written down if it is deemed that the "goodwill" has been permanently impaired. In our earlier example of American Funeral Supplies, Inc. it should be noted that the company has grown principally through acquisitions. When we begin the analysis of AFS' securities in Chapter 6, we will return to the issues addressed above at that point.

Special Industry Ratios

Although any industry has its own signature on its activity ratios, certain ones are so unique that we should discuss them in detail.

Railroads

Several industries require special ratios in addition to those listed above. The unique character of the railroads, for example, necessitates the computation of several financial and physical ratios that give a better picture of the operating characteristics of that industry than would be discerned from the standard core. The *maintenance ratio* indicates the effort the railroad is making in keeping its roadway and equipment in good repair. It is calculated by comparing the amount spent on maintenance to total operating revenues. This ratio is important because railroads tend to have heavy fixed charges (bond interest), and during lean times they are prone to let maintenance, which is postponable, lag behind. When the roads are "starving" their facilities, it is clear that expensive repairs may have to be done in the future, a fact that the analyst should know.

A second important railroad ratio is the *transportation* ratio. It is given by dividing transportation expenses by operating revenue and is a measure of the operating efficiency of the railroad. The physical measurement, *net ton-miles per train-hour*, is the best indicator of revenue efficiency and costs available to the analyst. Ton-miles are a good indicator of revenue efficiency. Such factors as car capacity utilized (tons per car), train size (cars per train), and miles per car-hour (train speed) are included in the ratio. Train-hours, similarly, are a convenient measure of cost.

Regulated (public) utilities

Analysis of public utility securities also requires several different ratios and some reinterpretations of the existing core. Many analysts believe, for example, that the operating ratio for public utilities should *exclude* depreciation allowances. This is a large item for most utilities, and differing estimations of plant life can significantly affect the amount charged to depreciation. Hence, comparisons of the operating efficiency of various utilities (control of wages, fuel costs, purchased power, operating taxes, maintenance, and so on) would be clouded if depreciation were included. With the separation of depreciation from the operating ratio, a new ratio, *depreciation as a percentage of operating revenue*, should be computed. This will indicate the consistency and relative size of depreciation in relation to operating revenues.

Physical ratios are also important for the public utilities. It is possible to compute the average *rate*, *usage*, and *bill* for residential and industrial users of electricity. These data are very useful in determining the factors underlying revenue patterns and can be crucial in assessing growth rates for public utilities. On the cost side, *system peak* and *load factors* are important, because the demand for electricity tends to be hourly and seasonal. If a utility has a capacity that is too small, consumer demand cannot always be accommodated (leading to brownouts or blackouts under severe conditions). This causes irritation of, and occasional trouble with, regulating authorities. On the other hand, too large a capacity is expensive and can eat into profits. One way the utility can reduce the effects of this phenomenon is through encouraging off-peak demand. Its ability to do this is given by the *load-factor* ratio:

$$\frac{\text{Total annual output}}{\text{Hours in a year}} \div \text{peak load}.$$

Thus, if a utility produces 1 million kwh (kilowatt hours) in a year and has a peak load of 200 kw, its load factor would be:

$$\frac{1,000,000}{8,760} \div 200 = 57\%.$$

Airlines

For the airlines, a *load factor* is also important. Two types of load ratios are usually computed. The *passenger load factor* indicates the percentage of seats occupied during the year. It is compared with the *break-even passenger load factor*, which is the percentage of occupied seats required for the coverage of total costs. (A variation of this ratio may be computed to determine the occupancy percentage required to cover fixed costs.) Load factors are useful to determine how much excess capacity the airline has. Because the airlines are a high-fixed-cost industry, profit rates tend to rise rapidly as the passenger load factor exceeds the break-even factor.

Airline analysts calculate two efficiency ratios that are useful in appraising costs. The *average length of trip* is calculated by dividing the total annual miles flown by the number of flights scheduled during the year. Longer trips are generally less costly per mile than short ones. Hence, higher values for this ratio imply more profitable operations. Another efficiency ratio is the average number of hours each plane is in the air. The ability of the firm to utilize its equipment intensively is usually considered favorable because depreciation and maintenance costs do not vary proportionately with the number of miles flown or the time each plane spends in the air.

Commercial banks

Financial institutions are unique and require special analysis. Commercial banks are highly levered, and the analyst must be careful to assess the *capital-to-deposits* ratio for them. In order to be profitable, a bank cannot maintain too large an amount of capital relative to its deposits. Nevertheless, if the ratio is too low, a small decline in the value of the bank's assets (through loan defaults or losses on its bond portfolio) can eliminate the stockholders' investment and even threaten the position of depositors. For this reason, regulatory authorities will put pressure on a bank with a low ratio. Institutions with high *risk-assets-to-capital* ratios (risk assets include loans, discounts, municipal bonds, corporate bonds, and miscellaneous assets) should be in the upper end of the range, and banks with low risk-assets-to-capital ratios could be in the lower end. A final ratio for banks that should be examined closely is the *net-loan-losses-to-net-operating-income* ratio. Losses on loans are usually not deducted from net operating income but are reported separately. It might be expected that highly profitable banks (making riskier loans) should have a larger net-loan-loss ratio than less-profitable banks, although this is not always the case. Since the 2008 collapse, commercial banks have been subject to greatly increased regulatory scrutiny. New ratios are being determined by the FDIC, Federal Reserve, Comptroller of the Currency, and so on to oversee bank solvency and survivability. Large banks still may be "too big to fail," but smaller ones certainly are not.

Life insurance companies

The reported profitability of life insurance companies depends to a large extent on the *legal reserves* that must be set aside out of premiums to meet future claims. This reserve will depend upon the mortality tables assumed by the company and the rate of interest it can earn on investments. If a conservative reserve policy is established by the company, it may report lower earnings than an equally profitable firm with a less-conservative policy. The analyst should examine the *mortality ratio* (ratio of actual mortality experienced to anticipated mortality) and the *interest ratio* (ratio of actual return on investment to expected return) to see if the reserves set aside have been excessive or insufficient.

Property and casualty companies

Three special ratios are required for analyzing property and casualty insurance companies. The *loss ratio* compares the loss and loss-adjustment expenses to net premiums earned. It gives some indication of the risk-selection ability of the firm. The *expense ratio* compares the commissions and acquisition expenses to net premiums written. It gives information about the cost-control abilities of the company. The *underwriting-gain-or-loss ratio* compares the loss and acquisition expenses to premiums earned. Underwriting gains or losses do not include investment income, which tends to be the major source of profits for stock property and casualty companies.

Mutual funds

For mutual funds, the *load* expresses the sales commission on the shares in terms of the gross amount paid. Thus, an 8.5 percent load would imply that an investor would pay $100 for shares with an asset value of $91.50; note that an 8.5 percent load corresponds to a ($8.50/$91.50) 9.3 percent *markup*. The *management fee*, usually expressed as a percentage of total assets per annum, is also of interest. *Brokerage fees to total income* (or, *securities sold to total assets*) will give some indications of the expenses generated by the managers in search of performance. The above factors are usually analyzed together, as the no-load funds are often run by brokerage firms and managed to generate sufficient management and brokerage fees in order to eliminate much of the advantage to investors of having no load. The *gross-redemption ratio* is given by (value shares redeemed/total value of shares); the *net-redemption ratio* is [(value of shares redeemed−value of new shares sold)/total value of shares]. Both these ratios give some indication of investor confidence in the fund; the latter also gives weight to management's ability to compensate for redemptions by the sale of new shares. The *cash ratio* for a fund is the cash and money-market instruments to total assets. A large ratio can imply (1) management bearishness on the market; (2) a preparation for anticipated net redemptions; or (3) a recent inflow of funds from the sale of new shares or portfolio liquidation that has not been employed. The most significant performance ratio is probably the annual return, which is given by:

$$\frac{\text{Assets per share (EOY)} + \text{dividend paid} - \text{assets per share (BOY)}}{\text{Assets (BOY)}}.$$

This return can then be compared over time to that of other funds or some market index.

In spite of the fact that as of 2015 there are over 9,500 publicly traded mutual funds (when there are only 5,500 stocks listed on the major exchanges), over the last decade, the growth in mutual funds and their investment has tapered, or become less popular. Instead, *exchange traded funds (ETFs)* have seen a huge increase in both ownership and investement opportunity. Since 2006, the number of available ETFs has exhibited a 17 percent compounded growth rate versus less than 1 percent for mutual funds. ETFs are like common stocks in that they are continually priced and can be bought or shorted anytime during the trading day through a broker-dealer by paying brokerage commissions. Often this is a flat fee or just a small percentage of the value of the investment.

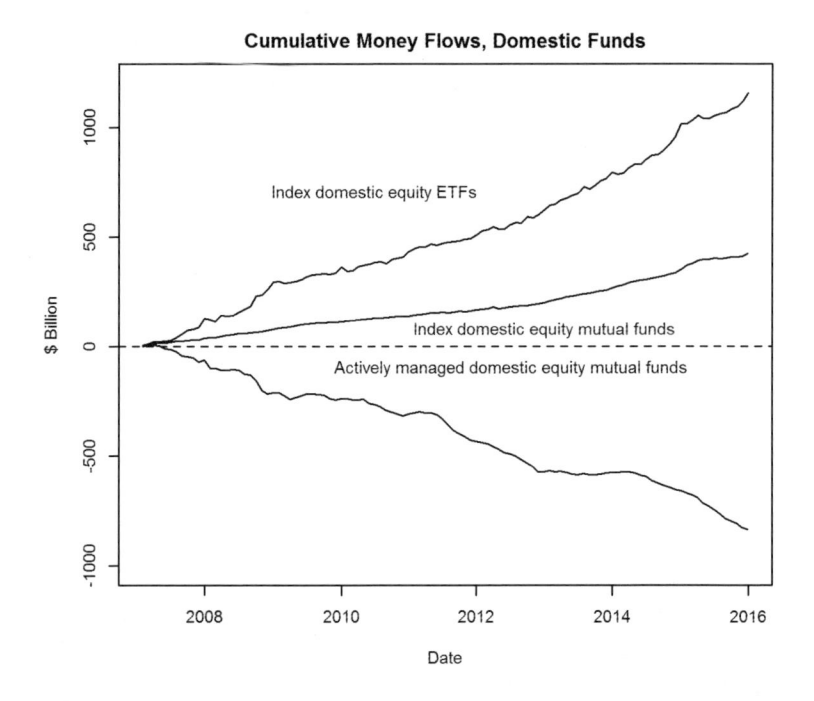

Cumulative Money Flows, Domestic Funds

Managers of the ETFs (often brokerage or investment banking firms) charge a fee for operating these entities. For managed index

ETFs, this fee is usually lower than a corresponding mutual fund fee; the average ETF fee is about 50 basis points (0.5 percent) annually, compared with the average 75 bps mutual fund fee. In the case of ETFs that "buy the market" (say the S&P 500 or Russell 2000), these fees can be extremely cheap, averaging less than 10 bps.

Summary

In this chapter, we began the process of analyzing individual securities. The culmination of our efforts will be the estimation of the variables needed to build an optimal portfolio: expected returns, variances, and covariances.

The art of financial analysis has depended for years on the computation of ratios of data from the published financial statements of corporations (for example, balance sheets, income statements, cash flow statements, and so on). The earliest attempts at evaluating a firm and its securities were mainly qualitative assessments and shrewd guesses. These early attempts were succeeded by the computation of a growing battery of comparative financial statistics.

Ratio comparisons may be made whenever it makes sense to examine the relationship between two or more financial numbers. There is nothing sacrosanct about any given set of ratios, and different comparisons may be necessary when conditions differ. Nevertheless, there is some advantage in attempting to standardize the computation of ratios whenever possible. Hence, financial analysts have developed a core set of ratios that may be used in determining such things as the current financial condition of the firm, the trend in the firm's financial condition, and the financial condition of the firm in relationship to the position of other firms.

By necessity, ratio analysis depends on the use of externally reported accounting data. To the extent that accounting data do not accurately depict the real economic condition of the firm, ratios do not give a good picture of the position of the firm. Accounting practices do not always produce numbers that the financial analyst regards as adequate or useful. Hence, adjustments have to be made frequently to accounting reports so that the analyst can get the information wanted. When accounting practices vary among firms or industries, the analyst must also make adjustments in order to get comparable results.

There are times when simply adjusting a firm's financial statements is insufficient to make them useful to the analyst. Even though the auditors may have certified a document as having been prepared "according to generally accepted accounting principles," this reassurance may mean very little. Unfortunately, accounting is an art and not a science, and there is no single "correct" way of recording business transactions. The accounting community frequently attempts to achieve verifiable results, which implies that reasonable people examining the same data would come to the same conclusions. These data are supposed to be supported by formal business documents that evidence "arm's-length" transactions and that leave little room for interpretation. Of course, if perfect verifiability were achieved (which never happens), it would be at the expense of the usefulness of statements. Many transactions do require interpretation for meaningful presentation, and judgment may play an important role. On the other hand, when opinions, estimates, and judgment become significant in interpreting financial events, the objectivity and consistency of reporting may suffer.

A major set of problems develops for the analyst when a merger or large acquisition occurs. It is clear that the combination of two firms during an accounting period may distort the financial reports of the surviving company, particularly with regard to such general figures as sales, net income, and so on. Arranging the figures on a per share basis may reduce some of the distortion; but even per share numbers can differ widely after a merger, even though the firm's position may not have altered considerably. The biggest problem for the analyst is making the figures comparable before and after the merger. This task is becoming more and more difficult as corporate acquisitions assume a more important role in business. Technically speaking, a combination of two or more companies in which one is the survivor is called a merger; if a totally new company absorbs the old companies, a consolidation has been effected. A combination of firms involved in different stages of the production of the same product is a vertical merger, and the combination of firms in totally unrelated lines of business is called a conglomerate merger. A combination of companies in the same business is called a horizontal merger.

The assets and liabilities of an acquired firm are reported after the merger on the books of the acquiring firm at their "fair market value" (usually determined by appraisal). Individual assets are carried at their separate "fair values," and liabilities are similarly appraised and carried. Any difference between the actual price paid for the acquisition and its net (assets less liabilities) fair value is reported as "goodwill from acquisitions." At the date of combination, the retained earnings balance of the surviving company is carried forward, and the balance of the acquired firm is eliminated. After the combination, future financial statements depict only the historical data of the acquiring company.

When the analyst encounters a merger, he or she is advised to examine the reasonableness of the transaction. The acquired assets may be worth a higher purchase price (than their book value) because of the synergism of the combination (the $2 + 2 = 5$ effect). Equally possible, however, is that inflation and higher replacement costs account for at least part of the difference. In any event, the analyst should accept the transaction (market) price of the assets. Under current accounting rules, "goodwill" is permanently placed on the books of the acquiring company, and "goodwill" is only written down if it is deemed that the "goodwill" has been permanently impaired.

Several industries require special ratios in addition to those listed in the main body of this chapter. The unique character of the railroads, for example, necessitates the computation of several financial and physical ratios that give a better picture of the operating characteristics of that industry than would be discerned from the standard core. Analysis of public utility securities also requires several different ratios and some reinterpretations of the existing core. Financial institutions are unique and require special analysis. Commercial banks are highly levered, and the analyst must be careful to assess certain key ratios. In order to be profitable, a bank cannot maintain too large an amount of capital relative to its deposits. The reported profitability of life insurance companies depends to a large extent on the *legal reserves* that must be set aside out of premiums to meet future claims. This reserve will depend upon the mortality tables assumed by the company and the rate of interest it can earn on investments. Special ratios are also required for analyzing property and casualty insurance companies. Finally for mutual funds, certain expense and performance ratios should be calculated on the shares in terms of the gross amount paid.

Problems

1. Below are income statements and balance sheets for the Wynn Corp. for the years 2013 and 2014.

Wynn Corp.
Consolidated Balance Sheets
(thousands)

	2013	2014
Net sales	$114,868	$170,356
Cost of goods sold	108,086	154,094
Operating depreciation	168	187
Gross income	$6,614	$16,075
Selling and administrative expenses	760	2,540
Net operating income	$5,854	$13,535
Other income	35	474
EBIT	$5,889	$14,009
Income taxes	2,660	6,720
Net income available for common	$3,229	$7.289
Common dividends	732	1,465
Balance carried to surplus	$2,497	$5,824
add surplus beginning period	7,115	9,612
Surplus end of period	$9,612	$15,436

Wynn Corp.
Consolidated Balance Sheets
(thousands)

	2013	2014
Current assets		
Cash	$3,625	$4,633
Receivables	13,896	20,468
Inventories	34,430	59,341
Total current assets	$51,951	$84,442
Net plant and equipment	$2,228	$3,084
Investment in subsidiaries	$1,253	$1,315
Total assets	$55,432	$88,841
Current liabilities		
Payables	$9,840	$20,707
Notes	15,000	27,000
Accruals	1,572	2,938
Reserves	2,498	5,851
Total current liabilities	$28,910	$56,496
Fixed liabilities	$–0–	$–0–
Net worth		
Common stock (1,000,000 shares)	$14,657	$14,657
Paid in surplus	2,252	2,252
Earned surplus	9,612	15,436
Total net worth	$26,521	$32,345
Total liabilities and worth	$55,432	$88,841

a. Prepare common size statements for the Wynn Corp.
b. Compute all the ratios required for the Wynn Corp. for 2013 and 2014. The following information will be required:

(1) Daily operating expenditures — about $500,000 (Note: this may be determined by dividing annual operating

expenditures by the number of days in the year. If operating expenses are expected to be higher in the next year than in the last one for which financial data are published, a budget for that year must be obtained. Also, the simple division of the number of days in the year into annual operating expenditures assumes that cash flows out evenly during the year. For seasonal business, this may not be a realistic assumption.)

(2) Market price of the stock as of the end of 2014 – $146 per share.

c. From the financial statements you have, try to decide what type of firm Wynn is. The asset mix of the enterprise should be of use in making this determination.

d. Analyze the position of Wynn. Would you consider it a profitable operation? Does the firm appear to be a risky venture?

2. Compute the following ratios for Raw Data (example problem in the chapter above) on an unadjusted and an adjusted basis:

a. Current ratio
b. Gross profit margin
c. Operating income ratio
d. EBIT ratio
e. Net profit margin
f. Total asset turnover
g. Earning-power-of-total-investment ratio
h. Net-profits-to-common-equity ratio
i. Total-debt-to-equity ratio

Which ratios differ when the statements are adjusted? Why? Does the position of the firm appear better or worse after the adjustments are made?

3. Hampstead Ltd. posted the following financial statements for 2014 (thousands):

Financial Statement Analysis

Income Statement		Balance Sheet	
Net sales	$100,000	Current assets	$50,000
Cost of goods sold[1]	50,000	Plant (net)	200,000
Gross income	50,000	Copyrights[3]	10,000
Other expenses[2]	40,000	Total assets	260,000
Net income before tax	10,000	Liabilities	$100,000
Tax	0	Net worth	160,000
Net income	$10,000	Total liabilities and net worth	$260,000

Notes to Financial Statements

[1] Includes depreciation charges of $10 million based on straight-line depreciation. For tax purposes, $20 million was deducted based on accelerated depreciation. The auditors feel the straight-line figure is an adequate figure for real economic depreciation.

[2] Includes an $8 million loss from litigation allowed as a tax deduction.

[3] Copyrights are valued at their acquisition price. A conservative appraisal of their economic value is about $100 million.

a. Prepare an adjusted income statement and balance sheet for Hampstead.
b. Reconcile the firm's tax payment. Assume the normal tax rate for Hampstead is 50 percent.
c. Compute these ratios for Hampstead on an unadjusted and an adjusted basis:
   (1) Gross profit margin
   (2) EBIT ratio
   (3) Net profit margin
   (4) Total asset turnover
   (5) Earning-power-of-total-investment ratio

(6) Net-profits-to-common-equity ratio
(7) Total debt-to-equity ratio.

4. A public utility has an annual output of 55 million kwh. Its peak load is 10,000 kw. Determine its load factor.

5. The Power and Wealth Fund has a net asset value of $20 per share, a management fee of 1 percent of assets per year, and the following marginal load schedule:

First $5,000	8.5 percent
Next 20,000	5
Next 40,000	3
Thereafter	0.5

If Sam pays a total of $100,000 for shares, how many will he get?

6. The Central Railroad has the following income statement (thousands):

Operating revenues:	
Freight	$95,097
Passenger (AMTRAK)	8,398
Other	4,905
Total operating revenue	$108,400
Operating expenses:	
Transportation	$45,500
Maintenance of way & structure	14,217
Maintenance of equipment	19,157
Traffic, other & special amortization	10,906
Total operating expenses	$89,780
Net railway operating income	$18,620
Less intermediate items:	
Payroll & other taxes	7,564
Net equipment & joint facility rents	5,207
Payments for guaranteed expenses	1,325

(*Continued*)

(*Continued*)

Rent for leased roads	1,121
Dividends and interest	(558)
Rent and miscellaneous (net)	(1784)
Net intermediate items	$12,875
EBIT	$5,745
Interest on debt	5,173
Earnings before taxes	$572
Taxes	272
Net Income	$300

Determine the following ratios for Central:

a. Transportation ratio
b. Total-maintenance ratio
c. Operating ratio
d. EBIT margin
e. Net margin.

7. As an investment analyst, you are reviewing the following income statement and balance sheet for the Boheme Corporation, a manufacturer of casual attire (figures in thousands):

Boheme Corporation
Statement of Income for the Year 2014

Sales		$200,000
Less:		
Cost of goods sold	$100,000	
Selling, general & admin. expenses	65,000	
Depreciation[1]	10,000	175,000
EBIT		$25,000
Less:		
Interest		5,000
Earnings before taxes		$20,000

(*Continued*)

(Continued)

Less:	
Taxes	4,000
Net Income	$16,000
Preferred dividends	1,000
Net income to common shareholders	$15,000
Common dividends	5,000
Earnings retained	$10,000

[1]For tax purposes, the firm uses accelerated depreciation. Charges amounting to $22,000 were deducted for 2014.

Boheme Corporation
Balance Sheet as of December 31, 2014

Current assets:	
Cash	$5,000
Receivables	5,000
Inventories	10,000
Total current	$20,000
Fixed assets:	
Gross plant	$100,000
Less:	
Accumulated depreciation	30,000
	$70,000
Other assets	10,000
Total assets	$100,000
Current liabilities	
Accounts payable	$10,000
Wages payable	6,400
Total current	$16,400
Bonds (10's '21)	50,000
Preferred stock (10%, $10 par)	10,000
Common stock ($1 par)	10,000
Retained earnings	13,600
	$100,000

a. You are considering the purchase of the Boheme 10's of 2021, which were issued when the firm was organized three years ago. The bonds are selling at 90¾ (that is, 90.75 percent of each $1000 par value). Interest is paid annually on December 31, and any purchase you make would be on January 2, 2015. The bonds mature on December 31, 2021. You have determined the following data from the 2012 and 2013 annual reports of the company:

	2012	2013
Sales	$50,000	$100,000
Gross margin	40.0%	45.0%
EBIT margin	14.0%	10.0%
Net margin	3.2%	4.0%
Asset turnover	0.625×	1.1×
Return on investment (EBIT/Total assets)	8.75%	11.0%
Total debt to total capital	0.75	0.74
Interest coverage	1.4×	2.0×

(1) Make any necessary adjustments to the 2014 statements.
(2) Reconcile the firm's tax payment. Assume a normal tax rate of 50 percent.
(3) Compute the above seven ratios for 2014.
(4) What favorable factors might influence your purchase of these bonds? What unfavorable ones?
(5) What other information might you wish to have in making your evaluation?
(6) What is the yield to maturity of the Boheme 10's '21?
(7) If you thought the firm was less risky today than it was when the bonds were issued, would you be willing to accept a return lower than 10 percent?
(8) How do you account for the current price of the bonds?

b. You are considering the purchase of Boheme common stock. In order to value the security, you have attempted to project future sales and earnings for 2015. You are convinced that sales will increase according to the past pattern (that is, up by 100 percent) and the EBIT margin will be about the same as it was in 2014. You assume debt levels and the tax rate will remain constant.

(1) Determine sales, EBIT, and net income to common shareholders for 2015.
(2) EPS of common were $0.16 in 2012 and $0.40 in 2013. Determine EPS for 2014 and projected EPS for 2015.
(3) The firm paid no dividend in 2012 or 2013 but did pay out one-third of the 2014 earnings. Cash DPS are expected to double in 2015. How much in dividends were paid in 2014? What projected pay-out rate is expected for 2015?
(4) The P/E multiple for Boheme averaged 20× in 2012 and 2013. What was the average price of the stock for each year?
(5) As of January 2, 2015, Boheme was selling at $15 per share. What is the current P/E multiple based on 2014 earnings?
(6) What may account for this change in the multiple?
(7) Based on the current price of Boheme and your expectations about the future of the company, would you buy it?

References

Bernstein, L. A., *Analysis of Financial Statements*, 5th edn. New York: McGraw-Hill, 1999.

Drake, P. P. and F. J. Fabozzi, "*Financial Ratio Analysis*," in Fabozzi, F. J., *Handbook of Finance*, Vol III, Chapter 54, pp. 581–595. New York: John Wiley & Sons, 2008.

Fabozzi, F. J., P. P. Drake, and R. S. Polimeni, *The Complete CFO Handbook: From Accounting to Accountability*. Hobobken, NJ: John Wiley & Sons, 2007.

Fridson, M. and F. Alvarez, *Financial Statement Analysis: A Practitioner's Guide*, 3rd edn. Hobobken, NJ: John Wiley & Sons, 2002.

Graham, Benjamin and D. L. Dodd, *Security Analysis*, 6th edn. New York: McGraw-Hill Book Company, 2009.

Peterson, P. P. and F. J. Fabozzi, *Analysis of Financial Statements*, 2nd edn. Hoboken, NJ: John Wiley & Sons, 2006.

Thompson, J. R., E. E. Williams, and M. C. Findlay, *Models for Investors in Real World Markets*. New York: John Wiley & Sons, 2003.

Chapter 5

Forecasting Techniques

History never repeats itself but it rhymes.

Mark Twain

Introduction to Forecasting

Forecasting can be defined as making a statement about an unknown event. It usually entails calculating and predicting future events, typically based on extrapolation from past experience. For physical systems, using past data is not a bad idea. For example, we have seen that the sunspot cycle follows a fairly regular 11-year pattern.

For the 3,179 months of sunspot numbers from 1749 through 2013, there is a definite cyclic component to the observations. When we look at a smaller window, we definitely can "eyeball" a 132-month period. Indeed, from peak-to-peak, we have an average of 131.25 months separation, with an average 132.5 months needed in the trough-to-trough undulation.

Again, using this rough technique, we can observe that the most recent sunspot peak activity occurred in Figure 5.1 at month 656, which corresponds to May 2012. We are fairly confident that the next trough in sunspot activity will occur around month 742, or August 2019. Although this example does not try to predict the number of sunspots, it does verify that May 2012 saw the lowest peak sunspot activity since about 1898.

Alas, the financial phenomenon that we wish to forecast is not governed by the same forces that make celestial observations predictable; however, the past is all we have to work with, so we will

172   Quantitative Financial Analytics

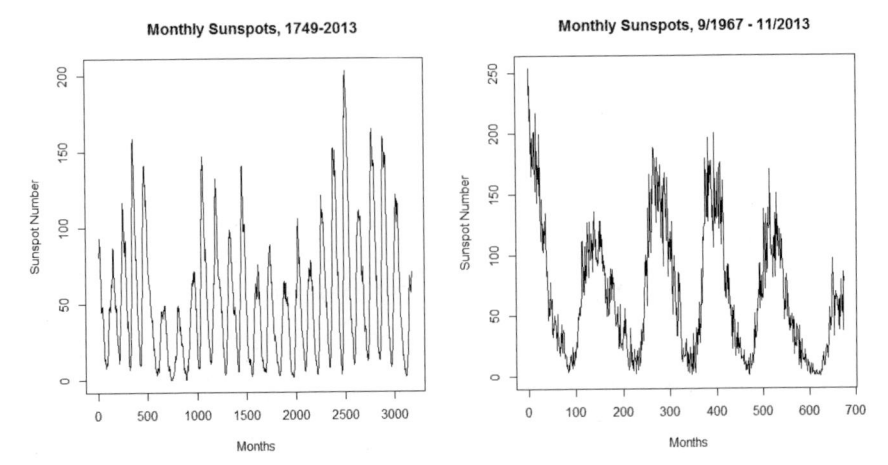

Figure 5.1. (Left) Sunspot Numbers, January 1749 to November 2013; Sunspot Numbers September 1967 to November 2013 (Right)

provide some overview of essential forecasting techniques, along with the caveat that their use might lead to disappointing results.

Forecast Accuracy Measures

Various measures to assess the accuracy of forecast numbers have been devised; we present three of the most common here. In all three cases, we desire that the total forecast error measure be as small as possible, indicating that each period forecast is as accurate as possible. In each case, absolutely accurate forecasts result in zero forecast error; the differences in these measures lie in how much to penalize the inevitable errors.

We define a prediction error at a time t as the difference between the forecast value F_t and the actual time series value X_t, for example, putting $E_t = F_t - X_t$. In each measure, we accumulate errors over the N-period forecast horizon. The following formulas define cumulative three error measures.

1. Mean absolute error (MAE).

$$\text{MAE} = \left(\sum_{t=1}^{N} |E_t|\right) \frac{1}{N}.$$

2. Root mean square error (RMSE).

$$\text{RMSE} = \left[\left(\sum E_t^2\right)\frac{1}{N}\right]^{1/2}.$$

3. Mean absolute percentage error (MAPE).

$$\text{MAPE} = \left(\sum_{t=1}^{N} |E_t/X_t|\right)\frac{1}{N}.$$

Note that both MAE and RMSE have the same units as the underlying time series, and that MAE is based on the absolute error versus the RMSE which relies on squared errors, and thus penalizes larger errors more than the MAE.

It can be seen that MAPE is expressed as a percentage, which some feel is a more natural way to summarize forecast errors. An intuitive description of interpreting various measures of error may be found in Basi et al. (1976). In any case, lower forecast errors result in lower summary measures, so once experience with one of these measures has been gained, the analyst may continue to use it in evaluating forecasts until there is a specific need to change evaluation techniques.

Naïve Forecasts

We will find in subsequent chapters that the most important variables indicating the worth and security of bonds and stocks were those relating to the future income-generating abilities of the firm. Because bond interest, sinking-fund payments, and common stock dividends are paid out of *future* rather than past revenues, it is imperative that the analyst forecast the position of the firm he or she is investigating as far into the future as possible.

Forecasting techniques vary from the simplest naïve projections to the development of complicated regression models of the firm's total activities. Budgets and financial statements play a role in almost every kind of forecasting technique, although the sophistication of the use of these data may vary considerably.

Analysts have been making naïve forecasts for years. Before the advent of the computer, practically all forecasts were simplistic by necessity. Some of the more common naïve techniques consist of making linear extrapolations of past performance. For example, if a firm's earnings have been growing at 20 percent compounded annually, the analyst may simply add this amount to current earnings in order to get next year's earnings. The main weakness of such an approach is obvious in that no consideration is given to the underlying determinants of earnings. Furthermore, the analyst is assuming blindly that past performance will always be repeated. (This assumption is explicit even in many of the more-sophisticated techniques.)

The use of ratios with naïve projections has long been the mainstay of financial analysis. A frequently used procedure is to project sales one or two years into the future and then apply historical ratios to generate *pro forma* income statements and balance sheets. When it appears to the analyst that various ratio patterns might change in the near future, these adjustments may be incorporated into the analysis.

We may consider an example. Suppose the Recensement Data Gathering Corporation has shown rapid growth in recent years. Sales have advanced by 30 percent annually, and profits have been growing by 40 percent. Ratios for Recensement for the past three years are given below:

Ratio	2012	2013	2014
Current	2.40	2.80	2.60
Gross margin	0.22	0.23	0.24
EBIT ratio	0.15	0.16	0.17
Net margin	0.06	0.07	0.09
Asset turnover	3.00	3.25	3.60
Long-term debt to capital	0.09	0.08	0.06

Sales for 2014 were $500,000. The analyst believes the past growth rate will continue for next year. He or she also feels that the current ratio will remain at about the 2014 level, that the long-run gross margin should be about 24 percent of sales, and that the earnings before interests and taxes (EBIT) and net margins will continue at 2014 levels. Long-run improvement in turnovers is anticipated, however, and the analyst feels 3.80 is an accurate total asset turnover projection. The firm has $10,000 in long-term debt (LTD) that should not change next year. The fixed asset investment should increase to about $150,000. Earnings for 2014 could be projected using a simple extrapolation of the earnings growth rate:

$$2014 \text{ earnings} = (0.09)(\$500,000) = \$45,000$$

$$(0.4)(\$45,000) = \$18,000$$

$$2015 \text{ earnings} = \$45,000 + \$18,000 = \$63,000.$$

A less naïve approach might be to prepare a *pro forma* income statement and balance sheet given the sales growth and ratio assumptions made above:

Rescentment Data
Pro forma Statement of Income

Sales [(500,000) + (.3)(500,000)]	$650,000
Cost of goods sold [(.76)(650,000)]	494,000
Gross margin	156,000
Other expenses	45,000
EBIT [(.17)(650,000)]	110,500
Interest and taxes	52,200
Net Income [(.09)(650,000]	58,250

Pro forma Balance Sheet

Current assets	$21,000
Fixed assets	150,000
Total assets [(650,000) ÷ (3.8)]	171,000
Current liabilities [(21,000) ÷ (2.6)]	8,000
Long-term debt	10,000
Net worth	153,000
	171,000

Notice that the earnings growth rate indicated by the second approach is less than that of the first:

$$(58{,}500 - 45{,}000) \div 45{,}000 = 30 \text{ percent}$$

This growth rate was implicit in the assumptions made in the second approach. If sales are growing by a given percentage and the net margin is assumed to be constant, then the earnings growth rate must equal the sales growth rate. In this instance, as in all examples in which ratio values are assumed, the analyst should be sure that internally inconsistent assumptions are not being made.

Some mention should be made as to the position of the firm with respect to the life-cycle business model. Growth for a company is usually described by an S-shaped curve, with startup/development, growth, rapid growth, maturity, and decline being typical divisions of this cycle. Knowing where the company is on this curve can help determine what naïve assumptions are applicable. Part of the *ceteris paribus* model is that the growth rate for earnings or sales remains relatively constant. This of course leads to an exponential level over time, which most recognize is not sustainable. Indeed, consideration needs to be given to the position of the firm in the growth life-cycle.

Figure 5.2 shows the sales and sales growth figures for both Polaroid (1962–2000) and for Intel (1972–2012). We note that Polaroid appears to be in the linear growth portion of the life-cycle curve. Polaroid's development, launch, and "rapid growth" phase would have occurred in the 1948–1980 period when its hallmark products came online. We do note the year-over-year growth for Polaroid was decreasing from 30 percent in the early 1960s down to negative growth (decline) prior to its bankruptcy in 2001.

Intel displays the development, launch, and rapid growth stages, and we would argue maturity through 2012. Naïve projections of the average 20 percent growth may be sustained in the near future as long as the growth in maturity is sustained.

In Figure 5.3, we see another example of changing life-cycle. Apple, Inc. (AAPL, formerly Apple Computer, Inc.) exhibits the launch and rapid growth phases from its 1980 initial public offering (IPO) until the mid-1990s, with an apparent maturing at that point.

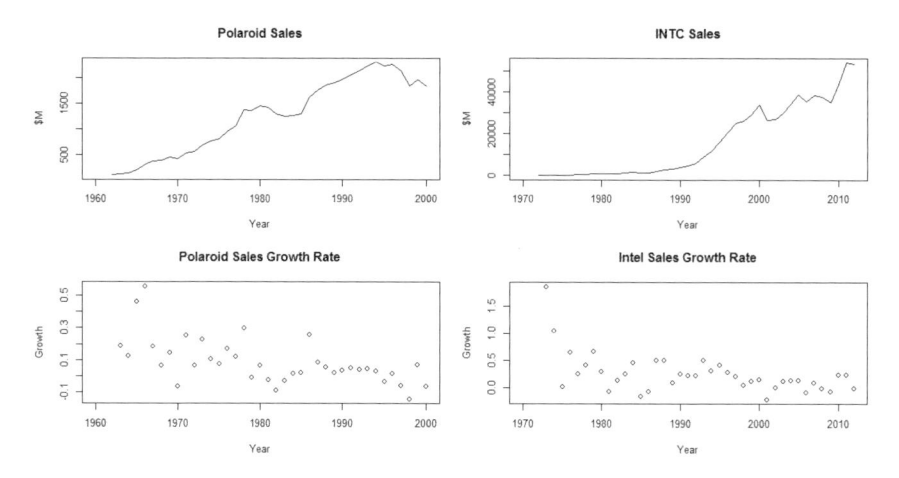

Figure 5.2. Sales and Sales Growth Percentages for Polaroid and Intel

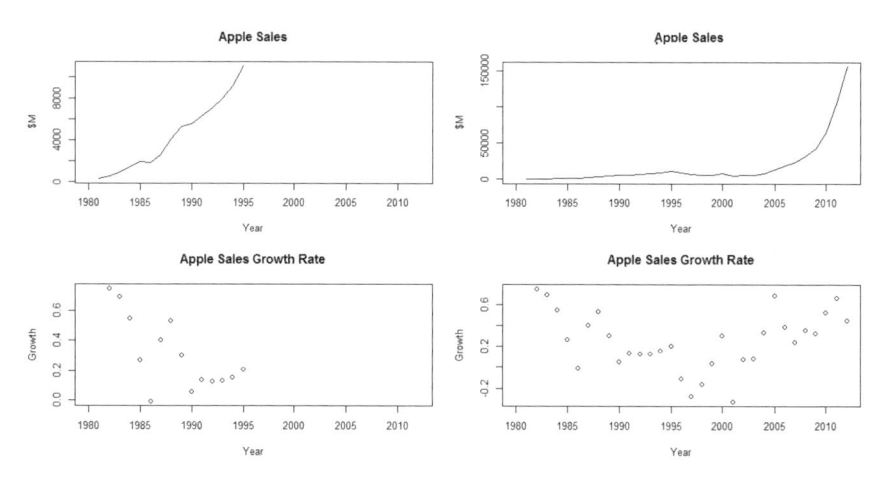

Figure 5.3. Apple, Inc. Sales and Sales Growth

This is easily seen from the declining growth rates until they hit negative in 1996–1998; however, the exponential peak of 1995 sales is dwarfed by its subsequent renaissance after the early 2000s.

Smoothing Techniques

Very popular forecasting techniques are based on smoothing of the data series. Smoothing takes out the seemingly random fluctuations and allows one to better quantify any underlying trends and so calculate some n-period look-ahead forecasts. Single dimensional smoothers are typically simple or exponential moving average filters.

Consider the sales figures for Solid Cyrogenics, Incorporated (SCI) for December 1988 through December 2010, superimposed with a three-year simple moving average (SMA) of sales. Note that the SMA smooths the sales figures. We would like to make a two-year ahead forecast, and given the trend reversals from 2000 to 2005 and vice versa, it makes most sense to forecast level sales of $2.133 billion based off on the smoothed average (Figure 5.4).

Compare this forecast with that based on the naïve approach. In it, we project using the average growth rate of recent periods which supposedly take into account the life-cycle of the firm. We see wide

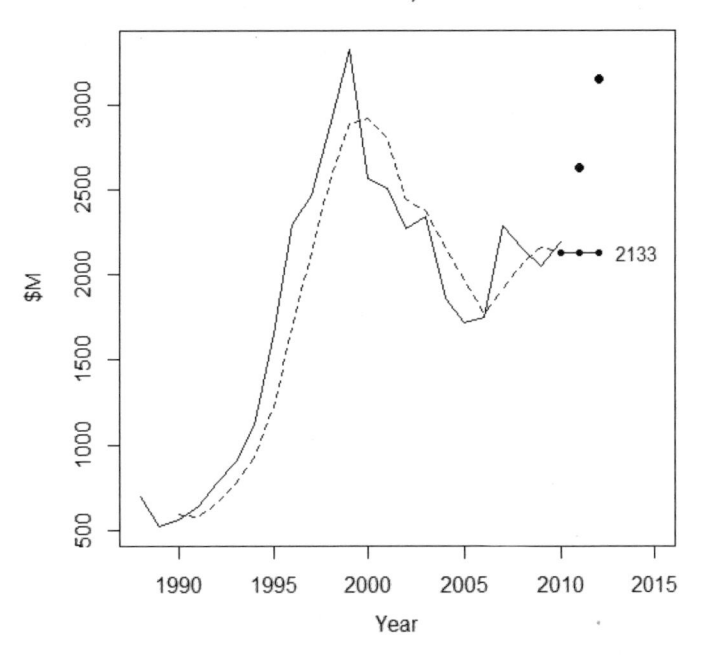

Figure 5.4. SCI Sales 1988–2010 with 2011 and 2012 Forecasts

variety depending if we use the previous 5, 10, 15, or ALL the sales growth data.

Naïve Forecasts Based on Average Growth Rates
(percent)

	5 years	10 years	15 years	29 years
	5.8%	−0.8%	−3.2%	10.0%
2012	2,451	2,156	2,332	2,653
2011	2,317	2,173	2,260	2,411

Since it is not immediately evident what constitutes a "fair" representation of the average growth rate over a business cycle, we plot all of the naïve forecasts, from which we may select an appropriate subset of growth values. One observes that these forecasts seem to be optimistic, so various *ad hoc* means of tapering off the calculations may be employed (such as expert opinion), but to be true to the process we leave the forecasts as they are.

If we were to forecast the *bottom* line, we would need in addition to forecast sales, estimates for future margins and expense ratios, as well as possibly some contingencies. We see from Figure 5.5 that the naïve assumption of rather stable margins might not be that helpful as a basis of a simple model. It will be necessary to devise a more adaptive model if we wish to forecast the bottom line.

Stochastic Modeling

Rather than relying on the naïve average growth values to make forecasts, it makes much more economic sense to incorporate the natural variability seen in the annual growth rates in making the estimates. There are two main ways to incorporate period variability in data of this sort. The first is so-called parametric simulation, and the second is non-parametric.

Parametric simulation attempts to model the variable of concern using a statistical probability distribution. The forecaster then draws

180   *Quantitative Financial Analytics*

SCI Margins, 1980-2010

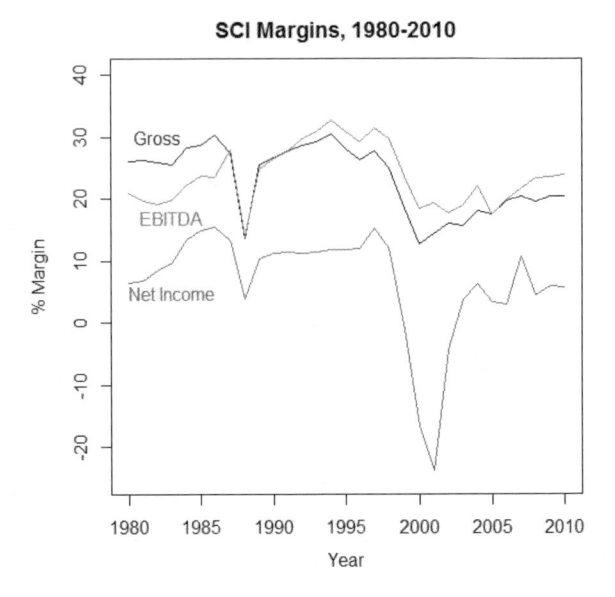

Figure 5.5. SCI Margins 1980–2010

from this distribution a sales growth figure, say, and then calculates the resulting sales value. This is done N times, corresponding to the number of forecast periods being attempted.

There are many considerations needed to create such a parametric model. The main challenge is its specification, which is determining which probability distribution to use for the data. It is well known that there are an infinite number of appropriate distributions, numbered either by the parameter values, or by the form of the distribution. Moreover, these distributions may be compound, for example, frequency and severity models. Additionally, a Bayesian approach might be warranted. In any case, blindly specifying, for example, a *normal* distribution for sales growth might be grossly wrong; considerable care (and experience) must be used in the model specification process.

Second to the distribution specification, the next problem is parameter estimation, which is how one determines what parameters are needed to specify the form of the distribution. In addition, there must be confidence bounds on these parameter estimates which can significantly affect the forecasts, showing the need for performing sensitivity analysis (see subsequent sections). There are many ways to estimate model parameters, but none of them work very well when the amount of historical data is small, which is usually the case in financial problems. It is almost certainly going to be a real problem for the entrepreneur in evaluating future outlook for a company given *no* track record, or at least very limited historical data.

For example, we use a parametric model for the sales forecast since some preliminary diagnostics on the sales growth values indicated that a normal model is not that bad, which conclusion is also borne out from comparison with a non-parametric approach (see next section). So the model for sales growth at time t is $G_t \sim N(\hat{\mu}, \hat{\sigma}^2)$. The mean and standard deviation parameters were estimated using the standard estimators[1] and found to be $\hat{\mu} = \text{avg}(G_t) = 10.04\%$ and $\hat{\sigma} = \sqrt{\text{var}(G_t)} = 18.6\%$, respectively. We conducted 500 simulations for each year 2011 and 2012, and obtained a terminal distribution of sales figures as shown in Figure 5.6 above. (The median forecast for each year is indicated with the open square □.)

Note that the forecast median and mean are very close to one another, again indicating that the normal distribution might not be all that wrong. Also note that the median forecasts of $2.425 and $2.603 billion (the open dots) seem more "intuitively" correct, or at least not too out of line. Lastly, it should be emphasized that the full range of variation is seen on the figure and in the summary statistics below.

Parametric Forecasts for FY 2011 and FY 2012 ($B)

	Min.	1st Qu.	Median	Mean	3rd Qu.	Max.
2011 Est.	1,216	2,135	2,425	2,418	2,703	3,593
2012 Est.	832	2,212	2,603	2,644	3,009	4,754

In *non-parametric simulation*, we let the data speak for themselves by resampling (with replacement) from the collection of sales

---

[1] See for example Thompson, Williams and Findlay (2003), pp. 229–231.

SCI Annual Sales, 12/88-12/2010

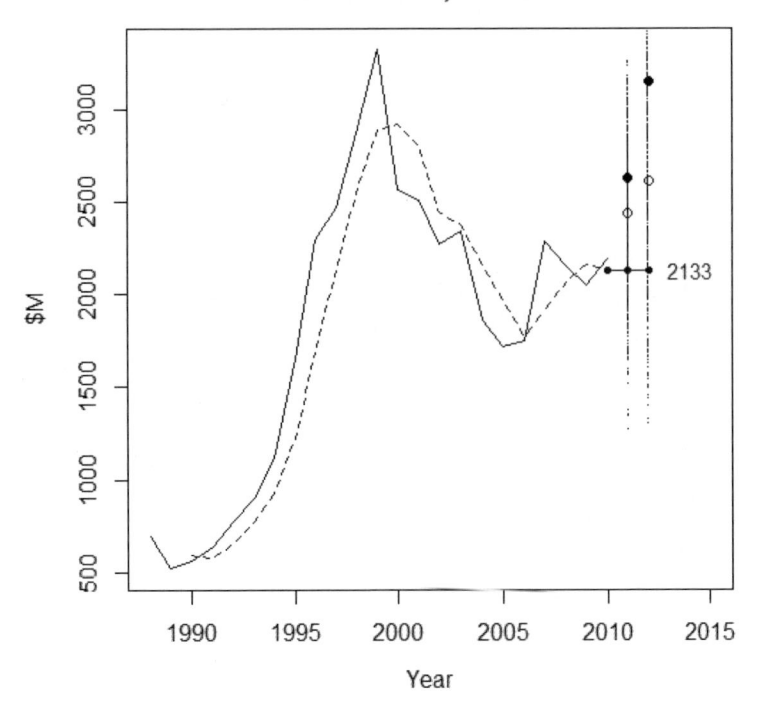

Figure 5.6. Parametric Forecast for SCI Sales 2011 and 2012

growths in our data sample. We then draw two annual growth factors and assemble the forecast sales levels for each year. This is repeated some large number of times (say 500) and a resulting distribution of sales levels is obtained for each year, *without* having to specify a model distribution or to estimate parameters.

The non-parametric approach is arguably the preeminent method of model building, but it certainly is so when there is no immediately apparent parametric model to fit, or when data are lacking, or both. As in the parametric approach, the outcome is a complete distribution of outcomes, from which the forecaster chooses a representative value for use in the forecast. Usually the mean or median is employed, and in cases where they differ substantially, the latter is preferred.

SCI Annual Sales, 12/88-12/2010

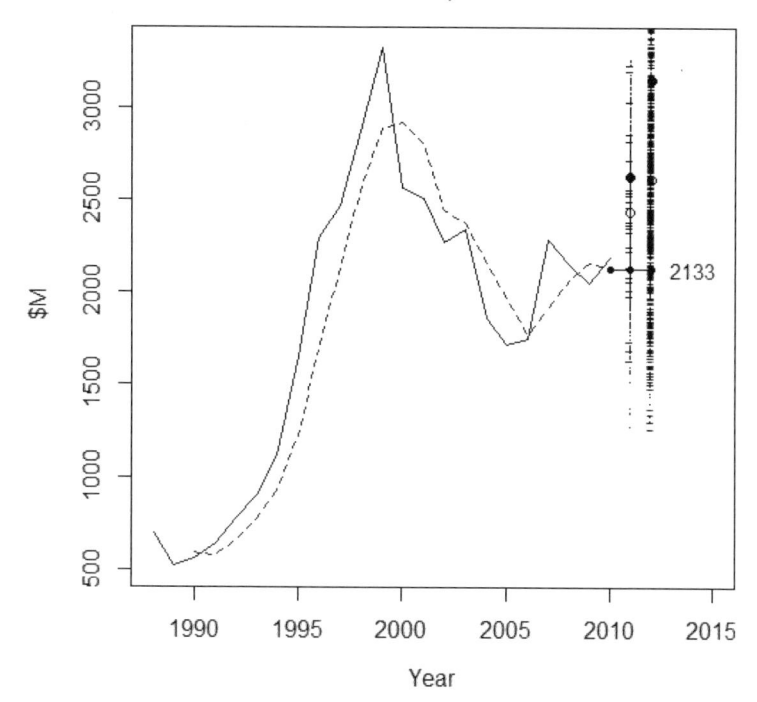

Figure 5.7. Non-Parametric Forecast for SCI Sales, 2011 and 2012 ("-") Superimposed on Parametric Forecasts (".")

The non-parametric forecasts are summarized below, and their complete distributions are plotted in Figure 5.7.

A quantitative assessment of forecast accuracy is given below, with *ex post* results of \$2.316 and \$2.410 billion obtained in FY 2011 and FY 2012. We note the stochastic approach is superior to the naïve approach under all accuracy measures, and that the median forecast is preferable to the mean forecast in both the parametric (Normal) and the non-parametric methods. Additionally, in the example, the parametric model is slightly better than the non-parametric model, but this is so only because the percentage sales growth data is symmetric and not significantly non-normal under diagnosis, reinforcing the adage that when a parametric model is indicated and available, then it is best to use it.

SCI Sales Forecast, 2011 and 2012, Performance Comparison

	2011	2012	MAE	RMSE	MAPE
SMA(3)	2,133	2,133	230	235	0.097
Avg. 10-Yr Growth	2,173	2,156	199	206	0.084
Median Normal	2,411	2,572	129	133	0.054
Mean Normal	2,397	2,631	151	166	0.063
Median Resampled	2,391	2,604	132	144	0.055
Mean Resampled	2,411	2,651	168	183	0.071
Actual Sales	**2,316**	**2,410**			
Sales Growth (percent)	5.73	4.08			

The same conclusions are reached when we attempt to perform a four-period forecast. Over this timeframe and compared with reality, the naïve and SMA forecasts returned about a 16 percent prediction error, compared with the stochastic error rates of about 6–7 percent.

SCI Sales Forecast, 2011–2014, Performance Comparison

	2011	2012	2013	2014	MAE	RMSE	MAPE
SMA(3)	2,133	2,133	2,133	2,133	435	507	0.161
Avg. 10-Yr Growth	2,173	2,156	2,139	2,122	420	504	0.155
Median Normal	2,411	2,572	2,807	3,115	159	170	0.062
Mean Normal	2,397	2,631	2,891	3,239	222	240	0.085
Median Resampled	2,391	2,604	2,896	3,071	173	205	0.068
Mean Resampled	2,411	2,651	2,948	3,267	252	274	0.097
Actual Sales	**2,316**	**2,410**	**2,551**	**2,994**			
Sales Growth (percent)	5.73	4.08	5.85	17.37			

There are a considerable number of enhancements to the stochastic modeling process that could be made. (1) For example, it could be argued that there is correlation in the growth rates for a firm; that is, for whatever econometric reason, declines in growth tend to be accompanied by follow-on declines, or *vice versa*. (2) In forecasting bottom line results, additional probabilistic models need to be specified. (3) Attempts can be made to model the processes involved in determining expense ratios and hence margins. However, we argue that a rather sophisticated forecast of future earnings before interest, taxes, depreciation, and amortization (EBITDA) or earnings can be made through this technique, which is much more tied to reality than that from the naïve forecasting approach, and is attainable without too much additional work.

Time Series Analysis

At the time this book was written, a simple Amazon.com book search for "Forecasting" returned 348,155 results, indicating that the subject is a timely, complex, and evolving one. Modern "Time Series Analysis" is rooted in the Autoregressive Integrated Moving Average model (ARIMA) methodology, although almost countless extensions and generalizations have been developed over the years.

The model is often written as ARIMA (p, d, q), with parameters p, d, and q. These parameters are non-negative integers that characterize the order of the autoregressive (AR), integrated (I), and moving average (MA) components of ARIMA model, respectively. The model is usually represented as follows:

$$\left(1 - \sum_{i=1}^{p} \phi_i L^i\right)(1 - L)^d X_t = \mu + \left(1 + \sum_{i=1}^{q} \theta_i L^i\right)\varepsilon_t, \qquad (5.1)$$

where X_t is the time series data, t is an integer, L is a lag operator (i.e., $L^k Z_t = Z_{t-k}$), μ is a grand mean, ϕ_i and θ_i are parameters of the autoregression and moving average, respectively, and ε_t are error terms.

ARIMA and its offspring and other relatives are extremely flexible and provide powerful insight into time series phenomena. They are quite strong in diagnosing and predicting trends and seasonality, all of which are important for the analyst doing forecasting. However, even an introductory review of the key concepts would be beyond the intended scope of this book and the interested reader can review the references at the end of this chapter for further edification. Most statistical and spreadsheet computer programs have some time series capability built into them since all the methods are computer-intensive.

Interestingly, academic research (as described in Givoly and Lakonishok, 1984) has shown the superiority of, for example, the Value Line Investment Survey estimates over sophisticated time series models. ARIMA models have consistently disappointed those trying to use them to forecast financial phenomena.

Regression and Correlation Analysis

Naïve forecasting techniques are reasonably satisfactory if the analyst is projecting only one or two years into the future. When longer forecasts are needed, however, more sophisticated approaches are required. For a number of firms, there are no underlying long-run trends in performance. If it appears to the analyst that a firm's activities are more or less stable (that is, sales, costs, and earnings do not vary by much), then there really is no forecasting problem. There are not many firms in this category, however. Much more likely is the case of the *cyclical* firm that evidences no long-run trends but that does have a consistent performance in the short run. Forecasting the position of a cyclical enterprise *may* be accomplished by the use of *regression and correlation analysis*, provided continuation of an upswing (or a downswing) in activities prevails. It must be remembered, however, that changes from an upswing to a downswing position (or vice versa) cannot be predicted with least-squares techniques. Statistical procedures are available for attempting this problem, but they are beyond the scope of this book.

The use of multiple regression and correlation analysis and corporate modeling allows the analyst to specify more accurately values for a far larger number of variables than the naïve methods. Like the naïve techniques previously discussed, however, regression analysis assumes some underlying trend in the data being examined. If no trend is there (short run or long run), the regression results will be of little value for forecasting purposes.

A typical analysis employing regression procedures will begin with a forecast of aggregate economic activity. Some securities analysts prepare their own predictions of such variables as gross domestic product (GDP), prices, the level of interest rates, and so on. Others depend upon the large econometric models, such as those developed at the University of Pennsylvania's Wharton School (now operated as IHS Global Insight), and the Brookings Institution, to generate aggregate predictions. Once the aggregate projection is made, the analyst then concentrates on developing a model of the industry of interest. Finally, a model is prepared for specific firms (or a firm) within that industry. Typically, the results of the aggregate forecast are fed into the industry model, and the output from the industry model is used as input for the firm projection. At each stage of developing the forecast, the analyst must be careful to select those independent variables that make *a priori* sense as determinants. Although it is possible to generate "good" statistical results (that is, high R^2 values that are also statistically significant) by correlating any two or more variables, it would be difficult for an analyst to defend a forecast that, say, based a prediction of sales on the phases of the moon. Even if high sales and a full moon correlated with a very good, statistically significant fit, one would be hard pressed to find an economic explanation for the phenomenon.

Examples

1. Peason-Jackson is a large, nationwide publisher of college textbooks. Textbook sales seem to depend on a number of factors, but two variables stand out as being particularly significant: family median income (Y) and the total college population (P). An analyst has determined the following equation to project total annual industry textbook sales:

$$S_i = 140.3 + 2.7(Y) + 5.94(P).$$

Where S_i is measured in millions, Y in thousands, and P in millions. For next year, if $Y = \$40,000$ and $P = 20,000,000$, a projection of S_i would be:

$$S_i = 140.3 + 2.7(40) + 5.94(20)$$
$$S_i = 367.10 \quad \text{or} \quad \$367,100,000.$$

2. Sales for Peason-Jackson are clearly a function of industry sales. It has also been determined that a high correlation exists between the firm's sales and one other variable, the number of salesmen employed by the firm (N). The following equation has been fitted:

$$S_p = -50.6 + 0.18(S_i) + 0.03(N).$$

where S_p is measured in millions. A prediction for Peason-Jackson sales for next year if $N = 1280$ would be:

$$S_p = -50.6 + 0.18(367.1) + 0.03(1280)$$

$$S_p = 53.878 \quad \text{or} \quad \$53,878,000.$$

Independent Variables and Sensitivity Analysis

Two major problems confront the analyst when using multiple regression analysis to forecast: (1) What are the key independent variables? And (2) How sensitive are the final forecasted results to changes in the values of the independent variables? The first of these questions is difficult to answer. Frequently, the analyst will try a number of combinations of variables, examining the coefficients of partial determination, R^2, and the statistical significance of the results in order to find the combination that yields the best prediction. The second problem can be handled through the use of *sensitivity analysis*. Simply explained, sensitivity analysis seeks to demonstrate how large a change in the value of a single independent variable is required to alter *significantly* the forecasted outcome. Because the values assigned to the exogenous variables in a system of forecasting equations are rarely known with certainty, it may be necessary for the analyst to try likely values first and then examine his results as less-likely values are used. It is clear, of course, that forecasted results for a dependent variable are no more accurate than the input assumed for the independent variables.

Sensitivity analysis may be employed in a number of contexts. The independent variables in any regression equation may be subjected to sensitivity tests. Many analysts have attempted to forecast stock prices directly without going through the extensive fundamental analysis that we recommend in this book. When such an approach (direct forecasting) is employed, sensitivity analysis may become a necessary supplement. Consider the case of the Second Philadelphia Corp., an investment banking house that attempts to forecast stock prices with regression analysis. The following equation is used:

$$P_t = f(P_{t-1}, D_{t-1}, S_t, L, r, i). \tag{5.2}$$

Where:

P_t is the stock price in period t.
P_{t-1} was the average stock price in the previous period.
D_{t-1} was the dividend in the previous period.
S_t is expected sales per share in period t.
L is the degree of financial leverage (debt to equity) for the firm expected in period t.
r is the rate of return on investment (EBIT to total assets) expected in period t.
i is the prime rate of interest expected in period t.

For this firm, the regression equation below has been determined:

$$P_t = -6.50 + (0.76)P_{t-1} + (0.15)D_{t-1} + (1.34)S_t \\ - (8.24)L + (12.54)r - (26.12)i.$$

Values for each independent variable have been estimated for period t as:

$$S_t = \$10$$
$$L = 0.40$$
$$r = 0.25$$
$$i = 0.06.$$

The average share price for Second Philadelphia during the previous period was $22. The firm paid a dividend of $1 per share in the previous period. A projection of the stock price would provide:

$$P_t = -6.50 + (0.76)(22.00) + (0.15)(1.00) + (1.34)(10.00)$$
$$- (8.24)(0.40) + (12.54)(0.25) - (26.12)(0.06)$$
$$= -6.50 + 16.72 + 0.015 + 13.40 - 3.30 + 3.14 - 1.57$$
$$= \$22.04.$$

Because future sales for Second Philadelphia are not known with certainty, sensitivity analysis may be employed to examine the differences in share prices produced by various sales estimates. If economic conditions are good, sales may be $11.00 per share. If they do not change from the past period, the $10.00 figure will prevail. If conditions deteriorate, sales per share could fall to $9.00. Sensitivity analysis could be applied to these three possible events:

1. If $S_t = \$11.00$, P_t becomes $23.38
2. If $S_t = \$9.00$, P_t becomes $20.70
3. Thus, a 10 percent deviation in sales per share can produce a 6 percent variation in forecasted price (that is, 1.34/22.04).

The analysis could be applied to other variables as well. Suppose i might be 0.05, 0.06, or 0.07. The best event ($i = 0.05$) would add $0.26 to the share price, and the worst one ($i = 0.07$) would reduce the price by $0.26. This does not appear to be a very sensitive variable.

The forecasting procedure used by Second Philadelphia, even when supplemented by sensitivity analysis, leaves much to be desired. We are not given R^2, the coefficients of partial determination, or F test values to measure statistical significance (see Appendix B for discussion of these concepts). Furthermore, one could suspect the presence of *serial correlation*, given the fact that one of the independent variables is a lagged version of the dependent variable. In any case, forecasting equations of this general sort should be used with great care. A more difficult, but also more adequate, method is to project stock "values" (rather than prices) using a series of equations indicating fundamental relationships such as company revenues to industry revenues, costs to revenues, and so on.

Summary

Forecasting can be defined as making a statement about an unknown event. It usually entails calculating and predicting future events, typically based on extrapolation from past experience. Unfortunately, the financial phenomena that we wish to forecast is not governed by the same forces that make physical observations predictable. The past is all we have to work with.

Various measures to assess the accuracy of forecast numbers have been devised; we presented three of the most common above. These are MAE, RMSE, and MAPE. In all three cases, we desire that the total forecast error measure be as small as possible, indicating that each period forecast is as accurate as possible. In each case, absolutely accurate forecasts result in zero forecast error; the differences in these measures lie in how much to penalize the inevitable errors.

Forecasting techniques vary from the simplest naïve projections to the development of complicated regression models of the firm's total activities. Budgets and financial statements play a role in almost every kind of forecasting technique, although the sophistication of the use of these data may vary considerably. The use of ratios with naïve projections has long been the mainstay of financial analysis. A frequently used procedure is to project sales one or two years into the future and then apply historical ratios to generate *pro forma* income statements and balance sheets. When it appears to the analyst that various ratio patterns might change in the near future, one may incorporate these adjustments into the analysis.

Very popular forecasting techniques are based on smoothing of the data series. Smoothing takes out the seemingly random fluctuations and allows one to better quantify any underlying trends and so calculate some n-period look-ahead forecasts. Single dimensional smoothers are typically simple or exponential moving average filters.

Rather than relying on the naïve average growth values to make forecasts, it makes much more economic sense to incorporate the natural variability seen in the annual growth rates in making the estimates. There are two main ways to incorporate period variability in data of this sort. The first is so-called parametric simulation, and the second is non-parametric.

Parametric simulation attempts to model the variable of interest using a statistical probability distribution. The forecaster then draws from this distribution a sales growth figure, say, and then calculates the resulting sales value. This is done N times, corresponding to the number of forecast periods being attempted.

In non-parametric simulation, we let the data speak for themselves by resampling (with replacement) from the collection of sales growths in our data sample. We then draw two annual growth factors and assemble the forecast sales levels for each year. This is repeated some large number of times (say 500) and a resulting distribution of sales levels is obtained for each year, without having to specify a model distribution or to estimate parameters.

Time series models (ARIMA) and their offspring and other relatives are extremely flexible and provide powerful insight into time series phenomena. They are quite strong in diagnosing and predicting trends and seasonality, all of which are important for the entrepreneur doing forecasting; however, even an introductory review of the key concepts would be beyond the intended scope of this chapter; the interested reader can review the references at the end of this section. Most statistical and spreadsheet computer programs have some time series capability built into them since all the methods are computer-intensive.

The use of multiple regression and correlation analysis and corporate modeling allows the analyst to specify more accurately values for a far larger number of variables than the naïve methods. Like the naïve techniques previously discussed, however, regression analysis assumes some underlying trend in the data being examined. If no trend is there (short run or long run), the regression results will be of little value for forecasting purposes.

Sensitivity analysis may be employed in a number of contexts. The independent variables in any regression equation may be subjected to sensitivity tests. Many analysts have attempted to forecast stock prices directly without going through the extensive fundamental analysis that we recommend in this book. When such an approach (direct forecasting) is employed, sensitivity analysis may become a necessary supplement.

Problems

1. Obtain the sunspot data for monthly mean total sunspot number (+13-month smoothed numbers [Jan 1749–now]. This is available from the Sunspot Index and Long-term Solar Observations (SILSO), provided by the Solar Influences Data Analysis Center (SIDC), which is the solar physics research department of the Royal Observatory of Belgium. The SIDC includes the World Data Center for the sunspot index and the ISES Regional Warning Center Brussels for space weather forecasting. You may obtain the data from the following internet site: http://sidc.oma.be/silso/datafiles.

    a. Censoring the most recent 250 months of sunspot activity data (approximately the last two sunspot cycles), forecast the time and intensity of the sunspot activity up through the present time. You should narrow your prediction to the nearest month. Your forecasting technique will be using what we call "in-sample" data to predict the "out-of-sample data" for 250 months ago to today.

    b. Comparing your forecast with the actual data, calculate your MAE, RMSE and MAPE for your predictions.

    c. Forecast the time and intensity of the next three peaks of sunspot activity.

2. Using the data in Appendix C, forecast select SCI Ratios and Supplementals for 12/31/13 through 12/31/18. You may validate your forecasts using financial statement data which has subsequently become available. Note that you will need to forecast the

stock price as well. If you use others' forecasts of the stock price, such as Valueline, or Thompson/Reuters, be sure and reference the source. Specifically, you should forecast:

Price/Earnings
Price/sales
Price/cash flow
Earnings per share (EPS)/(recurring)
Dividends per share (DPS)
Dividend Yield (percent)

3. Using a 20-day SMA, forecast three-period ahead stock price for three publicly traded stocks of your choice. Wait three days and record the actual price obtained, and calculate the MAE, RMSE, and MAPE for your predictions.

References

Albright, S. C., Wayne Winston, and Christopher Zappe, *Data Analysis and Decision Making*, 4th edn. Mason, OH: South Western Cengage Learning, 2011.

Basi, B. A., K. J. Carey, and D. T. Richard, "A Comparison of the Accuracy of Corporate and Security Analysts' Forecasts of Earnings," *The Accounting Review*, Apr. 1976, pp. 244–254.

Box, G. E. P., G. M. Jenkins, and G. C. Reinsel, *Time Series Analysis, Forecasting and Control*, 3rd edn. Englewood Cliffs, NJ: Prentice Hall, 1994.

Crichfield, T., Thomas Dyckman, and Josef Lakonishok, "An Evaluation of Security Analysts' Forecasts," *The Accounting Review*, Jul. 1978, pp. 651–668.

Evans, M. K., *Practical Business Forecasting*, Malden, MA: Blackwell Publishing, 2003.

Givoly, D. and Josef Lakonishok, "The Quality of Analysts' Forecasts of Earnings." *Financial Analysts Journal*, Sep.–Oct. 1984, pp. 40–47.

James, R. T., *Empirical Model Building: Data, Models, and Reality*, 2nd edn. Hoboken, NJ: John Wiley & Sons, Inc., 2011.

McMahon, E. K. and J. A., Dobelman, *A Market for Water: Constructing a Custom Weighted Water Index*. The Rice University, Statistics Department Technical Report TR-2014-02. Jan. 2014.

Thompson, J. R., E., E. Williams, and M. C. Findlay, *Models for Investors in Real World Markets*. Hoboken, NJ: John Wiley & Sons, 2003.

Chapter 6

Analysis of Fixed Income Securities

I am more concerned with the return of my money than the return on my money.

Will Rogers

Forecasts and Bond Analysis

Fixed-income securities are generally purchased because of the reduced risk associated with returns generated by these instruments. A *bond* obligates the issuing firm (or government) to pay interest at a specific rate, at a particular interval, and in a prescribed manner. Also, payments of principal are to be made periodically according to the terms specified in the *indenture* (the contractual agreement between the issuer and holder of the bond). The mere fact that a security takes the form of a fixed-income instrument does not insure the safety of the security. Indeed, the common stocks of some enterprises are less risky than the bonds of others. Nevertheless, the bond form does generally set a maximum payment ceiling (the coupon rate), and lesser amounts will be paid only if the issuer encounters financial difficulty.

Determining the probability that a firm (or other issuer) will be unable to meet coupon or principal payments is the primary responsibility of the bond analyst. Clearly, this task requires a complete analysis of the present and future financial position of the firm, and the bond analyst will employ the techniques outlined in the previous chapters to determine this position.

A recommended procedure is to forecast the earnings of the firm as far into the future as possible. In the ideal case, the analyst will be able to project throughout the life of the bond. Given this forecast, the analyst may then prepare annual probability distributions of interest (and principal) payments. From this set of distributions, the risk and return from purchasing the instrument may be determined.

We may consider an example of the appropriate methodology. An analyst has constructed a corporate model for the Consolidated Electric Appliance Corp. (CEA) He wishes to use this model in order to determine the risk and return associated with Consolidated's 5 percent subordinated debenture due on December 31, 2019. The bond pays interest semiannually, although the analyst is assuming annual payments to simplify his calculations.

Consolidated grossed $120 million in 2014. A revenue-forecasting equation has been generated with a reasonably good fit by means to multiple regression analysis:

$$R = 72.72 + 0.004(Y) + 4.26(P),$$

where:

R = annual revenue (in millions),
Y = per capita income of individuals in Consolidated's sales area,
P = population of Consolidated's sales area (in millions).

Analysis of past income statements has revealed that Consolidated incurs annual operating fixed costs of $80 million (including $40 million in depreciation) and has a variable cost ratio of about 0.2. Interest payments on the firm's bond indebtedness have totaled $5 million annually. The firm pays an average income tax of 40 percent.

1. Forecast total revenues for consolidated for 2015–2019 assuming the following values:

	Y	P
2015	$3,000	8.75M
2016	3,125	9.00
2017	3,300	9.40
2018	3,500	9.60
2019	3,800	10.00

The forecasted revenues would be:

2015	$72.72 + (0.004)(3{,}000) + (4.26)(8.75) = \$122.00$ million
2016	$72.72 + (0.004)(3{,}125) + (4.26)(9.00) = \$123.56$
2017	$72.72 + (0.004)(3{,}300) + (4.26)(9.40) = \$125.96$
2018	$72.72 + (0.004)(3{,}500) + (4.26)(9.60) = \$127.62$
2019	$72.72 + (0.004)(3{,}800) + (4.26)(10.00) = \$130.52$

2. Prepare simplified *pro forma* income statements for 2015–2019.

(in millions)

	2015	2016	2017	2018	2019
Revenues	$122.00	$123.56	$125.96	$127.62	$130.52
Fixed operating costs	80.00	80.00	80.00	80.00	80.00
Variable operating costs	24.40	24.71	25.19	25.52	26.10
Earnings before interest and taxes (EBIT)	17.60	18.85	20.77	22.10	24.42
Interest	5.00	5.00	5.00	5.00	5.00
Earnings before taxes (EBT)	12.60	13.85	15.77	17.10	19.42
Taxes	5.04	5.54	6.31	6.84	7.77
Net income	7.56	8.31	9.46	10.26	11.65

3. Compute the times-interest-earned ratio expected for 2015–2019.

$$2015: \frac{17.60}{5.00} = 3.52X$$

$$2016: \frac{18.85}{5.00} = 3.77X$$

$$2017: \frac{20.77}{5.00} = 4.15X$$

$$2018: \frac{22.10}{5.00} = 4.42X$$

$$2019: \frac{24.42}{5.00} = 4.88X.$$

4. How far would revenues have to decline before interest payments would be endangered in 2015?

Revenues	(X)	$106.25
Fixed operating costs	80.00	80.00
Variable operating costs	$(0.2)(X)$	21.25
EBIT	$5.00	$5.00

$$X - 80.00 - (0.2)(X) = 5.00$$

$$X = \$106.25 \text{ million}$$

Revenues would have to decline by 11.5 percent from 2014 revenues and be 12.9 percent under the 2015 projection before interest payments would be jeopardized.

5. What probability would one assign to the event: 2015 revenues are less than $106.25 million? This is the toughest question the analyst must answer, and it is obviously a very subjective matter. A decline in revenues of the magnitude indicated would be possible for firms in many industries. If Consolidated were a railroad, for example, the probability of such an event might be reasonably high. For a public utility, however, the chances of a decrease in revenues of over 3 or 4 percent is not great. Manufacturing concerns have varying patterns of revenue volatility, and the best guide may be to examine the experience of past years.

6. Does the regression result help the analyst in determining the probability of interest-payment jeopardization? One of the major characteristics of regression techniques is that they only indicate trends (positive or negative). Thus, a regression estimator will not, by itself, aid the analyst in determining the probability that a projection will be worse than expected.

However, the analyst may examine other statistics that will help in this determination. Initially one may inspect the R^2 value to check on the closeness of fit among the variables. A low R^2 might reduce the confidence in the estimated value and may cause the analyst to re-examine the historical data (the regression inputs) to determine whether large declines had been experienced in the past. Next, one should re-examine the standard error of the estimate. If the analyst believes the underlying distribution is essentially normal, then the standard error of the estimate may be used to determine the probability P ($R \leq$ \$106.25 million).

Suppose the revenue distribution for Consolidated is normally distributed with a standard error of \$2 million. Then, $P(R \leq$ \$106.25 million) $\cong 0$. For $R \leq$ \$106.25 million, a value almost 8 standard errors [that is $(122 - 106)/2$] from the expected value would have to occur. The probability of this event is extremely small.

7. What other variables, in addition to revenue variability, would the analyst have to examine in order to determine the probability that interest payments would be jeopardized? From the example above, the reader can recognize the importance of *operating leverage* on interest payments. A relatively small decline in revenues (11.5 percent) would completely wipe out EBIT for Consolidated. This is true because of the high level of fixed operating costs incurred by the company. For a firm with a lower degree of operating leverage, a larger decline in revenues could be tolerated before interest payments would be endangered. Thus, in addition to the stability of revenues, the analyst should examine the cost structure of the firm in order to determine the probability of interest-payment coverage as revenue declines.

8. Suppose revenues did indeed fall to \$106.25 million. Would the firm default on its bond interest payments? Not necessarily. Interest payments are made out of cash flows — not just earnings before interest and taxes. A firm may continue to pay interest on its indebtedness even though it is losing money. Several sources of funds other than earnings can be employed.

   (a) Cash generated from depreciation flows, for example, may be used to pay interest rather than replace plant and equipment.

When a firm uses depreciation flows for this purpose, of course, its long-run earnings potential is reduced.
(b) A firm may have built up a stock of cash that may be used to make interest payments. If the cash flows of the firm are independent over time, then the cash account may be used for interest payments during bad years and replenished during good years. If, as is more likely, the flows are dependent over time, then one bad year would follow another and the cash account would be soon depleted.
(c) The firm may borrow to meet interest obligations. Nevertheless, loans are granted for such purposes rarely, and then only when it appears that the firm is temporarily suffering an earnings decline.
(d) Historically, railroads had a habit of meeting debt charges by deferring maintenance of equipment and right of way. Hence, they allowed deterioration of facilities that eventually had to be repaired or replaced. Even today, the rail analyst examines the maintenance ratio when analyzing the position of a railroad. Although all these methods of continuing interest payments under depressed conditions may delay default, there is a tendency for them to be stopgap measures that only postpone the inevitable. Note that consolidation of the railroads (from over 90 Class I roads 50 years ago to just seven today) has significantly reduced the practice of deferring maintenance, and railroads like the Union Pacific and the BNSF (formerly the Burlington Northern Santa Fe and now a subsidiary of Warren Buffet's Berkshire Hathaway) are quite strong financially.

Coverage Ratios and Income Security

In addition to using the forecasting tools employed in the previous section, the analyst will also use several ratios to aid him or her in the determination of possible default. He will frequently compute the time-interest-earned ratio for past years and compare the firm's ratio with that of other firms in the same business. He will also examine the trend of the ratio for the firm over time. Of course, these ratios should not be substitutes in analysis for forecasting. Rather, they should serve as additional data to give added perspective to the results obtained from projections.

When a firm has several bond issues outstanding, it is possible to compute several variations of the times-interest-earned ratio. The simplest of these ratios is computed by adding all interest payments and dividing this sum into EBIT. The resulting ratio is called the *overall-interest-coverage ratio*. A second group of ratios, called *cumulative-deduction-coverage ratios*, attempts to differentiate among bonds on the basis of their claim on earnings (and assets in the case of liquidation in order to show a higher coverage for more secure obligations). The interest coverage of claims is computed in order of priority. First, the interest requirement for the most senior security is divided into EBIT to obtain its coverage ratio. Next, the claims of junior securities are added to the denominator of the coverage ratio successively in order to determine the coverage of each issue.

Although the exact arrangement of priorities can be ascertained only from the indentures of the relevant securities, the general order of priority is: first mortgage bonds and equivalents (for example, equipment trust certificates, collateral trust agreements, and so on), second mortgage bonds, debentures, subordinated debentures, junior subordinated debentures, preferred stock, and, finally, common stock. A third method of computing coverage ratios is the *prior deductions method*. Instead of adding the interest requirement of senior issues to the denominator as in the cumulative deduction method, this approach subtracts them from the numerator (EBIT). The coverage is then computed as [(EBIT − prior charges)/interest on security under analysis]. The computation may produce the absurd result that a junior obligation appears to be safer than a senior issue. Although this method gives no useful information, many investment banking houses once employed it to give a deceptively good picture for a bond they were about to underwrite. It should be avoided by the analyst. These three methods of computing coverage ratios are illustrated below.

The long-term debt (LTD) section of the balance sheet of the Atlantic and Pacific R.R. is as follows (in order of earnings claim):

First mortgage 5's of 2025	$24,200,000
Second mortgage 8 1/8's of 2019	20,000,000
Collateral trust notes 4's of 2025	50,000,000
Subordinated debentures 9's of 2030	6,000,000
	$100,200,000

Earnings before interest and taxes for Atlantic and Pacific is $10,750,000. The overall interest coverage would be:

$$
\begin{aligned}
(0.05)(24.2 \text{ million}) &= \$1,210,000 \\
(0.08125)(20 \text{ million}) &= 1,625,000 \\
(0.04)(50 \text{ million}) &= 2,000,000 \\
(0.09)(6 \text{ million}) &= \underline{540,000} \\
& \$5,375,000
\end{aligned}
$$

$$10{,}750{,}000/5{,}375{,}000 = 2.0X.$$

The cumulative coverage for each issue would be:

First mortgage bonds

$$(10{,}750{,}000)/(1{,}210{,}000) = 8.9X.$$

Second mortgage bonds

$$(10{,}750{,}000)/(1{,}210{,}000 + 1{,}625{,}000) = 3.8X.$$

Collateral trust notes

$$(10{,}750{,}000)/(1{,}210{,}000 + 1{,}625{,}000 + 2{,}000{,}000) = 2.2X.$$

Subordinated debentures

$$(10{,}750{,}000)/(1{,}210{,}000 + 1{,}625{,}000 + 2{,}000{,}000 + 540{,}000) = 2.0X.$$

Notice that the coverage for the most junior issue is the same as the overall coverage.

The prior deduction coverage for each issue would be:

First mortgage bonds

$$(10{,}750{,}000)/(1{,}210{,}000) = 8.9X.$$

Second mortgage bonds

$$(10{,}750{,}000 - 1{,}210{,}000)/(1{,}625{,}000) = 5.9X.$$

Collateral trust notes

$$(10{,}750{,}000 - 1{,}210{,}000 - 1{,}625{,}000)/(2{,}000{,}000) = 3.9X.$$

Subordinated debentures

$$(10{,}750{,}000 - 1{,}210{,}000 - 1{,}625{,}000 - 2{,}000{,}000)/(540{,}000) = 10.9X.$$

Note the absurd result here indicates *greater* security for the subordinated debentures than for the first mortgage bonds.

Protection in Case of Financial Difficulty

The major determinants of the firm's ability to make its interest payments are the volume of interest payments the firm owes in each period and the earnings available for those payments. Other tests used to determine the safety of the coupon and principal payments for a bond were discussed in Chapter 4. The degree of *financial leverage* possessed by the firm may be indicated by various debt-to-equity and debt-to-total-capital ratios.

The asset security of obligations may be tested by computing several asset-coverage ratios (such as the tangible asset debt coverage). Although the capital-structure and asset-coverage ratios do provide additional information about the position of the firm's debt obligations, they are most useful as indicators of what the holders might receive in case of liquidation or reorganization. Because the primary reason for bond purchases is the *avoidance* of any problems associated with payment default or delay, the analyst should be not be satisfied simply because a firm has little indebtedness or a bond is well secured by assets in case of difficulty. Of course, once the analyst is confident that coupon and principal payments are adequately protected by future earnings, added security provided by low indebtedness and large asset holdings can be considered a safety hedge in case a very poor state of events develops.

When financial difficulties do occur for a company, there are several courses of action available. If creditors believe that the firm will never be able to earn enough to repay its obligations, they may sue to place the firm in bankruptcy. If it is decided that the firm should be *liquidated*, a referee is appointed to sell the firm's assets at the best price he or she can obtain. The funds received are used first to pay for the cost of liquidation (legal fees and so on). Next, any back taxes, wages payable, and certain other claims are paid. Secured creditors are entitled to the proceeds obtained from the sale of the assets against which they have claims. In case their claims are not fully satisfied, they become general creditors for the balance owed them. Remaining funds are distributed to the general creditors. If funds are insufficient to meet all obligations, they are pro-rated by size of claim. When the general creditors are satisfied, distribution is made to subordinated creditors and then preferred stockholders. The balance, if any, goes to the common stockholders.

Because the process of bankruptcy is expensive administratively, many creditors will make great concessions to avoid the procedure. A frequently employed method is simply to give the debtor an *extension*, that is, more time to pay the obligation. This method is particularly attractive if interest payments are still being made (fully or partially) and only principal payments are being missed.

A second method, used generally where interest payments have been stopped, is the *composition*, by which less than the total amount due is accepted as full payment of the obligation. Many creditors are willing to accept such an arrangement, because the funds become available for investment elsewhere fairly quickly and also the settlement may be greater than that which could be obtained from legal proceedings.

It may be decided that a firm should be *reorganized* rather than liquidated under bankruptcy. This is almost always the case for companies engaged in providing a vital public service (such as public utilities and railroads). Under reorganization, a *receiver* is appointed by the courts to operate the business until a satisfactory plan can be worked out. This process may take months or even years. During the Great Depression of the 1930s, for example, many railroads were in receivership for 20 years before a reorganization could be accomplished. The reorganization plan is determined by a referee who decides upon a new capital structure for the firm.

The objective of the new structure is to make it possible for the firm to become viable again. This usually means that the firm will not be overly burdened with fixed charges. Because interest on income bonds must be paid only if earned, this security has become a standard part of many reorganizations. (The poor reputation generally accorded income bonds in the past is no doubt accounted for by its use in reorganizations.)

Reorganization may take place under two rules. The *absolute priority* rule settles claims with strict regard to their legal priority, and all senior claims must be satisfied in full before junior claims can be settled. Under *relative priority*, all claimants participate in the reorganization (including common stockholders), although heavier losses are apportioned to junior claims than senior. One method of distributing new securities under relative priority is to allocate on the basis of the market values of the old securities. We may consider a couple of examples.

The Singleton Publishing Co. is in financial difficulty. The company has been unable to meet interest payments on its subordinated debentures for two years, and preferred stock dividends have been passed for five years. Junior bondholders have granted two extensions of interest payments, but they are unwilling to grant a third. Lawyers for the company have polled the bondholders about the possibility of a composition, but full payment was demanded. Hence, the firm has petitioned to be declared bankrupt. A balance sheet for Singleton is given below (in 000's):

Cash	$ 50,000	Current liabilities	$ 200,000
Receivables	100,000	Mortgage bonds	300,000
Inventories	350,000	Subordinated debentures	300,000
Fixed assets	500,000	Preferred stock	100,000
	$1,000,000	Common equity	100,000
			$1,000,000

Receivables could be factored for 80 percent of their book value. Inventories can be sold at 70 percent of book value, and fixed assets could be liquidated at 40 percent of book value. It is expected that liquidation costs would be about $100 million. Among the firm's current liabilities are $50 million in wages payable, and $10 million in accrued taxes. Mortgage bondholders have a prior claim against all fixed assets. Upon liquidation, creditors would receive the following proceeds (in 000's):

Cash	$50,000
Receivables	80,000
Inventories	245,000
Fixed assets	200,000
	$575,000

(a) First mortgage bondholders would have claim to $200 million from the sale of fixed assets and would become general creditors for the balance of $100 million. (b) Liquidation costs, wages payable, and accrued taxes would have a claim against $160 million. (c) The balance ($575 million less $200 million less $160 million equals $215 million) would go to the general creditors. Other current liabilities are $140 million. Subordinated debenture holders have a claim of $300 million.

Thus, the payment to current liabilities would be 14/54 × $215 million ≅ $55 million, first mortgage bondholders would initially get an additional 10/54 × $215 million ≅ $40 million, and subordinated holders would claim 30/54 × $215 million ≅ $120 million. However, because the debentures are subordinated to the mortgage bonds, the bondholders are entitled to have satisfied any remaining claims against the portion due the debentures. Thus, $60 million would be transferred from the debenture claim to the mortgage bondholders. In sum, the mortgage bondholders would be paid in full, the other liability holders would be paid about 39 percent of their claim, and the debenture holders would receive about 20 percent of their claim.

The New York and Pennsylvania Railroad is being reorganized. Data from the trustee's files indicate:

	Current Book Value (in millions)	Trustee's Desired Structure (in millions)	Current Market Value (in millions)
First mortgage bonds	$100	$0	$ 80
Second mortgage bonds	150	0	90
Debentures	150	100	90
Subordinated notes	300	0	150
Income bonds	0	100	0
Preferred Stock	0	100	0
Common stock	300	200	90
	$1,000	$500	$500

Reorganization under absolute priority would result in the following: The $100 million first mortgage bonds would get $100 million of debenture bonds. First mortgage bondholders would thus get $1,000 in debentures for each $1,000 first mortgage bond held. Second mortgage bonds would get $100 million of income bonds plus $50 million of preferred stock. Second mortgage bondholders would thus get $667 in income bonds and $333 in preferred stock for each $1,000 bond held. Current debenture holders would get $50 million in preferred stock and $100 million in common stock, or $333 worth of preferred and $667 worth of common for each $1,000 debenture held. Subordinate note holders would receive $100 million in common, or $333 worth of common for each $1,000 in notes held. Common stock holders would get nothing.

Reorganization under relative priority would be somewhat more complicated. Because the total market value of securities is $500 million and securities to be distributed are valued at $500 million, each class of holder would get the following if the basis for reorganization were market values: (a) First mortgage bondholders would get $80 million in debentures, or $800 worth of debenture for each $1,000 first mortgage bond held. (b) Second mortgage bondholders would get $20 million in debentures plus $70 million in income bonds, or $133 worth of debenture and $467 worth of income bonds for each $1,000 second mortgage bond held. (c) Debenture bondholders would get $30 million in income bonds and $60 million in preferred stock, or $200 in income bonds and $400 in preferred stock for each $1,000 debenture held. (d) Subordinated note holders would receive $40 million in preferred stock plus $110 million in common stock, or $133 in preferred stock and $367 in common stock for each $1,000 note held. (e) Common stockholders would get $90 million in common stock, or three shares for every ten now held.

The Risk Structure of Interest Rates

In Chapter 3, we established that the structure of rates on long-term securities will be related to the expected future short-term rates. Furthermore, it seems reasonable to expect that the greater potential price volatility of long-term securities resulting from a change in the actual or expected level of interest rates should cause them to command a higher nominal rate of interest in the form of a risk premium. This risk (called *interest-rate risk*) is the result of bond price changes caused by interest rate changes and is considered a part of the liquidity preference version of term structure theory. It should be borne in mind that this is the one risk that exists even for government securities (except the very short term). It might be argued that inflation risk, or, more precisely, the change in expected rate of inflation risk, exists for all investments, including (especially) money. Indeed, it might be argued that there is no such thing as a riskless long-term investment. Even the investment in short-term securities involves risking the actual income to be earned in future periods. Thus, it might be even more correct to say that it is impossible to avoid all risks.

Once we depart from the world of federal government securities, *default risk* becomes quite prominent in our discussion of the structure of market returns. Although many readers might be tempted to view this risk as solely involving the probability of the security in question becoming worthless, such is not a general case. Even if an issuer enters bankruptcy, the securities generally command some positive market price on the basis of expected liquidation payments or a possible reorganization.

Thus, it is the possibility of partial payments and even full payments made behind schedule that constitute the difficult problems in the analysis of default risk. Consider the Ale Corp., which issued a five-year note at 6 percent with interest payments to be made annually. It is estimated that there is a 0.8 probability that the note will be paid on schedule, a 0.1 probability that the interest for years three and four will be skipped and paid at the end of year five, and a 0.1 probability that, aside from skipping interest in years three and four, the firm will enter bankruptcy in year five and the holder will receive a total liquidation payment of $1000 at the end of year seven. The expected return on this note would be:

a. 6 percent if the note is paid on schedule.
b. ≈5.8 percent if interest in years three and four is deferred until year five.

Year	CF	PV@ 2 percent	PV	PV@ 1 percent	PV
0	−1000	1.000	−1000	1.000	−1000
1+2	+60	1.859	+111.60	1.833	+110
5	+1000	0.784	+925.12	0.747	+881.46
			+36.72		−8.54

Year	CF	PV@ 2 percent	PV	PV@ 1 percent	PV
0	−1000	1.000	−1000	1.000	−1000
1+2	+60	1.942	+117	1.97	+118
7	+1000	0.871	+871	0.933	+933
			−12		+51

c. ≈ 1.8 percent if interest in years three and four is missed, and the firm enters bankruptcy in year five.

$$r = (0.8)(0.06) + (0.1)(0.058) + (0.1)(0.018) = 5.56\%.$$

Because the possibility of default, no matter how remote, exists for all non-U.S. federal government securities, it is necessary that they offer a nominal yield in excess of the riskless rate merely to possess an expected return equal to the riskless rate. As illustrated in the example above, the bond possessed a nominal yield of 6 percent and an expected yield of 5.56 percent. This factor alone would cause the yield curve for a homogeneous set of risky securities to lie above the yield curve for U.S. government securities. As a practical matter, however, risky securities generally offer an *expected* return in excess of the riskless rate. As a result, their nominal yield exceeds the riskless rate by a risk premium as well as the expected value of any default loss. In addition, this risk premium becomes larger as the security becomes riskier. Three hypothetical probability distributions of expected returns are given in Figure 6.1 (it is assumed the bonds are held until maturity). The certain return for U.S. government bonds is illustrated as case A. Case B is a moderately risky, and C a quite risky, bond. It will be observed that the distributions for both B and C are greatly skewed. Receipt of the nominal yield is generally the best possible outcome (sometimes a call above par will increase the return), with various degrees of default trailing down to the left. It should be noted that the distribution of returns becomes more symmetrical as the holding period considered becomes shorter. In this discussion, we have assumed that the bond is held until maturity. If we chose instead a one-year holding period, where return would be final price plus income compared to initial price, the probability distribution of returns would likely be close to normal. The figure has been drawn with the expected return on the risky bonds in excess of the riskless rate. The theoretical justification for this observed market behavior is based upon investor aversion to risk in general and, especially, to the direction of skewness.

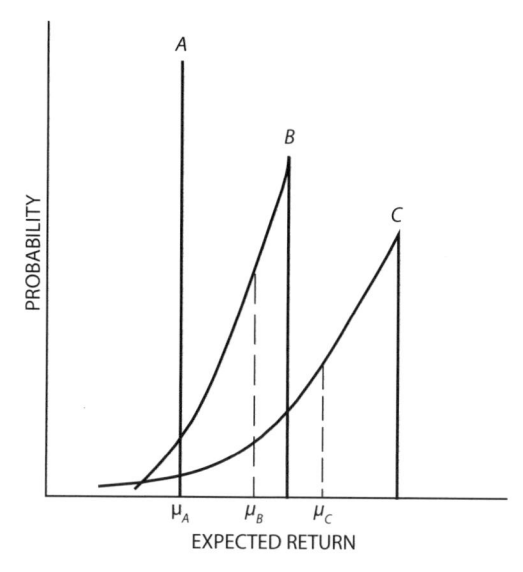

Figure 6.1. Probability Distributions of Return for Three Hypothetical Bonds of Varying Risk Held to Maturity

In terms of the analytical framework espoused by this book, default risk is a function of (1) the level and variation of gross revenues earned by the issuer; (2) the size of fixed charges against that income; and (3) the size of additional resources, such as working capital or bank credit, to meet the obligation. Let us begin by illustrating the difference in effect between variable and fixed charges against income. It should be noted that the effect of fixed charges is the same whether they are the result of operating (salaries and so on) or financial (interest) leverage.

Let:

$S_i = i^{\text{th}}$ possible level of sales

$\mu_s, \mu_{avc}, \mu_{afc}$ = expected value of sales, expected value of sales minus variable costs, expected value of sales minus variable and fixed costs

$\sigma_s, \sigma_{avc}, \sigma_{afc}$ = standard deviation of sales, standard deviation of sales minus variable costs, standard deviation of sales minus variable and fixed costs

VC = variable costs (a fixed percentage of sales)
FC = fixed costs, with reinvestment assumed equal to depreciation so that accrual and cash flow data are equal

$$Z = \left(1 - \frac{VC}{S}\right)$$

p_i = probability of ith level of sales occurring.

Then:

$$\mu_s = \sum_{i=1}^{n} S_i p_i \qquad (6.1)$$

$$\sigma_s = \sqrt{\sum_{i=1}^{n} (S_i - \mu_s)^2 p_i} \qquad (6.2)$$

$$\mu_{avc} = \sum_{i=1}^{n} (ZS_i) p_i = Z\left(\sum_{i=1}^{n} S_i p_i\right) = Z\mu_s \qquad (6.3)$$

$$\mu_{avc} = \sqrt{\sum_{i=1}^{n} (ZS_i - Z\mu_s)^2 p_i} = \sqrt{Z^2 \sum_{i=1}^{n} (S_i - \mu_s)^2 p_i} \qquad (6.4)$$
$$= Z\sigma_s.$$

Therefore:

$$\frac{\sigma_{avc}}{\mu_{avc}} = \frac{Z\sigma_s}{Z\mu_s} = \frac{\sigma_s}{\mu_s}. \qquad (6.5)$$

The point of Equations (6.1)–(6.5) is to demonstrate that the presence of variable costs does not change the risk of the cash flow. In other words, the probability that sales minus variable costs will be less than zero is the same as the probability that sales will be less than zero, assuming $VC/S < 1$. The variable costs reduce the mean value of the flow, of course, but they also tighten the dispersion of outcomes proportionally. Compare this with the result when fixed charges are also present:

$$\mu_{afc} = \sum_{i=1}^{n} (ZS_i - FC) p_i = Z \left(\sum_{i=1}^{n} S_i p_i \right) - FC = Z\mu_s - FC. \tag{6.6}$$

$$\begin{aligned}
\sigma_{afc} &= \sqrt{\sum_{i=1}^{n} [(ZS_i - FC) - (Z\mu_s - FC)]^2 p_i} \\
&= \sqrt{\sum_{i=1}^{n} [ZS_i - FC - Z\mu_s + FC]^2 p_i} \\
&= \sqrt{Z^2 \sum_{i=1}^{n} (S_i - \mu_s)^2 p_i} = Z\sigma_s.
\end{aligned} \tag{6.7}$$

Therefore:

$$\frac{\sigma_{afc}}{\mu_{afc}} = \frac{Z\sigma_s}{Z\mu_s - FC} > \frac{\sigma_s}{\mu_s}. \tag{6.8}$$

Thus, the presence of fixed charges will increase the risk of the firm's flows and the probability that the flow will be exhausted before a given security holder's claim is satisfied. If we redefine FC in Equation (6.8) as those fixed charges relating to a given holder's claim and all charges of greater priority, we can see how the variation increases as we move to more junior securities. We can also see that, because operating fixed charges generally have the highest priority, if these are large, *ceteris paribus*, even the most senior bondholder may be in a precarious position. Because the default upon even the most junior issue can throw the firm into bankruptcy, senior holders must join the junior and common-stock holders in being concerned that all fixed charges are met. For this reason, firms with large operating fixed charges may usually issue only a modest amount of debt without paying substantial risk premiums. Finally, however, it should be noted that some firms can have large operating and financial fixed charges (that is, FC large in relation to μ_s) at reasonable rates if the variation in revenue (σ_s) is small (for example, public utilities).

Recall that resources other than annual cash flow may be used to meet fixed-charge requirements. In any given year, the firm's cash balance, marketable securities held, and, in some cases, its unused lines of bank credit could be added directly to the cash flow in the denominator of Equation (6.8) in order to reduce the probability of funds available being inadequate to settle claims. The same statement could be made over the life of a bond issue if we could assume that the distributions of annual cash flows were independent over time (for example, the cash drawn down by an abnormally low sales figure in one year could be replenished by an equally high figure in subsequent years). When the flows are dependent, as they are likely to be in reality, one bad year follows another, and, the firm will soon run out of cash. The existence of liquidity balances, therefore, will afford protection to security holders against short-run fluctuations in the issuer's flows, but not against a long-run trend. Let us consider an example.

The Peel Corp. has $\mu_s = \$10$ million and $\sigma_s = \$3$ million, with sales normally distributed. The variable cost ratio (VC/S) is 0.6 and operating fixed costs are $1 million. Peel has senior bonds outstanding with interest requirements of $500,000 and junior bonds requiring $300,000. The probability that each will be fully paid is:

(1) $Z = 0.4$; $\dfrac{Z\sigma_s}{Z\mu_s - OFC - FC_s} = \dfrac{1.2M}{4M - 1M - .5M}$

$= \dfrac{1.2M}{2.5M}$; $P(X \geq 0) = P(X \geq \mu - 2.08\sigma) = 0.9812.$

(2) $\dfrac{1.2M}{2.2M}$; $P(X \geq 0) = P(X \geq \mu - 1.84\sigma) = 0.9671.$

If Peel had $1 million in cash that could be used to meet obligations, the probabilities would become:

(1) $\dfrac{1.2M}{3.5M}$; $P(X \geq 0) = P(X \geq \mu - 2.92\sigma) = 0.9982.$

(2) $\dfrac{1.2M}{3.2M}$; $P(X \geq 0) = P(X \geq \mu - 2.67\sigma) = 0.9962.$

Analysis of Fixed Income Securities 215

A generally reliable indicator of default risk is the bond rating assigned by Moody's, Standard & Poor's (S&P) or Fitch. Empirical work has shown that default loss has corresponded fairly well with these ratings. However, all the rating agencies were caught off guard during the 2008 financial crisis. S&P was sued by the federal government (along with several states) and negotiated a $1.4 billion settlement for having over-rated issues that subsequently collapsed in value. One of the authors of this book went to bed on a Friday night nervous but feeling fairly secured with his A-rated Lehman bonds only to find the firm declaring bankruptcy over the weekend. Much of this fiasco was engineered by the U.S. Treasury, and it is ironic that S&P is paying the price for the actions of the U.S. Government. Even more troublesome is the fact that only S&P was prosecuted until immense political pressure resulted in litigation against Moody's as well. This followed S&P's decision to downgrade the rating of the U.S. federal government from its coveted AAA status. Moody's (and Fitch) did not downgrade the U.S. debt (despite the explosion of debt created during 2008–2014) and were not originally prosecuted, causing many to feel the government had a vendetta against S&P. The irony is the government prosecuted S&P for NOT downgrading corporations with deteriorating financial conditions while it was furious that S&P did so as the U.S. government's finances were in shambles. One U.S. Treasury Secretary said S&P would rue the day they pulled the AAA rating from the federal government debt, and so it came to pass.

Despite the record in recent years, the rating agencies have done a fairly good job. Indeed, the Securities and Exchange Commission (SEC) essentially provides an oligopoly to these institutions. However, this does not imply that we can automatically class bonds with the same rating as being of equivalent risk; there are still bargains to be found by the diligent analyst. Nor does this mean that we can observe a neat AAA yield curve lying on top of the government yield curve (with an AA yield curve on top of it, and so on), all curves moving up and down and changing slope together. For one thing, it has been observed that the yield spread between high-grade and low-grade bonds narrows near the peak of the cycle (either because the good business has finally reached the marginal firm and made the interest payment more secure or else because euphoric investors are buying everything in sight) and widens at the trough (for the opposite reasons). It has also been argued that the yield curve for very risky securities may slope down, as the greatest risk of default occurs when the issue is near to maturity and can be neither repaid nor refunded.

There are other factors that prevent the market structure of returns from being a nice set of equal-risk yield curves lying on top of each other. The fact that municipal bond interest is generally tax exempt causes the nominal yield curve for at least high-grade municipals to lie under the government curve. The intercorporate dividend exclusion has also caused the apparent return on preferred stock to lie below the (less-risky) yield on bonds of the same issuer. The presence of a call feature may make the actual maturity of an issue indeterminate, thus confusing its location on any yield curve. In addition, market segmentation and other institutional factors affect the risk structure of yields as well as the term structure. The fact that many financial institutions are effectively precluded from investing in lower quality securities undoubtedly causes yield differentials (both nominal and expected) to be greater than they would otherwise be.

A concluding note should be made regarding equities. Because stock possesses a theoretically infinite life, the return on stocks of a given risk would appear as a point (at maturity $= \infty$) rather than an entire yield curve. Preferred stocks are rather well behaved in this regard, in that their yields should be comparable, after the adjustment for tax factors discussed above, to the yields on long-term bonds of similar risk, and the yields should move together. The case of common stock is more difficult, because the amount and timing of income is not contractual and can only be estimated. It is generally assumed that the return on common should be high, as it is the most risky security a firm can issue. Yet, this return cannot be precisely measured *ex ante* if the income stream is not known.

Finally, portfolio and capital market theory (to be discussed later in this book) suggest that security pricing and risk premiums should not be based upon an individual security's risk considered in isolation, but rather upon its contribution to portfolio risk. We must therefore defer further discussion on this point until then.

Methods of Principal Repayment

The security of coupon payments is clearly an important matter for the financial analyst. Nevertheless, the *security* of principal payments may be equally important. Legally, a bond may be considered in default if either interest or principal payments are in arrears. The repayment of principal may be accomplished in several ways. A common method for corporate bonds is repayment by way of a *sinking fund*. This arrangement obligates the issuer to begin repaying a certain percentage of the issue after some year in the life of the issue. Thus, a bond indenture may specify that no sinking fund payments be made for the first five years of the life of an issue, that 10 percent of the issue be paid over the next eight years, and that the remaining 20 percent be paid in the final (that is, fourteenth) year of the life of the issue.

Sinking-fund payments may be made by depositing the appropriate percentage of the par value with the trustee of the issue. In many cases, sinking-fund requirements may also be met by going out into the market and purchasing the equivalent par amount at market prices. Thus, if a bond is selling at a discount, the issuer may satisfy the sinking fund requirement by paying less than the amount that would be placed on deposit with the trustee. For example, a 10 percent sinking-fund requirement on a $10 million issue could be satisfied with $9 million if the bonds were purchased in the market at 90. Sinking-fund requirements of this form may exert upward pressure on bonds selling at a discount, as the presence of the issuer in the market decreases the supply of the obligation.

Funds placed on deposit with the trustee may be used to retire the appropriate part of the issue at par by lot drawing, or they may be invested in equivalent securities with comparable yields. In the latter case, funds accumulate until the issue matures. Then, the other securities are sold, and the issue is paid off. In the former case, the existence of the sinking fund reduces the average life of the bond issue, which in turn reduces the risk exposure of the investor. The redemption process under a lot-drawing sinking-fund arrangement is essentially random. The investor does not know when his or her bonds will be redeemed and thus cannot know the precise life of the debt.

Because the going rate of interest tends to be related to the maturity of the issue (see Chapter 3), the life of the bond is important to the investor. Analysts frequently compute the *yield to average life* of the bond, rather than the yield to maturity, when a lot-drawing sinking is used to pay off an issue. The yield to average life is computed by determining the *expected life* of a bond. The expected life is then substituted for the maturity of the obligation in making the yield calculation. Suppose a bond sells in the market at 90. It has a 6 percent coupon with sinking-fund payments equal to 10 percent of the issue coming due over each of the next five years. Fifty percent of the issue has already been repaid. The average life remaining for the bonds outstanding is given by:

Year	Probability	
1	0.2	0.2
2	0.2	0.4
3	0.2	0.6
4	0.2	0.8
5	0.2	1.0
		Average life 3.0 years

Thus, if the yield to maturity of the issue were computed, the results would be (using the shortcut formula of equation (3.4)):

$$\text{yield to maturity} = \frac{60 + \frac{1000 - 900}{5}}{\frac{1000 + 900}{2}} = \frac{80}{950} = 8.42\%,$$

or (using present-value tables):

Yield to maturity @ 8%
$$3.993(60) = 239.58$$
$$0.681(1000) = \underline{681.00}$$
$$920.58$$

@ 9%
$$3.890(60) = 233.40$$
$$0.650(1000) = \underline{650.00}$$
$$883.40$$

Interpolating, the yield $\cong 8.54\%$.

The yield to average life would provide the following yields, however:

$$\text{Yield to average life} = \frac{60 + \frac{1000-900}{3}}{\frac{1000+900}{2}} = \frac{93}{950} = 9.79\%,$$

Yield to average life @ 9%
$$2.531(60) = 151.86$$
$$0.772(1000) = \underline{772.00}$$
$$923.86$$

@ 10%
$$2.487(60) = 149.22$$
$$0.751(1000) = \underline{751.00}$$
$$900.22$$

Yield $\cong 10.0\%$.

The higher yield develops because the principal payment ($1,000) is five years away in the case of the yield to maturity calculation but only three years in the future (expected) in the yield to average life computation.

If the firm is required to satisfy the sinking-fund requirement by a lot drawing at par, then the yield to average life is the appropriate indicator of expected investor return. Furthermore, if the indenture requires that a premium over par be paid to investors whose bonds are chosen, this figure should be used in place of par value in the above computations. On the other hand, an indenture that allows the firm to satisfy its obligation either by lot drawings or by the purchase of bonds in the open market requires a more complicated analysis. In the case of bonds selling at a premium, it is to the corporation's advantage to employ a lot drawing at par.

This implies that yield to average life is the appropriate investor concept of expected return (assuming the current pattern of interest rates remains constant in the future). For bonds at a discount, the firm would presumably enter the market to satisfy its obligation. If bond markets were reasonably efficient, the purchases by the issuer would not affect the pattern of rates, and yield to maturity would reflect the investor's expected return; this result would also apply in the special case in which the investor chose to hold his bonds to maturity.

In "thin" markets, it is possible that the purchases by the issuer would force the price upward and result in a return greater than the yield to maturity to those investors who sold their bonds at the right time; it is unlikely that the expectation of this profit is great, however, and yield to maturity remains the best measure even in this case. It should be pointed out, additionally, that the coupon on a bond that does not allow the issuer the right to purchase in the market to satisfy sinking-fund requirements may be lower than for an equivalent bond that grants that privilege.

A second method of repaying principal is by means of *serial obligation*. In this case, a part of the issue is scheduled to mature each year until the entire issue is repaid. The investor knows in advance when his bond will mature, and coupon rates are adjusted according to maturities. Serial obligations are seldom used by corporate issuers, although government and municipal bonds are often of the serial type. Because the investor knows the maturity of a serial issue at the time of purchase, the yield to maturity on his bond is the appropriate return measure. The result may then be compared to yields on other bonds of the same specific maturity.

A final method of repayment is the *lump-sum payment*. In this case, the entire issue is repaid at the maturity date. This method is used frequently by public utilities that simply "roll over" debt (that is, replace a maturing issue with a new one). The federal government also tends to repay its debt on this basis. This form of repayment is satisfactory if the issuer is a top credit and has no difficulty in selling new bonds as old obligations come due. Lesser credits may have difficulty, however, in replacing debt, and the result may be detrimental to the holder of the maturing issue. It should be noted that bonds with an escrow sinking fund are technically lump-sum payment obligations from the standpoint of the investor. Nevertheless, this feature does provide additional lender protection. The yield to maturity is the appropriate return criterion for lump-sum payment bonds.

Prediction of Future Default

The security of interest and principal payments may be measured by use of an interest-and-sinking-fund-coverage ratio. The historical pattern of this ratio along with *pro forma* calculations of it based on projections of earnings before interest and taxes constitutes a good overall test of the ability of the firm to meet interest and sinking-fund payments.

Reconsider the EBIT projections for Consolidated Electric Appliance (described earlier in this chapter). Suppose the firm had $100 million outstanding in the 5 percent subordinated debenture, with sinking-fund payments of 5 percent due in 2015–2016, 10 percent in 2017–2018, and the balance (70 percent) due in 2019. The coverage of interest and sinking-fund payments, given the EBIT forecast, would be:

	2015
$\dfrac{\text{EBIT} + \text{depreciation}}{\text{Interest} + \text{sinking fund}}$	$\dfrac{17.60 + 40.00}{5.00 + 5.00} = 5.76X$
	2016
(Interest falls by 5 percent to 4.75 million)	$\dfrac{18.85 + 40.00}{4.75 + 5.00} = 6.04X$
	2017
(Interest falls by 5 percent to 4.50 million)	$\dfrac{20.77 + 40.00}{4.50 + 10.00} = 4.19X$

(*Continued*)

(Continued)

	2018
(Interest falls by 10 percent to 4.00 million)	$\dfrac{22.10 + 40.00}{4.00 + 10.00} = 4.44X$

	2019
$\text{Int.} + \dfrac{\text{EBIT} + \text{depreciation}}{\text{sinking fund} - (\text{tax rate})(\text{dep.})}$ $\overline{1-(\text{tax rate})}$	$\dfrac{24.42 + 40.00}{3.50 + \dfrac{70.00 - (0.4)(40.00)}{1-(0.4)}} = 0.69X.$

These ratios are respectable, although one might wonder whether interest or principal payments on the bonds would be in jeopardy in 2019. This prospect is unlikely. The firm will probably roll over its debt as it comes due. Given the stability of the firm's EBIT, it should have no difficulty refunding the issue in 2019.

Other ratios may be employed in a multiple discriminant analysis to predict possible default. The five ratios that best predicted eventual collapse are condensed to the following discriminant function:

$$Z = 0.012X_1 + 0.014X_2 + 0.033X_3 + 0.006X_4 + 0.999X_5, \quad (6.9)$$

where:

$X_1 = $ working capital/total assets
$X_2 = $ retained earnings/total assets
$X_3 = $ EBIT/total assets
$X_4 = $ market value equity/book value of total debt
$X_5 = $ sales/total assets.

X_1 through X_4 are expressed as whole numbers (10 percent = 10), and X_5 is expressed as a decimal (10 percent = 0.10). Firms with a Z value above 2.99 were "nonbankrupt" and those below 1.81 were "bankrupt." A value of $Z = 2.675$ as a cutoff provided the least misclassifications.

This function might be applied to Consolidated Electric Appliance. Suppose the firm is expected to have the following ratios in 2015:

Working capital/total assets	= 0.15
Retained earnings/total assets	= 0.20
EBIT/total assets	= 0.07
Market value equity/book debt	= 1.50
Sales/total assets	= 0.50

The Z value for the firm would be:

$$Z = (0.012)(15) + (0.014)(20) + (0.033)(7)$$
$$+ (0.006)(150) + (0.999)(0.5)$$
$$= 2.09.$$

Although this value is below the cutoff of $Z = 2.675$, it is unlikely that Consolidated is on the verge of collapse. In the first place, the universe to which Consolidated belongs (assets well over $25 million) is not the same as that upon which the given discriminant function was based. Equation (6.9) was determined for firms having a total asset size of $1 million to $25 million, and it might be misleading to use this equation for every case. The analyst should prepare his own discriminant function where circumstances warrant. Moreover, it would be unwise for an analyst to depend entirely on a discriminant function to determine a potential bankruptcy. All evidence should be considered, particularly the forecasts that have been made of the firm's future-earnings capacity. If a poor earnings forecast and generally weak ratios combine with a discriminant value below the cutoff, the analyst might expect trouble in the future.

Holding Period Risks

In addition to the factors previously considered in determining the yield and security of a bond, one other variable must be assessed: the desired holding period of the bond. It will be recalled from Chapter 3 that the aggregate level of interest rates may vary as economic conditions change, and that bond prices move inversely with the market rate of interest. Thus, there is a market risk in holding a bond as well as the business and financial risk associated with the issuer.

A precipitous decline in bond prices, caused by higher rates of interest, can reduce the flexibility of the bondholder and *force* him to hold an obligation until maturity (the so-called *lock-in effect*) in order to avoid realizing capital losses. Of course, an opportunity loss occurs whether or not it is realized. Moreover, if planning or necessity requires the sale of a bond prior to maturity, then the prevailing rate of interest at the time of sale can produce either a capital loss or gain for the holder. The extra risk resulting from interest rate changes that produce lock-ins or capital losses must be considered when a bond is purchased.

To some extent, the desired holding period for a bond may be affected by factors outside the control of the investor. It was mentioned earlier that sinking-fund requirements satisfied by lot drawing may reduce the holding period for the bondholder. Furthermore, most corporate bonds are *callable*. When a bond is called, the expected holding period may be reduced for the investor. Nevertheless, many bond indentures contain *deferred call protection* for a specified period of time (usually five to ten years). Moreover, bonds are called for refunding only when the issuing firm may refinance at a rate lower than the current coupon. Hence, the best call protection for the investor during high interest-rate periods is provided by purchasing bonds issued in the past at lower coupons. These bonds will sell at large discounts from par and thus would necessarily appreciate substantially before the market price of the issue approached the call price and made a call feasible for the issuer. Two similar bonds, one selling at a large discount and the other offering a large coupon, may sell at different yields to maturity because of this implicit difference in call protection.

Bonds are typically callable at prices somewhat above par, at least until near the maturity date, but a substantial drop in interest rates (causing bond prices to advance) may encourage the issuer to call an issue even at a premium. The result is to shorten the actual maturity of the bond. Also, the call possibility may prevent the bond from rising to a substantial premium in case interest rates do fall significantly after the issue date.

The bond indenture may contain several call price schedules that may affect the investor. One schedule will indicate call prices for refunding purposes. Another may specify call prices in future years for sinking fund purposes. A third schedule may indicate the prices at which all or part of the issue may be called if funds are raised by the debtor from sources other than a new issue sold at a lower cost (an asset conversion, for example). The premium on these schedules will usually decline to par as the set maturity date approaches.

Consider a bond that has 22 years remaining before maturity but is callable at 104 in two years. The bond is selling at a premium, and it is expected that the issue will be called at the first opportunity. The market price of the bond is 111, although equivalent risk bonds with similar coupons and maturities having longer call protection sell at higher prices. A non-callable bond of a similar credit with a 20-year maturity was recently sold to yield 6 percent, while the coupon on the bond under analysis is 9 percent. The yield to maturity on the callable bond would be:

$$\text{yield to maturity} = \frac{90 + \frac{1{,}000 - 1{,}110}{22}}{\frac{1{,}000 + 1{,}110}{2}} = \frac{80}{1{,}055} = 8.06\%.$$

The yield to first call would be:

$$\text{yield to first call} = \frac{90 + \frac{1{,}040 - 1{,}110}{2}}{\frac{1{,}040 + 1{,}110}{2}} = \frac{55}{1{,}075} = 5.12\%.$$

Which yield should the analyst use? The answer would depend on his or her long-run forecast of interest rates. If he or she believed that rates would continue as they are at the time of analysis, or if he or she believed they would fall further, the bond would almost certainly be called, and the correct yield would be the yield to first call. On the other hand, if the analyst expected rates to rise, particularly if he or she suspected an increase to a level beyond the current coupon on the bond, an argument could be made for using the yield to maturity.

Needless to say, if the analyst expected interest rates to fall, he or she might be advised to concentrate his attention on bonds with greater call protection (for example, deep discount bonds) that would not necessarily be called. The appropriate yield computation in this instance would, of course, be the yield to maturity. Furthermore, if the analyst expected rates to increase, the decision to purchase long-term bonds in the first place might be challenged.

The effect of the call privilege on corporate bond yields varies depending on money-market conditions. Yield differentials on bonds with different call characteristics (premiums offered and deferment periods) tend to increase during periods of high interest rates and to decline when interest rates are low. The overall effect of the call privilege has been to reduce realized yields on corporate bonds which were issued when interest rates have been high.

Bond Tables and Bond-Rating Agencies

The primary objective of the security analyst in evaluating a bond is the determination of the expected rate of return from the instrument and the risk associated with that return. Various yield calculations, including yields to maturity, average life, and first call, have been mentioned. Rarely will the analyst use either the shortcut formula we have discussed above or present-value tables in computing the yields on a bond. Instead, a complete set of bond tables are available (see Figure 6.2). Bond tables are based on present-value calculations such as those appearing in Appendix A, but they require absolutely no additional calculation. Indeed, using Microsoft Excel one can easily generate the entire bond table instantly, by using the cell formula:

$$= -\text{PV}(\text{Yield}, \#\text{Periods}, \text{Coupon}, \text{FV}).$$

The analyst looks up the yield on, say, a $7^3/_4$ percent coupon issue due in 18 years and six months selling at $95^3/_4$ and immediately finds a yield of 8.20 percent.

The analyst may also depend on rating agencies to help assess the riskiness of a bond issue. Moody's, S & Ps and Fitch rate the bonds

7.75%   **YEARS and MONTHS**

Yield%	18-6	19	19-6	20	20-6
6.00	119.40	119.68	119.96	120.23	120.49
6.20	116.92	117.16	117.40	117.63	117.85
6.40	114.52	114.72	114.92	115.11	115.30
6.60	112.18	112.35	112.51	112.67	112.82
6.80	109.92	110.05	110.18	110.30	110.42
7.00	107.71	107.82	107.91	108.01	108.10
7.20	105.57	105.65	105.72	105.78	105.85
7.40	103.50	103.54	103.58	103.62	103.66
7.60	101.48	101.50	101.51	101.53	101.55
7.80	99.51	99.51	99.50	99.50	99.49
8.00	97.61	97.58	97.55	97.53	97.50
8.20	95.75	95.70	95.66	95.61	95.57
8.40	93.95	93.88	93.82	93.75	93.69
8.60	92.20	92.11	92.03	91.95	91.88
8.80	90.49	90.39	90.29	90.20	90.11
9.00	88.84	88.72	88.61	88.50	88.40
9.20	87.22	87.09	86.97	86.85	86.73
9.40	85.66	85.51	85.37	85.24	85.12
9.60	84.13	83.97	83.83	83.68	83.55
9.80	82.64	82.48	82.32	82.17	82.02

Figure 6.2. A Bond Table

of seasoned companies, and much can be learned from comparing the respective ratings of various issues given by these independent agencies. Moody's rates the highest grade, non-speculative bond as Aaa. Such bonds have little risk of default and are of the highest quality. The equivalent S&P rating is AAA. Just under the highest rating is the Moody's Aa and the S&P AA. Double-A bonds are also of high quality, but they are somewhat less secure than the triple-A's. Medium quality bonds are rated A and Baa by Moody's and A and BBB by S&P's, the single A bond being a slightly better credit. Bonds rated Ba (Moody's) and BB (S&P) and below are considered to be speculative bonds that have some definite default possibility.

Although many analysts depend on the rating agencies for an independent, unbiased analysis of the credit-worthiness of a bond, the original analyst will do his own research into the risk condition of a bond issuer. Many analysts find that bonds with the same ratings tend to sell at nearly identical yields even though there may be risk differences within a rating class. Hence, the analyst who does an independent investigation may find opportunities that would go undiscovered. Furthermore, the analyst will always bear in mind that the price of even the highest-rated bonds will fall if the general level of interest rates increases. Indeed, the prices of low risk-bonds are *more* responsive to interest rate changes than those of high-risk obligations. The pure interest rate component of yield is higher for low-risk bonds than for high-risk ones (where the risk component is greater). Thus, an upward shift in the overall structure of rates will produce a larger proportional change in the yields of high-grade bonds than for lower-grade issues. Investors who bought $2\frac{1}{2}$ percent triple-A bonds in the early 1950s thinking that no decline in price could occur were very chagrined to see these issues quoted at 30- and 40-point discounts from par as a result of rising interest rates in the 1960s. Given the current low interest rate environment engendered by Federal Reserve Policy (QE-1, QE-2, etc.), history may be repeated.

Suppose an analyst is examining Royal Corp. bonds. He believes that 10 years from now there are six chances in 10 that yields will be higher than those currently prevailing (6.67 percent) on equivalent risk bonds. On the other hand, he or she feels that rates could be as much as 167 basis points (1.67 percent) lower. Given his yield forecast, the analyst could determine the price at which the Royal 5's of 2034 would sell in 2024 assuming the current year is 2014. If rates rose to 7.80 percent, the bond price would be:

$$7.80 = \frac{50 + \frac{1{,}000 - X}{10}}{\frac{1{,}000 + X}{2}} \quad X = 80,$$

or about $800. Notice that the number of years to maturity of the issue 10 years from now is 10 years (that is, 20 years minus 10 years). The analyst has used the yield-to-maturity calculation for 2024–2034 rather than the yield to average life because sinking-fund requirements can be met through market purchases. Because his forecast of interest of interest rates precludes a call (unless rates drop well below 5 percent between 2024 and 2034), the yield to first call has also been ignored. Thus, there would be a probability of 0.6 that the bond price *would not change*, because it currently sells for $800. If yields fell to 6.30 percent, the future bond price would be:

$$6.30 = \frac{50 + \frac{1{,}000 - X}{10}}{\frac{1{,}000 + X}{2}} \quad X = 90,$$

or about $900. If yields declined to 5.00 percent, the price of the bond 10 years hence would be:

$$5.00 = \frac{50 + \frac{1{,}000 - X}{10}}{\frac{1{,}000 + X}{2}} \quad X = 100.$$

Obviously, if yields fell to the coupon rate of the issue, it would advance to par.

Given his estimates of the future price of the Royal 5's of 2034, the analyst could determine the yield his clients would get if they bought the bond today (2014) and sold it in 10 years. If future yields rose to 7.80 percent and the price of the bond remained at 80, his clients' return would be:

$$\text{Yield} = \frac{50 + \frac{800 - 800}{10}}{\frac{800 + 800}{2}} = \frac{50}{800} = 6.25\%.$$

If future yields fell to 6.30 percent, and the price of the bond advanced to 90, the client's return would be:

$$\text{Yield} = \frac{50 + \frac{900 - 800}{10}}{\frac{900 + 800}{2}} = \frac{60}{850} = 7.06\%.$$

Finally, if yields declined to 5.00 percent (bond price at par), the clients' return would be:

$$\text{Yield} = \frac{50 + \frac{1{,}000 - 800}{10}}{\frac{1{,}000 + 800}{2}} = \frac{70}{900} = 7.78\%.$$

230   *Quantitative Financial Analytics*

Hence, the probability distribution of returns to the analyst's clients if they bought this issue is:

Probability	Yield (to 2024)
0.6	6.25 percent
0.3	7.06 percent
0.1	7.78 percent

Although the Royal Corp. is a good credit (double A), the analyst feels there is some slight chance that a default could occur. He has predicted the following default probabilities for the Royal 5's 2034:

Default (years hence)	Probability
1–9	0.00
10	0.02

If a default occurs in year 10, the analyst expects that liquidation would give debenture holders 40 percent of the par value of the investment plus the coupon. The expected return in the case of default would be:

$$\text{Yield} = \frac{50 + \frac{400 - 800}{10}}{\frac{400 + 800}{2}} = \frac{10}{600} = 1.67\%.$$

Because the shortcut equation does not always provide accurate results in the case of a deep discount situation (such as a price of 40), the analyst has verified the results using present-value tables:

@ 1%   (9.471)(50) = 473.55
       (0.905)(400) = 362.00
                      835.55

Analysis of Fixed Income Securities 231

@ 2% $\quad$ (8.983)(50) = 449.15
$\quad\quad\quad$ (0.820)(400) = 328.00
$\quad\quad\quad\quad\quad\quad\quad\quad\quad\;\;$ 777.15

Interpolating, $i = 1.60\%$.

Including the possibility of default, a refined probability distribution of returns could be computed. The expected return and standard deviation are also provided:

Return (X_i)	Probability (p_i)	Expected return
6.25%	(0.6)(0.98) = 0.588	3.6750%
7.06	(0.3)(0.98) = 0.294	2.0756
7.78	(0.1)(0.98) = 0.098	0.7624
1.60	(1.0)(0.02) = 0.020	0.0320
	1.000	$\bar{X} = 6.5450\%$
$X_i - \bar{X}$		$(X_i - \bar{X})^2 p_i$
6.25 − 6.55 = −0.30%		(0.09)(0.588) = 0.0529 × 10^{-4}
7.06 − 6.55 = 0.51		(0.26)(0.294) = 0.0764
7.78 − 6.55 = 1.23		(1.51)(0.098) = 0.1480
1.60 − 6.55 = −4.95		(24.50)(0.020) = 0.4900
		$\sigma^2 = 0.7673 \times 10^{-4}$

$$E(R) = 6.55\%$$
$$\sigma = \sqrt{0.00007673} = 0.88\%.$$

The analyst may conclude that although the Royal 5's of 2034 have a yield to maturity of 6.67 percent, the expected yield if the issue were held for 10 years would be only 6.55 percent. Furthermore, even though the issue is rated AA, there is a probability of 0.588 that only 6.25 percent would be earned (due to an increase in interest rates) and a probability of 0.020 that a meager 1.60 percent would be obtained (if the issue defaulted).

Analysis of Municipal Bonds

U.S. government obligations do not require the kind of analysis that has been discussed above. Indeed, it is generally assumed that short-term governments are virtually riskless, and the so-called pure rate of interest is approximated by the yield on short-term government obligations. Long-term U.S. governments (notes and bonds) do carry some price fluctuation (market) risk because the prices of all bonds vary as interest rates change. Hence, even the safest bonds regarding coupon and principal security can sell at large discounts. Even though the U.S. federal government is deeply in debt (so much so that if it were a private borrower, its bonds might even be in the "junk" category), it has one big advantage: it owns the printing press! Thus, it can be assumed that all U.S. federal debt will be repaid. Repayment may be made in vastly depreciated dollars (if the money supply grows too fast), but it will be repaid.

Analyzing municipal bonds requires a slightly different procedure from that employed in corporate bond evaluation. Unlike federal issues, municipals cannot be assumed to be default risk free. In addition to market price (interest rate) and default risks, many municipals are subject to liquidity risks. A number of these issues are quite thinly traded and may require considerable markdowns for quick sale. Although most state government issues, and bonds guaranteed by state governments, are for all practical purposes free of default risk, various city, country, and district bonds may have considerable coupon and principal risk associated with them. States with heavy pension liabilities (unionized teacher retirement obligations, for example) should be avoided. This includes states such as Illinois and California. Other states with propensities to elect left-wing "populist" officials who are inclined to be "big spenders" might also be considered risky. New York state and Massachusetts would fall into this category.

General obligation municipal bonds are secured by the "full faith and credit" of the issuer. There are several ratios that the analyst may examine to test the security of these obligations:

1. Municipal debt as a percentage of assessed valuation of taxable real estate. This ratio indicates the singular importance of

property taxes as a source of municipal finance. Ratios from 8 to 10 percent are considered acceptable by most analysts, although higher ratios may be approved when other taxation sources, such as sales and income taxes, are available. Recent court rulings in the United States have brought into doubt the long-run importance of property taxes in financing municipal governments. If other forms of taxation take the place of property taxes, new ratios to assess the security of municipal bonds will have to be devised. Furthermore, if federal revenue sharing becomes a significant source of funds to municipalities, it may be that the municipal bond will no longer be important as a financial instrument.
2. Per capita debt. This ratio indicates the total debt of the municipal authority per resident. To the extent that the number of taxpayers (rather than the value of property) is significant to a municipal's tax base, this ratio is important. Depending on the population of the issuing authority, per capita debt of the low thousands of dollars is acceptable, with larger amounts permitted for larger municipal issuers.
3. Debt service as a percentage of the municipal budget. When more than one-quarter of a municipal budget goes for debt service (interest plus debt retirement), the ability of the authority to meet its obligations is considered in jeopardy.

A second form of municipal is the *revenue bond*. The security of these issues depends upon the "profitability" of the project that the bond has financed. Revenue bonds may be analyzed in a similar manner to corporation issues, and earnings coverage becomes the most important element. Thus, the net revenue generated by a turnpike authority would be the best single factor to consider in appraising the riskiness of the issue. Public projects that are privately financed are not expected to earn large profits. Hence, coverage ratios should not be expected to be as high as those for corporate bonds. Ratios of $1\frac{1}{2}$ to 2 times charges are considered quite acceptable.

Municipal issues are generally tax exempt. That is, no federal income tax is due on the income earned from these bonds. Furthermore, state income taxes payable in the state of issue are generally waived. Thus, a purchaser of a New York City general obligation bond who lived there would pay neither federal, state, nor city income taxes on interest from the issue.

Suppose the New York City General Obligation 6's of 2031 are selling at par. A resident of the state is considering the purchase of the bonds. He is in the 40 percent marginal federal tax bracket (adjusted for the deduction of state income taxes) and the 12 percent State and City of New York bracket. The equivalent pretax yield he would have to earn to equal his tax-free New York City bond would be:

$$\text{Pretax yield} = \frac{\text{yield on municipal}}{1 - \text{marginal tax bracket}}$$
$$= \frac{0.06}{1 - 0.52}$$
$$= 12.5\%.$$

As it was suggested above, however, even 12.5 percent may be insufficient to compensate for the risk associated with the debt of a profligate state such as New York. Moreover, at the present time, New York bonds are providing gross yields at well under 6 percent.

Analysis of Preferred Stock

Preferred stock is considered to be a fixed income security because preferred dividends are usually paid at a specific rate. Participating preferreds may give preferred holders a return above the fixed payment after a specified amount has also been paid to common stockholders. These issues should be evaluated essentially as preferred stocks when the probability of extra payment is small and as common stocks when the probability is great.

Although preferred stocks are called stock and are treated legally as equity (preferred dividends must be paid out of after-tax dollars and preferred holders have a prior claim against earnings and assets only over common stock holders), the nature of the instrument makes it necessary to consider preferred stocks as essentially the most junior form of bond.

Hence, the analysis of preferred stocks proceeds very much like that discussed for corporate bonds. The basic tools of forecasting and ratio computations of profitability, income security, and asset security are the same. The only different ratio that is employed is the times-interest-earned-plus-preferred-dividends ratio.

We may reconsider the EBIT projections for Consolidated Electric Appliance Corp. Suppose that, in addition to the subordinated debenture issue, the firm had $20 million in $5 preferred stock (par $100). The total annual preferred dividend is ($20,000,000)(0.05) = $1,000,000. Times-interest-earned-plus-preferred-dividends coverage for the 2015 projection would be:

$$\frac{\text{EBIT}}{\text{Interest} + \frac{\text{preferred dividend}}{1 - \text{tax rate}}} = \frac{17.60}{5.00 + \frac{1.00}{1 - 0.4}} = \frac{17.60}{6.67} = 2.64X.$$

For years 2016–2019, we find:

$$2016: \frac{18.85}{6.42} = 2.94X \qquad 2018: \frac{22.10}{5.67} = 3.90X$$

$$2017: \frac{20.77}{6.17} = 3.37X \qquad 2019: \frac{24.42}{5.17} = 4.72X.$$

Consolidated $5 preferreds sell in the market for $75 per share. Assuming that the issue is not callable, the return would be:

$$\frac{5}{75} = 6.67\%.$$

If the issue were callable in 25 years at par, and if it were believed that Consolidated would call the issue, the return would become:

$$\frac{5 + \frac{100 - 75}{25}}{\frac{100 + 75}{2}} = \frac{6}{87.5} = 6.86\%.$$

Preferreds frequently yield less than the junior bonds of the same company. This is due to the fact that in the United States, most preferred dividends are 70 percent exempt from taxation for corporate holders to reduce the impact of the double taxation of dividends.

Continuing the Analysis of American Funeral Supplies

In Chapter 4, we examined income statements and balance sheets for American Funeral Supplies, Inc (AFS). Recall that this fictional company was founded in 1984 to supply various fluids, clothing, caskets, and burial markers and monuments to independent funeral directors. AFS went public in 2010, and has reported four complete years of statements filed with the SEC. Recall further that the company is headquartered in New Orleans and has sales of just under $7 billion. Over the past 30 years, revenues (sales) have grown from less than $10 million to the present levels, or a compounded rate of 24.4 percent. Much of this growth has come from acquiring smaller companies in the same line(s) of business. The remaining sales growth has been generated by organic revenue development efforts and extensive marketing. Local funeral directors are called on regularly by American salesmen. Extensive entertainment is also done to cement personal relationships which are vital in this business.

We began the analysis with the calculation of various ratios. First, we determined the five liquidity ratios for AFS from 2010 to 2013 as follows:

	2010	2011	2012	2013
Current	0.74	1.14	2.01	3.01
Cash	0.32	0.52	0.83	1.27
Quick	0.45	0.74	1.25	1.94
Basic defensive interval (BDI) (days)	102	121	113	128
WC/TA	(0.18)	0.07	0.30	0.46

Summarizing, the liquidity ratios suggests that AFS has become much more liquid over the past four years. The cash position has improved greatly, and the notes payables have been completely paid off. The current, cash, and quick ratios have all become substantially more positive. The BDI has increased as well and the net working capital position (current assets less current liabilities) has gone from being negative in 2010 to very positive in 2013. As a result, net working capital has become a fairly large percentage of total assets. All in all, it may be said that AFS has strong liquidity and could even reduce such if an attractive acquisition candidate came along.

Next, we turned our attention to AFS' profitability. The five profitability ratios for AFS from 2010 to 2013 as follows:

	2010	2011	2012	2013
Gross margin	0.38	0.40	0.40	0.37
Oper. profit	0.20	0.23	0.24	0.22
EBIT ratio	0.20	0.20	0.20	0.22
Oper. ratio	0.80	0.77	0.76	0.78
Net margin	0.13	0.12	0.15	0.12

An analysis of the profitability ratios indicates that AFS maintains fairly stable margins. These ratios should be compared with the same ratios for similar businesses to see if AFS is more, less, or about as profitable as its competitors.

AFS' turnover ratios were also considered. The six turnover ratios for AFS from 2010 to 2013 as follows:

	2010	2011	2012	2013
Total asset turnover	1.43	1.47	1.64	1.66
Receivables turnover	16.60	13.48	13.13	10.93
Average collection (days)	22	27	28	33
Inventory turnover	4.83	4.88	4.76	4.75
Average inventory (days)	76	75	77	77
Working capital turnover	N/A	21.30	5.48	3.65

An analysis of the turnover ratios portrays AFS as having fairly stable relationships. Once again, these ratios should be compared with those of similar businesses to see if AFS maintains more, less or similar sales generation per dollar of assets invested as its competitors. Note that the working capital turnover ratio is not applicable in 2010, due to the fact that net working capital is negative.

AFS' return on investment ratios were next calculated. The three return on investment ratios for AFS from 2010 to 2013:

	2010	2011	2012	2013
Net earning power	0.18	0.18	0.24	0.21
Earning power of total investment	0.28	0.33	0.43	0.37
Net profit to common equity	0.55	0.36	0.34	0.27

We established that the return on investment ratios for AFS are quite strong with few publicly-held companies earning as much money on their asset investment as does AFS. One of the reasons for this is the fairly strong profit ratios combined with almost equally strong asset turnovers. Put another way, the economic position of the company is such that it can charge reasonably high prices (resulting in strong profit margins) on an asset base that is relatively small. Not many firms are so fortunate. Lurking behind this positive situation is an indication that AFS may have relatively few competitors and those it has may have cost structures less efficient than that of AFS. Many businesses have high profit margins, but their asset base must be very high to earn those margins. Others have low profit margins but still make a good profit by turning over their asset base several times a year. One concern for AFS is the decline in all three ratios in the latest year.

AFS has no LTD outstanding, but it is considering a major acquisition which would be financed by borrowing. As AFS adds LTD to its capital structure, we shall return to a more extensive list of leverage and capital structure ratios. Note that the definition of "equity" in the AFS statements is the "capital stock" account plus accumulated retained earnings. Thus, total capital equals total assets in this case. At this point, we could determine certain leverage and capital structure ratios for AFS from 2010 to 2013 as follows:

	2010	2011	2012	2013
Total debt to equity	2.00	0.94	0.42	0.29
Total debt to total capital	0.67	0.48	0.30	0.23
Total debt to total assets	0.67	0.48	0.30	0.23

An analysis of the above ratios indicates that AFS has reduced its note payable over the past four years from $1.75 billion to zero. Additionally, it has increased its equity from $1.1 billion to $3.2 billion over the 2010 to 2013 period. As a consequence, all of the leverage ratios have improved dramatically. Indeed, it may be argued that AFS is insufficiently leveraged at this point. One way to balance this condition would be to borrow money to repurchase its common stock. Another would be to borrow to make future acquisitions. Both measures augur well for existing stockholders and are quite positive for the future of the company.

The five asset-relation ratios for AFS from 2010 to 2013 are as follows:

	2010	2011	2012	2013
Plant and equipment to total assets	0.03	0.02	0.02	0.02
Inventory to total assets	0.18	0.18	0.21	0.22
Receivables to total assets	0.09	0.11	0.12	0.15
Annual depreciation to plant and equipment	0.34	0.56	0.34	0.41
Approximate average asset life (in years)	2.94	1.79	2.94	2.44

The asset structure of AFS shows a heavy emphasis on inventories. Much of the inventory (fluids, clothing, and caskets) is purchased from other manufacturers, and AFS only makes a limited product line of cemetery grave markers. The company sells directly to funeral homes on terms (either cash up front, or for long-time customers, payment due 30 days after the shipment of goods). Receivables are not large given the sales volume of the business. There is very little in the way of fixed assets. Mostly this is office furniture, fixtures, etc. and vehicles. A small amount of manufacturing equipment is maintained for the production of grave markers. Given the nature of the operations, the fixed assets are depreciated over a fairly short time frame. This is true despite the fact that the actual physical life of much of the fixed assets is longer than that required for accounting (and tax) write-offs.

The asset and income security common stock ratios for 2010–2013 for AFS are indicated as follows:

	2010	2011	2012	2013
Book value per share of common stock	$10.86	$16.86	$25.62	$32.00
Net tangible assets per share	($0.14)	$6.86	$16.62	$24.00
EPS ratio	$5.95	$6.00	$8.76	$8.57
DPS ratio	Nil	Nil	Nil	$2.19
Cash flow per share	$6.02	$6.32	$9.06	$8.93
Payout ratio	Nil	Nil	Nil	0.26

These ratios suggest the asset and income security of AFS' common stock have improved over the past four years. Book value per share has tripled while tangible book has gone from a negative to a substantial positive. Earnings and cash flow per share have also advanced. The initiation of a dividend in 2013 seems prudent given the increasingly positive cash and earnings position of the company.

Analysis of Fixed Income Securities 241

The $2.19 dividend is protected by almost four times in earnings, such that the payout ratio is conservative at 0.26. Further dividend increases might be expected in the future. These ratios are important for fixed income security investors since solid equity performance and security may make it possible for AFS to issue more equity in the future which could serve to strengthen the position of debt holders.

We should also review AFS' yield and price ratios. Of the five ratios, only three are applicable since the company has no outstanding bonds or preferred stock. The remaining ratios for 2013 require information on the price of AFS common stock which was determined in Chapter 4. Assume we are examining the stock just after earnings were announced to the public early in 2014 and that high/low prices in the past were as follows (dollars per share):

	2010	2011	2012	2013
High	$47.86	$56.86	$65.62	$92.03
Low	$27.80	$36.06	$45.22	$52.09
Average	$37.83	$46.46	$55.42	$72.06

Based on the average prices, the yield and price are computed below (dollars figures in millions) from 2010 to 2013:

	2010	2011	2012	2013
Dividend yield of common stock	Nil	Nil	Nil	3.1%
Price to earnings ratio	6.4X	7.7X	6.3X	8.4X
Earnings yield ratio	15.7%	12.9%	15.8%	11.9%

At this point, we might want to make some projections for AFS. To do so, it is necessary to review the historical financial statements that were introduced in Chapter 4.

American Funeral Supplies, Inc.
Statement of income and retained earnings
for the year ending December 31
(Millions of Dollars)

	2013	2012	2011	2010
Net Sales	$6,883	$5,976	$4,814	$4,666
Cost of goods sold	4,320	3,600	2,882	2,895
Gross profit	$2,563	$2,376	$1,932	$1,771
Selling, general, and administrative expenses	874	788	677	648
Provision for amortization	173	128	170	175
Operating profit	$1,516	$1,460	$1,085	$948
Other income/expenses:				
Interest expense	(6)	(42)	(63)	(92)
Interest income	20	141	47	65
Earnings before taxes	$1,530	$1,559	$1,069	$921
Provision for federal income and state franchise tax	673	683	469	326
Net profit for the Year	$857	$876	$600	$595
Retained earnings, January 1	$2,542	$1,666	$1,066	$471
Dividends	219			
Retained earnings, December 31	$3,180	$2,542	$1,666	$1,066

American Funeral Supplies, Inc.
Balance sheet
as of December 31
(Millions of Dollars)

	2013	2012	2011	2010
ASSETS				
Current assets:				
Cash	$951	$898	$818	$706
Note receivable	239			
Accounts receivable (less allowance for doubtful collections)	630	455	357	281
Inventories	910	757	591	593
Prepaid expenses	91	61	47	22
Total current assets	$2,821	$2,171	$1,813	$1,602
Furniture, fixtures, machinery and equipment, motor vehicles	$227	$176	$153	$151
Less: Accumulated depreciation	139	103	96	64
	$88	$73	$57	$87
Patents and trademarks	$1,178	$1,077	$853	$753
Less: Accumulated amortization	751	578	450	280
	$427	$499	$403	$473
Goodwill	800	900	1,000	1,100
	$4,136	$3,643	$3,273	$3,262

(*Continued*)

244 Quantitative Financial Analytics

(Continued)

	2013	2012	2011	2010
LIABILITIES				
Current liabilities:				
Note payable	$0	$275	$1,000	$1,750
Accounts payable and accrued liabilities	224	196	118	100
Income tax payable	712	610	469	326
	$936	$1,081	$1,587	$2,176
Capital stock:				
Authorized 100,000,000 shares of common no par value — issued and outstanding	$20	$20	$20	$20
Retained earnings	3,180	2,542	1,666	1,066
Total capital stock and retained earnings	$3,200	$2,562	$1,686	$1,086
	$4,136	$3,643	$3,273	$3,262

Suppose we wish to project forward the income statement and the balance sheet. One procedure might be to review certain of the ratios from Chapter 4. For example, the sales growth rates would appear as follows:

2010–2011	$(4{,}814 - 4{,}666)/(4{,}666) =$	0.032
2011–2012	$(5{,}976 - 4{,}814)/(4{,}814) =$	0.241
2012–2013	$(6{,}883 - 5{,}976)/(5{,}976) =$	0.152
Average		0.142

Compounding over the four-year period suggests:

$$4,666(1 + g)^3 = 6,883$$

$$g = 0.138.$$

And various income statement ratios would be calculated as follows:

Ratio	2010	2011	2012	2013	Average
CGS/sales	0.62	0.60	0.60	0.63	0.613
SGA/sales	0.14	0.14	0.13	0.13	0.135
Op. inc./sales	0.20	0.23	0.24	0.22	0.223

Now we might make future projections given realistic assumptions. First, we are taking an aggressive view on sales based on the modest growth in 2010–2011. Second, we are assuming a conservative view of CGS/Sales due to the 2013 increase, and a slightly less one for SGA/Sales. Also, we adjust for the amortization expense after reviewing a footnote in the financial statements suggesting an expected decline in the investment in patents and trademarks. This reduction will improve operating income margins, which we shall assume to be 0.25 over the next five years.

1. Sales growth   at 0.14
2. CGS/sales   at 0.63
3. SGA/sales   at 0.13
4. Op. inc./sales at 0.25.

	2014	2015	2016	2017	2018
Sales (000)	7846	8945	10197	11625	13253
CGS	4943	5635	6424	7323	8349
SG&A	1020	1163	1326	1511	1723
Oper. Inc.	1962	2236	2549	2906	3313

To complete the income statement *pro formas*, we need to consider future interest income, interest expense, and federal and state income taxes. (Note that the so-called "franchise tax" is actually the collective state income taxes in all states where AFS operates.) At this point, it might be worth contemplating the Company's growth strategy. Discussions with management together with its publicly announced intentions suggest that a growth rate of 14 percent compounded annually must either involve a substantial investment in new capital, a major acquisition, or both.

Summary

Fixed-income securities are generally purchased because of the reduced risk associated with returns generated by these instruments. A *bond* obligates the issuing firm (or government) to pay interest at a specific rate, at a particular interval, and in a prescribed manner. Also, payments of principal are to be made periodically according to the terms specified in the *indenture* (the contractual agreement between the issuer and holder of the bond). The mere fact that a security takes the form of a fixed-income instrument does not insure the safety of the security. Indeed, the common stocks of some enterprises are less risky than the bonds of others. Nevertheless, the bond form does generally set a maximum payment ceiling (the coupon rate), and lesser amounts will be paid only if the issuer encounters financial difficulty.

Determining the probability that a firm (or other issuer) will be unable to meet coupon or principal payments is the primary responsibility of the bond analyst. Clearly, this task requires a complete analysis of the present and future financial position of the firm, and the bond analyst will employ the techniques outlined in the previous two chapters to determine this position.

A recommended procedure is to forecast the earnings of the firm as far into the future as possible. In the ideal case, the analyst will be able to project throughout the life of the bond. Given this forecast, the analyst may then prepare annual probability distributions of interest (and principal) payments. From this set of distributions, the risk and return from purchasing the instrument may be determined.

In addition to using the forecasting tools employed in Chapter 5, the analyst will also use several ratios to aid in the determination of possible default. The time-interest-earned and other similar coverage ratios for past years will be computed and compared with those of other firms in the same business. One would also examine the trend of these ratios for the firm over time. Of course, these ratios should not be substitutes in analysis for forecasting. Rather, they should serve as additional data to give added perspective to the results obtained from projections.

The major determinants of the firm's ability to make its interest payments are the volume of interest payments the firm owes in each period and the earnings available for those payments. The asset security of obligations is also important and may be tested by computing several capital structure and asset coverage ratios (such as tangible asset debt coverage). Although the capital structure and asset-coverage ratios do provide additional information about the position of the firm's debt obligations, they are most useful as indicators of what the holders might receive in case of liquidation or reorganization. Because the primary reason for bond purchases is the *avoidance* of any problems associated with payment default or delay, the analyst should not be satisfied simply because a firm has little indebtedness or a bond is well secured by assets in case of difficulty. Of course, once the analyst is confident that coupon and principal payments are adequately protected by future earnings, added security provided by low indebtedness and large asset holdings can be considered a safety hedge in case a very poor state of events develops.

It has been established that the structure of rates on long-term securities will be related to expected future short-term rates. Furthermore, it seems reasonable to expect that the greater potential price volatility of long-term securities resulting from a change in the actual or expected level of interest rates should cause them to command a higher nominal rate of interest in the form of a risk premium. This risk (called *interest-rate risk*) is the result of bond price changes caused by interest rate changes and is considered a part of the liquidity preference version of term structure theory.

It should be borne in mind that this is the one risk that exists even for government securities (except the very short term). Indeed, it might be argued that there is no such thing as a riskless long-term investment.

The security of coupon payments is clearly an important matter for the financial analyst. Nevertheless, the *security* of principal payments may be equally important. Legally, a bond may be considered in default if either interest or principal payments are in arrears. The repayment of principal may be accomplished in several ways. A common method for corporate bonds is repayment by way of a *sinking fund*. This arrangement obligates the issuer to begin repaying a certain percentage of the issue after some year in the life of the issue.

In addition to the factors previously considered in determining the yield and security of a bond, one other variable must be assessed: the desired holding period of the bond. The aggregate level of interest rates may vary as economic conditions change, and bond prices move inversely with the market rate of interest. Thus, there is a market risk in holding a bond as well as the business and financial risk associated with the issuer.

A precipitous decline in bond prices, caused by higher rates of interest, can reduce the flexibility of the bondholder and *force* one to hold an obligation until maturity (the so-called *lock-in effect*) in order to avoid realizing capital losses. Of course, an opportunity loss occurs whether or not it is realized. Moreover, if planning or necessity requires the sale of a bond prior to maturity, then the prevailing rate of interest at the time of sale can produce either a capital loss or gain for the holder. The extra risk resulting from interest rate changes that produce lock-ins or capital losses must be considered when a bond is purchased.

Problems

1. An analyst is attempting to value the 5 percent First Mortgage Bonds of the Central Railroad (C.R.R.). The bonds are due in

10 years and pay an annual coupon. The analyst has forecasted C.R.R. revenues as follows (in millions):

2015	$106	2020	$126
2016	108	2021	131
2017	114	2022	117
2018	105	2023	109
2019	118	2024	112

The analyst believes that revenues are normally distributed with a standard error of the estimate of $10 million.

An examination of past income statements has indicated that C.R.R. has annual fixed operating expenses of $50 million (including $10 million depreciation) and a variable operating cost ratio of 0.4. The company has several bond issues outstanding including $100 million of First Mortgage Bonds, $50 million of Second Mortgage Bonds, and $50 million of subordinated debentures that have coupons of 5 percent, 6 percent, and 8 percent, respectively. The firm pays 50 percent of earnings before taxes in corporate income taxes.

a. Prepare *pro forma* income statements for C.R.R. for 2015–2024.
b. Compute the expected times-interest-earned ratio (based on total interest) for 2015–2024.
c. How low could revenues be in the poorest year for the firm to be able to just meet interest payments out of earnings before interest and taxes?
d. What is the probability that the firm will earn less than its total interest payments in the poorest year?
e. Do you think the firm will default in this year? Why or why not?
f. What is the overall probability of default? (Use the average forecasted revenue figure.)

g. Suppose forecasted revenues were as follows (in millions):

2015	$126	2020	$108
2016	131	2021	106
2017	118	2022	105
2018	117	2023	109
2019	114	2024	112

Would this rearrangement of forecasted revenues influence your subjective judgment about the riskiness of the issue?

h. The probability computed in problem 1(f) assumes that revenues are independent from one year to the next. If revenues were in fact dependent, with poor years auguring poorer ones, would this influence your opinion about the probability of default?

2. Reconsider the Central Railroad (above).

   a. Compute the overall interest coverage, the cumulative deduction coverage, and the prior deduction coverage for 2015 (*pro forma*) for the road's indebtedness.
   b. Compute the overall interest coverage and the cumulative deduction coverage for 2018 and 2021 (*pro forma*).
   c. Suppose revenues for C.R.R. are $100 million. Compute the overall interest coverage and the cumulative deduction coverage. Is a default possible? What advantages would senior debt holders have?

3. A balance sheet for Ronald-Race Motors, Ltd. Is provided below (in millions):

Cash	$ 25	Current liabilities	$ 50
Receivables	75	Senior debentures	50
Inventories	100	Subordinated debentures	200
Fixed assets	300	Common equity	200
	$500		$500

The firm is in financial difficulty and has just omitted payment of interest on the subordinated debentures. If the firm were forced into liquidation by these bondholders, receivables and inventories could be collected and sold at 2/3 and 1/2 of their respective book values. Fixed assets could be sold at 1/3 of their book worth. Among the current liabilities are $20 million in accrued wages and $15 million in accrued taxes. Legal fees and liquidation costs would amount to $30 million.

The company has offered a composition of 80 percent in a new issue of income bonds that would have a coupon of 6 percent and a maturity of 50 years. The present subordinated debentures have a coupon of 8 percent. Should the subordinated debenture holders press for liquidation or accept the composition?

4. The Ronald-Race subordinated debenture holders have decided to sue for bankruptcy, but the courts have ruled that the firm is engaged in too vital an activity for liquidation. The firm will be reorganized under absolute priority according to the following structure:

	Trustee's Desired Structure (in millions)	Current Market Value (in millions)
Senior debentures	—	$40
Subordinated debentures	—	100
Preferred stock	$60	—
Common stock	120	100
	$180	$240

Current liabilities will be continued in the new structure at book value.

a. Determine what the other creditors would receive.
b. Determine what the long-term creditors would receive if the reorganization were done under relative priority.

c. Suppose the preferred stock issue paid 8 percent and sold in the market after reorganization at $10 per share. Suppose the new common stock began trading at $12. Would the old subordinated debenture holders have fared better by accepting the composition? What other alternative would they have had before reorganization?

5. The Baxter Corporation has issued a 10-year note at 7 percent with interest payments to be made annually. The following estimates have been made regarding payment.

Event	Probability
(1) All payments as due	0.75
(2) Interest in years six and following paid one year late — deficiency made up at end of life of issue	0.10
(3) Interest in years six and following paid one year late and only one-half amount due — deficiency made up at end of life of issue	0.05
(4) #3 with difference not made up	0.04
(5) Company in difficulty during year three-coupon negotiated down to 3 percent	0.03
(6) Company enters bankruptcy midway through year five — total bondholder recovery is 50 percent of par value	0.02
(7) Company enters bankruptcy now — no recovery	0.01
	1.00

a. What is the expected value of the return on this note?
b. Graph the probability distribution of possible rates of return.
c. Comment upon the dispersion and skewness of this distribution.

6. The Jet Corporation has μ_s = $100 million and σ_s = $30 million. Operating fixed costs are $50 million. The variable cost

ratio is 0.2. Senior debt has an annual interest requirement of $5 million and junior debt requires $8 million.

   a. What is the expected value of net income before interest and taxes?
   b. What is the probability that each issue will be fully paid?
   c. How would your answer to b. change if the firm held an extra $5 million in cash?

7. Rework problem 6 assuming that operating fixed costs are $20 million and the variable cost ratio is 0.5.

8. Assume the following data:

Issue	Yield
Treasury bills	5 percent
Government bonds (25 year.)	6$1/2$ percent
Aaa corporate bonds (25 year.)	7 percent
Aaa municipals (25 year.)	5 percent

Analyze the components of the 5 percent yield on municipals in terms of risk and tax premia to the marginal investor. Include a determination of his tax rate.

9. A firm has just floated a 15-year, 7 percent coupon bond at par. Sinking-fund payments of 10 percent must be made after the 10th year, with the balance being paid in the last year.

   a. If the firm could satisfy sinking-fund payments through purchase in the open market, what would the appropriate yield be?
   b. If the firm were forced to redeem at par by lot drawing, what yield would the issue have?
   c. Suppose the bond sold at a premium after issue and the firm could satisfy sinking-fund requirements either by market purchases or lot drawings. What yield would the analyst be most inclined to use?

10. a. The indenture of the 20-year Blue Corp. bonds provides for a sinking fund to retire 5 percent of the issue per year beginning

in year 11. What is the expected life of a Blue bond (also called the average life of the issue)?

b. If the Blue bonds are issued at $950 with an $80 coupon, compute the yield to maturity and the yield to average life.

11. The Central Railroad (see above) has a sinking-fund requirement on its 5's of 2019 (first mortgage bonds) beginning in 2015 of 20 percent. Equivalent payments must be made in 2016–2019. Determine the coverage of interest and sinking-fund payments over this period, given the EBIT projections.

12. Suppose C.R.R. plans to refund its 6's of 2030 (second mortgage) and 8's of 2040 (subordinated debentures) and has no sinking-fund requirements on these bonds. How would this information influence your judgment about the safety of the 5's of 2019? In any case, would you feel the first mortgage bond to be lacking in principal payment security?

13. In addition to its three bond issues, the Central Railroad has a $40 million, 7 percent preferred issue (par $100). Ignoring any sinking-fund payments on the railroad's debt obligations, compute the interest and preferred-dividends coverage for the projections made for 2015–2024.

14. C.R.R. preferred sells at $60. The issue is callable at par in 10 years. What is the current yield on the issue? What is the yield-to-call-date?

15. Evaluate the safety of the C.R.R. preferreds. What is the likelihood that the preferred dividend will be passed during 2015–2024?

16. Suppose C.R.R. passes the preferred dividend in 2015. Would it matter if the issue were a cumulative preferred (rather than a non-cumulative)?

17. What legal rights might the preferred stockholders have if the C.R.R. dividend were passed in 2015 and again in 2016?

18. An analyst has determined the following discriminant function for certain U.S. public corporations (assets over $100 million):

$$Z = 0.04X_1 + 0.09X_2 + 1.50X_3,$$

where:

X_1 = EBIT to total assets (times 100)
X_2 = EBIT to total interest payments (as calculated)
X_3 = sales to total assets (as calculated).

Determine Z for Consolidated Electric Appliance (see text discussion). Re-examine the times-interest-earned ratio for Consolidated as projected for 2015. If values greater than $Z = 0.99$ indicate a firm comes from the universe of "non-bankrupts," classify Consolidated.

19. a. Commercial Credit Ltd. 9's of 2029 were sold five years ago in 2009. The bond had 10-year call protection and is callable in 2019 at 105. The current price (2014) is 110. Compute the yield to maturity and first call for the issue.

   b. Which is the appropriate yield for the analyst to use if he or she expects interest rates on equivalent risk issues to be 8 percent in 2019?

20. A 7 percent, 25-year bond was issued two years ago with five years call protection. It may be called in year six at 107 and is currently selling for 109. Compute the yield to maturity and yield to first call.

21. Consider the bonds of the Net Corp.

   a. The bonds were issued seven years ago with a maturity of 25 years. The indenture provided for retirement of 6 percent of the issue per year beginning at the end of year 11. What is the average life of the issue now?

   b. Net bonds have a 5 percent coupon and sell for $900. Compute the yield to maturity and yield to average life.

   c. Instead of the above, assume that the Net bonds were issued with a 9 percent coupon, 10 years' call protection, callable at the end of year 11 at 106, and currently sell for 110. Compute the yields to maturity and to first call.

22. High Flyer Airlines has a set of collateral trust bonds due in eight years. We are considering recommending this Ba, BB rated issue for a three-year holding period for our speculative accounts. The

bonds carry a 6 percent coupon and can be bought at 84. We feel that the bonds should advance in price over the next three years, as interest rates fall, although there is some chance of decline. Our estimated price probability distribution is given as follows:

Probability	Price
0.1	81
0.3	87
0.6	93

The bonds carry some default possibility, because the cumulative-deduction-times-interest-earned multiple on forecasted income is only $2.4X$ for next year and $2.7X$ for the following two. The bonds are serial obligations, hence no sinking-fund payments are made. We estimate default yields to year three as follows:

Year	Default yield	Probability
1	−28.4%	0.03
2	−22.8	0.05
3	−17.0	0.08

a. If the bonds were purchased, what would be their yield to maturity?
b. Suppose the bonds were held for three years. Determine a probability distribution of expected returns, assuming the prices estimated above.
c. Assuming the probability-of-default schedule given above, determine the distribution of returns from purchasing the bond.

d. What is the expected return and standard deviation of returns from the bonds?
e. Do these bonds appear to be good speculative prospects? Why or why not?

23. Evaluate the New York City General Obligation 6 percent bonds due in 2031 (see above) in light of the following:

	Debt as a Percentage of Taxable Real Estate	Per Capita Debt	Debt Service Requirements as a Percentage of Budget
New York City	14	5,000	10
Atlanta	11	4,500	8
Houston	9	3,500	6

Atlanta bonds yield 6.45 percent to maturity and Houston bonds yield 5.45 percent. Would you expect the New York City bonds to sell at par in light of these alternative yields? Determine an appropriate yield employing the following formula:

$$\text{Yield} = i + (0.100)(D) + (0.0003)(P) + (0.250)(B),$$

where:

i = pure rate of interest
D = debt as a percentage of taxable real estate
P = per capita debt
B = debt as a percentage of budget.

Suppose $i = 0.02$ percent (tax-adjusted equivalent yield for taxable short-term governments).

24. Reconsider the position of Consolidated Electric Appliance. Assume the following projections of per capita income and

population for Consolidated's sales area:

	Y ($)	P (millions)
2015	3,000	8.75
2016	3,100	8.50
2017	3,200	8.30
2018	3,300	8.10
2019	3,400	8.00

a. Forecast total revenues for 2015–2019 and prepare *pro forma* income statements.
b. Compute the times-interest-earned ratio for each period.
c. How far would revenue have to fall to endanger interest payments? Is this very likely, given the revised projections?
d. Sinking-fund payments for Consolidated are given above. Determine the coverage of interest and sinking-fund payments for the revised projections.
e. Consolidated 5's of 2019 are selling at 90. Given the sinking-fund assumptions made above, determine the yield to maturity of the issue and the yield to average life. Assume the bond is bought in 2014.
f. The issue is callable today (2014) at 105, in 2015 at 104, in 2016 at 103, and in 2017 at 102. The probability that interest rates would fall enough to justify a call in 2015 and 2016 is considered remote, but a call might be possible in 2017 if interest rates fell below 4.5 percent on equivalent issues. Determine the yield to possible call for the issue.
g. Consolidated 5's are rated AA by S&P and Aaa by Moody. Default risks are considered minimal, but an increase in interest rates could produce a capital loss (or frozen position) before the issue matures. Interest rates for next year on equivalent risk issues are forecasted according to the

following distribution:

Probability	Yield (percent)
0.2	7.4
0.5	6.8
0.3	6.2

What is the probability that a capital loss would be incurred (on paper) by next year?

h. Suppose the issue were sold next year. Given the above probabilities, what would the expected return be? The standard deviation of returns?

References

Bierwag, G. O., G. C. Kaufman, and A. Toevs, eds., *Innovations in Bond Portfolio Management: Duration and Immunization.* Greenwich, CT: JAI Press, 1983.

Donaldson, G. G., *Corporate Debt Capacity: A Study of Corporate Debt Capacity and Determination of Corporate Debt Capacity.* Boston, MA: Harvard Graduate School of Business Administration, 1961.

Fabozzi, F. J., *Duration, Convexity, and Other Bond Risk Measures.* Hoboken, NJ: John Wiley & Sons, 1999.

Fabozzi, F. J., ed., *Investing in Asset-Based Securities.* Hoboken, NJ: John Wiley & Sons, 2000.

Fabozzi, F. J., *Fixed Income Securities.* Hoboken, NJ: John Wiley & Sons, 2002.

Fabozzi, F. J., A. K. Bhattacharya, and W. S. Berliner, *Mortgage-Backed Securities: Products Structuring and Analytical Techniques.* Hoboken, NJ: John Wiley & Sons, 2007.

Macaulay, F., *Some Theoretical Problems Suggested by the Movement of Interest Rates, Bond Yields, and Stock Prices in the United States Since 1856.* New York, NY: National Bureau of Economic Research, 1938.

Sharpe, W. F., G. J. Alexander, and J. V. Bailey. *Investments*, 6th edn. Upper Saddle River, NJ: Prentice Hall, 1999.

Chapter 7

Analysis of Common Stocks

> *The mature young lady is a lady of property. The mature young gentleman is a gentleman of property. He invests his property. He goes, in a condescending amateurish way, into the City, attends meetings of Directors, and has to do with traffic in Shares. As is well known to the wise in their generation, traffic in Shares is the one thing to have to do with in this world. Have no antecendents, no established character, no cultivation, no ideas, no manners; have Shares. Have Shares enough to be on Boards of Directors in capital letters, oscillate on mysterious business between London and Paris, and be great. Where does he come from? Shares. Where is he going to? Shares. What are his tastes? Shares. Has he any principles? Shares. What squeezes him into Parliament? Shares. Perhaps he never of himself achieved success in anything, never originated anything, never produced anything! Sufficient answer to all; Shares. O mighty Shares!*
>
> Charles Dickens, Our Mutual Friend (1865)

Common Stock Basics

The most difficult task of the security analyst is the appraisal of common stock. The variables involved are more numerous and complicated than in bond analysis, and the forecasting abilities of the analyst become far more crucial. Equities do not promise shareholders a fixed income, and the pattern of flows generated by common stocks is typically volatile.

Because equities are risky securities, the expected returns from purchasing them tend to be higher than those earned from bonds. Equity dividend yields have not equaled bond yields in recent years, but the combined returns from dividends and price appreciation have been somewhat greater on the average. Furthermore, all equities are not more risky than bonds. Indeed, the common shares of most blue-chip investment grade companies are *less* risky than the debt obligations of many other concerns. No one would argue, for example, that the shares of Johnson & Johnson are more risky than the mortgage bonds of many airlines. Of course, Johnson & Johnson common would be a bit more risky than its coveted AAA rated bonds (a rating shared only with Microsoft, Inc.). For decades, Exxon Mobil was the iconic AAA-rated U.S. company, but Standard and Poor's downgraded it in 2016 to AA+ due to low energy prices and increased debt load.

The basic procedure for evaluating equity securities begins very much like the one recommended for bond analysis. First, aggregate economic projections are made utilizing the techniques explained in Chapter 3. Next, a comprehensive evaluation of the industry in question is prepared. Finally, the future earnings position of the firm is forecasted as far as possible into the future. Probability estimates are attached where appropriate to such significant variables as sales, pertinent cost figures, and most importantly, net income. Because a major element of the cash return generated by a common stock is the dividend it pays, a careful projection of the future dividend policy of the firm must be made.

Ratio analysis can be a very useful supplement to the forecasting procedures outlined above (see Chapters 4 and 5). Various profit, turnover, and return-on-investment ratios may be computed for the firm in past years and for other comparable enterprises in the industry. These ratios may be used as performance criteria in evaluating the future prospects for the firm. A recommended policy is to compute *pro forma* ratios based on the projected data generated from the equations used to forecast sales, costs, and net income. These *pro forma* ratios may then be compared with past ratios and industry averages to measure relative performance. Ratios may also be used to verify the reliability of projections made with regression techniques. Thus, if the *pro forma* net profit margin resulting from a regression forecast was quite a bit higher than the firm had ever previously experienced, the analyst might wish to revise his projecting equations. The two sets of tools, forecasting equations and ratio analysis, should not be considered as mutually exclusive alternatives. Rather, they should be complementary methods of investigation.

Determining capital outlays and future financing

In order to illustrate a comprehensive procedure of analysis, we shall again consider Consolidated Electric Appliance (CEA) (see Chapter 6). We assume that the analyst has done all the background work that was required for bond analysis. These same data are used in the common-stock appraisal, and there is no need to repeat the explanation here. In the analysis of a common stock, however, two other projections must be made before an accurate forecast of future earnings may be determined. Capital investment is the lifeblood of the firm, and any growth predictions must by necessity include explicit forecasts of a company's asset acquisition policy. Furthermore, because capital investment requires financing, the analyst must project the sources of finance available to the firm in the future. Either capital investment or future financing policy may not be important enough to consider in bond analysis (we ignored both in Chapter 6 for the sake of convenience); however, they constitute a crucial part of the equity analysis.

Reconsider the revenue forecast and subsequent *pro forma* income statements made in Chapter 6 for CEA. Assume that the following data have been gathered from past CEA financial statements (in the manner described in Chapter 4):

CEA Selected Ratios, 2010–2014

	2010	2011	2012	2013	2014
Current ratio	3.2X	3.4X	3.9X	2.8X	3.3X
	0.133	0.145	0.159	0.124	0.133
Earnings before interest and taxes (EBIT) ratio					
Net profit margin	0.059	0.063	0.071	0.053	0.058
Fixed asset turnover	0.59X	0.65X	0.69X	0.57X	0.61X
Net-earning-power ratio	0.035	0.041	0.049	0.030	0.035
Total debt to equity	0.96	0.94	0.92	0.95	0.93
Dividend-payout ratio	0.77	0.78	0.79	0.85	0.81

From the *pro forma* statements, we can determine *pro forma* EBIT ratios and net profit margins for 2015–2019:

	2015	2016	2017	2018	2019
EBIT/sales	0.144	0.153	0.165	0.176	0.187
Net income/sales	0.062	0.067	0.075	0.082	0.089

We observe that there is a clear upward trend in both ratios for the *pro forma* data. The historical ratios, however, show an upward movement from 2010 to 2012 and then a sharp drop in 2013. All indications point to a substantial capital outlay in that year. Hence, the current ratio improves (as cash is built up), the profit margins advance (as sales increase faster than costs, which are mainly fixed), and the fixed asset turnover increases (as plant is depreciated while sales rise). In 2013, when the capital outlay seems to have been made, cash is expended (hence the decline in the current ratio), fixed costs increase (thus the decline in profit margins), and plant is added at a faster rate than sales increase (therefore the drop in asset turnover).

The analyst should realize that the extremely good initial results produced by his projection equations are to some extent due to the high degree of operating and financial leverage characteristic of the firm. When he/she forecasts an increase in sales and holds fixed costs and interest payments constant, he/she guarantees rather handsome improvements in profits. It would appear that an occasional capital addition would be required to sustain the improved sales pattern that the analyst foresees. Thus, the analyst's assumption of the constant level of fixed costs should be revised. Ideally, he could make a forecast of capital outlays (and subsequent higher fixed costs) from the long-run capital budget of the firm. If this information is unavailable to him, he will have to make estimates of the revenue-generating capacity of the plant and assume additions as forecasted output increases beyond the indicated capacity level.

In light of this further research, our analyst has decided that a large capital outlay will have to be made toward the end of the forecast period. The increased capacity resulting from the 2013 additions will be used by about 2018, it is believed. Thus, further improvements in revenues will depend on larger capacity. How might the analyst go about predicting the required capital outlay for 2018? The analyst has discovered from the history of the asset-turnover ratio that an extra dollar of sales requires about $1.61 in added fixed assets. This conclusion was reached by averaging the fixed asset turnover ratio from 2010 to 2014 and dividing the result into $1.00 of sales. Thus, the average turnover has been 0.62. This means that for each $1.61 in fixed assets purchased, annual sales have been able to advance by about $1.00 (that is, $1.00/$1.61 = 0.62). Of course, the analyst realizes that this is only a very crude method of determining necessary capital outlays and that it rests upon an assumption that the long-run relationship between fixed assets and sales is constant.

We know from our projections that sales are expected to increase from $120 million in 2014 to $127.62 million in 2018. If capacity is added in 2018 to accommodate a similar expansion from 2019 to

2023, CEA will have to make an outlay of $(1.61)(\$7.62 \text{ million}) = \$12.27$ million in that year. The added plant will raise fixed costs because depreciation charges will be higher. Suppose our analyst has determined that about one-half of fixed operating costs are depreciation charges. Further, he/she has found that fixed assets are depreciated on a straight-line basis over an average of five years (some plant lasts for 20 years, but most equipment is useful for only two or three years). The added depreciation charge for 2018 through 2023 would be:

$$(0.2)(\$12.27 \text{ million}) = \$2.45 \text{ million}.$$

An important question now must be raised concerning the method(s) the firm might employ to finance its required added plant. In order to sustain output at existing levels, it must be assumed that the company has at least reinvested depreciation flows (hence keeping the level of fixed assets constant from 2015 to 2017). The 2018 outlays could be financed from three sources, specifically: retention of earnings, the sale of new shares, and the sale of more bonds. How might the analyst decide what course CEA will follow? A check of the equity accounts from past balance sheets will reveal whether or not the firm has a history of stock issues. If it does not, chances are that it will not sell shares in the future. Computation of past dividend payout ratios will indicate something about the retention policy of the firm. A rather constant ratio might give some indication about future policy. Finally, a calculation of past debt-to-equity ratios may provide some information about the debt policy of the firm. Again, if a stable ratio is approximated, the analyst might get some indication about future debt levels. For CEA, the average dividend payout over 2010–2014 has been:

$$(0.77 + 0.78 + 0.79 + 0.85 + 0.81)/5 = 0.80.$$

Thus, the average retention rate has been 0.20. If this level of retention (payout) continues for 2015–2017, we can compute the amount that would be available for reinvestment as:

$$(0.20)(7.56 + 8.31 + 9.46) = \$5.07 \text{ million}.$$

Because the last major addition to capital was made in 2013, retained earnings for 2014 would also be available. Data from Chapter 6 allow us to reconstruct the 2014 income statement (in millions):

Revenue	$120.00
Fixed operating costs	80.00
Variable operating costs	24.00
EBIT	16.00
Interest	5.00
EBT	11.00
Taxes	4.40
Net income	$6.60

If the payout ratio was 0.81 in 2014, then retained earnings must be:

$$(0.19)(6.60) = \$1.25 \text{ million.}$$

Thus, the total amount of retention from 2014 to 2017 would be $5.07 million + $1.25 million = $6.32 million. It is likely that the analyst will find that the firm's current ratio will be increasing during 2014–2017, because retained earnings would take the asset form of added cash and/or marketable securities. In 2018, liquidity would be reduced as cash and marketable securities were converted into plant and equipment.

Now, if the firm maintains its past capital structure (about 0.94 debt to equity), it should be able to sell debt in 2018 to raise $(0.94)(\$6.32 \text{ million}) = \$5.94$ million. Adding this to the amount of retained earnings, we find:

$$\$6.32 \text{ million} + \$5.94 \text{ million} = \$12.26 \text{ million.}$$

This amount almost exactly equals the $12.27 million needed for expansion.

Thus, it is possible to recast the *pro forma* income statements for CEA over 2015–2019 making more accurate assumptions about the firm's future asset purchases, its future financing, and its future fixed cost structure. There may be long-run increases in other fixed cost items besides depreciation. These are ignored in this example, but the analyst should attempt to forecast them where possible. The projections are made below assuming: (1) the 2018 bond issue is sold at the beginning of the year at a 6 percent coupon cost; (2) the dividend payout remains at about 0.80; and (3) CEA has 1 million common shares outstanding.

Consolidated Electric Appliance Corp. *Pro forma* Statement of Income (in millions)

	2015	2016	2017	2018	2019
Revenues	$122.00	123.56	125.96	127.62	130.52
Fixed operating costs	80.00	80.00	80.00	82.45	82.45
Variable operating costs	24.40	24.70	25.19	25.52	26.10
EBIT	17.60	18.85	20.77	19.65	21.97
Taxes	5.00	5.54	6.31	5.72	6.64
Net income	7.56	8.31	9.46	8.57	9.97
Dividends	6.05	6.65	7.57	6.86	7.98
Retained earnings	$1.51	1.66	1.89	1.71	1.99
Earnings per share (EPS)	$7.56	8.31	9.46	8.57	9.97
Dividends per share (DPS)	$6.05	6.65	7.57	6.86	7.98

Common stock valuation models

Dollar returns from common stocks are derived from two sources; (1) the dividends paid by the firm, and (2) the price appreciation of the security. The ability of a firm to pay dividends, of course, depends upon its earning power. A firm that generates only a negligible return on its asset investment will obviously be in no position to pay dividends. Nevertheless, even firms that obtain very good returns on investment sometimes elect not to pay large dividends. Such firms may be able to benefit stockholders more by retaining earnings and reinvesting in profitable assets. This procedure will produce higher earnings in the future and improve the long-run dividend paying potential of the firm. Furthermore, such a policy may allow stockholders in high income-tax brackets a substantial tax saving. Cash dividends have normally been taxed at ordinary income rates, whereas capital gains have been given preferential treatment. (This has not been true in recent years, with dividends being accorded treatment more or less the same as capital gains.) When a firm retains earnings for reinvestment in profitable projects, it improves its long-run earnings stream. This improvement should be reflected in the price of the firm's shares. Thus, by retaining earnings, the firm may in effect raise the price of its stock. Investors would then have a capital gain rather than the ordinary income that they would get if a dividend were paid.

Common shares may be categorized by the above characteristics. The shares of firms that do not generate large returns on their investment in assets but that pay out in cash dividends most of what they do earn are called *income shares*. These stocks sell almost entirely on a pure dividend yield basis, because appreciation from retained earnings is limited. Income stocks may be above-average-risk securities issued by declining firms that have exhausted their most profitable reinvestment opportunities. Many fire and casualty insurance companies, undiversified tobacco equities, etc. would be included in this group. On the other hand, income stocks may also be lower-than-average-risk securities issued by firms that have their return on investment regulated by government. These equities, which are usually stable and relatively safe even during periods of recession, may retain earnings and show capital appreciation. Nevertheless, their growth rates are constrained by the regulated rate of return that they are allowed to earn on plant and equipment. The best examples of the low-risk income stock are the shares of American public utilities. Shares that are stable and relatively recession-proof are also called *defensive shares*. All defensive shares are not income stocks, however. Food and drug companies are considered to be defensive securities, and their dividend yields are generally low. Their shares also have growth potential. Gold-mining and distillery stocks are also typically classified as defensive stocks, and many of these securities (particularly the gold-mining shares) pay no dividends at all.

Equities that pay a rather constant dividend over time may be evaluated much like a preferred stock. One buys such a security for income, and its worth to the investor is the dividend stream that is produced. Hence, the return from purchasing such a stock is easily determined by the general yield equation for an asset:

$$P_0 = \frac{D_0}{(1+i)^0} + \frac{D_1}{(1+i)^1} + \cdots + \frac{D_\infty}{(1+i)^\infty}$$

$$P_0 = \sum_{t=0}^{\infty} \frac{D_t}{(1+i)^t}, \qquad (7.1)$$

where:

P_0 is the price of the stock
D_t is the dividend expected in year t
i is the rate of return earned on the stock.

In this equation, it is assumed that dividends are paid annually and that a dividend will soon be paid (hence the D_0 value). The first assumption is usually violated in the real world because firms have a tendency to pay quarterly dividends. In this case, the equation could be revised to:

$$P_0 = \sum_{t=0}^{\infty} \sum_{k=0}^{3} \frac{D_{t/4}}{(1+\frac{i}{4})^{4t+k}}. \qquad (7.2)$$

Nevertheless, the difference between Equations (7.1) and (7.2) is small, and for all practical purposes, the former may be used even if dividends are paid more often than once per year. Of course, the total dividend paid during the year (and not just the quarterly payment) should be used with Equation (7.1). The second assumption, that a dividend soon will be paid, may or may not be valid depending on the date of computation. If a dividend has just been paid, and another one will not come for a year, Equation (7.1) may be amended to become:

$$P_0 = \sum_{t=1}^{\infty} \frac{D_t}{(1+i)^t}. \tag{7.3}$$

Returning to Equation (7.1), if it is assumed that D_t is constant, the equation may be rewritten as:

$$P_0 = D \sum_{t=0}^{\infty} (1+i)^{-t}. \tag{7.4}$$

We know that:

$$\lim_{t \to \infty} \sum (1+i)^{-t} = \frac{1}{i}. \tag{7.5}$$

Thus,

$$P_0 = \frac{D}{i}. \tag{7.6}$$

Or,

$$i = \frac{D}{P_0}. \tag{7.7}$$

A similar proof obtains under conditions of continuous compounding. Here, $P_0 = \int_0^{\infty} D(t)e^{-it}dt$. Now, if $D(t)$ and i are assumed constant, then:

$$P_0 = D\left[-\frac{1}{t}e^{-it}\right]_{t=\infty} - D\left[-\frac{1}{i}e^{-it}\right]_{t=0} = \frac{D}{i}.$$

Equation (7.7) is the simplest form of yield expression. It only applies where the dividend payment is reasonably constant and will be paid for a very long time into the future. These are not totally unrealistic assumptions for some income stocks, particularly certain public utility equities. Thus, if the Elmira Gas Co. has paid a dividend of one dollar consistently over the past 30 years and expects to continue to do so in the future, its yield could be easily determined given the market price (P_0) of the stock. If Elmira common sold for $10, its yield would be:

$$\$1/\$10 = 10\%.$$

Similarly, assuming investors wished a 10 percent return from Elmira, the price of the stock could be determined, given the dividend payment:

$$\$1/0.10 = \$10.$$

Stocks that sell entirely on a dividend yield basis are becoming less important to investors. These stocks show no long-run growth in price, although gains (and losses) can be enjoyed (suffered) depending on movements in the overall rate of interest and changes in the risk position of the issuing company. Hence, an investor might buy Elmira Gas at $10 this year and see the price advance next year if the yield that investors expected from the stock declined. Suppose that overall rates of interest in the market fell such that investors required only a 9 percent rate of return on Elmira next year. Its price would become:

$$\$1/0.09 = \$11.11.$$

Thus, the investor who bought the stock this year at $10 would have his dollar dividend *plus* a capital gain of $1.11. It should be remembered, of course, that the gain had nothing to do with the growth of Elmira. It resulted entirely from a change in overall interest rates. A similar gain could have been earned on Elmira bonds. This point is explored more fully in the next section.

Holding-period returns

As in the case for bonds and preferred shares, the holding period for equities may be important. Because no one holds a security infinitely (as implied in Equation (10.1)), it is possible for capital gains (or losses) to occur if one sells the security. Changes in price may result from changes in the returns demanded by investors. Differences in demanded returns will occur: (1) if market interest rates change; (2) if the risk complexion of the firm alters; or (3) if expectations

Analysis of Common Stocks

about dividends beyond the holding period vary. Thus, if an investor paid P_0 for a stock today with the expectation of selling for P_n in n years, his return would be given by:

$$P_0 = \sum_{t=0}^{n} \frac{D_t}{(1+i)^t} + \frac{P_n}{(1+i)^n}. \qquad (7.8)$$

The best estimate at $t = 0$ of P_n is:

$$P_n = \sum_{t=n+1}^{\infty} \frac{D_t}{(1+i)^{t-n}}. \qquad (7.9)$$

Equation (7.8) is, of course, a restatement of Equation (7.1), because a substitution of 7.9 into 7.8 will produce 7.1. To see this point more clearly, consider the following example: Grand Union Power (GUP) pays a dividend of two dollars per share. The same dividend amount has been paid annually in the past for a number of years, and it is expected that this dividend will be paid in the future. The company is about ready to declare its annual dividend. Mrs. Ima Widow is considering a purchase of GUP common. She plans to hold the stock for five years. Her investment counselor has told her that interest rates should be lower then and that GUP should be in an even stronger financial position than it is now. The stock now sells for $23.375 per share. Her advisor believes that it will yield about 8 percent in five years. If this is the case, the price five years from now would be:

$$P_5 = \frac{\$2}{0.08} = \$25.$$

If Grand Union does sell at the expected price in five years, Mrs. Widow's expected return would be:

$$P_0 = \sum_{t=0}^{5} D_t(1+i)^{-t} + 25(1+i)^{-5}.$$

At $i = 12$ percent, $D_0 = 2(1.000) = 2.00$
$D_1 \ldots D_5 = 2(3.605) = 7.21$
$P_5 = 25(0.567) = 14.18$
$23.39.

Her return would be about 12 percent, as she paid $23.375 for the stock.

Notice that in the example, GUP was on the verge of paying its annual cash dividend. If it had just paid the dividend, we would expect the market price to be two dollars lower, or $21.375. If she bought just after the payment, her yield would still be about 12 percent:

$$P_0 = \sum_{t=1}^{5} D_t(1+i)^{-t} + 25(1+i)^{-5}.$$

At $i = 12$ percent,

$D_1 \ldots D_5 = 2(3.605) = 7.21$
$P_5 = 25(0.567) = 14.18$
$\$21.39.$

The dividend stream — Earnings multiplier model

Equities that evidence marked volatility in their sales, earnings, and dividend patterns are called *cyclical shares*. Aggregate economic activity has a distinct impact on the performance of these securities, and their evaluation depends on an accurate forecast of the business cycle. Typical cyclical shares include most steel, airline, automobile, railroad, and capital goods producer stocks.

An equation such as 7.8 may be used to determine the expected return on cyclical stocks. It must be remembered, however, that the dividend payments of these shares cannot be assumed to be constant. Thus, a projection of the expected dividend to be paid in each year of the holding period must be made. Furthermore, the anticipated price at the end of the holding period must be forecasted. Such a forecast is more difficult for a cyclical share than an income stock because factors other than the general level of interest rates and corporate risk are also important. In order to deal with terminal price expectations, we shall attempt to predict the price-earnings multiplier that will apply in the last year of the holding period.

A P/E multiple is simply the ratio of market price to earnings. It has been used by analysts in the past to determine the "value" of a security, and it can be a useful surrogate for expected return. Indeed, in the case of a firm that has a constant earnings stream and pays all earnings out in dividends, the P/E multiple is the inverse of the expected return. This can be seen by reconsidering Equation (7.7):

$$i = \frac{D}{P_0}.$$

If $D = E$, then

$$i = \frac{E}{P_0} \tag{7.10}$$

$$\frac{P_0}{E} = \frac{1}{i}. \tag{7.11}$$

When all earnings are not paid out in dividends and when earnings grow, the P/E multiple and the expected rate of return may differ. Nevertheless, there is a rough general relationship between the two.

The determinants of the P/E multiple may be given as follows:

$$M = f(i, \sigma, g), \tag{7.12}$$

where

M is the firm's P/E multiple
i is the general market rate of interest
σ is a measure of the riskiness of the firm
g is the growth rate in the firm's earnings stream.

Multiples can be expected to be negatively related to i and o and positively related to g. Many analysts feel that corporate risk is the primary determinant of multiples except for concerns with exceptionally high earnings growth rates (above 10 percent compounded annually for at least 10 years). For most firms, a general measure of this risk is indicated by their Standard & Poor (S&P) rating. These ratings may be used to select an appropriate multiple range for a given security. Whether a stock sells in the upper or lower end of the range will depend on the general level of interest rates and the growth potential of the firm. Historical multiples may also be used to establish a range of multiples for a firm. Thus, if a firm has sold between 12 and 14 times earnings for the past 10 years, it is likely that it will sell in that general range in the future (barring very large movements in the rate of interest and assuming the riskiness and growth potential of the firm do not change radically).

We may employ the expected terminal data multiple in a revised form of Equation (7.8):

$$P_0 = \sum_{t=0}^{n} \frac{D_t}{(1+t)^t} + \frac{(M)(E_n)}{(1+i)^n}. \qquad (7.13)$$

In this equation, M is the P/E multiple expected in year n (the terminal date of the holding period), and E_n is the forecasted EPS for year n. The value $(M)(E_n)$ should approximate the expected share price at period n. Thus, an investor can take his EPS forecast for year n, apply an appropriate multiple, and obtain a reasonable estimate of the price that he will receive when he sells his shares.

Two caveats should be indicated about the use of P/E multiples at a point in time. First, daily disturbances in stock market prices may produce wide ranges of multiples during any one year. Thus, if a stock sold between 20 and 30 during a year and earned two dollars per share, its multiple would range from 10 to 15 depending on the market price used. A good practice is to select a "normalized" price for computing the multiple. Where no clear growth pattern in price is indicated, the analyst may simply average the year's high and low prices to get a normalized value. In the above instance, the normalized price would be 25 and the resulting multiple would be 12–13. When a growth pattern is present, an argument may be made for using the year-end price or even the year's high price to compute the multiple.

The second caveat concerns the earnings figure used to estimate the stock price at the terminal holding date. For cyclical stocks, it may be that the earnings figure forecasted for the terminal year is substantially above (or below) average. Although there is a tendency for the prices of cyclical stocks to do well in above-average years and poorly in below-average ones, rarely do they match the extremes of the earnings pattern. Thus, multiples for cyclical stocks tend to fall in very good years (as earnings rise faster than stock prices) and rise in bad ones (as earnings fall faster than prices). This phenomenon should be borne in mind when forecasting the terminal price for these securities.

An illustration of estimating common stock returns

We may consider another major category of common shares — the *blue-chip stocks*. Equities of the largest concern that have long and unbroken records of earnings and dividend payments fall into this category. Blue-chip stocks are rated A+ and A by S&P and are considered to be the lowest overall risk form of common shares. The evaluation of most blue chips may be approached in the same manner as that described for the analysis of cyclical shares. The problems associated with terminal-date pricing are not so significant in the case of these stocks, however. Even those blue chips that are also cyclical stocks do not have wide movements in reported earnings per share. Many high-grade blue chips are income stocks and some are even *growth stocks* (discussed and analyzed below). The blue-chip companies are household names, such as Exxon Mobil, Johnson & Johnson, and Microsoft.

We may illustrate much of the discussion above with an example. Reconsider the earnings and dividend projections made for CEA (see example at the beginning of this chapter). Notice that CEA has a reasonably high dividend payout. This would tend to place the firm in the income stock category. If it is also a large, high quality company with a long record of earnings and dividend payment, it may also be considered a blue-chip stock. Notice further that the projected compounded annual growth rate for CEA is not terribly large. Comparing the projection in 2019 with that of 2015, we find a compounded annual growth rate of:

$$9.97(X) = 7.56$$
$$X = 7.56/9.97 = 0.758.$$

Examining the present value tables, a factor of 0.763 is found for four years (the time interval from the end of 2015 to the end of 2019) at a rate of 7 percent. Thus, the growth rate is just over 7 percent, which is not sufficient to classify the stock as a "growth" equity.

CEA common now (that is, the end of 2014) sells for $138 per share. The P/E multiple for CEA and the current dividend yield may be computed from examining the 2014 income statement (see earlier example). The firm earned $6.60 per share and paid a dividend of $5.35 ($6.60 − $1.25). The P/E multiple is thus:

$$\frac{138.00}{6.60} = 21X.$$

The current dividend yield is:

$$\frac{5.35}{138.00} = 3.9\%.$$

CEA is rated A+ by S&P. In the past, the stock has sold at a P/E multiple of 18–22X. It is expected that interest rates will be slightly lower in 2019 than they are currently, that the risk position of the firm will be more or less unchanged, and that growth prospects for the company beyond 2019 will be about the same as they were during 2015–2019. Given these expectations, we may determine a reasonable P/E multiple for 2019 earnings. An A+ rated industrial should have a multiple in the 14–15 range, although with some growth prospects a multiple above this range could be justified. The suggested range (14–15) is somewhat lower than the historical multiple at which CEA has been selling. The current multiple is 21. If risk and growth are unchanged over the 2015–2019 period but interest rates fall slightly, a very modest increase in the suggested multiple range might be allowed. A 2019 multiple of 20 would not be an unreasonable projection, considering the firm's historical multiple, its growth prospects, and the projected decline in interest rates.

Given the 2019 multiple selected above, we may estimate the stock price for 2019: $(20)(9.97) = \$199.40$.

Suppose a purchase of CEA were made today at 138. We may compute the compounded annual rate of return expected by an investor who projected the dividend stream outlined earlier and the terminal price indicated above. Assuming the dividend is paid annually and that the 2014 dividend has already been paid, we find:

at 12 percent,

$$\begin{array}{rl} (6.05) & (0.893) = 5.40 \\ (6.65) & (0.797) = 5.30 \\ (7.57) & (0.712) = 5.39 \\ (6.86) & (0.636) = 4.36 \\ (7.98) & (0.567) = 4.52 \\ (199.40) & (0.567) = \underline{113.06} \\ & 138.03 \end{array}$$

The expected return would be 12 percent.

Growth and Risk Analysis

An equity that evidences much better than average increases in sales and earnings for a consistent period of time is called a *growth stock*. These shares outperform the economy and most other equities in their respective industries. Growth companies typically pay negligible dividends because they can do better for their shareholders by retaining earnings and reinvesting in plant and equipment. They are aggressive in their search for new, profitable opportunities, and they typically spend a great deal on research and development. Many growth stocks are also blue chips, with such stock market stars as Apple and Microsoft as prime examples.

When a stock shows a sustained earnings growth pattern over a long period of time, the dividend paying potential of the security increases. For this reason, shareholders are willing to pay large P/E multiples for growth stocks. Indeed, some of the leaders among the growth equities have sold at 50 and even 100 times current earnings. Although most investors who pay these prices for growth securities believe that they are purchasing equities for capital gains, they are in fact buying a growing expected *future* dividend stream. Price appreciation occurs, of course, and this is due to the improved dividend paying abilities of the firm. Even though the firm may pay no dividend for years, as it retains earnings and grows, the fact that it *could* pay a larger dividend (and eventually will when its growth rate declines) produces the share price appreciation. Equation (7.8) is a very appropriate valuation model for growth shares. Reiterating,

$$P_0 = \sum_{t=0}^{n} \frac{D_t}{(1+i)^t} + \frac{P_n}{(1+i)^n} \qquad \text{(7.8 Restated)}$$

In general, the first term on the right-hand side of the equation will be small, because dividend payments in the near future will, in all likelihood, be negligible or even non-existent. The return to investors is produced by the price appreciation from P_0 to P_n; and, as we indicated above, P_n is determined by the dividend stream remaining beyond period n. Reiterating Equation (7.9):

$$P_n = \sum_{t=n+1}^{\infty} \frac{D_t}{(1+i)^{t-n}}. \qquad \text{(7.9 Restated)}$$

The relationship between share price movements and the timing of future dividend payments can be seen with an example. Suppose the Alpha, Beta, and Gamma Corporations are expected to maintain the following pattern of dividend payments:

Year	Alpha	Beta	Gamma
1	$1.00	$0.00	$0.00
2	1.00	0.25	0.00
3	1.00	0.50	0.00
4 and beyond	1.00	1.00	1.00

Shareholders desire a 10 percent return and will pay prices for each firm's shares that will produce a 10 percent yield. Notice initially that each company will pay $1 per year forever beginning in year 4. Thus, the price of each share should be ($1.00/0.1) = $10 at the beginning of year 4 and thereafter, with the 10 percent return represented by the $1 dividend in relation to the $10 price. For Alpha, the same analysis applies presently. The current price should be $10 and should remain there for the next three years. Within each year, the price of the stock would tend to rise as the dividend payment date approached. Theoretically, the price would be $10 right after a dividend payment and would rise to $11 just before the next payment. Once the dividend were declared (and shareholders as of a given record date were scheduled to receive their $1 per share), the stock would sell "ex-dividend" and would fall back to $10. For Gamma, the price pattern would be:

$$P_0 = 0 + \frac{P_3}{(1.10)^3} = \$10(0.751) = \$7.51$$

$$P_1 = \$10(0.826) = 8.26$$

$$P_2 = \$10(0.909) = 9.09$$

$$P_3 = 10.00.$$

Thus, Gamma holders receive their 10 percent return totally in the form of price increases for the first three years. It should be stressed that the price increase does not occur by magic, but rather because the present value of the future dividend stream rises as the stream moves nearer to the present by the passage of time. The Beta price pattern would be:

$$P_0 = 0 + \$0.25(0.826) + 0.50(0.751) + 10(0.751) = 8.09$$

$$P_1 = \$0.25(0.909) + 0.50(0.826) + 10(0.826) = 8.90$$

$$P_2 = \$0.50(0.909) + 10(0.909) = 9.54$$

$$P_3 = 10.00.$$

Thus, in year 1, the total return is from price change $(0.81/8.09 = 10\%)$. In years 2 and 3, it comes from both price change and dividends $[(0.64 + 0.25)/8.90 = 10\%]$; $[(0.46 + 0.50)/9.54 = 10\%]$. It will be recalled from above that substituting the price change Equation (7.9) into Equation (7.8) produces the basic dividend valuation model stated in Equation (7.1). Reiterating,

$$P_0 = \frac{D_0}{(1+i)^0} + \frac{D_1}{(1+i)^1} + \cdots + \frac{D_\infty}{(1+i)^\infty}. \qquad (7.1 \text{ Restated})$$

Rather than attempting to designate expected dividends over period $t = 0 - \infty$, it is operationally more feasible to estimate the approximate growth rate of dividends over time. Given an expected dividend growth rate g, we may revise Equation (7.1) to the following:

$$P_0 = \frac{D(1+g)^0}{(1+i)^0} + \frac{D(1+g)^1}{(1+i)^1} + \cdots + \frac{D(1+g)^\infty}{(1+i)^\infty}$$

$$P_0 = \sum_{t=0}^{\infty} \frac{D(1+g)^t}{(1+i)^t}. \tag{7.14}$$

In this instance, $D_0 = D(1+g)^0$, $D_1 = D(1+g)^1$, and so on. Under conditions of continuous compounding, Equation (7.14) becomes:

$$P_0 = \int_0^\infty D e^{gt} e^{-it} dt. \tag{7.15}$$

Which may be integrated, assuming g and i are constant and $g<i$, as follows:

$$P_0 = \int_0^\infty D e^{gt} e^{-it} dt = \int_0^\infty D e^{-t(i-g)} dt$$

$$= D\left[-\frac{1}{i-g} e^{-t(i-g)}\right] - D\left[-\frac{1}{i-g} e^{-t(i-g)}\right]$$

$$= D\left[-\frac{1}{i-g} e^{-\infty}\right] - D\left[-\frac{1}{i-g} e^{-0}\right]$$

$$= \frac{D}{i-g}. \tag{7.16}$$

Equation (7.16) is a useful summary of the variables determining the price of a growth stock. It can be rewritten in an even more informative way:

$$i = \frac{D}{P_0} + g. \tag{7.17}$$

This, in effect, tells us that the two components of the return on a growth stock are the dividend yield (D/P_0) and the growth in expected dividends. When the firm's retention rate (b) is expected to be constant, the dividend growth must equal the growth in earnings. Under these assumptions, the shares will sell at a constant P/E multiple (assuming interest rates also remain constant), and the earnings growth must equal the growth in share price. Thus, if D/E and P/E are constant, then Equation (7.17) indicates the total return to stockholders from dividends (D/P_0) and from capital gains (g).

The factors that determine the rate g are very important and should be understood by the analyst. Foremost in importance is the rate of return that the firm generates on its investment in assets. A broad indication of this rate may be obtained from examining the earning power of total investment ratio over time (EBIT/total assets). This ratio is the best single measure of the pretax return that the firm generates on its assets and should be scrutinized carefully for every growth stock. A second factor is the degree of financial leverage assumed by the firm and the spread between payments to bondholders and the earning power of total investment. The size of this spread will determine the residual return remaining for stockholders. A third factor that is also of crucial importance is the retention ratio $b(1-$ the dividend payout ratio). Every dollar retained and reinvested should be reflected in the growth rate.

We may be somewhat more specific about the determinants of g. Suppose a corporation is entirely financed by equity capital. Moreover, suppose that increases in equity come about solely from the retention of earnings. In this case, growth in earnings (dividends) before tax would be given by:

$$g = br. \tag{7.18}$$

where

b is the rate of earning retention
r is the return on assets (EBIT to total assets)

On an after-tax basis, 7.18 would become:

$$g = b(1-t)r. \tag{7.19}$$

This would follow because the growth in assets would be determined by b and the return on assets would be r. The after-tax return on assets would be $(1-t)r$. Multiplying $(1-t)r$ times the rate of growth of the asset base would produce the rate of growth of earnings. We may consider an example. Suppose International Copy Machines is a growth company. It now has the following income statement and balance sheet (simplified):

Income Statement Period $t = 0$		Balance Sheet As of $t = 0$	
Sales	$1,000,000	Assets	$1,000,000
Expenses	750,000		
EBIT	250,000	Bonds	– 0 –
Taxes	125,000	Equity	1,000,000
N.I.	$125,000		$1,000,000

In the steady state (all things remaining the same), the firm would have a return on its asset base (EBIT to total assets) of 0.25. The firm finances entirely by retaining earnings. If it elected to retain no earnings (pay out all earnings in dividends), the asset base could not grow, sales would not increase, and net income would remain the same over time (that is, the firm would *not* be a growth company). This can be verified through the use of Equation (7.6).

$$g = (0)(1 - 0.5)(0.25) = 0.$$

On the other hand, if the firm decided to retain, say, 40 percent of its earnings, the asset base would increase by $(0.4)(125,000) = \$50,000$. The new asset base would be $1,050,000. Given the extra assets, and assuming the return on investment continued at 0.25, the new income statement generated in period $t = 1$ would be:

Income Statement Period $t = 1$	
EBIT	$262,500*
Taxes	131,250
N.I.	$131,250

*(0.25) ($1,050,000)

This would represent a growth in net income of [(131,250 − 125,000)/125,000] = 5.0 percent. Equation (7.6) would give us the same result:

$$g = (0.4)(1 - 0.5)(0.25) = 0.05.$$

Suppose the firm retained all its earnings. The growth rate would be:

$$g = (1.0)(1 - 0.5)(0.25) = 0.125.$$

Of course, to use Equation (7.19) to determine corporate earnings growth rates, it must be assumed: (1) that the firm finances entirely with retained earnings; and (2) that the tax rate and the rate of return on investment remain constant. Neither of these assumptions may hold in the real world, although this fact should not be terribly important. Assumption (1) can be relaxed easily enough, and a revised equation can be formulated for a firm that employs debt as well as equity finance. The revised equation is:

$$G = [(1-t)(b)][L(r-c)+r]. \qquad (7.20)$$

where

L is the leverage ratio (debt to equity) employed by the firm
c is the average coupon rate of interest paid on corporate debt.

(Note that Equation (7.20) will be developed in the "Growth Rate Equations" section below.)

If it may be assumed that the tax rate, interest cost, and debt-equity ratio will be constant over time, then we may define $R = (1-t)[L(r-c)+r]$ as the after-tax return on equity and, furthermore, Equation (7.20) may be restated as $g = bR$. If we may further assume, as is often done in the case of regulated utilities, that earnings retained will earn at the required return on equity (i), then $R = i$. Solving Equation (7.17), we obtain:

$$i = \frac{D}{P_0} + g$$

$$i = \frac{D}{P_0} + bR$$

$$i = \frac{(1-b)E_0}{P_0} + bi$$

$$i - bi = (i-b)\frac{E_0}{P_0}$$

$$(1-b)i = (1-b)\frac{E_0}{P_0}$$

$$i = E_0 P_0.$$

Thus, in this special case, the inverse of the P/E ratio will provide the expected return on the stock.

The only difference between Equations (7.20) and (7.19) is that any extra return on investment above the interest payments made to bondholders is shown to influence the stockholders' earnings growth rate. Thus, if International finances half with bonds and half with equity $(L = 1)$, it would earn $(1-t)r$ on the asset investment made possible by equity sources (for example, $0.5 \times 0.25 = 12.5$ percent). If it retained b percent of its earnings, the growth produced by equity sources would be $b(1-t)r$. If $b = 0.4$ (60 percent dividend payout), $g = 0.4 \times 12.5 = 5.0$ percent. Bond financing would produce another $(r-c)$ return on the assets financed with debt sources. If $c = 6$ percent, $r-c$ would be $0.25 - 0.06 = 0.19$. Thus, the earnings growth resulting from debt finance would be $b(1-t)L(r-c)$, or $(0.4)(0.5)(1)(0.19) = 3.8$ percent. The total growth rate would be 5.0 percent (from equity sources) plus 3.8 percent (debt sources), or 8.8 percent. This example is presented numerically in Table 7.1.

Equation (7.20) can be used by the analyst to determine whether the firm is getting favorable or unfavorable leverage. If $r > c$, leverage would be favorable, and debt financing would improve the shareholders' net rate of return (net income to stockholders' equity) and earnings growth rate. If $r < c$, leverage would be unfavorable, and debt financing would reduce the return to shareholders and the earnings growth rate. In the case of International (above), suppose $r = 0.05$ and $c = 0.08$. If the firm retained all its earnings, but had no bond finance, the after-tax growth rate would be:

$$g = (1)(0.5)(0.05) = 0.025.$$

If the firm financed half with bonds and half with equity, however, the growth rate would be:

$$g = [(0.5)(1)][(1)(-0.03) + (0.05)]$$
$$= (0.5)(0.02)$$
$$= 0.01.$$

Thus, the rate of growth would be reduced from 2.5 percent to 1.0 percent.

Although Equation (7.20) is an improvement over Equation (7.19) in that debt finance is included as a variable, it still harbors the assumptions of a constant rate of taxation and a constant rate of return on investment. To the extent that tax rates fall, it should be obvious that earnings growth rates should improve. Similarly, if better cost controls (margins) or improved sales-asset relationships (turnovers) can be effected, higher growth rates could be obtained. The analyst should be very careful to use existing EBIT/total asset ratios as a surrogate for return on investment *only* if that relationship is expected to hold in the future. Equations (7.19) and (7.20) also assume that the only source of equity finance is the retention of earnings. Empirically, this is not a bad assumption because the sale of additional shares by existing (non-IPO) publicly held companies now account for only a negligible part of the total financing arranged by major U.S. corporations in any one year. Otherwise, *pro forma* expected ratios should be used.

Mergers and Growth

In many cases, it is possible for a company to grow and acquire assets over time by the acquisition of other firms (see Chapter 6). The attractiveness of such an acquisition is a function of the profitability of the assets (both tangible and intangible) to be acquired and the form and amount of payment to be made.

Mergers may occur for any number of reasons. Perhaps the oldest and strongest motivation is the simple desire to increase power over the market. The increased market power resulting from a merger may raise profits through "operating economies," such as bulk purchases, reciprocal purchases, advertising discounts, better channels of distribution (everything from more freight cars when needed to more shelf space), and better access to and bargaining position for external funds. Merger also allows a firm to acquire large numbers of talented management and research personnel and at the same time to gain increased market power to sell whatever they produce.

In other cases, mergers may occur because the acquired company is a bargain; poor management, inadequate capital, stock market disfavor, a poor year, or other factors may reduce the price of the stock to the point that the firm is worth a great deal more than the cost of acquiring it. The acquired firm may have liquid assets, such that the acquiring firm could raise more money by merging with it than by selling securities on the market. It is further possible that the acquired firm would have tax-loss carry-forwards that could be used to reduce future tax liabilities of the merged company.

There are two remaining arguments for merger that must be examined rather closely. The first is diversification. If a firm is able to acquire other firms whose earnings do not correlate very closely with its own (coefficient of correlation less than $+1$, and the closer to -1 the better), the probability distribution for earnings of the new firm should show less dispersion (be less risky) than for the old firm. If one dollar of earnings for the merged firm is less risky, it should be discounted at a lower rate in imperfect markets. This would result in an increase in the price of the stock and shareholder well-being. The merger would thus serve a valid economic function. It should be pointed out, however, that such diversification could also be achieved by shareholders in their own portfolios.

Much is written about the growth resulting from mergers. To the extent that the merged firms are able to interact and combine their talents to do things that neither could do before (the synergism or "$2 + 2 = 5$" effect), a valid justification for the merger, and perhaps an increase in stock price, may exist. On the other hand, the merger of firms in totally different lines of business with no subsequent

Table 7.1. Growth and the Levered Firm

International Copy Machines Balance Sheet Beginning Period $t = 0$

Assets	$1,000,000	Bonds (6%)	$ 500,000
		Equity	500,000
	$1,000,000		$1,000,000

International Copy Machines Income Statement For Period $t = 0$

EBIT	$250,000
Interest	30,000
EBT	$220,000
Taxes	110,000
N.I.	$110,000
Dividends	66,000
Retained Earnings	$ 44,000

International Copy Machines Sources and Uses of Funds For Period $t = 0$

Retained Earnings	$44,000
Bond Sale	44,000
	$88,000
Asset Purchases	$88,000

International Copy Machines Balance Sheet Beginning Period $t = 1$

Assets	$1,088,000	Bonds (6%)	$ 544,000
		Equity	544,000
	$1,088,000		$1,088,000

International Copy Machines Income Statement For Period $t = 1$

EBIT	$272,000*
Interest	32,640
EBT	$239,360
Taxes	119,680
N.I.	$119,680

Growth in Net Income

$$\frac{119{,}680 - 110{,}000}{110{,}000} = 8.8\%$$

*$(.25 \times 1{,}088{,}000)$.

interaction may create value through diversification but not through real growth, although growth may appear to occur. Consider the following:

Ming-Trico-Vaugn (MTV) is a conglomerate. It has 5 million shares outstanding and earns $6 per share. Because of MTV's growth characteristics, it sells at 40 times current earnings ($240 per share). The Stagnant Steel Co. has 4 million shares outstanding and earns $2 per share. Because of its poor growth prospects and inherent risk, the market will only pay 10 times current earnings ($20) for Stagnant stock. MTV has proposed a merger with Stagnant. No changes will take place in Stagnant's operations and the current management will remain intact. The merger will merely make Stagnant one of a growing list of companies controlled by MTV. A merger offer has been tendered giving Stagnant holders one new MTV share for each 10 Stagnant shares outstanding. Because this amounts to an offer of $240 for $200, virtually every Stagnant shareholder has accepted the proposal.

In contemplation of the merger, the chairman of MTV has his accountants prepare a new consolidated *pro forma* statement of income. In order to purchase Stagnant, 400,000 additional MTV shares will be issued. Thus, the new capitalization of the company should be 5,400,000 shares. Upon consolidating the net income of the two firms, the accountants report a revised total income of:

$$(6.00)(5,000,000) + (3.00)(4,000,000) = \$38,000,000.$$

Dividing this figure by the new capitalization of 5,400,000 shares produces an earning per share of:

$$(\$38,000,000/5,400,000) = \$7.04.$$

Thus, without changing operations at all, MTV has been able to show a fantastic increase in earnings of $[(7.04-6.00/(6.00)] = 17.3$ percent! Of course, an efficient and rational market would realize that the above transactions were merely financial, and unless the merger reduced the riskiness of MTV there should be no increase in the price of MTV shares. In fact, because MTV paid a premium of 20 percent above the value of Stagnant shares, it might be argued that the price of MTV shares should *fall*. Unfortunately, a few decades ago these transactions took place regularly (disproving once again the efficient market hypothesis) and it took a few years for the investors to realize that a conglomerate composed of no-growth organic components was not really a growth company.

Suppose that MTV and Stagnant had perfectly positive (+1) earnings correlations. Suppose further that rational markets prevailed and MTV stock did not increase after the "new" EPS had been announced. What would have happened to the earnings multiplier (P/E) of MTV stock?

$$\$240/\$7.04 = 34 \text{ times.}$$

Thus, the multiple would have fallen from $40X$ to $34X$. Of course, this would be quite rational, because the merged company would be riskier than the premerger MTV (Stagnant was riskier than MTV) and the future earnings growth rate from operations would be reduced (Stagnant had very poor earnings growth prospects).

In a less "efficient" market, the old multiple of $40X$ might hold (or even a higher one given the new "growth" in earnings). If this were the case, MTV common would advance to:

$$(40)(\$7.04) = \$281.60.$$

Assume that this did indeed happen, and MTV set about to find yet another merger partner. Suppose it found a company, call it Stagnant II, and consummated a merger on the same terms as with Stagnant I. What would be the effect on MTV earnings?

a. Price of Stagnant II stock: $20
b. Price markup given to effect merger: 20 percent
c. Price offer to Stagnant II: $24
d. Price of MTV stock: $281.60
e. Number of MTV shares given for each Stagnant II share: $24.00/281.60 = 0.085$
f. Number of new MTV shares issued: $(0.085)(4,000,000) = 340,000$
g. New total earnings: $38 million + $8 million = $46 million

h. New earnings per share: 46,000,000/5,740,000 = $8.01
i. Earnings growth: [(8.01 − 7.04)/(7.04)] = 13.8 percent.

We see in this example how it is possible to combine companies without growth in order to produce a "growth" company. As indicated in the discussion above, a company must find ever-larger merger partners if the apparent growth rate is not to decline. In addition, the market must be willing to assign a constant P/E ratio to earnings of ever-declining quality. On the other hand, if companies can be bought with convertible securities, warrants, or other kinds of "funny money," the apparent growth rate can be made even more spectacular.

The analyst should be aware of the difference between growth achieved from improved operations ("organic" growth) and growth induced from merger. Although the theoretical distinction between buying individual assets to increase output (and hopefully profits) and purchasing other firms to accomplish the same ends are not great, the practical differences may be enormous. Purely financial transactions (such as those illustrated in the example above) should be viewed with suspicion by the analyst unless there are clear-cut, real economic benefits accruing to the merging enterprise. Operating economies, improved market position, better managerial talent, and so on are all justifiable grounds for a merger. Unfortunately, these elements have not always been ingredients in the business combinations of recent years.

After-tax returns and growth

The after-tax return on an investment in common stock will depend on the tax position of the investor and the taxation climate in which he finds himself. For growth stocks, capital gains taxation becomes relatively more important than taxes levied on dividends. Employing the symbols of Equation (7.8), the after-tax dividend received in each period t is $(1 - m_t)D_t$ where m_t is the marginal income tax bracket of the investor in period t. The capital gain secured by the investor is simply $P_n - P_0$. His tax on the gain is $k_n(P_n - P_0)$ where k_n is the capital gains tax rate the investor is subject to at period n. His after-tax capital flow is thus: $P_n - [(k_n)(P_n - P_0)]$. His after-tax return would be given by i in the following equation.

$$P_0 = \sum_{t=0}^{n} \frac{(1-m_t)D_t}{(1+i)^t} + \frac{P_n - [k_n(P_n - P_0)]}{(1+t)^n}. \qquad (7.21)$$

An investor purchases a stock that pays a dividend of two dollars per year. He plans to hold the stock for five years. The stock now sells at $18X$ earnings of five dollars per share. It is expected that this multiple will apply in five years when EPS will be six dollars. The after-tax dividend return that the investor would get in periods $t = 1$ through $t = 5$ (the dividend in $t = 0$ has just been paid) depends upon his marginal tax bracket. If this is 40 percent, his after-tax return would be:

$$(1 - 0.4)(\$2) = \$1.20.$$

Suppose the investor pays capital gains taxes at one-half his marginal rate (this set of facts applied for many years prior to the passage of the Tax Reform Act of 1986); his after-tax capital flow would be:

$$\$108 - [(0.2)(108 - 90)] = \$104.40.$$

The investor's after-tax rate of return would be:

at 5 percent,   (4.329) (1.20) = \$5.19
(0.784) (104.40) = 81.85
\$87.04

at 4 percent,   (4.452) (1.20) = \$5.34
(0.822) (104.40) = 85.82
\$91.16

Or about 4.3 percent.

Notice how the differing tax rates on dividends and capital gains influence the results. In 1986, *the rules changed* such that all income was taxed at 28 percent. A few years later, rates advanced (under Presidents George H.W. Bush and Bill Clinton). Presently, both dividends (with certain exceptions) and capital gains are taxed at lower rates than other income; but all this will most likely change many times in the future. Readers are cautioned that politicians are fickle (and often stupid) and change the rules just to show they are "doing something" to deserve the money they are paid!

Riskiness of Stocks

In addition to the expected return estimate that the analyst has made, he needs to have some basic measure of the riskiness of the security he is analyzing. In the material to follow, we shall be attempting to measure the "absolute" or "total" risk associated with a common stock. Nevertheless, the important risk variable is the "non-diversifiable" or "systematic" element — that risk that cannot be diversified away in an efficient portfolio. When we begin constructing optimal portfolios in Chapter 9, the reader will observe that there are two parameters required for evaluation: (1) the expected return from holding a security; and (2) the covariances among returns of all securities in the portfolio. At this point, however, it should be noted that the variance is required before covariances may be estimated. Many analysts rely entirely on agency ratings to determine risk, and others use ratio analysis to discern the overall liquidity, profitability, leverage, and so on of the firm whose common stock is being considered. These methods are useful, but by themselves are inadequate. If the analyst has prepared probability distributions in estimating the expected return from the investment, he may use these distributions to determine the deviations around the expected values. A simple example will serve to explain. Suppose an analyst has specified a probability distribution for the sales of the Ace Co. He has also determined a conditional distribution of costs given each level of sales. (A more complicated set of conditional probability distributions could be prepared to take into account various categories of expenses.) Finally, he has calculated an overall distribution of net income and dividend payments.

Sales in (millions)	Total Expenses	Net Income
100 (.3)	70 (.2)	30 (.06)
	80 (.6)	20 (.18)
	90 (.2)	10 (.06)
90 (.5)	65 (.1)	25 (.05)
	75 (.7)	15 (.35)
	85 (.2)	5 (.10)
80 (.2)	60 (.2)	20 (.04)
	70 (.5)	10 (.10)
	80 (.3)	0 (.06)

If the firm has 10 million shares outstanding, the data may be grouped into a distribution of EPS:

EPS	Probability
$3.00	0.06
2.50	0.05
2.00	0.22
1.50	0.35
1.00	0.16
0.50	0.10
0.00	0.06
	1.00

From this, the analyst may construct a dividend payment distribution. Suppose he believes that management will pay a maximum dividend of two dollars but will distribute less if earnings are low. Within the range of EPS from one dollar to two dollars, he believes a 0.75 payout will take place. Below earnings of one dollar, no dividend will be paid. The DPS distribution would be:

DPS	Probability
$2.00	0.11
1.50	0.22
1.12½	0.35
0.75	0.16
0.00	0.16
	1.00

The expected value of EPS and DPS and their standard deviations may be computed. They equal:

EPS	DPS
$\mu = \$1.50$	$1.06
$\sigma = 0.72$	0.58

The analyst may repeat the above process for each year in the anticipated holding period of the security. Suppose he obtained the following:

Year	EPS	DPS
1	$\mu = \$1.50$	$1.06
	$\sigma = 0.72$	0.58
2	$\mu = 1.80$	1.20
	$\sigma = 0.85$	0.64
3	$\mu = 2.00$	1.40
	$\sigma = 0.95$	0.76.

Thus, he would have expected values and deviations for EPS and DPS over the three-year holding period. He could next determine a distribution of multiples to get the expected price in three years.

Assume he forecasts the following:

P/E Multiple	Probability
10×	0.6
12×	0.4

This distribution could be combined with the earnings distribution for year three to obtain a distribution of prices. Ideally, each multiple should be combined with each EPS to get the distribution. If the EPS distribution were:

EPS	Probability
$3.50	0.2
2.00	0.6
0.50	0.2

and if it were assumed that the P/E multiple was independent from the forecasted EPS (an assumption that may not hold), the price distribution would be:

Multiple	×	EPS	=	Price
10×(.6)		$3.50 (.2)		$35.00 (.12)
		2.00 (.6)		20.00 (.36)
		.50 (.2)		5.00 (.12)
10×(.4)		3.50 (.2)		42.00 (.08)
		2.00 (.6)		24.00 (.24)
		.50 (.2)		6.00 (.08)

Grouping the data:

Price	Probability
$42.00	0.08
35.00	0.12
24.00	0.24

(*Continued*)

Price	Probability
20.00	0.36
6.00	0.08
5.00	0.12
	1.00

The expected price and its standard deviation would be: $\mu = \$21.60$, $\sigma = \$10.50$.

In the example presented above, all the separate return distributions were assumed to be independent. Most likely, they will not be. Generally, if a firm does poorly in the early years of an investment-holding period, it will continue to do poorly. Thus, the dividend distributions of later years may well depend upon the outcomes in previous years. Furthermore, the EPS distribution in the terminal year will almost always be correlated with the dividend distribution of that year. Finally, the value of the P/E multiple in the terminal year will most likely be influenced by the earnings and dividend performance in earlier years. Thus, the analyst should attempt to construct conditional probabilities, where appropriate, for all the distributions involved.

Suppose an analyst has projected the following distributions for a stock that is to be held for two years:

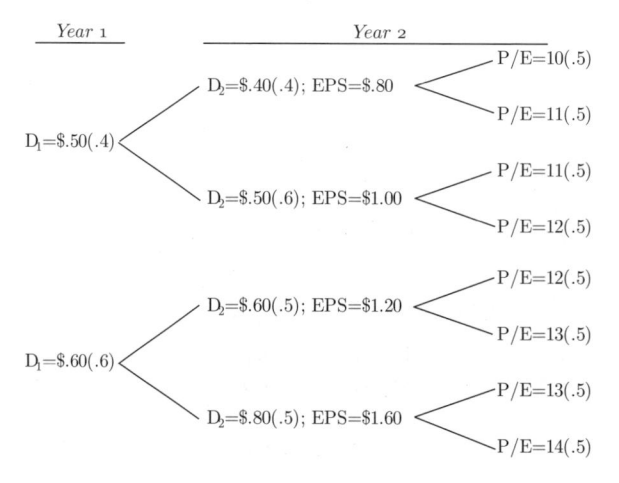

Year 1	Year 2	
$D_1=\$.50(.4)$	$D_2=\$.40(.4)$; EPS=\$.80	$P/E=10(.5)$
		$P/E=11(.5)$
	$D_2=\$.50(.6)$; EPS=\$1.00	$P/E=11(.5)$
		$P/E=12(.5)$
$D_1=\$.60(.6)$	$D_2=\$.60(.5)$; EPS=\$1.20	$P/E=12(.5)$
		$P/E=13(.5)$
	$D_2=\$.80(.5)$; EPS=\$1.60	$P/E=13(.5)$
		$P/E=14(.5)$

Eight outcomes (with associated probabilities) would be possible:

	D_1	D_2	P_n	Prob.
a.	$0.50	$0.40	$8.00	0.08
b.	0.50	0.40	8.80	0.08
c.	0.50	0.50	11.00	0.12
d.	0.50	0.50	12.00	0.12
e.	0.60	0.60	14.40	0.15
f.	0.60	0.60	15.60	0.15
g.	0.60	0.80	20.80	0.15
h.	0.60	0.80	22.40	0.15
				1.00

The yield from each combination (a–h) can be computed, given the current market price of the security, which is assumed to be $8, and placed in a probability distribution.

Combination	Yield (percent)	Probability
A	5.6	0.08
B	10.4	0.08
C	23.1	0.12
D	28.2	0.12
E	40.7	0.15
F	46.1	0.15
G	68.1	0.15
H	74.1	0.15

The expected yield from this distribution is 41.8 percent with a standard deviation of 22.6 percent.

For situations where more outcomes are designated (and where the time span is longer) many combinations are possible. In these instances, hand calculation becomes exceedingly tedious, and again the analyst must rely on the computer to do the computational work.

Risk Measures for Common Stock Returns

Once the analyst has specified his DPS and terminal price distributions for each year, he may compute an overall return-risk measure for the equity under investigation. If it is assumed that all distributions are independent, the following equations may be employed:

$$V_\mu = \sum_{t=0}^{n} \frac{\bar{D}_t}{(1+i)^t} + \frac{\bar{P}_n}{(1+i)^n}, \qquad (7.22)$$

and,

$$\sigma = \sqrt{\sum_{t=0}^{n} \frac{(\bar{D}_t^\sigma)^2}{(1+i)^{2t}} + \frac{(\bar{P}_n^\sigma)^2}{(1+i)^{2n}}}. \qquad (7.23)$$

where

- V_μ is the present value of the dividend stream and terminal selling price.
- $\bar{D}_t$ is the expected dividend in period t.
- $\bar{P}_n$ is the expected terminal price at period n.
- i is the rate of return from the investment.
- σ is the overall standard deviation around the present value.
- D_t^σ is the standard deviation of dividends in period t.
- P_n^σ is the standard deviation around the expected market price at period n.

Referring back to the first example constructed in the previous section (the Ace Co.), we may solve for V_μ and σ. Suppose an investor wished to determine the probability of earning at least 10 percent on the purchase of the stock. The present value of his projected return stream would be:

$$V_\mu = \frac{(1.06)}{(1.10)^1} + \frac{(1.20)}{(1.10)^2} + \frac{(1.40)}{(1.10)^3} + \frac{(21.60)}{(1.10)^3} = \$19.13.$$

If the current market price of the stock were $19.13, the investor would expect to obtain the 10 percent return. If the current market price were lower, he would expect a larger return. If it were higher, he would expect a lower return.

The risk from purchasing the stock would be:

$$\sigma = \sqrt{\frac{(0.58)^2}{(1+0.10)^2} + \frac{(0.64)^2}{(1+0.10)^4} + \frac{(0.76)^2}{(1+0.10)^6} + \frac{(10.50)^2}{(1+0.10)^6}}$$
$$= \$7.94.$$

If the stock were selling at $11.19 (that is, $19.13 − $7.94) and the underlying distributions were normal, the investor would determine the probability that he would earn less than 10 percent:

$$P(X|X \leq V_\mu - 1\sigma) \approx 0.16.$$

At the opposite extreme from having completely independent flows is the case of perfectly correlated returns. In this instance, any deviation from the mean value of a flow in any particular period would be matched by deviations in all other periods in exactly the same manner. The present value of the dividend stream and terminal selling price would be the same as in the independent case (Equation (7.22)), but the overall standard deviation around the present value would be given by:

$$\sigma = \sum_{t=0}^{n} \frac{D_t^\sigma}{(1+i)^t} + \frac{P_n^\sigma}{(1+i)^n}. \tag{7.24}$$

If the flows in the above example were perfectly correlated, the risk from purchasing the stock would be:

$$\sigma = \frac{0.58}{(1+0.10)^1} + \frac{0.64}{(1+0.10)^2} + \frac{0.76}{(1+0.10)^3} + \frac{10.50}{(1+0.10)^3}$$
$$= \$9.52.$$

Not surprisingly, the overall risk is greater when returns are perfectly correlated than when returns are independent.

In the real world, it will be unusual for returns to be either perfectly correlated or independent. A more likely situation would be a mixture of the two with parts of the return stream being independent and other parts being perfectly correlated. In this more realistic case, the present value of the stream would still be given by Equation (7.23), but the overall standard deviation would be much more complex:

$$\sigma = \sqrt{\left(\sum_{t=0}^{n}\frac{(D_t^\sigma)^2}{(1+i)^{2t}} + \frac{(P_n^\sigma)^2}{(1+i)^{2n}}\right) + \sum_{k=1}^{m}\left(\left[\sum_{t=0}^{n}\frac{(D_t^\sigma)^{(k)}}{(1+i)^t}\right] + \frac{(P_n^\sigma)^{(k)}}{(1+i)^n}\right)^2},$$
(7.25)

where D_t^σ and P_n^σ are the dividend-price standard deviations for the independent portion of the flow returns; and $(D_t^\sigma)^k$ and $(P_n^\sigma)^k$ are the dividend-price standard deviations for stream k of a perfectly correlated portion of the flow returns.

Reconsidering our example, suppose it can be determined that the dividend stream is perfectly correlated. That is, poor corporate performance in period $t = 1$ that results in a lower dividend payment than the expected value would also mean poor performance in period $t = 2$ and $t = 3$. Because the stock price at period $t = 3$ depends on future dividends (beyond $t = 3$), and these dividends would also be influenced by the poor performance of earlier years, at least part of the variation in stock price for $t = 3$ would be perfectly correlated with dividend-stream variations. Nevertheless, there may be other factors influencing stock prices (such as the overall level of interest rates or simply random events) so that part of the variation in stock price is also independent. Assume that we can determine that about 80 percent of the stock price variation in period $t = 3$ is traceable to the riskiness of the dividend stream, and 20 percent results from other (independent) factors. Given this information, we could reformulate Equation (7.25) to get the overall deviation for the investment:

$$\sigma = \sqrt{\frac{(P_3^\sigma)^2}{(1+0.10)^6} + \left(\sum_{t=1}^{3}\frac{(D_t^\sigma)^{(1)}}{(1+0.10)^t} + \frac{(P_3^{\sigma(1)})}{(1+0.10)^3}\right)^2}$$

$$= \sqrt{\begin{array}{c}(2.10)^2(0.564) + [(0.58)(0.909) + (0.64)(0.826) \\ +(0.76)(0.751) + (8.40)(0.751)]^2\end{array}}$$

$$= \$8.09.$$

Notice that the overall riskiness of the mixed case lies between the extremes of perfect correlation and independence.

The above formulations can also be used to generate a distribution of rates of return. The following steps should be employed:

1. Compute V_μ and σ for an initial value of i.
2. Determine the number of standard deviations that would equalize the present price of the stock and V_μ (that is, solve $V_\mu + Z\sigma = P_0$ for Z).
3. Find $P(X|X \leq V_\mu + Z\sigma)$ from Appendix C. This will be the probability that V_μ will be less than the present price of the stock at the given i and is, in turn, the probability that the rate of return will be less than i.
4. Plot the probability determined above on a cumulative probability distribution.
5. Iterate steps 1–4 above varying i in order to generate a complete cumulative probability distribution.
6. Convert the cumulative distribution to a discrete probability distribution of rates of return.
7. For a two-parameter description, the 15th percentile of the cumulative probability distribution will provide an estimate of the mean (expected) rate of return. Dividing the interquartile range by 1.35 will provide an estimate of σ.

Thus, the analyst would have a percentage rate of return expected from the purchase of a stock and the standard deviation around that percentage. There are other approaches to the problem of generating μ and σ statistics of rates of return. Below we consider one such method in detail. When the analyst has specified distributions with many more possible outcomes than we have dealt with above, manual calculations are not feasible and a computer must be employed. It is, of course, possible to attempt a deterministic solution on a computer that would merely compute a probability distribution of returns employing all observations from all distributions. Greater flexibility at less cost can usually be obtained by employing a Monte Carlo simulation. This method often provides an approximate solution when a deterministic solution is not possible by employing techniques of random sampling from the distributions of variables.

Monte Carlo simulation can perhaps best be explained by the case in which all variables are assumed to be independent of each other. The steps are as follows:

1. Determine a probability distribution for each variable (see Figure 7.1).
2. Transform any continuous distributions into discrete distributions, with each discrete interval representing 1 percent (or 0.1 percent or some other convenient interval) of the distribution.
3. Determine the midpoint of each interval in each discrete distribution.
4. Assign a number from 1 to n (where n represents the number of intervals into which each distribution was divided) to each interval. For example, if a distribution were divided into 100 intervals, the first percentile would be assigned the number 1, the second would be assigned 2, and the hundredth, 100.
5. The distribution of returns should also be divided into intervals (say, whole percentages) and counters defined (for example, 0.5 percent $\leq i_1 <$ 1.5 percent; 1.5 percent $\leq i_2 <$ 2.5 percent, and so on) which are initialized at zero (that is $i_1 = i_2 = \ldots i_n = 0$).
6. Generate from the computer, or select from a table, a two-digit (if fewer than 101 intervals are employed) random number for the first independent distribution.
7. Determine the interval on the distribution that was assigned a number corresponding to the random number generated and select the midpoint.
8. Repeat steps 6 and 7 for the remaining distributions such that there is one observation for each variable.

9. Compute the rate of return for this set of observations. For the example given, this would require inputting the simulated variables to the formula:

$$P_0 = \sum_{t=1}^{6} \frac{D_t}{(1+i)^t} + \frac{P_6}{(1+i)^6},$$

and solving for i.

10. The i computed in step 9 would then be assigned to the appropriate interval in the return distribution and the counter for that interval would be incremented by one. For example, if the first computation yielded an $i = 5.7$ percent, then i_6 would be incremented and, at the end of the first iteration, $i_{1-5} = i_{7-n} = 0$ and $i_6 = 1$.

11. Repeat steps 6–10 a large number of (N) times in order to generate a frequency distribution of i's.

12. Each counter can then be normalized to provide a distribution [for example, $i_1/N = P(i \mid .5 \text{ percent} \leq i < 1.5 \text{ percent})$].

13. From this distribution, μ_i, σ_i, or any other desired statistic may be computed. The larger N is, the better will be the resulting estimate (as in any random sampling situation).

Dependent relationships among variables may also be simulated. If two variables are perfectly correlated (positively or negatively) with each other, the distributions may simply be combined and simulated as one variable; the same result is obtained if the same random number is used for both distributions on each iteration.

Growth-rate equations for the levered firm

Here we further develop Equation (7.20). If a firm had debt as well as equity in its structure according to some optimal (or at least constant) combination, asset growth would result from earnings retention (and possibly stock sales, which we shall ignore) and bond flotations. Thus, asset growth would be dependent upon b (the retention rate) and the relationship between debt (B) and equity (S). We shall assume that earning assets (A) equal debt plus equity,

that is,
$$A = B + S. \qquad (7.26)$$

If the firm earns r on its asset base, then EBIT would be:
$$\text{EBIT} = rA. \qquad (7.27)$$

From EBIT, interest c is paid to bondholders, leaving for common shareholders before taxes:
$$E_b = \text{EBIT} - cB. \qquad (7.28)$$

After-tax earnings are given by:
$$E = (1-t)(\text{EBIT} - cB). \qquad (7.29)$$

If dividends (D) are paid to shareholders, $E - D$ is left to the firm for reinvestment in assets.

Now, we know that asset growth is:
$$\Delta A = \Delta B + \Delta S. \qquad (7.30)$$

Furthermore, retaining earnings will increase S such that:
$$\Delta S = E - D. \qquad (7.31)$$

If there is an optimal relationship (L) between the firm's debt and equity,
$$\Delta B = L\Delta S. \qquad (7.32)$$

We wish to know by how much earnings (E) will grow if earnings are retained and bonds are sold to maintain an optimal B/S combination. Let the growth rate in earnings be:
$$g = \Delta E/E. \qquad (7.33)$$

We have established the relationship between E and EBIT, thus:
$$\Delta E = (1-t)(\Delta \text{EBIT} - c\Delta B). \qquad (7.34)$$

Furthermore, we know from 7.27 that EBIT is simply the return on assets times the asset base. Extra EBIT resulting from expanding the asset base would thus be:

$$\Delta \text{EBIT} = r\Delta A. \tag{7.35}$$

Now, if we substitute (7.34) into (7.33), we find:

$$\Delta E = [(1-t)][(r\Delta A) - (c\Delta B)]. \tag{7.36}$$

We know ΔA from 7.30. Thus, by substituting that equation into 7.36, we find:

$$\Delta E = [(1-t)][r(\Delta B + \Delta S) - c\Delta B]. \tag{7.37}$$

This equation may be expanded,

$$\Delta E = [(1-t)][r\Delta B + r\Delta S - c\Delta B]. \tag{7.38}$$

Rewriting,

$$\Delta E = [(1-t)][r\Delta B - c\Delta B + r\Delta S]. \tag{7.39}$$

Factoring within the second term of the right-hand member of the expression, we find:

$$\Delta E = [(1-t)][(r-c)(\Delta B) + (r\Delta S)]. \tag{7.40}$$

We know ΔB from Equation (7.32) and ΔS from 7.30. Substituting these equations into 7.40, we find:

$$\Delta E = [(1-t)][(r-c)L(E-D) + (E-D)]. \tag{7.41}$$

Factoring within the second term of the right-hand member of the expression once again, we find:

$$\Delta E = [(1-t)][(E-D)][(r-c)L + r]. \tag{7.42}$$

Thus, the growth rate (Equation (7.33)) would be:

$$g = \Delta E/E = \frac{[(1-t)][(E-D)][L(r-c)+r]}{E}, \tag{7.43}$$

which may also be written as:

$$g = [(1-t)]\left[\left(1 - \frac{D}{E}\right)\right][L(r-c)+r]. \tag{7.44}$$

Because b equals $(1 - D/E)$, we can simplify to produce:

$$g = [(1-t)(b)][L(r-c) + r], \qquad (7.45)$$

which is also Equation (7.20) in the text.

Common stocks: Further considerations

Throughout the previous discussion of common stock returns, the focus was on the dividend paying ability of the equity and its possible price appreciation. Under very special circumstances, however, the analyst may wish to consider assets as well as earnings in computing the yield equation. There are instances in which a substantial volume of assets may not produce a large future earnings stream. If it is possible that these assets will be transformed into another form of higher yielding asset, or if it is conceivable that the assets will be distributed to stockholders, then the value of such assets should be assessed.

Firms that maintain large cash balances or that hold substantial amounts of liquid securities will often show a poor earnings record. If it appears possible that the liquidity of these firms will be reduced through the purchase of earning assets, the analyst should take this into account in projecting the future earnings stream for the firm. Also, if it is possible that the firm will pay a liquidating (or partially liquidating) cash dividend to shareholders, the amount of this distribution should be included in the analyst's yield equation. If a firm maintains its liquidity at the expense of earning assets and it appears that none of this surplus liquidity will be distributed to shareholders, the analyst should not consider the extra liquidity in evaluation except to the extent that substantial liquidity may reduce the riskiness of the firm. Note that high levels of liquidity frequently prompt tender offers to purchase controlling interest in the firm. The effect of these offers is usually to increase the price of the company's shares. If the probability of a tender offer looms significant, the analyst should attempt to quantify its expected value.

Financial companies (banks, insurance companies, and so on) frequently hold large volumes of liquid assets (cash, marketable securities). On occasion, a financial company will have a poor earnings record for this reason. Such firms offer an opportunity for an imaginative management to increase the firm's return on investment by reducing liquidity (switching from cash into mortgages or even consumer loans). When the analyst believes there is a strong chance for such a policy change, he should attempt to quantify the possible results. This is a very difficult task, and it sometimes requires assumptions about management behavior that are always difficult to make. Nevertheless, the analyst who can shrewdly make such judgments is often rewarded highly.

Certain non-financial concerns will have book values that exceed the market price of the firm's shares. Such firms rarely offer good investment returns to investors because their asset holdings are generally worth much less than the stated book values. Historically, American railroads sold at large discounts from book value. They did so because the earning power of their asset holdings was low. Furthermore, the possibility of converting into more profitable assets (or liquidating) was very small because of regulatory constraints. As the railroads consolidated into a few large concerns and as they were basically deregulated, they became very profitable. The surviving roads (especially Union Pacific and BNSF) have produced excellent returns for investors. Indeed, Warren Buffett's Berkshire Hathaway bought the BNSF because its asset values were converted to substantial earning power.

Manufacturing concerns that have substantial assets that produce little cash flow frequently cannot liquidate these assets, except at distress prices. Hence, for all practical purposes, their asset "values" have no real significance. An exception is the firm that generates a large cash flow but that shows negligible net income (perhaps due to substantial depreciation charges). Such a firm can use its cash flow to reinvest in more profitable ventures, or it can pay out partial liquidating dividends to shareholders. If it is likely that either of these events will transpire, the analyst should include the possibility in his appraisal. Firms that do not have a large cash flow but do have large working capital positions (particularly cash) may also have the option of converting into higher yielding assets or paying a liquidating dividend. It usually requires a change in management for this to occur, however.

Example

1. An analyst has projected the EPS stream for the Leafy Tobacco Co. for the next five years:

2015	$0.30
2016	0.28
2017	0.26
2018	0.28
2019	0.30

   The firm pays a $0.24 dividend per year and has done so for 10 years. The stock now sells for $3 per share, and the current P/E multiple is expected to be maintained in the future. The yield from purchasing Leafy shares for a five-year holding period would be, at 8 percent,

   $$(3.99)(\$0.24) + (0.681)(\$3) = \$3.00.$$

2. Leafy (above) has a book value of $5 per share and a net cash value (cash minus all liabilities) of $1.50 per share. The analyst feels that Leafy could pay out a partial liquidating dividend, but management shows no disposition toward this idea. Furthermore, there appears to be no chance that a new management team will take over in the near future. More likely, current management has shown some interest in diversifying into the manufacture of candy where it is felt that a return of at least 10 percent could be earned (net). Suppose the diversification took place in two years and the current net cash value per share were invested. Reprojected EPS would be:

   $$(0.10)(\$1.50) = \$0.15$$

2015	$0.30
2016	0.28
2017	0.41
2018	0.43
2019	0.45

3. The analyst believes Leafy would increase its dividend to $0.30 per share in 2018 if the diversification plan were accepted. Furthermore, he believes the market would value Leafy at 12Xearnings in 2019 if the firm diversified. Projected dividends and the 2019 market price given these assumptions would be:

	DPS	Market Price
2015	$0.30	
2016	0.28	
2017	0.26	
2018	0.28	
2019	0.30	(12) ($0.45) = $5.40

4. The return earned on Leafy stock if the diversification plan were adopted and the analyst's assumptions proved to be correct would be, at 20 percent:

(0.833) ($0.24) = $0.20
(0.694) (0.24) = 0.17
(0.579) (0.24) = 0.14   The return would be just
(0.482) (0.30) = 0.14   under 20 percent.
(0.402) (0.30) = 0.12
(0.402) (5.40) = 2.17
                 $2.94

5. The analyst believes the probability that the firm will diversify is 0.2. The expected return and the standard deviation of the two possible outcomes would be:

$$(0.8)(8.0) = 6.4 \qquad 8.0 - 10.4 = (-2.4)^2 = 5.76(0.8) = 4.61$$
$$(0.2)(20.0) = 4.0 \qquad 20.0 - 10.4 = (9.6)^2 = 92.16(0.2) = \underline{18.43}$$
$$\overline{10.4} \qquad\qquad\qquad\qquad\qquad\qquad\qquad 23.04$$
$$\mu = 10.4\%$$
$$\sigma = \sqrt{23.04} = 4.8\%.$$

Stock Prices and the Issuance of New Shares

The dynamic aspects of common stock analysis pose some of the more perilous problems for the analyst. This is particularly true because many analysts think in static terms and find it hard to cope with the secondary and tertiary effects of a change in a variable. Perhaps the greatest confusion is evidenced over the subject of issuing new shares. When a firm goes to the market to sell additional shares, the obvious short-run consequence is a reduction of current earnings per share. *Dilution* is the term applied to this phenomenon, and many analysts feel that the effect of issuing new shares (and the subsequent dilution) will depress share prices. Thus, if XYZ has 1 million shares outstanding selling at $20 per share and it sells another 100,000 shares, one might suppose that the price per share would fall (see Figure 7.1). Suppose XYZ earned $1.00 per share ($1 million). If another 100,000 shares were issued, the adjusted EPS would be:

$$1,000,000/1,100,000 = \$0.91.$$

If a multiple of $20X$ were applied to the adjusted earnings, a price of $(20)(0.91) = \$18.20$ would prevail. Thus, the shift in the XYZ share supply curve from S to S' would tend to depress the stock's price.

Of course, only part of the story has been told. It is usually the case that the secondary effects of selling new shares are very positive, and the real position of the firm may *improve* rather than deteriorate as a result of the issue. The sale of new shares may allow the firm to raise needed capital to expand facilities, improve sales, and increase long-run profits. If long-run EPS *increase* by an amount larger than the short-run dilution produced by the creation of new shares, the price of the firm's stock should *rise* rather than fall. Suppose XYZ earnings increased to a long-run EPS of $1.05 as a result of the new share issue. It might be expected here that demanders would begin *bidding up* share prices given these improved expectations.

In fact, if the multiplier of $20X$ held, we might expect the stock price to *rise* to: (20) ($1.05) = $21. This would be affected by a shift in the demand curve from D to D' (see Figure 7.1). Although it cannot be argued that every new issue of shares will produce increases in long-run earnings sufficient to offset the dilution effect, one should not merely assume that a new issue will depress prices. Rather, one should attempt to assess the long-run impact on earnings resulting from raising new capital.

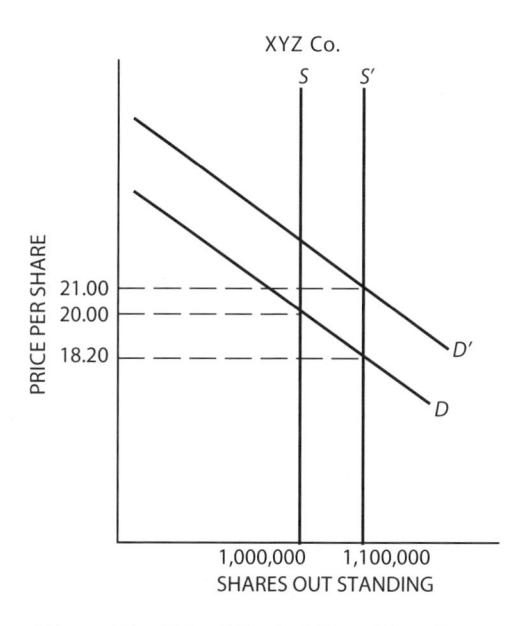

Figure 7.1. Price Effect of New Share Issue

Example

Cameo, Ltd. has 10 million shares outstanding. An analyst has forecasted revenues, EPS, and DPs for the next four years under the assumption that the firm's asset investment will grow only by the amount of earnings retained. His projections are given below:

Year	Revenue (000)	Total Expenses (000)	EPS	DPS
2015	$100,000	$80,000	$2.00	$1.00
2016	120,000	90,000	3.00	1.50
2017	150,000	105,000	4.50	2.00
2018	200,000	130,000	7.00	3.00

The firm has an asset investment of $50 million in 2015. Retained earnings for 2015 are projected at $10 million. Thus, the asset investment for 2016 is forecasted at $60 million. Retained earnings for 2016 are expected to be $15 million. The asset investment for 2017 is thus projected to be $75 million. Retained earnings are projected at $25 million for 2017. The asset investment for 2018 is forecasted to be $100 million. Notice that the analyst is assuming a constant asset turnover for each year:

Year	Revenue (000)	Total Assets (000)	Turnover
2015	$100,000	$50,000	$2X$
2016	120,000	60,000	$2X$
2017	150,000	75,000	$2X$
2018	200,000	100,000	$2X$

He is also using the following net income equation:

$$\text{Net income} = \text{sales} - (30{,}000{,}000 + 0.5\,\text{sales}).$$

Now, suppose Cameo sells at $105 per share. The analyst believes the current P/E multiple is high but justifiable in light of the earnings pattern predicted for 2015–2018. He does not feel the expected growth rate beyond 2018 will match the 50 percent compounded annual rate of earnings-per-share growth forecasted for 2015–2018, however. Thus, he expects the multiple to fall to about 20 times earnings in 2018. Given the analyst's expectations, the stock would yield: At 9 percent,

$$(0.917)(1.00) + (0.842)(1.50) + (0.772)(2.00)$$
$$+ (0.708)(3.00) + (0.70)(140.00) = \$104.96.$$

Cameo has announced an offering of 500,000 new shares to current stockholders at $100 per share. The dilution of projected EPS resulting from the offering would be:

		EPS
2015	20,000,000/10,500,000 =	$1.90
2016	30,000,000/10,500,000 =	2.86
2017	45,000,000/10,500,000 =	4.28
2018	70,000,000/10,500,000 =	6.67

Cameo plans to expand immediately with the $50 million it has raised. The analyst feels that the firm will have excess capacity for a while. He projects an asset turnover of $1.8X$ in 2015 and 2016, $1.9X$ in 2017, and $2.0X$ in 2018. His new net income equation is:

$$\text{Net income} = \text{sales} - (60,000,000 + 0.5 \text{ sales}).$$

Re-projected total assets, revenues, total expenses, EPS and DPS for Cameo over 2015–2018 assuming dividends are about one-half earnings would be:

Year	Total Assets (000)	Revenues (000)	Expenses (000)	EPS	DPS
2015	$100,000	$180,000	$150,000	$2.86	$1.43
2016	115,000	207,000	163,500	4.14	2.12
2016	136,750	259,825	189,913	6.66	3.33
2018	171,706	343,412	231,706	10.64	5.32

Suppose the market felt that the risk offered by investing in Cameo had not changed and that 9 percent was still an adequate return from the security. What price should the stock *advance to* at the time of the new offering, given the above forecast?

$$(0.917)(1.43) + (0.843)(2.12) + (0.772)(3.33) + (0.708)(5.32)$$
$$+ (0.708)(212.80) = \$160.10.$$

Thus, rather than declining, Cameo stock should in fact *rise* as a result of the new share offering.

Another area that presents problems for many analysts is the evaluation of *common stock dividends* and *stock splits*. The payment of a stock dividend is merely a method by which the firm "capitalizes" retained earnings into the permanent capital accounts (common stock, and common stock excess over par). For some firms, such as commercial banks, the transfer of retained earnings into permanent capital may be required by law. For most firms, however, the payment of a stock dividend is simply a way of distributing more shares to the existing stockholders. No real economic change occurs from the distribution. The net worth of the firm does not alter, and shareholders maintain the same percentage ownership in the firm after the declaration of a stock dividend that they had before it. The only real difference is that shareholders have a greater number of shares, which, of course, should be worth proportionately less per share.

Although there is no economic reason for most firms to pay stock dividends, many do pay them. Some managements believe they can fool shareholders by paying out stock rather than cash. Others contend that investors in high tax brackets prefer stock dividends to cash dividends because the extra stock accruing from a stock dividend may be sold if funds are needed. Nevertheless, it would not be necessary that a stock dividend be paid for the investor to obtain funds. He could simply sell some of his original holding of shares. Even if the stock had appreciated in value since his purchase, he would be equally well off by selling a percentage of his original holding as by receiving an equivalent percentage as a stock dividend which he would liquidate.

Splitting a firm's stock is similar to a stock dividend in that the real economic position of the investor does not change. He has more pieces of paper, but his percentage ownership in the firm is the same. The stock split does have an accounting effect in that the par value of the stock is reduced by the inverse of the split (a 2:1 split reduces the par value by one half), but this change is not terribly important. Par value has absolutely no meaning in terms of stock price value (except when a firm issues shares below their par value), and many companies no longer assign par values to their stock.

Three arguments are made to justify splits economically. The first is that splits are an omen of growth (or at least a "signal" that the firm's board of directors expects such). The second is that cash dividends may increase after a split. The third is that investors prefer shares selling in some optimal price range (usually $20 to $80). The first argument is without merit because the *rate* of sales and earnings growth will be the same regardless of the number of shares the firm has outstanding. Only the sale of *new* shares, which brings in added capital for investment, can affect sales and earnings growth. The second argument is behaviorally correct in that many firms do increase their dividend payout after a split. Nevertheless, an increase in payout can be accomplished without a split. Furthermore, if the firm is growing rapidly, a better policy would be to *reduce* the payout and reinvest in profitable projects. This might positively affect the well-being of shareholders more than the payment of a cash dividend! The third argument is the only real justification for a split. If investors really do prefer stocks selling in some given range, when a stock price advances out of that range it should be split. It is hard to imagine, however, that many investors would rather have 100 shares at $50 per share than 10 shares at $500. The investment is $5,000 regardless. Many of today's popular growth issues such as Google, Apple, Netflix, Baidu, and Berkshire Hathaway, trade at prices well over $100 per share, and the brokerage commission may be actually *less* for the same dollar investment in higher-priced shares than lower-priced ones. Of course, at very high prices (one share at $5,000, for example), share divisibility becomes impossible, and some investors are priced out of the market. There is little argument that shares selling at these prices should be split, unless management wishes to keep the shares out of the hands of small investors. The latter policy will undoubtedly produce a lower total market value for the firm.

Although the accounting and economic effects of the stock split are of questionable significance, many analysts and investors alike greet the news of a pending split enthusiastically. Of course, this fact in itself may justify the decision of a firm to split its shares by producing a self-fulfilling prophecy. Nevertheless, the only real effect of a split is the creation of more shares, which should sell at lower prices. It seems obvious that an investor who owns 100 shares of a stock selling at $10 per share, earning $1, and paying $0.50 in cash dividends would be no better off owning 200 shares of the same stock selling at $5 per share, earning $0.50, and paying $0.25 in dividends.

Example

1. A firm has the following capital structure:

Common stock ($10 par, one million shares)	$10,000,000
Common stock, excess over par	20,000,000
Retained earnings	70,000,000
	$100,000,000

The firm declares a 10 percent stock dividend. For stock dividends less than 20–25 percent, market price rather than book value is used to determine the recapitalization. The firm's market price is $150 per share. The transfer of the dividend from retained earnings into permanent capital is thus:

$$(0.10)(150,000,000) = \$15,000,000.$$

The new structure would be:

Common stock ($10 par, 1.1 million shares)	$11,000,000
Common stock, excess over par	34,000,000
Retained earnings	55,000,000
	$100,000,000

2. Suppose the firm above declared a 3:1 split. The capital structure would become:

Common stock ($3.33 1/3 par, 3 million shares)	$10,000,000
Common stock, excess over par	20,000,000
Retained earnings	70,000,000
	$100,000,000

Financial Analysis and Accounting Data

In this section, we issue a caveat to the analyst about the data that he has at his disposal for analysis. The historical numbers that he uses to prepare ratios and forecasting equations are generally based on figures that have been taken from the published financial statements of the firm being analyzed. Although these statements may have been prepared "according to generally accepted accounting principles," there may be significant variation in the real economic meaning of financial reports. Obvious inconsistencies in the methodology of preparation (for example, when a firm switches from LIFO to FIFO inventory valuation, or from accelerated depreciation to straight-line) require adjustments to the documents prepared by the accounting community (see Chapter 4). More subtle problems may exist, however, which cannot easily be handled by making simple adjustments.

One of the more plaguing difficulties with financial statements is that they are prepared on the assumption of stable prices. To the extent that prices change over time, the reported asset values on the firm's balance sheet (and perhaps the liability values as well) will be inaccurate. Further, because accounting costs are usually based on historical prices, a misstatement about the value of an asset may well result in an inaccurate depiction of net income. Moreover, net income in one period may not be equivalent to an identical net income in another if the aggregate level of prices has changed. If a firm earns $1.00 per share in 2014 and $1.05 in 2015, it really has shown no improvement if the overall price level has also risen by 5 percent.

Another problem is that the market values of a firm's assets may have no relationship to their book values. Price-level changes, variances from depreciation estimates, and the insistence of accountants upon valuing assets at the lower of cost or market (an example of the doctrine of "conservatism") make the balance sheet an unreliable statement about the value of the enterprise. Of course, the accountants themselves beg off, claiming that financial analysts expect too much from published statements. One respected former practitioner (Howard Ross, see references) has observed:

> "... accountants in their most solemn pronouncements have made it quite clear that the financial statements they prepare do not even purport to provide information about solvency and profitability. For instance, anyone might be pardoned for thinking that a conventional balance sheet is prepared to show the financial strength of a company by listing its obligations against its resources and to establish its net value. But this not at all how a balance sheet is defined in accounting texts" (p. 9).

Thus, when the analyst finds that return on total investment has increased from 20 percent to 21 percent, it is not clear that an improvement has taken place. Earnings figures from one year to the next (and across firms for any given year) are not strictly comparable, and total investment can become completely incomparable over time.

What is the unfortunate analyst to do under such circumstances? The answer, of course, is to make the best of the situation. Adjustments to published statements should be made whenever there is good justification to do so. Otherwise, the analyst should always bear in mind the limitations of the data that are being used in making an appraisal. A report based on less-than-perfect data is better than no report at all. Security analysis has always been a tentative undertaking. It is perhaps less so today than it was 50 years ago. Nevertheless, all the powerful statistical tools that the analyst now has at his disposal have not reduced the process to a scientific procedure. Analysis is an artful endeavor. It has been in the past and will always be a matter of rational guess work.

Convertible Securities

There are a variety of instruments that may be converted into or exchanged for common stock. Warrants, common stock subscription rights, purchase and sale options, and convertible securities are the most important examples. The valuation of any instrument that has the potential of becoming common stock must, of course, depend on initial evaluation of the common shares of the company in question. The underlying value of semi-equities also depends on other variables. In this chapter, we shall assume that a complete evaluation of the firm's common shares has been made according to the suggested methods outlined above. The other important variables will be considered as additional determinants of the value of the instrument being analyzed.

Debentures and preferred stocks may have a feature that allows the holder to convert these fixed-income securities into common stock. Convertible bonds and preferreds are very much alike in many respects. Nevertheless, it should be remembered that the interest on convertible bonds is deductible in the computation of the income taxes of the issuer like any other bond and that the coupon payments are a legal obligation that must be met along with sinking-fund requirements if any exist. Convertible preferreds, on the other hand, are similar to straight preferreds in that dividends are declared out of after-tax earnings. Furthermore, dividends on convertible preferreds may be passed during unprofitable years. Many convertible preferreds are cumulative, of course, and all arrearages on such issues must be paid before any common dividends may be issued. Because preferreds are considered to be equity securities, the use of a convertible preferred in a merger would usually constitute a tax-free exchange for the holder.

The convertible security is both a fixed-income instrument and potentially common equity. Thus, it must be analyzed as a bond (or preferred) *and* as common stock. All the evaluation techniques required for scrutinizing a fixed-income security (Chapter 6) plus those employed in this chapter must be called into play when a convertible is being considered. The convertible security contains several added characteristics that are not found in straight bonds or common stocks. A *conversion ratio* will be included in the indenture of the convertible bond (and in the share certificate of the preferred). This ratio indicates the number of common shares that may be obtained from surrendering the convertible instrument to the corporation. For example, a debenture with a conversion ratio of 20 would provide its holder with 20 common shares if the holder elected to convert the bond into common stock. If the bond were a $1,000 par issue, this would mean that for each $50 par amount, one common share would be obtained. The par value divided by the conversion ratio is termed the *conversion price*. Conversion ratios and prices are usually altered to reflect stock dividends and splits, although small stock dividends (3 percent or less) are sometimes ignored.

Because convertible security holders have the advantage over straight bond and preferred holders of sharing in the well-being of the firm if it is a profitable enterprise, one would expect that a price would be paid for the privilege. In general, convertible issues yield less than equivalent straight issues. The coupon on a convertible bond will always be set at a lower rate than would be the case if the issue were straight debt. This is also true for the dividend rate on a convertible preferred.

When a convertible security is sold, the conversion price is usually set somewhat above the current market price of the common stock. The difference between these prices is called the *conversion premium*. Expressed as a percentage, the conversion premium equals: (conversion price less the market price)/(market price). Conversion premiums vary from negligible amounts to more than 25 percent. Unseasoned firms may have to issue convertible securities in order to sell debt at all, and the conversion premium for bonds sold by such concerns would be small. Seasoned companies, on the other hand, will frequently sell convertibles at large premiums during very bullish periods.

The demand for convertibles is enhanced in bull markets by the presence of a number of institutional investors who are prohibited from holding common stocks but who can buy convertible debentures. The added demand from such purchasers tends to increase conversion premiums and to lower yields from what they otherwise might be. Another element of demand that has the same effect is induced by the greater borrowing power available through ownership of convertibles rather than pure equities. In the past, regulated margin requirements have been lower on convertibles than on common shares. Moreover, banks will frequently lend more on a convertible issue than on the underlying issue of common stock. The results may be favorable for the speculator who wishes to improve the leverage position of his portfolio, but they also imply higher premiums and lower yields for convertibles.

The dual nature of the convertible security means that it has two different fundamental values. The *conversion value* accrues from the right to convert the security into common stock. If a bond could be converted into 20 shares of common stock, and the price of the common were $60 per share, the conversion value of the bond would be $1,200. The bond would not sell for less than this price because arbitragers could always buy the bond and convert it into common. The *bond* (or *investment*) *value* derives from the income-generating power of the instrument. This value is the price at which the security would sell even if it had no conversion feature. The value of the instrument as straight debt (or straight preferred) constitutes another floor below which the price of the issue will not fall (regardless of the price of the common stock). A lower price would imply a higher yield than could be obtained on equivalent straight debt (or preferred) securities, and again arbitragers would bid up the price until yields were equalized.

We have observed that a convertible security cannot fall below the greater of its conversion or investment values. It can sell above either of these, however, and it frequently will because of the option value of the instrument. Premiums above floor values are limited for convertibles, however, because most convertibles are callable by the issuing corporation. A convertible may sell above the call price set by the issuer but only because the instrument can be converted into common stock. No one would pay a premium over the conversion value at such prices because a call by the issuer would force conversion. A bond selling well above its call price may very likely be called, and anyone who paid more than the conversion value of the bond would lose the difference.

The theoretical price behavior of a convertible security is illustrated in Figure 7.2. Suppose that a bond has a 10-year maturity remaining and is now callable at 105; it has a coupon of 5 percent and a conversion price of $50 per share; and equivalent straight-debt issues currently yield 6 percent.

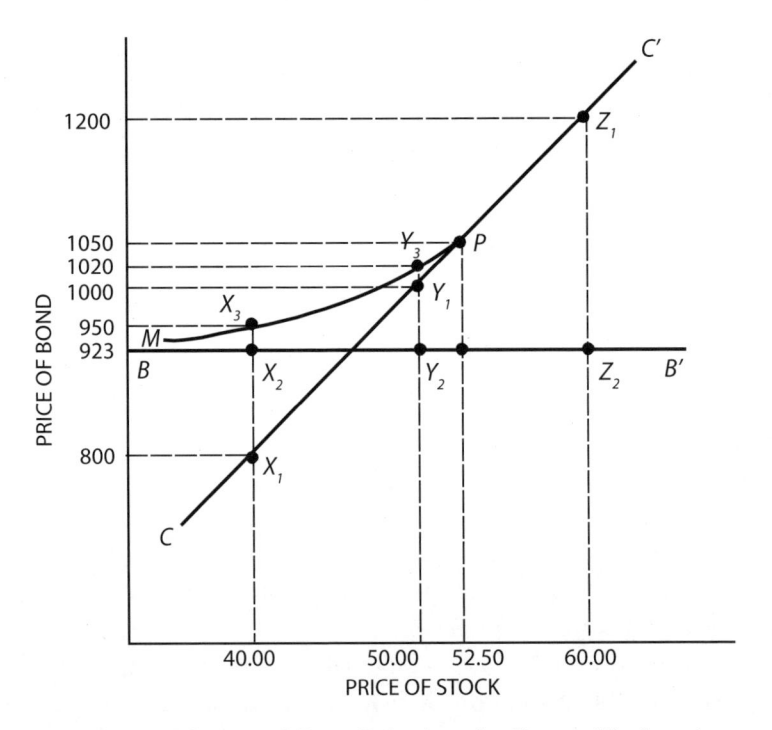

Figure 7.2. Theoretical Price Behavior of a Convertible Security

The investment value of the issue is:

$$0.06 = \frac{50 + \frac{1000-X}{10}}{\frac{1000+X}{2}}$$

$$X = \$923.$$

The bond would not sell below this value unless the yields on equivalent straight-debt issues also fell or the risk of the issuer increased. The bond value floor is given by line BB' in Figure 7.2. Now, let us suppose that the price of the common is $40 per share. The conversion value of the bond would be $(20 \times 40) = \$800$. In Figure 7.2, this is given as point X_1 on line CPC'.

Does this mean that the market price of the bond is $800? Definitely not. The investment value floor is $923 (point X_2 on line BB'). Furthermore, if the market wishes to pay premium for the option value of the bond, it may sell at an even higher price, say $950 (that is, point X_3 on the actual price line MPC').

What would happen at a common stock price of $50? The investment value would not change unless the increase in the price of the stock resulted from a reduction in the riskiness of the firm or a lowering of all market rates of interest. In either of these cases, the yield on equivalent straight-debt issues would fall, and the investment value of the bond would rise. Let us assume, however, that these variables are held constant and that the difference in the stock price occurs for other reasons (see the discussion on the determinants of stock prices above). At a price of $50, the conversion value of the bond would now be $(20\times) = \$1000$ (point Y_1 in Figure 7.2). The investment value would still be $923 (point Y_2). Let us suppose a slight premium continues to exist and that the market price of the bond is $1020.

What would develop at a common stock price of $60? The investment value would remain at $923 (point Z_2). The conversion value would become $(20 \times 60) = \$1200$ (point Z_1), and this would be the market price of the issue. No one would pay more because the issue would have been in the callable range beyond a price of $1050. Hence, at point P the market price line MPC' would join the conversion value line CPC'. When the market price of the common stock advanced to $52.50, the conversion value of the bond would exactly equal the call price. Market bond prices could be justified above this price only to the extent that the market price of the common stock also advanced.

The conversion of a security into common stock may occur for two reasons: (1) the convertible may be called by the issuing corporation; and (2) the yield from holding common stock may exceed the yield from holding the convertible. In the first instance, a convertible selling substantially above its call price may be called by the issuer. If this is done, the holder has the option of converting to common or accepting cash payment at the call price. Because the convertible would sell above its call price only if the conversion value of the bond exceeded the call price, the rational investor would always convert into common. Even if she did not (or could not for legal or institutional reasons) wish to hold common stock, it would be wise to convert and sell the common rather than accept the call price cash payment.

The second reason for conversion may best be considered with an example. Suppose an investor holds a convertible bond that has a conversion ratio of 10 and that the common stock of the issuing firm sells at 150. The conversion value of the bond would be $1500. Suppose further that the bond is now callable at 105 ($1050). The bond would sell in the market for $1500, because a call would be a definite possibility. Now, let us assume that the bond is a 4 percent coupon (and thus pays $40 per year in interest) and that the common stock pays a dividend of $5 per share. If one converted into common, the dividend return would be $(10 \times 5) = \$50$. Hence, many holders might decide to convert into common in order to obtain the larger dollar yield. No capital gain potential would be lost, because any percentage appreciation by the convertible would be matched by an exact percentage appreciation in the common. On the downside, however, the common stock could depreciate by a larger percentage than might be observed for the convertible. This is true because at some point a premium above the conversion value may tend to develop for the convertible (the area indicated by the MP segment of line MPC' in Figure 7.2). Furthermore, a lower limit on the price decline of the convertible may be set by the investment value of the security. Thus, if one expected a large percentage depreciation by the common, one might elect to hold the convertible. A wiser policy, of course, would be to sell the convertible if one were all that pessimistic. Indeed, one might also sell the stock short or buy a put (see Chapter 8).

A caveat should be issued concerning the lower limit on the price decline of a convertible. In the past, many investors have bought convertibles believing that the downside risk was minimized for the reasons mentioned above. They were very surprised to find their bonds selling at huge discounts as the price of the underlying common stock plummeted. Their error was in assuming a static situation in which the investment value of the bond did not change as the stock price fell. One reason for a decline in the price of a stock may be a deterioration in the earning capacity of the firm. This will increase the riskiness of the firm and will hence raise the rate that the firm would have to pay on straight-debt issues. This, in turn, will reduce the investment value of all the firm's bonds and thus will increase the downside potential of convertible issues. An increase in the general level of interest rates will produce the same effect. Additionally, price deterioration in the common stock may dampen investor enthusiasm about the future. This will manifest itself in the form of lower premiums above the conversion value. Hence, as stock prices fall, the premiums that convertible holders had been counting on to reduce any decline in convertible prices may tend to disappear.

A valuation model for convertible bonds that is similar to the bond-pricing equation developed in Chapter 6 may be constructed. Reiterating the straight-bond valuation formula:

$$P_0 = \sum_{t=1}^{n} \frac{C_t}{(1+i)^t} + \frac{P_n}{(1+i)^n},$$

where

P_0 is the current price of the bond
C_t is the annual dollar coupon paid on the bond
P_n is the par value of the bond

i is the yield to maturity of the bond
n is the number of years to maturity.

In the case of the convertible, the time horizon for holding the bond will be shorter than the number of years to maturity if the bond is converted. Thus, if a convertible is called, or if an investor elects to convert in order to get a higher dividend yield on the common, the bond would not be held to maturity. A revised equation taking conversion into account would be:

$$P_0 = \sum_{t=1}^{N} \frac{C_t}{(1+k)^t} + \frac{TV}{(1+k)^N}, \qquad (7.46)$$

where TV is the terminal value of the convertible, k is the expected rate of return from holding the convertible, and N is the expected holding period ($N \leq n$).

Two obvious problems develop when considering 7.46 as a valuation model. First, how does one estimate N, the expected holding period? And second, how is the terminal value (TV) of the bond determined? An approach to these problems may be developed. Suppose we let CV_t be the conversion value of a bond at period t. We know from the discussion above that this value must increase approximately linearly with increases in the stock price. Thus, if the current stock price is S_0, growth in the stock price over time would be given by:

$$S_t = S_0(1+g)^t, \qquad (7.47)$$

where S_t is the stock price at period t, g is the annual growth, and CV_t would be given by:

$$CV_t = S_0(1+g)^t R. \qquad (7.48)$$

In Equation (7.48), R is the conversion ratio. Now, if the issuing firm has a policy of calling bonds when the ratio of the market price of the common (S_t) to the conversion price (S_c) reaches a given level, 7.48 could be rewritten as:

$$CV_t = \frac{S_0}{S_c}(1+g)^t M, \qquad (7.49)$$

where M is the issue price of the bond. Notice that M/S_c equals R, the *conversion ratio*.

The TV of the bond would be that price prevailing when the bond is called. When the call takes place, the conversional value CV_t equals TV. Hence,

$$TV = \frac{S_0}{S_c}(1+g)^N M. \tag{7.50}$$

This equation can be solved to find N.

We may consider an example. Suppose the Grant Co. has outstanding an 8 percent debenture that is currently callable at 102. The bond will be callable at 101 in two years and at par in four years. The bond is also convertible into 20 shares of Grant common, which now sells for $25 per share. It is expected that the share price will grow at an annual rate of about 6 percent, and it is believed that the company will call the issue when the price of the common is 20 percent greater than the conversion price. Because the bond is convertible into 20 shares of stock, the conversion price is $1,000/20 = $50. If the current market price of the stock is $25, it will take:

$$\$50 = \$25(1+0.06)^t$$
$$t = 12.$$

years before the common reaches the conversion price. Because it is believed that the company will call the issue only after the price of the common is 20 percent greater than the conversion price (i.e., $60), it will require:

$$\$60 = \$25(1+0.06)^t$$
$$t = 15.$$

years before the bond is called. The conversion value of the bond will equal $(20)(\$60) = \$1,200$ at that time, and this amount must be the price at which the bond will be selling in 15 years. Because the bond is callable at par, no premium would be paid above the conversion value. Thus, the terminal value of the bond would have to equal the conversion value.

An investor who bought the Grant bonds today would expect the following stream over the next 15 years:

$$P_0 = \sum_{t=1}^{15} \frac{80}{(1+k)^t} + \frac{1200}{(1+k)^{15}}.$$

If the bond had a current price of $765, the investor would expect a return of about 12 percent: $(80)(6.811) + (1200)(0.183) = 544.88 + 219.60 = \$764.48$.

Summary

The most difficult task of the security analyst is the appraisal of common stock. The variables involved are more numerous and complicated than in bond analysis, and the forecasting abilities of the analyst become far more crucial. Equities do not promise shareholders a fixed income, and the pattern of flows generated by common stocks is typically volatile. Because equities are risky securities, the expected returns from purchasing them tend to be higher than those earned from bonds. Equity dividend yields have not equaled bond yields in recent years, but the combined returns from dividends and price appreciation have been somewhat greater on the average. Furthermore, all equities are not more risky than bonds. Indeed, the common shares of most blue-chip investment grade companies are less risky than the debt obligations of many other concerns. No one would argue, for example, that the shares of Johnson & Johnson are more risky than the mortgage bonds of many airlines. Of course, Johnson & Johnson common would be a bit more risky than its coveted AAA rated bonds (a rating shared only with Microsoft). Several more U.S. companies enjoyed AAA bond ratings until recent downgrades.

The basic procedure for evaluating equity securities begins very much like the one recommended for bond analysis. First, aggregate economic projections are made. Next, a comprehensive evaluation of the industry in question is prepared. Finally, the future earnings position of the firm is forecasted as far as possible into the future. Probability estimates are attached where appropriate to such significant variables as sales, pertinent cost figures, and most importantly, net income. Because a major element of the cash return generated by a common stock is the dividend it pays, a careful projection of the future dividend policy of the firm must be made. Ratio analysis can be a very useful supplement to the forecasting procedures. Various profit, turnover, and return-on-investment ratios may be computed for the firm in past years and for other comparable enterprises in the industry. These ratios may be used as performance criteria in evaluating the future prospects for the firm.

Dollar returns from common stocks are derived from two sources; (1) the dividends paid by the firm, and (2) the price appreciation of the security. The ability of a firm to pay dividends, of course, depends upon its earning power. A firm that generates only a negligible return on its asset investment will obviously be in no position to pay dividends. Nevertheless, even firms that obtain very good returns on investment sometimes elect not to pay large dividends. Such firms may be able to benefit stockholders more by retaining earnings and reinvesting in profitable assets. This procedure will produce higher earnings in the future and improve the long-run dividend paying potential of the firm. When a firm retains earnings for reinvestment in profitable projects, it improves its long-run earnings stream. This improvement should be reflected in the price of the firm's shares. Thus, by retaining earnings, the firm may in effect raise the price of its stock.

Common shares may be categorized by the above characteristics. The shares of firms that do not generate large returns on their investment in assets but that pay out in cash dividends most of what they do earn are called income shares. These stocks sell almost entirely on a pure dividend yield basis, because appreciation from retained earnings is limited. Income stocks may be above-average-risk securities issued by declining firms that have exhausted their most profitable reinvestment opportunities. Many fire and casualty insurance, undiversified tobacco equities, etc., would be included in this group. On the other hand, income stocks may also be lower-than-average-risk securities issued by firms that have their return on investment regulated by government. These equities, which are usually stable and relatively safe even during periods of recession, may retain earnings and show capital appreciation. Nevertheless, their growth rates are constrained by the regulated rate of return that they are allowed to earn on plant and equipment. The best examples of the low-risk income shares are those of American public utilities. Shares that are stable and relatively recession-proof are also called defensive shares. All defensive shares are not income stocks, however. Food and drug companies are considered to be defensive securities, and their dividend yields are generally low. Their shares also have growth potential. Gold mining and distillery stocks are also typically classified as defensive stocks, and many of these securities (particularly the gold mining shares) pay no dividends at all.

Equities that evidence marked volatility in their sales, earnings, and dividend patterns are called cyclical shares. Aggregate economic activity has a distinct impact on the performance of these securities, and their evaluation depends on an accurate forecast of the business cycle. Typical cyclical shares include most steel, airline, automobile, railroad, and capital-goods-producer stocks. Another major category of common shares is the blue-chip stocks. Equities of the largest concerns that have long and unbroken records of earnings and dividend payments fall into this category. Blue-chip stocks are rated A+ and A by S&P and are considered to be the lowest overall risk form of common share. The evaluation of most blue chips may be approached in the same manner as that for the analysis of cyclical shares. The problems associated with terminal-date pricing are not so significant in the case of these stocks, however. Even those blue chips that are also cyclical stocks do not have wide movements in reported earnings per share. Many high-grade blue chips are income stocks and some are even growth stocks. The blue-chip companies are household words, such as Exxon Mobil, Johnson & Johnson, and Microsoft.

An equity that evidences much-better-than-average increases in sales and earnings for a consistent period of time is called a growth stock. These shares outperform the economy and most other equities in their respective industries. Growth companies typically pay negligible dividends because they can do better for their shareholders by retaining earnings and reinvesting in plant and equipment. They are aggressive in their search for new, profitable opportunities, and they typically spend a great deal on research and development. Many growth stocks are also blue chips, with such stock market stars as Apple and Microsoft as prime examples.

When a stock shows a sustained earnings growth pattern over a long period of time, the dividend-paying potential of the security increases. For this reason, shareholders are willing to pay large P/E multiples for growth stocks. Indeed, some of the leaders among the growth equities have sold at 50 and even 100 times current earnings. Although most investors who pay these prices for growth securities believe that they are purchasing equities for capital gains, they are in fact buying a growing expected future dividend stream. Price appreciation occurs, of course, and this is due to the improved dividend paying abilities of the firm. Even though the firm may pay no dividend for years, as it retains earnings and grows, the fact that it could pay a larger dividend (and eventually will when its growth rate declines) produces the share price appreciation.

In many cases, it is possible for a company to grow and acquire assets over time by the acquisition of other firms. The attractiveness of such an acquisition is a function of the profitability of the assets (both tangible and intangible) to be acquired and the form and amount of payment to be made. Mergers may occur for any number of reasons. Perhaps the oldest and strongest motivation is the simple desire to increase power over the market. The increased market power resulting from a merger may raise profits through "operating economies," such as bulk purchases, reciprocal purchases, advertising discounts, better channels of distribution (everything from more freight cars when needed to more shelf space), and better access to and bargaining position for external funds. Merger also allows a firm to acquire large numbers of talented management and research personnel and at the same time to gain increased market power to sell whatever they produce.

In other cases, merger may occur because the acquired company is a bargain; poor management, inadequate capital, stock market disfavor, a poor year, or other factors may reduce the price of the stock to the point that the firm is worth a great deal more than the cost of acquiring it. The acquired firm may have large sums in the form of liquid assets such that the acquiring firm could raise more money by merging with it than by selling securities on the market. Other arguments for mergers must be examined rather closely. The first is diversification. If a firm is able to acquire other firms whose earnings do not correlate very closely with its own (coefficient of correlation less than $+1$, and the closer to -1 the better), the probability distribution for earnings of the new firm should show less dispersion (be less risky) than for the old firm. If one dollar of earnings for the merged firm is less risky, it should be discounted at a lower rate in imperfect markets. This would result in an increase in the price of the stock and shareholder well-being. The merger would thus serve a valid economic function. It should be pointed out, however, that such diversification could also be achieved by shareholders in their own portfolios.

Much is written about the growth resulting from mergers. To the extent that the merged firms are able to interact and combine their talents to do things that neither could do before (the synergism or "$2 + 2 = 5$" effect), a valid justification for the merger, and perhaps an increase in stock price, may exist. On the other hand, the merger of firms in totally different lines of business with no subsequent interaction may create value through diversification but not through real growth, although growth may appear to occur.

Under very special circumstances, the analyst may wish to consider assets as well as earnings in computing the yield equation. There are instances in which a substantial volume of assets may not produce a large future earnings stream. If it is possible that these assets will be transformed into another form of higher yielding asset, or if it is conceivable that the assets will be distributed to stockholders, then the value of such assets should be assessed.

Firms that maintain large cash balances or that hold substantial amounts of liquid securities will often show a poor earnings record. If it appears possible that the liquidity of these firms will be reduced through the purchase of earnings assets, the analyst should take this into account in projecting the future earnings stream for the firm. Also, if it is possible that the firm will pay a liquidating (or partially liquidating) cash dividend to shareholders, the amount of this distribution should be included in the analyst's yield equation. If a firm maintains its liquidity at the expense of earning assets and it appears that none of this surplus liquidity will be distributed to shareholders, the analyst should not consider the extra liquidity in evaluation except to the extent that substantial liquidity may reduce the riskiness of the firm. Note that high levels of liquidity frequently prompt tender offers to purchase controlling interest in the firm. The effect of these offers is usually to increase the price of the company's shares. If the probability of a tender offer looms significant, the analyst should attempt to quantify its expected value.

Financial companies (banks, insurance companies, and so on) frequently hold large volumes of liquid assets (cash, marketable securities). On occasion, a financial company will have a poor earnings record for this reason. Such firms offer an opportunity for an imaginative management to increase the firm's return on investment by reducing liquidity (switching from cash into mortgages or even consumer loans). When the analyst believes there is a strong chance for such a policy change, he should attempt to quantify the possible results. This is a very difficult task, and it sometimes requires assumptions about management behavior that are always difficult to make. Nevertheless, the analyst who can shrewdly make such judgments is often highly rewarded.

Certain non-financial concerns will have book values that exceed the market price of the firm's shares. Such firms rarely offer good investment returns to investors because their asset holdings are generally worth much less than the stated book values. Historically, American railroads sold at large discounts from book value. They did so because the earning power of their asset holdings was low. Furthermore, the possibility of converting into more profitable assets (or liquidating) was very small because of regulatory constraints. As the railroads consolidated into a few large concerns and as they were basically deregulated, they became very profitable. The surviving roads (especially Union Pacific and BNSF) have produced excellent returns for investors. Indeed, Warren Buffett's Berkshire Hathaway bought the BNSF because its asset values were converted to substantial earning power.

Manufacturing concerns that have substantial assets that produce little cash flow frequently cannot liquidate these assets, except at distress prices. Hence, for all practical purposes, their asset "values" have no real significance. An exception is the firm that generates a large cash flow but that shows negligible net income (perhaps due to substantial depreciation charges). Such a firm can use its cash flow to reinvest in more profitable ventures, or it can pay out partial liquidating dividends to shareholders. If it is likely that either of these events will transpire, the analyst should include the possibility in his appraisal. Firms that do not have a large cash flow but do have large working capital positions (particularly cash) may also have the option of converting into higher yielding assets or paying a liquidating dividend. It usually requires a change in management for this to occur, however.

There are a variety of instruments that may be converted into or exchanged for common stock. Warrants, common stock subscription rights, purchase and sale options, and convertible securities are the most important examples. The valuation of any instrument that has the potential of becoming common stock must, of course, depend on initial evaluation of the common shares of the company in question. The underlying value of semi-equities also depends on other variables. In this chapter, we have assumed that a complete evaluation of the firm's common shares has been made according to the suggested methods outlined in the previous chapters. Debentures and preferred stocks may have a feature that allows the holder to convert these fixed-income securities into common stock. Convertible bonds and preferreds are very much alike in many respects. Nevertheless, it should be remembered that the interest on convertible bonds is deductible in the computation of the income taxes of the issuer like any other bond and that the coupon payments are a legal obligation that must be met along with sinking-fund requirements if any exist. Convertible preferreds, on the other hand, are similar to straight preferreds in that dividends are declared out of after-tax earnings. Furthermore, dividends on convertible preferreds may be passed during unprofitable years. Many convertible preferreds are cumulative, of course, and all arrearages on such issues must be paid before any common dividends may be issued.

The convertible security is both a fixed-income instrument and potentially common equity. Thus, it must be analyzed as a bond (or preferred) and as common stock. All the evaluation techniques required for scrutinizing a fixed-income security plus those employed in this chapter must be called into play when a convertible is being considered. The convertible security contains several added characteristics that are not found in straight bonds or common stocks. A conversion ratio will be included in the indenture of the convertible bond (and in the share certificate of the preferred). This ratio indicates the number of common shares that may be obtained from surrendering the convertible instrument to the corporation. The par value divided by the conversion ratio is termed the conversion price. Conversion ratios and prices are usually altered to reflect stock dividends and splits, although small stock dividends (3 percent or less) are sometimes ignored. Because convertible security holders have the advantage over straight bond and preferred holders of sharing in the well-being of the firm if it is a profitable enterprise, one would expect that a price would be paid for the privilege. In general, convertible issues yield less than equivalent straight issues. The coupon on a convertible bond will always be set at a lower rate than would be the case if the issue were straight debt. This is also true for the dividend rate on a convertible preferred.

The primary goal of the stock analyst is not to determine the probability of firm bankruptcy, but rather to try to ascertain a fundamental valuation of the worth of the company into perpetuity, which should be reflected in the issue's stock price. This chapter has presented several ways to attempt this valuation. It should be cautioned however that even with the most sophisticated of means to determine this value, the share price will nonetheless vary quite a bit throughout the course of time, even when fundamental analysis shows a steady valuation. These stock market fluctuations are what make the business of investing in stocks so challenging. Fundamental notions of a long-time horizon outlook and diversification (see Chapter 10) will aid the investor in not chasing investment opportunities, but rather to be patient and reap the benefits of time and hard work spent analyzing the investibilty of stocks.

Problems

1. The 2013 and 2014 income statements and balance sheets for Winstone Inc., a manufacturer of ladies apparel (000's) are:

Winstone Inc. Statements of Profit and Loss

	2013	2014
Net sales	$11,486,842	$17,035,617
Less operating expenses:		
Cost of goods sold	10,808,614	15,494,047
Selling expenses	16,871	38,520
Administrative expenses	49,736	57,067
Interest on short-term debt	26,333	92,444
Total operating expenses	10,901,554	15,682,078
Net operating income	585,288	1,353,539
Other income (net)[1]	3,651	47,456
Net income before income taxes	588,939	1,400,995
Less income taxes	266,000	672,000
Net available for common	322,939	728,995
Less common dividends	73,287	146,575
Balance carried to surplus	249,652	582,420
Add surplus beginning of period	711,549	961,201
Surplus end of period	$961,201	$1,543,621

[1] Includes $56,938 in federal taxes refunded in 2013, and $56,996 in taxes refunded in 2014.

Winstone Inc. Balance Sheets

	2013	2014
Current assets:		
Cash	$362,572	$464,360
Accounts receivable	1,389,676	2,046,867
Inventories	3,443,137	5,934,183
Total current assets	$5,195,385	$8,445,410
Fixed assets:		
Net property	$143,803	$223,233
Tools and dies, net	28,415	3,345
Investment in subsidiaries	50,591	81,910
Total fixed assets	$222,809	$308,488
Deferred expenses:		
Prepayments	$46,722	$30,619
Other assets:		
Leasehold improvements	$41,044	$44,708
Misc. deposits, etc.	37,322	46,873
Long-term receivables	—	8,022
Total other assets	$78,366	$99,603
Total assets	$5,543,282	$8,884,120
Current liabilities:		
Accounts payable	$ 984,061	$2,070,703
Notes payable	$1,500,000	2,700,000
Accrued expenses	157,173	293,548
Tax reserve	223,833	545,193
Other current liabilities	26,000	40,000
Total current liabilities	$2,891,066	$5,649,484
Fixed liabilities:	—	—
Net worth:		
Common stock (1 billion shs.)	$1,465,749	$1,465,749
Paid in surplus	225,266	225,266
Earned surplus	961,201	1,543,621
Total net worth	$2,652,216	$3,234,636
Total liabilities and worth	$5,543,282	$8,884,120

Key ratios for Winstone for 2010–2012 and for the industry in 2014 are given as follows:

Ratio	2010	2011	2012	Industry Average
Current	1.4X	1.7X	1.9X	2.6X
Gross margin	0.02	0.03	0.04	0.07
Net margin	(loss)	0.01	0.02	0.03
Total asset turnover	2.1X	2.0X	2.0X	2.0X
Net-earning-power ratio	—	0.02	0.04	0.06
Total debt to equity	0.86	0.94	1.00	0.75
Book value per share	$2.18	$2.27	$2.40	—
Dividend payout	nil	nil	0.30	0.48
P/E multiple	—	42X	20X	14X
EPS	($0.02)	$0.09	$0.19	—

a. Adjust the income statements and balance sheets for 2013 and 2014. Prepare adjusted statements. Reconcile the firm's tax payment in light of the fact that expected taxes should be 50 percent of net income before taxes.
b. Compute the above ratios for 2013 and 2014. Use adjusted data where it is appropriate to do so (that is, net margin, net earning power, dividend payment, and P/E multiple). Compute EPS on an unadjusted and an adjusted basis. The average market price for Winstone shares was $5 in 2013 and $9.375 in 2014.
c. What favorable and unfavorable trends do you observe for Winstone?
d. An analyst has determined the following projection equation for the ladies apparel industry:

$$S_I = 240 + (0.07)\text{CS} + (1.23)\text{WOM}$$

where S_I = industry sales (in millions)

CS = clothing sales (in billions)
WOM = number of women between ages of 14 and 65 (in millions).

The analyst has obtained CS and population forecasts from the Departments of Commerce and Labor. (Note: the numbers are assumed and do not represent actual forecasts by either the U.S. Dept. of Commerce or the Dept. of Labor).

Year	CS (billions)	Women 14–65 (million)
2015	$1,553	90.5
2016	1,620	91.3
2017	1,710	92.1
2018	1,806	91.0
2019	1,926	90.5

Given the above, project industry sales from 2015 to 2019.

e. The following projection equation for Winstone has also been computed:

where

$S_W = -1.54 + (0.05)S_I + (0.02)SEL$
S_W = Winstone sales (in millions)
S_I = industry sales (in millions)
SEL = Winstone selling expenditures (in thousands).

The analyst has found out from Winstone's management that they plan a continued aggressive campaign to increase their share of the market. The selling expense budget is expected to double each year from 2015 to 2019. From this information, forecast Winstone's sales for 2015–2019.

f. Since Winstone entered the apparel business 12 years ago, its market share has averaged 3.7 percent. In recent years

(2010–2014), there has been a distinct upward trend, however, and the analyst believes the firm could achieve 10 percent of the market eventually. From the forecasts of industry and firm sales, compute Winstone's projected market share from 2015 to 2019. Are these figures consistent with the analyst's expectations about Winstone's eventual potential?

g. The analyst notes that Winstone operated near the break-even point from its inception in 2002 until 2011. The firm lost money during its first five years of operations and also incurred deficits in 2009 and 2010. He is convinced that the enterprise has passed the critical stage, however, and that future years will be profitable. He recognizes that the large improvements in margins experienced from 2010 to 2014 cannot continue and were characteristic of a firm moving away from its break-even point. He feels that the firm should be able to achieve the industry average gross margin in the future, however. If this is true, what would the dollar gross margin be for 2015–2019?

h. In order to make possible the rather large increases in sales that are projected, it is clear that the firm's asset base will have to expand. The firm must carry larger volumes of receivables and inventories in order to compete, and these items will increase along with necessary additions to fixed plant. The analyst expects the asset turnover to be steady at about $2.0X$. If this is the case, how much in added assets will be required from 2015 to 2019?

i. The analyst believes that the short-term debt position of the firm is dangerously high. Management argues, however, that the high percentage of current to fixed assets allows the firm to have substantial amounts of short-term liabilities. Management points to the low cost of this source of finance (only $92 thousand was paid in interest in 2014, even though liabilities equaled $5.6 million). It appears that management will not consider a long-term debt issue and will finance future growth out of retained earnings and increases in current liabilities. The analyst has prepared *pro forma* statements for 2015 with this in mind:

Winstone Inc. Pro forma Statement Profit and Loss, 2015 (in millions)		Winstone Inc. Pro forma Balance Sheet, 2015 (in millions)	
Sales	$23,000	Total assets	$11,500
CGS	21,390		
Gross margin	1,610		
Selling expense	77	Current liabilities	$ 7,726
Adm. Expense	50	Fixed liabilities	—
Interest	112	Common stock	1,466
Net operating income	1,371	Paid in surplus	225
Other income (net)	(23)	Earned surplus	2,083
Net income before tax	1,348		$11,500
Taxes (50%)	674		
Net available for common	674		
Less common dividends	135		
Balance to surplus	539		
Add surplus, BOY.	1,544		
Surplus, EOY	$ 2,083		

Note:

(1) Gross margin equals 0.07 sales.
(2) Selling expense is assumed equal to the budgeted amount (as projected above).
(3) Administrative expenses are assumed to be $50,000 for 2015 and are expected to increase by about $20,000 annually.
(4) Interest is assumed to equal 2.0 percent of the total current liabilities of the previous year.

(5) Other income is assumed to be -$23,000 in 2015, and zero thereafter.
(6) Taxes equal 50 percent of NIBT.
(7) The dividend payout ratio is assumed to be 0.20.
(8) Total assets equal 0.5 sales.
(9) Common stock and paid in surplus are assumed constant.

From the above data, construct *pro forma* income statements and balance sheets for 2016–2019.

j. Recapitulate EPS and DPS as follows:
   (1) Reported, 2011–2014
   (2) Adjusted, 2013–2014
   (3) Projected, 2015–2019.

k. Categorize Winstone as an income, defensive, cyclical, blue-chip, and/or a growth stock.

l. What is Winstone's current dividend yield (2014)?

m. Winstone has an S&P rating of B+. Between now and 2019, it is expected that the firm will become a much larger firm and will be somewhat less risky. The high level of current liabilities will leave the firm more risky than others in the same industry, however. It is expected that interest rates will not change appreciably by 2019. Determine a reasonable P/E multiple for 2019 earnings.

n. Price the stock for 2019, given the multiple you selected above.

o. Winstone may be purchased today at $9.375. From the projections made above, what rate of return would an investor expect from Winstone during 2015–2019? (Assume the dividend is paid annually and that the 2014 dividend has already been paid).

2. Amalgamated Telephone pays an annual dividend of five dollars. The firm has a stable earnings record and does not anticipate changing the dividend in the future.

   a. If an investor wished to earn 8 percent on Amalgamated, how much would he pay per share?

   b. Suppose the market price of Amalgamated were $50 per share. How much would it yield?

c. If market rates of interest increased such that investors felt Amalgamated should yield 12.5 percent, at what price would it sell?
d. Suppose an investor bought Amalgamated at 50. He held the stock for 10 years and earned a return of 10 percent. If the stock just paid a dividend, at what price did the investor sell the stock at the end of 10 years?
e. Amalgamated was purchased at 50. The lowest possible return an investor would accept on the investment is 6 percent. If the dividend were maintained, how far could the price of the stock decline in 10 years so that just 6 percent would be realized? What would have to be the expected return on Amalgamated from year 10 onward for the price to prevail?

3. Supergrow, Ltd., is expected to pay no dividends for 10 years. From year 11 and thereafter, the firm is expected to pay three dollars per share annually. If investors require a 12 percent return for holding Supergrow, what price pattern would the stock evidence? What pattern would prevail if the firm paid a dividend of one dollar for years one to five, two dollars for six to ten, and three dollars thereafter? What pattern would prevail if the firm paid three dollars throughout?

4. The Uni Corp. currently has the ability to pay a dividend of two dollars per year forever. By retaining all earnings for 10 years, however, a dividend of $10 per year forever could be paid beginning in year 11. If Uni shareholders require a 15 percent return, what would be the current price of the stock under each of the policies?

5. A firm pays a dividend of one dollar per share. The market price of the firm's shares is 20, and the market expects dividends to grow by 10 percent annually. What return would investors obtain from purchasing this security, assuming a constant future dividend payout ratio and P/E multiple?

6. Equatoroid, Ltd., is a growth company. The firm is primarily financed by retained earnings, pays 50 percent of earnings in taxes, and earns 25 percent on its asset investment. If the firm retains 80 percent of its earnings, what is its rate of growth?

7. Suppose Equatoroid finances with debt as well as equity. The firm tries to maintain a debt-equity ratio of 0.4. What would its growth rate be if it paid bondholders a rate of 6 percent?

8. A simplified income statement and balance sheet for Dynamic Sinculator is given below:

Income Statement		Balance Sheet	
Revenues	$100,000,000	Assets	$50,000,000
Expenses	59,000,000		
EBIT	41,000,000	Bonds	$20,000,000
Interest	1,000,000	Net worth	30,000,000
EBT	40,000,000		$50,000,000
Taxes	20,000,000		
N.I.	20,000,000		
Dividends	4,000,000		
R.E.	$16,000,000		

Other data

    Market price per common share $80
    Number of shares outstanding   5 million

a. Compute the following relationships:

(1) EBIT/Total assets
(2) Debt/Equity
(3) Retention rate
(4) Average tax rate
(5) EPS
(6) DPS
(7) P/E multiple
(8) Dividend yield
(9) Coupon rate on bonds

b. Assuming that all the relationships are constant in the future, determine the dividend growth rate for Dynamic Sinculator.

c. What would the earnings growth rate be? The rate of growth in the share price?
d. What would the annual growth in assets be?
e. What would the growth in sales be, given a constant total-asset turnover?
f. What return would investors expect from a purchase of Dynamic, given the above assumptions?
g. Would this sort of return be a feasible expectation? What difficulties might arise?

9. International Transportation and Telecommunication has 10 million shares outstanding and earns $2 per share. As a "growth" conglomerate, the firm's stock sells at 50 times current earnings. The Sinking Offshore Shipping Co. has 5 million shares outstanding and sells at $10 per share based on current EPS of $1. International plans to merger with S.O.S. by offering shares in the ratio of current market prices.

a. What is the ratio of exchange of International shares for S.O.S. shares?
b. How many International shares would be outstanding after the merger?
c. What will be the new International EPS?
d. What apparent "growth" has taken place?
e. Given the fact that International is heavily engaged in transportation, what diversification effects might the merger make possible?
f. Suppose the merged company were riskier than the premerger International. What price and P/E multiple might an efficient market pay for the merged company's stock?
g. Suppose the market retained the old P/E multiple that existed for premerger International. What would the new market price of the merged company be?
h. Trace the "growth effect" if International could find yet another Sinking Offshore Shipping Co.

10. An investor is in the 50 percent marginal income tax bracket. She pays capital gains taxes at a rate of 25 percent. She is considering

the purchase of a stock that now sells at $100 per share. The stock has an EPS of $4, which should grow by 10 percent compounded annually. The stock pays a dividend of $1, which should be increased to $1.20 after two years and to $1.50 for the fifth year of holding. The investor believes the current P/E multiple will prevail in five years when she plans to sell the stock. If the investor wants to earn at least 6 percent on her investment *after taxes*, should she purchase the shares?

11. An analyst has prepared the following sets of probability distributions for a stock (sales and costs in millions):

	Years 1–2	Year 3
Sales	25 (0.4)	30 (0.3)
	30 (0.6)	40 (0.7)
Costs	0.6 of sales (0.5)	0.6 of sales (0.5)
	0.7 of sales (0.5)	0.7 of sales (0.5)

a. Prepare net income and EPS distributions for the three years. The firm has 10 million shares outstanding.
b. The analyst expects the firm to pay out one-third of earnings in dividends. Determine the expected dividend and its standard deviation for years 1–3.
c. The following P/E multiple distribution is anticipated by the analyst for year 3.

P/E Multiple	Probability
16X	0.4
18X	0.6

Determine the distribution of market prices for year 3.
d. Compute the expected market price and standard deviation for year 3.

e. Suppose an investor wished to earn 20 percent on this stock. What maximum price would she pay today, given the expected values of the dividend and terminal price distributions?
f. Assume the stock currently sells at the price to yield 20 percent. Determine the standard deviation of the present value price distribution if the returns are assumed to be independent. Determine overall σ assuming the returns are perfectly correlated.
g. Assume the stock sells at $16. What is the probability that a return below 20 percent will be earned?

12. An investor expects the following returns from an investment:

Year	Dividend	Terminal Selling Price
1	$\mu = \$10, \sigma = \$1$	
2	$\mu = 10, \sigma = 1$	
3	$\mu = 10, \sigma = 1$	
4	$\mu = 10, \sigma = 1$	
5	$\mu = 10, \sigma = 1$	$\mu = \$100, \sigma = \$10$

a. For $i = 8$ percent, what is the present value of the returns, assuming the distributions are independent?
b. What is standard deviation of the distribution?
c. If the current price of the security is $94, what is the probability that the investor will earn less than 8 percent?

13. An analyst has simulated the future performance of a security. She has obtained a distribution with $\mu_i = 12$ percent and $\sigma = 4$ percent.

a. If the distribution is approximately normal, what is the probability that the investment will lose money?
b. What is the probability that the return will be 12 percent or greater?
c. What is the probability that the return will exceed 20 percent?

d. Suppose the distribution of returns for the security were positively skewed. Might this influence the analyst's judgment about the riskiness of the security? What if it were negatively skewed? Can you suggest a better measure of risk in these instances?

14. The Old Conservative National Bank has demonstrated the following earnings and dividend pattern for the past 10 years:

	EPS	DPS
2005	$1.18	$0.90
2006	1.20	0.90
2007	1.23	0.90
2008	1.19	0.90
2009	1.23	0.90
2010	1.27	0.90
2011	1.30	1.00
2012	1.24	1.00
2013	1.26	1.00
2014	1.30	1.00

The 2014 balance sheet for the bank is given below (in millions):

Cash	$20	Demand deposits	$50
Marketable securities	50	Term deposits	60
Loans	50	Common stock (1 million shs)	20
Investments	30	Surplus	10
Banking house	10	Undivided profit	20
Total assets	$160	Total liab. & worth	$160

The bank earned an average of 5 percent on its marketable securities in 2014, 10 percent on its loans, and 8 percent on its investments. It also earned $1 million in gains on its portfolio and grossed $3.5 million from customer services. The bank incurred operating costs of $9.9 million and paid an average rate of 2.18 percent on its demand and term deposits. Its average tax rate is 50 percent.

a. Reconstruct the bank's 2014 income statement.
b. Old Conservative maintains a 20 percent reserve requirement against demand deposits and a 4 percent reserve against term deposits. What are its excess reserves? (Note: Legal reserves consist of bank vault cash plus deposits held with the district Federal Reserve Bank.)
c. Suppose the bank placed its excess reserves in new loans. What would be its added net return?
d. In addition to placing its excess reserves in new loans, suppose the bank generated $1,000,000 in new demand deposits, set aside the appropriate reserves, and invested the balance in new loans. If the cost of generating the new accounts and making the new loans were $40,000, what added return would the bank earn?
e. Suppose the bank reduced its marketable security investment by $20 million and placed $20 million more in loans. How much added net income would be earned?
f. Old Conservative now sells for $20 per share. The stock price has increased at the same rate as long-run earnings (about 2 percent per year). What return have investors been getting?
g. An analyst believes there is a chance that a change in corporate control with a new management team is about to take over at Old Conservative. If this happens, the policies outlined in c, d, and e above will be adopted. Forecast 2015 earnings assuming the new management takes over (assume all other variables except those affected by the policy changes will remain constant).
h. What factors positively affecting the bank's P/E multiple would exist if the policy changes were made? What negative factors?
i. Suppose the P/E remained constant. Project the price of the shares at the end of 2015 if the policy changes are made.

j. What return would an investor earn from purchasing the shares if the price indicated above were obtained? Assume an increase in the dividend for 2015 to $1.50 per share.
k. The analyst feels the probability that management will change is about 0.4. Determine the expected return and the standard deviation of the two possible outcomes.

15. Jiminex, Inc., earned $30 million in 2014. Projections for 2015 indicate a net income of $33 million. The firm has 5 million shares outstanding, pays out about three-quarters of net income in common dividends, and sells at $60 per share.

    a. Compute EPS and DPS for 2014 and projected EPS and DPS for 2015.
    b. Investors expect Jiminex to evidence earnings increases at about 10 percent annually for a long time. What is the current return from purchasing Jiminex shares?
    c. Suppose Jiminex sells 1 million new shares at the current market price. What earnings and dividend dilution would result?
    d. An analyst believes that the capital raised by Jiminex will increase its earnings growth rate to 12.5 percent. If the market agrees with this analysis and is willing to continue to accept the same return as before (calculated in b above), what must happen to the price of Jiminex shares?

16. An investor bought 100 shares of Amalgamated Rubbish two years ago. He paid $90 per share then, and the stock now sells at $100. The stock paid a $5 cash dividend last year and will soon do so again.

    a. When the stock pays its cash dividend, what should happen to the stock price?
    b. Suppose Amalgamated declares a 5 percent stock dividend in place of the cash dividend. What should happen to the price of the stock?
    c. What tax would the investor pay on his cash dividend if he is in the 25 percent marginal tax bracket for qualified dividends?

d. Suppose a stock rather than a cash dividend were declared. If the stock dividend were 5 percent and the investor elected to sell the extra shares, what would his after-tax return be? (He pays capital gains taxes at a rate of 25 percent).
e. Compare this with his return if a cash dividend were paid.
f. Would your calculation above justify the payment of a stock dividend for tax reasons?

17. Suppose Amalgamated (above) were split 5 for 1. What should the new market price be? (Assume no dividends, cash or stock, are paid.)
18. Jones owns a ZEX convertible bond, 6s2032. The bond is convertible into 50 shares of ZEX common and is now callable. The current price of ZEX common is $25 per share. The company has just announced the call of the 6s92 at 108. What should Jones do?
19. Smith owns an SPC convertible, 3s2018. The bond is convertible into 20 SPC shares. The bond is callable at 110, although the current price of the bond is only 89. SPC common pays a dividend of $2 per share and sells for $40 per share. Should Smith convert?
20. The Iowa Corporation has issued 4 percent convertible debentures (par value $1,000), which may be exchanged for 20 shares of common. The price of the common is $40 per share. What are the conversion ratio, conversion price, and conversion premium of the bond?
21. The Bravo Corporation has issued convertible debentures at a par of $500. They may be exchanged for 20 shares of stock currently selling for $22. What are the conversion ratio, price, and premium?
22. The Smetina Corp. has outstanding a 10-year, 6 percent coupon debenture that is convertible into 100 shares of common. The common stock of Smetina sells for $7 per share, and an equivalent straight-debt issue now yields 8.9 percent to maturity.

a. What is the conversion value of the convertible? The bond (investment) value?

b. The market price of Smetina common when the convertible was sold was $8. If the convertible was sold at par ($1,000), what conversion premium was paid by purchasers?
c. The Smetina convertible sells now at 85. What premium are investors paying beyond the greater of the conversion or investment value of the bond? What accounts for this premium?
d. The Smetina convertible is callable at 104 in two years. If the price of Smetina common rose to $11, at what price would the convertible sell? Would a premium be possible?
e. Suppose Smetina common increased in price over the next year from $7 to $11. Suppose further that the convertible sold in the market at its conversion value. What percentage gain would each security evidence?
f. Suppose Smetina common fell in price to $3 and that the investment value of the convertible did not change. What percentage loss would each security show?
g. Assume that the decline in the price of Smetina common was due to a deterioration in the fundamental position of the firm (an increase in risk) and an increase in general level of interest rates. If the Smetina straight-debt issue now yields 12.5 percent to maturity, what are the new conversion and investment values of the bond?
h. Given the conditions in g above, what percentage loss would the convertible evidence if it sold at no premium over the greater of its investment or conversion value?

23. An analyst has forecasted the following EPS for the Cote Co.:

2015	$1.00
2016	1.20
2017	1.50
2018	2.00
2019	2.50

Cote has typically sold at a P/E multiple of 20X and the analyst expects this multiple to hold in the future. The firm has a policy of paying out about half of its earnings in dividends. Cote has a 4 percent convertible debenture outstanding due in 2019. The bond may be converted into 50 shares of common and would currently yield 6.3 percent as straight debt. The bond is currently callable at 108. The price of Cote common now (2014) is $16 per share.

a. What are the conversion and bond values of the 4s2019?
b. If the bond is called, what should the investor do?
c. Suppose the bond is not called. What annual return would convertible holders expect over the five years remaining to maturity? The current (2014) price of the bond is $962.50.

24. Select a firm from one of the following Global Industry Classification Standard (GICS) industries for analysis:

Aerospace & Defense	Diversified Financial Services
Air Freight & Logistics	
Airlines	Diversified Telecommunication Services
Auto Components	
Automobiles	
Banks	Electric Utilities
Beverages	Electrical Equipment
Biotechnology	Electronic Equipment, Instruments and Components
Building Products	
Capital Markets	
Chemicals	Energy Equipment & Services
Commercial Services & Supplies	
	Food & Staples Retailing
Communications Equipment	Food Products
Construction & Engineering	Gas Utilities
Construction Materials	Health Care Equipment & Supplies
Consumer Finance	
Containers & Packaging	Health Care Providers & Services
Distributors	
Diversified Consumer Services	Health Care Technology

(*Continued*)

(Continued)

Hotels, Restaurants & Leisure	Real Estate Investment
Household Durables	Trusts (REITs)
Household Products	Real Estate Management &
Independent Power Producers	Development
Industrial Conglomerates	Road & Rail
Insurance	Semiconductors &
Internet & Catalog Retail	Semiconductor Equipment
Internet Software & Services	Software
IT Services	Specialty Retail
Leisure Products	Technology Hardware,
Life Sciences Tools & Services	Storage & Peripherals
Machinery	Textiles, Apparel & Luxury
Marine	Goods
Media	Thrifts & Mortgage Finance
Metals & Mining	Tobacco
Multiline Retail	Trading Companies &
Multi-Utilities	Distributors
Oil, Gas & Consumable Fuels	Transportation
Paper & Forest Products	Infrastructure
Personal Products	Water Utilities
Pharmaceuticals	Wireless Telecommunication
Professional Services	Services

a. Examine financial statements for the firm for the past five years. Make appropriate adjustments to the financial statements, and reconcile the firm's actual tax payment with expected taxes.
b. Compute all significant ratios for the firm over the five-year period.
c. Determine a least-squares forecasting equation for the sales of the industry. Use this equation, if appropriate, in preparing a sales forecasting equation for the firm.
d. Project revenues for the industry and the firm for the next five years.

e. Forecast expenses for the firm for the next five years using either least-squares equations or ratio analysis. Estimate net income, EPS, and DPS.
f. Prepare *pro forma* income statements and balance sheets for the forecasting period. Determine probable additions to plant and equipment, and estimate possible sources of finance.
g. Compute the ratios calculated above from the *pro forma* statements. Reconcile any discrepancies between historical patterns and the projected values.
h. Categorize your firm as an income, defensive, cyclical, blue-chip, or growth stock.
i. Determine the current dividend yield for the stock.
j. Examine the historical P/E multiples for the firm. Try to assess the level of interest rates, the riskiness of the firm, and the growth potential for the stock in five years. From these data, project a P/E multiple for earnings at the end of the five-year holding period.
k. Given the current price of the firm's stock and the dividend and terminal price projections made above, compute the return expected from a purchase of the security.

References

Bacon, C. R., *Practical Portfolio Performance Measurement and Attribution*, 2nd edn., Hoboken, NJ: John Wiley & Sons, Inc., 2008.

Cootner, Paul, ed., *The Random Character of Stock Market Prices*. Cambridge: The MIT Press, 1964.

Damodaran, A., *Investment Valuation*, 2nd edn., Hoboken, NJ: John Wiley & Sons, 2002.

Graham, B., D. Dodd, and S. Cottle, *Security Analysis*, 6th edn. New York, NY: McGraw-Hill Book Company, 2009.

Jagannathan, R., A. Malakhov, and D. Novikov, "Do Hot Hands Exist among Hedge Fund Managers? An Empirical Evaluation," *Journal of Finance*, February 2010, pp. 217–255.

Jegadeesh, Narasimham and Sheridan Titman, "Returns to Buying Winners and Selling Losers: Implications for Stock Market Efficiency" *Journal of Finance*, March 1993, pp. 65–91.

Lakonishok, Josef, Andrei Shleifer, and Robert W. Vishny, "Contrarian Investment, Extrapolation, and Risk," *Journal of Finance*, December 1994, pp. 1541–1578.

Malkiel, B. G., *A Random Walk Down Wall Street*, 12th edn., New York, NY: Norton, 2015.

Ross, Howard, *The Elusive Art of Accounting*. New York, NY: The Ronald Press Company, 1966.

Rubinstein M., *A History of the Theory of Investments*. New York, NY: John Wiley & Sons, 2006.

Sharpe, William F., Gordon J. Alexander, and Jeffery V. Bailey, *Investments*, 6th edn., Upper Saddle River, NJ: Prentice Hall, 1999.

Taleb, N., *The Black Swan*. New York: Random House, 2007.

Thompson, J. R., E. E. Williams, and M. C. Findlay, *Models for Investors in Real World Markets*. New York, NY: John Wiley & Sons, 2003.

Williams, E. E. and M. C. Findlay, *Investment Analysis*. Englewood Cliffs, NJ: Prentice Hall, Inc., 1974.

Williams, J. B., *The Theory of Investment Value*. Cambridge, MA: Harvard University Press, 1938.

Chapter 8

Futures and Options

We can easily represent things as we wish them to be.

Aesop

Introduction

This chapter is about futures, options and other derivatives, which might be more aptly described as *speculative securities*. A *futures contract* is a legally binding agreement to buy or sell a commodity or financial instrument at a later date. Futures contracts may be traded on an organized exchange, or on the "over-the-counter (OTC)" market. Exchange-traded contracts are standardized according to the quality, quantity, and delivery time and location for each commodity. The only variable is price. An *option* on a security gives the option buyer the right — but not the obligation — to buy or sell a particular asset at a stated price at any time prior to a specified date. There are two fundamental types of options: *calls* and *puts*. A call option conveys to the option buyer the right to purchase a particular security at a stated price at any time during the life of the option. A put option conveys to the option buyer the right to sell a particular asset at a stated price at any time during the life of the option.

In general, a "derivative" security is simply a contract whose value is determined by the performance of an underlying asset. A philosophical example could be common stock, which is a security laying claim to the earnings and net assets of a corporation. Derivatives may be written or bought on other derivatives, such as an option on a futures contract, or an option on an option.

Examples of speculative securities include:

- A credit default swap (CDS) is essentially an insurance product which pays off if a debt issuer defaults on its obligations. Buying 3-year credit default swaps on Greek sovereign debt back in 2007 would have cost about 15 bps annually, or about $150,000 per annum for CDS on $100 million of Greek debt. At the height of the Greek financial crisis, these CDS were selling for around 5,000 bps (yielding in a 3,333 percent profit). Note that the par value (principal amount) of each bond is 10,000 bps. Thus, no CDS would ever be valued more than that. It is interesting that, in the Greek case cited, purchasers were willing to pay 1/3 of the par value of the instrument simply for insurance.
- Buying puts on UAL and AA the week before the 9–11 attack would have resulted in another tremendous profit opportunity.
- One could have purchased deep out of the money calls (200 points) on AAPL for $14.50 back in January 2012, and in September 2012, they could have been sold for $100+, less the premium paid. Profit on a 10-call position: $85,500 on an investment of $14,500, or about 589 percent return. Profit if buying an equivalent amount of stock (36 shares): $25,375/$14,500 = 175 percent return.
- An option seller on expiration day in January 2013, sells 10 of the February AAPL 450 puts for 70¢, for income production. These were 65 points out of the money, a safe bet for AAPL. Four trading days later, these very puts had to be bought back at $15.06, resulting in a loss of $14.36 per contract, a $14,360 loss on potential gain of only $700, a 1,950 percent flummoxing. Had the trader been foolish enough to sell the February 500 puts at $8.00 each, she would have had to repurchase them at $53.50, for a loss of $45,500.
- Buying 6-month puts on cotton in April 2012, five cents out of the money, would have cost 1.64¢ per contract ($820); 5 months later cotton had dropped 20¢ and each contract had increased in value by $10,000, for a return of 1,219 percent.
- In 2005, when gold broke above $500/oz, the "smart money" loaded up on gold futures and exchange-traded funds (ETF's).

The steady rise of gold from $400 to almost $1,800/oz in 7 years with its compound growth rate of 23.5 percent has been a major success story of alternative investing.

From these examples, it can be seen that fabulous profits (and losses) have been obtained through speculating in common stock and index options, futures and other derivatives. Although it is unlikely that too many people actually bought or sold these instruments at the times indicated in the above illustrations, it is nonetheless true that price movements of large magnitudes have occurred for many derivatives in the past, and the risk-seeking investor, albeit ruin-averse, should consider these instruments as a potentially attractive speculative vehicle.

A famous example

When Ted Turner shocked the world on September 18, 1997 by promising to give $1 billion of his wealth to the United Nations programs over 10 years, he was not going to take any chances that it could cost more than $1 billion. In fact, given his basis in the stock, some could argue that it only cost him around $3 million; indeed, others have mused that his after-tax position *increased* by $100 million. Mr. Turner was quoted as saying "the donation will be made in ten annual installments of $100 million in Time Warner stock". His August 1997 net worth was reportedly about $3.2 billion, and TWX stock was trading at $51.50 per share, so he was figuring on selling around 20 million shares of the stock.

Sometime before the announcement, on May 12, 1997, Mr. Turner had already established a collar on two million shares, when TWX common was trading around $45; he bought 3-year put[s] with a strike price of $39.63 and sold 3-year call[s] with a strike of $60.90. This was presumably done on the over the counter market, as that is the venue for deals such as these. This collar could have been a debit position, i.e., it had a net positive cash flow, but even if it didn't, the cost was not that much. Moreover, he could also borrow up to 90 percent of the put's strike for additional liquidity if he needed to. Given his likely negligible cost basis in Time Warner, Turner could have simply sold covered calls on the position until he had to pay a periodic payment; however, his cash flow planning would benefit from a calculated downside of $39.63.

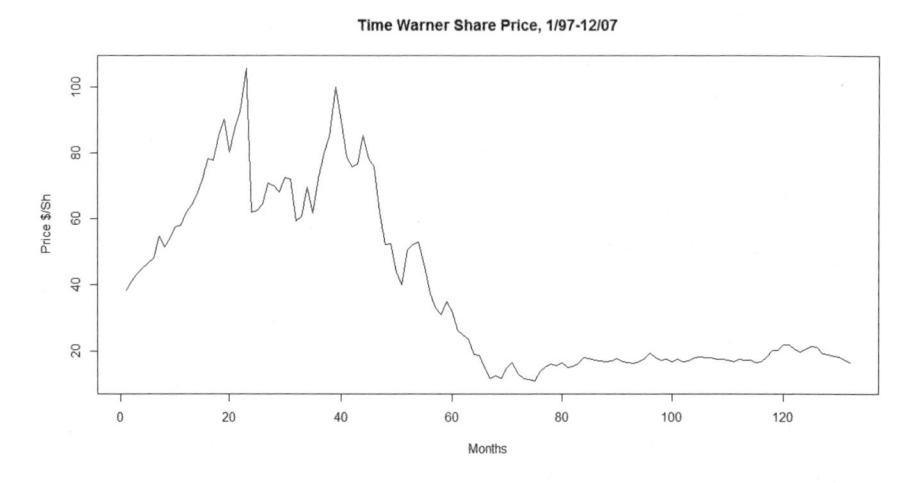

Time Warner Share Price, 1/97-12/07

Eight months later in December 1997, when TWX was trading around 62, on the way up to 100, it is likely that some or all of his position would have been called, and he would have had to sell at $60.90. Suppose the entire position was called. His profit on the upside was about (2,000,000)($15.90) = $31,800,000 (The $15.90 was the gain from $45 to $60.90). We don't know his cost on the puts, but assuming conservatively that it was a zero-cost collar, his little profit during this uptick was about $32 million. He could then establish another collar further up the scale. By the time next year's installment was due, TWX had risen to 68 AFTER a stock split! This pattern of higher and higher prices continued until about 2–3 months prior to the AOL merger of January 11, 2001, after which the opposite price performance was realized. The price languished around $15 to $20 per share; during the good years Ted was making his payments using only about one and a half to two million shares per year, but from 2002 through 2006, his progress payments required some five million shares apiece, for a total of up to 35 million shares.

Unfortunately, we have no way of knowing exactly how the Turner deal played out, but the fact remains that he was able to lock in his commitment at presumably no real transaction cost, especially given his likely extremely low cost basis in the stock.

Futures

It is logical to begin our discussion with futures since the commodities of life were the first traded goods. Beer production was sold forward as far back as in the time of Uruk III, Sumer, 31st century B.C. Indeed, our record of this contract is a pictographic script tablet which has all the elements of a futures contract. Beer production is still being sold forward today, and other commodities surround our daily experience. Consider the humble cup of coffee; to produce it requires five futures contracts: coffee, sugar, lumber (for the stirring stick), crude oil (for the Styrofoam cup or plastic stirring stick), and milk. If one uses powdered creamer, one also needs various other chemicals and industrial products, which trade futures but in the OTC markets.

Organized futures exchanges were observed in history beginning in 1570. This is when forward contracts began trading on London's Royal Exchange. Stock options were traded on London joint stock companies and government gilts ("stocks") as early as 1690. Most of the U.S. commodity exchanges were established in the mid-19th century, with new ones emerging and mergers/consolidations occurring ever since. The economic *raison d'être* for futures contracts is to offset commodity price risk from commercial operators to speculators who are willing and able to assume the market price risk. Organized exchanges permitted the standardization of forward contracts which allowed producers, users, and speculators much improved access to markets and pricing transparency to the underlying values.

Futures contract specifications include the contract size, product description, pricing unit, tick size (minimum fluctuation), daily price limits, trading hours, contract months (e.g., Mar, Jun, Sep, Dec), settlement procedure (cash or physical delivery), position limits and ticker symbols. For example, one can trade rainfall index futures and options on the Chicago Mercantile Exchange (CME), which are contracts on inches of rainfall for 10 U.S. cities. The contract size is $500 times the respective CME rainfall index; the pricing unit is

$1 per index point (1 point = 1 inch of rainfall); there are no price limits; settlement procedure is by cash (we do not have to deliver rainfall); contract months are Mar, Apr, May, Jun, Jul, Aug, Sep, Oct. Trading is done by the automated trading system GLOBEX, with a daily rest period of 3:15–5:00 p.m. Options on the rainfall contract are traded by open outcry in the pits, Monday through Friday, 8:30 a.m.–3:15 p.m.

Although traditionally the exchanges were established to facilitate trade in the agricultural commodities, today there is much wider variety of tradable products. A sample of these futures products include interest rates, equities, commodities, foreign exchange rates, weather products, real estate products (S&P/Case-Shiller Home Price Index), and alternative investments, along with associated options. Trading in futures can be a highly sophisticated venture, especially if one wishes to become a clearing member or engage in a seat on one of the exchanges. Clearly, commercial users would like to lock in supply or a future sales price for their commodities. But it is the allure to the speculator which keeps the market inefficiency holes filled in. One could open a miniscule account at a futures brokerage (say $5,000) and begin trading crude oil, for example.

The exchanges also establish margin requirements to trade the products, and the brokers have their margin requirements as well. Futures margins are not like stock margin accounts, which are really loans of cash to the account holder by the brokerage (called "call money" in the past); futures margins are actually performance bonds deposited by the trader, and profits and losses are marked-to-market (MTM) each day with a corresponding debit or credit of cash to the account. For example, the Crude Oil West Texas Intermediate contract trades for all months on CME/New York Mercantile Exchange (NYMEX), with a trading unit of 1,000 bbl (42,000 gallons), and physical delivery. The settlement type is important, many financial products are cash-settled, but many commodity contracts are still settled physically, in this case, one would need to provide 42,000 gallons of crude oil to the designated delivery point. Price adjustments can be made for other types of oil besides WTI. At a time when the price of crude oil is $100, a typical trading margin is $3,400. So if we are long one contract and the price of oil goes up by $1/bbl, we have made $1,000, a 20 percent return on our "investment" (margin). This is tempting to the speculator. Note that this $3,400 performance bond is 3.4 percent of the 1,000 bbl contract, indicating a leverage of over 9:1 on the asset.

After the initial margin has been deposited with the broker, a "maintenance" level must be maintained before additional margin is required. For example, the initial/maintenance margin for gold might be $4,400/$4,000. Hence, a long gold contract can sustain a $4 drop in the price of gold before additional margin must be provided.

Some authors quote an infinite return in this case since "futures do not involve an exchange of funds" at inception. Although this is true, there is a definite opportunity cost of having one's funds tied up in margin in order to trade futures. For example, to trade a single S&P 500 index futures contract requires a margin in 2014 of $24,000. With a point size of $250 per S&P 500 index point, this represents only a 1.04 percent return; however, 10 points returns $2,500, or 10.4 percent. We prefer to and will henceforth use the real-world calculations. On the other hand, if oil drops $5/bbl in a day, then the trader will receive a margin call to deposit more money into the account. Brokers do not think lightly about margin calls, they will close the account's positions, at a loss sometimes, and they can still demand more money. If there are several positions in the account, profitable ones will be closed out first as well as the losing ones; the trader sometimes has no control. Caveat emptor! The salient elements of futures contracts are the contract symbol, the trading (expiration) month, and the contract volume and open interest (see Figure 8.1).

The contract months are designated using the symbols:

F	G	H	J	K	M	N	Q	U	V	X	Z
Ja	Fb	Mr	Ap	Ma	Je	Jl	Ag	Se	Oc	Nv	Dc

Futures volume is quoted with *the previous day's* volume and open interest unless a real-time screen is available. It is evident that trading volume drops off for the further out months; the highest volume is for the "spot" month, in this case the February contract

Crude Oil WTI

Daily Prices As of :- Monday, 2 January, 2017

Symbol:CL

Contract	Close	Change	Open	High	Low	Prev. Settle	Prev. Volume	Prev. Open Int.
CASH	5375	-3		5375	5375	5378	0	0
CLG17	5372	-5	5387	5409	5341	5377	360194	457983
CLH17	5466	-6	5481	5502	5437	5472	128316	327402
CLJ17	5543	-6	5553	5578	5517	5549	59365	150761
CLK17	5605	-6	5633	5638	5581	5611	32881	113161
CLM17	5649	-6	5668	5684	5624	5655	41040	227315
CLN17	5676	-6	5702	5704	5656	5682	17697	51573
CLQ17	5690	-6	5695	5719	5669	5696	9163	49607
CLU17	5699	-5	5720	5728	5680	5704	11939	73010
CLV17	5703	-5	5722	5728	5681	5708	5212	40632
CLX17	5705	-5	5716	5730	5692	5710	4372	37511
CLZ17	5706	-5	5709	5736	5679	5711	23949	207020
CLF18	5699	-4	5718	5718	5690	5703	1832	36928
CLG18	5691	-4		5691	5691	5695	448	14962
CLH18	5682	-4		5682	5682	5686	1035	23529
CLJ18	5673	-3		5673	5673	5676	286	7153
CLK18	5664	-3		5664	5664	5667	191	5415
CLM18	5659	-2	5669	5679	5631	5661	4072	57326
CLN18	5650	-2		5650	5650	5652	467	4878

Figure 8.1. Crude Oil Futures Quotes, January 2, 2017 (Source: Barchart.com, Chicago, IL)

(CLG17). For a less-actively traded product, this front-month volume drop-off is very clearly seen.

Investing in futures and options is an oxymoron since all derivatives contracts have varying active months and fixed expiration dates; most "investing" is therefore in fact trading. Professional futures traders use a combination of fundamental and technical analysis techniques. Fundamental analysis includes research into the factors affecting (worldwide) supply and demand, since indeed, price is supposed to be at the intersection of supply and demand. Typical factors in an agricultural commodity trader's analysis include expected harvest, yield per acre, the status of stored supply, weather, global climate change, and even includes the political sphere (e.g., corn and fuels). Econometric models of commodity prices are quite complex, all of these factors and more go into cattle prices, for example, as well as do current (worldwide) trends in dining.

Other fundamental techniques include seasonality studies, such as those for July lean hogs, the prices tend to be a minimum in August and steadily climb to a peak in the following month of May. Actual trading results over 15 years for a strategy such as "Buying August lean hogs on Feb 12 and sell May 1 results in profits over 80 percent of the time." There are many seasonal strategies which have seen 100 percent profitable results.

Another fundamental technique is to trade spreads. These positions are the result of buying one contract and selling another related future. It is believed that although prices may not be predictable, the spread between either calendar contracts or related commodity contracts is more predictable. Much research has borne this out. A typical example might be buy Jul lean hogs and sell Jun lean hogs on March 9 and hold until May 8; this strategy has been successful in 100 percent of the cases from 1993 to 2008. (See CME Group Commodity Products. *2008 Moore Research Report, Pork.* Chicago, IL).

Rober Robens (see Williams and Noseworthy, 1987) summarizes these concepts as follows:

> *"Seasonal price movements are a function of 'normal' market conditions and relationships that economists and analysts often rely upon for recommendations and projections. For seasonals to be reliable it is important to identify the significant variables that are the primary motivating forces for change. In commodities, these variables often center around crop production and harvest considerations, free stocks and inventories, domestic consumption and export demand.*
>
> *"Spreads are simply price relationships which exist in change between commodities futures contract months of between different commodities. These price relationships often have characteristic behavioral patterns resulting from certain repeated fundamental considerations."*

Because of the temporal nature of the futures asset, and the time it takes for market fundamentals to change (hopefully in the direction of the analyst's belief), futures and options are most often traded using technical analysis, which we discuss in more detail later in this book. Technical analysis comprises a vast toolkit of market price and volume indicators in order to give position entry and exit guidance. These tools range from simple moving averages, to visual behavioral patterns, to sophisticated statistical calculations. Academic research holds that all such techniques have no value; operationally, even the purely fundamental futures traders use a collection of technical indicators to inform their positions.

The most successful class of futures operator is the commercial class. They are the ones who have a need for 112,000 pounds of (non-domestic) sugar at 13¢ per pound. The second most successful class of futures trader is the broker and managed funds class. Another successful group is the authors who make their income from selling books, newsletters, and seminars on trading. It is considered unusual for an individual small commodity speculator to survive more than five years in the markets.

Warrants

A *common stock warrant* is simply a legal instrument issued by a corporation that grants the holder the right to purchase the common stock of the corporation at a stated price within a stated period of time. Thus, there are three basic elements to the common stock warrant. The first of these, the *privilege of exchange*, is the most essential element. This privilege usually entitles the holder to exchange the warrant for common stock, on the basis of one warrant for one share of stock, although multiple or fractional shares are sometimes specified. The second, the stated *price of exchange* or *option price*, is the price for common above which the warrant becomes mathematically valuable. This option price may be fixed over the life of the warrant or may change, usually rising as the age of the warrant increases. The final element, the stated *period of time*, is the duration of the life of the warrant. This period may vary from a few days to perpetuity.

Prior to the introduction of exchange-traded stock options in 1973, a healthy market in warrant trading was offered by the major stock exchanges (NYSE, AMEX, NASDAQ, TSX), covering companies such as AT&T, Ford Motor Company, AIG, General Motors, etc. Warrants were a major source of speculative leverage. Since then, the market has thinned considerably, with warrants trading mostly on smaller issues. According to the advisory service http://commonstockwarrants.com, as of January 2017, there were 183 publicly traded warrants on 164 U.S. and Canadian companies; this compares to approximately 12,000 options traded on 3,817 US companies. Due to the thin nature of the warrants markets, there are usually large spreads between the bid and ask prices. Listed stock options on the other hand trade on the organized options exchanges, such as the Chicago Board Options Exchange (CBOE) and several others. This is one difference between warrants and exchange-traded options. The other main distinction is the availability of longer expiration horizons, as opposed to a maximum of 3 years with options on a smaller sampling of stocks. Yet another difference is that the number of outstanding warrants is limited by their offering and cannot be increased; but, option open interest can be increased any time two parties wish to create another contract.

An example will illustrate these three elements. Suppose ABC Co. has an issue of $3^3/_4$ perpetuals that have been outstanding for quite some time. Each warrant of this issue is exchangeable for one share of common stock at $3.75 for the remainder of the life of the company. Thus, when the price of ABC common advances beyond $3^3/_4$, the warrant assumes a mathematical value. This mathematical value is precisely the difference between the price of the stock and $3.75.

In 1942, the common stock warrants of RKO were selling for $0.0625 each. Four years later, they were selling for $13, representing a 208-fold increase. In 1948, Hoffman Radio warrants were priced at a nickel apiece. Two years later, they sold as high as $25 each — a 500-fold increase. Universal Picture warrants sold at $39 in 1945, but by 1947, they had fallen to $1.50. Between August 1956 and December 1959, General Tire common advanced from $50 to $280 (adjusted) — a 460 percent increase. The General Tire $60 warrants went from $7.25 to $215, however, in the same span — a 2,865 percent increase. More spectacularly, the $70 warrants went from $4.50 to $205, for a 4,455 percent increase. The most dramatic performance in the history of common stock warrants was the 123,077 percent increase in the price of Tri-Continental warrants witnessed from 1942 to 1962. Although most of the trading activity today is in *options* on common stocks and futures, the analysis is similar.

Common stock warrants may come into being in various ways. The most typical of these include the following:

1. Through the sale of common stock and the warrants together as a unit.
2. Through exchange as a result of a reorganization.
3. Through sale to underwriters at a nominal price — part of their actual compensation.
4. Through separate public sale (rare).
5. Through attachment as a bonus to senior securities or preferred stock.

The way a warrant comes into being may give some indication as to the future performance of the common stock of the company in question and, consequently, to the future value of the warrant. Warrants that result from bankruptcy reorganizations, where stockholders and other junior-security holders are given warrants in the reorganized company for their old securities, may be suspect. The fact that the company had to be reorganized might give some indication as to the future uncertainty for the common and hence the warrant. Although amazing comebacks in such cases have been witnessed (for example, the St. Louis Southwestern R.R. many years ago), during the period after reorganization warrants tend to be depressed.

When warrants are used as a partial compensation for investment bankers or as a "sweetener" for other issues, no indication is given about the future performance of the warrant. Many well-established firms employ the second of these practices, and on occasion, both are employed by established firms. The use of the warrant as a sweetener for the sale of another issue, particularly debentures or other forms of bond issue, is an alternative to issuing a convertible security. Several advantages exist for the purchaser of the senior security with warrants attached over the senior issue convertible into common stock. First, the holder has the option of selling the warrant and retaining the original issue. The convertible holder obviously cannot do this. Second, the life of the warrant cannot be reduced or terminated at the option of the company, whereas many convertible issues are callable after a period of time. Finally, because of the speculative attractiveness attaching to warrants alone they usually command a greater premium in the market over their realizable value than would a comparable convertible issue.

Determining the worth of a warrant would be a simple matter if warrants sold at their mathematical value. Because there is value associated with the option element of a warrant, however, warrants generally sell above their mathematical worth. There is a tendency for the actual price of a warrant to approach its mathematical value as the price of the common stock rises significantly beyond the exercise price, however. The determinants of the price of a warrant are:

$$P_w = f(P_o, T_n, P_c, D_i, F_c), \qquad (8.1)$$

where:

P_w = market price of the warrant
P_o = option or exercise price of the common
T_n = duration of the issue, that is, time remaining before expiration
P_c = current price of the common
D_i = potential dilution, that is, ratio of the number of warrants outstanding to the number of common shares outstanding
F_c = the future common stock price

From the discussion above, we may observe that P_o and P_c have a definite quantifiable relationship to the value of the warrant. These two variables determine the mathematical value of the warrant, which may be expressed as follows:

$$V = (P_c - P_o)N, \qquad (8.2)$$

where:

V is the mathematical value of the warrant
N is the number of shares that may be purchased with one warrant
P_c and P_o are as in Equation (8.1)

To consider a simple example, if the stock of the XYZ Co. were currently selling in the market place at $25 per share, and each warrant allowed the purchase of one share of common stock at $15 per share, the mathematical value of the XYZ Co. warrants would be $10 per warrant.

The variables T_n, D_i, and F_c determine the premium that one would be willing to pay above the pure mathematical value of the warrant. T_n suggests something quite important regarding the nature of a stock warrant: a warrant is really nothing more than a long-term option enabling its owner to obtain the common stock at a fixed price in the future. Obviously, this option has a value that exists even when the common stock is selling substantially below the option price. This is true because the stock *might* rise above the option price at some point during the life of the warrant. The value related to the variable T_n might appear to be intuitively obvious: the longer the time remaining in the life of the warrant, the more valuable the option privilege becomes. Unfortunately, the empirical relationship is not so easily discerned. Attempts to quantify the effects of longevity on the value of the warrant have produced some evidence to suggest that this variable becomes important only as the warrant approaches expiration. It has also been observed that maturity differences are not important beyond a specific number of years. It may be argued, however, that although isolated empirical investigations have found a truncation effect, there are no theoretical grounds for such a phenomenon. This view is adopted by many financial economists, who maintain that warrants often expire with the price of the common below the option price, although given more time the common *could* rise to produce a mathematical value for the warrant. Given two price relatives, common price to option price and warrant price to option price, empirical data are fitted to functions of the form $Y = aX^b$, and a graphical representation similar to Figure 8.1 is depicted. In this diagram, the warrant price relative (P_w/P_o) is the dependent (Y) variable, and the common-stock price relative (P_c/P_o) is the independent (X) variable. The maximum relative is given where $(P_w/P_o) = (P_c/P_o)$. Values where $(P_w/P_o) > (P_c/P_o)$ are not possible, because this would imply $P_w > P$ (that is, the warrant price exceeded the common stock price).

The minimum relative is given where $[(P_c/P_o) - 1] = [(P_w/P_o)]$. Values where $[(P_c/P_o) - 1] > [(P_w/P_o)]$ imply $(P_c - P_o) > P_w$. This condition is not possible because if the mathematical value of the warrant exceeded its market price, arbitragers would buy the warrant, exercise it, and sell the common until $(P_c - P_o) = P_w$.

Possible relatives are given by functions A, B, and C. These functions represent warrants of specific maturity categories with increasing slopes corresponding to longer maturities. Thus, if function A were the fit of warrants with maturities of one year or less and B were the fit of warrants with maturities of one to two years, the latter group would command a larger premium than the former.

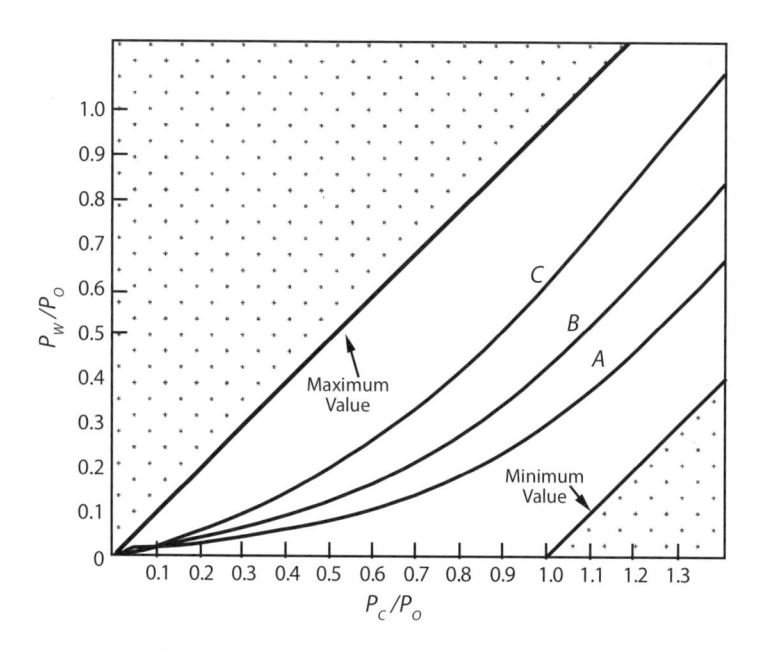

Figure 8.2. Warrant Longevity Value Model

Symbolically,

$$\frac{P_{w(B)}/P_{o(B)}}{P_{c(B)}/P_{o(B)}} > \frac{P_{w(A)}/P_{o(A)}}{P_{c(A)}/P_{o(A)}},$$

thus:

$$P_{w(B)}/P_{c(B)} > P_{w(A)}/P_{c(A)}.$$

This sort of relationship has been observed empirically where the functional relationship ranged from $Y = 0.2753(X)^{1.8545}$ for warrants of six-month to one-year maturities to $Y = 0.5509(X)^{1.2155}$ for perpetual warrants. The R^2 exceeds 0.94 for four of six functions, indicating an excellent empirical fit.

The second of the key variables in the determination of the value of the premium applied to a given warrant issue is D_i, the potential dilution of earnings and dividends resulting from the exercise of warrants after the option price is reached. Because common stock warrants do not receive dividends, holders of warrants may elect to exercise their option to buy common stock in order to enjoy the income from dividends that the common pays. This, of course, assumes that the common stock is paid a dividend, and many of the companies that issue common-stock warrants do not pay dividends. It also assumes that the premium has become insignificant relative to the dividends that are paid. Thus, if XYZ common is selling at $25 per share, its outstanding warrants are selling at $10.25, and the exercise price is $15, some holders would exercise the purchase option if the dividend were large enough. The fact that additional shares are issued at less than the market price per share may produce a long-run dilution in earnings per share. This would occur if the present value of earnings generated from plant and equipment purchased with the funds obtained from the sale of new shares to warrant holders were less than the price paid by warrant holders for their shares. A dilution in long-run earnings would affect the market price of the common stock and hence the value of the warrant. In this instance, the presence of a substantial volume of warrants might serve to depress the market price per warrant.

It can be argued in this case that exercise would not take place because the rational holder of the warrants would simply sell at the market price of $10.25 and buy the common at $25, for a cost of $14.75 per share, a price lower than the $15 option price. This would indeed be true if it were not for the "turn of the market" (brokerage commissions, taxes, and so on). In this example, if the "turn" were larger than the $0.25 differential, the option to purchase at $15 would be exercised. Thus, if the differential, which is actually the premium, is less than the turn, exercise may occur. If it is larger than the turn, exercise will not occur.

All this assumes, of course, that the extra dividends received from holding common are more valuable to the holder than the prospective return from holding the warrant. In the above case, if the common rose in price by 20 percent (from 25 to 30), the warrant would have to rise to at least 15 (the mathematical value of the warrant), which is almost a 50 percent increase. Thus, the speculator who expected higher prices for XYZ common would probably prefer to hold the warrant regardless of the XYZ dividend. This illustrates the major attraction of warrants to the risk-seeking investor. Price movements for warrants are generally magnified in percentage terms from a given change in the price of common. The phenomenon operates both positively and negatively. If XYZ fell by 20 percent, from 25 to 20, the warrant could fall by as much as 50 percent because the mathematical value of the warrant would now be only 5. Even if a larger premium developed at the lower warrant price, which frequently happens, the percentage decline in the price of the warrant would be magnified.

There is empirical evidence to demonstrate that firms with the high dividend payouts tend to have slower rates of earnings growth. This retardation of earnings growth may tend to reduce the attractiveness of warrants that may be exercised for high-yield common stocks. The negative impact of high cash payouts on warrant values has been recognized in studies that have found dividend yields to have a negative regression coefficient, with higher yields indicating lower warrant values.

The final key variable in the determination of the value of the premium to be applied to a given issue of common-stock warrants is

F_c, the future price of the common stock. In many ways, this variable is the most important one for the determination of the value of the warrant, and undoubtedly it is the most difficult to handle. The ideal way of approaching this variable is to follow the procedures indicated previously for analyzing a common share. The important factors here are the expected future earnings of the company, the expected future dividends, and the expected future multiplier to apply to the earnings of the company per common share when the stock is to be sold. The analysis proceeds in the manner described earlier in this book.

Suppose an analyst has forecasted the following earnings-per-share pattern for the Keystone Corp. for the next five years:

2014	$1.00
2015	$1.20
2016	$1.50
2017	$2.00
2018	$2.50

The analyst expects an earnings multiple of 20 to hold in 2018, and he believes the firm will maintain a dividend payout of about 50 percent over the period. Keystone common sells at $26 1/4$. If a purchase were made at the beginning of 2014 for holding until 2018, the following return would be expected:

	2014	2015	2016	2017	2018
Dividends per share (DPS)	$0.50	$0.60	$0.75	$1.00	$1.25
Market price at terminal date					20 × 2.50 = 50.00
Dollar returns	$0.50	$0.60	$0.75	$1.00	$51.25
@ 16 percent	0.826	0.743	0.641	0.552	0.476
Annual present value	$0.41	$0.45	$0.48	$0.55	$24.40

Total present value = $26.29.

Thus, if the stock were purchased at $26.25, a return of about 16 percent could be earned.

Keystone Corp. also has a set of warrants expiring in 2020. The warrants give the holder the right to buy one share of common for each warrant held at a price of $30 per share. The mathematical value of the warrant currently is:

$$V = (P_c - P_o)N$$
$$= (\$26.25 - \$30.00)(1)$$
$$= -\$3.75.$$

although the warrant sells in the market for $5. Thus, investors are paying a premium of $8.75 over the mathematical value of the warrant. Investors evidently feel that the future prospects for Keystone are sufficiently bright to produce a stock price substantially above the exercise price during the life of the warrant. Is this optimism justifiable?

To answer this, we may determine the price of Keystone warrants in 2018, given the above assumptions. If there were no premium existing then, the warrant price would be:

$$P_w - V = 0$$
$$P_w = V = (P_c - P_o)N$$
$$P_w = (50 - 30)1 = \$20.$$

and it could be higher if a premium continued. An investor who bought the warrant would have an expected return of at least:

$$(X)(\$20) = \$5$$
$$X = 0.25.$$

At 32 percent, a dollar received five years hence is worth $0.25 today. Thus, the expected return would be about 32 percent. This compares with an expected return of only 16 percent for the common.

Suppose, however, that the analyst is incorrect in his estimates and that the following EPS pattern and multiple prevail:

2014	$0.80
2015	$1.00
2016	$1.20
2017	$1.40
2018	$1.50 (multiple in 2018 = 17 times earnings)

Common-stock holders would earn only 1.7 percent rather than the expected 16 percent:

Dollar return	@2%			@1%		
.40	×	.980 =	.39	×	.990 = $	.40
.50	×	.961 =	.48	×	.980 =	.49
.60	×	.942 =	.57	×	.971 =	.58
.70	×	.924 =	.65	×	.961 =	.67
.75	×	.906 =	.68	×	.951 =	.71
25.50[a]	×	.906 =	23.10	×	.951 =	$24.25
			$25.87			$27.10

$$\text{return} = 1.7 \text{ percent}$$

[a] 17 × 1.50 = 25.50

Given the revised data, warrant holders would *lose* even if the premium remained constant:

(a) $V = (P_c - P_o)N$
$= (25.50 - 30.00)1$
$= -\$4.50$

(b) Premium $= P_w - V$
$\$8.75 = P_w - (-\$4.50)$
$P_w = \$4.25$

(c) at -3 percent, $(.863)(\$5.00) = \$4.31$.

Thus, we observe that under favorable conditions, the warrant return would be double that of the common stock (32 percent versus 16 percent). Under unfavorable ones, however, the common stock investment earned 1.7 percent, and the warrant investment lost 3 percent. Warrants are thus seen to be riskier than common stocks because their returns are levered. That is, good returns on a common stock produce better ones for warrants. Poor returns produce poorer ones.

In the U.S., the prevalence of warrant trading has greatly decreased after the introduction of exchange-traded stock options in 1973. Warrants today tend to be thinly traded but are promoted by various speculative investment newsletters. Finding them takes work and is worth the cost of the advisory services if the investor is so inclined. These securities appear in mutual funds and other institutional holdings. Warrants are still actively traded in some foreign markets such as the Deutsche Borse and the Hong Kong Stock Exchange. Like options, active investor attention is required around warrant expiration time, and in monitoring early buyback activity by the issuing company.

Although the diminished size of warrant trading may make one wonder why this chapter dwells on the subject, the justification is both historical and practical. From a historical point of view, warrant trading in the 1930s through the 1960s laid the foundation for the incredible use of options trading today. This chapter returns to options shortly. It is also important to note that the valuation models of warrants just presented are the same as in options valuations. A second reason is included in the previous paragraph. Warrants still do exist and the nature of that market provides those looking for inefficiency opportunities to profit. Moreover, some rather large companies still have warrants outstanding. One example is the AIG warrant expiring January 19, 2021 (symbol AIGWS) listed on the NYSE. The warrant has an exercise price of $45. This price is subject to anti-dilution adjustment. The instrument creating the warrant states:

> "The initial exercise price is subject to anti-dilution adjustment for certain events, including (i) future stock dividends, distributions, subdivisions or combinations; (ii) the issuance of below market

rights, options or warrants entitling the holder to purchase AIG common stock for a period of sixty days or less; (iii) dividends or other distributions of capital stock (other than AIG common stock); rights to acquire capital stock, debt or other assets (subject to certain exclusions); (iv) per share cash dividends in excess of $0.675 in the aggregate in any twelve-month period; and (v) certain above-market issuer tender offers for more than 30 percent of the then-outstanding AIG common stock."

Why would one buy the warrant? In early 2017, AIG common was selling for around $66 per share. The warrant had a mathematical (intrinsic) value of ($66 − $45 = $21). Suppose the warrant sold at a premium of $4 (or $25). Suppose further that AIG rose to $99 over the next four years. The stock appreciation would be 50 percent ($99 − $66). At a minimum (no premium), the warrant would be worth: $99 − $45 = $54. Thus, the warrant would have more than doubled in value. On the other hand, if AIG fell to, say, $45 at the expiration date, the stock would have depreciated by $21. This would be a decline of about 32 percent (from $66 to $45). The warrant would expire worthless, however, for a loss of 100 percent. As the old sayings goes, "You pays your money and you takes your chances."

Common stock subscription rights

Common stock subscription rights are a unique form of warrant that comes into being when a company sells additional shares to its own stockholders through a rights offering. New shares must be sold in this manner when stockholders have retained the *preemptive right* in the firm's charter to maintain their proportionate ownership share of the company. When a firm plans a rights offering, each shareholder receives rights according to the number of shares held. These rights allow the purchase of new shares at a stated subscription price. Thus, rights are simply warrants with a very short maturity. They have value because the stated subscription price is always set below the then-existing market price of the firm's shares. Hence, shareholders will generally exercise their rights by buying new shares, or they will sell them to someone else who may exercise them. Only foolish investors will allow their rights to expire without exercising or selling them, although such people do exist. (If the market price of shares falls below the subscription price during the offering and stays there until the expiration date, the rights will have no value and nothing would be lost by not exercising them. Indeed, in this instance, shares might be bought more cheaply in the market than through subscription.)

The mechanics of a rights offering are quite simple. First, the board of directors of the company announces a rights offering to shareholders listed on the books as of the record date. These shareholders will receive rights to buy additional shares that may be exercised any time between the date of the rights distribution and the expiration date. In the period between the announcement and the last date, one may purchase the stock to become a shareholder by the record date (the former is called the "ex" date and is five business days before the record date), the common stock is said to be selling "rights-on" or "cum-rights." This means that any purchase of the common stock between those dates carries with it the right to buy additional new shares. After the ex date, the common stock sells "rights-off" or "ex-rights." Then, the common stock and warrants trade as separate instruments (a market for the warrants on a "when issued" basis generally is established soon after the announcement date), and the purchase of a share in the open market no longer carries with it the right to buy new shares from the company. On the ex date, when the common stock begins to sell ex-rights, its price must fall by the value of the right. If it does not, then we may conclude that the price of the common stock would have risen during that trading day had it not been the ex date. Thus, suppose a stock is selling at $15 the day before the ex date and has rights attached worth $1. If the stock still sells at $15 the next day, while the rights trade separately at $1, then the stock would otherwise have gone from $15 to $16.

During the period when the stock is selling cum-rights, the theoretical or mathematical value of each right is:

$$R_o = \frac{P_c - P_s}{N+1}, \qquad (8.3)$$

where:

R_o = the theoretical or mathematical value of a right when the stock is selling cum-rights
P_c = the market price of the stock rights-on
P_s = the subscription price per share
N = the number of rights required to purchase one new share of stock

On the ex date, the price per share should fall to:

$$P_x = \frac{(P_c \times N) + P_s}{N+1}, \qquad (8.4)$$

where: P_x = price of the stock ex-rights.
And the value of the right becomes;

$$R_x = \frac{P_x - P_s}{N}, \qquad (8.5)$$

where:

R_x = the theoretical or mathematical value of a right when the stock is selling ex-rights

The theoretical value of a right is very much like the mathematical value of a warrant. Frequently, investors are willing to pay a premium for the option value of the right. These premiums are usually smaller than those paid for a warrant because the exercise life of a right is usually short.

Example

The Edmundston Co. has announced a rights offering that will allow shareholders to subscribe to one new share for each 20 now held (20 rights to buy one new share). The firm's stock now sells for $101, and the subscription price will be $80 per share.

(a) The theoretical value of each right is:

$$R_o = \frac{P_c - P_s}{N + 1}$$
$$= \frac{101 - 80}{21}$$
$$= \$1.$$

(b) When the stock goes ex-rights, its price should fall to:

$$P_x = \frac{(P_c \times N) + P_s}{N + 1} = \frac{(101)(20) + 80}{21} = \$100.$$

(c) If the price of the stock is $100 when it goes ex-rights, the theoretical value of each right would be:

$$R_x = \frac{P_x - P_s}{N}$$
$$= \frac{100 - 80}{20}$$
$$= \$1.$$

Warrants, convertibles, and dilution

The exercise of warrants and the conversion of convertible securities result in a dilution of the short-run per share earnings of the firm. In the case of warrants, the effect may be reduced in the long run because funds raised from the sale of additional shares to warrant holders may be used to buy assets that will generate a larger future income stream per share. In the case of convertible debentures, the issuer is relieved of making interest payments once conversion has taken place. This will increase reported earnings before taxes and will free funds for reinvestment in the firm. In both instances, the long-run effect of exercise and conversion will not be negative if the extra funds made available for reinvestment produce a large enough per share future income stream. Furthermore, the current market price per share of common need not fall even if short-run dilution exceeds the extra stream generated by reinvestment. This is true because the exercise of warrants increases the firm's equity base (hence reducing its riskiness). The conversion of debentures reduces the outstanding debt of the firm and also increases the equity base (again, reducing the firm's risk position).

Because the existence of warrants and convertibles implies potential dilution of per share earnings, the accountants require that earnings per share be computed under the assumption of conversion of all securities that are common stock equivalents. Such securities include all stock options issued by the firm to management and others, all outstanding warrants, and convertibles. Statements are to be presented that also include a fully diluted EPS figure.

The dilution effect from the sale of common stock to warrant holders is similar to that of the sale of new shares except that the price obtained is lower. The effect of a debenture conversion may be illustrated with a simple example. A firm has $100 million of 5 percent debentures outstanding that are convertible into common at $20 per share. The before and after conversion income statements are given below.

	Before Conversion	After Conversion
Earnings before interest and taxes (EBIT)	$28,000,000	$28,000,000
Interest on debentures	5,000,000	—
EBT	23,000,000	28,000,000
Taxes (@50 percent)	11,500,000	14,000,000
Net income	11,500,000	14,000,000
Number of shares	10,000,000	15,000,000
EPS	$1.15	$0.93

The EPS number would be reported as "primary earnings" ($1.15) and the after-conversion number would be deemed "fully diluted earnings" ($0.93).

Options

There exists a form of option that is not sold by a corporation on its own shares but rather by other individuals on shares that they hold (or promise to acquire). A *call* option gives the purchaser the right to buy a certain common stock (or other security) at a stated price for a given period of time. A *put* option allows the holder to sell a stock at a stated price for a given period of time. A *straddle* is the purchase of a put and call on the same security for the same period of time at the same price. A *spread* is similar to a straddle except the put price is set below the call price. If the option is written at the current market price of the stock, which is usually the case, the spread put would be below the market price, and the call would be above it. Combinations of options are also possible. A *strip* is a straddle plus a put. A *strap* is a straddle plus a call.

A call option is analyzed like a warrant. Because options are usually written with the exercise price at the current market price of the stock, an option usually has no mathematical (or *intrinsic*) value at that time (that is, $V = P_c - P_o = 0$). Buyers pay positive prices for options because they believe the price of the stock optioned will rise sufficiently at some time during the option period to recover the cost of the option and provide an acceptable rate of return. This is called the *time value* of the option. On occasion, options are written at prices below the current market price of the optioned shares. In this case, the option does have a mathematical value. Such options, of course, are sold at prices above this value. The mathematical value is added to the time value to get the option premium (market price).

Options are typically written for 30, 60, 90, and 120 days; longer-cycle options are also traded which expire each year in January. These are called *long-term anticipation securities (LEAPS)*. The price of an option will depend upon supply and demand factors in the market for the option. If speculators believe an upward movement in a common stock's price is imminent, they will bid up the price of options on that stock. Because the probability of an upward movement increases with time, longer options usually sell for higher prices than short-period ones (often in a relation approximating a square root function, for example, six-month options at $1.4X$ the cost of three-month options on the same stock).

Options are also traded on underlying stock market indexes such as the S&P 100, S&P 500, NASDAQ, etc. Indeed, the most active exchange-traded options market in the world presently in terms of contracts traded is that for the Korea Composite Stock Price Index KOSPI 200 index options, which are traded on both the Korean stock and futures exchange.

Unfortunately, many people tend to view the option market strictly in terms of a small investor buying a call on a volatile stock in the hope of achieving a leveraged gain. Although such things do occur, they present a very limited view of the role of the market. Paper gains can be locked in by the purchase of a put if the investor has doubts about the short-term price movement of the stock. Furthermore, a portfolio that must hold a stock for tax or other reasons but has little enthusiasm for its short-run price performance can earn a tidy profit (20 percent or more) selling calls against the security. If, on the other hand, the portfolio manager is enthusiastic about a security, he can make money writing puts. Although this is hardly an area for the novice, it should be iterated that options, properly employed, can increase the return and reduce the risk of the portfolio. Consider the following examples:

1. A stock sells for $40 per share. A 90-day call option can be purchased for $200 on 100 shares. What profit would be made if the stock sold for $45 within 90 days? For $42? $41? $38?

    at $45: $4500 − ($4000 + 200) = $300; = 150 percent gain
    at $42: $4200 − ($4000 + 200) = 0; = 0 percent (breakeven)
    at $41: $4100 − ($4000 + 200) = $100; = 50 percent loss
    at $38: $3800 − ($4000 + 200) = $400; = 100 percent loss
    (in this case, the call would not be exercised).

2. Suppose a stock sells for $40 and can be straddled at a price of $400 per 100 shares for one year. What returns will be generated if the stock sells at $30 during the year, assuming the option is exercised? At $36? At $40? At $42? At $46?

    at $30: ($4000 − 3000) − $400 = $600; = 150 percent gain
    at $36: ($4000 − 3600) − $400 = 0; = 0 percent (breakeven)
    at $40: ($4000 − 4000) − $400 = −$400; = 100 percent loss (no exercise)

at $42: $4200 − ($4000 + 400) = −$200; = 50 percent loss
at $46: $4600 − ($4000 + 400) = $200; = 50 percent gain.

All options trading was done on an over-the-counter basis, until April 1973, when the first organized options exchange opened. This was made possible by the publication of the Black-Scholes-Merton option pricing model (see Chapter 10 below). The CBOE has added a degree of standardization to option trading in that all CBOE contracts expire on the third Friday of the month. There are also "Weeklies" which are options in the front months which expire weekly. In the over-the-counter market, an option can expire on any day; thus, an option written on one day is not interchangeable with one written the following day. The CBOE also has standardized exercise prices that are introduced at predetermined price intervals approximating the current market of the underlying stock. The premium (which is the market price of the option) is obtained through electronic transactions (formerly on the exchange floor), where competing market-makers (specialists) are assigned to each option to help assure a fair and orderly market. Thus, an investor can obtain the most recent option prices of the thousands of stocks on which contracts are written. This market has proven to result in the world's most liquid securities market, with over 1.2 billion contracts being traded in 2015.

To illustrate an example of trading a CBOE option, assume that an investor decided on May 4 to purchase the ABC Co. October $40 option. The closing price of the option for that day was $7, while the stock closed at $41.75. Since the mathematical value of the option was $1.75 ($41.75 − $40.00), if the investor purchased at the closing price he would have paid a premium of $5.25 ($7.00 − $1.75) for the privilege of being able to buy ABC common stock at $40 per share until October 31 (179 days). This is the so-called *time value* of the option. If ABC advanced during that period, the investor most likely would not exercise his option. Rather, he would sell it on the exchange to another buyer. Thus, if ABC sold at 50 on August 15, and the price of the option were 14, the investor could close out his position at a 100 percent profit. The purchaser on August 15 would have paid a time value premium of $4 (since the mathematical value of the option was then $10) for the option. During the final trading day, options would be exercised assuming the market price of the stock exceeded the option price.

Several empirical studies have been made of the profitability of trading in options, although the results are mixed. In a simulated experiment of put and call purchases, it was found that in the great bull market after the Second World War calls yielded handsome returns, but puts lost money. Nevertheless, the profits that could have been made from holding common stocks *exceeded* those that purchasing options would have produced. An analysis of the period 1957–1960 discovered that large losses (60–80 percent per year) would have been suffered by option purchasers. It was also found that individuals who wrote options (against stock they owned or promised to acquire) could have earned between 18 and 32 percent per annum if their investment commitment were sufficiently large and if they frequently revised their offerings. Although these results are not terribly encouraging to the prospective options purchaser, it should be remembered that these studies were simulations of a large number of holdings. To the extent that one is very optimistic about a stock he is considering buying, or very pessimistic about a security he is considering selling (selling short), the option can be an attractive speculative vehicle. The biggest danger in purchasing an option, however, is being right in the long-run but wrong in the short-run. Many speculators have bought call options on stocks that they were very bullish about, only to have the stock do nothing until their option expired and then show a remarkable advance. Since speculators have a tendency to buy heavily (holding little or no cash reserves), they are unable to purchase a second option at the expiration of their initial option. Thus, they lose all (or most) of their investment, even though their basic "hunches" were correct.

Summary

This chapter is about futures, options, and other derivatives, which may be described as speculative securities. Fabulous profits (and losses) have been obtained through speculating in common stock and index options, futures and other derivatives.

Futures contract specifications include the contract size, product description, pricing unit, tick size (minimum fluctuation), daily price limits, trading hours, contract months (Mar, Jun, Sep, and Dec), settlement procedure (cash or physical delivery), position limits and ticker symbols. Although, traditionally the exchanges were established to facilitate trade in the agricultural commodities, today there is a much wider variety of tradable products.

Investing in futures and options is an oxymoron since all derivatives contracts have varying active months and fixed expiration dates; most "investing" is therefore in fact trading. Professional futures traders use a combination of fundamental and technical analysis techniques. Fundamental analysis includes research into the factors affecting (worldwide) supply and demand, since indeed, price is supposed to be at the intersection of supply and demand. Typical factors in an agricultural commodity trader's analysis include expected harvest, yield per acre, the status of stored supply, weather, global climate change, and even includes the political sphere (e.g., corn and fuels). Econometric models of commodity prices are quite complex, all of these factors and more go into cattle prices, for example, as well as do current (worldwide) trends in dining.

A common stock warrant is a legal instrument issued by a corporation that grants the holder the right to purchase the common stock of the corporation at a stated price within a stated period of time. Thus, there are three basic elements to the common stock warrant. The first of these, the privilege of exchange, is the most essential element. This privilege entitles the holder to exchange the warrant for common stock, usually on the basis of one warrant for one share of stock. The second, the stated price of exchange or option price, is the price for common above which the warrant becomes mathematically valuable. This option price may be fixed over the life of the warrant or may change, usually rising as the age of the warrant increases. The final element, the stated period of time, is the duration of the life of the warrant. This period may vary from a few days to perpetuity.

Common stock subscription rights are a unique form of warrant that comes into being when a company sells additional shares to its own stockholders through a rights offering. New shares must be sold in this manner when stockholders have retained the preemptive right in the firm's charter to maintain their proportionate ownership share of the company. When a firm plans a rights offering, each shareholder receives rights according to the number of shares held. These rights allow the purchase of new shares at a stated subscription price. Thus, rights are simply warrants with a very short maturity. They have value because the stated subscription price is always set below the then-existing market price of the firm's shares. Hence, shareholders will generally exercise their rights by buying new shares, or they will sell them to someone else who may exercise them. Only foolish investors will allow their rights to expire without exercising or selling them, although such people do exist.

The exercise of warrants and the conversion of convertible securities result in a dilution of the short-run per share earnings of the firm. In the case of warrants, the effect may be reduced in the long run because funds raised from the sale of additional shares to warrant holders may be used to buy assets that will generate a larger future income stream per share. In the case of convertible securities, the issuer is relieved of making interest payments (or dividends in the case of preferred stock) once conversion has taken place. This may increase reported earnings before and/or after taxes and will free funds for reinvestment in the firm. In both instances, the long-run effect of exercise and conversion will not be negative if the extra funds made available for reinvestment produce a large enough per share future income stream. Furthermore, the current market price per share of common need not fall even if short-run dilution exceeds the extra stream generated by reinvestment. This is true because the exercise of warrants increases the firm's equity base (hence reducing its riskiness). The conversion of debt securities reduces the outstanding debt of the firm and also increases the equity base (again, reducing the firm's risk position). Like options, active investor attention is required around warrant expiration time, and in monitoring early buyback activity by the issuing company.

A call option is very much like a warrant. Because options are usually written with the exercise price at the current market price of the stock, an option usually has no mathematical value at that time (that is, no intrinsic value), only time value. Buyers pay positive prices for options because they believe the price of the stock optioned will rise sufficiently at some time during the option period to recover the cost of the option and provide an acceptable rate of return. On occasion, options are written at prices below the current market price of the optioned shares. In this case, the option has an intrinsic (mathematical) value in addition to its time value.

Problems

1. The Mason Company has warrants outstanding that may be used to purchase one share of common at $30. If Mason common is at $40, what is the theoretical value of the warrant? What happens if the stock rises by 25 percent to $50?

2. The Jarvis Co. has warrants outstanding to purchase 5.3 shares of common at $50 per share.

    a. If Jarvis Common is at $200, what is the theoretical value of the warrant?
    b. What happens to the theoretical value if the common rises by 20 percent to $240?
    c. What happens if it rises another 20 percent to $288?
    d. What implications can you draw from this example?

3. This problem has four parts.

    a. Warrants issued by the Racine Corp. allow the holder to buy five shares of Racine common for each warrant held. The stock sells for $18 per share and the option price is $15. What is the mathematical value of the warrant?
    b. Racine warrants sell at $20 each. What premium are investors paying for the warrant?
    c. Suppose Racine common advances by 50 percent. By what percentage would the warrant advance if it maintained its premium? If the premium disappeared?

d. Let the stock fall by 50 percent. By what percentage would the warrant fall if it maintained its premium? What premium would have to develop to keep the decline in the price of the warrant to 50 percent?

4. Reconsider the Keystone Co. (in the chapter) changing the exercise price from $30 to $21.50.

   a. What is the new mathematical value of the warrant?
   b. What is the premium?
   c. Given the assumptions of the problem, would it pay to exercise the warrants to buy common stock?

5. This problem has five parts.

   a. Lucerne Ltd. Common sells for $49 per share. The firm has just announced a rights offering whereby its shareholders may subscribe for one new share for each eight now held. The subscription price will be $46 per share. What is the theoretical value of each right?
   b. Suppose Lucerne common advances to $52 per share. What would the new theoretical value of each right be? Compare the price increases of the common and the rights.
   c. Suppose Lucerne common fell to $46 per share. What would the theoretical value of each right be?
   d. Lucerne common has gone ex-rights. The stock is selling for $50 per share. What is the theoretical value of each right? At what price should the common have sold just before it went ex-rights?
   e. After Lucerne common went ex-rights, the stock continued to sell for $50 per share. The rights sold for $1. Can this phenomenon be explained?

6. The Continental Company, whose stock is currently selling for $30, has announced a rights offering by which its shareholders may subscribe for one new share for each 10 held at $20.

   a. What is the theoretical value of each right?
   b. To what value should the price of the stock fall when it goes ex-rights?

c. If the price stays at $30 when it goes ex-rights, what is the theoretical value of each right?

7. The Sinco Corporation, whose stock sells at $150, has announced a rights offering by which its shareholders may subscribe for one new share for each four held at $125.

   a. What is the theoretical value of the right?
   b. To what value should the price of the stock fall when it goes ex-rights?
   c. If the price in fact falls to $135 when it goes ex-rights, what is the theoretical value of the right? What is it if the price falls to $100?

8. A stock sells for $98 per share. A one-year option to buy 100 shares may be purchased for $1,000. The future price of the common stock is expected to be given by the following distribution:

Price	Probability
$ 90	0.1
$ 95	0.2
$100	0.3
$110	0.3
$120	0.1

   The stock will pay a dividend of $3 per share. The option contract requires that the exercise price be reduced by the amount of any dividends paid to the common shareholders during the period of the option.

   a. Compute the expected return if the common stock were purchased today and sold in one year.
   b. Compute the expected return from purchasing the call option.

9. A straddle on 100 shares of a volatile stock may be purchased at $400 for six months. The stock pays no dividend and now

sells at $20 per share. Price expectations for the six-month period are:

Price	Probability
$25	0.3
$20	0.4
$15	0.3

Compute the expected return from purchasing the straddle.

10. A call on the stock mentioned in number 9 above could be bought for $200. Compute the expected return and the standard deviation if the common stock were purchased today and sold in six months. Compute the expected return and standard deviation from purchasing the call option.

11. The stock of Albert, Inc., is currently selling for $50 per share. At the end of three months, there is a 0.5 probability that it will sell at $60, and a 0.5 probability it will sell for $40.

   a. What is the expected value, ignoring taxes and commissions, of buying 100 shares of Albert, Inc.?
   b. What is the expected value of selling 100 shares short?
   c. What is the expected value of buying a 90-day, 100 share put on Albert at $50 for $200?
   d. What is the expected value of buying a 90-day, 100 share call on Albert at $50 for $200?
   e. Explain the above.

12. The Shumann Corp. plans to raise $50 million of debt funds either with a 5 percent bond (convertible at $100 per share) or a 6 percent issue with warrants attached to each $1,000 debenture to subscribe to six shares of common at $100 each. The present capital structure for Shumann is given below:

Debentures	$ 50,000,000
Common stock ($10 par)	100,000,000
Excess over par	100,000,000
Retained earnings	250,000,000
	$500,000,000

Construct capital structures before and after conversion, assuming the convertible bonds are issued, and before and after exercise, assuming bonds with warrants are sold. (The prime rate at the time of debenture issue is 6 percent.)
13. Shumann (above) earns $100 million before interest and taxes. The debenture issue now outstanding is a 7 percent straight-debt issue. The firm is in the 50 percent tax bracket. Prepare before and after conversion income statements assuming the convertible bonds are issued. Prepare similar statements assuming the straight bonds with warrants are sold.

References

CME Group Commodity Products. *"Moore Research Report, Pork."* Chicago, IL: 2008.

CNN Interactive, "Ted Turner Donates $1 Billion to U.N. Causes," URL: http://edition.cnn.com/US/9709/18/turner.gift/, September 19, 1997.

Duff, R., "Charitable Contributions, Collars and Covered Calls In Wealth Preservation," *Journal of Financial Planning*, Dec. 1997, pp. 36–37.

Fried, S., *The Speculative Merits of Common Stock Warrants*. New York, NY: R.H.M. Associates, 1961.

Hull, J. C., *Options, Futures, and Other Derivatives*, 7th edn. Upper Saddle River, NJ: Pearson Prentice-Hall, 2009.

Ip, G. "Collars Give Insiders Way to Cut Risk," *Wall Street Journal*, September 17, 1997, C1:6.

McMillan, L. G., *McMillan on Options*, 2nd Ed. Hoboken, NJ: John Wiley & Sons, 2004.

National Futures Association, *Opportunity and Risk: An Educational Guide to Trading Futures and Options on Futures*. Chicago, IL: National Futures Association, 2006.

Williams, L. R. and M. L. Noseworthy. *Sure Thing Commodity Trading — How Seasonal Factors Influence Commodity Prices*. Brightwaters, NY: Windsor Books, 1987.

Woodard, C., "Ted Turner Gift Poised to Boost UN," *Christian Science Monitor*, April 22, 1998, p. 1.

Chapter 9

Risk, Uncertainty, Utility and Portfolio Theory

A man who seeks advice about his actions will not be grateful for the suggestion that he maximize expected utility.

A. D. Roy

Utility Theory

Before we can proceed with the analysis and selection of portfolios, it is necessary to establish criteria of choice. In other words, what attribute(s) of a particular security or portfolio of securities make(s) it more desirable than another security or portfolio? The reader might be tempted to suggest that return (or income or wealth — three measures that tend to move in the same direction and are thus used somewhat interchangeably in this discussion) is the appropriate criterion. This statement appears to be unambiguously true in at least two cases, which we shall now consider.

All the writers we can find on the subject agree in one way or another that more wealth is preferable to less, other things being equal. Therefore, if security A promised a certain return of 20 percent, but security B promised a certain return of only 10 percent, A would be unambiguously preferred to (in terminology used later "is said to dominate") B, and return would be a satisfactory criterion. The crucial point to remember, however, is that we are discussing *certain* increments to wealth.

If we now assume that the returns on the securities discussed above are not certain but rather subject to probability distributions with the mathematical expectations of 20 percent and 10 percent, it is still possible to salvage the return criterion. To do so, we must assume it possible to engage in an infinite number of independent trials of A and B, each trial involving an infinitely small proportion of our total wealth. The law of large numbers tells us that the actual return will approach the expected return, A will be preferred to B, and the expected return will be an appropriate ranking criterion.

Unfortunately, we rarely encounter certainties or infinitely divisible and replicable events in the real world. The difficulties involved in the employment of the expected return criterion in other situations are easy to illustrate. Suppose that one were offered the following options: (1) receive $1; (2) bet $100 against $102 on the flip of a fair coin; (3) bet $100,000 against $100,002 on the same flip. The expected return of each option is $1 and, by this criterion, one would be indifferent among them. Yet it seems unlikely that any real person would be indifferent as to which option was chosen. It would appear that more refined selection criteria are required.

Perhaps the most famous illustration of the limitations of the expected return criterion is the Petersburg Paradox. The original work on this subject was published almost three centuries ago (Daniel Bernoulli, 1954) This article was a translation from Latin into English by Louise Sommer. The original article appeared in the *Papers of the Imperial Academy of Sciences in Petersburg*, 1738, pp. 175–192.) The paradox can be stated as follows:

> Peter tosses a coin and continues to do so until it should land "heads" when it comes to the ground. He agrees to give Paul one ducat if he gets "heads" on the very first throw, two ducats if he gets it on the second, four if on the third, eight if on the fourth, and so on, so that with each additional throw the number of ducats he must pay is doubled. Suppose we seek to determine the value of Paul's expectation (p. 31 of translation).

The expected return of this proposition is $[(1/2) (1 \text{ ducat}) + (1/4) (2 \text{ ducats}) + (1/8) (4 \text{ ducats}) + \ldots] = (1/2 \text{ ducat} + 1/2 \text{ ducat} + 1/2 \text{ ducat} + \ldots) = \sum_{n=1}^{\infty} \frac{2^{n-1}}{2^n} = \infty$. Yet it was noted that no one would ever pay a very large sum, much less an infinite sum, to play the game. Therein lay the paradox.

Because it was apparent in this example and numerous others that individuals were not consistent maximizers of expected wealth, an analytical problem arose. In order to make statements and predictions about human behavior in economic decision-making, it is necessary to assume some consistency in goal seeking. It is especially desirable to assume that humans act in order to maximize happiness, satisfaction, and so on. Expected wealth had served as a satisfactory surrogate for these goals, but its limitations became too great (as in the above case). Instead of seeking another measurable surrogate, the writers of the period simply identified an abstract concept, *utility*, as that which everyone sought to maximize. By definition, therefore, everyone is a utility maximizer, because the only meaning of utility is that bundle of happiness, satisfaction, and so on that one directs all of one's actions toward maximizing. It then follows that whichever course of action provides the greatest utility is the one to be undertaken.

Unfortunately, this analysis has solved no problems. In order to determine which course of action provides the greatest utility, it is necessary to measure the utility. This, in turn, requires identifying those measurable variables of which utility is a function and specifying the function. In view of the measurement problems, it is not surprising that early writers chose to assume that utility was simply a function of wealth (although not a linear function — which would obviate the advantages of identifying utility as a separate concept).

Daniel Bernoulli approached the problem by assuming that the same proportional additions to the initial level of wealth should have the same absolute utility. Thus, $100,000 would have the same utility to a millionaire as $1 to the same person when he only possessed $10. Operationally, this approach assumes that the utility of a money gain is a log function of the size of the gain. In general, if initial wealth (α) is set at the origin on a utility scale, then the utility of an increase in wealth (Θ) can be shown as a constant times $\log \frac{\alpha+\Theta}{\alpha}$. Specifically, Bernoulli demonstrated that the value of the Petersburg game, under these assumptions, would be $\sqrt{\alpha+1} \times \sqrt[4]{\alpha+2} \times \sqrt[8]{\alpha+4} \cdots - \alpha$. If initial wealth of the player (α) were 0, this would reduce to $\sqrt{1} \times \sqrt[4]{2} \times \sqrt[8]{4} \cdots = 2$, implying that he would be indifferent between the right to play the game and a gift of two ducats. (Bernoulli, *op. cit.*, p. 32.) Other indifference points were 3 for $\alpha = 10$, 4 for $\alpha = 100$, and 6 for $\alpha = 1000$.) Bernoulli posits the following example:

> Suppose Caius, a Petersburg merchant, has purchased commodities in Amsterdam which he could sell for ten thousand rubles if he had them in Petersburg. He therefore orders them to be shipped there by sea, but is in doubt whether or not to insure them. He is well aware of the fact that at this time of year, of one hundred ships which sail from Amsterdam to Petersburg, five are usually lost. However, there is no insurance available below the price of eight hundred rubles a cargo, an amount which he considers outrageously high. The question is, therefore, how much wealth must Caius possess apart from the goods under consideration in order that it be sensible for him to abstain from insuring them?
>
> If X represents his fortune, then this together with the value of the expectation of the safe arrival of his goods is given by
>
> $$\sqrt[100]{(X+10{,}000)^{95} X^5} = \sqrt[20]{(X+10{,}000)^{19} X}.$$
>
> In case, he abstains. With insurance, he will have a certain fortune of $X + 9{,}200$. Equating these two magnitudes we get: $(X+10{,}000)^{19} X = (X+9200)^{20}$ or, approximately, $X = 5{,}043$. If, therefore, Caius, apart from the expectation of receiving his commodities, possesses an amount greater than 5043 rubles he will be right in not buying insurance. If, on the contrary, his wealth is less than this amount he should insure his cargo (*Ibid.*, p. 29).

There have been many interesting extensions, refinements, and contradictions of the Bernoulli analysis. It has been shown, for example, that under certain circumstances, Bernoullian utility assumptions can be used to avoid utility analysis altogether. It will be recalled that Bernoulli suggested that decisions be made on the basis of the expected (arithmetic mean) utility, which was in turn based on the logs of the returns. If we assume that long-run wealth maximization is a desirable goal, then it can be shown that the arithmetic mean of the logarithms (utilities) of returns is maximized when the geometric mean of returns is maximized. Therefore, the criteria of choice may in this case revert to maximization of return, defined as the geometric mean.

Bernoulli presented the case of a poor man who came into possession of a lottery ticket promising a 50–50 chance of 20,000 ducats or nothing and asked if he would be considered unwise to sell the ticket to a rich man for 9,000 ducats. Let us further assume that the poor man has wealth of 1,000 ducats and the rich man 100,000 ducats. From these data, the following table may be constructed:

	Future Occurences		Criterion	
Strategy	Ticket Wins	Ticket Loses	Arith. Mean	Geo. Mean
Poor Man				
(Hold)	2.1	0.1	1.1	0.46
(Sell)	1.0	1.0	1.0	1.0
Rich Man				
(Buy)	1.11	0.91	1.01	1.005
(Don't Buy)	1.00	1.00	1.00	1.00
Probabiltiy	0.5	0.5		

The case of the rich man is fairly simple. If he wins, his return is $(100{,}000 + 20{,}000 - 9{,}000)/100{,}000 = 1.11$; if he loses it is $(100{,}000 - 9000)/100{,}000 = 0.91$. If the poor man sells the ticket, he has a 10,000 certainty; to hold the ticket then becomes a gamble which pays a $(10{,}000 - 9{,}000 + 20{,}000)/10{,}000 = 2.1$ return if he wins and $(10{,}000 - 9{,}000)/10{,}000 = 0.1$ if he loses. As shown in the table, the rich man would want to buy and the poor man would want to hold the ticket on the basis of the arithmetic mean, but the transaction would be desirable for both on the basis of the geometric mean. Bernoulli would claim the latter result valid from a utility standpoint and it could also be argued the same from a long-run wealth maximization standpoint.

A solution to the paradox was also offered and published by Bernoulli along with his own. In the solution, it was assumed that the utility of wealth was equal to the square root of its quantity. As such, the utility of the Petersburg game was:

$$1/2\sqrt{1} + 1/4\sqrt{2} + 1/8\sqrt{4} + \cdots = \frac{1}{2-\sqrt{2}},$$

and its value in certain money was $[1/(2-\sqrt{2})]^2$, or slightly less than three ducats (Bernoulli, *op. cit.*, pp. 32–34.).

A second solution was also suggested. In this case, it was assumed that the utility of wealth remained constant beyond a certain point. For argument, it was assumed that the utility of all sums greater than 2^{24} was the same as that of 2^{24}. The value of the Petersburg game then became $1/2 + 1/2 + (24 \text{ times}) + 1/2 + 1/4 + 1/8 + \cdots = 12 + 1 = 13$. The utility function implied by this solution is linear to 2^{24} and horizontal beyond; as such, it is bounded upward. This is important because it can be shown that an unbounded function (like Bernoulli's log function) can still give an infinite value. See Karl Menger, quoted in Arrow (1971), p. 23.

On the other hand, a bounded function is probably unrealistic and violates the assumption that more wealth is always preferred to less. Menger's contention has to do with the fact that the inclinations of many people to disregard very small probabilities, very small probability differences, and also very small amounts of money cannot be fitted into an orderly axiomatic system.

Finally, some authorities assume that the utility function is quadratic, of the form $U_x = a + bx - cx^2$ where a, b, and c are constants and b and c are positive. A limitation of quadratic utility functions is that they are not only bounded upward but, indeed, have a maximum beyond which utility declines; it is generally assumed that only the portion to the left of the maximum constitutes the relevant range. A major advantage of quadratic utility functions is that they are completely consistent with the assumption that assets are chosen on the basis of only the first two moments about the mean of the distribution of returns. We shall return to the significance of this attribute.

Von Neumann–Morgenstern Utility

Early writers on utility theory often claimed that it was possible to measure utility on an absolute scale, whereby the joy or pain of money gains and losses could be exactly computed and even compared among individuals. This group, identified as the neoclassical cardinal utility theory school, was essentially discredited by the ordinal utility theory writers. The latter agreed that, through revealed preference, it was possible to detect which goods or combinations of goods were preferred (or were a matter of indifference) to other goods or combinations by the individual under analysis. The point of disagreement, however, was that the ordinalists contended that it was impossible to say by how much one combination of goods was preferred to another. They further insisted that interpersonal comparisons of utility gains and losses could not be made, and that all the writing about the absolute measurement of joy and pain (going back to Bentham's hedonist calculus, if not earlier) was, at best, non-operational.

Modern cardinal utility theory dates from the work of von Neumann and Morgenstern (John von Neumann and Oskar Morgenstern, 1944). They contend only that, given certain assumptions and certain data about an individual's preferences, it is possible to predict his choices in certain risky situations. The method is called cardinal only because it employs numbers in making these predictions; it makes no pretense of absolute measures and has essentially nothing in common with the earlier cardinal school.

In general, it is assumed that the individual is intelligent, rational, and fully understands the implications of the alternatives being presented to him. In addition, the following five axioms must be assumed for von Neumann–Morgenstern utility calculations to hold:

1. *Transitivity.* If the subject is indifferent between outcomes A and B and also between B and C, he must be indifferent between A and C.
2. *Continuity of preferences.* If A is preferred to B and B is preferred to no change, there must be a probability $\alpha (0 < \alpha < 1)$, such that the individual is indifferent between αA and B.
3. *Independence.* If A is preferred to B, then for any probability $\alpha (0 < \alpha < 1)$, $\alpha A + (1 - \alpha)B$ is preferred to B. Or, viewed another way, if one is indifferent between A and B, then one is also indifferent between αA and αB.
4. *Desire for high probability of success.* If A is preferred to no change and if $\alpha_1 > \alpha_2$, then $\alpha_1 A$ is preferred to $\alpha_2 A$.
5. *Compound probabilities.* If one is indifferent between αA and B, and if $\alpha = \alpha_1 \times \alpha_2$, then one is indifferent between $\alpha_1 \alpha_2 A$ and B. In sum, if the outcomes of one risky event are other risky events, the subject should act on the basis of final outcomes and their associated probabilities alone.

If these assumptions can be made, the analyst may then begin to chart the utility of wealth function of his subject. The first step is to define arbitrarily in terms of *utils* (the cardinal utility unit of measurement) two end points of the range of wealth to be tested; it is important to use end points because the methodology is one of interpolation but it may *not* be used for extrapolation. Suppose, for example, we defined $0 as 0 utils and $1 million as 1000 utils and the following conversation ensued:

Q. How much would you be willing to pay for a lottery ticket offering a 50–50 chance of $1 M or $0?
A. $250,000 [0.5 (0 utils) + 0.5 (1000 utils) = 500 U].
Q. How much would you pay for a 50–50 chance of $250,000 or nothing?
A. $62,500 [0.5 (0 U) + 0.5 (500 U) = 250 U].

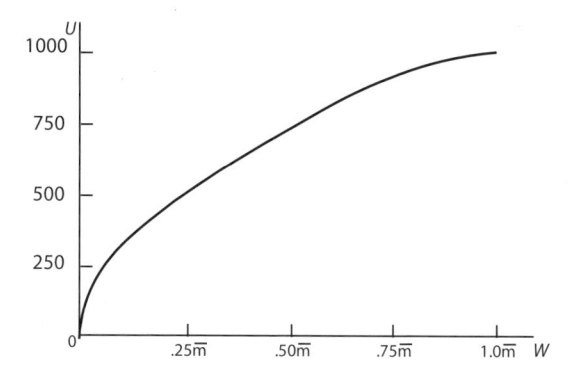

Figure 9.1. Utility as a Function of Wealth ($U = \sqrt{W}$)

We have thus assumed two points on the utility versus wealth graph (see Figure 9.1) and have been able to compute two more. In so doing, and in various applications we will make of this analysis, we have employed the expected utility maxim of von Neumann–Morgenstern analysis:

The utility of the game (risky event) is not the utility of the expected value of the game but rather the expected value of the utilities associated with the outcomes of the game.

To be specific, in our first question above, the utility of the lottery ticket was not the utility of its expected value ($500,000) but rather the expected value of the utilities of the two outcomes ($0 and $1 M̄). If the utility of the game were the utility of its expected value, then the individual would be indifferent between the lottery and a gift of $500,000, and we would be back in the Petersburg Paradox.

It will be noted that in the numerical example, the utility of wealth is a square root function. In practice, of course, it is not likely to be so well behaved. But, by asking enough lottery-type questions, it should be possible to plot a curve and from the curve to determine the utility associated with every wealth outcome within the relevant range of a risky situation.

Suppose that our subject in the above example (for whom $U = \sqrt{W}$) is faced with a risky situation with the possible outcomes enumerated below:

Outcome	Probability	EV
+10,000	.3	3,000
+90,000	.5	45,000
+490,000	.2	98,000
		$\mu = \overline{\overline{146,000}}$

The certain sum for which he would be willing to sell his interest is given by:

W	$U = \sqrt{W}$	Probability	EU
+10,000	100 U	.3	30
+90,000	300 U	.5	150
+490,000	700 U	.2	140
			$\overline{320 \text{ U}}$

$W = U^2 = (320)^2 = \underline{\underline{\$102{,}400}}$.

This game possesses the same utility to the subject as a certain $102,400.

Indifference Curves

Let us return to our subject in the last section for whom the utility of wealth was equal to the square root of his wealth position. Again defining $0 as 0 utils and $1 $\bar{\text{M}}$ as 1000 utils, we may conclude that having $250,000 possesses ($\sqrt{250{,}000}$) = 500 utils for the subject, as shown by point A on Figure 9.2. A 50–50 chance, represented by point D, of having $90,000($\sqrt{90{,}000}$ = 300 U), point B, or $490,000($\sqrt{490{,}000}$ = 700 U), point C, also provides [(0.5)(200 U) + (0.5)(700 U)] = 500 utils for the subject. Furthermore, a 50–50 chance, represented by point G of having $10,000($\sqrt{10{,}000}$ = 100 U),

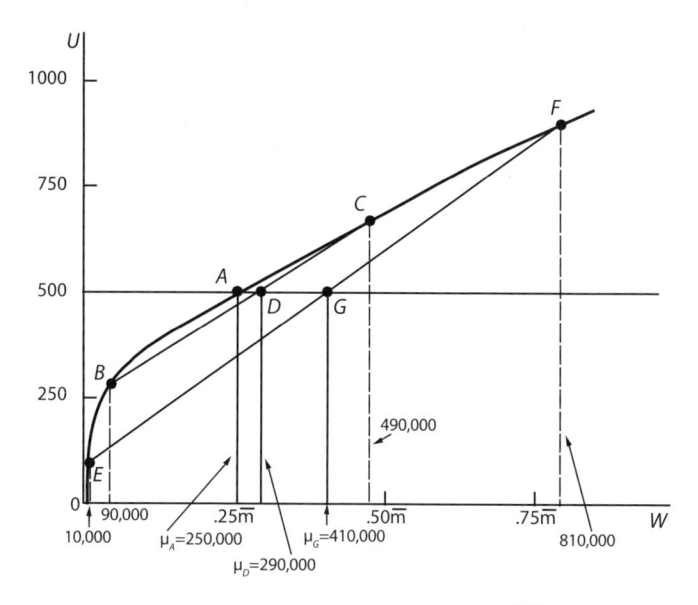

Figure 9.2. Utility as a Function of Wealth ($U = \sqrt{W}$), Specific Values

point E, or $\$810{,}000(\sqrt{810{,}000} = 900\text{ U})$, point F, also provides [(0.5) (100 U) + (0.5) (900 U)] 500 utils.

Therefore, because the opportunities represented by points A, D, and G provide the same utility, the subject should be indifferent among them. Note, however, the following differences in the expected value and standard deviation of opportunities A, D, and G.

(1) $\mu_A = \$250{,}000(1.0) = \$250{,}000$

$\sigma_A = \sqrt{(250{,}000 - 250{,}000)^2(1.0)} = 0.$

(2) $\mu_D = (\$90{,}000)(0.5) + (490{,}000)(0.5) = \$290{,}000$

$\sigma_D = \sqrt{(\$90{,}000 - 290{,}000)^2(0.5) + (490{,}000 - 290{,}000)^2(0.5)}$
$= \$200{,}000.$

(3) $\mu_G = (\$10{,}000)(0.5) + (\$810{,}000)(0.5) = \$410{,}000$

$\sigma_G = \sqrt{(\$10{,}000 - 410{,}000)^2(0.5) + (810{,}000 - 410{,}000)^2(0.5)}$
$= \$400{,}000.$

408   Quantitative Financial Analytics

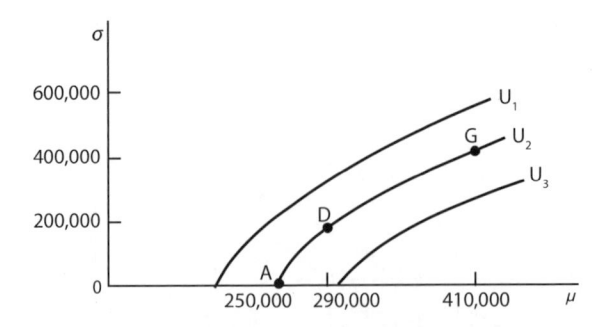

Figure 9.3. Risk Averse Indifference Curves

Because we have decided that each of these three opportunities provides equal utility let us graph them in (μ, σ) space, as shown in Figure 9.3 as curve U_2.

What we have generated, of course, is an *indifference curve*, the locus of all points on the graph providing the same utility as a $250,000 certainty. (It is possible also to derive indifference curves from utility functions mathematically by the expansion of a Taylor series.) Because we are depicting a three-dimensional graph (μ, σ, U) in two-dimensional (μ, σ) space, there are an infinite number of indifference curves that could be drawn, one corresponding to each certain sum (U_1 and U_3 are representative examples on Figure 9.3).

In dealing with indifference curves, it is important to remember that: (1) each point on a given indifference curve provides the same utility as all other points on the same curve, and (2) each point on a second given indifference curve (for the same person at the same time) provides a constant amount of greater (or less) utility than each point on the first curve.

Now observe that the indifference curves are concave and positively sloped in (μ, σ) space since $dU/dW > 0$ and $d^2U/dW^2 < 0$, then $d\sigma/d\mu > 0$. This implies that our subject requires a greater expected return (μ) in order to tolerate a greater dispersion of possible outcomes (σ) and be equally satisfied. Because dispersion of possible outcomes about the mean has been defined as a measure of risk, we may say, in the popular parlance, that our subject is a *risk averter*.

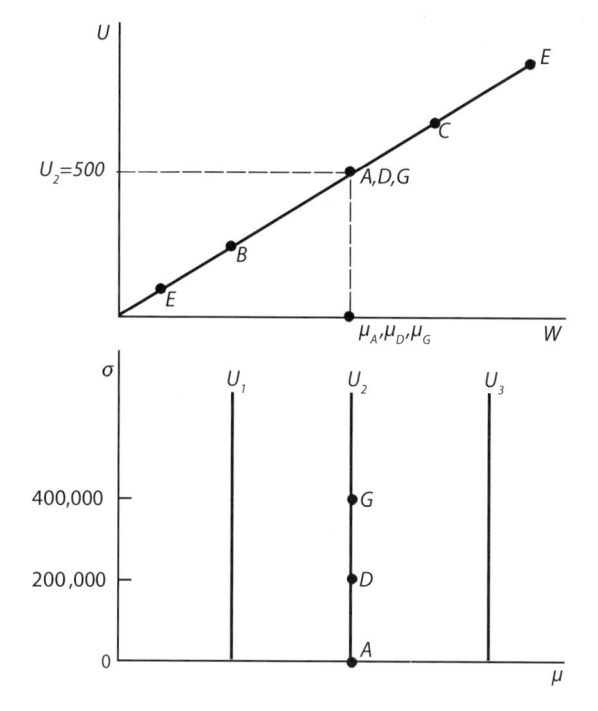

Figure 9.4. Risk Neutral Indifference Curves

Suppose, instead of the above situation, that our subject had a linear total utility of wealth function; this is the same thing as assuming a constant marginal utility of wealth function or that $200,000 is exactly twice as desirable as $100,000. The resulting utility-of-wealth function and indifference curves are given in Figure 9.4. Because the expected utility of the outcomes equals the utility of the expected value, all opportunities having the same expected value will have the same utility, regardless of risk. The indifference curves are therefore vertical, since $dU/dW > 0$ and $d^2U/dW^2 = 0$, then $d\sigma/d\mu = \infty$. A person possessing such a function is called *risk neutral*.

Finally, suppose our subject had an increasing marginal utility of wealth function, such that $200,000 was more than twice as desirable as $100,000. We observe, in Figure 9.5 that risky combinations D and G provide the same utility as certainty A, but with a lower expected value. The corresponding indifference curves for the

410   *Quantitative Financial Analytics*

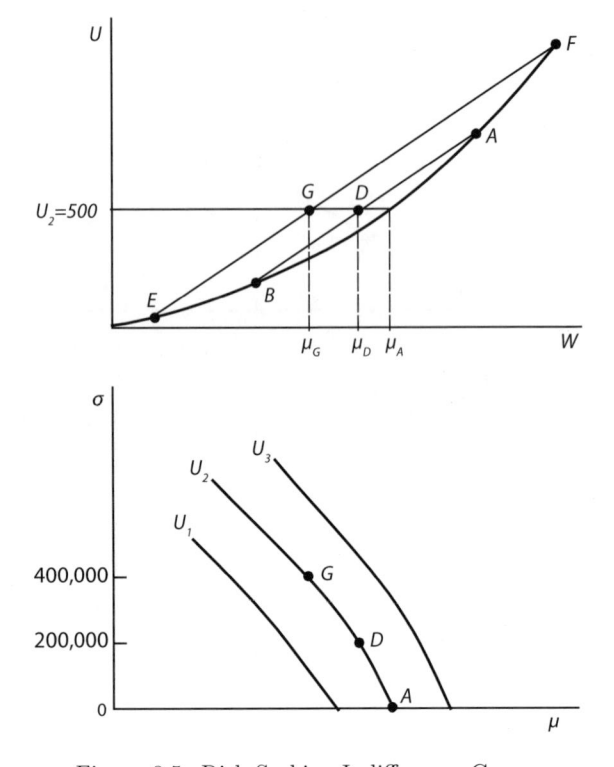

Figure 9.5. Risk-Seeking Indifference Curves

subject are concave but negatively sloped. Since $dU/dW > 0$ and $d^2U/dW^2 > 0$, then $d\sigma/d\mu < 0$. Such a person is called a *risk seeker*.

Now that the indifference curves have been geometrically derived from their respective utility-of-wealth functions, it becomes convenient to switch the axes in their graphs for subsequent discussion. It will be observed that this task is accomplished in Figure 9.6, and we shall henceforth deal with the indifference curves in (σ, μ) space. Furthermore, we shall concentrate our attention upon the risk averter. It has been demonstrated that the risk averter's indifference curves in (σ, μ) space will be positively sloped and concave from above. The actual shape of the curves, of course, depends upon the corresponding utility-of-wealth function.

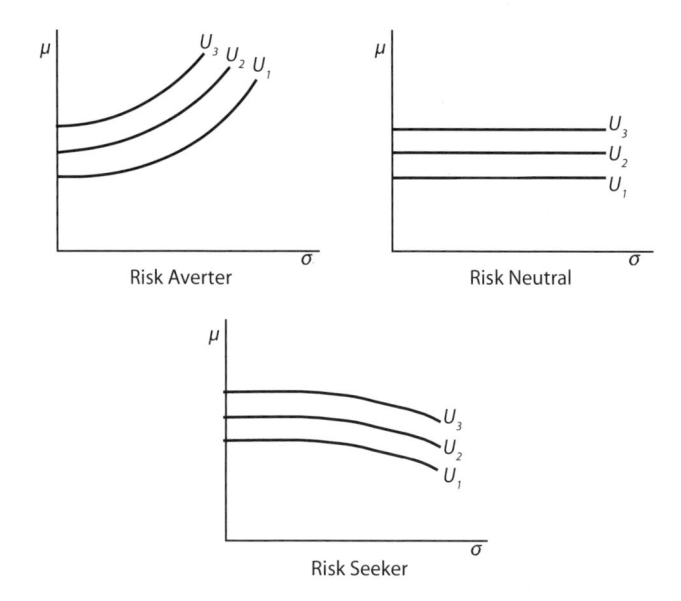

Figure 9.6. Indifference Curves in (σ, μ) Space

If the utility function happens to be quadratic ($U = a + bx - cx^2$), it has also been shown that the indifference curves will be concentric circles with the center at $\sigma = 0$ and $\mu =$ the value of X which maximizes the utility function ($-b/2c$). The indifference curves corresponding to other types of utility functions are not nearly so simple to specify.

In a famous article (Milton Friedman and Leonard J. Savage, 1948.), the authors set about to rationalize the following observable phenomena:

1. People buy fire insurance, thus preferring a certain small loss to the small probability of a large loss coupled with the large probability of no loss. This game is undertaken at unfair odds (the premium pays for costs and profits of the insurance company as well as loss coverage) indicating that the individual will pay a premium to avoid risk in this range of his wealth function and is thus risk averse.

2. The same people also buy lottery tickets or engage in other forms of gambling, thus preferring a large probability of a small loss

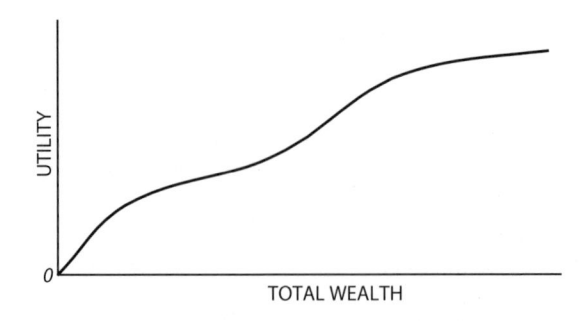

Figure 9.7. Friedman-Savage Utility Function

combined with the small probability of a large gain to no change in their wealth. Because such gambles are also undertaken at unfair odds (the house profit), the behavior implied is risk seeking over this range of the wealth function.

3. Finally, the lotteries considered in 2 are observed to have more than one prize, implying that people would prefer a greater probability of winning a smaller prize and thus are risk averse at wealth levels beyond some point.

The utility function implied by such behavior is shown in Figure 9.7.

The Friedman–Savage conclusions help to explain the tendency of people to risk "excess" funds at unfair odds in the hope of making a "killing." Unfortunately, however, the risk-seeking range will differ for different individuals and over time. As such, predictions about behavior are almost impossible to make under this system and few practical application have been devised.

In another famous article, some similar questions were considered (Harry Markowitz, 1952b). The utility function he derived is shown in Figure 9.8. Present or accustomed wealth is placed at the origin. Small increases in wealth are shown to give increasing satisfaction (implying risk-seeking behavior), although diminishing marginal utility does eventually occur. In like manner, small losses are not too bothersome.

Large losses do create large disutilities, but these tend toward a limit below some level of loss. One possible cause of the latter is that

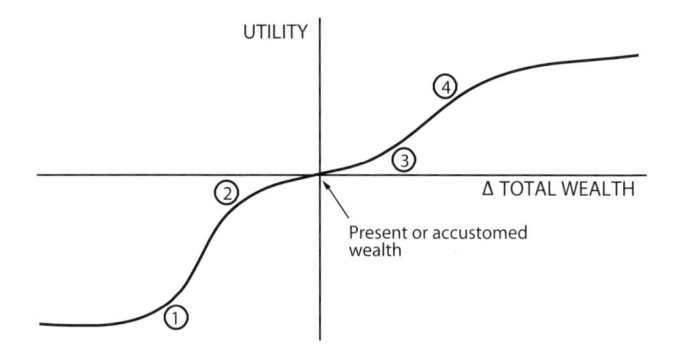

Figure 9.8. Markowitz Utility Function

the probability of catastrophic loss is generally so low and the cost of insurance relatively so high that most people ignore the possibility (for example, the likelihood of being killed in an auto accident on a single trip to the grocery store).

As a generalization, it may be said that an individual will ignore outcomes falling to the left of inflection point 1 in Figure 9.8 and insure against those falling between points 1 and 2. Between points 2 and 3, the individual may gamble (or speculate at unfavorable odds); if, however, he wins or loses enough to fall outside this range, he will quit. Between points 3 and 4 (often viewed as the investment range), the individual will show increasingly risk-averse behavior. Beyond point 4, the risk aversion becomes rather severe, as there is little increase in utility associated with any gain in wealth (perhaps implying a well-diversified portfolio of treasury bills). Obviously, the Markowitz analysis is even more difficult to apply operationally than the Friedman–Savage, even though it may be more descriptive of real behavior than the simple models presented above.

Several difficulties with utility analysis remain. Utility functions that are bounded upward (implying a zero marginal utility of wealth), as in the alternative solution to the Petersburg Paradox, not only violate the basic notion that more wealth is preferable to less, but also cause risky situations to be indeterminate. As long as all the possible outcomes of a risky event lie on the horizontal portion of the utility function, not only is the risky event as desirable as a certainty equal to the expected value of the risky event (which is true for all linear utility functions) but it is also as desirable as a certainty equal to its worst (or best!) possible outcome.

Furthermore, if the slope of the utility function becomes negative at some point (implying a negative marginal utility of wealth), as in the case of the quadratic, utility can be increased by throwing money away; such pathological implications for behavior do not articulate well with the basic rationality assumptions.

The assumptions of extreme risk aversion (corresponding to very low or even negative marginal utilities of wealth) at high levels of wealth do not appear to correspond terribly well to observed individual behavior. Many very rich individuals continue working well beyond the point when one might expect that extra contributions to wealth would produce almost no extra utility. Consider Warren Buffett as an example. The entire idea that "money is merely the way you keep score" argues against the notion of zero marginal utility.

In another vein, the history of families such as the Kennedys and Rockefellers may indicate that the utility derived from the power of wealth may supplant consumption requirements at high levels of wealth. The theoretical basis of these assumptions is obscure, and empirical justification of them is virtually non-existent. One defense often raised is that wealth exhibits diminishing marginal utility in the way any consumer good does. The point ignored, of course, is that wealth represents command over *all* goods and, although enough ice cream cones may satisfy one's craving and even cause illness beyond a point, the application of the same logic to imply total satiation of wants of all goods and services is not necessarily justified.

Indeed, one of the longest standing assumptions of risk aversion seems to be in the field of public finance, where the underlying notion of a diminishing marginal utility of wealth is a necessary condition to develop a normative case for progressive income taxation. Given then that the notion of risk aversion existing at all levels of wealth is open to some question, the idea of its increasing with wealth (as implied by most of the standard functions introduced in the chapter) is even more suspect. The idea of utility reaching a maximum and thereafter declining (or even remaining constant) appears even more divorced from reality. Additional measures seem required.

The implications of risk aversion varying over wealth levels and especially, diminishing as wealth increases have been investigated. A measure of local risk aversion (for small changes in wealth) $r(W)$, equal to the following:

$$r(W) = -\frac{U''(W)}{U'(W)}.$$

The argument continues on to demonstrate that local risk aversion is a decreasing function of wealth if and only if the premium required to undertake any given risk declines as assets rise. It further demonstrates that this requirement, $r'(W) \leq 0$, is equivalent to the condition $U''(W)U'(W) \geq [U^*(W)]^2$. A measure of proportional risk aversion, $r^*(W) = W \times r(W)$ may also be introduced along with an analysis and clarification of various functions in terms of constant, increasing, or decreasing proportional and absolute risk aversion. One example of constant risk aversion (the special case of no aversion) is $U(W) = f(W)$; an example of constant proportional risk aversion is $U(W) = f(\log W)$.

Portfolio Theory

For the last 70–80 years, a very clear division has existed between the work of the security analyst and that of the portfolio manager. The analyst attempts to divide the universe of securities into three parts: (1) underpriced (recommended purchase); (2) fully priced (recommended long-run hold); and (3) overpriced (no longer recommended). The portfolio manager then constructs groups of securities into recommended holdings based on risk/return characteristics. The first decision to be made usually involves the breakdown between stocks and bonds; a general heuristic is to place enough of the portfolio in bonds so that the interest payments, plus a token dividend from the remainder in stocks, would meet the minimum income requirement of the portfolio in all but the very worst of years. Beyond this consideration, the ratio of bonds to stocks might also be varied depending upon the manager's view of the cycle (more bonds at the peak of a boom, and so on). The bond portfolio would then be divided among governments, municipals (depending upon the portfolio's tax status), industrials, utilities, and transportation issues according to perceived risk or the manager's tastes; diversification by maturity was also obtained (to avoid the necessity of reinvesting large sums at any future point in time). The stock portfolio would be apportioned among cyclical, defensive, and growth issues on the basis of income required, state of the market, and the ability to bear risk. Among the three stock categories, further allocations by industry might be made. Finally, with the bond portfolio apportioned by type and maturity range and the stock portfolio apportioned by industry, the manager would select the appropriate securities in the apportioned amounts from the analyst's list of recommendations.

Following the above sequence, the proverbial widow (in a pre-Fem-lib era) who had just received a bequest would generally have minimum income needs that would be quite large in relation to her principal and extend over a long time. Because a failure to earn the required income would quickly exhaust her capital and make her a public charge (in the days before receiving welfare became fashionable), the portfolio manager would apportion most, if not all, of her portfolio to bonds (and governments at that); any equities purchased would also be of a defensive-income variety. On the other hand, the proverbial successful businessman (or businesswoman in today's more egalitarian world) would generally have enough other assets and income to make no current income requirements of his or her portfolio and also to be able to endure a fair amount of risk. Thus, the portfolio manager would allocate most of the funds to equities and, with no income constraint, much of that to growth companies. Therefore, the resulting portfolios of government bonds for widows and of high-risk growth stocks for businesspeople were derived by the systematic application of the same decision framework to differing individual circumstances.

Institutional portfolio regulations and policies were derived in a similar manner. Because banks' assets represent the funds of depositors and life insurance companies' investments represent policyholders' reserves, it was felt that little risk could be undertaken; portfolio regulation of these institutions reflects this philosophy. On the other hand, institutions like mutual funds are closer to the concept of "businessman's risk," and, consequently, they are not as severely regulated in regard to the risk of the assets they may hold.

The major difficulty with the approach outlined above is that it is based upon the assumption that portfolio risk is a weighted sum of the total risk of the component securities, considered in isolation; as demonstrated in the next section of this chapter, this is simply untrue. Another unfortunate assumption of the above methodology is that the "interior decorator" approach to security selection ("a little of this, a little of that") results in efficient diversification; as indicated below, this contention is also incorrect.

The impact of the modern theory upon the role of security analysis has been implied in the previous chapters. It will be noted that securities have not been "priced" in this book, because securities cannot be priced upon the basis of their risk considered in isolation from other securities; furthermore, security purchasers are price takers, not price makers. The function of the security analyst has been viewed here to be the estimation of security return, risk, and covariance with the returns of the securities (perhaps employing a market index, as considered later in this chapter). Thus, the portfolio manager should no longer be provided with a buy, hold, or sell recommendation, but rather an estimate of the parameters of the distribution of security returns. At least, this is true in theory. In fact, most analysts today still "price" stocks and provide recommendations accordingly. Stocks have "price" objectives; and when they are reached or the objective is changed, a "sell" or "fully priced" recommendation is issued.

The considerations of client-required return and ability to bear risk should be treated in the form of utility function determination. The goal is the same, but the use of a utility framework is more precise and also allows for trade-offs between risk and return. The proverbial widow would have a very risk-averse function (which, as demonstrated in the rest of this chapter, will cause a low-risk portfolio to be chosen), and the proverbial businessperson will have a less risk-averse function (and a riskier portfolio). Under the modern theory, then, the manager takes the analyst's parameters, determines for each level of risk that portfolio with the highest attainable return (the efficiency frontier, derived in the next section), compares the market's trade-off of risk and return to his client's preferences, and selects the utility-maximizing portfolio.

The goal of portfolio management, like all other human endeavors, is thus assumed to be utility maximization. It has further been demonstrated that this goal is operationally similar to the more traditional goals (for example, income, limited income with growth, and so on), because it will have different operational implications for individuals in differing circumstances and of differing risk predilections. In addition, the goal of institutional portfolio management should be the maximization of beneficiary utility. If markets are efficient, the last goal can be achieved by an institutional portfolio policy designed to place the parameters of its own securities on the highest attainable market (risk-return trade-off) line; this policy will maximize the market value of investors' holdings, from which point they can go about the maximization of their own utility in isolation. If markets are not efficient, the institution will need to adopt a "clientele" approach, estimate a utility function representative of its beneficiaries, and work to put the parameters of its own securities on the highest attainable indifference curve of the posited utility function.

In theory, the goal of portfolio management is utility maximization, and the institutional objective is the maximization of the market value of the wealth of the portfolio beneficiary. The first step in this process is an understanding of the effects of diversification upon risk and return. The simplest way to begin is with an examination of the two-asset portfolio.

Suppose that we were offered the opportunity to bet $1 against $2 on a fair coin being flipped "heads," or the same odds on "tails." The expected value of such an opportunity is $[(0.5)(+2)+(0.5)(-1) = 50$ cents] and, because of the small sum involved, we would probably overlook the risk $[\sigma = \sqrt{(2.00 - 0.50)^2(0.5) + (-1.00 - 0.50)^2} = \$1.50]$ and undertake the bet. If, however, the stakes were raised to

$100,000 against $200,000, our enthusiasm for the $50,000 expected value might well be tempered by the $150,000 standard deviation; at the least, some reference to utility considerations would be required.

These difficulties could be overcome if we were allowed to subdivide our $1 (or $100,000) bet into one-half on "heads" and one-half on "tails" of the same coin. In this case, we would lose $0.50 on one bet and win $1.00 on the other each time. Thus, the expected value of the game would remain $0.50, but the risk would be totally eliminated. The reduction in risk is effected because our winning is contingent upon the outcome of several events that do not always occur together (are not perfectly positively correlated). Indeed, we were able to eliminate risk in our example because our events (both sides of the same coin) were perfectly negatively correlated. The existence of events (that is, the return on securities) that are less than perfectly positively correlated with each other gives rise to the concept of diversification for risk reduction that underlies portfolio theory.

The expected return on a portfolio of assets is simply the weighted average of their individual expected returns, or

Let: μ = expected return on portfolio
α_i = proportion of portfolio invested in ith asset
μ_i = expected return on ith asset
n = number of assets in portfolio

Then: $$\mu = \sum_{i=1}^{n} \alpha_i \mu_i. \qquad (9.1)$$

Therefore, a portfolio composed 50 percent of an asset with a 10 percent expected return and 50 percent of an asset with a 20 percent expected return would have an expected return of $[(0.5)(10 \text{ percent}) + (0.5)(20 \text{ percent})] = 15$ percent. It is important to note that risk does not enter the computation of expected return; the example above has $\mu = 15$ percent regardless of the standard deviations of the two securities. Because of the effects of correlation upon risk, the standard deviation of the portfolio is not as easily computed as the expected value.

Let: $C_{ij} = r_{ij}\sigma_i\sigma_j$ $C_{ij} = r_{ij}\sigma_i\sigma_j$ be the covariance between the returns of securities i and j, where r_{ij} is the correlation coefficient of returns between securities i and j, and σ = standard deviation of portfolio returns.

$$\text{Then:} \quad \sigma = \sqrt{\sum_{i=1}^{n}\sum_{j=1}^{n} \alpha_i \alpha_j C_{ij}}, \tag{9.2}$$

$$\text{or} \quad \sigma = \sqrt{\sum_{i=1}^{n}\sum_{j=1}^{n} \alpha_i \alpha_j \sigma_i \sigma_j r_{ij}}. \tag{9.3}$$

Note that the correlation coefficient, r, plays a major role in Equations (9.2) and (9.3). Briefly, $r_{ij} = \frac{E[(I-\mu_j)(J-\mu_j)]}{\sigma_i \sigma_j}$ and, therefore, C_{ij} may be restated as $E[(I-\mu_i)(J-\mu_j)]$ or $[E(IJ) - \mu_i\mu_j]$. It should be noted that if $i = j$, then $r_{ij} = 1$ and C_{ij} is the variance $(\sigma^2_{i=j})$.

Let us now consider the simple two-security case. The expected return will be (for $n = 2$):

$$\mu = \alpha_1\mu_1 + \alpha_2\mu_2, \tag{9.4}$$

and the standard deviation will be:

$$\sigma = \sqrt{\alpha_1^2\sigma_1^2 + 2\alpha_1\alpha_2\sigma_1\sigma_2 r_{12} + \alpha_2^2\sigma_2^2}. \tag{9.5}$$

Beginning with the assumption that both securities are risky, let us examine the importance of r_{12} in determining the risk of the portfolio. Assume the following data:

Security	μ_i	σ_i
1	10 percent	3 percent
2	20 percent	7 percent

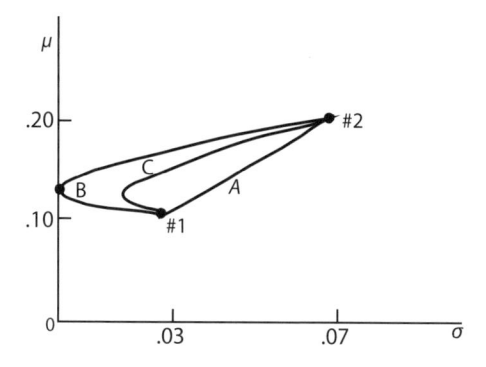

Figure 9.9. The Two-asset Portfolio (Risky Securities)

Case A: $r_{12} = +1.00$. In this instance, Equation (9.5) becomes:

$$\sigma = \sqrt{(\alpha_1^2 \sigma_1^2) + 2(\alpha_1 \sigma_1)(\alpha_2 \sigma_2) + (\alpha_2^2 \sigma_2^2)}$$

which is of the general algebraic form $(a+b)^2 = a^2 + 2ab + b^2$. Thus, $\sigma = (\alpha_1 \sigma_1) + (\alpha_2 \sigma_2)$, and risk, like return, increases linearly in (σ, μ) space. Such a case is graphed as A in Figure 9.9 and illustrates that risk cannot be reduced without accepting a lower return (no gains from diversification) in the case of perfect positive correlation.

Case B: $r_{12} = -1.00$. In this instance, Equation (9.5) becomes:

$$\sigma = \sqrt{(\alpha_1^2 \sigma_1^2) - 2(\alpha_1 \sigma_1)(\alpha_2 \sigma_2) + (\alpha_2^2 \sigma_2^2)}$$

which is of the general algebraic form $(a-b)^2 = a^2 - 2ab + b^2$. Thus, $\sigma = |(\alpha_1 \sigma_1) - (\alpha_2 \sigma_2)|$, and $\sigma = 0$ where $\alpha_1 = \sigma_2/(\sigma_1 + \sigma_2)$.

Combinations of two securities under this assumption are graphed as B in Figure 9.9. Here, the gains from diversifying a portfolio composed entirely of security 1 at least to the riskless point are obvious.

Case C: $r_{12} = 0$. In this instance, the equation becomes:

$$\sigma = \sqrt{(\alpha_1^2 \sigma_1^2) + (\alpha_2^2 \sigma_2^2)}.$$

(Note that, assuming normal returns, $r_{12} = 0$ is the same thing as statistical independence of returns, that is, $[(P(I|J) = P(I)]$.)

This combination is graphed as C in Figure 9.9 and exhibits gains from diversification. For the specific data given above, the curve reaches a minimum σ at $\mu = 11.55$ percent. In general, the minimum σ point in the two-asset case is given by $d\sigma/da_1 = 0$, with $\alpha_I = (\sigma^2 - \sigma_1\sigma_2 r_{12})/(\sigma_1^2 + \sigma_2^2 - 2\sigma_1\sigma_2 r_{12})$. Furthermore, as the number of assets with statistically independent returns grows larger, and the proportion invested in each becomes increasingly smaller, the law of large numbers (or more precisely, the central limit theorem) implies that risk can be essentially eliminated in the limit, leaving us in the simple case of dominance discussed earlier.

If we may assume the investor to be rational and risk-averse, then certain combinations of securities 1 and 2 may be immediately eliminated. In case B of Figure 9.9 (where $r_{12} = -1$), for example, it will be noted that for every portfolio from the all 1 portfolio to the $\sigma = 0$ portfolio, which has the same σ and a larger μ. Thus, regardless of the specific shape of one's utility function, one would be foolish to invest in any of the former set of portfolios with the latter available. This notion leads directly to the concept of *efficiency*. A portfolio is "efficient" when it is impossible to obtain a greater average return without incurring greater standard deviation and it is impossible to obtain smaller standard deviation without giving up return on the average. Therefore, all the portfolios below minimum σ on curves B and C of Figure 9.9 are inefficient. All the points on curve A are efficient. The points representing the coordinates of all efficient portfolios form a curve called the *efficiency frontier*. The efficiency frontier for C from Figure 9.9 has been graphed as EF in Figure 9.10. Although it cannot be known at this stage which portfolio is optimal for a given investor, it is known from the above logic that for a rational, risk-averse investor, the optimal portfolio will be on the efficiency frontier.

The selection of an optimal portfolio follows in a straightforward fashion, however. Indifference curves (derived above) are applied, and the optimal portfolio is found at the point of tangency of EF with the highest attainable indifference curve (point X in Figure 9.10). This point is preferable to any other on the curve (for example, E or F) because it provides a higher level of utility (that is, $U_2 > U_1$).

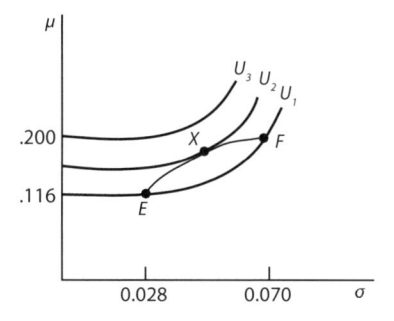

Figure 9.10. Portfolio Selection

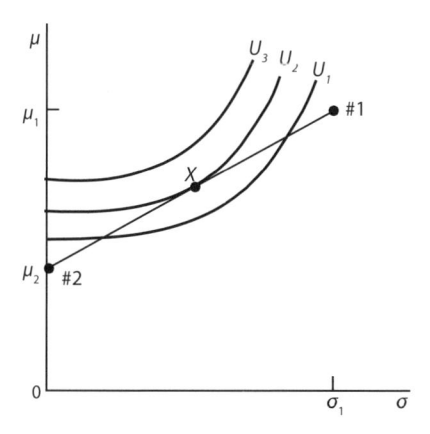

Figure 9.11. The Two-asset Portfolio (Including a Riskless Security)

A point on a higher indifference curve (for example, on U_3) would be even better, but by the definition of an efficiency frontier given above, points above EF do not exist.

We may consider the special case in which one of the securities (assume security 2) is riskless. Then $\sigma_2 \equiv 0$ and Equation (9.5) becomes $\sigma = \alpha_1 \sigma_1$, such that the risk of the portfolio is proportional to the investment in the risky asset. Thus, any combination of securities 1 and 2 could be drawn as a straight line in (σ, μ) space, as shown in Figure 9.11. Furthermore, if 1 were a portfolio of securities with parameters (σ_1, μ_1), the same result would be obtained if a riskless security with return μ_2 were added to the portfolio. The optimal combination of the risky security or portfolio and the riskless asset may also be determined by the application of indifference curves (point X). We shall return later to the implications of this phenomenon.

When we move from the two-security case to the many (or, n) security case, the theoretical problems are not very great. We could merely say that the investor (1) takes all the opportunities available to him; (2) combines them in various proportions to form several (or several million) hypothetical portfolios; (3) computes the μ and σ for each of these portfolios; (4) for each level of μ, selects the portfolio with the least σ; (5) generates the efficiency frontier that is ready for application of his indifference curves; and (6) selects the optimal portfolio. This, conceptually speaking, is all there is to the n-security portfolio analysis case.

From a practical standpoint, however, the problems are enormous. Aside from computing the μ and σ for each security to be analyzed, we would also estimate the covariance for each security with every other security (a matter of $(n^2 - n)/2$ covariances, or 499,500 in the $n = 1000$ security case). Furthermore, to follow the above-suggested method, we would then compute the parameters of a very large number of portfolios; if we limited our position in a security to even multiples of 1 percent of our portfolio, in the 1000-security case there are $(1000,000!)/[(99,900!)(100!)]$ possible portfolios to analyze. Even with the aid of modern computers, such a task is impossible.

A first step in the simplification of the task is to reduce the number of portfolios to be analyzed. Because we are only interested in the portfolios that form the efficiency frontier, it is only the parameters of these portfolios that should be computed. Such a problem may be approached by reference to Figure 9.12. Here dots represent security parameters and the boxes represent portfolio parameters. The objective is to minimize a function of the type $\sigma^2 - \theta\mu$.

By initializing the procedure at $\theta = \infty$, the highest return security (F) is obtained; note that, because diversification cannot increase return, the highest return portfolio will be composed entirely

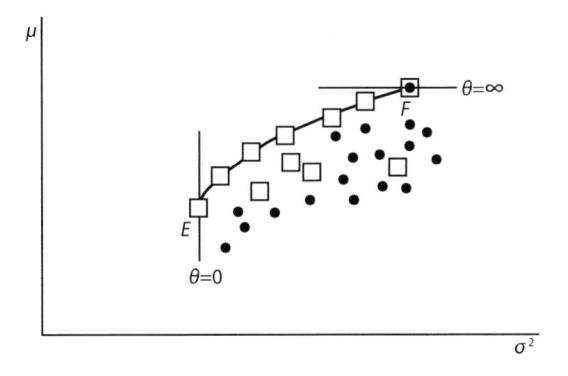

Figure 9.12. Efficiency Frontier Generation

of the highest return security. From this point, one may employ a quadratic programming algorithm to trace the efficiency frontier by allowing θ to decrease to 0 (at which point E, the minimum-variance portfolio, is obtained). In actuality, the iterative procedures only determine "corner" portfolios, which are those points at which a security enters or leaves the efficient portfolio; the efficiency frontier between two corner portfolios is a linear combination of the corner portfolios. Aside from the objective function, these techniques also generally involve constraints, such as the requirement that the weights assigned to securities be non-negative and/or sum to one.

It is also possible to generate an efficiency frontier employing calculus. The following formulation provides the minimum-risk portfolio subject to an expected return μ^* and full investment ($\Sigma\alpha = 1$).

Minimize Z, where

$$Z = \sum_{i=1}^{n}\sum_{j=1}^{n} \alpha_i \alpha_j C_{ij} + \lambda_1 \left(\sum_{i=1}^{n} \alpha_i \mu_i - \mu*\right) + \lambda_2 \left(\sum_{i=1}^{n} \alpha_i - 1\right), \tag{9.6}$$

and minimum Z is found where $\partial Z/\partial \alpha_i = 0$, $\partial Z/\partial \lambda_k = 0$ for all i and k, and second order conditions are met. The λ's are Lagrangian multipliers and are conceptually equivalent to a dual in programming or a shadow price (or opportunity cost) in more common parlance. A calculus maximization may also be employed.

Maximize Z where

$$Z = \phi \sum_{i=1}^{n}(\alpha_i \mu_i) - \left(\sum_{i=1}^{n}\sum_{j=1}^{n}\alpha_i \alpha_j C_{ij}\right) + \lambda\left(1 - \sum_{i=1}^{n}\alpha_i\right). \quad (9.7)$$

And again, maximum Z is found where $\partial Z/\partial \alpha_i = \partial Z/\partial \lambda = 0$ and ϕ is an indicator of return-risk preference.

To illustrate the hand solution for one point on the efficiency frontier (and also the need for access to a computer if one plans to do much work in this area), suppose that the efficient portfolio at $\mu^* = 15$ percent were desired for the two-asset case below.

Security	μ_i	σ_i	
A	10 percent	3 percent	
B	20 percent	7 percent	$r_{AB} = 0$

Although there are certainly easier solutions, employing Equation (9.6), we obtain:

$$Z = \alpha_A^2 \sigma_A^2 + \alpha_B^2 \sigma_B^2 + \lambda_1(0.1\alpha_A + 0.2\alpha_B - 0.15) + \lambda_2(\alpha_A + \alpha_B - 1)$$
$$= \alpha_A^2 \sigma_A^2 + \alpha_B^2 \sigma_B^2 + 0.1\alpha_A \lambda_1 + 0.2\alpha_B \lambda_1 - 0.15\lambda_1 + \alpha_A \lambda_2$$
$$+ \alpha_B \lambda_2 - \lambda_2.$$

Taking partial derivatives and setting them equal to zero, we obtain:

(1) $\dfrac{\partial Z}{\partial \alpha_A} = 2\alpha_A \sigma_A^2 + 0.1\lambda_1 + \lambda_2 = 0.$

(2) $\dfrac{\partial Z}{\partial \alpha_B} = 2\alpha_B \sigma_B^2 + 0.2\lambda_1 + \lambda_2 = 0.$

(3) $\dfrac{\partial Z}{\partial \lambda_1} = 0.1\alpha_A + 0.2\alpha_B - 0.15 = 0.$

(4) $\dfrac{\partial Z}{\partial \lambda_2} = \alpha_A + \alpha_B - 1 = 0.$

Finally, we substitute algebraically for a solution (if the problem were any larger, matrix algebra at least would be necessary).

(4) $\alpha_A + \alpha_B - 1 = 0$
$\alpha_A = 1 - \alpha_B$.

(3) $0.1(1 - \alpha_B) + 0.2\alpha_B - 0.15 = 0$
$0.1 - 0.1\alpha_B + 0.2\alpha_B - 0.15 = 0$
$0.1\alpha_B = 0.05$
$\alpha_B = 0.5$
$\therefore \alpha_A = 0.5$.

(2) $2(0.5)(0.07)^2 + 0.2\lambda_1 + \lambda_2 = 0$
$0.0049 + 0.2\lambda_1 + \lambda_2 = 0$
$\lambda_2 = -0.0049 - 0.2\lambda_1$.

(1) $2(0.5)(0.03)^2 + 0.1\lambda_1 + (-0.0049 - 0.2\lambda_1) = 0$
$0.0009 + 0.1\lambda_1 - 0.0049 - 0.2\lambda_1 = 0$
$-0.1\lambda_1 - 0.004 = 0$
$\lambda_1 = -0.04$
$\therefore \lambda_2 = -0.0049 - 0.2(-0.04) = 0.0031$.

Therefore, the weights are 50 percent security A and 50 percent security B. The two Lagrangian multipliers are interpreted as ∂ (optimal Z satisfying other constraints)$/\partial$ (given constraint), the denominators being 0.15 for λ_1 and 1 for λ_2.

In general, the quadratic programming method can deal with inequalities as constraints but cannot handle negative variables, such as leverage or short sales; the opposite is true in both cases for the calculus methods. The use of artificial variables or additional Lagrangian constraints can eliminate these limitations, however. The input data (μ_i, σ_i, C_{ij}) are the same in all cases, and computer programs are available to solve problems by many of these methods. A hand solution to any but the simplest problem is very tedious and involves mathematics well beyond the scope of this book.

Not only do the methods discussed thus far require that a covariance matrix (for each security with every other security) be estimated, but also the computational procedures generally require that this matrix be inverted for each portfolio to be analyzed. The inversion of large matrices (our $n = 1{,}000$ case would provide a $1{,}000 \times 1{,}000$ covariance matrix), even with the aid of a computer, is extremely time consuming. To deal with both the problems of estimation and inversion, Professor Sharpe devised a simplified model of portfolio analysis that seems to provide reasonably accurate results.

Sharpe (1963), in his seminal paper, introduced the Sharpe Diagonal Model which assumes that the return on a security may be related to an index (such as the Dow-Jones, S&P 500, gross domestic product (GDP), or whatever) as follows:

$$\text{Return}_i = a_i + b_i \text{Return}_I + c_i \qquad (9.8)$$

$$\mu_i = a_i + b_i \mu_I + c_i, \qquad (9.9)$$

where:

a_i and b_i are constants

μ_I is the return (including dividends) on the index

c_i is an error term with $\mu_{c_i} = 0$ and $\sigma_{c_i} = a$ constant.

It is further assumed that c_i is not correlated with μ_I, with itself over time, nor with any other security's c (the last implying that securities are only correlated through their common relationship to the index). Therefore, μ_i can be estimated as $(a_i + b_i \mu_I)$. The parameters a_i and b_i can either be estimated, computed by regression analysis, or both. Furthermore, σ_{c_i} can be viewed as the variation in μ_i not caused by its relationship to the index, while $\sigma_i - \sigma_{c_i}$ is that portion of the total variation in μ_i caused by variation in μ_I.

The return on the portfolio becomes:

$$\mu = \sum_{i=1}^{n} \alpha_i (a_i + b_i \mu_I + c_i)$$

$$\mu = \sum_{i=1}^{n} \alpha_i (a_i + c_i) + \left(\sum_{i=1}^{n} \alpha_i b_i \right) \mu_I, \qquad (9.10)$$

where the first term is viewed as an investment in the essential nature of the securities, and the second term is an investment in the index. The risk of the portfolio is:

$$\sigma = \sqrt{\sum_{i=1}^{n}(\alpha_i \sigma_{c_i})^2 + \left(\sum_{i=1}^{n} \alpha_i b_i\right)^2 \sigma_I^2}, \qquad (9.11)$$

where, again, the first term may be viewed as the risk of the portfolio attributable to the particular characteristics of the individual securities, and the second term as the risk attributable to the index.

Thus, the Sharpe model greatly simplifies the input problem by making it directly amenable to regression analysis. In addition, by assuming that securities are only related through the index, the non-zero elements in the covariance matrix are reduced to those on the diagonal, thus easing the computational burden.

To illustrate the Sharpe approach, assume that the index currently stands at 1000 and, with reinvestment of dividends, it is expected to be at 1100 at the end of the year. Given the following data, suppose we wished to determine portfolio μ and σ for $\alpha_1 = 0.2$, $\alpha_2 = 0.5$, and $\alpha_3 = 0.3$.

$$\sigma_I = 0.10$$
$$\mu_1 = 0.06 + 0.1\mu_I, \quad \sigma_{c_1} = 0.03$$
$$\mu_2 = 0.03 + 2\mu_I, \quad \sigma_{c_2} = 0.20$$
$$\mu_3 = 0.00 + \mu_I, \quad \sigma_{c_3} = 0.10.$$

Employing Equation (9.10) we obtain:

$$\mu = (0.2)(0.06) + (0.5)(-0.03) + (0.3)(0.00)$$
$$+ [(0.2)(0.1) + (0.5)(0.3)(1)](0.10)$$
$$\mu = 0.012 - 0.015 + (1.32)(0.10) = 12.9 \text{ percent.}$$

Employing Equation (9.11):

$$\sigma = \sqrt{\begin{array}{c}[(0.2)(0.03)]^2 + [(0.5)(0.2)]^2 + [(0.3)(0.1)]^2 \\ + [(0.2)(0.1) + (0.5)(2) + (0.3)(1)]^2(0.1)^2\end{array}}$$

$$\sigma = \sqrt{(0.006)^2 + (0.1)^2 + (0.03)^2 + (1.32)^2(0.1)^2}$$

$$\sigma = \sqrt{0.000036 + 0.01 + 0.0009 + 0.017424}$$

$$= \sqrt{0.02836} = 16.8 \text{ percent.}$$

The three-security case of portfolio analysis has historically been analyzed graphically and, because it provides some useful insights, we shall consider it briefly.

1. We initially set a conservation condition that the entire portfolio will be invested ($\alpha_1 + \alpha_2 + \alpha_3 = 1$). The amount invested in the third security (α_3), therefore, is the amount not invested in the other two ($\alpha_3 = 1 - \alpha_1 - \alpha_2$), and it is possible to conduct the analysis in two-dimensional space.
2. We then set α_1 on the abscissa and α_2 on the ordinate, as shown in Figure 9.13. Point A represents the all 1 portfolio ($\alpha_1 = 1$, $\alpha_2 = \alpha_3 = 0$), point B the all 2 portfolio ($\alpha_2 = 1$, $\alpha_1 = \alpha_3 = 0$), and point C the all 3 portfolio ($\alpha_1 = \alpha_2 = 0$, $\alpha_3 = 1$). If we further add non-negativity conditions ($\alpha_1 \geq 0$; $\alpha_2 \geq 0$; $\alpha_3 \geq 0$), then triangle ABC becomes the attainable set of portfolios.

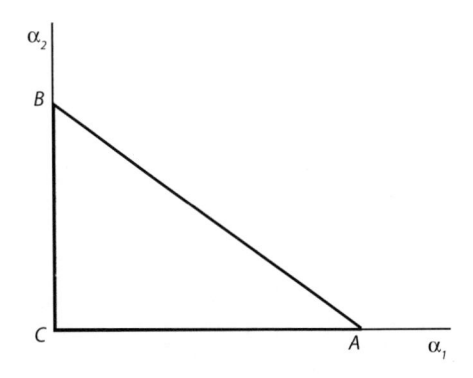

Figure 9.13. Three Asset Portfolios

3. The mean of any portfolio in this system is thus:

$$\mu = \alpha_1 \mu_1 + \alpha_2 \mu_2 + \alpha_3 \mu_3$$

$$\mu = \alpha_1 \mu_1 + \alpha_2 \mu_2 + (1 - \alpha_1 - \alpha_2) \mu_3$$

$$\mu = \mu_3 + \alpha_1 (\mu_1 - \mu_3) + \alpha_2 (\mu_2 - \mu_3).$$

Then, if $\mu_2 \neq \mu_3$

$$\alpha_2 = \frac{\mu - \mu_3}{\mu_2 - \mu_3} - \frac{\mu_1 - \mu_3}{\mu_2 - \mu_3} \alpha_1, \tag{9.12}$$

in the familiar $Y = a + bX$ form.

Equation (9.12) is significant because it provides the combinations of α_1 and α_2 (and implicitly α_3) that will return a given μ. It is also significant because it is the equation for a line with slope of $-(\mu_1 - \mu_3)/(\mu_2 - \mu_3)$ and intercept of $(\mu - \mu_3)/(\mu_2 - \mu_3)$; it will be noted that as the given return, μ, changes, the intercept of the line changes but the slope does not. From this observation derived the concept of *isomean lines*, which are a series of parallel lines with each point on a given line promising the same return, and return increasing from one isomean line to the next in the direction of the security having the greatest expected value. A system of such lines has been drawn in Figure 9.14 under the assumption that $\mu_3 > \mu_2 > \mu_1$.

4. The variance of the three-security portfolio is:

$$\sigma^2 = \alpha_1^2 \sigma_1^2 + \alpha_2^2 \sigma_2^2 + \alpha_3^2 \sigma_3^2 + 2\alpha_1 \alpha_2 C_{12} + 2\alpha_1 \alpha_3 C_{13} + 2\alpha_2 \alpha_3 C_{23},$$

which upon substitution and expansion is:

$$\sigma^2 = \alpha_1^2 (\sigma_1^2 - 2C_{13} + \sigma_3^2) + \alpha_2^2 (\sigma_2^2 - 2C_{23} + \sigma_3^2)$$
$$+ 2\alpha_1 \alpha_2 (C_{12} - C_{13} - C_{23} + \sigma_3^2) + 2\alpha_1 (C_{13} - \sigma_3^2)$$
$$+ 2\alpha_2 (C_{23} - \sigma_3^2) + \sigma_3^2,$$

which is, in turn, the equation for an ellipse. Therefore, the points representing all the portfolios having the same σ_2 will form an ellipse, a so-called *isovariance curve*. Other sets of portfolios all having the same variance but larger than the first set will form a larger ellipse that has the same center.

432   *Quantitative Financial Analytics*

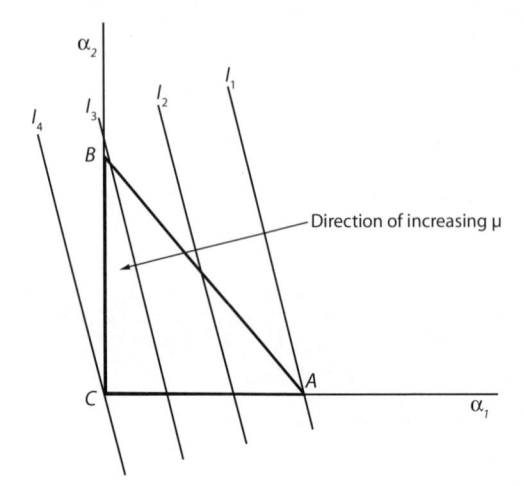

Figure 9.14. Isomean Curves

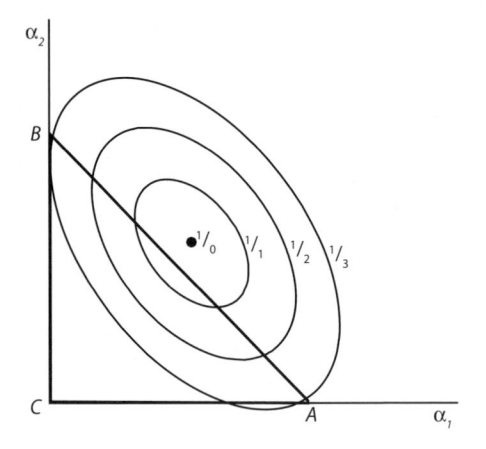

Figure 9.15. Isovariance Curves

The isovariance curves are therefore said to be a series of concentric ellipses. The center of these ellipses is, of course, the minimum-variance portfolio. A series of isovariance curves is shown in Figure 9.15.

5. A moment's reflection should indicate that (a) the highest return to be found on any isovariance curve is at its point of tangency with the highest attainable isomean curve (the tangent on the

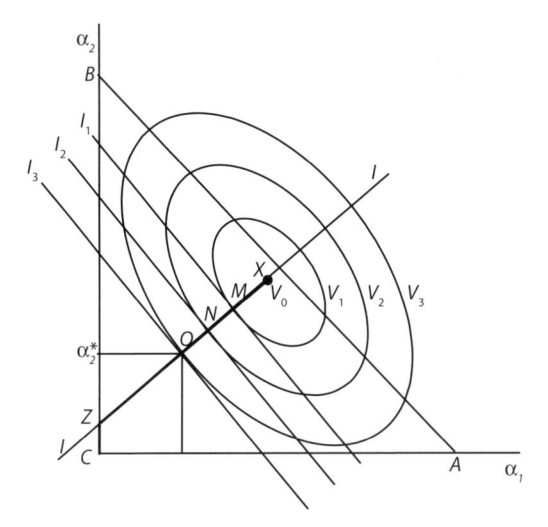

Figure 9.16. The Efficiency Frontier in (α_1, α_2) Space

other side of the isovariance curve will give the lowest attainable return), and (b) the lowest attainable risk on any isomean curve is at its point of tangency with an isovariance curve. The locus of these points of tangency is called the *critical line* and shown as ll in Figure 9.16. The critical line is a straight line that always passes through the center of the isovariance ellipses (the minimum-variance portfolio) and is, by definition, the locus of optimal portfolios. Not all these portfolios are attainable, however. The set of efficient portfolios, therefore, tends to follow the critical line where possible and to select the minimum-variance portfolio in the direction of increasing return otherwise.

6. The set of efficient portfolios (or the efficiency frontier) can be observed in Figure 9.16 to follow the critical line from X, the minimum-variance portfolio, to Z, the boundary of the attainable set, and then along the boundary to C. Because points on the critical line beyond Z are not attainable, those on ZC give the best available trade-off of σ^2 for μ.

7. Finally, it is possible to transfer the efficiency frontier from (α_1, α_2) space of Figure 9.16 to (σ^2, μ) space in Figure 9.17.

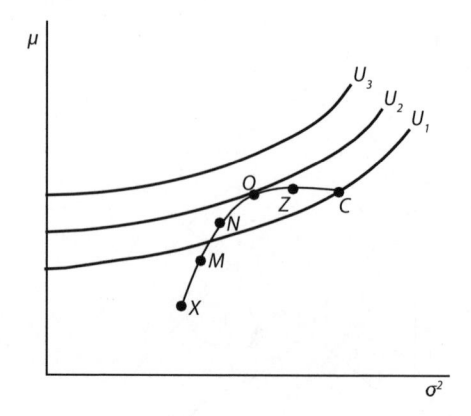

Figure 9.17. The Efficiency Frontier in (σ^2, μ) Space

8. The final step in portfolio selection is then to place the investor's indifference curves on the same axes and select that portfolio represented by the point on the efficiency frontier that is tangent to the highest indifference curve. In the case illustrated, this would be point O which is tangent to U_2. Referring to Figure 9.17, it can be seen that portfolio O is composed of α_1^* of 1, α_2^* of 2, and $1 - \alpha_1^* - \alpha_2^*$ of 3.

Example

The efficiency frontier for the following diagram may be traced:

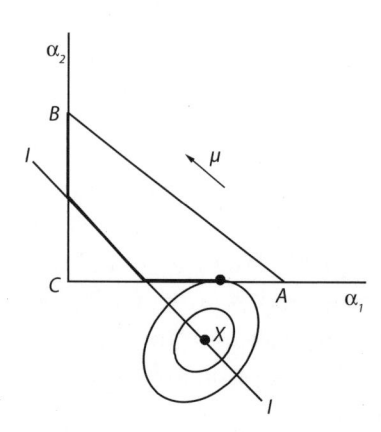

The smallest variance portfolio attainable is the point of tangency of the isovariance curves with the α_1 axis. From there, the efficiency curve moves along the boundary to the critical line, up the critical line to the α_2 boundary, and then along the α_2 boundary.

Summary

In order to proceed with the analysis and selection of portfolios, it is necessary to establish criteria of choice. In other words, what attribute(s) of a particular security or portfolio of securities make(s) it more desirable than another security or portfolio? One might be tempted to suggest that return (or income or wealth — three measures that tend to move in the same direction and are thus used somewhat interchangeably) is the appropriate criterion. This statement appears to be unambiguously true in at least two cases. Experts agree in one way or another that more wealth is preferable to less, other things being equal. Therefore, if security A promised a certain return of X percent, but security B promised a certain return of only Y, where X >Y, A would be unambiguously preferred to (in terminology used later "is said to dominate") B, and return would be a satisfactory criterion. The crucial point to remember is that certain increments to wealth are being portrayed.

If it is assumed that the returns on securities A and B are not certain but rather subject to probability distributions with the mathematical expectations of X percent and Y percent, it is still possible to salvage the return criterion. To do so, it must be assumed that it is possible to engage in an infinite number of independent trials of A and B, each trial involving an infinitely small proportion of our total wealth. The law of large numbers tells us that the actual return will approach the expected return, A will be preferred to B, and the expected return will be an appropriate ranking criterion. Unfortunately, we rarely encounter certainties or infinitely divisible and replicable events in the real world.

Perhaps the most famous illustration of the limitations of the expected return criterion is the Petersburg Paradox formulated over 275 years ago by Daniel Bernoulli. A solution to the paradox was provided by Bernoulli and a contemporary. These solutions depended on the use of utility functions of logarithmic and quadratic form.

Early writers on utility theory often claimed that it was possible to measure utility on an absolute scale, whereby the joy or pain of money gains and losses could be exactly computed and even compared among individuals. This group, identified as the neoclassical cardinal utility theory school, was essentially discredited by the ordinal utility theorists. The latter agreed that, through revealed preference, it was possible to detect which goods or combinations of goods were preferred (or were a matter of indifference) to other goods or combinations by the individual under analysis. The point of disagreement, however, was that the ordinalists contended that it was impossible to say by how much one combination of goods was preferred to another. They further insisted that interpersonal comparisons of utility gains and losses could not be made, and that all the writing about the absolute measurement of joy and pain (going back to Bentham's hedonist calculus, if not earlier) was, at best, non-operational. Modern cardinal utility theory, which dates from the work of von Neumann and Morgenstern contends only that, given certain assumptions and certain data about an individual's preferences, it is possible to predict his choices in certain risky situations.

Several difficulties with utility analysis have persisted over the years. Utility functions that are bounded upward (implying a zero marginal utility of wealth), as in the alternative solution to the Petersburg Paradox, not only violate the basic notion that more wealth is preferable to less, but also cause risky situations to be indeterminate. As long as all the possible outcomes of a risky event lie on the horizontal portion of the utility function, not only is the risky event as desirable as a certainty equal to the expected value of the risky event (which is true for all linear utility functions) but it is also as desirable as a certainty equal to its worst (or best) possible outcome. Furthermore, if the slope of the utility function becomes negative at some point (implying a negative marginal utility of wealth), as in the case of the quadratic, utility can be increased by throwing money away; such pathological implications for behavior do not articulate well with the basic rationality assumptions.

The assumptions of extreme risk aversion (corresponding to very low or even negative marginal utilities of wealth) at high levels of wealth do not appear to correspond terribly well to observed individual behavior. The theoretical basis of these assumptions is obscure, and empirical justification of them is virtually non-existent. One defense often raised is that wealth exhibits diminishing marginal utility in the way any consumer good does. The point ignored, of course, is that wealth represents command over all goods and, although enough ice cream cones may satisfy one's craving and even cause illness beyond a point, the application of the same logic to imply total satiation of wants of all goods and services is not necessarily justified.

The point of tracing through the various arguments in utility theory is that such constitute the very basis of modern portfolio theory. For the last 70–80 years, a very clear division has existed between the work of the security analyst and that of the portfolio manager. The analyst attempts to divide the universe of securities into three parts: (1) underpriced (recommended purchase); (2) fully priced (recommended long-run hold); and (3) overpriced (no longer recommended). The portfolio manager then constructs groups of securities into recommended holdings based on risk/return characteristics. The impact of the modern theory upon the role of security analysis has been implied by the previous chapters.

It will be noted that securities have not been "priced" in this book, because securities cannot be priced upon the basis of their risk considered in isolation from other securities; furthermore, security purchasers are price takers, not price makers. The function of the security analyst has been viewed here to be the estimation of security return, risk, and covariance with the returns of the securities. Thus, the portfolio manager should no longer be provided with a buy, hold, or sell recommendation, but rather an estimate of the parameters of the distribution of security returns. At least, this is true in theory. In fact, most analysts today still "price" stocks and provide recommendations accordingly. Stocks have "price" objectives; and when they are reached or the objective is changed, a "sell" or "fully priced" recommendation is issued.

The considerations of client-required return and ability to bear risk should be treated in the form of utility function determination. The goal is the same, but the use of a utility framework is more precise and also allows for trade-offs between risk and return. The proverbial widow would have a very risk-averse function, and the proverbial businessperson will have a less risk-averse function (and a riskier portfolio). Under the modern theory, then, the manager takes the analyst's parameters, determines for each level of risk that portfolio with the highest attainable return, compares the market's trade-off of risk and return to his client's preferences, and selects the utility-maximizing portfolio. The goal of portfolio management, like all other human endeavors, is thus assumed to be utility maximization. It has further been demonstrated that this goal is operationally similar to the more traditional goals (for example, income, limited income with growth, and so on), because it will have different operational implications for individuals in differing circumstances and of differing risk predilections. In addition, the goal of institutional portfolio management should be the maximization of beneficiary utility.

If markets are efficient, the last goal can be achieved by an institutional portfolio policy designed to place the parameters of its own securities on the highest attainable market (risk-return trade-off) line; this policy will maximize the market value of investors' holdings, from which point they can go about the maximization of their own utility in isolation. If markets are not efficient, the institution will need to adopt a "clientele" approach, estimate a utility function representative of its beneficiaries, and work to put the parameters of its own securities on the highest attainable indifference curve of the posited utility function.

Problems

1. Bernoulli provided solutions to the following problems. See if you can do as well.

a. What minimum fortune should be possessed by the man who offers to provide the insurance to Caius in order that he be rational in doing so?

b. Sempronius owns goods at home worth a total of 4,000 ducats and in addition possesses 8,000 ducats of commodities in foreign countries from where they can be transported only by sea. However, our daily experience teaches us that of 10 ships, one perishes.

 (1) What is Sempronius' expectation of the commodities?
 (2) By how much would his expectation improve if he trusted them equally to two ships?
 (3) What is the limit of his expectation as he trusted them to increasing numbers of ships?

2. Under the Bernoulli criteria, would a rational individual ever enter a risk venture that had any finite probability of costing all his wealth? Why? How might this result be rationalized? Why, in modern society, might it be said that it is impossible to lose all one's wealth?

3. Suppose that a man were offered either (1) a certain $230 or (2) a 50–50 chance of $400 or 100. Which option would he take if:

a. He possessed a square root of money gain utility function?
b. A Bernoulli function with initial wealth of $1,000?
c. The same as b with initial wealth of $100?

4. With regard to the material in the section on von Neumann–Morgenstern utility:

a. Determine the certain sum for which the subject in the example would relinquish the following opportunity:

W	Probability
40,000	0.3
160,000	0.5
250,000	0.2

b. Explain how von Neumann–Morgenstern axiom 5 treats the utility derived from gambling itself (that is, deals with the existence of Las Vegas).
c. Compute the mean and standard deviation of outcomes in the example and in "a" above.

   (1) What is the mean and standard deviation in each case of the certain dollar value for which the subject would be indifferent?
   (2) We now have two sets of (σ, μ) for each of the two opportunities. Which of the two games (example of "a") would the subject prefer to play?
   (3) For what probability α would he be indifferent between $\alpha \times$ (game he prefers) and the game he does not prefer?
   (4) Graph each game in (σ, μ) space under the assumption that we have enough intermediate points besides the two for each game computed above to generate two curves. What statements might be made about the curves and the points on them?

5. For this question, assume $U = \sqrt{W}$ and $\$0 = 0$ U and $\$1$ M $= 1000$ U.

   a. For what $\alpha (0 \leq \alpha \leq 1)$ would the subject be indifferent between α ($\$1$ million) and a certain $\$250,000$?
   b. For what α would the subject be indifferent between (α) ($\$500,000$) and (0.3) ($\$200,000$)?
   c. For what α would the subject be indifferent between (α) ($\$500,000$) and $(1-\alpha)$ $200,000$?

6. What do you imagine it means to say that von Neumann–Morgenstern utility functions are unique up to a linear (proportionate) transformation?
7. Draw the total utility-of-wealth function and selected indifference curves for an individual for whom $U_W = -1000 + 100W - 0.001W^2$.

8. Using the data in Figures 9.2 and 9.3, determine which of the following risky propositions would be the most desirable:

Proposition	μ	σ
A	100,000	100,000
B	290,000	200,000
C	400,000	500,000
D	300,000	300,000
E	200,000	0

9. "Under von Neumann-Morgenstern propositions, utility is a linear function of wealth only for those who are risk neutral, but utility is assumed to be a linear function of probability for everybody." Discuss this statement.

10. Using the data given in the example in the chapter for securities 1 and 2, complete the following:

	α_1	α_2	r_{12}	σ	μ
(a)	0.5	0.5	1.0	_____	
(b)	0.7	0.3	1.0	_____	
(c)	0.5	0.5	1.0	_____	
(d)	0.6	0.4	0.0	_____	
(e)	0.5	0.5	0.5	_____	

11. Using the data for α_1 given above and assuming 2 to be a riskless security with $\mu = 5$ percent, compute (σ, μ) for the 5 portfolios in 10.

12. Given the data below, graph the portfolios of A and B in (σ, μ) space and determine the efficient portion:

Security	σ	μ	
A	10 percent	30 percent	$r_{12} = 0.4$
B	1 percent	5 percent	

13. Rework the calculus example in the chapter separately for:

    a. $\mu^* = 11$ percent
    b. Security C with $\mu_C = 15$ percent, $\sigma_C = 5$ percent, $r_{AC} = r_{BC} = 0.5$.

14. Rework the Sharpe example in the chapter under each of the following assumptions separately and comment upon the effect:

    a. $\sigma_I = 0.2$
    b. $\sigma_{c3} = 0.2$
    c. $\sigma_{c2} = 0.5$.

15. The Beta Fund has computed returns on three securities over the past 10 years. It also has available the average annual level (including dividend reinvestment) of the Metropolis Stock Exchange:

	Return on Security A	B	C	Index Level (End of Year, including dividend reinvestment)
20X1	0.10	0.05	0.15	300
20X2	0.15	−0.05	0.25	350
20X3	0.10	0.10	0.05	300
20X4	0.20	0.00	0.20	400
20X5	0.00	0.40	−0.20	250
20X6	0.25	−0.10	0.15	500
20X7	0.30	−0.10	0.20	550
20X8	0.20	0.15	0.10	400
20X9	0.25	0.00	0.15	500
20X0	0.30	0.00	0.20	550

a. What is the arithmetic mean return on each security over the 10-year period? The geometric mean?

b. What are the slope and intercept parameters for the regression line of each security's return against the index?

c. Using Sharpe's model and an index estimate next year of 600, what are portfolio σ and μ if $\alpha_A = 50$ percent, $\alpha_B = 30$ percent, and $\alpha_C = 20$ percent?

16. Find the efficiency frontier in the following three cases:

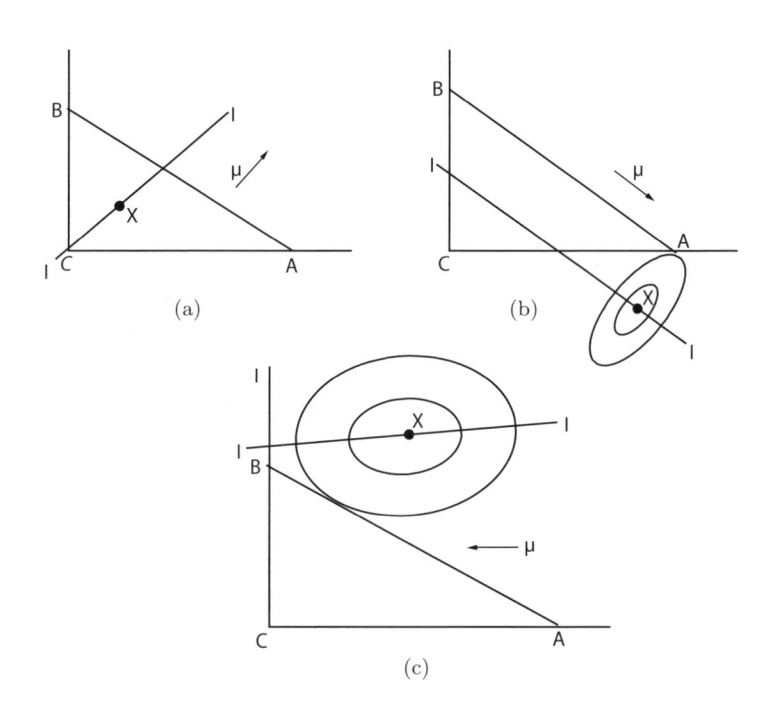

(a)

(b)

(c)

17. If $\mu_1 = 10$ percent, $\mu_2 = 5$ percent, and $\mu_3 = 20$ percent, what is the slope of the isomean curves? If $\mu = 15$ percent, what is the intercept?

References

Amenc, N. and V. Le Sourd, *Portfolio Theory and Performance Analysis*. Hoboken, NJ: John Wiley & Sons, Inc., 2003.

Arrow, Kenneth, *Essays in the Theory of Risk Bearing*. Chicago: Markham Publishing Co., 1971.

Bacon, C. R., *Practical Portfolio Performance Measurement and Attribution*, 2nd edn. Hoboken, NJ: John Wiley & Sons, Inc., 2008.

Banz, R. W., "The Relationship Between Returns and Market Value of Commons Stocks," *Journal of Financial Economics*, March 1981, pp. 3–18.

Bernoulli, Daniel., "Exposition of a New Theory on the Measurement of Risk" (Louise Sommer, trans.), *Econometrica,* January 1954, pp. 23–36 (first published 1738).

Blume, M. C. and Friend, Irwin,, "Risk, Investment Strategy and the Long-Run Rates of Return," *Review of Economics and Statistics*, August 1974, pp. 259–269.

Elton, E. J., Gruber, M. J., et al., *Modern Portfolio Theory and Investment Analysis*, 9th edn. New York, NY: John Wiley & Sons, Inc., 2014.

Findlay, M. C. and E. E. Williams, "A Note on Risk Seeker Portfolio Selection and Lender Constraints," *Southern Economic Journal,* Jan. 1976, pp. 515–520.

Friedman, Milton, and Leonard Savage., "The Utility Analysis of Choices Involving Risk," *Journal of Political Economy,* August 1948, pp. 279–304.

Markowitz, Harry., "Portfolio Selection," *Journal of Finance,* March 1952a, pp. 77–91.

Markowitz, Harry., "The Utility of Wealth," *Journal of Political Economy,* April 1952b, pp. 151–58.

Markowitz, Harry., "The Optimization of a Quadratic Function Subject to Linear Constraints," *Naval Research Logistics Quarterly,* March-June 1956, pp. 111–133.

Markowitz, Harry., *Portfolio Selection.* New York, NY: John Wiley for the Cowles Foundation, 1959.

Sharpe, William F., "A Simplified Model for Portfolio Analysis," *Management Science,* January 1963, pp. 277–93.

Sharpe, William F., Gordon J. Alexander, and Jeffery V. Bailey., *Investments*, 6th edn. Upper Saddle River, NJ: Prentice Hall, 1999.

Tobin, James., "Liquidity Preference as Behavior Towards Risk," *Review of Economic Studies*, February 1958, pp. 65–87.

Treynor, Jack L. and Fisher Black., "How to Use Security Analysis to Improve Portfolio Selection," *Journal of Business*, Vol. 46, No. 1. Januray 1973, pp. 66–86.

Von Neumann, John and Oskar Morgenstern., *Theory of Games and Economic Behavior.* Princeton, NJ: Princeton University Press, 1944.

Chapter 10

Capital Market Theory, Efficiency, and Imperfections

Interestingly, professional economists appear to think more highly of professional investors than do other professional investors.

William Sharpe

Capital Market Theory

In the last chapter, we briefly considered the two-asset portfolio with one of the assets riskless. We concluded, designating the riskless security as 2, that:

$$\mu = \alpha_1\mu_1 + \alpha_2\mu_2 \tag{10.1}$$

and

$$\sigma = \alpha_1\sigma_1. \tag{10.2}$$

We further decided that the same conditions would hold if 1 were a portfolio, instead of a security, and a riskless security were added to it. Figure 10.1, repeated from the last chapter, designates all combinations of portfolio 1 and riskless security 2. The combination of portfolios so depicted is called the *lending case* because in essence a portion of the funds available is being lent at the pure or "riskless" rate of interest, while the remainder is invested in portfolio 1. The riskless rate is often approximated by the yield on short-term US Treasury Bills.

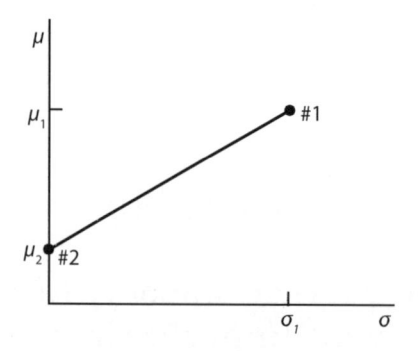

Figure 10.1. Lending Case

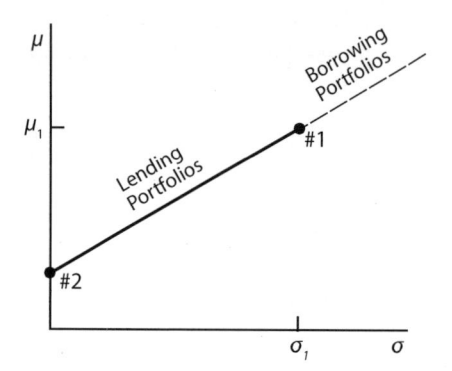

Figure 10.2. Borrowing and Lending Cases

Using the simple construct developed above, it is also possible to consider the case of borrowing against, or leveraging, the portfolio. Because positive α_i's are used to indicate securities bought and included in the portfolio, it does not seem unreasonable to use negative α_i's to indicate liabilities sold against the portfolio. The same result would be obtained by making the μ's negative (to indicate a cost rather than a return) but would undermine our convention that $\Sigma \alpha_i = 1$.

In the example above, if α_2 becomes negative, then α_1 becomes >1 and $\alpha_1 \sigma_1$ also increases linearly. Making the rather unrealistic assumption that the individual can also borrow at the riskless rate, our borrowing line becomes merely an extension of the lending line beyond 1, as shown in Figure 10.2.

Therefore, beginning with all our funds in portfolio 1, we can either lend some of the funds at the pure rate and move down the line in the direction of μ_2 or borrow at the pure rate to invest more funds in portfolio 1 and move up the line.

Given the effects of borrowing and lending at the riskless rate, it then becomes necessary to determine which of the available portfolios should be so employed. It would seem reasonable, as a first principle, to borrow or lend against that portfolio which provided the greatest increase in return for a given increase in risk; in other words, we should desire that borrowing–lending line with the greatest available slope. The cases are illustrated in Figure 10.3. The efficiency frontier is shown as EF. Borrowing and lending against either portfolio A or D (which gives the same line $= \mu_2 - D - A$) is inefficient because a better risk–return trade-off is given by B. Portfolio C would appear even better, except that by definition no security or portfolio exists above EF. Therefore, the optimal attainable borrowing–lending portfolio is found by extending a straight line from the pure rate of interest tangent to the efficiency frontier. The geometry of this conclusion is demonstrated more rigorously below in the discussion of the excess return criterion.

Let us take another look at such an optimal line, shown in Figure 10.4 as $r - O - Z$, through portfolio O. It will be observed

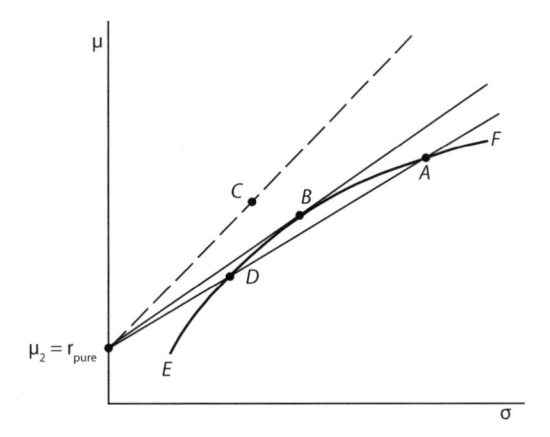

Figure 10.3. Determination of the Optimal Borrowing and Lending Portfolio ($r_L = r_B$)

448 *Quantitative Financial Analytics*

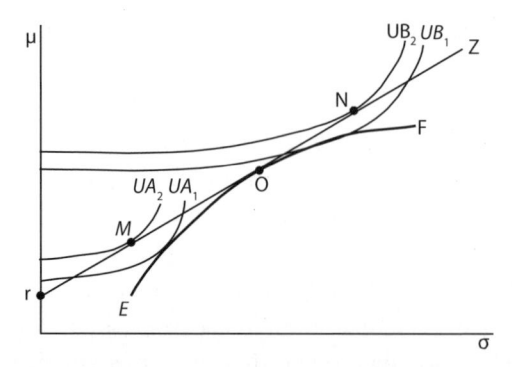

Figure 10.4. Determination of the Optimal Portfolio for Individuals with Varying Risk Preferences

that for every portfolio on the efficiency frontier between E and O, there exists some combination of portfolio O and the riskless security (given by the lending line $r - O$) that is more desirable (lower σ for the same μ, and so on). In like manner, every point on the efficiency frontier between O and F is dominated by some borrowing against O (given by the line OZ). It would therefore appear that the revised efficiency frontier is $r - O - Z$. If this were the case, then all efficient portfolios would be composed of portfolio O plus borrowing or lending.

A very risk-averse person, such as Mr. A, might choose portfolio M (see Figure 10.4) composed of portfolio O plus riskless loans, while a less risk-averse person, such as Mr. B, might choose portfolio N, which involves leveraging portfolio O. (For completeness, it is noted that a risk-neutral investor will choose that combination of securities and loans with the highest expected return, while a risk seeker will either select the same or a portfolio of even greater risk, depending upon the slope of his indifference curves.)

Even the more realistic case of the individual who can only borrow at a higher rate than he can lend is fairly easy to handle in this framework. In this situation, we can draw lines from both the borrowing rate (r_B) and the lending rate (r_L) tangent to the efficiency frontier (see Figure 10.5) to obtain lending portfolio O and borrowing portfolio U. The revised efficiency frontier then becomes

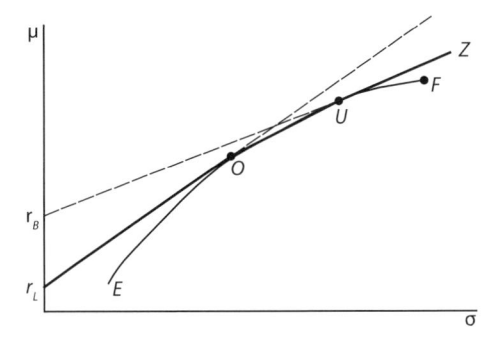

Figure 10.5. Determination of the Optimal Borrowing and Lending Portfolio ($r_L = r_B$)

(1) lending from r_L to O; (2) movement along the efficiency frontier itself from O to U; and (3) borrowing from U on out along UZ. The indifference curves would then be applied as before.

A crucial assumption is implicitly made above, that is, that the separation theorem holds in this case. The separation theorem essentially posits that the investment decision is independent of the financing decision. In our case, it would imply that investors would select portfolio O without regard to whether they would then borrow against it or buy riskless securities with excess funds. The theorem also implies that a portfolio with a given μ and σ would possess the same utility no matter whether it were composed of (1) 100 percent securities; (2) less than 100 percent securities plus some riskless loans; or (3) more than 100 percent securities plus some borrowing. It is quite unlikely that the separation theorem holds in the real world but the models in the rest of this chapter, which are based on it, provide sufficient insight that we shall choose to ignore this practical difficulty temporarily.

The effects of lending part of the funds in the portfolio and leveraging (borrowing against) the portfolio may be illustrated with a simple example. Suppose a risky portfolio of securities has a $\mu = 15$ percent and $\sigma = 10$ percent, and the pure rate of interest $= 6$ percent. The parameters of a holding of (1) 50 percent in the portfolio and 50 percent lending, and (2) 150 percent in the portfolio and 50 percent borrowing would be determined as follows:

$$
\begin{aligned}
(1)\quad & \mu = \alpha_1\mu_1 + \alpha_2\mu_2 \\
& \mu = .5(.15) + .5(.06) = 10.5 \text{ percent} \\
& \sigma = \alpha_1\sigma_1 = .5(.10) = 5 \text{ percent} \\
(2)\quad & \mu = 1.5(.15) + (-.5)(.06) = 19.5 \text{ percent} \\
& \sigma = 1.5(.10) = 15 \text{ percent.}
\end{aligned}
$$

Notice that in the case of lending both expected return and risk are reduced; conversely, in the case of borrowing each parameter is increased.

The Capital Market Line (CML)

If we may assume that investors behave in a manner consistent with the prior chapter and the first section of this chapter, then certain statements may be made about the nature of capital markets as a whole. Before a complete statement of capital market theory may be advanced, however, certain additional assumptions must be presented:

1. The μ and σ of a portfolio adequately describe it for the purpose of investor decision making $[U = f(\sigma, \mu)]$. Technically, this condition requires either that the distribution of security returns be normal or that the investor's utility function be quadratic.
2. Investors can borrow and lend as much as they want at the pure rate of interest.
3. All investors have the same expectations regarding the future, the same portfolios available to them, and the same time horizon. Technically, homogeneity of expectations is not required if a weighted average of divergent expectations may be employed. In the latter case, however, it is necessary that the weights be stable as well as the proportional response of each divergent expectation to new information, and so on. This condition is often referred to as "idealized uncertainty."
4. Taxes, transaction costs, inflation, and changes in interest rates may be ignored.

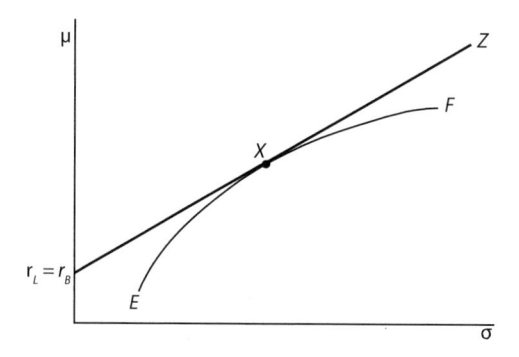

Figure 10.6. The Capital Market Line

Under the assumptions above, all investors will have identical efficiency frontiers (EF), borrowing and lending rates ($r_L = r_B$) and, thus, identical optimal borrowing–lending portfolios (X). (see Figure 10.6). Because all investors will lend to move along $r-X-Z$, it must follow for equilibrium to be achieved that all existing securities be contained in the portfolio (X). In other words, all securities must be owned by somebody, and any security not initially contained in X would drop in price seeking to acquire the same portfolio (X), and will then borrow until it did qualify. Therefore, the portfolio held by each individual would be identical to all others and a microcosm of the market, with each security holding bearing the same proportion to the total portfolio as that security's total market value would bear to the total market value of all securities. In no other way could equilibrium be achieved in the capital market under the assumptions stated above.

The borrowing–lending line for the market as a whole ($r-X-Z$ in Figure 10.6) is called the capital market line (CML). The securities portfolio (X) employed is the total universe of available securities (called the market portfolio) by the reasoning given above. The CML is linear by the logic of the first section of this chapter because it represents the combination of a risky portfolio and a riskless security. One use made of the DML is that its slope provides the so-called market price of risk, or, that amount of increased return required by market conditions to justify the acceptance of an increment to risk, that is,

$$\frac{\mu_{\text{market}} - r_{\text{pure}}}{\sigma_{\text{market}}}.$$

The Security Market Line (SML)

A major question raised by the CML analysis of the last section involves the means by which individual securities would be priced if such a system were in equilibrium. Throughout this book, we have generally assumed that markets are not in equilibrium; therefore when we combine securities into a portfolio that has the average return of the component securities but less than the average risk, we simply ascribe this "gain from diversification" to our own shrewdness. In the type of market assumed in the last section, however, everyone will be doing the same thing, and the prices of securities will adjust to eliminate the windfall gains from diversification.

Sharpe (1964) has suggested a logical way by which such security pricing might take place. If everyone were to adopt a portfolio theory approach to security analysis, then the risk of a given security might be viewed as not its risk in isolation but rather the change in the total risk of the portfolio caused by adding this security. Furthermore, because capital market theory assumes everyone to hold a perfectly diversified (that is, the market) portfolio, the addition to total portfolio risk caused by adding a particular security to the portfolio is that portion of the individual security's risk that cannot be eliminated through diversification with all other securities in the market. Students of statistics will recognize this concept of the nondiversifiable portion of the individual security's risk as the covariance of returns between the security and the market as a whole $(C_{i_M} = \sigma_i \sigma_M r_{iM})$.

Because the concept of individual security pricing is rather elusive, let us restate it. Sharpe contends that the price (and thus return) of a given security should not be determined in relation to its total risk, because the security will be combined with other securities in a portfolio and some of the individual risk will be eliminated by diversification (unless all the securities are perfectly positively

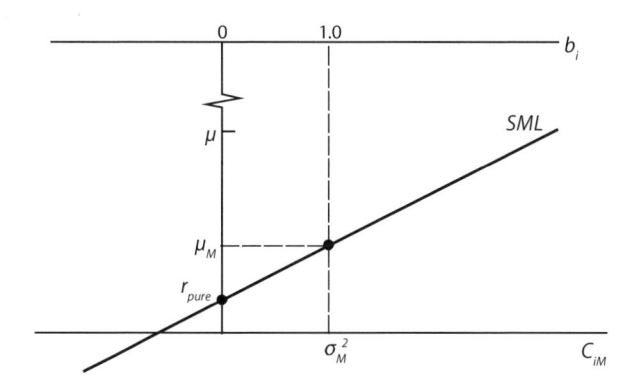

Figure 10.7. The SML

correlated). Therefore, the return of the security should only contain a risk premium to the extent of the risk that will actually be borne (that is, that portion of the total risk which cannot be eliminated by diversification — which is variously called *nondiversifiable risk* or *systematic risk*).

If this logic is accepted, it is then possible to generate a security market line (SML), as shown in Figure 10.7, where the return on individual securities is related to their covariance with the market. If capital markets are in equilibrium and all the other assumptions of this chapter hold, then the parameters of each security should lie on the SML. Furthermore, because the risk of a portfolio is the weighted sum of the nondiversifiable risk of its component securities, all portfolios should also fall on the SML in equilibrium. It should be noted that although all portfolios will fall on the SML, as a general rule no individual securities will fall on the CML (they will all lie to the right of the CML).

Several additional points may be made regarding the SML. In the first place, several authors differentiate between *defensive* and *aggressive* securities on the basis of whether the covariance of the security with the market is less or greater than the variance of the market return itself. If $C_{iM} < \sigma_M^2$, then the changes in the security's return caused by market changes are less than the market changes themselves and the security is considered defensive. If $C_{iM} > \sigma_M^2$, then the security responds more than proportionally to market changes and is considered aggressive.

It is also possible to discuss the SML in terms of Sharpe's index model (see Chapter 9), where:

$$\mu_i = a_i + b_i \mu_I + c_i. \quad (10.3)$$

The b_i term (called Sharpe's *beta coefficient*), given μ_I, is equal to:

$$(b_i|\mu_I) = \frac{C_{iI}}{\sigma_I^2} = C_{iI}\left(1/\sigma_I^2\right). \quad (10.4)$$

which, if the index is a valid depiction of the market:

$$(b_i|\mu_I) = \frac{C_{iM}}{\sigma_M^2} = C_{iM}\left(1/\sigma_M^2\right). \quad (10.5)$$

Under these assumptions, the abscissa of a point on the SML expressed in terms of b_i is merely $1/\sigma_M^2$ times that of the same point expressed in terms of C_{iM} and the two are directly comparable. Viewed another way, the risk premium an individual security would exhibit in equilibrium is:

$$(\mu_i - r_{\text{pure}}) = \left[\frac{\mu_M - r_{\text{pure}}}{\sigma_M^2}\right] C_{iM} = (\mu_I - r_{\text{pure}}) b_i. \quad (10.6)$$

It is further possible to say that defensive securities would have a b_i less than, and aggressive securities greater than, unity. A major advantage of transferring the discussion into beta terminology is that the regression coefficient can be used directly to estimate the systematic risk of the asset.

Unfortunately, the beta concept also possesses serious pitfalls. In the first place, its very simplicity and popularity cause it to be used by many people who fail to understand its limitations. Because the concept is subject to all the assumptions of both regression analysis and the efficient capital market hypothesis, statistical problems and economic imperfections may undermine its usefulness. Many investors are unaware of these limitations and have blithely employed the beta as a new get-rich-quick scheme. The notion that one need only fill his portfolio with securities possessing large betas and wealth shall surely follow has been adopted in many quarters by individuals who do not appreciate the fact that at best the beta is a risk-measure surrogate and *not* an indicator of future returns. The idea that the assumption of large amounts of risk will generate large returns only approaches being correct over the long run in reasonably efficient markets, and even then it ignores utility considerations.

A further difficulty with the beta concept follows from empirical findings that betas for small portfolios (and, of course, individual securities) over short periods can be highly unstable, although there is evidence of reasonable stability for the betas of large portfolios over long holding periods. It would thus appear that one of the few valid applications of the beta concept would be as a risk–return measure for large portfolios. An example of how betas can be used in this regard is presented in the next section.

Portfolio Evaluation

Several measures directly related to capital market theory have been developed for the purpose of a portfolio evaluation. The latter is essentially a retrospective view of how well a particular portfolio or portfolio manager did over a specified period in the past. Most of the published research in this area has dealt with mutual funds, seemingly because they are controversial, economically important in certain financial markets, and possessed of long life with readily available data. Much of the early work in this area (including the advertisements of the funds themselves) was of a simple time-series nature, showing how well an investor could have done over a given period in the past if he had invested then or else comparing these results to what the investor could have earned in other funds or the market as a whole. The more recent work considers both return and its variability, contending that mutual funds that invest in riskier securities should exhibit higher returns.

One result of this work, considered subsequently, has been the finding that investors do as well or better on average by selecting securities at random as they could with the average mutual fund. Another implication, of more relevance here, is the growing feeling that the managers of any kind of portfolio should be rated not on the return they earn alone but rather on the return they earn adjusted for the risk to which they subject the portfolio.

Before proceeding, however, a caveat is in order about the nature of *ex post* risk and return measures. As in any problem in measurement, one must delineate (1) why a measurement is being made, (2) what is to be measured, (3) which measurement technique is appropriate, and (4) the import of the results of the measurement. If one is not careful, *ex post* return measurements can easily result in the "if only I had..." syndrome, which is a waste of time and effort as far as making an investment in the present is concerned. For such measures to be of use, one must assume that the ability of a manager or fund to earn greater-than-average returns in the past is some indication of ability to do so in the future.

As the empirical work cited below indicates, there is little evidence to support this contention. As far as risk is concerned, there is some doubt about what the concept of *ex post* risk means. Most of the writers in this area are careful to stress the term "return variability" instead of risk per se. Because the outcomes of all past events are currently known with certainty, the use of return variability as a measure of risk in this instance involves a different notion of risk than we have been using. Again, to make operational investment decisions, it would seem necessary to assume that past risk–return behavior of managers or portfolios either could or would be maintained in the future. Deferring judgment for the moment on the above reservations, let us consider the proposed evaluation measures. Sharpe (1966) has proposed the use of a reward-to-variability ratio related to the slope of the CML:

$$\frac{\mu_i - r_{\text{pure}}}{\sigma_i}. \tag{10.7}$$

In effect, Sharpe is computing the slope of the borrowing–lending line going through the given portfolio and arguing that a greater slope is more desirable. In terms of Figure 10.8, Sharpe demonstrates

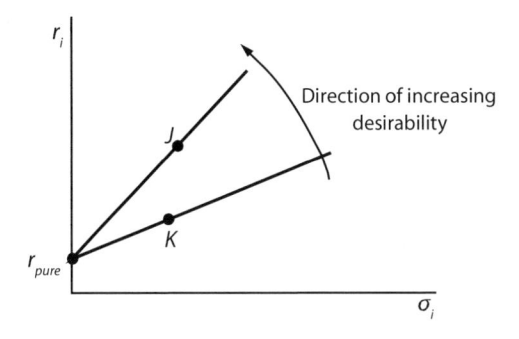

Figure 10.8. Sharpe's Return-to-Variability Criterion

that no *a priori* judgments about the performance of portfolios J and K can be made until the borrowing–lending lines are added. Subsequently, it is possible to note that a combination of the greater return to variability portfolio J and riskless loans dominates any combination of K and loans. Equation (10.7) has become quite famous among practitioners and is now known as the "Sharpe Ratio." It is regularly employed to adjust portfolio returns for risk and to compare these risk-adjusted returns with market averages (S&P 500, DJIA, etc.).

A second measure based on the SML has been proposed by Treynor:

$$\frac{\mu_i - r_{\text{pure}}}{b_i}. \qquad (10.8)$$

The line in (beta, return) space $= r_{\text{pure}} + (\mu_i - r_{\text{pure}})/(b_i) = $ *characteristic line* of security or portfolio i (Figure 10.9). See Treynor (1965) and Treynor and Mazuy (1966).

The implications of this analysis for the determination of the relative performance of portfolios J and K are shown in Figure 10.9. The methodology is fairly similar to that of Sharpe, except that by using the SML instead of the CML, the Treynor measure is capable of evaluating individual security holdings as well as portfolios. A disadvantage is that the accuracy of the rankings depends in part upon the assumption (implicit in the use of the SML) that the fund

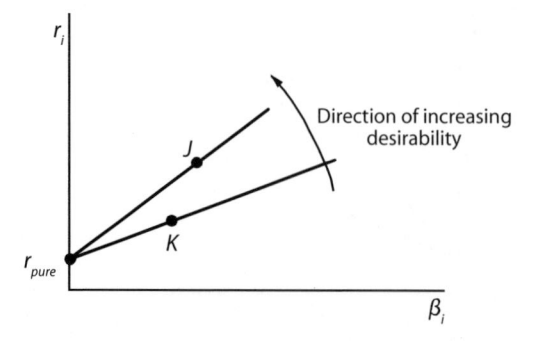

Figure 10.9. Treynor's Characteristic Line Analysis

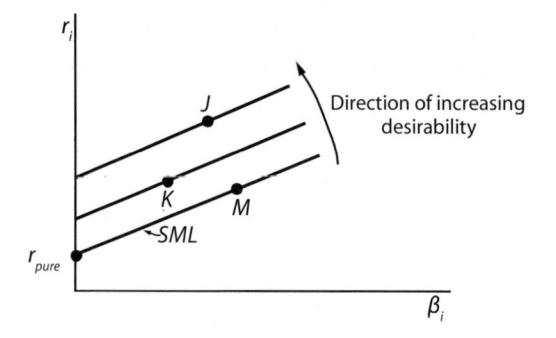

Figure 10.10. Jensen's Measure

evaluated would have been held in an otherwise perfectly diversified portfolio.

A third measure, also based on the SML but different from Treynor's, has been proposed by Jensen (1968, 1969):

$$(\mu_i - r_{\text{pure}}) - b_i(\mu_M - r_{\text{pure}}). \tag{10.9}$$

This measure is expressed in units of return above or below the pure rate of a line drawn through the parameters of the security or portfolio parallel to the SML, as illustrated in Figure 10.10. This measure does allow comparisons of a portfolio to the market and is also amenable to estimation by regression; because of its treatment of differential risk, however, direct comparisons between funds or portfolios generally cannot be made. Furthermore, it has been suggested that all three of the above measures are biased against high-risk portfolios by failing to recognize the inequality of borrowing and lending rates and the resulting nonlinearity of the SML and CML.

Both the Sharpe and the Treynor ratios measure excess return per unit of risk. The Sharpe ratio provides this per unit of total risk (standard deviation), and the Treynor measures the excess return per unit of systematic risk (beta). It is clear, however, that upside variance is a positive outcome for portfolio returns, but that downside deviation with respect to some target return is the harmful component. This distinction is an attempt to better define "risk" as opposed to "volatility." As Markowitz (1959) noted (p. 194, 1st edition),

> Analysis based on semi-variance tends to produce better portfolios than those based on variance. Variance considers extremely high and extremely low returns equally desirable. An analysis based on variance seeks to eliminate both extremes. An analysis based on semi-variance, on the other hand, concentrates on reducing losses.

In the early 1980s' Frank Sortino's research developed a relative risk ratio which bears his name, based on the downside semi-variance relative to a target rate of return. He originally wanted to call the measure the "mean-lower partial moment ranking ratio," but instead it was coined the *Sortino ratio*. It is calculated as:

$$\frac{\mu_i - r_{\text{DTR}}}{\sigma_{\text{D}}}, \qquad (10.10)$$

where DTR = desired target return (formerly known as MAR, minimum acceptable return);

$$\sigma_{\text{D}} = \sqrt{\frac{1}{n} \sum_{t=1}^{n} (\mu_t - r_{\text{DTR}})^2 \cdot I(\mu_t < r_{\text{DTR}})}$$

is the downside deviation (lower semi-variance); and $I(x)$ is the indicator function, i.e. $I(x) = 1$ if $x \geq 0$ and

$$I(x) = 0 \quad \text{if } x < 0.$$

Professor Sortino has collaborated with Robert van der Meer and Auke Plantinga to advocate their Upside Potential Ratio (UPR), calculated as upside potential divided by downside deviation (Sortino et al., 1999). In this framework reward is measured not in expected return but in upside potential (exceeding DTR); and risk is measured as downside volatility of returns failing to meet DTR.

Another measure introduced earlier that seems to hold some promise as an evaluation tool is the geometric mean. Over a given time period, the geometric mean portfolio return could be compared to that of other portfolios or some market index. There are several advantages to such a measure. Assuming that the interval considered is "sufficiently" long (and if it is not, one may doubt the validity of any evaluation technique), then undue risk-taking should manifest itself in numerous low period returns and, thus, a reduced geometric mean (or terminal wealth, which is an equivalent concept in this context). If such is not the case, then the equivalence of historical variability and risk becomes increasingly dubious.

The geometric mean also facilitates the use of very short investment periods (because funds value their holdings from one to four or more times a day, up to one thousand observations per year could be obtained). It provides a cumulative effect if desired by simply including each new set of observations without discarding any of the old which could, in turn, be used to determine a cumulative management performance fee (some of which would be withheld against poor future performance).

Depending upon the information desired by the investor, therefore, several measures of portfolio performance are available. We must again stress, however, that the past is generally a "sunk cost" and unless certain continuity assumptions appear valid, the predictive power of these measures is seriously questionable.

Additional Topics in Portfolio Management

The portfolio selection methodology described in Chapter 9 requires a complete enumeration of the parameters of available investments and of the investor's utility function. Because of the costs of obtaining such information and the fact that some information may be unavailable at any price, any methodology that further delimits the area of investigation is that of value. A major breakthrough was accomplished when Markowitz devised the quadratic programming algorithm to generate the efficiency frontier (see Chapter 9). Another advance was made when Sharpe employed an index model to simplify input generation (Chapter 9). This section considers additional techniques for reducing the number of portfolios under consideration.

A criterion that is more an addendum to the concept of efficiency than a selection criterion, but nevertheless provides a good introduction to the discussion, may be considered. Portfolios with low μ and σ may not be eliminated by the concept of efficiency in comparison with portfolios having much higher μ and only slightly larger σ, even though the probability that the best outcome of the former would ever exceed the worst outcome of the latter was very small. Therefore a lower *confidence limit* could be set at $\mu - K\sigma$ and low-return portfolios dominated by this rule could be dropped from the efficiency frontier. The parameter K would be a function of the investor's degree of risk aversion and, if return could be assumed to be normally distributed, could be determined on a one-tail test of the percentage of the time the investor would tolerate a shortfall of actual returns (for example, 16 percent for $K = 1$, 2 percent for $K = 2$, and so on).

For example, suppose that an investor was prepared to ignore low returns that occurred no more than 2 percent of the time. This percentage would correspond to the portion remaining in the left tail of a normal distribution at a point two standard deviations below the mean; thus, $K = 2$. Now consider the following points on an efficiency frontier:

	A	B
μ	4 percent	10 percent
σ	1	3
$\mu - 2\sigma$	2	4

Neither point can be termed inefficient, as B has a higher return but at greater risk. It may be noted, however, that the investor's perceived worst outcome of B (the lower confidence limit of B) is greater than the same for A (that is, 4 percent >2 percent). Thus, portfolio A, and other portfolios in the lower range of the efficiency frontier, could be eliminated by the confidence-limit criterion.

A far more comprehensive concept, called *stochastic dominance*, allows for the elimination from further consideration of securities or portfolios on the basis of known characteristics of entire classes of utility functions. *First-degree stochastic dominance* (FSD) requires only the assumption that more wealth is preferable to less (that is, $dU/dW > 0$). It may then be said that investment B exhibits FSD over investment A if, for each possible level of return, the cumulative probability of B falling below the level of return is less than or equal to the same for A (and the strict inequality holds in at least one case). Consider the following example:

r_i	Prob. (A)	Prob. (B)
5 percent	0.2	0.1
10	0.3	0.2
15	0.4	0.3
20	0.1	0.4
	1.0	1.0
μ	12 percent	15 percent
σ	4.6	5.0

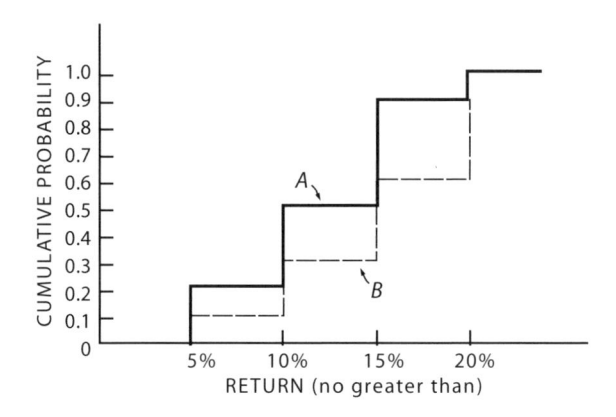

Capital Market Theory, Efficiency, and Imperfections 463

Figure 10.11. First-Degree Stochastic Dominance

The cumulative probability distributions of returns for A and B are shown in Figure 10.11. The FSD decision rule is shown as follows:

r_i	Cumulative Probability $A = A(r_i)$	Cumulative Probability $B = B(r_i)$	$A(r_i) - B(r_i)$
5 percent	0.2	0.1	+.1
10	0.5	0.3	+.2
15	0.9	0.6	+.3
20	1.0	1.0	0

For investment B:

$$\text{FSD}(r_i) = A(r_i) - B(r_i) \geq 0 \quad \text{for all } r_i, \text{ and}$$
$$> 0 \quad \text{for at least one } r_i.$$

Thus, investment B exhibits FSD over investment A and would be preferred by anyone to whom more wealth was preferable to less (that is, all rational persons, including risk seekers and neutrals, as well as averters).

Second-degree stochastic dominance (SSD) requires the assumption of risk neutrality or aversion ($d^2U/dW^2 \leq 0$) as well as rationality ($dU/dW > 0$). Under these assumptions, it is possible to make selections between certain investments that do not exhibit FSD. Consider the following investment alternatives:

r_i	Prob. (A)	Prob. (B)
5 percent	0.2	0.1
10	0.3	0.4
15	0.3	4.0
20	0.2	0.1
	1.0	1.0
μ	12.5 percent	12.5 percent
σ	5.1	4.03

The FSD analysis would provide:

r_i	Cumulative Probability $A = A(r_i)$	Cumulative Probability $B = B(r_i)$	$A(r_i) - B(r_i) = FSD(r_i)$
5 percent	0.2	0.1	+.1
10	0.5	0.5	0
15	0.8	0.9	−.1
20	1.0	1.0	0

Thus, neither investment would exhibit FSD over the other. SSD, in effect, considers the cumulative difference between the two cumulative probability distributions employed in FSD. Again considering investment B:

$$\text{SSD}(r_i) = \text{SSD}(r_{i-1}) + (r_i - r_{i-1})[A(r_{i-1}) - B(r_{i-1})]$$
$$\text{SSD}(r_i) = \text{SSD}(r_{i-1}) + (r_i - r_{i-1})\text{FSD}(r_{i-1}).$$

Capital Market Theory, Efficiency, and Imperfections

(1) i	(2) r_i	(3) $r_i - r_{i-1}$	(4) $FSD(r_{i-1})$	(5) (3) × (4)	(6) $SSD(r_{i-1})$	(7) $SSD(r_i)$
1	5 percent	—	—	—	—	0
2	10	0.05	+.1	+.005	0	+.005
3	15	0.05	0	0	+.005	+.005
4	20	0.05	−.1	−.005	+.005	0

By the SSD equation, col (7) = col (5) + col (6) and, in turn, becomes the entry in col (6) on the next row. Thus, investment B is preferred by SSD if $SSD(r_i) \geq 0$ for all i and the strict inequality holds in at least one case.

Finally, if neither FSD nor SSD will allow a choice to be made between two investments, *Third-degree stochastic dominance* (TSD) may be employed. In addition to the first and second order conditions for the utility of wealth function discussed above, TSD also requires that $d^3U/dW^3 \geq 0$. Following the parallelism previously established, TSD is essentially concerned with the cumulative functions employed in SSD. We present our final investment comparison with regard to showing the dominance of B:

r_i	Prob. (A)	Prob. (B)
5 percent	0.1	0
10	0	0.3
15	0.9	0.6
20	0	0.1
	1.0	1.0
μ	14 percent	14 percent
σ	3	3

r_i	$A(r_i)$	$B(r_i)$	$FSD(r_i)$
5 percent	0.1	0.0	+.1
10	0.1	0.3	−.2
15	1.0	0.9	+.1
20	1.0	1.0	0

(1)	(2)	(3)	(4)	(5)	(6)	(7)
i	r_i	$r_i - r_{i-1}$	$FSD(r_{i-1})$	(3) × (4)	$SSD(r_{i-1})$	$SSD(r_i)$
1	5 percent	—	—	—	—	0
2	10	0.05	+0.1	+0.005	0	+0.005
3	15	0.05	−0.2	−0.01	+0.005	−0.005
4	20	0.05	+0.1	−0.005	−0.005	0

Because neither FSD nor SSD can be shown, the TSD for B is given by:

$$\text{TSD}(r_i) = \text{TSD}(r_{i-1} + (r_i - r_{i-1}))[\text{SSD}(r_i) + \text{SSD}(r_{i-1})]/2.$$

For B to be preferred, then, $TSD(r_i) \geq 0$ for all i (with the strict inequality holding for at least one i) and, furthermore, $\mu_B \geq \mu_A$. The TSD of B over A is shown in Figure 10.12.

At this writing, there exist no algorithms for the generation of stochastic dominance (SD) efficient portfolios and the analysis implied has remained dormant for decades. The work done has been of a sampling nature, primarily to demonstrate the differences between SD and (σ, μ) efficient portfolios. The Sharpe mutual-fund studies (see above) were replicated for 34 funds between 1954 and 1963, and it was found that no fund dominated the Dow Jones Industrial Index although the latter exhibited SSD over six funds and TSD over nine. The ability to select optimal portfolios with a

(1)	(2)	(3)	(4)	(5)	(6)
i	r_i	$r_i - r_{i-1}$	$FSD(r_{i-1})$	$(3) \times (4)$	$SSD(r_{i-1})$
1	5 percent	—	—	—	—
2	10	0.05	+0.1	+0.005	0
3	15	0.05	−0.2	−0.01	+0.005
4	20	0.05	+0.1	−0.005	−0.005

(7)	(8)	(9)	(10)	(11)
$SSD(r_i)$	$\dfrac{(6) \times (7)}{2}$	$(8) \times (3)$	$TSD(r_{i-1})$	$TSD(r_i) = (9) + (10)$
0	—	—	—	0
+0.005	+0.0025	+0.000125	0	+0.000125
−0.005	0	0	+0.000125	+0.000125
0	−0.0025	−0.000125	+0.000125	0

Figure 10.12. Worksheet for TSD

minimal knowledge of individual preferences provided by SD holds great promise, but many problems of implementation remain to be solved.

In addition to stochastic dominance, several authors have attempted to provide other portfolio selection criteria that avoid the necessity of collecting utility data from the investor. If such techniques could prove satisfactory, numerous problems could be avoided. Among them are those cases in which an investor's risk aversion is not known, when risk aversion changes over time, or when more than one person is the beneficiary of a portfolio. A specific technique for portfolio selection, on the basis of minimizing the probability of the occurrence of some disastrous level of loss (D), was presented over 60 years ago by Roy (1952). He employed Chebyschev's inequality, which does not require the assumption of a special form of probability distribution for returns. Expressed in our terminology, the relevant form of the inequality is:

$$P(X|X \leq D) \leq \frac{\sigma^2}{(\mu - D)^2}. \tag{10.11}$$

which, when differentiated, set equal to zero, and solved, provides a minimum probability at $\sigma/(\mu - D)$. In Figure 10.12, it will be observed that any line connecting point D to the efficiency frontier will have slope $\sigma/(\mu - D)$ but only at the point of tangency will the point itself have the requisite slope. The point of tangency is thus the safety-first portfolio associated with a given minimum required return. Two such points are illustrated in Figure 10.13.

An approach similar in methodology has been suggested by John Lintner (1965). If we let r_{pure} represent the rate to be earned on some

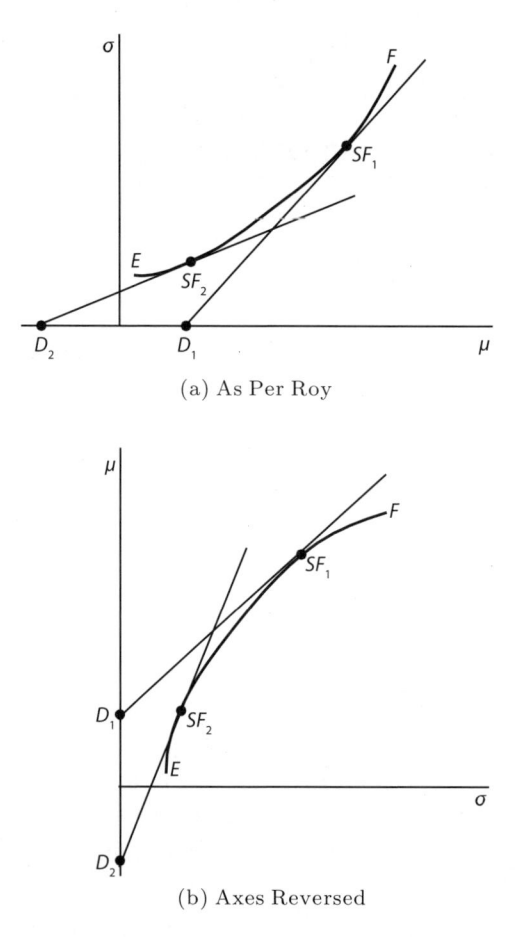

(a) As Per Roy

(b) Axes Reversed

Figure 10.13. Safety-First Portfolio

riskless asset then Lintner defines the excess return (X) to be earned on a given risky asset as:

$$X_i = \mu_i - r_{\text{pure}}.$$

It will be recalled that the parameters for the two-asset portfolio when security 2 is riskless are:

$$\mu = \alpha_1 \mu_1 + \alpha_2 \mu_2, \quad \text{and} \quad \sigma = \alpha_1 \sigma_1$$

thus:

$$\alpha_1 = \frac{\sigma}{\sigma_1}.$$

Bear in mind all the while that asset 1 can be a risky portfolio as well as a security. But:

$$\mu_2 = r_{\text{pure}} \quad \text{and} \quad \alpha_2 = 1 - \alpha_1,$$

therefore:

$$\mu = \alpha_1 \mu_1 + (1 - \alpha_1) r_{\text{pure}}$$
$$\mu = \alpha_1 \mu_1 + r_{\text{pure}} - \alpha_1 r_{\text{pure}}$$
$$\mu = r_{\text{pure}} + \alpha_1 (\mu_1 - r_{\text{pure}}),$$

and substituting the relationships defined above:

$$\mu = r_{\text{pure}} + \frac{\sigma}{\sigma_1} X_1$$

$$\mu = r_{\text{pure}} + \frac{X_1}{\sigma_1} \sigma$$

$$\mu = r_{\text{pure}} + \theta \sigma, \quad \text{where} \quad \theta = \frac{\mu_1 - r_{\text{pure}}}{\sigma_1}. \tag{10.12}$$

An examination of Equation (10.12) will indicate that a portfolio that maximizes θ will also maximize μ for a given σ and r_{pure}. The verbal sense of this is that we are trying to maximize excess return per unit of risk. The geometric equivalence to the Roy approach is shown in Figure 10.14. Here again, any line connecting r_{pure} with a risky security or portfolio will possess the requisite slope, but a

470 *Quantitative Financial Analytics*

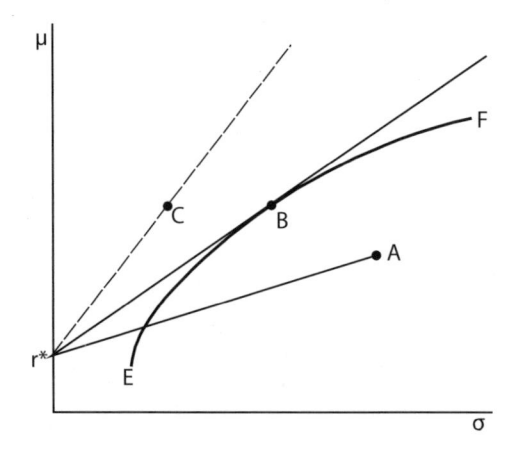

Figure 10.14. Excess-return Criterion Portfolio

maximum slope is desired. Thus, it follows that the risk-excess return trade-off is better in the case of B than A, and further that C would be even better except that, by definition, no securities or portfolios exist above the efficiency frontier. Further reflection should indicate that the optimal portfolio by the excess-return criterion is found at the point of tangency between a ray emanating from r_{pure} and the efficiency frontier. The similarity to the Roy technique is further illustrated by the fact that, if the Roy disaster level (D) is set equal to r_{pure}, the two approaches will select the same portfolio.

In comparing the Roy and Lintner approaches, several points should be made. The safety-first model, from its basis in Chebyschev's inequality to its goal of minimization of probability of outcomes below one specific point, seems to come as close to decision making under uncertainty as any technique presented in this book; very little is assumed to be known about either the risk preferences of the investor or the distribution of returns on investment. This lack of specification is an advantage in many real-world situations, and this is one reason the model was included here. On the other hand, if more complete information is available, more precise models may be employed. Surprisingly enough, given their technical similarity, the Lintner model is on the other end of the spectrum in regard to equilibrium and perfection assumptions. To be universally applicable for risk averters, the excess-return criterion requires the separation theorem (discussed earlier) to hold, which assumes, among other things, that the portfolio can borrow or lend at the same rate (specifically, at r_{pure}). The excess-return criterion essentially involves the application of the basic capital market theory model to the selection of individual portfolios. Although this application does not require all the equilibrium assumptions of capital market theory, the likely inapplicability of the separation theorem is enough to raise doubts regarding its general adoption.

A final criterion for portfolio selection without specific reference to utility considerations that has been suggested is the maximization of geometric mean. If it may be assumed that (1) the same investment opportunities are available in each investment period; (2) the outcomes of these opportunities are independent over time; and (3) all income is reinvested, then the terminal wealth at the end of n periods associated with investment in any given portfolio is given by the following equations. Let $W_{i,n}$ = wealth in period n associated with investment in portfolio i; $\rho_{i,j}$ = return earned in period j on portfolio i; W_0 = initial wealth; N = number of periods.
Then

$$W_{i,n} = W_0(1+\rho_{i,1})(1+\rho_{i,2})\cdots(1+\rho_{i,n})$$

$$W_{i,n} = W_0 \prod_{j=1}^{n}(1+\rho_{i,j}) \tag{10.13}$$

$$\frac{W_{i,n}}{W_0} = \prod_{j=1}^{n}(1+\rho_{i,j})$$

$$\left(\frac{W_{i,n}}{W_0}\right)^{\frac{1}{n}} = \left[\prod_{j=1}^{n}(1+\rho_{i,j})\right]^{\frac{1}{n}}$$

$$E\left[\left(\frac{W_{i,n}}{W_0}\right)^{\frac{1}{n}} - 1\right] = E\left[\left(\prod_{j=1}^{n}(1+\rho_{i,j})\right)^{\frac{1}{n}} - 1\right]. \tag{10.14}$$

The right side of Equation (10.14) is the expected geometric mean return on portfolio i. The portfolio that maximizes this expectation thus will maximize the expectation of terminal wealth. It can also be shown (by the central-limit theorem) that the probability of the maximum geometric mean portfolio resulting in greater terminal wealth than any other available portfolio approaches unity as n approaches infinity.

All the above, however, are simply mathematical tautology. It was shown earlier that the maximization of the geometric mean of returns is consistent with the maximization of a log utility-of-wealth function. Thus, if the investor possesses a log utility function or, given the central limit theorem, if the number of investment periods is infinite, the geometric-mean criterion is sufficient. In some other cases, it has been found to be a reasonable approximation. However, Samuelson has shown that as long as n is finite, there exist classes of utility functions for which the proposed criterion is not even a good approximation. Indeed, he also demonstrated that there are classes of utility functions for which no uniform strategy is optimal (see Paul Samuelson, 1971) Even without Professor Samuelson's argument, there is a good question as to whether assumptions (1)–(3) above are very realistic. The problems of multiperiod optimization are indeed great, however, and are considered subsequently. It will soon be apparent that the other techniques are sufficiently troublesome that geometric mean maximization becomes a very attractive alternative if the assumptions are anywhere close to being fulfilled.

It should be noted from the outset that the portfolio and capital market theory outlined above remains essentially unimplemented even in the security investment field. This result follows despite the facts that: (1) securities are homogeneous and divisible; (2) the returns from securities do not vary greatly with the holder (little management and relatively simple tax effects, at least at the margin); (3) the markets for securities are relatively efficient (in terms of transaction costs, liquidity, and so on); (4) the returns from securities appear to be independent over time (little if any serial correlation) and, thus, independent of holding period; (5) a great deal of publicly available, machine-accessible information exist on most securities; and (6) most securities of significance trade in one national market. Because none of the above analytical advantages apply as well (if at all) to alternative investments such as real estate, private equity holdings, etc., it should not be surprising to learn that, given the current state of the art, it is impossible to integrate these investments into portfolio selection in a completely satisfactory manner.

A very serious hindrance would appear to involve input generation. The difficulties with the determination of σ, μ for alternative investments are considerable. For a Markowitz approach, it would be necessary to estimate the covariance of returns between each holding and every other holding. Obviously, an index approach would be required. The Sharpe single index is probably too broad for mixed asset portfolios, because no single index (such as gross domestic product (GDP) or the prime rate of interest) could relate to all assets and yet not include a great deal of "noise." An intermediate approach that offers some promise is the use of a multiple index model, which comes in two basic forms: (1) a model that relates the returns on each class of asset to its appropriate index and then relates the indices by means of a Markowitz covariance approach; and (2) a model that relates index returns to another index (often GDP), in the form of one index model on top of another. The latter is the easier to solve because it essentially involves running the Sharpe model twice (first on the assets and then on the indexes); the difficulty arises because of the amount of "noise" created by such a two-level estimation procedure.

Finally, we are faced with the fact that prospective returns on alternative investments cannot be estimated in the same way as security returns. Because securities trade in reasonably good markets, it is possible to employ the fiction of an "annual holding period," from which holding-period returns may be computed and regressed against index (market) returns. Because of the assumption of independence of securities' returns, it then becomes possible to employ the expected value of these historical relationships as a future estimate of the risk and return of the security.

In conclusion, the inclusion of alternative investments in a theoretically correct system of portfolio selection is hindered by

1. the lack of a quadratic integer programming algorithm;
2. the lack of an adequate index of returns;
3. the individualistic nature of such investments (with regard to taxes, holding period, and so on) that makes the estimation of returns from a general index (even a good one) difficult;
4. the lack of market data to provide even *ex post* estimations of risk and return;
5. the lack of independence of asset returns and non-replicability of deals; and
6. portfolio restrictions, information imperfections, and so on that preclude anyone from holding a perfectly diversified portfolio.

Over the course of time, expectations regarding the earning power and dividend-paying potential of the firm, the risk of the same, and the firm's stock's covariance with other securities will change. Furthermore, the market price of the stock and the level of interest rates will undoubtedly change. Finally, the investor's utility function itself may change or else changes in his level of wealth may cause his degree of risk aversion to change. Any of these factors will tend to cause the investor's portfolio to be suboptimal. It then becomes necessary to revise the portfolio.

Portfolio revision may be viewed as the general case of asset acquisition and disposition, with portfolio selection representing the special case of revision of the all-cash portfolio. As such, revision involves all the problems of portfolio selection and some additional difficulties as well. Any asset sold at a profit, for example, becomes subject to taxation that, in turn, reduces the amount of funds available for reinvestment; it might thus be desirable to maintain a position in a slightly inferior security if the capital gains taxes would wipe out any advantage. Also, the purchase or sale of any security will incur transaction costs, which also reduce the amount to be invested. This problem could be ignored in portfolio selection because it was assumed that the costs would be incurred no matter what was bought. A simple one-period revision model is presented below to illustrate these effects.

Let

μ_i = expected return on ith asset
C_{ij} = covariance of return between ith and jth security
α_i = amount invested in ith security at beginning of period
β_i = amount invested in ith security at end of period before portfolio revision
γ_i = amount in ith security after portfolio revision (decision variable)
$\delta_i(\omega_i)$ = increase (decrease) in amount of ith asset held from existing to revised portfolio
$b_i(s_i)$ = buying (selling) transfer cost of ith asset ($b_0 = s_0 = 0$ for cash) and assumed proportional for convenience
r_i = realized return on ith asset, composed of cash dividend return (r_i^c) and capital gain return (r_i^g). By definition,

$$r_i = r_i^c + r_i^g$$

t_c, t_g = ordinary income and capital gain tax rates for investor

The cash account at the end of the year is equal to beginning cash plus all dividends after taxes:

$$\beta_o = \alpha_o + \left(\prod_{i=1}^{n} r_i^c \alpha_i\right)(1 - t_c), \qquad (10.15)$$

and the amount invested in each risk asset is:

$$\beta_{i(i=1,\ldots,n)} = (1 + r_i^g)\alpha_i. \qquad (10.16)$$

From this point, short sales and borrowing are excluded:

$$\alpha_i, \beta_i, \gamma_i \geq 0, \quad \text{for all } i, 0 \text{ to } n. \qquad (10.17)$$

By definition, the net change in holdings of the ith asset is given by the difference between holdings in the end of period portfolio and the revised portfolio:

$$\delta_i - \omega_i = \gamma_i - \beta_i, \quad \delta_i, \omega_i \geq 0$$

$$\text{and } \delta_i \text{ or } \omega_i \text{ or both} = 0. \tag{10.18}$$

The total value of the portfolio after revision must equal the value prior to revision less any transaction costs and taxes realized:

$$\sum_{i=0}^{n} \gamma_i = \sum_{i=0}^{n} \beta_i - \sum_{i=1}^{n} \left[\delta_i b_i + \omega_i \left(s_i + \left(1 + r_i^g\right)^{-1} \left(r_i^g - s_i - r_i^g s_i\right) t_g \right) \right]. \tag{10.19}$$

Subject to these constraints, the objective function then becomes:

Maximize Z,

$$Z = \sum_{i=0}^{n} (1 + \mu_i) \gamma_i - \lambda \left[\sum_{i=1}^{n} \sum_{j=1}^{n} \gamma_i \gamma_j C_{ij} \right]. \tag{10.20}$$

Multiperiod revision models generally involve dynamic programming, in which the last-period portfolio is optimized first and then the model works backward to the present. Various limitations have prevented the practical applications of such models except for very small portfolios over a limited number of periods.

Two final points should be made. One of the reasons that dynamic programming is necessary stems from the contention that one-period portfolio planning tends to be "myopic" (suboptimal over many periods) unless the underlying utility function is a log or power function. It has been shown, however, that if investors may be assumed to be risk-averse and markets perfect, one-period investment planning is consistent with long-run optimization. Finally, models of the sort presented above include taxes and transaction costs, but not information costs. But for the latter, the model could be run (and revision take place) continuously. Because gathering information and running the model do require time and money, however, the question of how often to revise (or more precisely, consider revision) appears to be unanswered at this time.

The reader will observe that much of the analysis (and citations provided) above go back for five decades. Since then, research has gone off in other directions (see below) but the seminal efforts remain the cornerstone of modern portfolio theory. Most Ph.D. students in financial economics have never actually read these early papers and take for granted that the versions provided and embellished upon are correct. It may be suggested that enterprising doctoral candidates (especially in heterodox fields like statistics) could profit by doing further work suggested by these ancient papers.

Capital Markets: Efficiency and Imperfections

One of the major assumptions underlying capital market theory presented so far was that investors possessed either homogeneous (or a stable weighted average of) expectations regarding the future. One implication of this assumption is that a change in expectations will occur either unanimously or else in some stable average way that is an operational equivalent of unanimity. Thus, if markets are in equilibrium, a change in expectations will cause them to move in a rapid and unbiased fashion to a new equilibrium. Markets that behave in this manner will always "fully reflect" available information, which is the definition of an efficient market. Various empirical tests have been made of the efficiency of the securities markets, and these form the basis of the following discussion. A point to be borne in mind, however, is that any proof of capital market efficiency does not validate all the assumptions in Chapter 9. Efficiency is a necessary condition for equilibrium, but it is not altogether sufficient; we shall return to this point in the latter part of the chapter.

It will be recalled, that, even in a world of perfect certainty, prices of securities could be expected to change over time as long as the income stream was not instantaneous and constant. Indeed, price change would be necessary in such a case to cause the expected return for each holding period to be obtained, that is,

$$P_1 + D_1 \equiv P_0(1 + r_1), \qquad (10.21)$$

or

$$P_1 - P_0 \equiv r_1(P_0) - D_1.$$

In a world of less-than-perfect certainty, changes in expected income or the required rate of return (caused, in turn, by changes in the pure rate or the perceived risk of the issue) could also cause the prices of securities to change over time. It is argued, however, that only the availability of new information or better analysis of already available information should cause the expectations regarding income, risk, and interest rates to change and, thus, prices to change for these reasons. If it may be assumed that: (1) all relevant information is available to all market participants; (2) any new information is spread and assimilated immediately; and (3) vast numbers of market participants employ the most sophisticated analytical techniques, then the securities market may be viewed as a "fair game" where:

$$E[(\tilde{P}_1 + \tilde{D}_1)|I_0] = P_0[1 + E(\tilde{r}_1|I_0)]. \qquad (10.22)$$

The above merely states that the expected price of a security in period one given the information available in period zero (assuming all dividends or interests are reinvested) is equal to the price in period zero times one plus the expected rate of return, given available information. (This formula and material in this section are discussed in more detail in Eugene F. Fama (1970). This hypothesis also implies that (1) the excess market value of a security or (2) the excess expected return to be earned by holding the security both have, given available information, an expected value of zero.

Several points should be noted. Equation (10.22) does not imply that prices need to be stable. Indeed, to the extent that $E[\tilde{D}_1] \neq E[\tilde{r}_1](P_0)$, then $E[\tilde{P}_1] \neq P_0$. Thus, we have a probabilistic model with implications similar to the certainty model (Equation (10.21)). A major difference, however, is indicated by the presence of the expectations operator and tildes for both the $(\tilde{P}_1 + \tilde{D}_1)$ and $\tilde{r}_1$ terms, implying that they are random variables at time zero. Thus, although the certainty model would indicate a constant rate of price change over time (that is, linear on semilog graphs), the expectations model indicates that price could be expected to vary about such a line. Such a possibility is also reflected by the error term in the various capital-market estimation models.

Finally, it will be noted that both $(\tilde{P}_1 + \tilde{D}_1)$ and $\tilde{r}_1$ are conditioned by available information, I_o. To the extent new information or better analysis becomes available, $E[\tilde{P}_1 + \tilde{D}_1]$ and can alter, and the expected rate of price change over time can shift. Adding the assumption that the timing of the arrival of new information in the market is a random variable, we see that shifts in the expected-price-change line, as well as movement about it, can be treated as random events. We shall now examine various efforts to prove or refute the efficient markets hypothesis. This analysis answers some of the questions that were suggested in Chapter 1 at the very beginning of this book.

The earliest empirical work was produced by the "random walk" hypothesis researchers primarily to attack the "technical analysts." Technical analysts have for many years contended that by analyzing only the past price movements of a security, it is possible (or, "they are able" — depending upon the size of the ego of the technical analyst involved) to predict future price movements and thus make greater-than-normal profits. The distress of the random-walk followers is perhaps best expressed by Paul Cootner (1964, p. 232):

> If any substantial group of buyers thought prices were too low, their buying would force up the prices. The reverse would be true for sellers. Except for appreciation due to earnings retention, the conditional expectation of tomorrow's price, given today's price, is today's price.
>
> In such a world, the only price changes that would occur are those that result from new information. Since there is no reason to expect that information to be nonrandom in appearance, the period-to-period price changes of a stock should be random movements, statistically independent of one another.

The early random walk writers, then, concerned themselves with demonstrating that successive price changes were statistically independent of each other, that various mechanical trading rules based upon price changes did not yield profits statistically superior to a simple "buy-and-hold" strategy, and that "price changes from transaction to transaction are independent, identically distributed random variables with finite variances" implying, by the central limit theorem, that for numerous transactions price changes will be normally distributed (see Fama, *op. cit.*, p. 399). The Cootner volume contains many of the earlier studies and the Fama article has an extensive bibliography, so one is not reproduced here. Selected references are included at the end of the chapter.

More recent theorists have refined certain parts of the basic random-walk argument. In the first place, it is suggested that price changes do not follow a true random walk (with an expected value of zero), but rather a submartingale (with an expected value greater than zero). A martingale is a process in which the conditional expectation of the $(n+1)$th observation, given a set of data, is the nth observation. Rates of return are often assumed to follow a martingale, such that the expected value of the price given information up to a point $t-1$ (I_{t-1}) equals the price at time $t-1$, or $E(P_t|I_{t-1}) = P_{t-1}$. A submartingale is a similar concept with $E(P_t|I_{t-1}) \geq P_{t-1}$; stock prices are generally assumed to follow a submartingale process. A random walk is a very strict form of martingale that assumes not only the mean but the entire distribution to be the same.

Thus, the theory can take long-run price trends into account and accept a very modest amount of serial correlation in successive price changes. In view of the general upward trend of prices over time, it was surprising to many observers that the statistical case against absolute independence of successive price changes was as weak as it was. The challenge to the technicians has become to demonstrate that their rules can earn greater-than-normal profits.

It has also been contended that price changes are not normally distributed about an expected trend but rather belong to the broader family of stable Paretian distributions of which the normal is only a limiting case. The implication for our purposes is that the "fat-tailed" stable distributions have an infinite variance, such that the usual portfolio approach employing σ and cannot be used if prices (and, thus, returns) are so distributed. Fama has demonstrated, however, that a similar form of analysis, employing a different dispersion parameter, can be employed. See Eugene F. Fama (1965).

Although the weak tests of capital market efficiency dealt with the inability to make profitable predictions of future prices from past prices, a second form of testing (called the "semi-strong efficient market hypothesis") attempted to prove that prices reflect all available information. These tests sought to demonstrate that new information results in a rapid adjustment to a new equilibrium price that, by implication, is taken to demonstrate that the price at any time must reflect available information. Specifically, the tests took events such as announcements of stock splits, earnings, dividends, interest-rate changes, and so on, and studied (1) how rapidly a price adjustment was made and (2) whether the price adjustment was an unbiased evaluation of the information (such that subsequent adjustments were as likely to be in one direction as the other). The results of the tests confirmed that price adjustments occur rather quickly after the first public announcement of the information, implying that at least a significant portion of the market receives and interprets the information quickly. It follows, then, that the initial price adjustment has been generally found to be unbiased. A price trend caused by the slow spread and interpretation of new information could result in a profitable return for swift action; that such a trend does not occur seems affirmed.

In a crude sense, it could be said that the weak tests indicate that one cannot become wealthy as a technician (forecasting price or return movements based on past behavior), and the semi-strong tests indicate that, by the time one reads some new information, it is too late to profit from it. The theory still allows a person possessing superior information or analytical techniques to expect a better-than-normal return. A third form of testing (called the "strong efficient market hypothesis") went all the way to asking if there can be any information not reflected in the price of a security such that anyone can expect above-average profits. During the 1920s, it was claimed that "any day is a good day to buy a good stock." If the strong form of the efficient capital market hypothesis held, then, "any day is as good as any other day to buy any stock (or bond, or mutual fund, and so on)."

The rationale for the strong tests lies in a combination of the semi-strong tests (information assimilated in a rapid and unbiased fashion) and the fact that a great many supposedly knowledgeable and trained people are engaged in the securities business. It is argued that with so many people and so much information, there should be few if any true "sleepers." Studies have indicated that corporate insiders may have superior information and thus higher expected returns. Other investors, however, have not been shown to produce consistently higher returns. In particular, numerous studies of mutual funds have shown that their average performance is, if anything, inferior to the market as a whole.

It also appears that, even for individual funds, past success is an unreliable guide to future performance. In sum, it has been shown that the investor could do better picking securities at random than with the average mutual fund. And, because mutual funds are viewed as possessing as much information, analytical skill, and diversification as any investor, their inability to out-perform the market is taken as very compelling evidence in support of the strong form of the efficient markets hypothesis. It should be noted, however, that even in academic circles, the strong form has a much smaller following than the other two tests.

Capital Markets and the Real World

In order to justify the time and money spent on the study of investments (including the purchase price of this book), it is necessary to come to terms with the strong form of the efficient capital markets hypothesis. Indeed, if the consumer groups gain additional strength, it may soon be necessary to place on the dust jacket of all investments books "Caution: Studies have shown that contents provide no advantage over random selection." Nevertheless, it should be remembered that the strong-form tests are based almost entirely on mutual-fund performance. Some may question the use of these institutions as absolute proof that, if they cannot outperform the market, no one can.

For several reasons, it may be argued that mutual funds are an unconvincing choice for a test of the strong form of the efficient capital markets hypothesis. First, *the level of training and education of a number of fund managers is not terribly high.* Although many funds are operated by competently trained managers, many more are not. Second, *The compensation scheme employed by most funds encourages suboptimal behavior.* Small funds take excessive risks in order to achieve the top of the annual performance lists. This is done in order to gain new shareholders and the subsequent profits derived from percentage-of-assets management fees. Third, *large funds cannot acquire substantial amounts of any promising issue without influencing market price unless their position is accumulated over time.* Moreover, when a fund has acquired a large holding of a thinly traded issue, the position cannot be liquidated easily without influencing price. Fourth, *even if large funds could find small companies whose stock evidenced very lucrative future potential, the shares of these firms would represent only a small percentage of a large fund's assets.* Hence, the fund could not increase its return significantly even if it did find securities that significantly outperformed the market. Fifth, *legal requirements constrain open-ended (mutual) funds to hold over-diversified portfolios.*

There are a number of legal and institutional arrangements that tend to undermine many of the assumptions required for a capital market theory in addition to those that produce market inefficiency. In particular, it appears unlikely that market portfolios are (or can be) maintained by a substantial part of the investment community. In the first place, we can observe that legal and institutional arrangements eliminate some securities from consideration, much less selection, by certain investors. Banks and savings associations, for example, are effectively prohibited from owning any stock (with a few insignificant exceptions). Banks, savings banks, and some other institutional investors are also effectively precluded from owning low-grade (Ba or lower) bonds. Thus, whole classes of securities do not appear in the investment universe for the affected institutions.

More pervasive still than the outright prohibitions of securities are the various limitations on holdings. Thus, although most life insurance companies may legally purchase stock, they may only do so to a very small extent (5–10 percent of total portfolio). The legally required "crude" diversification also applies to banks. Many of the above restrictions, and others, reflect a rather curious legal philosophy that completely ignores portfolio concepts. It is generally agreed that most financial institutions serve a public purpose that requires that they continue to exist and avoid insolvency. It is then contended that this goal is best served by requiring the institutions to have a low-risk portfolio (this assertion alone is questionable). Moreover, it is felt that a low-risk portfolio is composed of a large number of low-risk securities. Hence, some institutions are provided with a "legal list" of high-rated, low-risk securities from which to select their portfolios.

Others, especially trust departments, operate under the "prudent man rule" (requiring them to exhibit the care a prudent man would in managing his own affairs). Unfortunately, the courts seem to feel that this philosophy represents prudence. Thus, the investment manager must be concerned not only that the portfolio succeed but also that no individual security fail lest he be sued. "Prudence" usually prevails. It is an unfortunate truism that no trustee has been successfully sued for portfolio dissipation because he invested in government bonds. It should be observed that recent court actions indicate that the prudent man rule may eventually be abandoned. However, the growing demand that funds be channeled to "socially desirable" investments (which can include mortgages, municipals, minority loans, pollution control equipment loans, or loans to whatever other powerful special-interest group desires cheap money) is causing an entirely new set of constraints to arise to take its place.

A second set of legal and institutional constraints also mitigates against the validity of some necessary assumptions of capital market theory. It appears very likely that the separation theorem probably does not apply in the real world. In addition to all the investment constraints already considered, it should be noted that many institutions are prohibited from selling short, while individuals are limited in this regard. Both institutions and individuals are also quite restricted in borrowing against their portfolios. Some institutions can have only a limited (or no) debt outstanding, and individuals are subject to Federal Reserve margin requirements. It thus cannot even be pretended that the crucial assumption that the investment decision is independent of the financing decision holds.

It seems clear that many investors cannot hold the market portfolio. It is also clear that the separation theorem does not apply. Can it be argued, consequently, that capital market theory (and efficiency implying equilibrium) is invalid? Economists would say no. As long as some participants can borrow and others can lend and every security can be held by at least some participants, the efficiency proponents can bring forth their stable weighted average arguments. The latter then becomes an argument in positive economics: markets behave *as though* they were in static equilibrium with all participants having free access and homogeneous expectations, even though this is not indeed the case. This argument will fail to hold to the extent that changes in the distribution of wealth alter the weights or different participants do not revise their expectations proportionately to new information.

Expectations, Convergence, and the Efficient Market Hypothesis

In most areas of economics, dynamic theory is the most complicated form of analysis. This is true because expectations, rather than existing conditions, are the main determinants. Equilibrium is based on a given state of expectations, and any changes in those expectations will force a movement to a new equilibrium. Unfortunately, "the adjustments needed to bring about equilibrium take time." See J. R. Hicks (1946). When markets are inefficient, time becomes the most important variable to the analysis. But when markets are efficient, the adjustments occur rather quickly and time is not terribly important. A perfectly efficient market will return to equilibrium immediately. Proponents of the efficient-capital-market hypothesis maintain that timing is not important in analyzing investments because the market digests new information instantaneously, redetermines expectations, and recalculates prices accordingly.

A condition of static equilibrium can cease to exist if new information concerning systematic risk, expected dollar returns, or the market price of systematic risk (that is, the slope of the SML) is perceived. For example, let us assume a market in which all dividends are reinvested so that returns over the next period ($t = 1$) are given by:

$$\tilde{r}_1 = \frac{\tilde{P}_1 - P_0}{P_0}, \qquad (10.23)$$

where $\tilde{r}_1$ is the expected return one period hence; $\tilde{P}_1$ the expected market price of the stock one period hence (with dividends reinvested), and P_0 the current market price ($t = 0$).

We further assume that time periods are very short (that is, they are too short to act between $t = 0$ and $t = 1$). Finally, we assume that R is the appropriate return for a given level of systematic risk (taken from the SML). In equilibrium,

$$E(\tilde{r}_1|I_0) = R = r_0. \qquad (10.24)$$

If R changes because of either a shift in the SML or a change in the systematic risk of a stock, there exists a new R^* ($R^* \neq R$) which will produce the potential for a windfall gain between $t = 0$ and $t = 1$ of ω.

$$E(\tilde{r}_1|I^*) = R + \lambda \omega$$
$$= R + \lambda \left(\frac{\tilde{P}_1^* - \tilde{P}_1}{P_0} \right) \qquad (10.25)$$

$$E(\tilde{r}_2|I^*, \lambda = 1) = R^*, \qquad (10.26)$$

where I_0 = available information at period $t = 0$; I^* = new information becoming available between $t = 0$ and $t = 1$; R^* = the new equilibrium return, given new information about either the level of risk evidenced by the shares or the position of the SML; P_0 = the share price at $t = 0$; $\tilde{P}_1$ = the share price at $t = 1$ corresponding to information; $\tilde{P}_1^*$ = the share price at $t = 1$ corresponding to information; λ = a one-period price adjustment coefficient; and ω = the potential windfall gain which would occur between $t = 0$ and $t = 1$ assuming complete adjustment (that is, where $\lambda = 1$).

If markets are efficient, $\lambda = 1$ and adjustment takes place immediately. Because time periods are assumed to be short, only those holding the security when new information reaches the market will receive the windfall (that is, ω will result too quickly for anyone to act on the information profitably). Beyond period $t = 1$, the only return expected would be the new equilibrium rate R^*. If markets are inefficient, $\lambda \neq 1$ and adjustment will not take place immediately. In the case $0 < \lambda < 1$, the entire windfall gain will not be allocated before profitable action can be taken. Indeed, if $\lambda < 0$ (which corresponds to a complete misinterpretation of the new information), then a potential windfall even greater than ω could be possible to the extent that the market eventually interprets the information correctly. If $\lambda > 1$, the market overreacts, and a windfall in the opposite direction is possible.

We have considered two of the conditions that will produce a disturbance in the static equilibrium of stock prices. The third condition (a change in expected dollar returns) will initially manifest itself as $\tilde{P}_1^* \neq \tilde{P}_1$ whereas, in the former conditions, the disturbance was introduced by $R^* \neq R$. The analysis proceeds along similar lines, with Equation (10.23) remaining intact. The expected return for $t = 2$, however, becomes:

$$E(\tilde{r}_2 | I^*, \lambda = 1) = R. \qquad (10.27)$$

In all three instances, empirical evidence suggests that λ is close to 1. Nevertheless, all the semi-strong studies have examined I^* of a fairly obvious sort (earnings announcements, stock splits, and so on). They do not address themselves to the fact that analysts may obtain other kinds of I^* that cannot be neatly measured. The analyst who has a better forecasting method, for example, may be able to discern information that no simple sort of empirical investigation could detect, and his long-term returns could be expected to surpass the market return.

Of course, determining better I^* is what security analysis is all about. The analyst should be cautioned, however, that his returns will be above the market's only if what he knows eventually becomes known by the market (hence, producing a new equilibrium). If he envisages a disequilibrium that will produce a windfall gain (ω) and the market never "learns" ($\lambda = 0$ in all future periods), he is better off only to the extent that his superior insight allows him to earn higher returns for a given level of risk than would be provided by the market's perception of equilibrium risk–return relationships.

He does not earn the windfall adjustment return, however, that would follow if the market eventually came to agree with his superior insight. On the other hand, if the market received and correctly interpreted new information at the same time as the analyst ($\lambda = 1$), no above-normal returns would be expected. Thus, the analyst must be rather sure that his insight is indeed superior, and that the market will eventually agree with him, in order to derive the most benefit from his prognostications.

Expectations about future dollar returns (and estimated risk) may be even more important than expectations about future rates of return for making above-average profits. If an analyst foresees better prospects for a security than the market, he may get even greater returns if the market eventually comes around to his view. Suppose an analyst expects security C (Figure 10.15) to produce a future stream that will yield 12 percent, given the current market price ($100), but the market only forecasts a 10 percent return, which is the equilibrium yield. The analyst expects a perpetual earnings stream (perhaps in the form of dividend payments) of $12, whereas the market only expects $10. If the analyst turns out to be correct,

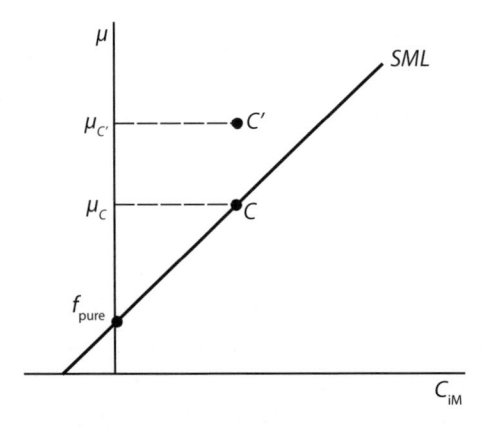

Figure 10.15. Differences in Expected Rates of Returns

the price of the security will rise to $12/0.1 = $120, assuming the stock is still in the 10 percent risk class. If the market moves toward the analyst's position within one year, his return would not only be better than the equilibrium 10 percent, but also exceed his expected 12 percent. His yield, in fact, would be $(120 + 12 - 100)/100 = 32$ percent.

This result can be found by using Equation (10.24). Assuming the reinvestment of dividends, the stock price at $t = 1$ would be $120 + $12 = 132. The price that would prevail without market recognition would be expected to be $110 (the market anticipates $10 in dividends, rather than $12, for reinvestment). Hence, when recognition occurs $\lambda = 1$ and:

$$E(\tilde{r}_1|I^*) = R + \lambda \left(\frac{\tilde{P}_1^* - \tilde{P}_1}{P_0} \right)$$

$$= 10 \text{ percent} + (1)\left(\frac{132 - 110}{100}\right)$$

$$= 32 \text{ percent.}$$

Again, the time required for convergence is seen to be very important. If it took the market three years to converge (suppose the stock paid $12 in years one and two, but the market only became convinced that this dividend could hold in the long run in period $t = 3$), his return would be:

at 18 percent
$t = 0$ $-$100(1.000) = -\ 100.00
$t = 1$–3 $+\ 12(2.174) = +\ \ \ 26.09$
$t = 3$ $+\ 120(0.609) = +\ \ \ 73.08$
                                $-\ $\ \ 0.83,$

or just under 18 percent. If the market never came to accept the analyst's judgment (and the yield, in fact, was 12 percent), he would still earn a larger return than that expected by the market. On the other hand, if the analyst's view were adopted by the market, his return would be far greater still. Thus, having better insight than the market would have given the analyst a 2 percent higher return in our example (12 percent − 10 percent), whereas having insight about patterns of market expectations could produce a 20 percent additional return (that is, 32 percent − 12 percent).

The movement of stock prices from expected levels to those that the analyst thinks are justifiable is called *convergence*. The principle of convergence has been recognized by conventional authorities for years, and the importance of timing in convergence has been given renewed consideration. It is clear that rapidity of convergence will greatly influence returns, and the longer the time required for the market to recognize the superior insight of the analyst, the lower will be his annual rate of return. In terms of the SML, convergence takes place as the market realizes that a security is under (or over) priced and that the security moves toward the line. In Figure 10.16, two securities are shown. The first, A, is seen to be "under" priced. That is, the return from is greater than it should be given A's risk characteristic. Once the market agrees that A is under priced, demanders will bid up prices until the security reaches the SML at A'. At this point, the rate of return will be μ'_A, which, of course, is lower than μ_A. In the process of reaching equilibrium, the security rises in price, and investors who bought A when its yield was μ_A receive a windfall gain. Similarly, security B is over priced, given its risk characteristic. Its price will be bid down (expected returns rising

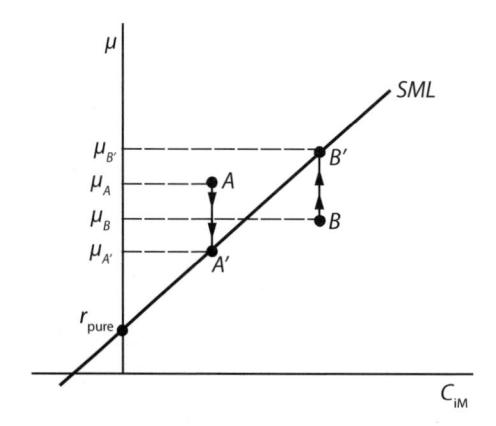

Figure 10.16. Convergence and the SML

from B to B') until it reaches the SML, if the analyst is correct in his appraisal. Investors who sold B short would reap a windfall gain as the price of B falls to yield μ'_B.

The investor who wishes to achieve returns above the market must consistently find securities that are under (over) priced, buy (sell short), and hope that the market soon agrees with him. Efficient-market proponents would argue that no one could repeatedly find securities off the SML, and even if he could, this would not constitute "beating the market." It is suggested that even if a true disequilibrium security is found and a capital gain is obtained, the market has not been "beaten." The equilibrating mechanism of the market is what allowed the capital gain. Notwithstanding the semantics of the argument, it seems only logical that one who could find securities off the SML frequently would enjoy above-average returns.

Expectations play a major role in convergence. Furthermore, it is *changes in expectations*, rather than simply new information, that influence returns. This distinction is important because all new information does not change expectations. A stock split, for example, does not change the fundamental position of the firm, and it should not be surprising that the long-run effect of a split on investor returns is nil. On the other hand, expectations can change *even though new information does not develop*.

Although all three conditions producing disequilibrium can affect future expectations, we will focus our attention on the market price of risk (that is, shifts in the SML) and not the parameters of an individual security. Examination of market factors, rather than unique security characteristics, is more conducive to generalization and comparison to prior theoretical work. Extending a Hicksian scheme over the entire SML (Hicks, *op. cit.*, p. 205), it could be argued that there exists an elasticity of expectations about equilibrium rates of return at a given level of systematic risk that may be defined as:

$$\varepsilon_x = \frac{E[\tilde{R}_{t+1} - R_t]}{(R_t - R_{t-1})}, \qquad (10.28)$$

for the simple one-period forecasting model. ε_x may be negative, zero, positive, positive and unity, or positive and greater than unity. If $\varepsilon_x = 0$, we have the case of rigidly inelastic expectations, where changes in historical returns do not cause changes in expected future returns. This case would most closely correspond to the efficient market hypothesis. Properly defined, R_t is the cost of equity capital to a firm in the given systematic risk class. Thus, when firms apply a given discount rate (that is, cost of capital) to all future flows generated by a capital budgeting proposal, they are implicitly assuming $\varepsilon_x = 0$.

If $\varepsilon_x = 1$, expectations about changes in future returns do depend on changes in historical returns, and patterns of historical changes will alter expected future returns in the same direction and in the same proportion. If $\varepsilon_x = 1$, this historical pattern will "make people feel that they can recognize a trend, so that they try to extrapolate." Hicks outlined his elasticities in terms of commodity prices initially, but they are later applied to his discussion of interest rates (*Ibid.* pp. 260–262, 281–282).

Finally, if $\varepsilon_x < 0$, people make "the opposite kind of guess, interpreting the change as the culmination point of fluctuation." Although a reasonably strong *a priori* case can be made for $\varepsilon_x = 0$, empirical tests using expectations are very difficult to construct. Hicks felt that the interest elasticity of expectations was small if not zero (*Ibid.* p. 282). It may be that other elasticities do exist at times (when interest rates have been advancing or declining very rapidly), and the analyst who can properly judge expectations about future rates will earn superior returns. We address this possibility below in a Graham and Dodd framework by completing our analysis of American Funeral Supplies, Inc. (AFS).

Example: AFS, A Graham & Dodd approach

In order to finish this book, we need to see how the securities analysis framework we constructed in earlier chapters integrates into portfolio and capital asset pricing theory. In order to do so, we shall return to the AFS example which has been marbled throughout earlier chapters. We urge the reader to go back and follow the example, especially the materials in Chapter 4 (Financial Statement Analysis), Chapter 6 (Analysis of Fixed Income Securities), and Chapter 7 (Analysis of Common Stocks).

We left AFS in Chapter 6 with projections of future growth. These projections could only be sustained by either a major acquisition or internal (organic) growth stimulated by increasing market share. In its most recent conference call with investors and securities analysts, the company announced its choice would be the acquisition of a major competitor for $1 billion. In order to finance this acquisition, AFS has proposed issuing $700 million in 10 year notes at a 6 percent yield. The company would further employ $300 million of the $951 million in cash it had on hand as of December 31, 2013. The company's investment bankers have suggested that the notes could be issued at par with no discount but also with no call provision (see Chapter 6 discussion). Interest on the notes would be paid in semi-annual coupons with annual cost of: (0.06)($700 million) = $42 million.

It was thought that the present lack of indebtedness of the company would assure an investment grade rating on the issue, but the lack of required payments to reduce the principal of the debt (sinking fund, etc.) together with the relatively small size of the issue and the market capitalization of the company (100 million shares outstanding at the most recent market price of $84.23, or $8.4 billion) would allow for a rating of no higher than BBB (S&P) and Baa (Moody's). The bankers also pointed to the excellent coverage ratios which would result (see Chapter 6 for the means of calculating these ratios), and a pro forma debt to equity ratio of (in millions): $700/$3,200 = 0.22 as further evidence that the issue should result in an investment grade rating. Although BBB/Baa are barely in that category, many potential investors in such debt (such as insurance companies) are severely constrained to have mostly investment grade securities in their portfolios.

The company does not make forecasts of its future earnings, but one analyst took the projections he had made for sales growth, etc.

(see Chapter 6) and determined the following for 2014 (in millions of dollars except per share amounts):

Sales	$7,846	(14 percent growth over 2013)
CGS	(4,943)	(see Chapter 6)
SG&A	(1,020)	"
Other	79	"
Operating Income	1,962	—
Interest	(42)	(interest on the new notes)
Earnings before Income Tax	1,920	—
Income Tax	(845)	(44 percent state and federal)
Net Income	$1,075	—
EPS	$10.75	(100,000,000 shares outstanding)
DPS	$2.80	(26 percent payout ratio)

The analyst continues with the following commentary: "We expect great things from the recently announced acquisition of National Burial by AFS. Last year's EPS of $8.57 should advance by about 25 percent to $10.75 in 2014. In light of the current market price of approximately $84, the stock looks cheap at a PE multiple of only 7.8X. Although AFS has historically sold at well below market multiples (averaging 7.2X over the past four years), we believe the company is due for a growth spurt. Part of the explanation of the lower multiple in past years has been the flat death rate in the United States. This should pick up substantially in the near future as the baby boomers (born in huge numbers right after WW II) begin to die. Moreover, Wall Street has always felt AFS was far too conservative by having little to no debt and was insufficiently aggressive in promoting internal growth. We have argued with that view in the past since earnings have grown from $5.95 to $8.57 per share since 2010. Also, the payment of a dividend this past year has been a very positive signal to the market.

The yield of over 2.5 percent at the present market price adds a further inducement to purchase the shares. Based on our projections for 2014, we see a value in the $100 per share range for 2014. This should be supported by an increase in the dividend from $2.19 per share to about $2.80. At $100, the stock would still be selling for a PE of only 9.3X, which is well below current market averages."

The sort of discussion provided by the analyst is what could be described as a "pure Graham and Dodd" approach (Graham and Dodd, 1934). Going back to their seminal book in 1934, this view of the market argued that some stocks were "over-priced," some "under-priced," and some "correctly-priced." The job of the analyst was to find the bargains and sell the expensive stocks. Of course, this view was at complete odds with the Efficient Market Hypothesis. In terms of the capital asset pricing theory discussion earlier in this chapter, such stocks would be incorrectly priced (riding either above or below the SML) and valuations should be corrected quickly. We will return to this form of analysis shortly, but for the time being it is important to follow the Graham and Dodd logic. This is true for a couple of reasons. First, it is the approach taken by most real world analysts. They look for bargains (or losers to sell) and hope to convince the market they are right. Second, most investors also take this approach. The Graham/Dodd method has been the cornerstone of the success of Warren Buffett and numerous other people who have made themselves (and others) rich in the process. The analyst is arguing that AFS is "under-priced" and should be bought until it approaches $100 per share. His opinion will eventually be built into the share price unless other analysts disagree. The procedure he follows is very much in keeping with the methodology of most analysts in today's world.

Now let us see how the dynamics of the analyst method might play out in a capital assets pricing/portfolio theory context. In the first place, we might go back to the Securities Market Line discussed above. If AFS were indeed "under-priced," it would appear above the SML. Eventually, the mis-pricing would cause the stock to rise until it rested on the SML. At this point, it would appear like all other stocks in the SML and would be incorporated into the capital asset pricing model (CAPM). Further, it would be a constituent portfolio holding in the universe of stocks. In other words, it would fit precisely into the portfolio theory models described above. The riskiness of the security would also have to be reflected, and this might be accomplished by the use of Sharpe's beta method described earlier in this chapter. The analyst mentioned above has calculated the beta for AFS using the S&P 500 (with dividends included) and with monthly data over a period of 10 years (120 data points) and finds AFS' beta to be about 1.00. This means AFS has risk characteristics that approach the market in general. Capital asset pricing has been empirically evaluated over many years (going back to the 1920s). The results find the so-called riskless rate of interest to be about 3 percent, the rate of inflation just about the same, and the total return (dividends and capital gains) to be between 9 and 10 percent for large capitalization equities. If AFS' market price were "in equilibrium" and was correctly priced, it should also return about this amount.

If the analyst is correct, however, AFS's market price is below its fundamental value. We may discover this by projecting the future income statements forward for AFS from 2015 to 2018 using the same assumptions as made by the analyst (all numbers in millions except per share figures).

	2015	2016	2017	2018
Sales	8,945	10,197	11,625	13,253
CGS	(5,635)	(6,424)	(7,323)	(8,349)
SG&A	(1,163)	(1,326)	(1,511)	(1,723)
Other	89	102	115	132
Operating Income	2,236	2,549	2,906	3,313
Interest	42	42	42	42
Earnings before Income Tax	2,194	2,507	2,864	3,271
Income Tax	965	1,103	1,260	1,439
Net Income	1,229	1,404	1,604	1,832
EPS	$12.29	$14.04	$16.04	$18.32
DPS	$3.20	$3.65	$4.17	$4.76

Referring back to the basic common stock valuation equation in Chapter 7, we may portray the future dividend income stream a shareholder in AFS might expect over the next five years. Given the projections above, the dividend stream would be:

Year	Dividend
2014	$2.80
2015	3.20
2016	3.65
2017	4.17
2018	4.76

Projecting the future stock price is a bit more difficult. Given the growth in earnings and dividends expected over the next five years, a PE multiple higher than the past average of about 7.2X might be in order. Indeed, the analyst argues for a multiple expansion to 9.3X for 2014. At 10X projected earnings in 2018, the stock price would be: $(10)(\$18.32) = \$183.20$. We might try several multiple prospects (as we did in Chapter 7), but the procedure would be the same. Given the present stock price of $84.23, we could solve for the expected return if one bought the stock at today's price, received the dividends forecasted above, and sold the stock in five years for $183.20. Given these cash flows, we could use a computer, or hand calculator, or even a present value table (with interpolation), to find that the return would be approximately 20 percent.

	Cash Flow	20 percent PV Factor	PV CF
t = 1	2.80	0.833	2.33
t = 2	3.20	0.694	2.22
t = 3	3.65	0.579	2.11
t = 4	4.17	0.482	2.01
t = 5	4.76	0.402	1.91
	$183.20	0.402	73.65
			$84.23

r = 20 percent
$\beta = 1.00$

Now let us consider what a return of 20 percent and a beta of 1.00 means in a portfolio theory/capital asset pricing framework. The beta suggests that the stock should return about what the market is expected to yield. Over the long term, this should be in the 9–10 percent range. A 20 percent return is double that, meaning AFS stock lies well above the SML and should rise in price until the expected return is 9–10 percent. At this point the stock price would be "in equibilrium" and it should find a home in the basket of stocks held by the market. Not every portfolio would have to own the stock, of course, but those who held it would own a stock in a diversified portfolio which was priced in accordance with its actual risk. With its beta equal to that of the market (the S&P 500 in this case), the return would equal the market return.

In a Graham/Dodd setting, it would be argued that the stock is substantially undervalued and it should eventually (say, in the next five years) increase from its present price of $84.23 to $183.20. Adding in the expected dividends over the next five years would provide a total return (capital gains and dividends) of 20 percent for a stock whose risk characteristics indicate a required return of less than half of that amount. Graham and Dodd investors (like Warren Buffett) would buy the stock today and keep it at least until its price reached the five-year target. Some Graham and Dodd followers (Buffett again) might even hold the stock beyond the price target, or at least until it became well "over-valued." In Buffett's case, he might like AFS so well that he would establish a large ownership position over time and then perhaps buy the entire company. This is what he has done many times (see, for example, the acquisition of the publicly held BNSF Railway which is now wholly -owned by Berkshire Hathaway). Returns far above 20 percent might even be earned in the near future on AFS if the stock were to make a major upward move toward its "equilibrium value" in the next year or two.

In conclusion, the AFS example demonstrates that both the portfolio theory/capital asset pricing approach to investing and the Graham and Dodd fundamental appraisal method should produce similar results. It might be argued that, in a truly efficient market, such mis-pricing should never happen. Indeed, for many years finance academics argued just that, but numerous examples of mis-pricing have finally convinced many professors that the securities markets are just not perfectly efficient. Some have tried to redefine the notion of efficiency to comport with the real world facts, but that is simply sophistry and of interest only to those engaged in the esoteric subject of the history of financial thought. For our purposes here, we will conclude that securities markets are *not* efficient; and that is a good thing. It makes it possible to invest for profit using the sort of data we have presented in this book.

Capital Allocation Effects

As a final note, businesses grow by purchasing assets through their capital budgeting process. They may also acquire other companies as the AFS example above suggests. The methods employed to accomplish this task are detailed in numerous books on corporate finance, financial management, and capital budgeting. Since the results of these activities are very germane to our discussion above, we might review the steps taken by AFS in making its $1 billion acquisition.

The first step is for AFS to compute its weighted average after tax cost of capital, or WACC. This is done by calculating the cost of debt and equity sources employed by the firm. The cost of debt usually involves an inspection of the so-called "capitalization" table available in the firm's 10Q and 10K SEC filings. In the case of AFS, its only source of debt is its new 6 percent bond issue. Since the interest on this debt is tax deductible and AFS pays federal and state income tax (t) at 44 percent, its after tax cost of debt would be: $(0.06)(1-t)$, or $(0.06)(0.56) = 0.034$. The cost of equity is readily available by using the CAPM. CAPM tells us that the long-run return (since 1926) of medium to large cap equities (the "market") has been in the 9–10 percent range (including dividend and capital gains). The riskless rate of interest has been about 3 percent, providing a "risk premium" of 6–7 percent for the market. Some companies are riskier (as measured by beta — see discussion above) and some less risky than the market. AFS has a beta of 1.0 so it is as risky as the market and should thus have a 9–10 percent return. Obviously, the return to AFS' stockholders is also the cost of equity to the company. So we shall use a cost of equity of 9.5 percent (averaging the 9 percent and 10 percent figures). Notice that there is no tax deductibility for equity returns. (As an aside, it might be noted as well that the very low interest rates of recent years may have reduced these costs somewhat.)

Now we can compute the WACC. The total capitalization (debt and equity) of AFS is as follows: debt ($700 million) and equity (100,000,000 shares at $84.23 = $8.42 billion), or ($0.7 billion + $8.42 billion = $9.12 billion. Debt as a percentage of total capital would be: $(0.7/9.12) = 0.08$ and the equity percentage would be: $(8.42/9.12) = 0.92$. Given the after-tax cost of debt at 3.4 percent and the after tax cost of equity at 9.5 percent, the WACC would be: $(0.08)(3.4 \text{ percent}) + (0.92)(9.5 \text{ percent}) = (0.3 \text{ percent}) + (8.7 \text{ percent}) = 9.0$ percent.

The WACC is then used as a discount rate to evaluate capital investment projects, acquisitions, etc. The reason the WACC is the appropriate discount rate is that it is the opportunity cost to the firm. That is, in lieu of investing in new assets, the firm could always buy back its shares and reduce its debt in the same proportions as its capital structure. There is an implicit assumption here, as well, that the assets (acquisitions) be considered for purchase are of the same overall risk as the company itself. In AFS' case, when we review its $1 billion acquisition we are positing that it is of the same risk as the company.

AFS is considering the purchase of a competitor, Federated Funeral Supply Co. (FFS), a privately owned company. The stockholders of FFS are prepared to sell their stock such that FFS would be merged into AFS for $1 billion in cash. An extensive review ("due diligence") of FFS indicates the company has a strong history with recent revenue of about $600 million, cost of goods sold of $360 million, and general and administrative expenses of about $90 million. Thus, the operating income of the business would be (in millions): $600 - $360 - $90 = 150. Taxes are paid at 44 percent (federal and state) or $66, leaving net income of $84. Now, at this point, if AFS were buying a depreciating asset with a finite life, the depreciation expense could be added back to net income to obtain free cash flow. In the case of an acquisition, the depreciation would be added back but the capital expenditures required to keep the business moving forward would have to be subtracted. In the case of FFS, the firm is expected to remain at a steady state with no growth such that depreciation flows and capital expenditures would be cancelled out. Thus, the free cash flow of FFS would be the same as net income, or about $84 million per year.

AFS believes an addition $15 million per year in after-tax income could be added to this amount due to synergies from the acquisition. This would include savings from office overhead (officer salaries, etc., plus expenses incurred by the former owners which could be eliminated without affecting the operating income of the business). Purchasing expenditures could also be reduced, and combining the selling forces of the two companies would be possible as well. Now adding the synergies to the expected free cash flow would produce an adjusted amount of $99 million per year.

At this point we need to value the free cash flow of $99 million over a very long period of time. If the cash flows were variable per year, it would be necessary to discount each flow for each year and discount each by to the present value. In this cash, since the flows are equal for each year, we could use the perpetual growth formula derived earlier in this book to value common stock. Recalling the formula (Equation (2.13)), we find $PV = D/i$.

That is, the present value of a stock is its future dividend stream (here assumed constant each year) divided by the expected rate of return. For present purposes, the equation becomes: $PV = FCF/WACC$ or in the case of the FFS deal, $PV = \$99/0.09 = \$1,100$ or $1.1 billion. Subtracting the $1 billion paid by AFS would produce a net present value (NPV) of $1.1 billion minus $1.0 billion, or $100 million. Thus, the deal should be worth about $100 million in extra value to AFS.

Of course, one might object that the NPV of the deal was entirely due to the synergies (the NPV without them would be $84 million/0.09 or $93 million). This is true but it might also be argued that the WACC for AFS is high due to its lack of leveraging. If future acquisitions were done with debt, the capital structure might eventually become, say, 50 percent debt and 50 percent equity. Were the respective costs of capital to remain the same, the WACC would fall to $(0.5)(3.4 \text{ percent}) + (0.5)(9.5 \text{ percent}) = 6.45$ percent and even at a cash flow of $88 million (no synergies), the present value would be (in millions): $88/0.0645 = \$1,364$ or $1 billion and 364 million. It should be pointed out, however, that leverage is not free. In general, leverage increases the riskiness of the firm to both the debt holders and the stockholders and both costs will typically rise as more debt is incurred. At some point, the advantage of substituting cheaper debt for more expensive equity will be offset by the rising costs of both.

For the purposes herein described, it is probably safe to say that AFS should acquire FFS for $1 billion. The extra profit resulting from the purchase would be $88 million, or added EPS of $88 million/200 million = $0.44. This amount would raise 2013 EPS of $8.57 to about $9.01 per share for 2014, or an increase of just over 5 percent. The analyst (see above) has forecasted 2014 EPS of $10.75 so some organic (internal) growth plus a few more acquisitions would be necessary to achieve this result. It may be the case that the analyst's projections are too optimistic given the pricing of the FFS deal. If so, the entire projecting process would have to be repeated. Perhaps it would be determined that the stock was still "cheap" but maybe not nearly so cheap as the analyst at first thought. It is clearly the case that AFS is NOT in a growth business although the death rate should be increasing in the future as the baby boomers move along in age. Also, there may still be a number of acquisitions for AFS to make. A lesson here may be that markets are most definitely not perfectly efficient but maybe they are not as inefficient as the analyst hypothesized in the example we examined above.

Summary

This chapter outlines what has become known as the capital asset pricing model, or CAPM. The CAPM is essentially a means of identifying an investor's optimal portfolio. In order to perform this task, it is necessary to estimate expected returns and variances for all possible securities. In addition, the covariances among all such securities must be determined along with the risk-free rate of interest. At this point, the investor can pinpoint a tangency portfolio along with its expected return and standard deviation and be able to identify an optimal portfolio by examining where one of his indifference curves touches (but does not intersect) the efficiency set of portfolios. This portfolio requires an investment in the tangency portfolio together with borrowing or lending at the risk-free rate along a linear function (because the efficient set is linear).

The CAPM is based on certain assumptions about the behavior of investors together with an assumption about the existence of perfectly competitive security markets. Based on these assumptions, it turns out that all investors hold the same efficient portfolio of risky assets. Investors only differ in the amount of risk-free borrowing or lending they choose to undertake. This risky portfolio held by all investors is called the market portfolio. The market portfolio includes all securities in the investment universe with each being weighted proportionally by its market value in comparison to all other securities.

The linear efficient set of the CAPM is called the CML. It is the equilibrium relationship between the expected return and the standard deviation of all efficient portfolios. In the CAPM framework, the relevant risk measure is a security's expected return relative to its covariance with the market portfolio. The relationship between market covariance and expected return is called the SML. Due to the difficulty of measuring these relationships, alternatives have been derived. One such is the so-called "beta" of a security which measures the covariance between the returns of the security and those of the market portfolio in relation to the variance of the market portfolio. The CAPM beta is like the market one except it is not a market equilibrium model. Also, the market model employs a market index which is a subset of the CAPM market portfolio. Finally, the CAPM allows the separation of the total risk of a security into its market and non-market components. One part of this risk may be diversified away while the other cannot be.

We conclude this chapter (and the book) with a discussion of the Graham and Dodd approach to buying (and selling) securities. We find that this method is employed regularly in the real world of finance and has been since the mid-1930s. The chapter attempts to graft the CAPM on the Graham and Dodd framework, and concludes that such may be accomplished without assuming that markets are efficient.

Problems

1. Compute the parameters of the following holdings, given a risky portfolio (1) with $\mu = 20$ percent and $\sigma = 25$ percent and a pure rate of 5 percent.

	α_1	α_1
(a)	0.0	1.0
(b)	0.5	0.5
(c)	1.0	0.0
(d)	1.5	−0.5
(e)	2.0	−1.0

2. Assume an efficiency frontier composed of only the following discrete points:

Portfolio	μ	σ
A	10 percent	5 percent
B	15	10
C	20	20
D	25	30
E	30	50

a. If $r_L = r_B = 6$ percent, which of the above portfolios would be optimal for borrowing and lending?
b. If $r_L = 6$ percent, but $r_B = 10$ percent, how would your answer change?

3. What general relationship would you expect to find among r_L, r_B, and r_{pure}? Why? What are the implications of these relationships for the individual's efficiency frontier?

4. a. Assuming that the market portfolio has $\mu = 12$ percent and $\sigma = 15$ percent and the pure rate of interest is 6 percent, draw the CML.
b. How much expected return would be demanded under this system at a σ level of 20 percent?
c. How much would μ increase if a σ level of 25 percent were adopted?
d. State, in general terms, the relationship between $\Delta\mu$ and $\Delta\sigma$ in this system.

5. Classify the following securities as aggressive or defensive if $\sigma_M = 0.10$:

a. $b_1 = 1.2$
b. $C_{2M} = 0.02$
c. $b_3 = .7$
d. $C_{4M} = -0.001$.

6. Complete both parts:

a. Compute C_{1M} and C_{3M} from 5a and c above. What assumptions must be made?
b. If $\mu_M = 0.10$ and $r_{\text{pure}} = 0.03$, determine μ_i for the four securities in 5.

7. From the data in 5 and 6:

a. Plot the four securities on an SML using b_i.
b. Do the same thing using C_{iM}.

8. Rank the three securities described in the chapter by the Treynor and Jensen criteria, assuming a pure rate of 5 percent. Explain your results.

9. Assume that portfolios with the parameters given below lie along an efficiency frontier. Which would be eliminated if a lower confidence limit (K) of 1.0 were applied? If limits of 0.5, 2, and 3 were applied?

Security	A	B	C	D	E	F	G	H	I
μ	0.30	0.25	0.20	0.15	0.13	0.11	0.08	0.06	0.03
σ	0.50	0.31	0.19	0.10	0.07	0.05	0.03	0.02	0.01

10. Graph the efficiency frontier from the coordinates given in problem 1 above.

    a. If the pure rate of interest were 2 percent, which portfolio would be selected by the excess-return criterion?
    b. Which would be the safety-first portfolio if the disaster level (D) were set at 10 percent? At 5 percent?

11. Determine which of the following portfolios would be an optimal choice by stochastic dominance for an investor whose utility function possesses the requisite first-, second-, and third-order characteristics:

		Probability		
Return	A	B	C	D
−5 percent	0.2	0.1	0	0
0	0.2	0.3	0.3	0.4
5	0.0	0.0	0.2	0
10	0.1	0.1	0	0
15	0	0	0.1	0.3
20	0.5	0.5	0.4	0.3
μ	0.10	0.105	0.105	0.105

12. Reconsider the four portfolios described in problem 11 above. Which could be eliminated as inefficient? Which would be selected by the geometric-mean criterion?
13. Review the graphical presentation of the three-security portfolio in the chapter. For this question, security A should be graphed on the abscissa, B on the ordinate, and C equal to the remainder by convention. Begin with the simple triangular attainable set. Demonstrate the effects upon the attainable set as the following constraints are added:

    a. Debt may be incurred up to 10 percent of the total investment.
    b. $\alpha_A \leq .25$ (total investment).
    c. 0.3 (total investment) $\leq \alpha_C \leq 0.7$ (total investment).

14. a. The shares of the Serita Corporation are expected to pay a dividend of $1 per year forever and possess a degree of systematic risk corresponding to a return of 10 percent on the SML. At what price should Serita shares sell?
    b. Suppose that markets are not in equilibrium and the data in part a only refer to the expectations of a particular group of investors, while another group of investors expects a dividend of $1.50 per year forever and has a SML indicating an 8 percent return for Serita shares. What may now be said about the price of Serita shares? What would you expect to happen to the price of Serita if the first group of investors became wealthier while the second group became poorer, *ceteris paribus*? What do you imagine to be the impact of a new issue of shares by Serita?
15. In his review of Jensen's work on mutual-fund evaluation, Fama states: "...regardless of how mutual-fund returns are measured (i.e., net or gross of loading charges and other expenses), the number of funds with large positive deviations of returns from the market line...is *less than* the number that would be expected by chance with 115 funds under the assumption that fund managements have no special talents in predicting returns." (Fama, "Efficient Capital Markets," *op. cit.*, p. 413; emphasis

added.) Comment on the implications of the above for the evaluation of strong form tests.
16. Obtain biographical data on well-known mutual-fund managers. Study especially the education and training of these managers in line with the ability to assimilate and analyze all available information. Also check to see if investment decisions by one manager may be reviewed as independent of decisions made by others. Can you then find any other interpretation of mutual-fund performance than capital market efficiency? Do the same analysis for prominent hedge fund managers.

References

Amenc, N., and V. Le Sourd, *Portfolio Theory and Performance Analysis.* Hoboken, NJ: John Wiley & Sons, Inc., 2003.

Bacon, C. R., *Practical Portfolio Performance Measurement and Attribution*, 2nd edn. Hoboken, NJ: John Wiley & Sons, Inc., 2008.

Cootner, P., ed., *The Random Character of Stock Market Prices.* Cambridge: The MIT Press, 1964.

Fama, E. F., "Portfolio Analysis in a Stable Paretian Market," *Management Science*, January 1965, pp. 404–419.

Fama, E. F., "Risk, Return, and Equilibrium: Some Clarifying Comments," *Journal of Finance*, March 1968, pp. 29–40.

Fama, E. F., "Efficient Capital Markets: A Review of Theory and Empirical Work," *Journal of Finance*, May 1970, pp. 383–417.

Fama, E. F., "Efficient Capital Markets: II," *Journal of Finance*, December 1991, pp. 1575–1617.

Fama, E. F. and K. R. French, "The Cross-Section of Expected Stock Returns." *Journal of Finance*, June 1992, pp. 427–465.

Fama, E. F. and K. R. French, "Common Risk Factors in the Returns on Stocks and Bonds." *The Journal of Financial Economics*, 1993, 33, pp. 3–56.

Fama, E. F. and K. R. French, "Multifactor Explanations of Asset Pricing Anomalies." *The Journal of Finance*, March 1996, 51, No. 1, pp. 55–84.

Findlay, M. C. and E. E. Williams, "Better Betas Didn't Help the Boat People", *Journal of Portfolio Management*, Fall 1986, pp. 4–9.

Findlay, M. C. and E. E. Williams, "A Fresh Look at the Efficient Market Hypothesis: How the Intellectual History of Finance Encouraged a Real 'Fraud on the Market'." *Journal of Post Keynesian Economics.*, Spring 2000–2001, pp. 181–199.

Graham, B. and D. Dodd, *Security Analysis*. New York: McGraw-Hill, 1934.
Grossman, S. J. and J. E. Stiglitz, "On the Impossibility of Informationally Efficient Markets," *American Economic Review*, June 1980, pp. 393–408.
Hicks, J. R., *Value and Capital*, 2nd edn. London: Oxford University Press, 1946.
Jagannathan, R., A. Malakhov, and D. Novikov, "Do Hot Hands Exist among Hedge Fund Managers? An Empirical Evaluation." *Journal of Finance*, February 2010, pp. 217–255.
Jegadeesh, N. and Sheridan Titman, "Returns to Buying Winners and Selling Losers: Implications for Stock Market Efficiency." *Journal of Finance*, March 1993, pp. 65–91.
Jensen, M. C., "The Performance of Mutual Funds in the Period 1945-1964." *Journal of Finance*, May 1968, pp. 389–416.
Jensen, M. C., "Risk, the Pricing of Capital Assets, and the Evaluation of Investment Portfolios." *Journal of Business*, April 1969, pp. 167–247.
Lakonishok, Josef, Andrei Shleifer and Robert W. Vishny, "Contrarian Investment, Extrapolation, and Risk." *Journal of Finance*, December 1994, pp. 1541–1578.
Lintner, J., "Security Prices, Risk, and Maximal Gains from Diversification." *Journal of Finance*, December 1965, pp. 587–615.
Malkiel, B. G., *A Random Walk Down Wall Street*, 12th edn. New York: Norton, 2015.
Markowitz, Harry, *Portfolio Selection*. New York, NY: John Wiley for the Cowles Foundation, 1959.
Roy, A. D., "Safety First and the Holding of Assets." *Econometrica*, July 1952, pp. 431–449.
Rubinstein, M., "Rational Markets: Yes or No? The Affirmative Case." *Financial Analysts Journal*, May–June 2001, pp. 15–29.
Rubinstein, M., *A History of the Theory of Investments*. New York: John Wiley & Sons, 2006.
Samuelson, P., "The 'Fallacy' of Maximizing the Geometric Mean in Long Sequences of Investing or Gambling." *Proceedings of National Academy of Science USA*, October 1971, pp. 2493–2496.
Sharpe, W., "Capital Asset Prices: A Theory of Market Equilibrium under Conditions of Risk." *Journal of Finance*, September 1964, pp. 425–442.
Sharpe, W., "Mutual Fund Performance." *Journal of Business*, January 1966, pp. 119–138.
Sortino, F., van der Meer, R. and Plantinga, A. "The Dutch Triangle." *Journal of Portfolio Management*, Fall 1999, 26(1), pp. 50–58.
Sortino, F., *The Sortino Framework for Constructing Portfolios: Focusing on Desired Target ReturnTM to Optimize Upside Potential Relative to Downside Risk*, Elsevier Science, 2009.

Taleb, N., *The Black Swan.* New York: Random House, 2007.
Thompson, J. R., E. E. Williams and M. C. Findlay, *Models for Investors in Real World Markets.* New York: John Wiley & Sons, 2003.
Treynor, J. L. "How to Rate Management of Investment Funds." *Harvard Business Review*, January–February 1965, pp. 63–75.
Treynor, J. L. and K. K. Mazuy, "Can Mutual Funds Outguess the Market?" *Harvard Business Review*, July–August 1966, pp. 131–136.
Treynor, J. L., "Toward a theory of market value of risky assets." Written in 1962 but published only recently in *Asset Pricing and Portfolio Performance*, edited by Robert A. Korajczyk (London: Risk Publications, 1999), pp. 15–22.
Whitmore, G. A., "Third-Degree Stochastic Dominance." *American Economic Review*, June 1970, pp. 457–459.

Appendix A

Time Value of Money

Numquam poneda est pluralitas sine necessitate.

William of Occam

Present and Future Value Factors

As we saw in Chapter 2, the time value of money (TVoM) axiom requires some additional algebra in order to value a stream of payments or dividends realized in future time periods. Table A1 provides some basic time value equivalence factors needed to evaluate the economic value of these income/expense streams. Traditionally this has been accomplished with the use of factor tables; this is generally unnecessary given the ubiquitous computer power available today. We provide a brief description, generating and summary formulas, a cash-flow diagram, and pseudo-code needed for the analyst to calculate her own equivalency factors. Most of these formulas are available in spreadsheet programs such as Microsoft Excel as well.

There are also calculators for these factors which can be found on the Internet; a small sample includes:

- www.financeformulas.net
- www.calculator.net/financial-calculator.html
- www.ultimatecalculators.com
- www.thecalculatorsite.com/finance/

Table A.1. Time Value Equivalency Factors

Factor Name	Generator or Formula	Pseudo-Code	Cash Flow Diagram
Future value (compound amount factor)	$F = P \times (1+r)^N$	same	
Present value factor	$P = F \times (1+r)^{-N}$	same	
Capital recovery factor	$P = \sum_{t=1}^{N} \frac{A}{(1+i)^t}$ $A = P / \sum (1+i)^{-t}$ $= P \frac{i(1+i)^N}{(1+i)^N - 1}$	```function(i,n){ t=seq(1,n) 1/sum((1+i)^-t) }```	
Present value of an annuity factor	$P = \sum_{t=1}^{N} \frac{A}{(1+i)^t}$ $= A \sum (1+i)^{-t}$ $P = A \frac{(1+i)^N - 1}{i(1+i)^N}$	```function(i,n){ t = seq(1,n) sum((1+i)^-t) }```	
Uniform series compound amount factor	$F = A \sum_{t=1}^{N} (1+i)^{t-1}$ $= A \frac{(1+i)^N - 1}{i}$	```function(i,n){ t = seq(0,n-1) 1*sum((1+i)^t) }```	
Sinking fund factor	$A = \frac{F}{\sum_{t=1}^{N} (1+i)^{t-1}}$ $= F \frac{i}{(1+i)^N - 1}$	```function(i,n){ t = seq(0,n-1) 1/sum((1+i)^t) }```	

It is perhaps more reasonable to code one's own formulas which will free the analyst from having to have access to the internet in order to accomplish her job.

In Table A.1, i is the annual interest rate (in percent), and n and t are usually the time index, with N being the total number of (equally spaced) periods. We usually assume payments are at the end of the (annual) periods; periods with more granularity are treated in Chapter 2. Factor tables normally present the required factors corresponding to $1 in future or present values.

Microsoft Excel formulas can be specified from the intrinsic or online help for the present value and payment functions, PV and PMT.

Internal Rate of Return (IRR) Calculation

When the payment streams are not identical, we must use the more general equation $PV = \sum_{t=1}^{n} \frac{P_t}{(1+r)^t}$, where r is the discount rate (or the to-be-determined IRR) and P_t are the net cash flows each period. The net present value (NPV) takes into account the initial investment and can be expressed as $NPV = -P_0 + PV(P_t) = -P_0 + \sum_{t=1}^{n} \frac{P_t}{(1+r)^t}$. Chapter 5 discusses the forecasting skills needed to estimate future cash flows, but it is usually the case that we are trying to solve for the target rate of return r. Unlike the constant payment formulas in Table A.1, in the general case, there are no closed-form solutions, and the IRR must be solved iteratively.

Solution of the IRR arises from finding the roots of the nth order polynomial that the NPV formula generates. Consider the case where the initial investment is $10,000 and there are 2 periods of cash flow. With $PV = P_0$ we have $\frac{P_1}{(1+r)} + \frac{P_2}{(1+r)^2} = P_0$, or $P_1(1+r) + P_2 = P_0(1+r)^2$. Continuing, this is $(P_1 + P_2 - P_0) + (P_1 - 2P_0)r - P_0 r^2 = 0$ which defines a parabola and can be written as $C + Br + Ar^2 = 0$. The nature of the two roots depends on the discriminant value, $B^2 - 4AC$.

Suppose the two cash flows are $3,000 and $4,000, respectively. Our quadratic may be written as $10r^2 + 17r + 3$, with resulting discriminant $B^2 - 4AC = 169 = 13^2 > 0$, yielding the two real roots identified on Figure A.1. Indeed, for $n = 2$ we have the quadratic

Quantitative Financial Analytics

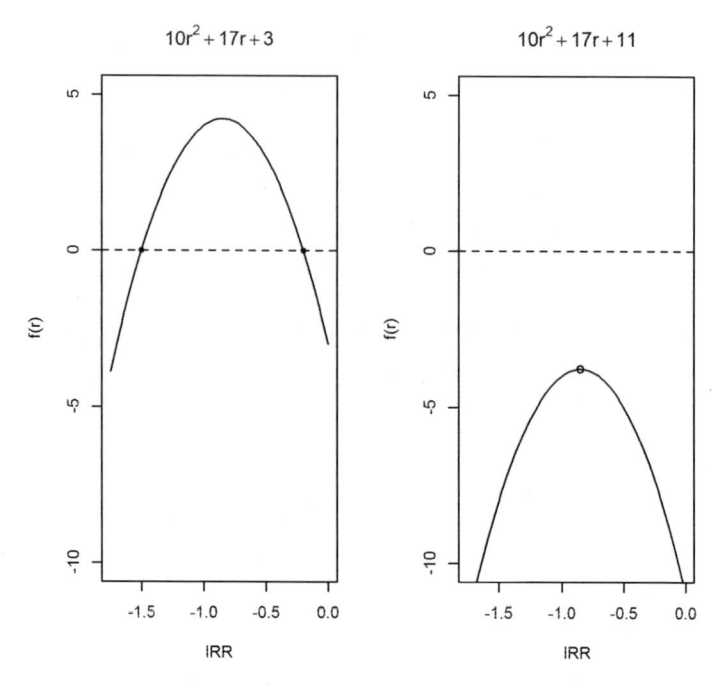

$$10r^2 + 17r + 3 \qquad 10r^2 + 17r + 11$$

Figure A.1. Quadratic IRR

formula giving the solution $r = (-0.20, -1.5)$. Note that the first solution, -20 percent IRR, represents a loss on investment. The second solution is not feasible and hence is disregarded.

Now let us suppose we have a negative cash flow of \$4,000 in year two; the new IRR equation becomes $10r^2 + 17r + 11$ with a negative discriminant, which has the imaginary roots $r = -0.85 \pm 0.614i$. As can be seen from the figure, its graph does not cross zero, but merely has an inflection and functional minimum at $r = -0.85$.

In almost all practical problems, the number of cash flows is non-trivial, and the IRR equation must be solved iteratively. Multiple roots can be obtained. Consider a project with four cash flows:

$$\frac{P_1}{(1+r)} + \frac{P_2}{(1+r)^2} + \frac{P_3}{(1+r)^3} + \frac{P_4}{(1+r)^4} = P_0$$

$$P_1(1+r)^3 + P_2(1+r)^2 + P_3(1+r) + P_4 = P_0(1+r)^4$$

$$(P_1 + P_2 + P_3 + P_4 - P_0) + (3P_1 + 2P_2 + P_3 - 4P_0)r$$
$$+ (3P_1 + P_2 - 6P_0)r^2 + (P_1 - 4P_0)r^3 - P_0 r^4 = 0.$$

These can be expressed as $f(r) = z_1 + z_2 r + z_3 r^2 + z_4 r^3 + z_5 r^4 = 0$ and we wish to solve for the resulting IRR value(s).

Project NPV with Uneven Cash Flows
Discount rate = 18.50115 percent

Year	1	2	3	4
Net Cash Flow	3,000	4,000	6,000	2,000
Discount rate	0.185	0.185	0.185	0.185
x PV factor	0.8439	0.7121	0.6009	0.5071
Present Value Cash Flows	2,531.62	2,848.49	3,605.65	1,014.24
Total PV of Cash Flows	10,000.00			
Less Initial Investment	−10,000.00			
Net Present Value	0.00			

Using this data, we obtain two real and two complex roots, i.e., $r^* = (0.1850115, -1.258 \pm 0.6258i, -1.36812)$. We use the realistic value of 18.5 percent in the table since the others are not feasible (Figure A.2).

The three indicated inflection points (one real and two complex) are obtained by:

$$\frac{d}{dr} f(r) = z_2 + 2z_3 r + 3z_4 r^2 + 4z_5 r^3 = 0, \text{ giving}$$
$$r^*_{f'} = (-0.24595, -1.2645 \pm 0.359i).$$

The quartic polynomial is the highest degree that can be solved algebraically; indeed Ferrari's 1540 solution for the four roots requires an entire page to transcribe. The discriminant alone is quite complex

Polynomial of Degree 4

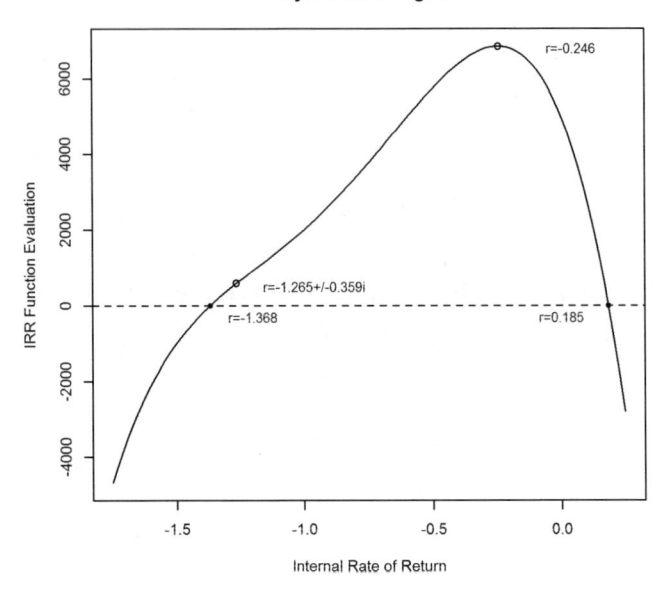

Figure A.2. Quartic IRR

and can be used to determine which of nine cases the roots will satisfy. In this appendix, we use the R language `polyroot` function, which is an instance of the Jenkins–Traub (1972) iterative algorithm. Other software such as the HP-12C's financial functions, Excel's Solver, and various other programs and apps can also solve these higher order problems.

Since many *pro forma* financial statements typically forecast out 5 periods, let us see what sort of roots the quintic polynomials possess. We look at two possible scenarios outlined below.

Project NPV with Uneven Cash Flows

Year	1	2	3	4	5
Scenario 1	3,000	4,000	6,000	2,000	5,000
Scenario 2	3,000	4,000	−2,000	2,000	−1,000

The roots for Scenario 1 (r_5^*) and Scenario 2 ($r_{5'}^*$) calculate to be:

$$r_5^* = (+0.273, -0.835 \pm 0.717i, -1.651 \pm 0.549i)$$

$$r_{5'}^* = (-1.87, -0.393 \pm 0.66i, -1.018 \pm 0.552i).$$

We note that for all positive cash flows, there is a single positive IRR value (27.3 percent), but for the case of 2 negative values, there are no positive real roots. In another case (not shown), with a single negative cash flow, there were two negative roots. Thanks to Descarte's "Rule of Signs," as can be seen from the polynomials labeled on Figure A.3, the number of sign changes in Scenario 1 is one, which means there is one positive real root (which there indeed is); in the second scenario, there are no sign changes and hence we see no positive real roots.

There is much current and historical interest in solving, finding bounds for, or simply analyzing the roots of polynomials, and

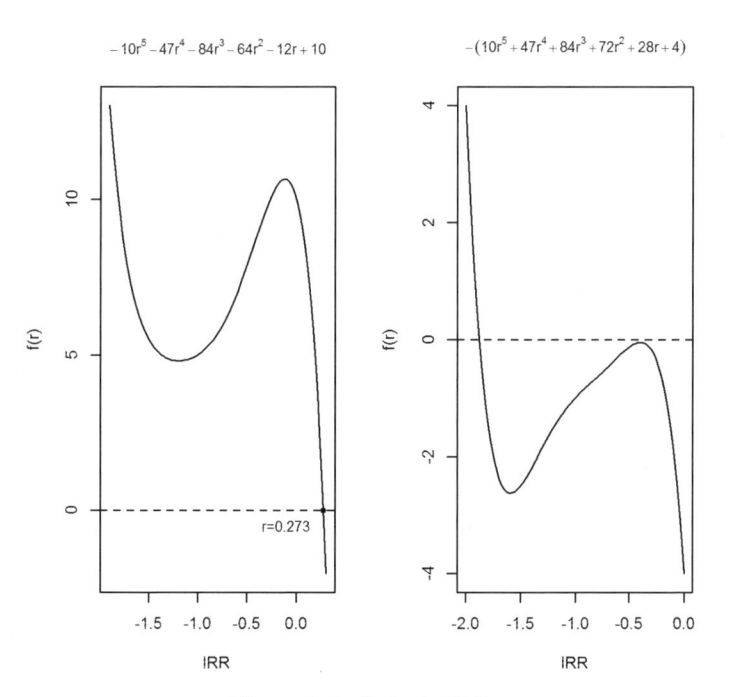

Figure A.3. Quintic IRR

the interested reader is directed to any convenient encyclopedia of mathematics for further knowledge.

Problems

1. The sum of $5,000 is placed in a savings account that pays interest of 4 percent compounded annually. How much will be in the account after 25 years?
2. What would your result be in the problem above if interest were compounded quarterly (at the same 4 percent annual rate)?
3. Suppose this savings account paid interest of 4 percent (annually) compounded daily. What would be the approximate amount in the account after 25 years? What is the exact amount? What is the exact amount net of annual income tax on earnings of 25 percent?
4. What is the annuity value of 25 payments of $100 at a rate of 10 percent per period?
5. What is the present value of $1,000 received 10 years from now if interest is compounded annually at a rate of 6 percent?
6. What is the present value of $250 received in nine years if interest is compounded annually at a rate of 8.5 percent?
7. The Atlantic Share Corp. has purchased stock in the Lambert Co. It is expected that Lambert shares will be selling for about $100 in 10 years and that Lambert will pay a dividend of about two dollars per share over the next 10 years. If Atlantic wished to earn 20 percent on its investment, how much should it have paid for the Lambert shares?
8. The Ludmilla Corp. pays a dividend of one dollar per share and expects to increase the dividend by ten cents per year for the next five years. Ludmilla now sells for $20 per share. If an investor wished to earn 10 percent on Ludmilla shares, at what price would the stock have to sell in five years?
9. The Daland Shipping Corp. has paid a dividend of three dollars per share to common stockholders for the past 20 years and plans to continue doing so in the future. Prospects for growth in the firm are negligible because the firm merely reinvests annual

depreciation flows and does not retain earnings or seek external financing. If investors believe Daland should yield 6 percent, determine the market price of the shares.

10. A mortgage has a term of 25 years. The face value of the mortgage is $30,000, and it has a yield to maturity of 4 percent. Assuming continuous compounding, what annual payment should be made on the mortgage?

Appendix B

Financial Statistics

And Satan stood up against Israel, and provoked David to number Israel... And David's heart smote him after that he had numbered the people. And David said unto Hashem, I have sinned greatly in that I have done: and now, I beseech thee, O Hashem, take away the iniquity of thy servant; for I have done very foolishly.

1 Chronicles 21:1, 2 Samuel 24:10

Probability, Random Variables, and Measures of Location, Dispersion and Shape

A variable that eludes predictability but that has a specific range or set of possible values and a definite probability associated with each value is called a *random variable*. In finance, one makes use of random variables frequently because many of the values determined are based on future events. These are rarely known with certainty, but with effort, it may be possible to attach probabilities to each possible outcome of a given future event. The assignment of probabilities is generally a subjective matter, although the use of statistical methods may reduce the uncertainty associated with obtaining relative likelihoods.

An exhaustive set of probabilities attaching to all possible outcomes of a given future event is called a *probability distribution*. Suppose x_i is the ith outcome of event X; then $p(x_i)$ is the probability that X will take on the value $p(x_i)$. The probability distribution for event X is given by $p(x)$. For example, let event X be the price of a stock in 10 years. If we can make educated guesses about the range of prices at which the stock may sell and the relative likelihood for each price, this range and the attaching probabilities constitute a probability distribution.

One may generate several important measures from a probability distribution. Perhaps the most important is the mean or *expected value*, which is defined as:

$$E(X) = \sum_i x_i p(X_i). \tag{B.1}$$

For an exhaustive distribution (where all possible values are specified), $\sum_i p(x_i) = 1$.

The expected value is a measure of *central tendency* and is frequently the best value to assume for X for decision-making purposes. There are other measures of central tendency, however, that may be useful for specific types of decisions. The *mode* of a distribution is that value of X with the largest $p(x_i)$. The *median* is the value that is the midpoint in the distribution; that is, it is the value that divides the distribution in half.

A second important characteristic that may be generated from a probability distribution is the *variance*. The variance is defined as:

$$V(X) = E(X - E(X))^2 = \sum_i [x_i - E(X)]^2 p(x_i). \tag{B.2}$$

The variance is a least-squares measure of the degree of deviation about the mean. Hence, it is often used as an indicator of the "riskiness" of a distribution. The square root of the variance, the *standard deviation*, is sometimes used in place of the variance as a measure of deviation. (The symbols μ and σ are used to indicate mean and standard deviation in many finance texts, although for samples the symbols $\bar{x}$ and s are more appropriate.) Note that the units of the standard deviation are the same as for the data itself, which is one reason it is so often used to describe spread of the values of X.

Dispersion and risk are frequently used interchangeably in finance. More concretely, however, three states of future events should be delineated. In the first state, that of *certainty*, we know which value X will take. In this instance, $[x_i - E(X)] = 0$, because $x_i = E(X)$. When $[x_i - E(X)] = 0, V(X)$ also equals zero. This is the best of all possible worlds, but it rarely prevails in the real world. The second state is that of *uncertainty*. This state exists when $\sum p(x_i) < 1$ or when probabilities cannot be assigned to given values. When $\sum p(x_i) < 1$, all possible outcomes are not known; the distribution is not exhaustive; and $V(X)$ is undefined. This is an intolerable state that must be altered if decisions are to be made. The final state, *risk*, obtains when $p(x_i) \neq 1$, but $\sum p(x_i) = 1$. In this case, we do not know which value X will take on, but we can specify the probabilities that $(X = x_i)$, and all possible outcomes are known (the distribution is exhaustive). Under conditions of risk, it is clear that the greater $V(X)$ becomes, the poorer estimate of the ultimate outcome will be $E(X)$, or any x_i. Therefore, the greater the dispersion of the distribution, the riskier the distribution becomes.

The variance and standard deviation are absolute measures of dispersion. As such, they do not always provide a basis for good comparisons. For example, suppose two stocks had expected prices of $10 and $100, respectively, and standard deviations of $1 and $5. If we examined only the standard deviation, the second stock might appear riskier than the first. On the other hand, the expected value of the second is much greater than that of the first. The relative dispersion, hence, is actually larger for the first stock. A good measure of relative dispersion is the *coefficient of variation*, which is given by:

$$CV(X) = \frac{\sqrt{V(X)}}{E(X)}. \tag{B.3}$$

or σ/μ in terms of other frequently employed symbols. When we compute the coefficient of variation, we find that for the first stock, $\sigma/\mu = 1/10$; whereas for the second, $\sigma/\mu = 5/100$. Using this relative measure of dispersion, the first stock is clearly the riskier.

Another type of relative measure of dispersion is the *semivariance*. This statistic indicates only the variability in the negative direction and places the following constraint on the variance equation:

$$[x_i - E(X)] < 0. \tag{B.4}$$

As a measure of risk, the semi-variance has the advantage of not penalizing values that are better than expected.

The variance is known technically as the second moment about the mean. There are higher-degree moments that may also be significant in financial analysis. Associated with the third moment is the notion of *skewness*. Skewness is a measure of the *symmetry* of a distribution about its mean. A distribution that is not skewed is said to be symmetrical. A distribution with a long left tail is said to be negatively skewed. One with a long right tail is said to be positively skewed (see Figure B.1). A measure of skewness is provided by computing the third moment about the mean and dividing it by the cube of the standard deviation:

$$SK = E\left(\frac{X-\mu}{\sigma}\right)^3 = \frac{\sum_i [X_i - E(X)]^3 p(x_i)}{(\sqrt{V(X)})^3}. \quad (B.5)$$

In general, positive values for SK are preferred to negative ones. One practical application is that positive skewness has been shown to be a necessary but not sufficient condition for preference, *ceteris paribus*, for all families of utility functions that meet the requirements for third-degree stochastic dominance (defined in Chapter 10).

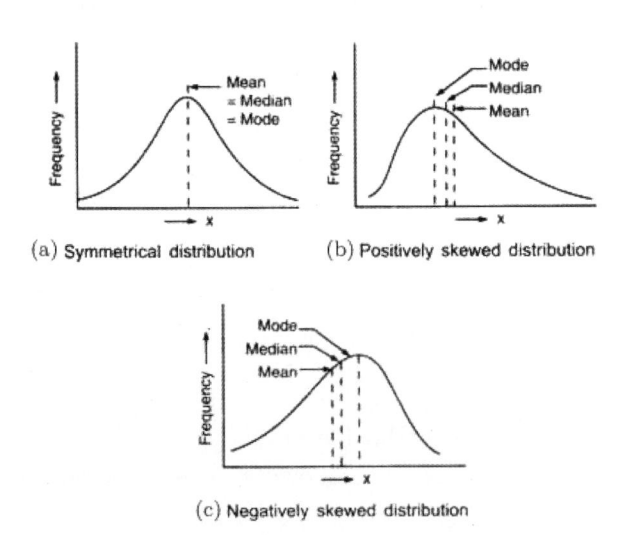

Figure B.1. Examples of Skewness

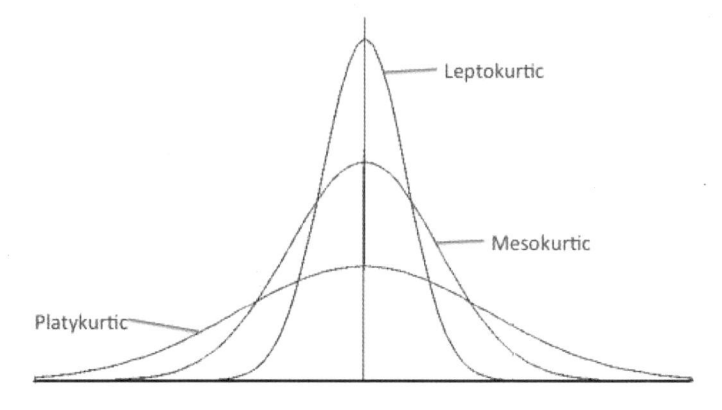

Figure B.2. Comparisons of Heterokurtotic Distributions

A final measure that may be important is associated with the fourth moment about the mean. *Kurtosis* measures the peakedness of a distribution and the tail behavior.

A normal, bell-shaped distribution is said to be *mesokurtic*. One that is flatter than the bell-shaped curve is said to be *platykurtic*, and one that is steeper is said to be *leptokurtic* (see Figure B.2). A common measure of kurtosis is computed by dividing the fourth power of the standard deviation (square of the variance) into the fourth moment about the mean:

$$KU = E\left(\frac{X-\mu}{\sigma}\right)^4 = \frac{\sum_i [x_i - E(X)]^4 p(x_i)}{[V(X)]^2}. \tag{B.6}$$

Larger values for KU indicate a more peaked distribution. KU for a mesokurtic distribution is $+3$. Lower values indicate a platykurtic distribution, and higher ones suggest a leptokurtic distribution. There seems to be no general agreement on the relative desirability of the degree of kurtosis, except that highly platykurtic distributions may have infinite moments which makes financial analysis difficult to perform.

Examples

An analyst is attempting to forecast the earnings per share of Dynamo Quebec Power Ltd. for next year. He believes that four values are possible and that the relative likelihood of each is described as follows:

$$x_1 = \$2.50; \quad p(x) = 0.3$$
$$x_2 = \$2.00; \quad p(x) = 0.4$$
$$x_3 = \$1.70; \quad p(x) = 0.2$$
$$x_4 = \$1.10; \quad p(x) = 0.1.$$

1. What is the expected value of earnings for next year?

$$(\$2.50) \times (0.3) = \$0.75$$
$$(\$2.00) \times (0.4) = \$0.80$$
$$(\$1.70) \times (0.2) = \$0.34$$
$$(\$1.10) \times (0.1) = \underline{\$0.11}$$
$$E(X) = \$2.00.$$

2. What are the mode and median values of the distribution? The mode is the most likely value. At $x_i = \$2.00$, $p(x_i)$ is greatest. The median divides the distribution in half. This occurs at $x_i = \$2.00$.
3. What is the standard deviation of the distribution?

$$2.50 - 2.00 = 0.50; (0.50)^2 \rightarrow (0.250) \times (0.3) = 0.075$$
$$2.00 - 2.00 = 0.00; (0.00)^2 \rightarrow (0.000) \times (0.4) = 0.000$$
$$1.70 - 2.00 = -0.30; (-0.30)^2 \rightarrow (0.090) \times (0.2) = 0.018$$
$$1.10 - 2.00 = -0.90; (-0.90)^2 \rightarrow (0.810) \times (0.1) = \underline{0.081}$$
$$V(X) = 0.174$$

$$\sigma = \sqrt{0.174} = \$0.42.$$

4. What is the coefficient of variation of Dynamo Quebec earnings?

$$CV(X) = \frac{\$0.42}{\$2.00} = 0.21.$$

5. What is the semi-variance of earnings?

$$x_i - E(X) < 0$$
$$\$0.018 + \$0.081 = \$0.099.$$

6. Determine the symmetry of the distribution.

$$\begin{aligned}(0.50)^3 &\to (0.125) \times (0.3) = 0.0375\\ (0)^3 &\to (0) \times (0.4) = 0\\ (-0.30)^3 &\to (-0.027) \times (0.2) = -0.0054\\ (-0.90)^3 &\to (-0.729) \times (0.1) = \underline{-0.0729}\\ & -0.0408\end{aligned}$$

$$SK = \frac{-0.0404}{0.0730} = -0.56.$$

The distribution is negatively skewed.

7. Compute the kurtosis of the distribution.

$$\begin{aligned}(0.50)^4 &\to (0.0625) \times (0.3) = 0.01875\\ (0)^4 &\to (0) \times (0.4) = 0\\ (-0.30)^4 &\to (0.0081) \times (0.2) = 0.00162\\ (-0.90)^4 &\to (0.6561) \times (0.1) = \underline{0.06561}\\ & 0.08598\end{aligned}$$

$$KU = \frac{0.08598}{0.03066} = 2.80.$$

The distribution is slightly platykurtic.

The Normal Distribution

A very important distribution for decision-making purposes is the *normal* distribution. This distribution describes continuous value data, and has the characteristics of being perfectly symmetrical and mesokurtic. The mean, median, and mode for this distribution are identical, because it is not skewed. Probability calculations involving the normal distribution are easily made with tables such as the one provided in Table B.2.

One convenient feature of the normal distribution is that about 2/3 of the distribution lies within one standard deviation of the mean. Within two standard deviations is about 95 percent of the distribution, and all but a fraction of 1 percent of the distribution lies within three standard deviations of the mean (see Figure B.3).

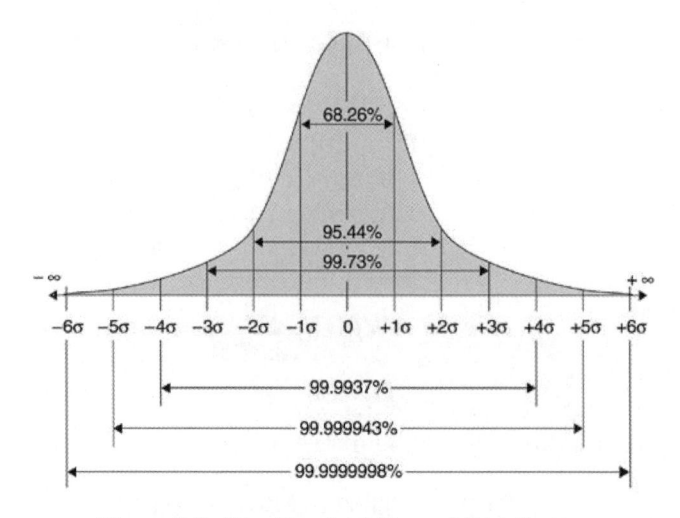

Figure B.3. The Standard Normal Distribution

Another important data transformation usually associated with the normal distribution is that of *standardization*. For a random variable X, we subtract its mean $E(X)$ and divide by its standard deviation to obtain a new random variable Z whose mean is zero and variance unity. That is, $Z = \frac{X-\mu}{\sigma} = \frac{X-E(X)}{\sqrt{V(X)}}$. In the case of normal data, the standardized data is also normal, with commensurate $(\mu, \sigma) = (0, 1)$. Standardized data values are sometimes referred to as *z-scores*. Care should be taken with non-normal data, however, in that while it can be standardized with mean zero and unity variance, its distribution will often be unknown.

A rather underappreciated property of the normal distribution is the very low probabilities it assigns to rare events. For example:

z	$P(Z \leq z)$	z	$P(Z \leq z)$
-6	9.8659E-10	3	0.998650102
-5	2.8665E-07	4	0.999968329
-4	3.1671E-05	5	0.999999713
-3	1.3499E-03	6	0.999999999

Examples

1. The short-run price (over the next month) of a stock is assumed to be normally distributed with a mean of $20 and a standard deviation of $3. The current price of the stock is $15. What is the probability that the purchase of the stock will result in a loss by next month?

    This example shows the usefulness of standardization. We need $P(x_i < 15)$. By standardizing the normal data we have

    $$P(X < 15) = P\left(\frac{X - \mu}{\sigma} < \frac{15 - 20}{3}\right) = P(Z < -1.67),$$

    which is easily obtained from Table B.2 as 0.0475. $15 is 1.67σ below the mean, giving a z-score of -1.67. Values below $15 will occur with a probability of about 5 percent.

2. It is believed that interest rates on high-grade utility bonds are normally distributed. It is felt that the mean value for the first quarter of next year will be 8 percent with a standard deviation of 1 percent. What is the probability that the rate on these bonds will be no lower than 7 percent?

    $$P(X \geq 0.07) = 0.84.$$

    This may be taken directly from Table B.1. The value 7 percent is exactly one standard deviation from the mean. Hence, values less than 7 percent will occur with a probability of about 0.16, and values 7 percent or greater will occur with a probability of $1.00 - 0.16 = 0.84$.

    Notice that since the distribution is continuous, there is no probability associated with a single point value, so that $P(X \leq x) = P(X < x)$, or $P(X > x) = 1 - P(X \leq x)$.

Sampling and the *t*-Distribution

Except when dealing with elicited probabilities, it is almost always the case that the analyst is using samples from a probability distribution, whose parameters are in reality unknown. Therefore, in most practical work, calculated parameters such as the mean and variance must be determined (estimated) from the sample. Examples of estimators would include the sample mean $\bar{X} = \frac{1}{n}\sum_{i=1}^{n} X_i$ and sample standard deviation $S = \sqrt{\frac{1}{n-1}\sum_{i=1}^{n}(X_i - \bar{X})^2}$; analogues for the skewness and kurtosis are calculated similarly. These statistics are easily calculated in software. Statistical inference on many problems such as the population mean is facilitated using the so-called *t-distribution*. Suppose we have normal data for X, and we are interested in testing for or finding confidence limits for the true population mean $E(X) = \mu$. It turns out that the sample mean is unbiased, that is, $E(\bar{X}) = \mu$ also. Additionally, recall that the standard deviation of the sample mean is $\sigma/\sqrt{n}$. If we standardize the sample mean as $Z = \frac{\bar{X}-\mu}{\sigma/\sqrt{n}}$, we find that Z is normally distributed with mean zero and unity variance, so it is easy to evaluate statistical statements about the sample mean by using the z-table in Table B.2.

Unfortunately, we do NOT KNOW σ! If we used the sample standard deviation s, the resulting standardized distribution is NOT normal. It is, however, easy to work with since we can use a t-table to do the job. The t-distribution is very similar to the normal distribution except that it has no parameters other than the degree of freedom ν. In the case of $\bar{X}$, the $\nu = n-1$. Algebraically, $Z = \frac{\bar{X}-\mu}{s/\sqrt{n}}$ is distributed t_{n-1}. For very large sample sizes, the t-distribution approaches the standard normal. For small sample sizes, it becomes more platykurtic until at $n = 1$ it becomes what is known as the Cauchy distribution, with no finite moments at all; see Figure B.4 for a graphical comparison.

Examples

1. Suppose that the mean interest rate value on the high-grade utility bonds for the first quarter of next year is expected to be 8 percent, and that the sample standard deviation of $s = 1$ percent has been obtained based on a sample of size 10. What is the probability that the rate on these bonds will be no lower than 7 percent?

$$P(X > 0.07) = P\left(\frac{X - 0.07}{0.01} > \frac{0.07 - 0.08}{0.01}\right) = P(T > -1).$$

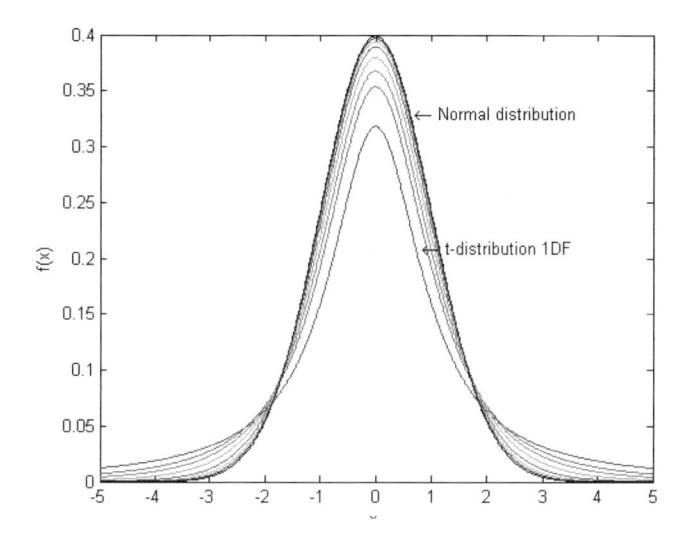

Figure B.4. Normal and t-Distributions Compared

Note that the t-score is equal to the z-score in the previous example, but since we have substituted s for σ in the standardization, the t-distribution is required. Since we did, we need the probability that $t_{10} \leq -1$. In Table B.2, the closest probability corresponding to 1.0 in the $\nu = 10$ row is 0.15, giving an answer of 85 percent. A more exact value could be obtained from interpolation in the table, or better, from using software to look up the actual value of 0.1705, giving a final result of 83 percent. This is slightly lower than the 84 percent probability obtained in the previous normal example, reflecting the greater variability of the t statistic due to the introduction of another statistic, s, in the denominator of the standardization.

Differences of many multi-millions of dollars can be based on a single decimal place value, indicating that, as in this case, it is vastly superior to use the t-distribution when the population standard deviation is not known. Since software is ubiquitous and required in most cases anyway, one should almost always use the t-distribution in numerical work.

2. It is believed that daily percent stock market returns of CAT stock are normally distributed. Suppose we have observed 20 days of

market activity (1 month), and have estimated the sample mean (daily) return to be 0.0716 percent, or 7.16 basis points (bps), with sample standard deviation of 2.212 percent. Obtain a 90 percent confidence interval for the unknown mean population return based on the original data.

A common confidence interval formula for t-distributed data can be written as $\mu \in \bar{x} \pm (t_{n-1,\frac{\alpha}{2}})(s/\sqrt{n})$. In this case, $\bar{x} = 0.000716, s/\sqrt{n} = 0.02212/\sqrt{20} = 0.00507$, and the $t_{19,.05}$ critical value is obtained from Table B.2 as 1.729, giving the 90 percent confidence interval as $\mu \in 0.0716 \pm 1.729(0.5074) = (-0.81\%, 0.95\%)$. Since the confidence interval spans zero, we cannot be statistically certain that the true mean return itself is different than zero. A larger sample size would be required to better answer the question. Using a year of trading data ($\nu = 251$) gives a standard error $s/\sqrt{251} = 0.0014$ versus 5.07 bps, resulting in a 90 percent confidence interval for μ of 6.9–7.4 bps.

Covariance

The *covariance* of two random variables Y and X is defined as:

$$\text{Cov}(X,Y) = E[(X - \mu_X)(Y - \mu_Y)]. \tag{B.7}$$

Expanding, we find:

$$\begin{aligned}\text{Cov}(Y,X) &= E[(XY - Y\mu_X - X\mu_Y + \mu_X\mu_Y)] \\ &= E(XY) - \mu_X\mu_Y - \mu_X\mu_Y + \mu_X\mu_Y \\ &= E(XY) - \mu_X\mu_Y. \end{aligned} \tag{B.8}$$

The covariance gives some indication of how two random variables will vary together.

The correlation coefficient and the covariance of two random variables are related in the following way:

$$\rho_{xy} = \frac{\text{Cov}(X,Y)}{\sigma_x \sigma_y}, \tag{B.9}$$

which may be rewritten as:

$$\text{Cov}(X,Y) = \rho_{xy}\sigma_y\sigma_x. \tag{B.10}$$

Suppose the future performance of two stocks, X and Y, is being considered. Stock X is believed to perform quite favorably under bull market conditions, and an investment in it should produce a handsome profit. Under bear market conditions, however, this stock should do very badly, and the investment would show a sizeable loss in this case. Stock Y, on the other hand, will do moderately well in a bull market, but will remain at current levels even if the market in general does rather poorly. A return matrix under the two possible market conditions is given below:

Market Condition	Probability	Profit Stock X	Profit Stock Y
Bull Market	.5	$4,000	$1,000
Bear Market	.5	−2,000	–0–

The independent expected value and variance for each stock would be:

$$\begin{aligned}\text{Stock } X: (0.5)(4{,}000) &= 2{,}000 \\ (0.5)(-2{,}000) &= \underline{-1{,}000} \\ E(X) &= 1{,}000\end{aligned}$$

$$\begin{aligned}(4{,}000) - (1{,}000) = (3{,}000)^2 &\to 9{,}000{,}000(0.5) = 4{,}500{,}000 \\ (-2{,}000) - (1{,}000) = (-3{,}000)^2 &\to 9{,}000{,}000(0.5) = \underline{4{,}500{,}000} \\ &\phantom{\to 9{,}000{,}000(0.5) = }V(X) = 9{,}000{,}000\end{aligned}$$

$$\begin{aligned}\text{Stock } Y: (0.5)(1{,}000) &= 500 \\ (0.5)(0) &= \underline{0} \\ E(X) &= 500\end{aligned}$$

$$\begin{aligned}(1{,}000) - (500) = (500)^2 &\to 250{,}000(0.5) = 125{,}000 \\ (0) - (500) = (-500)^2 &\to 250{,}000(0.5) = \underline{125{,}000} \\ &\phantom{\to 250{,}000(0.5) = }V(X) = 250{,}000.\end{aligned}$$

The covariance between the two investments would be:

$$\text{Cov}(X, Y) = E(XY) - \mu_X \mu_Y$$

$$E(XY) = (4{,}000)(1{,}000)(0.5) + (-2{,}000)(0)(0.5) = 2{,}000{,}000$$

$$\mu_X \mu_Y = (1{,}000)(500) = 500{,}000$$
$$\text{Cov}(X, Y) = 2{,}000{,}000 - 500{,}000 = 1{,}500{,}000.$$

The correlation coefficient between the investments is given by:

$$\rho_{xy} = \frac{\text{Cov}(X,Y)}{\sigma_x \sigma_y} = \frac{1{,}500{,}000}{(3{,}000)(500)} = \frac{1{,}500{,}000}{1{,}500{,}000} = 1.00.$$

Notice that when the two variables are correlated using only two values for each variable, the loss of degrees of freedom forces a correlation coefficient of unity.

In the case of samples, we define the sample covariance as:

$$S_{XY} = \frac{1}{n-1} \sum_{i=1}^{n} (X_i - \bar{X})(Y_i - \bar{Y}).$$

With simplifying formula:

$$(n-1)S_{XY} = \sum X_i Y_i - \bar{X} \sum Y_i - \bar{Y} \sum X_i + n\bar{X}\bar{Y}$$
$$= \sum X_i Y_i - n\bar{X}\bar{Y}.$$

. We can then define the sample correlation coefficient as the ratio of the sample covariance divided by the product of the sample standard deviations; i.e., $r_{xy} = \frac{S_{xy}}{S_x S_y}$.

Regression and Correlation Analysis

The relationship between two or more random variables may be described through the use of a technique called *regression* analysis. When only two variables are involved, the analysis is referred to as *simple* regression. When more than two variables are involved, the term *multiple* regression is applied. In order to determine the closeness of the relationship between variables, one variable must be selected as the *dependent* variable. This choice is important and will depend on the nature of the variables. The other variables are said to be *independent*. With the establishment of the dependent and independent variables, a least-squares trend line may be computed. This line may take the form of a linear equation, if it is believed that the relationship between the variables is linear, or it may take the form of a non-linear equation.

Suppose we wish to establish the relationship between two variables, Y and X. Suppose further that we believe X to be the independent variable and Y to be the dependent one. We may establish a general equation of the form $Y = f(X)$. Now, let us try to decide what form the equation should take. One method of doing this would be to prepare a simple *scatter diagram* plotting pairs of points representing Y and X values (see Figure B.5). In the case of our general equation above, we shall assume that the relationship appears to be more or less linear. Thus, we shall be fitting a linear least-squares trend line when we *regress* Y against X.

The properties of the least-squares trend line may be described by two equations:

$$\sum(Y - \hat{Y}) = 0$$

$$\sum(Y - \hat{Y})^2 = \text{minimum},$$

where Y are original observations, and $\hat{Y}$ are trend-line computed values.

The first equation assures that the positive and negative deviations of observed values Y from trend values $\hat{Y}$ exactly balance out. The second equation guarantees a "best fit" in that the sum of the squares of the deviations about this line is smaller than for any other line. It should be noted that the properties of the least-squares trend line are the same as those of the arithmetic average (mean) for a probability distribution.

The equation for a straight line (linear relationship) is of the form $Y = a + bX$. Hence, we need to find values for a and b that will satisfy the properties detailed in Equations (B.7) and (B.8). This may be done by solving two additional equations called *normal* equations. The first normal equation is obtained by multiplying the general equation through by the coefficient of the first constant and summing (note that the coefficient of a is one):

$$Y = a + bX$$

$$\sum Y = \sum a + \sum bX.$$

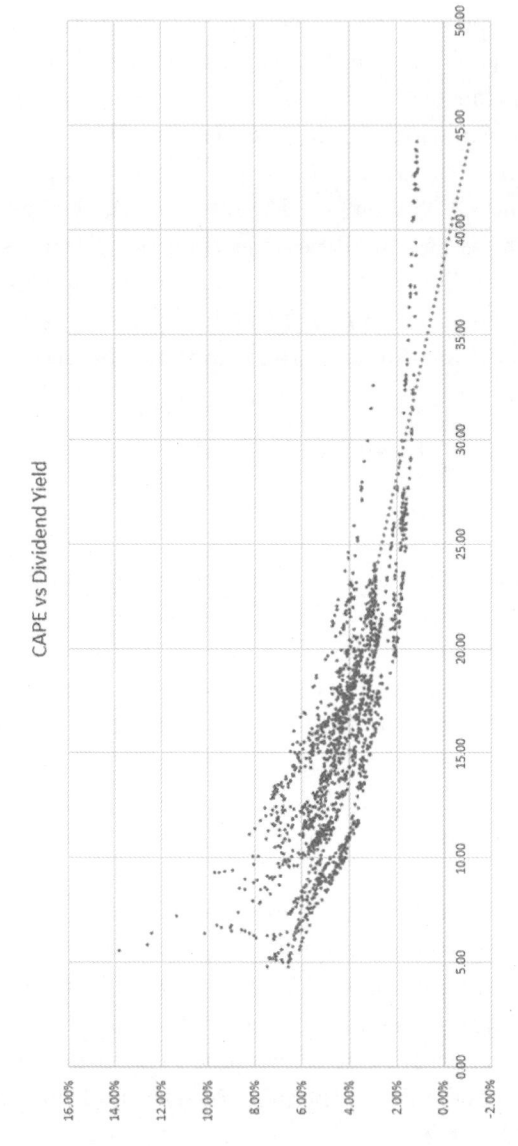

Figure B.5. Scatterplot of Cyclically Adjusted P/E Ratio vs. Dividend Yield[1]

---

[1]Fun with CAPE (Don't cry for me Argentina), http://www.dollarwisefl.com/tag/greece, accessed 2/23/15

Because a is a constant, $\sum a = na$. Also, because b is a constant, $\sum bX = b\sum X$. Thus,

$$\sum Y = na + b\sum X.$$

The second normal equation may be found by multiplying the general equation through by the coefficient of the second constant and summing:

$$Y = a + bX$$
$$XY = aX + bX^2$$
$$\Sigma XY = \Sigma aX + \Sigma bX^2$$
$$\Sigma XY = a\Sigma X + b\Sigma X^2.$$

Year	Sales (million)	Net Income (millions)
2009	10	0
2010	12	1
2011	13	2
2012	11	3
2013	14	4

Suppose the Alberich Mining Corp. wished to regress its sales activity and the net income it earns. Data for the past five years are given below:

A least-square regression equation for Alberich could be determined by using the normal equations:

$Y = f(X)$, where Y is net income and X is sales.

$$\Sigma Y = 10$$
$$\Sigma X = 60$$
$$\Sigma XY = 127$$
$$\Sigma X^2 = 730$$
$$\Sigma Y = na + b\Sigma X$$

$$10 = 5a + 60b$$
$$\Sigma XY = a\Sigma X + b\Sigma X^2$$
$$127 = 60a + 730b.$$

Solving simultaneously, we find:

$$\begin{aligned} 127 &= 60a + 730b \\ 120 &= 60a + 720b \end{aligned}$$

$$\begin{aligned} 7 &= 10b & b &= 0.7 \\ 10 &= 5a + 60(0.7) & a &= -6.4. \end{aligned}$$

Thus, the least-squares regression equation is:

$$Y_c = -6.4 + 0.7X.$$

The computation of least-squares trend lines may be done more efficiently than through the use of Equations (B.9) and (B.10). The intercept a may be computed by:

$$a = \frac{\Sigma Y - b\Sigma X}{n} = \bar{Y} - b\bar{X}.$$

and the slope b by:

$$b = \frac{(\Sigma XY) - (\Sigma X \Sigma Y)/n}{\Sigma X^2 - (\Sigma X)^2/n} = r_{xy}\left(\frac{s_y}{s_x}\right).$$

The solution to the problem posed above would be (solving for b first because it is required to compute a):

$$b = \frac{[127] - [(60)(10)]/5}{(730) - (60)^2/5} = 0.7$$

$$a = \frac{10 - (0.7)(60)}{5} = -6.4.$$

The simplest method of computing least-squares equations is by use of the computer. Programs exist that can handle large amounts of correlated data. Computations involving more than 20 or so inputs become onerous when calculations are made manually, and few analysts rely on calculators any longer to fit least-squares trend lines. Computers can also perform the more complicated computations associated with multiple regression analysis and non-linear least-squares equations. Because few analysts use hand methods anymore, the calculations presented above should serve as an explication of the mathematical process underlying regression and correlation analysis rather than as a tool to provide solutions.

Once the least-squares trend line is established, the analyst may wish to know just how good the fit is between the variables. Thus, a measure of the closeness of the relationship between the variables must be sought. The first step in this process requires the determination of the *standard error of the estimate*, which is a measure of the deviation of actual values around the estimated trend line. The standard error of the estimate is given by the following equation:

$$s_{y \cdot x} = \sqrt{\frac{\Sigma(Y - \hat{Y})^2}{n-1}}.$$

If $s_{y \cdot x} = 0$, we know that all actual values lie on the trend line, and there is a clear linear relationship between Y and X. On the other hand, if there were no linear relationship between the variables, the standard error of the estimate would equal the standard deviation of the dependent variable $s_{y \cdot x} = s_y$.

Determination of the standard error of the estimate allows us to compute an index of the closeness of the relationship between the variables. This index, called the *coefficient of correlation*, is given by:

$$r_{y \cdot x} = \sqrt{1 - \frac{s_{y \cdot x}^2}{s_y^2}}.$$

The square of the coefficient of correlation, r^2, is called the *coefficient of determination*. Its value is the percentage of the variation explained by the liner regression model. Values for r^2 may be between 0 and 1. If two random variables are perfectly correlated, $s_{y \cdot x} = 0$. Hence, $r^2 = 1 - \frac{0}{s_y^2} = 1$. If two variables are completely uncorrelated,

$s_{y \cdot x}^2 = s_y^2$. In this case, $r^2 = 1 - \frac{s_{y \cdot x}^2}{s_y^2} = 0$. Thus, when two variables are highly correlated, r^2 will be a large decimal. When they are poorly correlated, r^2 will be a small decimal.

The equation for multiple regression is one of the form:

$$Y = a \pm bX_1 \pm cX_2 \pm dX_3.$$

In this instance, several independent variables are correlated with the dependent variable, and a general measure of the closeness of the relationship between the dependent variable and the joint simultaneous configuration of the independent variables is required. This measure, designated the *coefficient of multiple determination*, or R^2, is complicated to compute by hand. Although a number of basic statistics books present short-cut equations for the calculation, the statistic is always provided by computer programs that compute multiple-regression equations. Because the analyst will rarely perform these calculations, we shall omit a detailed listing of the equations required to determine R^2.

Coefficients of partial determination measure the relationship between the dependent variable and any one of the independent variables, while the other independent variables are *held constant*. These coefficients are distinct from the separate coefficients of determination of each independent variable with the dependent variable. An interpretation of a coefficient of partial determination may be made by considering an example multiple-regression equation with partial coefficients given under the independent variables:

$$Y = a + bX_1 + cX_2 + dX_3$$
$$(0.82) \quad (0.91) \quad (0.41)$$
$$R^2 = 0.86.$$

In this example, 82 percent of the variation in Y that is not associated with X_2 or X_3 is incrementally associated with X_1.

There are several problems that develop in interpreting regression results. High R^2 values may occur when n is very small simply because too few inputs are included to demonstrate variability. Also, it should be remembered that R^2 measures covariation, *not* causality. If green lights are highly associated with moving automobiles, this does not mean that green lights *cause* automobiles to move. There are further problems of inference from sample data to populations. It may be necessary to test the hypothesis that the R^2 determined is significantly different from zero. The F test may be used for this purpose, and its application is discussed in most statistics texts. Other problems develop when serial correlation is suspected among the disturbance terms. This phenomenon is particularly associated with the use of time-series data, and the analyst should be aware of the fact that the presence of serial correlation reduces the efficiency of his estimators. Tests such as that developed by Durbin–Watson may be used to discern serial correlation, although the problem is beyond the scope of this book.

Conditional Probability Distributions

Two random variables are said to be *independent* if and only if:

$$P(X, Y) = P(X) \times P(Y).$$

In this case, the probability of X assuming any value is not affected by any value Y might take on, and vice versa.

Statistical independence may be illustrated with a set of *conditional* probabilities. Consider the following *joint* probability distribution:

Possible Outcomes for X	Possible Outcomes for Y		Total Probability
	$Y_1 = \$10$	$Y_2 = \$500$	
$X_1 = \$100$	.30	.10	.40
$X_2 = \$200$	.20	.40	.60
Total Probability	.50	.50	1.00

There are two possible outcomes for X (that is, X_1 and X_2) and two for Y (Y_1 and Y_2). Variable X may take on either of its values without being influenced by or influencing Y. Thus, given the fact that $X = X_1$, we may observe that $P(Y = Y_1) = 0.30/40 = 0.75$. Given the fact that $X = X_1$, it is also clear the $P(Y = Y_2) = 0.10/0.40 = 0.25$. Because Y can only be Y_1 or Y_2, the sum of the probabilities $(0.75 + 0.25)$ must equal 1.00. Similarly, given the fact that $X = X_2$, $P(Y = Y_1) = 0.20/0.60$ and $P(Y = Y_2) = 0.40/0.60$, and $1/3 + 2/3 = 1.00$. The mathematical relationship of the variables is described by:

$$P(Y|X) = \frac{P(Y,X)}{P(X)},$$

where

$P(Y|X)$ is the conditional probability of event Y, given that the event X has occurred.

$P(X)$ is the probability of event X occurring.

$P(Y,X)$ is the joint probability of Y and X both occurring.

In Table B.1, the probability that X will take on value X_1 [that is, $P(X = X_1)$] is simply 0.4. The probability that $X = X_1$, *given that* $Y = Y_2$, however, is:

$$P(X_1|Y_2) = 0.10/0.50 = 0.20.$$

The probability that $X = X_1$ and $Y = Y_1$ would be:

$$P(X_1, Y_1) = P(Y_1) \times P(X_1|Y_1)$$
$$= (0.50)(0.30/0.50)$$
$$= 0.30.$$

If we assume that X will occur before Y (that is, X is assumed to be given before Y takes on values), a tree diagram may be drawn to indicate all possible outcomes (Figure B.6):

Note if we are concerned with the probability of Y_1 occurring in any event, the tree diagram clearly shows that $P(Y_1) = P(Y_1, X_1) + P(Y_1, X_2) = 0.3 + 0.2 = 0.5$.

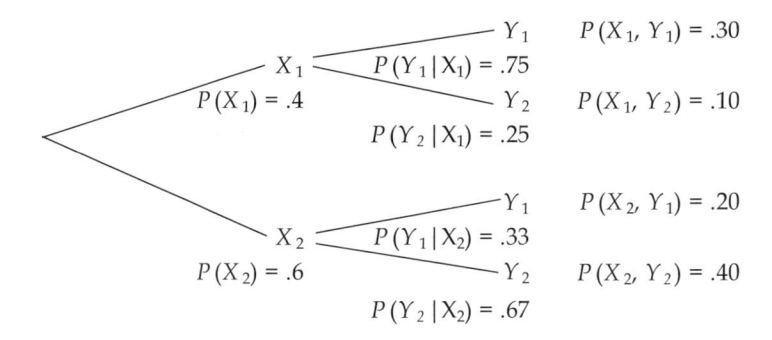

```
                                    Y₁      P(X₁, Y₁) = .30
              X₁    P(Y₁|X₁) = .75
    P(X₁) = .4                       Y₂      P(X₁, Y₂) = .10
                    P(Y₂|X₁) = .25

                                    Y₁      P(X₂, Y₁) = .20
              X₂    P(Y₁|X₂) = .33
    P(X₂) = .6                       Y₂      P(X₂, Y₂) = .40
                    P(Y₂|X₂) = .67
```

Figure B.6. Tree Diagram

Expected Values and Variances of Two or More Random Variables

The expected value of two (or more) random variables is simply the sum of the respective expected values, or:

$$E(Y + X) = E(Y) + E(X).$$

The variance of two or more random variables is given by:

$$V = \sum_{i=1}^{N} \sum_{j=1}^{N} \rho_{ij} \sigma_i \sigma_j.$$

For two random variables, we find:

$$V = \rho_{yy}\sigma_y\sigma_y + \rho_{yx}\sigma_y\sigma_x + \rho_{xy}\sigma_x\sigma_y + \rho_{xx}\sigma_x\sigma_x.$$

Now, we know $\rho_{yy} = 1$ and $\rho_{xx} = 1$. We also know that $\rho_{xy} = \rho_{yx}$. Hence, we may calculate the variance as:

$$V = \sigma_y^2 + \sigma_x^2 + 2\sigma_y\sigma_x\rho_{xy}.$$

In covariance form, we have:

$$V = V(Y) + V(X) + 2\text{Cov}(X, Y).$$

When random variables are percentages (such as in the case of rates of return), the expected value of two or more random variables is the weighted average of the respective expected returns:

$$E = \sum_{i=y}^{N} \alpha_i E_i,$$

where α_i is the proportion of the total placed in the ith investment. In this case, the variance becomes:

$$V = \sum_{i=1}^{N} \sum_{j=1}^{N} \alpha_i \alpha_j \rho_{ij} \sigma_i \sigma_j.$$

For two random variables,

$$V = \alpha_y^2 \sigma_y^2 + \alpha_x^2 \sigma_x^2 + 2\alpha_y \alpha_x \rho_{xy} \sigma_y \sigma_x,$$

which, in covariance form, is:

$$V = \alpha_y^2 V(Y) + \alpha_x^2 V(X) + 2\alpha_y \alpha_x \text{Cov}(Y, X).$$

Reconsider the two stocks X and Y that were examined in the section on Covariance. There, we found Stock X had an expected profit of $1,000 and a variance of $9 million. Stock Y had an expected profit of $500 and a variance of $250,000. The covariance between the two investments was $1,500,000. Suppose an investor purchased *both* stocks. His expected return from the portfolio would be:

$$E(X+Y) = 1{,}000 + 500 = 1{,}500.$$

The variance of the total portfolio would be:

$$V(X+Y) = 9{,}000{,}000 + 250{,}000 + 2(1{,}500{,}000)$$
$$= 12{,}250{,}000.$$

In the above case, we may assume that an equal investment of $10,000 had been made in each stock (total investment of $20,000). If all the dollars had been put into Stock X, the expected return and variance would be:

$$E(X) = (2)(1{,}000) = 2{,}000$$

$$V(X) = 8{,}000 - 2{,}000 = (6{,}000)^2 \rightarrow 36{,}000{,}000(0.5) = 18{,}000{,}000$$
$$-4{,}000 - 2{,}000 = (-6{,}000)^2 \rightarrow 36{,}000{,}000(0.5) = \underline{18{,}000{,}000}$$
$$V(X) = 36{,}000{,}000.$$

A comparison of the return-variance pattern from each portfolio would show:

$$E(X+Y) = 1{,}500 \qquad E(X) = 2{,}000$$
$$V(X+Y) = 20{,}000 \qquad V(X) = 36{,}000{,}000.$$

Thus, the diversified portfolio would provide a lower expected return and a lower risk.

Problems

1. An analyst is attempting to predict the price of a bond next year. The bond currently sells at 90, has six years to maturity, and has a 6 percent coupon. The analyst has obtained predictions from the economics department of his firm about the prime rate of interest for next year. They feel the chances are about 0.5 that the prime rate will be 6 percent, about 0.3 that it will be 5 percent, and about 0.2 that it will be 4 percent. The analyst believes that the bond he is analyzing should yield about 200 basis points (a basis point equals 0.01 percent) more than the prime rate.

   a. Formulate a probability distribution for the price of the bond next year. (Use the short-cut yield formula given in Chapter 3 and compute the price to the nearest dollar.)
   b. Determine the expected value of the price.
   c. Compute the mode and median prices.
   d. What is the standard deviation of the distribution? The coefficient of variation?

e. Determine the semi-variance of the distribution. Comment on the efficacy of this statistic as a measure of risk in this instance.

f. Describe the symmetry and kurtosis of the distribution.

2. The dividend payment for next year of the Elsa Company is expected to be one dollar per share with a standard deviation of ten cents. What is the probability that the dividend will be greater than one dollar? What is the probability that no dividend will be paid? What is the minimum dividend that one might reasonably expect? Assume that dividend payments by Elsa are normally distributed.

3. Jones bought a call on 100 shares of Ionocon Corp. this week. His call entitles him to buy the shares at a price of $10 per share for the next six months. The shares are now $10.50 per share, and Jones' call cost him a total of $150. He believes the price of Ionocon shares for the near future is normally distributed with a mean of $15 and a standard deviation of $5. What is the probability that Jones will lose money?

4. Glamour Glow, Ltd. is a growth stock. The price of its shares moves with the market. When stock prices are up, Glamour Glow generally outperforms the averages. Alchemy Mining is a contracyclical stock. When the market is up, Alchemy does not do very well because investment dollars are chasing up stocks like Glamour Glow. When the market is down, particularly if the negative movement is the result of an international money panic, Alchemy does extremely well. A return matrix for investment in Glamour Glow and Alchemy under three market conditions is given below:

Market Condition	Probability	Profit-Glamour	Profit-Alchemy
Prosperity	.6	$3,000	−$1,000
Recession	.3	−1,000	0
Money panic	.1	−2,000	5,000

a. Calculate the independent expected value and variance for each stock.
b. What is the covariance between the two? The correlation coefficient?

5. Compute the standard error of the estimate, the coefficient of correlation, and the coefficient of determination for the Alberich Mining Corp. (See discussion earlier in chapter.) Interpret your results.

6. The Rheingold Jewelry Co. is attempting to correlate its sales (Y) with several independent variables. It is felt that such variables as national income (X_1), the retail price level (X_2), and the level of interest rates (X_3) might influence sales. After gathering data for 20 years, the firm has determined the following equation:

$$Y = 186 + 0.038(X_1) - 0.124(X_2) - 1.81(X_3)$$
$$(0.84) \qquad (0.22) \qquad (0.45)$$
$$R^2 = 0.64.$$

a. If sales are in thousands, what are the likely units for national income, the retail price level, and the level of interest rates?
b. Let

$$X_1 = 1{,}000$$
$$X_2 = 126$$
$$X_3 = 7.$$

Determine the trend value of sales.

c. Interpret the R^2 value and the coefficients of partial determination.
d. Suppose data had been gathered for only five years. What would you expect to happen to R^2? Why?

7. Using the joint probability table below, assume that Y will occur before X. Draw a tree diagram indicating all possible outcomes.

| | Possible Outcomes for Y | | Total |
Possible Outcomes for X	$Y_1 = \$10$	$Y_2 = \$500$	Probability
$X_1 = \$100$	.30	.10	.40
$X_2 = \$200$	.20	.40	.60
Total Probability	.50	.50	1.00

8. Let the outcomes in the above table take on the numerical values given (that is, $X_1 = \$100$, and so on). Calculate the following:

   a. The independent expected value and variance for X and Y.
   b. The covariance between them.
   c. The correlation coefficient between them.
   d. The expected return and variance of the combination.

9. Two investments have the following characteristics:

   $\mu_X = \$30,000 \quad \sigma_X = \$10,000$
   $\mu_Y = \$20,000 \quad \sigma_Y = 0.$

   What are the covariance and correlation coefficient between the investments?

10. Reconsider the prospective prices of Glamour Glow, Ltd., and Alchemy Mining.

    a. Determine the expected return and variance if both stocks are bought.
    b. Given the miserable expected performance of Alchemy, is there any argument for including it in the portfolio?

11. A portfolio contains two stocks, A and B. The expected yield from A is 10 percent, with a variance of 25 percent. The expected yield from B is 8 percent, with a variance of 9 percent. The correlation between returns from A and B is zero. If 1/5 of the portfolio is in A and 4/5 in B, what is the expected return and variance from the portfolio?

Table B.1. Standard Normal Probabilities

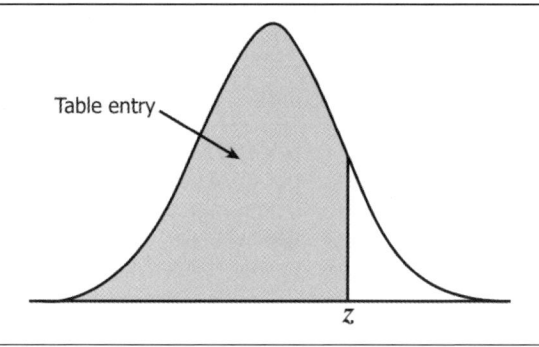

Left Tail Probabilites

z	0.00	0.01	0.02	0.03	0.04	0.05	0.06	0.07	0.08	0.09
0.00	0.500	0.504	0.508	0.512	0.516	0.520	0.524	0.528	0.532	0.536
0.10	0.540	0.540	0.548	0.552	0.556	0.560	0.564	0.567	0.571	0.575
0.20	0.579	0.583	0.587	0.591	0.595	0.599	0.603	0.606	0.610	0.614
0.30	0.618	0.622	0.626	0.629	0.633	0.637	0.641	0.644	0.648	0.652
0.40	0.655	0.659	0.663	0.666	0.670	0.674	0.677	0.681	0.684	0.688
0.50	0.691	0.695	0.698	0.702	0.705	0.709	0.712	0.716	0.719	0.722
0.60	0.726	0.729	0.732	0.736	0.739	0.742	0.745	0.749	0.752	0.755
0.70	0.758	0.761	0.764	0.767	0.770	0.773	0.776	0.779	0.782	0.785
0.80	0.788	0.791	0.794	0.797	0.800	0.802	0.805	0.808	0.811	0.813
0.90	0.816	0.819	0.821	0.824	0.826	0.829	0.831	0.834	0.836	0.839
1.00	0.841	0.844	0.846	0.848	0.851	0.853	0.855	0.858	0.860	0.862
1.10	0.864	0.867	0.869	0.871	0.873	0.875	0.877	0.879	0.881	0.883
1.20	0.885	0.887	0.889	0.891	0.893	0.894	0.896	0.898	0.900	0.901
1.30	0.903	0.905	0.907	0.908	0.910	0.911	0.913	0.915	0.916	0.918
1.40	0.919	0.921	0.922	0.924	0.925	0.926	0.928	0.929	0.931	0.932
1.50	0.933	0.934	0.936	0.937	0.938	0.939	0.941	0.942	0.943	0.944
1.60	0.945	0.946	0.947	0.948	0.949	0.951	0.952	0.953	0.954	0.954
1.70	0.955	0.956	0.957	0.958	0.959	0.960	0.961	0.962	0.962	0.963
1.80	0.964	0.965	0.966	0.966	0.967	0.968	0.969	0.969	0.970	0.971
1.90	0.971	0.972	0.973	0.973	0.974	0.974	0.975	0.976	0.976	0.977
2.00	0.977	0.978	0.978	0.979	0.979	0.980	0.980	0.981	0.981	0.982
2.10	0.982	0.983	0.983	0.983	0.984	0.984	0.985	0.985	0.985	0.986
2.20	0.986	0.986	0.987	0.987	0.987	0.988	0.988	0.988	0.989	0.989
2.30	0.989	0.990	0.990	0.990	0.990	0.991	0.991	0.991	0.991	0.992
2.40	0.992	0.992	0.992	0.992	0.993	0.993	0.993	0.993	0.993	0.994

(*Continued*)

Table B.1. (*Continued*)

Left Tail Probabilites

z	0.00	0.01	0.02	0.03	0.04	0.05	0.06	0.07	0.08	0.09
2.50	0.994	0.994	0.994	0.994	0.994	0.995	0.995	0.995	0.995	0.995
2.60	0.995	0.995	0.996	0.996	0.996	0.996	0.996	0.996	0.996	0.996
2.70	0.997	0.997	0.997	0.997	0.997	0.997	0.997	0.997	0.997	0.997
2.80	0.997	0.998	0.998	0.998	0.998	0.998	0.998	0.998	0.998	0.998
2.90	0.998	0.998	0.998	0.998	0.998	0.998	0.998	0.999	0.999	0.999
3.00	0.999	0.999	0.999	0.999	0.999	0.999	0.999	0.999	0.999	0.999
3.10	0.999	0.999	0.999	0.999	0.999	0.999	0.999	0.999	0.999	0.999
3.20	0.999	0.999	0.999	0.999	0.999	0.999	0.999	0.999	0.999	0.999
3.30	1.000	1.000	1.000	1.000	1.000	1.000	1.000	1.000	1.000	1.000
3.40	1.000	1.000	1.000	1.000	1.000	1.000	1.000	1.000	1.000	1.000

Table B.2. t-Distribution Critical Values

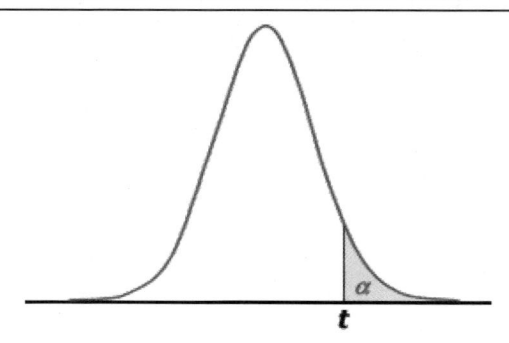

Right Tail Probability α

df	0.25	0.20	0.15	0.10	0.05	0.025	0.02	0.01	0.005
1	1.000	1.376	1.963	3.078	6.314	12.71	15.89	31.82	63.66
2	0.816	1.061	1.386	1.886	2.920	4.303	4.849	6.965	9.925
3	0.765	0.978	1.250	1.638	2.353	3.182	3.482	4.541	5.841
4	0.741	0.941	1.190	1.533	2.132	2.776	2.999	3.747	4.604
5	0.727	0.920	1.156	1.476	2.015	2.571	2.757	3.365	4.032
6	0.718	0.906	1.134	1.440	1.943	2.447	2.612	3.143	3.707
7	0.711	0.896	1.119	1.415	1.895	2.365	2.517	2.998	3.499
8	0.706	0.889	1.108	1.397	1.860	2.306	2.449	2.896	3.355
9	0.703	0.883	1.100	1.383	1.833	2.262	2.398	2.821	3.250
10	0.700	0.879	1.093	1.372	1.812	2.228	2.359	2.764	3.169

(*Continued*)

Table B.2. (*Continued*)

				Right Tail Probability α					
df	0.25	0.20	0.15	0.10	0.05	0.025	0.02	0.01	0.005
11	0.697	0.876	1.088	1.363	1.796	2.201	2.328	2.718	3.106
12	0.695	0.873	1.083	1.356	1.782	2.179	2.303	2.681	3.055
13	0.694	0.870	1.079	1.350	1.771	2.160	2.282	2.650	3.012
14	0.692	0.868	1.076	1.345	1.761	2.145	2.264	2.624	2.977
15	0.691	0.866	1.074	1.341	1.753	2.131	2.249	2.602	2.947
16	0.690	0.865	1.071	1.337	1.746	2.120	2.235	2.583	2.921
17	0.689	0.863	1.069	1.333	1.740	2.110	2.224	2.567	2.898
18	0.688	0.862	1.067	1.330	1.734	2.101	2.214	2.552	2.878
19	0.688	0.861	1.066	1.328	1.729	2.093	2.205	2.539	2.861
20	0.687	0.860	1.064	1.325	1.725	2.086	2.197	2.528	2.845
25	0.684	0.856	1.058	1.316	1.708	2.060	2.167	2.485	2.787
30	0.683	0.854	1.055	1.310	1.697	2.042	2.147	2.457	2.750
35	0.682	0.852	1.052	1.306	1.690	2.030	2.133	2.438	2.724
40	0.681	0.851	1.050	1.303	1.684	2.021	2.123	2.423	2.704
45	0.680	0.850	1.049	1.301	1.679	2.014	2.115	2.412	2.690
50	0.679	0.849	1.047	1.299	1.676	2.009	2.109	2.403	2.678
75	0.678	0.846	1.044	1.293	1.665	1.992	2.090	2.377	2.643
100	0.677	0.845	1.042	1.290	1.660	1.984	2.081	2.364	2.626
200	0.676	0.843	1.039	1.286	1.653	1.972	2.067	2.345	2.601
300	0.675	0.843	1.038	1.284	1.650	1.968	2.063	2.339	2.592
400	0.675	0.843	1.038	1.284	1.649	1.966	2.060	2.336	2.588
500	0.675	0.842	1.038	1.283	1.648	1.965	2.059	2.334	2.586
1000	0.675	0.842	1.037	1.282	1.646	1.962	2.056	2.330	2.581
∞	0.674	0.842	1.036	1.282	1.645	1.960	2.054	2.326	2.576
	50%	60%	70%	80%	90%	95%	96%	98%	99%

Confidence Level C

References

Hogg, R. V. and E. A. Tanis, *Probability and Statistical Inference,* 8th edn. Upper Saddle River, NJ: Prentice Hall, 2010.

Thompson, J. R., E. E. Williams, and M. C. Findlay, *Models for Investors in Real World Markets.* Appendix A ("A Brief Introduction to Probability and Statistics"). New York, NY: John Wiley & Sons, Inc., 2003.

Vickers, A., *What is a p-Value, Anyway?* Boston, MA: Addison Wesley, 2010.

Weisberg, S., *Applied Linear Regression,* 2nd edn. New York, NY: John Wiley & Sons, Inc., 1985.

Appendix C

Company Data

Many shall be restored that now are fallen and many shall fall that now are in honor.
Horace – Ars Poetica

Importance of Real World Data

A primary tenet of this book is that appropriate analysis of financial data from a company under scrutiny will reveal its innate fundamental valuation. Such analysis thus allows an investor a fighting chance to buy undervalued stocks and sell overvalued ones. Although this valuation may or may not be reflected in the market quotation for a publicly traded firm, the Graham and Dodd principles outlined in Chapter 10 depend on its determination. Similarly, accurate company historical data are required as a basis for any material forecasts of future results.

Service Corporation International (SCI)

We provide 37 annual fiscal year periods of historical data for Service Corporation International (SCI) common stock, CUSIP 81756510, for the period 1980 through 2016 in the tables that follow. SCI became a publicly held stock in 1969 and has been listed on the New York Stock Exchange (NYSE) since 1974. The company has been the largest publicly traded death care provider (funeral homes and cemetery operations) for most of this period. It originally traded under the NYSE ticker SRV until 2004 when the symbol changed to

SCI. Note that all the data are from publicly available sources such as company 10-K SEC filings, company website press releases, or other primary sources, and are retrieved using the FactSet Research Systems Inc. workstation. These figures are final, as-filed, non-restated, and all in millions of U.S. dollars, except for ratios and per share amounts. Definitions of applicable accounting ratios are found in Chapter 4. SCI neither endorses nor has verified the authenticity of these data.

The majority of the data reflects a December fiscal year, although until 1988, SCI had a fiscal year ending in April. Note that for the year change (April 1987 through December 1988) a 20-month time frame accounting period is reflected.

Figure C.1 shows a monthly stock price chart for SCI. The solid line plots the actual prices seen in the time frame indicated; we have overlaid split-adjusted prices in the dashed line. Recall that stocks never trade at "adjusted" prices at actual dates in the past.

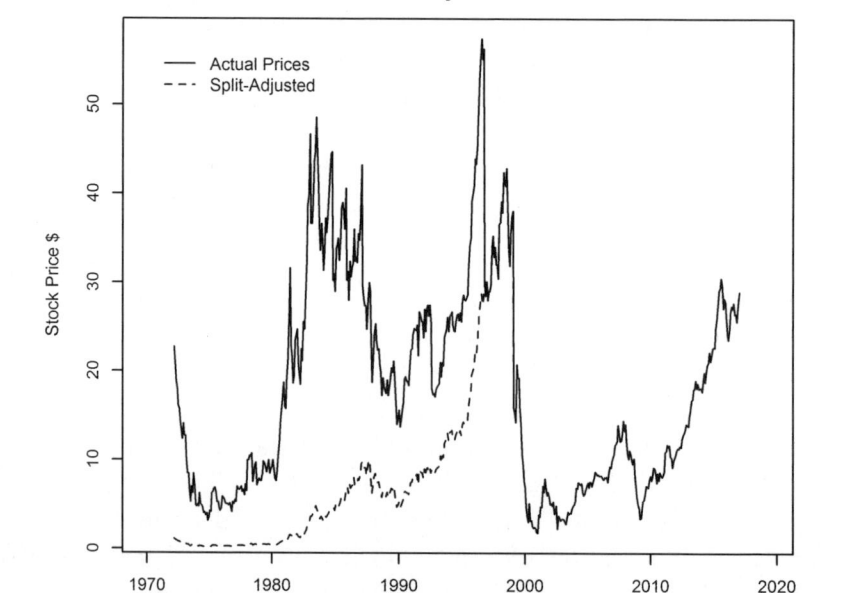

Figure C.1. SCI Monthly Price History

There have been seven stock splits since 1981. They are listed below:

Stock Splits

Date	Amount
03-Sep-1996	2 For 1
01-Jul-1992	3 For 2
02-Feb-1987	3 For 2
01-Nov-1985	3 For 2
31-Oct-1984	3 For 2
21-Jan-1983	3 For 2
12-Jun-1981	4 For 3

The company has paid a continuous (increasing) dividend (Figure C.2) since 1977, suspending it only for FY2000–2005 while it was regrouping from a series of overseas acquisitions.

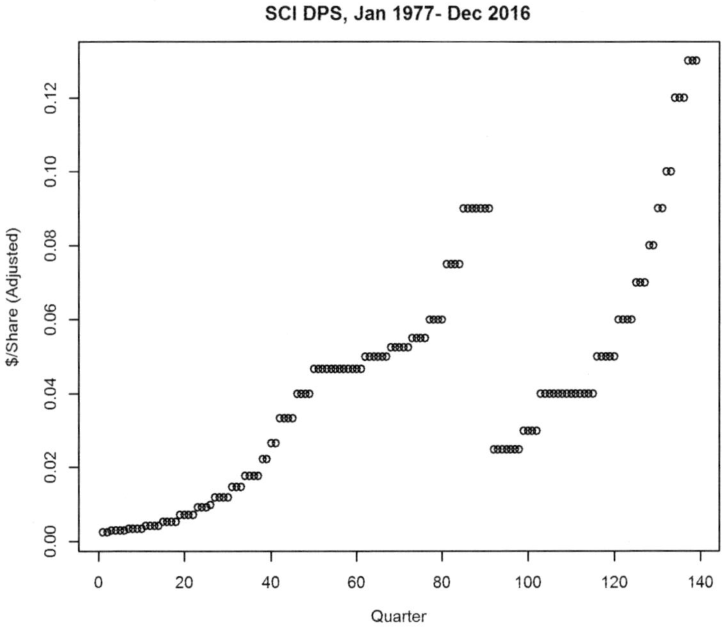

Figure C.2. SCI Split-Adjusted Quarterly Dividend History

Non-restated financial statement data are presented in Tables C.1–C.30.

Table C.1. SCI Income Statement Items, 2013–2016

Income Statement	Dec'16	Dec'15	Dec'14	Dec'13
Sales/Revenue	3,031.1	2,986.4	2,994.0	2,556.4
Sales/Revenue Growth (%)	1.50	−0.25	17.12	6.05
Gross Income	676.4	671.9	675.8	549.6
Gross Income Growth (%)	0.67	−0.57	22.97	4.63
Gross Margin (%)	22.32	22.50	22.57	21.50
EBIT	539.5	550.5	558.2	422.8
EBIT Growth (%)	−1.99	−1.39	32.02	5.36
EBIT Margin (%)	17.80	18.43	18.65	16.54
EBITDA	784.4	785.8	795.3	615.6
EBITDA Growth (%)	−0.17	−1.20	29.19	4.28
EBITDA Margin (%)	25.88	26.31	26.56	24.08
Net Income	177.0	234.2	170.3	143.8
Net Income Growth (%)	−24.40	37.51	18.38	−5.70
Net Margin (%)	5.84	7.84	5.69	5.63

Table C.2. SCI Balance Sheet Items, 2013–2016

Balance Sheet	Dec'16	Dec'15	Dec'14	Dec'13
Cash & Short Term Investments	194.99	147.19	206.26	151.42
Cash & ST Investments Growth (%)	32.48	−28.64	36.22	60.76
Cash & ST Investments/Total Assets	1.62	1.26	1.73	1.17
Total Assets	12,038.15	11,718.89	11,923.64	12,906.07
Total Assets Growth (%)	2.72	−1.72	−7.61	33.28
Asset Turnover (x)	0.26	0.25	0.24	0.23
Return on Assets (%)	1.49	1.98	1.37	1.27
Total Debt	3,286.59	3,188.73	3,082.52	3,307.06
Total Debt Growth (%)	3.07	3.45	−6.79	67.85
Total Debt/Total Assets (%)	27.30	27.21	25.85	25.62
Total Debt/Total Equity (%)	300.77	269.16	225.21	233.84
Net Debt	3,091.60	3,041.54	2,876.26	3,155.64
Net Debt Growth (%)	1.65	5.75	−8.85	68.20
Net Debt/Total Equity (%)	282.93	256.74	210.14	223.13
Total Liabilities	10,942.90	10,529.49	10,546.27	11,481.69
Total Liabilities Growth (%)	3.93	−0.16	−8.15	37.99
Total Shareholders' Equity	1,092.71	1,184.69	1,368.73	1,414.23
Total Shareholders' Equity/Total Ass	9.08	10.11	11.48	10.96
Return on Equity (%)	15.55	18.34	12.24	10.43

Appendix C: Company Data 557

Table C.3. SCI Cash Flow Items, 2013–2016

Cash Flow	Dec'16	Dec'15	Dec'14	Dec'13
Net Operating Cash Flow	463.60	472.19	317.36	384.71
Net Operating Cash Flow Growth (%)	*−1.82*	*48.79*	*−17.51*	*4.19*
Cash Flow Return on Invested Capital	*10.85*	*11.00*	*7.13*	*9.83*
Capital Expenditures	−193.45	−150.99	−144.50	−113.08
Capital Expenditures Growth (%)	*−28.12*	*−4.49*	*−27.78*	*2.20*
Net Investing Cash Flow	−218.09	−166.42	257.29	−1,156.79
Net investing Cash Flow Growth (%)	*−31.05*	*−164.68*	—	*−561.20*
Net Financing Cash Flow	−186.97	−338.48	−537.97	825.12
Net Financing Cash Flow Growth (%)	*44.76*	*37.08*	*−165.20*	—
Free Cash Flow	270.15	321.20	172.86	271.63
Free Cash Flow Growth (%)	*−15.89*	*85.82*	*−36.36*	*7.10*
Free Cash Flow Yield (%)	*4.85*	*6.04*	*3.55*	*6.94*

Table C.4. SCI Ratios and Supplementals, 2013–2016

Ratios (x)	Dec'16	Dec'15	Dec'14	Dec'13
Price/Earnings	31.56	22.71	28.02	27.06
Price/Sales	1.84	1.78	1.62	1.53
Price/Book Value	4.92	4.30	3.40	2.72
Price/Tangible Book Value	—	—	—	—
Price/Cash Flow	12.01	11.27	15.32	10.18
Price/Free Cash Flow	20.61	16.56	28.13	14.42
Dividend Yield (%)	1.80	1.69	1.50	1.49
Enterprise Value/EBIT	15.71	14.79	13.50	16.59
Enterprise Value/EBITDA	10.80	10.36	9.47	11.39
Enterprise Value/Sales	2.80	2.73	2.52	2.74
EBIT/Interest Expense (Int. Coverage)	3.33	3.18	3.14	3.23
Pension				
Pension Funded Status	—	−32.31	−36.92	−37.50
Pension Expense	—	−0.13	3.69	−0.43
Supplemental				
Stock Option Comp Exp (Net of Tax)	—	8.78	7.88	7.24
Operating Lease Commitments	—	113.97	114.97	122.28
Long Term Debt Maturities	89.97	95.18	90.93	146.36

Table C.5. SCI Per Share Data, 2013–2016

Per Share	Dec'16	Dec'15	Dec'14	Dec'13
Sales per Share	15.46	14.61	13.98	11.83
Sales per Share Growth (%)	*5.85*	*4.50*	*18.11*	*7.55*
EPS (recurring)	—	1.22	1.50	0.81
EPS (recurring) Growth (%)	—	*-18.91*	*84.82*	*3.51*
EPS (diluted)	0.90	1.15	0.81	0.67
EPS (diluted) Growth (%)	*-21.44*	*41.43*	*20.90*	*-4.29*
Dividends per Share	0.51	0.44	0.34	0.27
Dividends per Share Growth (%)	*15.91*	*29.41*	*25.93*	*17.39*
Book Value per Share	5.77	6.05	6.68	6.66
Book Value per Share Growth (%)	*-4.66*	*-9.43*	*0.30*	*4.67*
Tangible Book Value per Share	-3.73	-5.01	-4.08	-4.38
Tangible Book Value per Share Growth (%)	*25.62*	*-22.89*	*6.88*	*-211.29*
Cash Flow per Share	2.36	2.31	1.48	1.78
Cash Flow per Share Growth (%)	*2.39*	*55.88*	*-16.81*	*5.66*
Free Cash Flow per Share	1.38	1.57	0.81	1.26
Free Cash Flow per Share Growth (%)	*-12.29*	*94.68*	*-35.82*	*8.61*
Diluted Shares Outstanding	196.04	204.45	214.20	216.01
Basic Shares Outstanding	*193.09*	*200.36*	*210.74*	*211.81*
Total Shares Outstanding	189.41	195.77	204.87	212.32
Basic Shares Outstanding	215.71	234.24	248.87	251.71
Dividend Yield (%)	1.67	1.88	1.94	1.95

Table C.6. SCI Income Statement Items, 2007–2012

Income Statement	Dec'12	Dec'11	Dec'10	Dec'09	Dec'08	Dec'07	Dec'06
Sales/Revenue	2,410.48	2,316.04	2,190.55	2,053.52	2,155.62	2,285.30	1,747.30
Sales/Revenue Growth (%)	*4.08*	*5.73*	*6.67*	*-4.74*	*-5.67*	*30.79*	*1.85*
Gross Income	525.23	478.54	449.22	421.18	418.77	468.50	344.67
Gross Income Growth (%)	*9.76*	*6.53*	*6.66*	*0.58*	*-10.61*	*35.93*	*15.34*
Gross Margin (%)	*21.79*	*20.66*	*20.51*	*20.51*	*19.43*	*20.50*	*19.73*
EBIT	401.32	374.68	349.23	318.89	331.32	329.25	249.77
EBIT Growth (%)	*7.11*	*7.29*	*9.51*	*-3.75*	*0.63*	*31.82*	*16.71*
EBIT Margin (%)	*16.65*	*16.18*	*15.94*	*15.53*	*15.37*	*14.41*	*14.29*
EBITDA	590.38	558.36	523.24	482.36	501.81	495.50	346.45
EBITDA Growth (%)	*5.73*	*6.71*	*8.48*	*-3.88*	*1.27*	*43.02*	*14.92*
EBITDA Margin (%)	*24.49*	*24.11*	*23.89*	*23.49*	*23.28*	*21.68*	*19.83*
Net Income	152.55	144.90	126.42	123.10	97.45	243.32	52.60
Net Income Growth (%)	*5.27*	*14.62*	*2.70*	*26.33*	*-59.95*	*362.54*	*-7.20*
Net Margin (%)	*6.33*	*6.26*	*5.77*	*5.99*	*4.52*	*10.65*	*3.01*

Table C.7. SCI Balance Sheet Items, 2007–2012

Balance Sheet	Dec'12	Dec'11	Dec'10	Dec'09	Dec'08	Dec'07	Dec'06
Cash & Short Term Investments	94.19	132.71	170.85	179.75	128.40	168.59	39.88
Cash & ST Investments Growth (%)	−29.02	−22.32	−4.95	39.99	−23.84	322.75	−91.07
Cash & ST Investments/Total Assets (%)	0.97	1.42	1.86	2.02	1.58	1.89	0.41
Total Assets	9,683.57	9,327.81	9,190.54	8,890.98	8,110.88	8,932.24	9,729.39
Total Assets Growth (%)	3.81	1.49	3.37	9.62	−9.20	−8.19	29.09
Asset Turnover (x)	0.25	0.25	0.24	0.24	0.25	0.24	0.20
Return on Assets (%)	1.60	1.56	1.40	1.45	1.14	2.61	0.61
Total Debt	1,970.29	1,899.98	1,870.46	1,908.73	1,870.55	1,884.39	1,958.87
Total Debt Growth (%)	3.70	1.58	−2.00	2.04	−0.73	−3.80	63.79
Total Debt/Total Assets (%)	20.35	20.37	20.35	21.47	23.06	21.10	20.13
Total Debt/Total Equity (%)	146.71	136.48	126.43	128.73	144.65	126.29	122.83
Net Debt	1,876.10	1,767.27	1,699.62	1,728.98	1,742.16	1,715.80	1,918.99
Net Debt Growth (%)	6.16	3.98	−1.70	−0.76	1.54	−10.59	156.16
Net Debt/Total Equity (%)	139.69	126.95	114.88	116.60	134.72	114.99	120.33
Total Liabilities	8,320.74	7,915.62	7,710.59	7,408.19	6,817.70	4,143.28	4,698.69
Total Liabilities Growth (%)	5.12	2.66	4.08	8.66	64.55	−11.82	45.12
Total Shareholders' Equity	1,343.03	1,392.09	1,479.46	1,482.78	1,293.18	1,492.08	1,594.78
Total Shareholders' Equity/Total Assets (%)	13.87	14.92	16.10	16.68	15.94	16.70	16.39
Return on Equity (%)	11.15	10.09	8.54	8.87	7.00	15.76	3.31

Table C.8. SCI Cash Flow Items, 2007–2012

Cash Flow	Dec'12	Dec'11	Dec'10	Dec'09	Dec'08	Dec'07	Dec'06
Net Operating Cash Flow	369.25	388.11	354.38	372.07	350.18	356.18	324.22
Net Operating Cash Flow Growth (%)	*−4.86*	*9.52*	*−4.75*	*6.25*	*−1.68*	*9.86*	*3.70*
Cash Flow Return on Invested Capital (%)	*11.34*	*11.82*	*10.68*	*11.56*	*10.90*	*10.45*	*10.34*
Capital Expenditures	−115.63	−118.38	−97.90	−83.79	−154.10	−157.01	−99.53
Capital Expenditures Growth (%)	*−2.32*	*20.92*	*16.84*	*−45.63*	*−1.85*	*57.76*	*0.11*
Net Investing Cash Flow	−174.95	−190.26	−279.71	−152.49	−151.27	378.12	−1,297.50
Net Investing Cash Flow Growth (%)	*8.04*	*31.98*	*−83.43*	*−0.80*	*−140.01*	—	*−858.71*
Net Financing Cash Flow	−231.51	−238.67	−88.19	−178.43	−230.51	−607.53	565.21
Net Financing Cash Flow Growth (%)	*3.00*	*−170.64*	*50.58*	*22.59*	*62.06*	*−207.49*	—
Free Cash Flow	253.62	269.74	256.48	288.28	196.08	199.17	224.69
Free Cash Flow Growth (%)	*−5.98*	*5.17*	*−11.03*	*47.02*	*−1.55*	*−11.36*	*5.37*
Free Cash Flow Yield (%)	*8.38*	*10.70*	*12.41*	*13.94*	*15.15*	*4.88*	*7.37*

Table C.9. SCI Ratios and Supplementals, 2007–2012

Ratios (x)	Dec'12	Dec'11	Dec'10	Dec'09	Dec'08	Dec'07	Dec'06
Price/Earnings	19.73	17.46	16.50	16.71	13.43	16.53	56.94
Price/Sales	1.26	1.09	0.94	1.01	0.60	1.79	1.74
Price/Book Value	2.17	1.71	1.34	1.40	0.96	2.48	1.88
Price/Tangible Book Value	—	—	—	12.66	248.42	21.02	18.33
Price/Cash Flow	8.19	6.49	5.83	5.56	3.70	11.46	9.40
Price/Free Cash Flow	11.93	9.34	8.06	7.17	6.60	20.49	13.57
Enterprise Value/EBIT	11.99	11.11	10.56	11.95	9.00	26.44	33.47
Enterprise Value/EBITDA	8.15	7.45	7.05	7.90	5.94	17.57	24.13
Enterprise Value/Sales	2.00	1.80	1.68	1.86	1.38	3.81	4.78
EBIT/Interest Expense (Int. Coverage)	2.97	2.80	2.72	2.47	2.47	2.24	2.02
Pension							
Pension Funded Status	−28.67	−29.21	−31.38	−32.89	−32.95	−37.10	−65.44
Pension Expense	2.53	1.02	2.03	4.05	1.75	15.47	3.66
Supplemental							
Stock Option Comp Exp (Net of Tax)	6.59	5.93	5.14	5.98	5.53	5.39	—
Operating Lease Commitments	89.51	87.95	86.39	79.75	82.92	98.20	114.02
Long Term Debt Maturities	31.43	23.55	22.50	49.96	27.10	36.59	46.18

Table C.10. SCI Per Share Data, 2007–2012

Per Share	Dec'12	Dec'11	Dec'10	Dec'09	Dec'08	Dec'07	Dec'06
EPS (recurring)	0.78	0.79	0.62	0.74	0.53	0.91	0.31
EPS (recurring) Growth (%)	*-0.82*	*26.62*	*-15.42*	*39.88*	*-41.79*	*190.24*	*12.77*
EPS (diluted)	0.70	0.61	0.50	0.49	0.37	0.85	0.18
EPS (diluted) Growth (%)	*14.75*	*22.00*	*2.04*	*32.43*	*-56.47*	*372.22*	*-5.26*
EPS (basic)	0.71	0.62	0.51	0.49	0.38	0.87	0.18
EPS (basic) Growth (%)	*14.52*	*21.57*	*4.08*	*28.95*	*-56.32*	*383.33*	*-5.26*
Sales per Share	11.00	9.79	8.74	8.13	8.28	7.87	5.88
Sales per Share Growth (%)	*12.44*	*11.95*	*7.47*	*-1.73*	*5.19*	*33.91*	*5.06*
Dividends per Share	0.23	0.20	0.16	0.16	0.16	0.13	0.11
Dividends per Share Growth (%)	*15.00*	*25.00*	*0.00*	*0.00*	*23.08*	*23.81*	*5.00*
Book Value per Share	6.36	6.24	6.14	5.84	5.18	5.68	5.44
Book Value per Share Growth (%)	*1.92*	*1.73*	*5.15*	*12.61*	*-8.68*	*4.37*	*0.94*
Tangible Book Value per Share	-1.41	-1.00	-0.17	0.65	0.02	0.67	0.56
Tangible Book Value per Share Growth (%)	*-40.96*	*-472.04*	*-126.98*	*3,134.56*	*-97.01*	*19.53*	*-57.87*
Cash Flow per Share	1.69	1.64	1.41	1.47	1.34	1.23	1.09
Cash Flow per Share Growth (%)	*2.78*	*15.97*	*-4.04*	*9.60*	*9.64*	*12.48*	*6.97*
Free Cash Flow per Share	1.16	1.14	1.02	1.14	0.75	0.69	0.76
Free Cash Flow per Share Growth (%)	*1.58*	*11.36*	*-10.36*	*51.66*	*9.79*	*-9.24*	*8.69*
Diluted Shares Outstanding	219.07	236.67	250.60	252.48	260.45	290.44	297.37
Basic Shares Outstanding	215.71	234.24	248.87	251.71	257.48	284.97	292.86
Dividend Yield (%)	1.67	1.88	1.94	1.95	3.22	0.93	1.02

Table C.11. SCI Income Statement Items, 1999–2005

Income Statement	Dec'05	Dec'04	Dec'03	Dec'02	Dec'01	Dec'00	Dec'99
Sales/Revenue	1,715.61	1,859.31	2,341.65	2,272.42	2,510.34	2,564.73	3,321.81
Sales/Revenue Growth (%)	−7.73	−20.60	3.05	−9.48	−2.12	−22.79	15.54
Gross Income	298.83	334.50	365.80	363.92	359.39	327.64	613.76
Gross Income Growth (%)	−10.66	−8.56	0.52	1.26	9.69	−46.62	−14.61
Gross Margin (%)	17.42	17.99	15.62	16.01	14.32	12.77	18.48
EBIT	214.02	264.70	281.17	274.16	289.08	247.71	531.17
EBIT Growth (%)	−19.15	−5.86	2.56	−5.16	16.70	−53.37	−18.52
EBIT Margin (%)	12.47	14.24	12.01	12.06	11.52	9.66	15.99
EBITDA	301.46	410.00	442.23	402.71	483.01	471.74	783.32
EBITDA Growth (%)	−26.47	−7.29	9.81	−16.63	2.39	−39.78	−8.30
EBITDA Margin (%)	17.57	22.05	18.89	17.72	19.24	18.39	23.58
Net Income	56.69	117.01	85.08	−101.22	−596.63	−425.52	−34.30
Net Income Growth (%)	−51.56	37.53	—	83.03	−40.21	−1,140.70	−110.02
Net Margin (%)	3.30	6.29	3.63	−4.45	−23.77	−16.59	−1.03

Table C.12. SCI Balance Sheet Items, 1999–2005

Balance Sheet	Dec'05	Dec'04	Dec'03	Dec'02	Dec'01	Dec'00	Dec'99
Cash & Short Term Investments	446.78	287.79	239.43	200.63	29.29	47.91	88.22
Cash & ST Investments Growth (%)	*55.25*	*20.20*	*19.34*	*584.91*	*-38.86*	*-45.69*	*-75.37*
Cash & ST Investments/Total Assets (%)	*5.93*	*3.51*	*2.14*	*1.87*	*0.25*	*0.37*	*0.60*
Total Assets	7,536.69	8,199.20	11,202.67	10,723.79	11,579.94	12,898.47	14,601.60
Total Assets Growth (%)	*-8.08*	*-26.81*	*4.47*	*-7.39*	*-10.22*	*-11.66*	*10.07*
Asset Turnover (x)	*0.22*	*0.19*	*0.21*	*0.20*	*0.21*	*0.19*	*0.24*
Return on Assets (%)	*0.72*	*1.21*	*0.78*	*-0.91*	*-4.87*	*-3.09*	*-0.25*
Total Debt	1,195.93	1,253.96	1,711.57	2,001.19	2,560.62	3,322.22	4,084.58
Total Debt Growth (%)	*-4.63*	*-26.74*	*-14.47*	*-21.85*	*-22.92*	*-18.66*	*5.80*
Total Debt/Total Assets (%)	*15.87*	*15.29*	*15.28*	*18.66*	*22.11*	*25.76*	*27.97*
Total Debt/Total Equity (%)	*75.29*	*67.65*	*112.09*	*153.49*	*178.71*	*168.14*	*116.86*
Net Debt	749.15	966.18	1,472.13	1,800.56	531.33	3,274.31	3,996.36
Net Debt Growth (%)	*-22.46*	*-34.37*	*-18.24*	*-28.87*	*-22.69*	*-18.07*	*14.10*
Net Debt/Total Equity (%)	*47.16*	*52.12*	*96.41*	*138.10*	*176.66*	*165.72*	*114.34*
Total Liabilities	3,237.78	3,544.86	9,675.71	9,420.01	10,147.08	10,922.65	11,106.33
Total Liabilities Growth (%)	*-8.66*	*-63.36*	*2.71*	*-7.17*	*-7.10*	*-1.65*	*9.83*
Total Shareholders' Equity	1,588.49	1,853.58	1,526.96	1,303.77	1,432.86	1,975.82	3,495.27
Total Shareholders' Equity/Total Assets (%)	*21.08*	*22.61*	*13.63*	*12.16*	*12.37*	*15.32*	*23.94*
Return on Equity (%)	*3.29*	*6.92*	*6.01*	*-7.40*	*-35.01*	*-15.56*	*-1.03*

Table C.13. SCI Cash Flow Items, 1999–2005

Cash Flow	Dec'05	Dec'04	Dec'03	Dec'02	Dec'01	Dec'00	Dec'99
Net Operating Cash Flow	312.66	107.81	374.11	352.17	383.34	368.24	432.85
Net Operating Cash Flow Growth (%)	*190.02*	*−71.18*	*6.23*	*−8.13*	*4.10*	*−14.93*	*31.31*
Cash Flow Return on Invested Capital (%)	*10.79*	*3.54*	*11.98*	*10.16*	*8.68*	*6.03*	*6.16*
Capital Expenditures	−99.42	−96.01	−116.00	−100.05	−74.16	−83.37	−211.48
Capital Expenditures Growth (%)	*3.55*	*−17.24*	*15.95*	*34.90*	*−11.04*	*−60.58*	*−16.48*
Net Investing Cash Flow	171.02	289.52	−37.42	326.93	325.41	193.07	−423.98
Net Investing Cash Flow Growth (%)	*−40.93*	—	*−111.45*	*0.47*	*68.55*	—	*60.00*
Net Financing Cash Flow	−326.19	−349.64	−300.15	−505.48	−727.44	−564.46	−266.76
Net Financing Cash Flow Growth (%)	*6.71*	*−16.49*	*40.62*	*30.51*	*−28.87*	*−111.60*	*−125.61*
Free Cash Flow	213.24	11.80	258.11	252.13	309.17	284.87	221.37
Free Cash Flow Growth (%)	*1,707.44*	*−95.43*	*2.37*	*−18.45*	*8.53*	*28.69*	*189.66*
Free Cash Flow Yield (%)	*8.50*	*0.46*	*15.92*	*25.78*	*21.73*	*59.73*	*11.65*

Table C.14. SCI Ratios and Supplementals, 1999–2005

Ratios (x)	Dec'05	Dec'04	Dec'03	Dec'02	Dec'01	Dec'00	Dec'99
Price/Earnings	43.05	20.69	19.25	—	—	—	—
Price/Sales	1.46	1.38	0.69	0.43	0.57	0.19	0.57
Price/Book Value	1.52	1.30	1.07	0.76	1.02	0.24	0.54
Price/Tangible Book Value	6.16	3.98	4.91	8.25	61.90	—	1.85
Price/Cash Flow	8.03	23.82	4.33	2.78	3.71	1.30	4.39
Price/Free Cash Flow	11.77	217.65	6.28	3.88	4.60	1.67	8.58
Enterprise Value/EBIT	27.43	23.33	11.03	10.16	13.80	15.14	11.08
Enterprise Value/EBITDA	19.48	15.06	7.01	6.92	8.26	7.95	7.51
Enterprise Value/Sales	3.42	3.32	1.32	1.23	1.59	1.46	1.77
EBIT/Interest Expense (Int. Coverage)	2.09	2.24	1.96	1.70	1.37	0.88	2.23
Pension							
Pension Funded Status	−50.28	−60.05	−70.10	−65.38	—	—	—
Pension Expense	8.40	54.55	11.21	6.32	—	—	—
Supplemental							
Stock Option Comp Exp (Net of Tax)	—	—	—	—	—	—	—
Operating Lease Commitments	204.76	212.70	173.98	179.65	267.90	295.61	959.42
Long Term Debt Maturities	20.47	75.08	182.68	100.33	220.64	176.78	423.95

Table C.15. SCI Per Share Data, 1999–2005

Per Share	Dec'05	Dec'04	Dec'03	Dec'02	Dec'01	Dec'00	Dec'99
EPS (recurring)	0.28	0.57	0.57	0.34	−0.52	−0.38	0.80
EPS (recurring) Growth (%)	−51.56	−0.20	66.85	—	−37.12	−147.06	−38.76
EPS (diluted)	0.19	0.36	0.28	−0.34	−2.09	−1.51	−0.13
EPS (diluted) Growth (%)	−47.22	28.57	—	83.73	−38.41	−1,061.54	−109.94
EPS (basic)	0.19	0.37	0.28	−0.34	−2.09	−1.51	−0.13
EPS (basic) Growth (%)	−48.65	32.14	—	83.73	−38.41	−1,061.54	—
Sales per Share	5.59	5.39	7.79	7.72	8.80	9.41	12.13
Sales per Share Growth (%)	3.68	−30.71	0.90	−12.37	−6.44	−22.44	10.78
Dividends per Share	0.10	0.00	0.00	0.00	0.00	0.00	0.27
Dividends per Share Growth (%)	—	—	—	—	—	−100.00	−25.00
Book Value per Share	5.39	5.73	5.06	4.39	4.90	7.25	12.85
Book Value per Share Growth (%)	−6.04	13.43	15.17	−10.50	−32.36	−43.56	5.58
Tangible Book Value per Share	1.33	1.87	1.10	0.40	0.08	−0.69	3.75
Tangible Book Value per Share Growth (%)	−29.15	70.71	172.60	399.48	—	−118.27	−27.53
Cash Flow per Share	1.02	0.31	1.24	1.20	1.34	1.35	1.58
Cash Flow per Share Growth (%)	225.88	−74.85	4.02	−11.06	−0.49	−14.54	25.90
Free Cash Flow per Share	0.70	0.03	0.86	0.86	1.08	1.05	0.81
Free Cash Flow per Share Growth (%)	1,930.94	−96.01	0.24	−21.05	3.74	29.27	177.74
Diluted Shares Outstanding	306.75	344.68	300.79	294.53	285.13	272.54	273.79
Basic Shares Outstanding	302.21	318.74	299.80	294.53	285.13	272.17	272.28
Dividend Yield (%)	1.22	0.00	0.00	0.00	0.00	0.00	3.89

Table C.16. SCI Income Statement Items, 1992–1998

Income Statement	Dec'98	Dec'97	Dec'96	Dec'95	Dec'94	Dec'93	Dec'92
Sales/Revenue	2,875.09	2,468.40	2,294.19	1,652.13	1,117.18	899.18	772.48
Sales/Revenue Growth (%)	*16.48*	*7.59*	*38.86*	*47.88*	*24.24*	*16.40*	*20.09*
Gross Income	718.77	687.61	604.45	465.22	341.20	263.32	222.06
Gross Income Growth (%)	*4.53*	*13.76*	*29.93*	*36.35*	*29.57*	*18.58*	*24.39*
Gross Margin (%)	*25.00*	*27.86*	*26.35*	*28.16*	*30.54*	*29.28*	*28.75*
EBIT	651.93	620.83	541.24	411.62	289.50	219.61	183.36
EBIT Growth (%)	*5.01*	*14.71*	*31.49*	*42.19*	*31.82*	*19.77*	*28.17*
EBIT Margin (%)	*22.68*	*25.15*	*23.59*	*24.91*	*25.91*	*24.42*	*23.74*
EBITDA	854.21	778.38	671.06	510.05	365.57	277.83	230.73
EBITDA Growth (%)	*9.74*	*15.99*	*31.57*	*39.52*	*31.58*	*20.41*	*29.59*
EBITDA Margin (%)	*29.71*	*31.53*	*29.25*	*30.87*	*32.72*	*30.90*	*29.87*
Net Income	342.14	378.93	276.08	194.37	131.58	103.09	86.54
Net Income Growth (%)	*−9.71*	*37.26*	*42.04*	*47.71*	*27.64*	*19.13*	*17.94*
Net Margin (%)	*11.90*	*15.35*	*12.03*	*11.76*	*11.78*	*11.47*	*11.20*

Table C.17. SCI Balance Sheet Items, 1992–1998

Balance Sheet	Dec'98	Dec'97	Dec'96	Dec'95	Dec'94	Dec'93	Dec'92
Cash & Short Term Investments	358.21	46.88	44.13	29.74	218.34	20.82	31.25
Cash & ST Investments Growth (%)	664.15	6.22	48.41	−86.38	948.61	−33.38	−18.66
Cash & ST Investments/Total Assets (%)	2.70	0.45	0.50	0.39	4.23	0.57	1.20
Total Assets	13,266.16	10,306.86	8,869.77	7,663.81	5,161.89	3,683.30	2,611.12
Total Assets Growth (%)	28.71	16.20	15.74	48.47	40.14	41.06	22.97
Asset Turnover (x)	0.24	0.26	0.28	0.26	0.25	0.29	0.33
Return on Assets (%)	2.90	3.95	3.34	3.03	2.98	3.28	3.66
Total Debt	3,860.66	2,729.25	2,210.93	1,854.28	1,607.89	1,087.20	990.63
Total Debt Growth (%)	41.46	23.44	19.23	15.32	47.89	9.75	23.75
Total Debt/Total Assets (%)	29.10	26.48	24.93	24.20	31.15	29.52	37.94
Total Debt/Total Equity (%)	122.40	100.12	91.82	86.33	117.44	122.92	145.02
Net Debt	3,502.45	2,682.37	2,166.79	1,824.55	1,389.55	1,066.38	959.38
Net Debt Growth (%)	30.57	23.79	18.76	31.31	30.30	11.15	25.89
Net Debt/Total Equity (%)	111.04	98.40	89.99	84.95	101.49	120.56	140.45
Total Liabilities	10,112.06	7,580.86	6,461.95	5,515.97	3,792.77	2,798.79	1,928.03
Total Liabilities Growth (%)	33.39	17.32	17.15	45.43	35.51	45.16	27.88
Total Shareholders' Equity	3,154.10	2,726.00	2,407.82	2,147.85	1,369.12	884.51	683.10
Total Shareholders' Equity/Total Assets (%)	23.78	26.45	27.15	28.03	26.52	24.01	26.16
Return on Equity (%)	11.64	14.76	12.12	11.05	11.68	13.15	13.32

Table C.18. SCI Cash Flow Items, 1992–1998

Cash Flow	Dec'98	Dec'97	Dec'96	Dec'95	Dec'94	Dec'93	Dec'92
Net Operating Cash Flow	329.65	299.44	209.86	90.70	162.44	130.95	145.52
Net Operating Cash Flow Growth (%)	*10.09*	*42.69*	*131.36*	*−44.16*	*24.05*	*−10.01*	*164.34*
Cash Flow Return on Invested Capital (%)	*5.37*	*6.10*	*5.03*	*2.76*	*6.99*	*7.26*	*9.49*
Capital Expenditures	−253.22	−230.53	−193.15	−125.23	−81.09	−59.59	−66.82
Capital Expenditures Growth (%)	*9.84*	*19.35*	*54.24*	*54.43*	*36.09*	*−10.83*	*73.61*
Net Investing Cash Flow	−1,059.88	−633.44	−480.13	−844.34	−352.46	−274.38	−182.77
Net Investing Cash Flow Growth (%)	*−67.32*	*−31.93*	*43.14*	*−139.56*	*−28.46*	*−50.12*	*−12.96*
Net Financing Cash Flow	1,041.56	336.75	256.92	565.03	387.53	132.99	30.08
Net Financing Cash Flow Growth (%)	*209.29*	*31.08*	*−54.53*	*45.80*	*191.40*	*342.18*	*−76.39*
Free Cash Flow	76.42	68.90	16.71	−34.53	81.35	71.37	78.70
Free Cash Flow Growth (%)	*10.91*	*312.48*	—	*−142.44*	*13.99*	*−9.32*	*375.18*
Free Cash Flow Yield (%)	*0.76*	*0.73*	—	—	—	—	—

Table C.19. SCI Ratios and Supplementals, 1992–1998

Ratios (x)	Dec'98	Dec'97	Dec'96	Dec'95	Dec'94	Dec'93	Dec'92
Price/Earnings	29.06	25.00	25.45	24.44	18.38	21.17	16.15
Price/Sales	3.48	3.84	2.94	2.72	2.16	2.43	1.82
Price/Book Value	3.13	3.41	2.96	2.61	2.20	2.52	2.05
Price/Tangible Book Value	7.36	7.57	7.70	6.27	6.82	4.88	5.14
Price/Cash Flow	30.31	31.64	—	—	—	—	—
Price/Free Cash Flow	130.75	137.49	—	—	—	—	—
Enterprise Value/EBIT	20.51	19.29	16.54	17.39	14.49	15.00	12.89
Enterprise Value/EBITDA	15.65	15.39	13.34	14.03	11.47	11.86	10.24
Enterprise Value/Sales	4.65	4.85	3.90	4.33	3.75	3.66	3.06
EBIT/Interest Expense (Int. Coverage)	3.68	4.54	3.91	3.48	3.61	3.68	3.37
Pension							
Pension Funded Status	—	—	—	—	—	—	—
Pension Expense	—	—	—	—	—	—	—
Supplemental							
Stock Option Comp Exp (Net of Tax)	—	—	—	—	—	—	—
Operating Lease Commitments	226.37	262.89	286.41	228.66	163.34	114.49	101.51
Long Term Debt Maturities	96.07	64.57	113.88	122.24	277.71	24.98	10.60

Table C.20. SCI Per Share Data, 1992–1998

Per Share	Dec'98	Dec'97	Dec'96	Dec'95	Dec'94	Dec'93	Dec'92
EPS (recurring)	1.31	1.47	—	—	—	—	—
EPS (recurring) Growth (%)	−11.04	—	—	—	—	—	—
EPS (diluted)	1.31	1.47	—	—	—	—	—
EPS (diluted) Growth (%)	−11.04	—	—	—	—	—	—
EPS (basic)	—	—	—	—	—	—	—
EPS (basic) Growth (%)	—	—	—	—	—	—	—
Sales per Share	10.95	9.58	9.51	8.09	6.43	5.39	5.03
Sales per Share Growth (%)	14.37	0.66	17.54	25.94	19.16	7.30	11.60
Dividends per Share	0.36	0.30	0.24	0.22	0.21	0.20	0.20
Dividends per Share Growth (%)	20.00	25.00	9.09	4.76	3.70	2.96	5.36
Book Value per Share	12.17	10.78	9.46	8.42	6.31	5.21	4.44
Book Value per Share Growth (%)	12.90	13.88	12.37	33.53	21.03	17.35	9.60
Tangible Book Value per Share	5.17	4.85	3.64	3.51	2.03	2.69	1.77
Tangible Book Value per Share Growth (%)	6.56	33.54	3.59	72.55	−24.43	51.74	−7.71
Cash Flow per Share	1.26	1.16	—	—	—	—	—
Cash Flow per Share Growth (%)	8.10	—	—	—	—	—	—
Free Cash Flow per Share	0.29	0.27	—	—	—	—	—
Free Cash Flow per Share Growth (%)	8.91	—	—	—	—	—	—
Diluted Shares Outstanding	262.52	257.78	—	—	—	—	—
Basic Shares Outstanding	256.27	245.47	—	—	—	—	—
Dividend Yield (%)	0.95	0.82	0.86	1.00	1.51	1.54	2.16

Table C.21. SCI Income Statement Items, 1985–1991

Income Statement	Dec'91	Dec'90	Dec'89	Dec'88	Apr'87	Apr'86	Apr'85
Sales/Revenue	643.25	563.16	518.81	692.82	386.63	263.95	234.17
Sales/Revenue Growth (%)	14.22	8.55	−25.12	—	46.48	12.72	9.13
Gross Income	178.51	149.92	132.78	94.62	105.77	80.12	67.00
Gross Income Growth (%)	19.07	12.91	40.33	—	32.01	19.58	10.51
Gross Margin (%)	27.75	26.62	25.59	13.66	27.36	30.36	28.61
EBIT	143.06	121.88	104.35	65.33	90.88	50.48	45.37
EBIT Growth (%)	17.37	16.80	59.74	—	80.03	11.26	18.31
EBIT Margin (%)	22.24	21.64	20.11	9.43	23.51	19.13	19.38
EBITDA	178.05	149.07	128.59	96.46	107.94	62.21	55.50
EBITDA Growth (%)	19.44	15.92	33.31	—	73.50	12.10	16.54
EBITDA Margin (%)	27.68	26.47	24.79	13.92	27.92	23.57	23.70
Net Income	73.37	63.53	53.62	27.12	51.60	40.95	34.94
Net Income Growth (%)	15.49	18.49	97.71	—	26.01	17.22	20.50
Net Margin (%)	11.41	11.28	10.33	3.91	13.35	15.51	14.92

Table C.22. SCI Balance Sheet Items, 1985-1991

Balance Sheet	Dec'91	Dec'90	Dec'89	Dec'88	Apr'87	Apr'86	Apr'85
Cash & Short Term Investments	38.42	17.79	36.93	38.14	39.90	128.59	43.63
Cash & ST Investments Growth (%)	116.00	-51.83	-3.17	—	-68.97	194.76	-19.24
Cash & ST Investments/Total Assets (%)	1.81	1.08	2.31	2.04	4.63	22.66	10.91
Total Assets	2,123.45	1,653.69	1,601.47	1,871.82	862.40	567.38	400.03
Total Assets Growth (%)	28.41	3.26	-14.44	—	52.00	41.84	19.47
Asset Turnover (x)	0.34	0.35	0.30	0.51	0.54	0.55	0.64
Return on Assets (%)	3.89	3.90	3.09	1.98	7.22	8.47	9.51
Total Debt	800.51	584.58	494.35	465.95	234.43	171.60	63.96
Total Debt Growth (%)	36.94	18.25	6.09	—	36.62	168.28	-4.22
Total Debt/Total Assets (%)	37.70	35.35	30.87	24.89	27.18	30.24	15.99
Total Debt/Total Equity (%)	130.00	134.60	88.63	90.23	48.99	57.39	25.03
Net Debt	762.09	566.80	457.42	427.81	194.53	43.01	20.34
Net Debt Growth (%)	34.46	23.91	6.92	—	352.34	111.46	59.36
Net Debt/Total Equity (%)	123.76	130.50	82.01	82.84	40.65	14.38	7.96
Total Liabilities	1,507.68	1,219.37	1,043.69	1,355.40	383.82	268.37	144.52
Total Liabilities Growth (%)	23.64	16.83	-23.00	—	43.02	85.69	17.00
Total Shareholders' Equity	615.78	434.32	557.78	516.42	478.58	299.02	255.51
Total Shareholders' Equity/Total Assets (%)	29.00	26.26	34.83	27.59	55.49	52.70	63.87
Return on Equity (%)	13.97	12.81	9.98	5.45	13.27	14.77	14.97

Table C.23. SCI Cash Flow Items, 1985–1991

Cash Flow	Dec'91	Dec'90	Dec'89	Dec'88	Apr'87	Apr'86	Apr'85
Net Operating Cash Flow	55.05	90.62	100.89	63.18	100.15	—	—
Net Operating Cash Flow Growth (%)	*−39.25*	*−10.19*	*59.70*	—	—	—	—
Cash Flow Return on Invested Capital (%)	*4.56*	*8.82*	*10.02*	*7.55*	*17.17*	—	—
Capital Expenditures	−38.49	−30.26	−26.15	−32.06	−71.69	−35.59	−16.23
Capital Expenditures Growth (%)	*27.19*	*15.72*	*−18.44*	—	*101.42*	*119.29*	*−20.91*
Net Investing Cash Flow	−161.80	113.11	−112.83	−113.17	−61.06	−32.52	−13.08
Net Investing Cash Flow Growth (%)	*−243.05*	—	*0.29*	—	*−87.77*	*−148.60*	*25.65*
Net Financing Cash Flow	127.39	−222.86	13.56	85.58	−15.15	92.90	−11.05
Net Financing Cash Flow Growth (%)	—	*−1,743.89*	*−84.16*	—	*−116.30*	—	*−11.45*
Free Cash Flow	16.56	60.35	74.74	31.11	65.96	—	—
Free Cash Flow Growth (%)	*−72.56*	*−19.25*	*140.23*	—	—	—	—
Free Cash Flow Yield (%)	—	—	—	—	—	—	—

Table C.24. SCI Ratios and Supplementals, 1985–1991

Ratios (x)	Dec'91	Dec'90	Dec'89	Dec'88	Apr'87	Apr'86	Apr'85
Price/Earnings	17.53	17.58	15.17	38.05	22.63	19.60	15.15
Price/Sales	2.00	1.89	1.45	1.21	3.03	3.05	2.26
Price/Book Value	2.22	2.38	1.36	1.63	2.60	2.73	2.11
Price/Tangible Book Value	4.68	3.25	1.64	2.30	2.60	2.96	2.11
Price/Cash Flow	—	—	—	—	—	—	—
Price/Free Cash Flow	—	—	—	—	—	—	—
Enterprise Value/EBIT	14.89	13.12	11.63	19.47	15.82	17.00	12.30
Enterprise Value/EBITDA	11.96	10.73	9.44	13.18	13.32	13.79	10.06
Enterprise Value/Sales	3.31	2.84	2.34	1.84	3.72	3.25	2.38
EBIT/Interest Expense (Int. Coverage)	3.32	3.33	3.17	1.91	6.03	7.71	7.59
Pension							
Pension Funded Status	—	—	—	—	—	—	—
Pension Expense	—	—	—	—	—	—	—
Supplemental							
Stock Option Comp Exp (Net of Tax)	—	—	—	—	—	—	—
Operating Lease Commitments	100.60	45.99	46.00	56.67	—	—	—
Long Term Debt Maturities	13.83	7.21	8.68	11.01	—	—	—

Table C.25. SCI Per Share Data, 1985–1991

Per Share	Dec'91	Dec'90	Dec'89	Dec'88	Apr'87	Apr'86	Apr'85
EPS (recurring)	—	—	—	—	—	—	—
EPS (recurring) Growth (%)	—	—	—	—	—	—	—
EPS (diluted)	—	—	—	—	—	—	—
EPS (diluted) Growth (%)	—	—	—	—	—	—	—
EPS (basic)	—	—	—	—	—	—	—
EPS (basic) Growth (%)	—	—	—	—	—	—	—
Sales per Share	4.50	3.98	3.58	4.80	3.01	2.31	2.13
Sales per Share Growth (%)	13.19	11.09	−25.41	—	30.20	8.41	8.05
Dividends per Share	0.19	0.18	0.14	0.15	0.10	0.09	0.07
Dividends per Share Growth (%)	3.71	28.57	−8.69	—	10.00	30.43	21.05
Book Value per Share	4.05	3.16	3.84	3.57	3.51	2.59	2.29
Book Value per Share Growth (%)	28.38	−17.85	7.64	—	35.72	13.18	16.38
Tangible Book Value per Share	1.92	2.31	3.18	2.53	3.51	2.39	2.29
Tangible Book Value per Share Growth (%)	−16.64	−27.43	25.44	—	47.27	4.30	16.38
Cash Flow per Share	—	—	—	—	—	—	—
Cash Flow per Share Growth (%)	—	—	—	—	—	—	—
Free Cash Flow per Share	—	—	—	—	—	—	—
Free Cash Flow per Share Growth (%)	—	—	—	—	—	—	—
Diluted Shares Outstanding	—	—	—	—	—	—	—
Basic Shares Outstanding	—	—	—	—	—	—	—
Dividend Yield (%)	2.07	2.40	2.69	2.63	1.07	1.26	1.42

Appendix C: Company Data 579

Table C.26. SCI Income Statement Items, 1980–1984

Income Statement	Apr'84	Apr'83	Apr'82	Apr'81	Apr'80
Sales/Revenue	214.58	208.54	161.73	134.76	115.01
Sales/Revenue Growth (%)	*2.90*	*28.94*	*20.01*	*17.17*	—
Gross Income	60.63	53.30	41.81	35.32	30.12
Gross Income Growth (%)	*13.75*	*27.47*	*18.39*	*17.28*	—
Gross Margin (%)	*28.25*	*25.56*	*25.85*	*26.21*	*26.19*
EBIT	38.35	33.24	24.77	21.54	19.01
EBIT Growth (%)	*15.36*	*34.20*	*15.00*	*13.33*	—
EBIT Margin (%)	*17.87*	*15.94*	*15.32*	*15.98*	*16.53*
EBITDA	47.62	41.60	30.85	26.42	24.20
EBITDA Growth (%)	*14.47*	*34.86*	*16.77*	*9.17*	—
EBITDA Margin (%)	*22.19*	*19.95*	*19.07*	*19.60*	*21.04*
Net Income	28.99	20.53	13.61	9.30	7.40
Net Income Growth (%)	*41.23*	*50.87*	*46.27*	*25.63*	—
Net Margin (%)	*13.51*	*9.84*	*8.41*	*6.90*	*6.44*

Table C.27. SCI Balance Sheet Items, 1980–1984

Balance Sheet	Apr'84	Apr'83	Apr'82	Apr'81	Apr'80
Cash & Short Term Investments	54.02	46.15	13.80	7.00	8.66
Cash & ST Investments Growth (%)	*17.04*	*234.38*	*97.13*	*−19.14*	—
Cash & ST Investments/Total Assets (%)	*16.13*	*14.89*	*5.26*	*4.12*	*5.35*
Total Assets	334.84	310.00	262.54	169.79	161.86
Total Assets Growth (%)	*8.01*	*18.08*	*54.63*	*4.90*	—
Asset Turnover (x)	*0.67*	*0.73*	*0.75*	*0.81*	—
Return on Assets (%)	*8.99*	*7.17*	*6.29*	*5.61*	—
Total Debt	66.78	70.22	95.42	73.62	73.19
Total Debt Growth (%)	*−4.89*	*−26.41*	*29.62*	*0.58*	—
Total Debt/Total Assets (%)	*19.94*	*22.65*	*36.35*	*43.36*	*45.22*
Total Debt/Total Equity (%)	*31.60*	*37.60*	*79.15*	*106.38*	*116.52*
Net Debt	12.76	24.06	81.62	66.62	64.54
Net Debt Growth (%)	*−46.96*	*−70.52*	*22.52*	*3.22*	—
Net Debt/Total Equity (%)	*6.04*	*12.88*	*67.70*	*96.26*	*102.74*
Total Liabilities	123.52	123.23	141.98	100.59	99.05
Total Liabilities Growth (%)	*0.24*	*−13.20*	*41.15*	*1.56*	—
Total Shareholders' Equity	211.32	186.76	120.56	69.20	62.82
Total Shareholders' Equity/Total Assets (%)	*63.11*	*60.25*	*45.92*	*40.76*	*38.81*
Return on Equity (%)	*14.57*	*13.36*	*14.34*	*14.09*	—

Table C.28. SCI Cash Flow Items, 1980–1984

Cash Flow	Apr'84	Apr'83	Apr'82	Apr'81	Apr'80
Net Operating Cash Flow	—	—	—	—	—
Net Operating Cash Flow Growth (%)	—	—	—	—	—
Cash Flow Return on Invested Capital (%)	—	—	—	—	—
Capital Expenditures	−20.52	−18.36	−43.20	−12.15	−7.20
Capital Expenditures Growth (%)	11.76	−57.50	255.71	68.59	—
Net Investing Cash Flow	−17.59	−16.30	−38.54	−9.98	−6.23
Net Investing Cash Flow Growth (%)	−7.95	57.71	−286.17	−60.32	—
Net Financing Cash Flow	−9.91	20.48	30.33	−8.44	−6.35
Net Financing Cash Flow Growth (%)	−148.40	−32.46	—	−32.96	—
Free Cash Flow	—	—	—	—	—
Free Cash Flow Growth (%)	—	—	—	—	—
Free Cash Flow Yield (%)	—	—	—	—	—

Table C.29. SCI Ratios and Supplementals, 1980–1984

Ratios (x)	Apr'84	Apr'83	Apr'82	Apr'81	Apr'80
Price/Earnings	13.19	20.16	8.06	9.28	3.67
Price/Sales	1.78	1.99	0.68	0.64	0.24
Price/Book Value	1.79	2.46	1.12	1.11	0.43
Price/Tangible Book Value	1.79	2.46	1.12	1.11	0.43
Price/Cash Flow	—	—	—	—	—
Price/Free Cash Flow	—	—	—	—	—
Enterprise Value/EBIT	10.20	14.55	8.74	6.66	4.83
Enterprise Value/EBITDA	8.21	11.63	7.02	5.43	3.79
Enterprise Value/Sales	1.82	2.32	1.34	1.06	0.80
EBIT/Interest Expense (Int. Coverage)	6.18	4.18	2.84	3.03	2.89
Pension					
Pension Funded Status	—	—	—	—	—
Pension Expense	—	—	—	—	—
Supplemental					
Stock Option Comp Exp (Net of Tax)	—	—	—	—	—
Operating Lease Commitments	—	—	—	—	—
Long Term Debt Maturities	—	—	—	—	—

Table C.30. SCI Per Share Data, 1980–1984

Per Share	Apr'84	Apr'83	Apr'82	Apr'81	Apr'80
EPS (recurring)	—	—	—	—	—
EPS (recurring) Growth (%)	—	—	—	—	—
EPS (diluted)	—	—	—	—	—
EPS (diluted) Growth (%)	—	—	—	—	—
EPS (basic)	—	—	—	—	—
EPS (basic) Growth (%)	—	—	—	—	—
Sales per Share	1.97	2.17	2.18	2.04	1.59
Sales per Share Growth (%)	*−9.19*	*−0.29*	*6.89*	*28.17*	—
Dividends per Share	0.06	0.05	0.03	0.03	0.02
Dividends per Share Growth (%)	*23.93*	*30.17*	*28.50*	*32.55*	—
Book Value per Share	1.97	1.76	1.32	1.18	0.87
Book Value per Share Growth (%)	*11.92*	*32.58*	*12.30*	*35.79*	—
Tangible Book Value per Share	1.97	1.76	1.32	1.18	0.87
Tangible Book Value per Share Growth (%)	*11.92*	*32.58*	*12.30*	*35.79*	—
Cash Flow per Share	—	—	—	—	—
Cash Flow per Share Growth (%)	—	—	—	—	—
Free Cash Flow per Share	—	—	—	—	—
Free Cash Flow per Share Growth (%)	—	—	—	—	—
Diluted Shares Outstanding	—	—	—	—	—
Basic Shares Outstanding	—	—	—	—	72.23
Dividend Yield (%)	1.60	1.05	2.36	2.08	5.44

Appendix D

Selected Snapshot Data

A wise man changes his mind, a fool never.

Spanish proverb

Selected Snapshot Data

For convenience and historical purposes, this appendix provides snapshot constituent data as of one week after the inauguration of President Donald J. Trump. The Dow Jones Industrial Average (DJIA) stood at 20,093, the Standard & Poor's (S&P) 500 was at 2,294, the NASDAQ index was 5,660, Berkshire Hathaway traded at $247,000 per share, and the VIX was 11.27. The 30-year, 10-year, and 5-year US Treasury bonds were returning yields of 3.06, 2.48, and 1.94 percent, respectively; the 13-week Treasury bill yielded 49.8 basis points (bps), and the Switzerland 10-year bond had a yield of negative 6.66 bps.

The DJIA broke 1,000 in 1981, and surpassed the 10,000 level on March 29, 1999. When the latter occurred, "Dow 20,000" became a rallying cry to fuel the continued exuberance in the dot.com expansion. On May 7, 1999, Salomon Smith Barney Senior Vice President Alan R. Shaw stated their analysis showed "The Dow industrials could reach 20,000 by 2003." Another fund manager in April of that year predicted the industrials would broach 20,000 in the next five years. He said that the surge won't "be in a straight line, on balance the market will remain very strong" through at least

2004. The DJIA peaked at 11,287 and began its 2½-year crash and 10-year depression one year after that beginning March 2000. Since then, we experienced the 25 percent decline to 7,524 (post dot.com high) and the run-up to the Global Financial Crisis (GFC) to 14,093, subsequent crash to 6,594, and recovery to this post-inaugural level. We note that the time it took the DJIA to recover its year prior all-time high was 10 years and 6 months.

The market capitalization of the Dow Jones Industrials when that index surpassed 10,000 was $2.65 trillion, and at the 20,000 level it has increased to $5.74 trillion. Nominally, this is a 116 percent increase; in real terms, the market capitalization actually increased from $2.65 to $3.81 trillion, or 45 percent. Approximately half of the constituents in this index have changed in this period, with 13 old stocks leaving and new stocks entering. Of the remaining 17 stocks which have continuously traded, it is constructive to note how their performance has fared. Figure D.1 depicts the change in

Surviving DJIA Companies - Market Capitalization ($000's) and % Share

Company Symbol and Name		1999	2017	
MMM	Minnesota Mining & Mfg Company	28,678,108	105,906,930	0.71
CVX	Chevron Corp	58,475,294	214,809,235	0.70
CAT	Caterpillar Inc	16,948,008	57,916,376	0.58
UTX	United Technologies Corp	30,267,259	90,327,638	0.38
BA	Boeing Company	34,719,907	103,498,738	0.38
DIS	Walt Disney Company	67,969,623	173,112,728	0.18
JNJ	Johnson & Johnson	126,314,844	308,453,918	0.13
XOM	Exxon Mobil Corp	177,479,717	354,583,718	-0.08
PG	Procter & Gamble Company	134,268,618	232,062,113	-0.20
MCD	McDonald's Corp	61,566,869	102,028,350	-0.23
AXP	American Express Company	55,809,018	70,337,347	-0.42
KO	Coca Cola Company	159,769,488	178,772,151	-0.48
DD	E.I. Du Pont De Nemours and Company	64,455,542	67,547,873	-0.52
IBM	International Business Machines	162,916,958	168,586,592	-0.52
WMT	Wal-Mart Stores	211,228,035	201,785,655	-0.56
MRK	Merck & Company	194,738,801	170,253,272	-0.60
GE	General Electric Company	367,005,520	265,480,164	-0.67

Figure D.1. Change in Percent of Share of Total Market Capitalization between 3/29/1999 and 1/27/2017 for Surviving DJIA Companies

percent of share of total market capitalization between 3/29/1999 and 1/27/2017 for these surviving companies. We note that the majority of surviving companies are declining in relative market share of capitalization; this is in favor of the new entrants, who include AAPL, CSCO, HD, INTC, GS, etc.

The 20 most popular stocks as of February 2017 (compiled from a variety of sources) may be listed as in Table D.1. A more quantitatively derived list made from the 100 highest volume stocks on various U.S. exchanges is presented in Table D.2. The S&P 100 constituents are presented in Table D.3, and various commodity prices are found in Table D.4.

Table D.1. The Most Popular U.S. Stocks, February 2017

Symbol	Company Name	Price	MktCap ($B)	Avg. Volume
ACN	Accenture pic	115.35	71.55	2,515,200
BABA	Alibaba Group Holding Limited	102.07	255.175	12,837,400
GOOG	Alphabet Inc.	823.31	576.44	1,761,510
AMZN	Amazon.com, Inc.	835.77	397.13	4,253,000
AAPL	Apple Inc.	121.95	641.19	30,287,900
BIDU	Baidu, Inc.	174.1	60.4	2,113,050
CMG	Chipotle Mexican Grill, Inc.	416.6	12.06	1,128,320
FB	Facebook, Inc.	132.18	380.97	23,115,200
GE	General Electric Company	30.01	265.48	33,224,600
GWPH	GW Pharmaceuticals pic	115.75	2.92	476,677
IBM	International Business Machines Cc	177.3	168.59	3,766,130
MSFT	Microsoft Corporation	65.78	511.46	26,170,900
PSO	Pearson pic	7.6	6.287	528,076
SHLD	Sears Holdings Corporation	7.42	794.16M	1,264,990
SIRI	Sirius XM Holdings Inc.	4.75	22.92	32,337,300
GLD	SPDR Gold Shares	113.49	31.15	9,015,320
SFM	Sprouts Farmers Market, Inc.	18.72	2.66	2,697,650
TSLA	Tesla Motors, Inc.	252.95	40.69	4,654,480
PCLN	The Priceline Group Inc.	1602.92	79.1	450,056
TWTR	Twitter, Inc.	16.57	11.755	16,826,900

Table D.2. U.S. Exchanges, Top Trading Stocks, February 2017

Symbol	Company Name	Price	6-Month Avg. Daily Volume	Shares Oustanding (MM)
ABT	Abbott Laboratories	41	9,121,247	1,721
ATVI	Activision Blizzard, Inc.	39.61	8,521,688	743
AMD	Advanced Micro Devices, Inc.	10.67	43,282,516	927
AKS	AK Steel Holding Corporation	8.07	18,485,826	314
AAPL	Apple Inc.	121.95	33,290,375	5,258
AMAT	Applied Materials, Inc.	35.04	11,512,409	1,077
ARIA	ARIAD Pharmaceuticals, Inc.	23.68	8,540,968	194
T	AT&T Inc.	42.01	22,606,970	6,141
BAC	Bank of America Corporation	23.36	100,765,260	10,124
ABX	Barrick Gold Corporation	17.79	17,408,539	1,165
BSX	Boston Scientific Corporation	23.87	8,278,875	1,362
BMY	Bristol-Myers Squibb Company	47.74	13,375,521	1,671
SCHW	Charles Schwab Corporation	42.31	8,324,027	1,326
CHK	Chesapeake Energy Corporation	6.92	51,105,965	887
CSCO	Cisco Systems, Inc.	30.98	21,817,911	5,020
C	Citigroup Inc	57.11	19,649,656	2,850
CLF	Cliffs Natural Resources Inc.	9.02	12,752,815	231
KO	Coca-Cola Company	41.45	12,770,326	4,313
CMCSA	Comcast Corporation Class A	75.95	9,670,226	2,383
GLW	Corning Inc	26.68	8,952,083	951
COTY	Coty Inc. Class A	19.5	9,190,734	746
CSX	CSX Corporation	48.06	9,186,894	937
DAL	Delta Air Lines, Inc.	49.7	9,254,461	749
DNR	Denbury Resources Inc.	3.68	10,384,875	398
DB	Deutsche Bank AG	20.46	8,133,729	1,379
EBAY	eBay Inc.	32.51	10,337,874	1,118
ECA	Encana Corporation	13	14,639,154	973
ESV	Ensco plc	11.37	9,608,105	303
XOM	Exxon Mobil Corporation	85.51	11,091,274	4,147
FB	Facebook, Inc. Class A	132.18	20,514,023	2,341
FCAU	Fiat Chrysler Automobiles N.V.	11.08	9,283,856	1,528
FIT	Fitbit, Inc. Class A	7.21	10,337,348	170
F	Ford Motor Company	12.49	35,988,663	3,903
FCX	Freeport-McMoRan, Inc.	16.37	30,808,365	1,362
FTR	Frontier Communications Corporation	3.54	21,359,150	1,173

(*Continued*)

Table D.2. (*Continued*)

Symbol	Company Name	Price	6-Month Avg. Daily Volume	Shares Oustanding (MM)
GE	General Electric Company	30.01	31,543,493	8,846
GM	General Motors Company	37.01	13,607,336	1,512
GNW	Genworth Financial, Inc. Class A	3.43	9,079,497	498
GILD	Gilead Sciences, Inc.	71.26	9,884,996	1,317
GG	Goldcorp Inc.	15.76	8,750,855	853
GRPN	Groupon, Inc.	3.45	11,512,678	571
HAL	Halliburton Company	58.21	8,146,881	864
HL	Hecla Mining Company	6.34	11,650,765	395
HPE	Hewlett Packard Enterprise Co.	22.55	10,638,074	1,665
HST	Host Hotels & Resorts, Inc.	18.59	9,979,522	740
HPQ	HP Inc.	14.8	12,173,165	1,705
HBAN	Huntington Bancshares Incorporated	13.78	13,953,379	1,086
IAG	IAMGOLD Corporation	4.47	11,124,170	451
INTC	Intel Corporation	37.98	20,751,907	4,739
JCP	J. C. Penney Company, Inc.	6.45	17,399,746	308
JPM	JPMorgan Chase & Co.	86.93	15,895,693	3,578
KEY	KeyCorp	18.3	16,002,644	1,079
KMI	Kinder Morgan Inc Class P	22.38	14,612,791	2,232
KGC	Kinross Gold Corporation	3.61	15,729,898	1,245
KR	Kroger Co.	33.36	9,912,118	938
LC	LendingClub Corp	6.14	8,233,458	394
MRO	Marathon Oil Corporation	17.41	15,875,474	847
MRK	Merck & Co., Inc.	61.75	10,964,904	2,757
MU	Micron Technology, Inc.	23.97	25,454,237	1,103
MSFT	Microsoft Corporation	65.78	25,573,145	7,775
MDLZ	Mondelez International, Inc. Class A	44.2	7,950,950	1,544
MS	Morgan Stanley	43.65	11,814,900	1,852
NFLX	Netflix, Inc.	142.45	8,547,234	429
NKE	NIKE, Inc. Class B	53.19	9,094,339	1,325
NE	Noble Corporation plc	7.2	11,239,886	243
NVAX	Novavax, Inc.	1.33	12,875,970	271
NVDA	NVIDIA Corporation	111.77	13,474,419	539
OAS	Oasis Petroleum Inc.	14.89	11,900,101	236
ORCL	Oracle Corporation	40.23	12,276,876	4,106
PFE	Pfizer Inc.	31.42	23,732,515	6,068

(*Continued*)

Table D.2. (*Continued*)

Symbol	Company Name	Price	6-Month Avg. Daily Volume	Shares Oustanding (MM)
PG	Procter & Gamble Company	86.72	15,515,087	2,676
QCOM	QUALCOMM Incorporated	54.24	10,502,522	1,478
RF	Regions Financial Corporation	14.54	19,494,180	1,215
RAD	Rite Aid Corporation	6.93	18,283,380	1,052
SDRL	Seadrill Ltd.	2.86	9,439,352	504
SIRI	Sirius XM Holdings, Inc.	4.75	41,326,530	4,825
SWN	Southwestern Energy Company	9.42	14,083,878	495
S	Sprint Corp.	9.22	19,368,082	3,981
SBUX	Starbucks Corporation	56.12	8,632,578	1,455
SYMC	Symantec Corporation	27.35	8,420,294	623
FTI	TechnipFMC Plc	35.3	11,445,579	467
RIG	Transocean Ltd.	14.9	14,580,376	389
FOXA	Twenty-First Century Fox, Inc. Class A	31.29	10,991,199	1,057
TWTR	Twitter, Inc.	16.57	26,678,934	715
X	United States Steel Corporation	33.77	17,818,687	172
VRX	Valeant Pharmaceuticals International	13.47	20,146,978	341
VER	VEREIT, Inc. Class A	8.41	7,840,680	974
VZ	Verizon Communications Inc.	49.6	14,045,129	4,077
V	Visa Inc. Class A	83.77	9,033,784	1,855
WMT	Wal-Mart Stores, Inc.	65.66	8,700,682	3,073
DIS	Walt Disney Company	109.3	7,850,292	1,584
WFT	Weatherford International plc	5.26	23,845,406	981
WFC	Wells Fargo & Company	56.59	26,008,020	5,016
WLL	Whiting Petroleum Corporation	11.5	22,256,302	284
WMB	Williams Companies, Inc.	28.5	9,216,190	816
WPX	WPX Energy, Inc. Class A	14.28	8,684,644	396
XRX	Xerox Corporation	6.98	9,692,368	1,014
YHOO	Yahoo! Inc.	44.42	10,330,336	954
AUY	Yamana Gold Inc.	3.19	17,200,329	1,007
ZNGA	Zynga Inc. Class A	2.57	11,394,686	775

Table D.3. S&P 100 Constituents (January 27, 2017)

Symbol	Company Name	Price	Volume
AAPL	Apple Inc	121.95	20,562,900
ABBV	Abbvie Inc Common Stock	60	14,151,200
ABT	Abbott Laboratories	41	7,033,600
ACN	Accenture Plc	115.35	2,545,100
AGN	Allergan Plc	213.2	2,397,500
AIG	American International Group	65.21	5,612,800
ALL	Allstate Corp	75.59	1,275,400
AMGN	Amgen	157.16	4,885,100
AMZN	Amazon.Com Inc	835.77	2,998,700
AXP	American Express Company	76.85	3,530,900
BA	Boeing Company	167.7	4,883,200
BAC	Bank of America Corp	23.36	54,590,102
BIIB	Biogen Inc Cmn	278.21	1,353,300
BK	Bank of New York Mellon Corp	44.78	5,863,700
BLK	Blackrock	375.06	686,800
BMY	Bristol-Myers Squibb Company	47.74	22,918,600
BRK.B	Berkshire Hath Hld B	164.4	2,520,300
C	Citigroup Inc	57.11	17,074,201
CAT	Caterpillar Inc	98.99	6,371,400
CELG	Celgene Corp	113.62	4,069,800
CL	Colgate-Palmolive Company	64.68	14,874,801
CMCSA	Comcast Corp A	75.95	11,663,300
COF	Capital One Financial Corp	89.15	2,195,100
COP	Conocophillips	49.43	5,408,000
COST	Costco Wholesale	162.06	2,341,100
CSCO	Cisco Systems Inc	30.98	18,461,900
CVS	CVS Corp	77.75	10,924,300
CVX	Chevron Corp	113.79	11,698,801
DD	E.I. Du Pont De Nemours and Company	77.7	2,109,100
DHR	Danaher Corp	80.96	2,277,200
DIS	Walt Disney Company	109.3	5,578,200
DOW	Dow Chemical Company	61.31	5,262,000
DUK	Duke Energy Corp	76.94	2,562,000
EMR	Emerson Electric Company	60.14	3,260,600
EXC	Exelon Corp	35.08	3,247,200

(*Continued*)

Table D.3. (*Continued*)

Symbol	Company Name	Price	Volume
F	Ford Motor Company	12.49	34,613,801
FB	Facebook Inc	132.18	19,539,500
FDX	Fedex Corp	195.92	1,991,300
FOX	21St Centry Fox Class B	30.85	1,815,000
FOXA	21St Centry Fox Class A	31.29	8,259,200
GD	General Dynamics Corp	185.14	4,340,100
GE	General Electric Company	30.01	30,005,602
GILD	Gilead Sciences Inc	71.26	6,939,700
GM	General Motors Company	37.01	10,228,601
GOOG	Alphabet Class C	823.31	2,965,700
GOOGL	Alphabet Class A	845.03	3,752,400
GS	Goldman Sachs Group	236.95	3,253,100
HAL	Halliburton Company	58.21	6,892,900
HD	Home Depot	138.33	3,149,400
HON	Honeywell International Inc	118.42	3,873,800
IBM	International Business Machines	177.3	3,482,300
INTC	Intel Corp	37.98	44,368,500
JNJ	Johnson & Johnson	113.38	8,886,000
JPM	JP Morgan Chase & Co	86.93	12,535,399
KHC	Kraft Heinz Co Cmn	89.43	1,842,900
KMI	Kinder Morgan	22.38	10,606,899
KO	Coca-Cola Company	41.45	12,967,300
LLY	Eli Lilly and Company	75.38	3,132,700
LMT	Lockheed Martin Corp	253.5	2,597,700
LOW	Lowe's Companies	73.25	4,183,600
MA	Mastercard Inc	109.84	2,591,500
MCD	McDonald's Corp	122.86	3,592,600
MDLZ	Mondelez Intl Cmn A	44.2	9,441,400
MDT	Medtronic Inc	74.95	4,903,000
MET	Metlife Inc	55.61	5,007,400
MMM	3M Company	177.48	1,623,600
MO	Altria Group	71.03	5,915,700
MON	Monsanto Company	109.4	1,747,200

(*Continued*)

Appendix D: Selected Snapshot Data 591

Table D.3. (*Continued*)

Symbol	Company Name	Price	Volume
MRK	Merck & Company	61.75	6,653,200
MS	Morgan Stanley	43.65	7,635,500
MSFT	Microsoft Corp	65.78	44,817,898
NEE	Nextera Energy	121.37	3,135,100
NKE	Nike Inc	53.19	7,362,000
ORCL	Oracle Corp	40.23	9,232,601
OXY	Occidental Petroleum Corp	68.95	3,836,400
PCLN	Priceline Group	1602.92	428,500
PEP	Pepsico Inc	103.48	4,248,200
PFE	Pfizer Inc	31.42	24,054,699
PG	Procter & Gamble Company	86.72	9,332,300
PM	Philip Morris International Inc	96.32	3,055,300
PYPL	Paypal Holdings	40.27	22,749,100
QCOM	Qualcomm Inc	54.24	23,474,299
RTN	Raytheon Company	145.88	3,698,700
SBUX	Starbucks Corp	56.12	28,884,900
SLB	Schlumberger N.V.	84.5	4,758,100
SO	Southern Company	48.48	4,255,200
SPG	Simon Property Group	179.51	2,194,000
T	AT&T Inc	42.01	19,018,201
TGT	Target Corp	63.7	7,471,900
TWX	Time Warner Inc	96.38	2,720,700
TXN	Texas Instruments	78.03	9,737,500
UNH	United health Group Inc	162.99	3,110,300
UNP	Union Pacific Corp	109.2	3,555,400
UPS	United Parcel Service	118.09	2,284,100
USB	U.S. Bancorp	52.99	6,893,300
UTX	United Technologies Corp	109.7	2,829,900
V	Visa Inc	83.77	5,445,900
VZ	Verizon Communications Inc	49.6	18,369,201
WBA	Walgreens Boots Alliance	81.5	4,613,000
WFC	Wells Fargo & Company	56.59	17,186,201
WMT	Wal-Mart Stores	65.66	13,433,600
XOM	Exxon Mobil Corp	85.51	10,947,801

Table D.4. Futures Prices (January 27, 2017)

Commodity	Contract	Close
U.S. Dollar Index	DXH17 (Mar'17)	100.195
British Pound	B6H17 (Mar'17)	1.2598
Canadian Dollar	D6H17 (Mar'17)	0.7621
Japanese Yen	J6H17 (Mar'17)	0.87555
Euro FX	E6H17 (Mar'17)	1.07525
Mexican Peso	M6H17 (Mar'17)	0.04764
Eurodollar	GEH17 (Mar'17)	98.91
T-Bond	ZBH17 (Mar'17)	150-19
10-Year T-Note	ZNH17 (Mar'17)	124-105
5-Year T-Note	ZFH17 (Mar'17)	117-260
2-Year T-Note	ZTH17 (Mar'17)	108-127
30-Day Fed Funds	ZQJ17(Apr'17)	99.285
Crude Oil WTI	CLH17 (Mar'17)	53.01
Gasoline RBOB	RBH17(Mar'17)	1.547
Natural Gas	NGH17 (Mar'17)	3.321
Wheat	ZWH17 (Mar'17)	418-0
Corn	ZCH17 (Mar'17)	361-2
Soybeans	ZSH17 (Mar'17)	1042-0
S&P 500 E-Mini	ESH17 (Mar'17)	2281.25
Nasdaq 100 E-Mini	NQH17 (Mar'17)	5145.75
Dow Indu 30 E-Mini	YMH17 (Mar'17)	19954
S&P 500 VIX	VIG17 (Feb'17)	12.85
Live Cattle	LEJ17 (Apr'17)	117.325
Lean Hogs	HEJ17 (Apr'17)	68.3
Gold	GCG17 (Feb'17)	1193.7
Silver	SIH17 (Mar'17)	17.195
High Grade Copper	HGH17 (Mar'17)	2.6915
Platinum	PLJ17 (Apr'17)	988.3
Paladium	PAH17 (Mar'17)	751.4
Cotton #2	CTH17 (Mar'17)	74.85
Orange Juice	OJH17 (Mar'17)	173.2
Coffee	KCH17 (Mar'17)	152.4
Sugar#11	SBH17 (Mar'17)	20.33
Cocoa	CCH17 (Mar'17)	2,095
Lumber	LSH17 (Mar'17)	324.2

Index

accounting data, 132, 157
acid test, 115, 124
airlines, 72, 153, 262
American Funeral Supplies, Inc., 112, 113, 236, 242, 243
annuity, 43
ARIMA, 185, 186
arm's-length transactions, 138, 158

balance sheet, 73, 111, 115, 129, 134, 136, 137, 140, 163, 165, 175, 202, 205, 244, 250, 284, 319, 320, 346, 350
bankers' acceptance, 62
bankruptcy, 24, 71, 72, 115, 176, 204, 209, 210, 213, 223, 251
basic defensive interval (BDI), 124
Bernoulli, Daniel, 398, 399, 435
beta, 454, 455, 457, 496, 498, 503
bidding up, 313
blue-chip stocks, 277, 332
bond, 6, 16, 18, 20, 21, 38, 40, 46, 60, 61, 63, 66–72, 82, 85, 89, 93, 94, 96, 99, 102–107, 122, 151, 153, 166, 173, 195, 196, 199, 201, 203, 207, 208, 210, 211, 214–218, 220, 223–227, 228, 229, 232–234, 246–249, 253–256, 258, 261–263, 268, 284, 286, 305, 321–330, 336, 337, 346, 353–355, 365, 371, 394, 416, 481
boot, 26, 148, 149
brokerage, 13, 155
businessman's risk, 417

call money, 364
call option, 359, 384–386, 391, 393, 394
call privilege, 226
capital gain, 141, 149, 150, 269, 272, 292, 475, 491
capital market, vii, viii, 3, 59, 65, 73, 106, 216, 450–452, 454, 455, 471, 472, 477, 480, 481, 483–485, 508
capital market line (CML), 451
capital market theory, 445
capitalization, 46
cemetery, 553
central limit theorem, 422, 472, 480
certificates of deposit, 63
certified public accounting (CPA), vii
Chebyschev's inequality, 467, 470
Chicago Board Options Exchange (CBOE), 387

593

Chicago Mercantile Exchange (CME), 363
coefficient of determination, 539
coefficient of multiple determination, 540
coefficient of partial determination, 540
collar, 361, 362
collateral trust bond, 72
commercial banks, 153
commercial paper, 63
commodities, 99, 363, 364, 367, 400, 439
common size analysis, 123
common stock, 73, 121–123, 129–132, 135, 140, 168, 173, 201, 207, 208, 216, 239–241, 252, 261–263, 292, 294, 316, 321–327, 330, 331, 336, 337, 353, 361, 368–372, 374, 376, 379, 381, 384, 385, 387, 393, 394, 553
common stock security ratios, 121
common stockholders, 74, 204, 205, 234
compound average growth rate (CAGR), 52
compound interest, 41
conditional probability distributions, 541
confidence limit, 461, 462, 506
conglomerate, 139, 159, 290, 347
consolidation, 139, 144, 145, 158
continuous compounding, 42
cost of capital, 79, 492
covariance, 417, 420, 424, 428, 429, 452, 453, 473–475, 503, 532
crash of 1929, 20, 23, 34
credit (default) risk, 61
cumulative preferred, 73

debentures, 72, 207, 321, 394
default risk, 208–210, 215, 232

derivatives, viii, 359, 361, 366, 395, 426
dilution, 312, 313, 315, 352, 371, 374, 383, 384, 390
discounting, 44, 45
dividends, 38, 70, 73, 115, 120, 133, 135, 160, 166, 173, 205, 234, 235, 254, 262, 268–270, 273, 275, 279, 281–284, 292, 300, 302, 306, 309, 311, 315–318, 321, 322, 330, 331, 333, 336–338, 345, 348, 352, 353, 355, 374–376, 393, 428, 429, 475, 478, 481, 486, 489, 496

efficiency, viii, 17, 18, 20, 34, 68, 81, 151–153, 418, 422–426, 433–435, 443, 445, 447–449, 451, 461, 462, 468, 470, 477, 480, 485, 499, 503–506, 508
Efficiency Frontier, 422, 425
efficient market hypothesis (EMH), 6–8, 492
equation of exchange, 87
equilibrium, 78, 80–83, 89, 93, 103, 451–454, 470, 477, 481, 485–488, 490, 491, 503, 507
equipment trust certificate, 72
Eurodollar, 64
Excel, 226
excess-return, 470, 471, 506
exchange traded fund (ETF), 156

Federal Deposit Insurance Company (FDIC), 5
Federal Deposit Insurance Corporation (FDIC), 63
Federal National Mortgage Association, 68
Federal Reserve, 23, 35, 60, 82, 103, 154, 228, 351, 484
Fibonnacci, 41

Financial Accounting Standards Board (FASB), 112
financial statements, 20, 109, 111, 112, 129, 131, 133–135, 138, 150, 157–159, 162, 173, 242, 264, 319, 320, 356
First-Degree Stochastic Dominance (FSD), 462
Fisk, Jim, 10
floating supply, 16
forecasting, 171, 173, 185, 186
Funeral Supplies, Inc., 111, 123, 151, 492
futures, viii, 38, 359–361, 363–368, 386, 395
futures contract, 359, 363, 365, 367

general obligation bonds, 69
Generally Accepted Accounting Principles (GAAP), 112
geometric mean, 52, 94, 97, 401, 442, 460, 471, 472
goodwill, 130, 135, 150, 151, 159
Gould, Jay, 10
Government National Mortgage Association, 68
Graham and Dodd, 7
Great Depression, 11, 74
gross returns, 47
gross-redemption ratio, 155
growth stocks, 277, 279, 292, 332, 333, 416

Hicks, Sir John, 96
Hicksian, 96, 491
HP-12C, 37
HP12C, 111

income bonds, 72, 207
income statement, 111, 129, 133–137, 163–165, 175, 244, 245, 267, 278, 284, 338, 346, 351

indenture, 21, 71–73, 195, 217, 219, 225, 246, 253, 255, 322
indifference curve, 408, 418, 422, 434
initial public offerings (IPO), 18
installment sale method, 141
institutional pressure, 98
interest-rate risk, 208, 247
isomean lines, 431
isovariance curve, 431

Keynes, John Maynard, 11
Keynesian, viii, 76, 78, 80, 82, 84, 85, 90, 103
kurtosis, 525

law of large numbers, 398, 422, 435
least-squares, 186, 356, 357, 522, 534, 535, 538, 539
lending portfolio, 447, 449
leptokurtic, 525
leverage and capital structure ratios, 118
life insurance companies, 154, 159, 416, 483
limit order, 19
Liquidity, 114, 117, 444
load factors, 152
lock-in effect, 224, 248
long-term anticipation securities (LEAPS), 385
long-term debt securities, 59

Mackay, Charles, 8
margin, 22
margin calls, 365
margin requirements, 23, 35, 323, 364, 484
marginal propensity to consume, 77, 103
market order, 19
market segmentation, 98, 216

Markowitz, Harry, viii, 412, 413, 444, 461, 473
mean absolute error (MAE), 172
mean absolute percentage error (MAPE), 173
merger, 139, 144, 145, 150, 158, 159, 288, 290–292, 321, 347, 362
mesokurtic, 525
monetary policy, 84, 85, 88, 91
money supply, 83–85, 87–91, 100, 103
Monte Carlo, 37, 304
mortgage bond, 71, 72, 207, 208, 254
mortgage bonds, 71, 205
municipal securities, 61
munis, 61, 62
mutual funds, 155, 160, 417, 455, 482

naïve, 173–175, 178, 179, 183, 185, 186
net-redemption ratio, 155
New York Mercantile Exchange (NYMEX), 364
New York Stock Exchange (NYSE), 17
no-call period, 71
nominal yield, 210, 216
non-parametric, 179, 181–183
normal distribution, 180, 181, 461, 527, 528, 530
normal equations, 535

operating leverage, 199
options, viii, 24, 321, 336, 359, 361, 363, 364, 366, 368, 384–388, 395, 398
over-the-counter (OTC), 17, 359

P/E, 168, 274–276, 278, 279, 282, 286, 291, 292, 297, 298, 310, 315, 333, 340, 344–348, 351, 354, 357
parameter estimation, 180
parametric model, 180–183
parametric simulation, 179
Paretian distributions, 480
participating preferred, 73
perpetual life, 59
Petersburg Paradox, 398, 405, 413, 435, 436
platykurtic, 525
portfolio management, 418, 438
preemptive right, 380
preferred stock, 73, 166, 205, 234
present value, 44
probability distribution, 51, 179, 180, 192, 210, 230, 231, 252, 256, 288, 294, 299, 303, 304, 334, 467, 521, 522, 529, 535, 545
probability distribution, 541
profit ratios, 115
prudent man rule, 484
public utility, 152, 159, 164, 198, 271
pure expectations hypothesis, 92–95, 97–99, 105
put option, 359, 385

quantity theory of money, 87

railroads, 10, 70, 72, 127, 151, 159, 204, 205, 309
random variable, 521
random walk, 479, 480
random walk hypothesis, 479
rate of return, 50
ratio analysis, 109
regression, 173, 186, 188, 189, 196, 198, 199, 263, 375, 428, 429, 442, 454, 458, 534

reorganization, 145, 147–149, 203–205, 207, 209, 247, 251, 252, 370
resampling, 37, 181
return on investment ratios, 117
rights-off, 381
rights-on, 381, 382
risk seeker, 410
risk-averse, 413, 417, 422, 438, 448, 476
root mean square error (RMSE), 173
Royal Exchange, 363

Second-Degree Stochastic Dominance (SSD), 463
Securities Act (1933), 20, 34
Securities Exchange Act (1934), 21, 23, 27, 34, 35
security market line (SML), 453
self-regulatory organization (SRO), 112
semi-equities, 321
semivariance, 523, 524, 526, 546
separation theorem, 449, 471, 484, 485
Service Corporation International (SCI), 553
Sharpe Ratio, 457
Shorting, 26
simple moving average (SMA), 178
sinking-fund, 119, 120, 173, 217–221, 224, 229, 253, 254, 256, 258, 321, 336
skewness, 210, 524
smoothing, 177
Solid Cryogenics, Incorporated, 178
Sortino ratio, 459
South Sea Bubble, 9
spread, 17, 19, 60, 65, 215, 283, 367, 385, 478, 481

standard error, 532, 547
Standard & Poor's, 13
stochastic dominance, 462, 466, 467, 506
stock split, 317, 318, 362, 491
stop order, 19
straddle, 385, 393, 394
Subchapter "C", 74
subordinated debentures, 72, 202, 203, 205, 250, 251
sunspot, 172
system peak, 152

t-distribution, 529, 550
t-score, 531
tax liabilities, 134, 288
taxes, 61, 62, 69, 70, 74, 76–79, 81, 92, 102, 116, 133, 134, 142, 147, 152, 160, 164, 165, 168, 199, 202, 204, 206, 221, 233, 234, 246, 249, 251, 253, 292, 293, 306, 321, 338, 340, 345, 347, 353, 356, 375, 383, 394, 395, 474–476
term structure of interest rates, 92, 101
Third-Degree Stochastic Dominance (TSD), 465
Thompson, Williams and Findlay, 4, 23
time, 38
time value, 65, 385, 387, 391, 511
Time Warner, 361
transactions costs, 92, 450, 472, 474, 476
transfer payments, 76, 78
treasury bill, 60–62, 92, 101
treasury bonds, 67
treasury notes, 67
tulipomania, 10
turnover ratios, 116, 117, 120, 126, 237, 238

utility, 39, 152, 153, 397, 399, 400, 402–414, 417–419, 422, 436–441, 449, 450, 455, 461, 462, 465, 467, 471, 472, 474, 476, 506

Value Line, 13
variance, 294, 420, 425, 431–433, 435, 453, 480, 503
von Neumann and Morgenstern, 403, 436

Wall Street, 14, 20, 26, 395, 494
Wall Street Journal, 27

warrant, 223, 292, 368–381, 382–385, 389–392, 394, 395
Warren Buffett, 2
World Bank, 69
World War II, 98
Wynn Corp., 160, 161

yield and price ratios, 122
yield curve, 92, 97, 98, 106, 107, 210, 215, 216

z-score, 528